D1286695

BRITAIN AND JAPAN

1858–1883

Court Scene, New Year Ceremony at the Emperor's Shrine, 1878
By Yamazaki Toshinobu

BRITAIN
AND JAPAN
1858–1883

GRACE FOX

OXFORD
AT THE CLARENDON PRESS
1969

Oxford University Press, Ely House, London W. 1

GLASGOW NEW YORK TORONTO MELBOURNE WELLINGTON
CAPE TOWN SALISBURY IBADAN NAIROBI LUSAKA ADDIS ABABA
BOMBAY CALCUTTA MADRAS KARACHI LAHORE DACCA
KUALA LUMPUR SINGAPORE HONG KONG TOKYO

PRINTED IN GREAT BRITAIN

TO THE MEMORY OF
JACOB J. WEAVER JR.
AND
JAMES T. SHOTWELL

ACKNOWLEDGEMENT

MANY persons in England, Japan, and the United States helped me in this study of British influence on the development of modern Japan. They fall into three main groups: those who helped me in locating the evidence, those who translated Japanese sources, and those who criticized portions of my manuscript. In England, I am indebted to Mr. E. K. Timings and the staff of the Public Record Office, Mr. A. Taylor Milne of the Institute of Historical Research, Professor W. G. Beasley of the University of London, and to the archivists or librarians at Windsor Castle, the Foreign Office, the Admiralty, the Board of Trade, University College, London, the Bodleian, University Library, Cambridge, the Royal Society, the Royal Institution, the Bank of England, the Society for the Propagation of the Gospel, and the Church Missionary Society: in Japan, to those at the Ministry of Foreign Affairs, the National Diet Library, Tokyo and Waseda Universities, Tōyō Bunko and the Municipal Libraries at Hakodate and Nagasaki: in the United States, to Dr. Hugh Borton, former President of Haverford College, to Mr. Andrew Y. Kuroda, the Head of the Japanese Section, and to Mrs. Jeffie Bennett Smith and Mrs. Eileen C. Donahue of the Reference Staff, of the Library of Congress, and to the staffs of the Widener, Houghton, and Baker Libraries of Harvard University, of the United Church Board for World Ministries Library and Archives, Boston, and of Rutgers University Library.

I am especially indebted to Mr. John Keswick of Matheson & Co. Ltd. for making possible my use of the Jardine Matheson Archive at Cambridge, to Messrs. John and A. C. Swire for the Butterfield and Swire material; to Mr. J. Leighton-Boyce for sources on British banks, to Commander Sir Michael Culme-Seymour and the late Florence, Lady Culme-Seymour, for access to the Seymour Papers at Rockingham, to Mr. George B. Endacott, formerly of Hong Kong University, for guidance to the records at Hong Kong, to Mr. Paul C. Blum of Tokyo and Mr. Harold S. Williams of Kobe for the privilege of working in their private collections of books and papers on Japan, and to Professor Higasi Keniti, a former member of Hokkaido University, and his wife whose combined help in locating and translating Japanese records made possible my chapter on British influence on Japanese science.

Others who gave me help in the translation of Japanese sources were: Mr. Aoki Arata and Mr. Mizusawa Kōsaku, formerly of the Japanese Diplomatic Service, Mr. Maruyama Takamitsu and Mrs. Hashimoto Ikuko of Tokyo, Mr. Tabata Kōsaburō and Miss Okada Hiroko of the Hakodate Municipal Library, and Mr. Bobbie T. Matsui of the Japan-American Cultural Center at Hakodate, Mr. Kuroda and his staff, Mr. Key K. Kobayashi, Mr. Hisao Matsumoto, Mr. Shojo Honda and Mr. Tetsuo Yoshikawa at the Library of Congress, Mr. George Whittall and Mr. and Mrs. Robert Flershem of Washington, and Messrs. Kiogama Tetsuo, Sadanaga Masayasu, Yoneda Morio, Nishikawa Masao, and Tominaga Yukio during their sojourns in Washington.

For constructive criticism of portions of my manuscript I am indebted to Professor Emeritus Oka Yoshitake of Tokyo University, Professor Higasi Keniti, Dr. Arthur W. Hummel of Washington, Professor Emeritus Charles R. Whittlesey of the University of Pennsylvania, Associate Professor Hugh T. Patrick of Yale University, Dr. William G. Welk of the Export-Import Bank of Washington, Professor Theodore H. McNelly of the University of Maryland, Assistant Professor John C. Perry of Carleton College, Northfield, Minnesota, and Mr. John Phillip Emerson of Oxon Hill, Maryland.

I had the dependable and imaginative assistance of Mrs. Duncan Macrae Taylor of London in my search in the British archives and the help of the late Miss Janice Macrae Taylor in the papers of the Scottish missionary societies. Mr. Herbert J. Bruder, Engineering Draughtsman of the United States Army Coastal Engineering Research Center, Washington, D.C., made the original drawings of the maps and Mrs. John Fanfani of Washington, and Mrs. Robert Wilde of Westminster, Maryland, gave me valued secretarial help.

I wish to acknowledge the gracious permission of Her Majesty Queen Elizabeth II to use the letter referred to on page 215 of this book and the permission of Her Majesty's

Stationery Office to reproduce Crown Copyright material of which the numbers and dates of the manuscripts concerned are given. Finally I am grateful for Grants-in-Aid from the Social Science Research Council and from the American Philosophical Society which furthered my work in the British archives.

GRACE FOX

Washington, D.C.
28 February 1968

CONTENTS

PART TWO

ECONOMIC AND TECHNOLOGICAL DEVELOPMENTS

PART THREE

BRITISH INFLUENCE ON JAPANESE CULTURE

ILLUSTRATIONS

MAPS

TABLES

NOTE ON NAMES AND THEIR SPELLING

JAPANESE personal names are given in the usual Japanese order with the family name first and with macrons to mark the long vowels, except in citing English works by Japanese authors where macrons do not appear. And except where macrons are a part of a transliterated title of a book or article, I have omitted them on the well-known place names, Tokyo, Osaka, Kyoto, and Hokkaido, and on the Japanese nouns, shogun and daimyo, since these words are now given this way in English dictionaries. Contrary to Japanese custom which places a feudal title between the family name and the given name, e.g. Date, Iyo- no- kami, Muneki, I have given the feudal title last, e.g. Date Muneki, Iyo-no-kami, to avoid possible confusion for Western readers. Some inconsistencies in the spelling of both Japanese and English names have shown up during the preparation of the index owing to irregularities in their spelling in the original sources and to unfortunate oversights in the proof reading. I have therefore indicated in the index the correct spelling. I wish also to mention here for the benefit of my American readers that the word 'until' is used in my text according to its English meaning which is 'as far as and including' before the year month, week, or day given.

GRACE FOX

ABBREVIATIONS

A.B.C.	American Board of Commissioners for Foreign Missions
Ad.	Admiralty Manuscript in the Public Record Office
Adm.	The Admiralty Board
Ad. R.O.	Manuscript in the Admiralty Record Office
B. and F.	British and Foreign Bible Society
B.G.K.M.	*Bakumatsu Gaikoku Kankei Monjo* (Documents relating to Foreign Affairs in the Last Days of the Shogunate)
Brit. Mus.	British Museum
B. and S.	Butterfield and Swire Ltd.
B.T.	Board of Trade
C.M.S.	Church Missionary Society
Conf'l.	Confidential
Cons. Report	Consular Report
D.N.G.M.	*Dai Nihon Gaikō Monjo* (Japanese Foreign Office Archives)
D.N.B.	*Dictionary of National Biography*
F.O.	Foreign Office
J.M.	Jardine, Matheson and Company
L.C.	Library of Congress
N.B.S.S.	National Bible Society of Scotland
P.P. H. of C.	Parliamentary Papers, House of Commons
P.R.O.	Public Record Office, London
S.P.G.	Society for the Propagation of the Gospel in Foreign Parts.
T.A.S.J.	*Transactions of the Asiatic Society of Japan*
U.P.S.	United Presbyterian Church of Scotland

PART ONE

DIPLOMATIC RELATIONS

I

THE TWO ISLAND EMPIRES

Britain and Japan, 1858. The two island empires had little in common when at Britain's demand their representatives met that August to negotiate a commercial treaty. Britain, a world-wide empire dedicated to free trade; Japan, a group of four islands, almost isolated from the world for more than two centuries by a self-imposed seclusion policy. Britain, a constitutional monarchy run by a parliamentary system; Japan, a decadent military dictatorship. Britain, a rich manufacturing nation; Japan, a traditionally feudal society undermined by a developing money economy. Britain, a stronghold of Protestant evangelism; Japan, since 1616 the declared persecutor of Christians. Britain, the advocate of an informed public opinion; Japan, a nation without a press, her masses generally denied political knowledge. Each people had a rich but vastly different cultural heritage, intense national consciousness, and an assurance of superiority. Each had long felt the security of insularity while profiting by the cultural influences of a neighbouring continent. To understand their relations with each other for the next twenty-five years, a review of their institutions and previous policies is needed.

Britain in the 1850s

In 1858 Britain was politically the most advanced nation in western Europe. Since the Reform Act of 1832 manufacturers, financiers, and men of letters sat beside the gentry in Parliament which as a result now represented about half the middle classes of the kingdom in addition to the landed aristocrats. Many political, social, economic, and religious reforms had been effected. More were in the making. Royal commissions, investigations, and reports sparked new legislation. Public opinion in favour of drastic changes had become a force no statesman or politician could ignore without peril.

The statesmen of the next three decades had already come

to the front. In 1858 Benjamin Disraeli, the rising commander of the Conservative Party, was leader of the House of Commons and Chancellor of the Exchequer in Lord Derby's second Conservative government—a government which was to give place, before the impending Anglo-Japanese treaty could come into operation, to the last ministry of Viscount Palmerston. A Whig aristocrat and genial 'man of the people', Palmerston was then seventy-five. In fifteen parliaments and many cabinets since 1807, he had proved himself a consummate politician, rarely gifted in appraising the temper of the nation. His coalition Cabinet of Whigs and Liberals of June 1859 rested on a solid parliamentary majority for the next six years. The ageing reformer Lord John Russell, dedicated to peace and the extension of the franchise, claimed the Foreign Office to the exclusion of the Earl of Clarendon who had superior diplomatic skills.[1] And William E. Gladstone, a free trader, a financial genius, and the 'rising hope of the younger Liberals', was again Chancellor of the Exchequer.[2]

Above these parties was the stabilizing institution of the British crown. Victoria had been Queen since 1837. She was a conservative, hard-working monarch, well versed in the constitutional precepts of the period, who had won new respect for the crown. With her husband and most influential adviser, Prince Albert, she took a lively interest in all important matters of government, constantly demanding accurate and detailed information from every department.[3] She felt a great concern about British relations with other countries and made it clear that she expected to be informed of the proposed policies of her ministers in advance of granting the Royal sanction.[4]

Every ministry took just pride in the nation's economic

---

[1] Clarendon entered Palmerston's cabinet in 1864 for the Duchy of Lancaster and became Foreign Secretary in Russell's cabinet (1865-6) which followed Palmerston's death in Oct. 1865. He was again Foreign Secretary from Dec. 1868 until his death in June 1870 while serving in Gladstone's first cabinet.

[2] G. M. Trevelyan, *British History in the Nineteenth Century* (New York, 1933), p. 325.

[3] *The Greville Memoirs, A Journal of the Reign of Queen Victoria from 1852–1860*, 2 vols. (London, 1867), ii. 126.

[4] Memo. from the Queen to Lord John Russell, 12 Aug. 1850, in G. M. Young and W. D. Handcock, Editors, vol. 12, pt. I. *English Historical Documents, 1833–1874* (New York, 1956), 71, which is in David C. Douglas, Gen. Ed., *English Historical Documents*, 12 vols. (New York, 1953-9).

progress. The industrial revolution to which Britain had given birth had produced great wealth and vast technological improvements. In the 1850s the British people were approaching the crest of a hitherto unknown agricultural and industrial prosperity which they reached in 1873. Profiting by the peace which revolution and wars of liberation had denied the rest of Europe, Britain had become the only industrialized state with a spectacular leadership in manufactures, trade, and finance.[1] Her textile mills were working at full speed, offering improved conditions for her employees and producing more linen, silk, wool, and cotton goods than the United Kingdom could consume. The age of iron was giving place to steel. Britain had connected her farms with her cities by a network of railways and was supplying the demand for rails and locomotives abroad. She was also developing her mines to build ironclad steamships and to supply them as well as her railroads with coal. She had the largest mercantile marine and the most powerful navy afloat which gave her citizens an assured, even when unwarranted, protection, wherever they might be.

A dynamic faith in free trade replaced the old mercantilist doctrines. By 1850 Parliament had abolished protective tariffs, repealed the Navigation Acts, and supported the expansion of British commercial interests in China, South Africa, and India —all in an effort to meet Britain's need for more raw materials for her factories, wider markets for her manufactures, and extra food for her increasing population.[2] Success soon seemed assured. From 1855 through 1859, the total value of British imports and exports rose from £260 million to £335 million with steady increases ahead.[3]

London was not only the centre of world trade but the centre of world finance. British currency was based on gold. The Bank of England had assumed the functions of a central bank and led the international money markets. It alone could issue bank

[1] Although Britain had fought Russia in the Crimea 1854–6, the war was carried on at a distance and did not seriously disturb her economy.

[2] In 1855 the number of people in England and Wales was estimated at 18,787,000 to which Scotland added 2,962,500, while the number in Ireland was unknown. By 1883 the population of the whole United Kingdom reached 35,951,865. Great Britain (Board of Trade), *Statistical Abstract for the United Kingdom in each of the Last Fifteen Years from 1850–1864*, 12thNo. (London, 1865), p. 96; 31st No., 1869–83 (London, 1884), p. 160.

[3] Ibid., 12th No., p. 12.

notes and these, on demand, were convertible into gold. Its discount rate gave the lead to short-term interest rates throughout the world. Its power and effort to keep credit stable was contributing much to the steadier development of the national economy which characterized the mid nineteenth century.[1] The discovery of gold in California (1849) and in Australia (1851) had vastly increased the amount of currencies in the world, thus enabling foreign nations to import more British goods by paying for them in gold, and bringing more gold into the Bank of England than ever before. Great insurance companies, like Lloyd's, merchant bankers, shipping services, and merchant houses of all kinds organized activities at home and overseas which added to the incoming wealth of Britain and encouraged further expansion of her markets.[2]

A large number of English and Scottish missionary and Bible societies were also concerned with the areas overseas. Many Protestant organizations sought to compete with the Roman Catholic and Orthodox churches for the faith of the natives. Work among the American Indians, the South Sea Islanders, and in Africa and India was in progress. Among the societies which would soon take an interest in the Far East was the Society for the Propagation of the Gospel in Foreign Parts (founded in 1701) and the Church Missionary Society (1799) representing the 'High' and 'Low' branches of the Anglican Church, the British and Foreign Bible Society (1804), the United Presbyterian Church of Scotland Missionary Society (1835), and the Edinburgh Medical Missionary Society (1841). By the middle of the century these organizations were generally concerned with both primary and higher education, medical service, and the translation of the Bible into the vernacular, as part of an overall effort to build 'self-governing, self-supporting, and self-propagating' native churches.[3]

An independent and highly nationalistic press—daily newspapers, weekly and monthly journals, and scholarly quarterly reviews—informed, directed, and voiced Britain's thinking on all public issues. Great editors fought political, philosophical,

[1] W. H. B. Court, *A Concise Economic History of Britain* (Cambridge, 1954), pp. 102, 190.
[2] Ibid., p. 79.
[3] Definition of aim of missions given by Henry Venn of England and Rufus Anderson in the United States.

and personal battles anonymously through these channels. *The Times* under John Thadeus Delane (1841–75) was the recognized leader of them all.[1] It was the first paper to establish a universal news service and the first to introduce a parliamentary sketch or leading article. It kept in touch with home politics at the centre and had agents and correspondents abroad with such skilful means of transmitting dispatches that the news of *The Times* occasionally anticipated that of the government.[2] With such information at hand criticism could be fearless; men and policies made and broken.

The ideals, conflicting ambitions, contradictory moral values, self-satisfaction, and self-criticism of the British people at this period are all apparent in the pages of their press. Nationalists[3] and internationalists,[4] pacifists[5] and jingoes,[6] free traders[7] and protectionists,[8] anti-imperialist voices,[9] advocates of colonial self-government,[10] defenders of expansion in Asia and Africa,[11] all had their say. Every faction was concerned with British glory and prosperity even if by way of a minority interest. In general it was an age of great optimism fortified in 1859 by Darwin's theory of human evolution. With free trade, individual enterprise, *laissez-faire*, and an increasingly democratic government, Britain looked forward to unlimited progress—not for herself alone—but through the spread of her institutions for the rest of mankind. Such was the nation which in 1858 confronted Japan.

[1] *Saturday Review*, 3 Nov. 1855, quoted by L. M. Salmon, *The Newspaper and Authority* (New York, 1923), p. 384. Arthur Irwin Dasent, *John Thadeus Delane, His Life and Correspondence*, 2 vols. (New York, 1908), i. 34. The Times, London, *The History of The Times*, 4 vols. (London, 1935–52), ii. 57–58.

[2] R. A. Scott-James, *The Influence of the Press* (London, 1919), pp. 104–5. J. S. R. Phillips, 'The Growth of Journalism', in *The Cambridge History of English Literature*, 14 vols. (Cambridge, 1916), xiv, 167–211.

[3] *The Times*, Editorials 17 Jan., 2 Mar. 1850, 3 Jan. 1851.

[4] Ibid., Editorials 1 May, 9 Aug. 1851. *Examiner*, 3 May 1851. *Punch*, xx. 198, 233; xxi. 5.

[5] *The Times*, Editorials 1 Jan., 30 Oct., 31 Dec. 1850. *Punch*, xix. 121.

[6] *The Times*, Editorials 28 Jan., 6 Feb. 1852. *Examiner*, 24 Jan., 2 Feb. 1852.

[7] Ibid., Editorial 27 Mar. 1852. *The Times*, 4 Mar. 1853.

[8] *Punch*, xx. 141. *Examiner*, account of speech of Earl of Malmesbury, 27 Apr. 1850.

[9] *The Times*, Editorials 26 Sept., 20 Dec. 1851, 22 Jan., 30 June, 14 July, 17 Aug., 19 Sept. 1852. *Examiner*, 31 May 1851, 16 Mar., 3 Apr. 1852.

[10] *The Times*, 9 Feb. 1850, Russell's speech on Colonial Policy; Editorial 24 Apr. 1851.

[11] Ibid., Editorials 22 Apr., 23 July 1850, 23 Mar. 1853. *Examiner*, Editorials 14 June 1851, 10 Jan. 1852.

The Diplomatic Prelude: British Relations with China and Japan,
  1833–1858

As British action in China set patterns and gave warnings of
her policies in Japan, its consideration is necessary here. In
1833 pressure from the free traders and dissatisfaction with
the more than century-old administration of the East India
Company led the British government to abolish the Company's
monopoly of the China trade at Canton. Conflicts with the
anti-foreign Chinese bureaucracy over establishing official
relations with the newly appointed British Superintendent of
Trade and over the suppression of the growing opium trade with
India precipitated war in 1839. Britain's overwhelming victory
led to the Treaty of Nanking, 29 August 1842, the first treaty
China had concluded with a Western maritime nation.

By this and a supplementary treaty in 1843, Britain forced
China to cede to her the island of Hong Kong to become a crown
colony; to open in addition to Canton four ports (Amoy,
Foochow, Ningpo, and Shanghai), of which Shanghai soon
gained the greatest commercial prominence; to permit the
appointment of consuls at all ports (with the right of direct
communication on a basis of equality with Chinese officials of
equal rank); to pay huge indemnities; to establish a duty of
five per cent. *ad valorem* on China's imports and exports; and to
grant her extraterritorial and most-favoured-nation privileges.[1]

These treaties launched a network of British authority in the
Far East. Her Majesty's Plenipotentiary and Superintendent
of Trade became also the Governor of Hong Kong. He was
chief of the consuls at the treaty ports and the final authority
in all matters concerning British citizens in China. The consuls
in turn, owing to the limited communication and travel facilities
between their posts and Hong Kong, were given responsibilities
unknown to those in Europe. They communicated directly
with the local Chinese officials and exercised extensive judicial
powers in addition to acting as 'security for any British
merchantships'. Both the Plenipotentiary and the consuls had
the assistance of a permanent squadron of the Royal Navy in
protecting the rights of British citizens and restraining distur-

---

[1] Godfrey E. P. Hertslet, *Hertslet's China Treaties*, 2 vols., 3rd ed. (London,
1908), i. 7–13, 24, 26. G. F. Hudson, 'The Far East', in *The New Cambridge Modern
History*, 12 vols. (Cambridge, 1957–60), x. 692.

bances at the ports—a support too readily solicited by merchants, missionaries, and diplomats alike. The government in London, aware of its ignorance of the area and in the absence of rapid mails and telegraphic communication, left many decisions to its officials on the spot in accordance with very general instructions.[1] These emphasized, however, its desire for peace with the Chinese people. For example, the Board of Admiralty ordered its naval officers to study Chinese wishes and feelings in order to preserve amicable relations 'with so peculiar a country as China where actions indifferent in themselves and which among European nations would lead to little or no inconvenience, might produce an impression highly unfavourable to the British character and destructive of that wholesome influence which it is so important should attach in China to everything connected with Great Britain'.[2]

France and the United States soon exacted treaties from China similar to those of Britain. France went even further by securing in 1844 an edict for the toleration of Catholicism which was later extended to Protestantism. But neither British traders nor French missionaries were content with the rights provided by the treaties since the anti-foreign Chinese authorities interpreted them as narrowly as possible. The British especially wanted the right of entry into the walled city of Canton, permission to travel freely in the territory beyond the treaty ports, and diplomatic contacts with the Imperial government at Peking. Having to negotiate solely with an Imperial commissioner at Canton, who was usually the local viceroy, had proved less than satisfactory. Since the American and French treaties granted the right to propose revision in twelve years, the British in 1856 looked forward to gaining these additional rights through their treaty guarantee of most-favoured-nation treatment.[3]

Although friction over the British treaty with China was intense the Foreign Office and its representative in China planned to seek similar arrangements with some additional rights and to rely on the presence of an impressive naval force

[1] Grace Fox, *British Admirals and Chinese Pirates 1832–1869* (London, 1940), pp. 35–36.
[2] Ad. 13/3, Adm. to Inglefield, 3 Aug. 1846, Art. 2.
[3] Hudson, op. cit., p. 694.

when considering the opening of commercial relations with
Japan. There was only a limited and spasmodic interest in
Japan before 1854, however, as the potential Japanese trade
seemed trifling in comparison with the often exaggerated
prospects in China. Instructions from London and schemes of
the British Superintendent of Trade to open negotiations with
the Japanese empire in 1846 were abandoned because the
naval force at hand was considered inadequate to assure their
success.[1]

By 1854 the British had been glad to let Commodore Perry,
acting for the United States, take the risk of opening Japan to
the West and hoped to profit by the results.[2] Perry's success
had been limited. Even at the threat of war, Japan yielded
only to America's most pressing demands in the Treaty which
she signed at Kanagawa 31 March 1854. These included: the
opening of the remote ports of Shimoda and Hakodate to
provide essential supplies and relief to American ships and
crews solely through the agency of Japanese officials; the
promise of most-favoured-nation treatment; and a vague
arrangement for an American consul to reside at Shimoda
eighteen months after the signing of the treaty, which was
Perry's device for insuring a future commercial treaty.[3]

Reports of this achievement prompted Lord Clarendon, then
Foreign Secretary, to authorize Dr. John Bowring (later Sir
John Bowring), the new Superintendent of Trade, to co-
operate with the French representative at Hong Kong on a
mission to Japan, when he could safely be away from China,
then in the throes of the T'aip'ing rebellion. The outbreak of
war with Russia in the Crimea, however, necessitated the use
of the entire China squadron to observe and, if possible,
capture the Czar's Pacific fleet which operated from bases in
Kamchatka and the Sea of Okhotsk. Hence the diplomatic
mission of Bowring and his French colleague with the support
of the ships under the naval Commander-in-Chief, Sir James
Stirling, was postponed.[4]

---

[1] W. G. Beasley, *Great Britain and the Opening of Japan 1854–1858* (London, 1951),
ch. III and pp. 97–98, 102–3.   [2] Ibid., pp. 93–97.

[3] W. G. Beasley, *Select Documents on Japanese Foreign Policy, 1853–1868* (London,
1955) (hereafter cited as *Documents*), pp. 119–22. Hugh Borton, *Japan's Modern
Century* (New York, 1955), p. 37.

[4] Beasley, *Great Britain and the Opening of Japan*, pp. 97–102.

Rear-Admiral Stirling then took matters into his own hands. Aboard his flagship H.M.S. *Winchester* and accompanied by three other ships he entered the port of Nagasaki on 7 September 1854 with the hope of rounding up the Russians and making arrangements with the Japanese to forestall the Russians from using Japanese ports and resources to equip or repair their cruisers and to harbour prizes.[1] He considered a commercial treaty impossible at that time. Furthermore, he believed Japan was more important for political than commercial reasons and he wanted to establish the groundwork of a cordial understanding with the Japanese officials. But he had no authority from London to make any treaty.[2]

The details of his negotiations have been covered elsewhere.[3] There were serious mistakes by the ill-equipped interpreters on both sides and exasperating delays by the alarmed Japanese. More generous terms resulted from Japan's misunderstanding of Stirling's original request for information regarding Japan's 'intentions concerning the admission into its ports of the ships of war of the belligerent parties in the present conflict', not only in reference to Nagasaki, 'but also in regard to all other ports and places within the Japanese territory'.[4] Because of the garbled translation, the Japanese understood this to mean a request for the opening of all Japanese ports for British use in prosecuting the war against Russia. Naturally the authorities at Yedo refused to risk Russian hostility in such a manner. They were willing, however, to grant to British ships admission to Nagasaki and Hakodate for replenishing wood, water, and other supplies and for making repairs.[5] They recognized no difference between emergencies arising from naval warfare and those from other causes. Under no circumstances would they consider the use of either port for war purposes of any kind.

On 14 October after several conferences on drafts where clauses concerning revision and most-favoured-nation treatment

[1] Ad. I/5629, Stirling to Adm., 26 Oct. 1854.

[2] Ad. I/5657, Stirling to Graham, 27 Oct. 1854. Beasley, *Great Britain and the Opening of Japan*, pp. 114–15.

[3] Ibid., ch. V. Grace Fox, 'The Anglo-Japanese Convention of 1854', *Pacific Historical Review*, 1941, x. 411–34. The Japanese officials were the Nagasaki commissioner (*bugyō*), called governor by the British, and a censor (*metsuke*).

[4] Ad. I/5657, Stirling to Governor of Nagasaki, 7 Sept. 1854, encl. in Stirling to Graham, 27 Oct. 1854.

[5] Beasley, *Great Britain and the Opening of Japan*, p. 119.

were debated and not clearly settled,[1] the negotiators agreed on the terms to be submitted for ratification to their respective governments. The text provided for the opening of Nagasaki and Hakodate for effecting repairs and obtaining essential provisions and supplies for British ships but required them to comply with the rules and regulations of each port. Only ships in distress could enter other ports without permission from the Imperial government. All British ships in Japanese ports were obliged to conform to Japanese laws. If officers broke them, the ports could be closed; inferior persons were to be handed over to the ship's commanders for punishment. British ships and subjects were granted the advantages of the most-favoured nation, excepting those accruing to the Dutch and the Chinese from their existing relations with Japan.[2] Finally, ratification by the two governments was to take place in twelve months and when ratified could not be changed by any 'high officer coming to Japan'.[3]

Stirling's agreement met harsh criticism from Bowring and the merchant communities in China who were angered at his indifference to the extension of trade.[4] The Foreign Office, however, applauded his initiative and tact. In spite of the disapproval of the Board of Trade, Her Majesty's Government ratified the Convention promptly. Even Stirling's proposal that the Queen send a yacht to the Japanese ruler met with favour. Lord Clarendon, then Foreign Secretary, signed this treaty instead of the Queen since the Governor of Nagasaki had stated that a high officer but not the Shogun would sign for Japan.[5]

Stirling exchanged ratifications of the Convention with the Japanese at Nagasaki on 9 October 1855, well supported by two French and eleven British warships. His unauthorized subsequent efforts to secure changes favourable to the British in both the treaty and the port regulations through Japanese agreement to his written explanation of the articles of his Convention accomplished little. Although the British government ratified what Stirling did, it never accepted his glorified

[1] Beasley, *Great Britain and the Opening of Japan*, pp. 122–9.
[2] See below, pp. 20–21.
[3] Beasley, *Great Britain and the Opening of Japan*, pp. 205–6.
[4] Ibid., pp. 130, 145–6.
[5] Ibid., p. 147. Fox, *Pacific Historical Review*, 1941 x. 422–3.

interpretation of the treaty as a prelude to a new maritime empire which had already proved its value to the British fleet at Hakodate during the summer of 1855. Lord Clarendon and the Board of Trade regarded the Convention merely as an entering wedge which could lead to the expansion of commercial relations with Japan. For that purpose Clarendon preferred to send not the Admiral but Sir John Bowring.[1]

The most-favoured-nation clause of the Convention, however, soon resulted in Britain's claim to further privileges in Japan, not only those secured by the United States but also by Russia.[2] In August 1855 Clarendon had instructed Bowring to claim for England whatever advantages, commercial or otherwise, Perry's treaty had gained for the United States, but later left the timing of Bowring's now authorized expedition to Japan to the Superintendent's judgement. Reports of Japan's refusal to admit Americans to either residence or trade, his hostility to Stirling, and desire for diplomatic authority over the China squadron made Bowring hesitant about undertaking the mission at once. Instead, in March 1856 he proposed to his superiors in London that the British and French initiate a joint expedition to Yedo, impressively escorted by an Anglo-French squadron.[3]

The arrival of Admiral Sir Michael Seymour as Stirling's successor with orders to fulfil what Stirling had initiated regarding the British interpretation of the terms of the Convention and to secure promised copies of the Russian treaty meant that again a naval commander-in-chief reached Nagasaki before Bowring. On 3 September 1856 with only three ships, Seymour demanded the right to enter the inner harbour of Nagasaki in accordance with Stirling's exposition of Article I of the treaty, and did so without opposition. He reported the end of the Anglo-Russian war, secured a copy of the Russian treaty with Japan, and wrangled fiercely for days with the Nagasaki

---

[1] Ibid. 424–6. Beasley, *Great Britain and the Opening of Japan*, pp. 136–44.

[2] J. H. Gubbins, *The Progress of Japan 1853–1871* (Oxford, 1911), pp. 63–64 and Appendix 5. On 7 Feb. 1855 Japan signed a treaty with Russia which was ratified 7 Dec. 1856. Here Japan opened Shimoda, Hakodate, and Nagasaki to Russian ships, permitted free arrangements for acquiring supplies at the first two ports, allowed the appointment of consuls, defined the Russo-Japanese boundary in the Kurile Islands and recognized the principle of extraterritoriality.

[3] Beasley, *Great Britain and the Opening of Japan*, pp. 149–55.

officials over the British interpretation of the treaty. In the end he gained permission for British officers accompanied by Japanese guides to land at Nagasaki within territory administered by the Shogunate but not in the neighbouring fiefs. They were forbidden to separate, to enter private homes, or to purchase goods. New port regulations merely added the provision for a depot, already built at Nagasaki, to be used for the purchase and storing of supplies, and recreation space for British seamen. Seymour accepted these concessions temporarily, implying that he expected the restrictions to be lifted the following year. The Foreign Office approved his work while Bowring rejoiced in his firm methods and preparation for smoother relations with Japan.[1]

Instructions from London to Bowring to proceed to Japan and orders to Seymour to supply the naval escort needed to secure for Britain a treaty at least as liberal as Russia's would have been carried out in the spring of 1857 had not the outbreak of hostilities with China in 1856 and the Indian Mutiny in 1857 demanded Britain's total attention elsewhere.[2]

Anglo-Indian relations not only suffered from the mutiny but fear and hatred of Britain for this and other reasons increased in the Far East. This was especially true in China where tensions over relations with Britain and France were already at the breaking-point. Difficulties caused by Western missionaries determined to evangelize and teach in the interior beyond the treaty ports under the protection of extraterritoriality were added to those resulting from British demands for the most liberal enforcement of the treaties in operation and efforts to extend their rights in China through treaty revision. Furthermore the enormous growth of the opium trade of which British consuls were under orders to take no legal notice, and the development of an inhuman Western traffic in coolie labour increased the grievances and hostility of the intensely antiforeign Manchu authorities. The fact that both trades flourished with the connivance of many Chinese, especially Cantonese, complicated their control by both British and Chinese. The weak government at Peking not only did little to enforce its prohibition of the two traffics but continued to refuse to communicate on any questions with the official representatives

[1] Beasley, *Great Britain and the Opening of Japan*, pp. 158–62.   [2] Ibid., p. 164.

of the treaty powers except through a commissioner at Canton. Here bitterness against Britain was intense because of the hostilities of 1841 and the decline in foreign trade owing to the development of Shanghai.[1] Furthermore in 1856 the British consul was the energetic, fearless Harry S. Parkes, bent on the full enforcement of the treaties and the protection of British honour. A minor incident, even an unwarranted one, was all that was needed to bring the two nations again into open conflict. Neither side understood the law and conventions of the other; each felt contemptuous and overwhelmingly superior towards its adversary.

In October 1856 the British and French governments sought their long-range objectives in China by precipitating on slight provocation a second war. Sir John Bowring found grounds for military reprisals in the refusal of the Imperial Commissioner at Canton 'Yeh Ming-ch'en' to meet in full the demands of Consul Parkes for redress for a still debatable violation of treaty rights and an insult to the British flag. He hastily sanctioned naval action without reference to London. Both sides were guilty of outrageous destruction and trade was stopped. The forces at Admiral Seymour's command, however, were not large enough to capture Canton. A stalemate had resulted when news of Bowring's policy reached the London Foreign Office.[2]

Palmerston's government endorsed Bowring's policy with some misgivings.[3] But opposition in Parliament caused the question of war with China to be taken to the British people. During four evenings of debate, beginning 26 February 1857, a combination of Conservatives and Liberals led by Disraeli, Gladstone, Russell, and Richard Cobden attacked Bowring's actions as dishonest, illegal, and impolitic. In consequence the Commons defeated the government by a vote of 263 to 247 on 3 March 1857—a clear indication of the pacifist sentiment in

[1] John K. Fairbank, Edwin O. Reischauer, Albert M. Craig, *A History of East Asian Civilization*, 2 vols. (Boston, 1960–5), ii. 150–5. British and American imports of opium amounted to at least 50,000 chests a year in the 1850s, thus doubling the quantity brought to Canton in the early 1830s.

[2] W. C. Costin, *Great Britain and China, 1833–1860* (Oxford, 1937), pp. 206–16, 286. For a sympathetic account of Parkes's policy see Stanley Lane-Poole and F. V. Dickins, *The Life of Sir Harry Parkes*, 2 vols. (London, 1891–4), i. 216–41.

[3] Costin, op. cit., pp. 217–18, 229.

Britain and of an active conscience concerning the methods by which British rights should be upheld.[1]

The voters, however, returned Palmerston to power with a verdict to continue the war. But, in the light of Bowring's rashness, the Cabinet transferred plenipotentiary power in China to a special envoy, James Bruce, the eighth Earl of Elgin, in April 1857.[2] A practised diplomat formerly in Canada and Jamaica, Lord Elgin was now instructed to proceed to the Peiho River and to negotiate at Tientsin with the emissaries of the Court. He was to procure China's agreement to an uncompromising execution of the treaties at Canton and elsewhere, and to the making of reparations for recent injuries and the destruction of property. If granted, he was empowered to strive with no threat of force for the right of direct communication with the Chinese government and access for British trade to the interior of China. He could resort to coercive measures should the Court refuse to negotiate or deny Britain's first requirements, and in penalty for such refusals he could then demand with force the additional rights. Britain now knew that her claim for the revision of the treaty could not be legally sustained. Elgin could insist, however, that recent events had proved the need for a better basis for Anglo-Chinese relations. In addition to this difficult assignment, he was instructed to negotiate a commercial treaty with Japan while in the Far East.[3]

Meanwhile, France decided to co-operate in the British demands on China. A series of persecutions of native Christians had culminated in 1856 in the execution of a French missionary, Chapdelaine, on charges of subversive activities in an area of the rebellion. Yeh's indifferent response to the French insistence on amends gave Napoleon III his grounds for coercion.[4] Anglo-French action, however, was delayed until late in 1857. Lord Elgin had to divert his expeditionary forces to India because of the mutiny. The late arrival of Baron Gros, the new French plenipotentiary, and of British military reinforcements also kept Elgin from going directly to Peking. By October he had orders to settle with the local authorities at Canton first. Heavy pressure for revenge from merchants exiled from the city

---

[1] *Hansard's Parliamentary Debates*, 3rd Series, cxliv, cols. 1391–1485, 1495–1585, 1590–1684, 1726–1850, 26, 27 Feb., and 2, 3 Mar. 1857.

[2] Costin, op. cit., p. 218. [3] Ibid., pp. 231–2. [4] Ibid., pp. 202–4.

and now at Hong Kong strengthened his decision to give up a preliminary effort towards diplomatic negotiations with Peking. The forces of England and France conquered and occupied Canton with a minimum of disorder in the last days of December. And they set up a provisional government under the former Provincial Governor, Pih Kwei, supervised by a foreign military tribunal and assisted by a combined Anglo-French and Chinese police corps. Trade began again in February.[1]

Elgin and Gros, accompanied by representatives of the United States and Russia, then turned to treaty-making at Tientsin. Many difficulties and delays attended the British negotiations. The expedition had taken on a highly belligerent character when on 30 May 1858 it finally reached Tientsin after capturing the Taku forts at the mouth of the Peiho— a precaution demanded by the British and French admirals. Horatio Nelson Lay, Inspector of Customs at Canton, acting on instructions from Elgin, was harsh and rude in making his demands on the Chinese. Among the concessions which Elgin forced upon China were: a resident minister at Peking; the right to travel in the interior of China; the opening of eleven new ports; the downward adjustment of tariff rates; the payment of indemnities; and the protection of missionaries by Chinese authorities. They were embodied in the Treaty of Tientsin, signed 26 June 1858, and became the model for China's agreements of 3 July with the other three powers.[2]

Baron Gros considered these terms 'exorbitant and perhaps even dangerous for England'. He openly predicted that the British government would be compelled 'to use force to secure the execution of the concessions obtained by force alone'.[3] Aware of this judgement Elgin set out to negotiate a commercial treaty with Japan before concluding the tariff and related questions with the Chinese at Shanghai.

Tokugawa Japan

Japan, divided and bankrupt, was ill prepared to resist the demands of the greatest power on earth. Political, economic, and intellectual forces were challenging her military dictatorship.

---

[1] Ibid., pp. 234–41.
[2] G. E. P. Hertslet, op. cit., i. 18–35. Hudson, op. cit., p. 703.
[3] Costin, op. cit. p. 272.

The interdependent relationships of her once rigid feudal order had broken down. Money values dominated her agrarian economy. Her social classes were violating their boundaries. Nevertheless the administrative structure and arbitrary laws which the first three Tokugawa Shoguns established between 1603 and 1651 had endured. Equally persistent were the early Tokugawa aims to maintain peace, prevent change, and keep the Tokugawa in control.[1]

Although by the last half of the eighteenth century the hereditary Shoguns[2] were no longer men of ability, their government, the *Bakufu*,[3] clung to the absolute power which the Emperor had delegated to its founder, Tokugawa Ieyasu, in 1603. The Emperor was merely the symbol of supreme authority, reverenced by all according to tradition but exercising no governing powers. The fiction of his investing each successive Shogun as his deputy, however, was kept alive in one of the elaborate ceremonies to which his duties were then restricted. He and his courtiers, the *kuge*, were even dependent upon the Shogun for their financial support. In consequence, they lived in secluded and Spartan simplicity at Kyoto while the Shogun and his vassals indulged in luxuries and wantonness in their great capital at Yedo.[4]

Weak, devious, and often corrupt men surrounded the Shogun in the nineteenth century and performed the functions of government. Among policy makers the most powerful were the *Rōjū*, the four or five senior councillors, chosen from the

---

[1] George Bailey Sansom, *The Western World and Japan* (New York, 1950), p. 180. 'Shogun' comes from *Sei-i-tai-shōgun*, literally, 'Barbarian-subduing generalissimo'. The title was first taken in 1192 to indicate the *de facto* ruler of Japan. Beasley, *Documents*, p. 328.

[2] The successor to a Shogun who died without heirs could be chosen from only two groups of Tokugawa descendants; the *Sanke*, the three senior branches of the Tokugawa family, descendents of the younger sons of Ieyasu whose fiefs were Owari, Kii, and Mito; or the *Sankyō*, members of the houses of Tayasu and Hitotsubashi, descendants of the eighth Shogun and the house of Shimizu, the heirs of the ninth Shogun. The *Sankyō* had no fiefs but lived in Yedo, receiving an income of 100,000 *koku* from the Shogun's estates. Beasley, *Documents*, p. 328.

[3] *Bakufu*, literally 'tent government', signifying military headquarters.

[4] Yedo was the name for Tokyo at this time. It is used throughout this study in accordance with the practice of the British Foreign Office, even after the name of the city was officially changed to Tokyo. As early as the 1720s Yedo had a population of about 1,000,000. E. S. Crawcour, 'Japanese Commerce in the Tokugawa Period', *The Journal of Asian Studies*, xxii (Aug. 1963), 395.

Shogun's vassals-in-chief whose *han* (fiefs) annually yielded
50,000 *koku*.¹ They had supervision over the administration,
the great daimyo (feudal lords), monasteries and shrines, and
Court-*Bakufu* relations. Beneath them in order of importance
were the four to six members of a junior or second council who
were concerned with the feudal class beneath daimyo rank;
the governors of Kyoto and Osaka; a number of *bugyō* (commissioners or magistrates); and the *ōmetsuke* and *metsuke* (chief
and subordinate censors). There were several ranks of *bugyō*: at
the top the *jisha-bugyō* had responsibility for both Buddhist
and Shinto establishments; two *machi-bugyō* administered the
Shogun's capital; the *kanjō-bugyō* directed the government's
finances; lesser *machi-bugyō* were the governors of Nagasaki and
other key cities under Tokugawa control; and after August
1858, *gaikoku-bugyō* were appointed to conduct relations with
foreign diplomats at home and abroad. The *ōmetsuke* were
responsible for detecting disloyalty or maladministration among
the feudal lords and officials of daimyo status, while the *metsuke*
supervised those of lower rank. In times of crisis or during the
minority of a Shogun, a *tairō* or regent, chosen from the four
families in the Tokugawa vassalage whose fiefs yielded a
minimum of 100,000 *koku*, could be appointed over all these
officials to conduct important matters of State.²

It was an inefficient system of administration, rigid in its
regulation of rank and seniority and often confusing, especially
to incoming Westerners, regarding the relative functions of
the officials and where the power of decision rested.³ In the
opinion of its nineteenth-century critics, it operated primarily
for the benefit of the *Bakufu*.

The determination of the first three Tokugawa to maintain
peace and entrench their own power led to the exclusion
policy. This isolated Japan from the economic and military
competition of the West after a period of expansion, foreign
trade, and the acceptance of Roman Catholic missionaries in
the sixteenth century. Fearing not only foreign conquest in the

---

¹ *Koku*: 4·96 English bushels, used as the standard measure before 1868 to assess
the rice revenues of feudal lands and the capacity of ships.
² Beasley, *Documents*, pp. 322–30. George Bailey Sansom, *A History of Japan*,
3 vols. (Stanford, 1958–63) (hereafter cited as *History*), iii. 23.
³ W. G. Beasley, *The Modern History of Japan* (New York, 1963) (hereafter cited
as *History*), p. 5.

wake of the missionaries and merchants but also the co-operation of those representatives of Spain and Portugal with local disaffected vassals to undermine their authority, the early Tokugawa sought to limit all foreign intercourse to an area which they alone controlled. Laws which banned and persecuted Christianity throughout Japan and restricted foreign trade to a few Dutchmen and Chinese in the vicinity of Nagasaki were the result.[1] Anti-Christian instructions began in 1611. Foreign missionaries were expelled in 1614. Two years later a decree from the *Rōjū* ordered all daimyo to prohibit all their people down to the farmers from accepting the Christian faith. A hideous persecution of native Christians followed so that by 1639 Christianity was exterminated in Japan, except for some persistence underground. The *Bakufu* then established a kind of inquisition with Buddhist priests as agents to ferret out converts—a system duplicated in the *han* in 1664.[2]

In conjunction with this policy the *Bakufu* restricted all foreign trade to Nagasaki and Hirado in 1616—a great blow to the British East India Company, which had had the run of the country since 1613 and which closed its factory in 1623 because of financial losses owing to more *Bakufu* prohibitions. All Spanish and Portuguese merchants were expelled from Japan between 1624 and 1639. Two years later the restriction of the Dutch traders to a prison-like existence on the small island of Deshima at the head of Nagasaki Bay brought them under Tokugawa control.[3] Laws in the 1630s prohibiting Japanese subjects from going abroad, punishing with death those who did so and returned, forbidding the construction of ships above 500 *koku* capacity, and requiring reference to Yedo

[1] Sansom, *The Western World and Japan*, pp. 169–70, 178–9; *History*, iii. 42–43. Takekoshi Yosoburo, *Economic Aspects of the History of the Civilization of Japan*, 3 vols. (London, 1930), ii. 16, 257.

[2] Shihōshō (Ministry of Justice), *Tokugawa Kinrei Kō* (Collection of the Tokugawa Prohibitions), First Series, 6 vols. (Tokyo, 1895), v. 120–3, for text of first decrees. Sansom, *History*, iii. 39–42. James Murdoch in collaboration with Yamagata Isoh, *A History of Japan*, 3 vols. (London, 1925–6), ii. 498–502, 624–5.

[3] Peter Pratt, *History of Japan*, compiled from Records of the East India Company at the Instance of the Court of Directors, 1822, ed. by M. Paske-Smith, 2 vols. (Kobe, 1931), i. 137, 195. Tokyo University Shiryō Hensanjo (Historiographical Institute), Ed., *Dai Nippon Shiryō* (Japanese Historical Materials), Pt. XII, 34 vols. (Tokyo, 1925), xxv. 96–97, East India Company Letters, William Eaton to Sir Thomas Smythe, Hirado, 18 Dec. 1616. Sansom, *History*, iii. 37–38, 41–42. Murdoch, op. cit. ii. 663–4, 677.

regarding the treatment of foreign ships which applied for entry in Japanese ports, finalized Japan's isolation.[1] Foreign trade, however, did not stop with the one or several ships annually permitted the Dutch at Deshima. Some commerce was still possible with Korea through the liaison officers of the Daimyo of Tsushima and a small Japanese settlement at Pusan.[2] Furthermore, since the Ming Emperors banned direct trade with Japan, the Tokugawa made temporary concessions to satisfy their desire for Chinese luxuries, silks, and medicines, formerly supplied by the Portuguese through Macao. They permitted the sale of Chinese goods which semi-piratical Chinese merchantmen brought in, having received for themselves in 1635 a monopoly of all raw silk, the most valuable item among the imports.[3] More surprising still, they recognized the suzerainty and trade monopoly in the Ryūkyū Islands[4] which the Daimyo of Satsuma had secured by conquest in 1609 and encouraged the resumption of the ancient tribute-bearing trade missions from Ryūkyū to China. Through this channel additional Chinese luxuries were sold throughout Japan in violation of the Shogun's monopoly at Nagasaki while Satsuma gained strength and profits.

Conditions changed with the lifting of the ban on direct trade with China in 1684. Many Chinese junks bringing rich cargoes to Japan caused such a serious outflow of Japanese metallic currency that in 1715 the *Bakufu* reduced the number of Chinese ships allowed annually in Japan, limited the amount of money to be spent on foreign trade, and restricted Chinese traders to residence in Nagasaki under conditions similar to

[1] Sansom, *History*, iii. 36–37. Ōkurashō (Finance Ministry), *Nihon Zaisei Keizai Shiryō* (Materials on Japanese Finance and Economy), 11 vols. (Tokyo, 1922), iv. 1096–7. The law of 1635 limiting the capacity of ships to 500 *koku* was amended to apply to military ships only in 1638 and vessels of 1,000 *koku* were used in the rapidly growing sea trade in the eighteenth and nineteenth centuries between Hokkaido and the ports along the Japan and Inland Seas as far south as Kagoshima. Robert G. Flershem, 'Some Aspects of Japan Sea Trade in the Tokugawa Period', *The Journal of Asian Studies*, xxiii (May 1964), 405–7.

[2] Hilary Conroy, *The Japanese Seizure of Korea: 1868–1910* (Philadelphia, 1960), p. 22.

[3] Sansom, *History*, iii. 36–37.

[4] Ryūkyū (modern Okinawa) is the Japanese romanization and pronunciation for the same characters, *kanji*, which the Chinese call L'iu Ch'iu and the English in the nineteenth century spelled in many ways, e.g., Lūchū, Loochoo, Lewchew, etc.

those of the Dutch at Deshima. At the same time the Yedo government clamped down on the Satsuma–Ryūkyū tribute trade with China, hoping to bring it under its monopoly at Nagasaki. The government's increasing restrictions on Satsuma's profits during the eighteenth century led Satsuma and Ryūkyū merchants to extensive smuggling operations off the Satsuma coast in spite of the heavy penalties which the *Bakufu* placed on the illicit traffic.[1] And smuggling was still a common practice when the British reopened trade with Japan.

The Shogun, no matter how dissolute, was not only the recognized head of the government and the monopolist of legitimate foreign trade but the most powerful lord in Japan's rigidly stratified feudal order. He and his family owned *han* which provided an income of one-fourth of Japan's average annual rice crop and monopolized the mining of the nation's precious metals. He commanded the allegiance of approximately 260 daimyo who held lands of varying size and value in accordance with the rewards or penalties given to their ancestors after Ieyasu's military victories or as gifts from his successors when lands were confiscated or escheated. Two classes of daimyo, the *fudai* and *tozama*, resulted. The *fudai* (hereditary vassals) were those whose ancestors had supported Ieyasu in his rise to supremacy. Their fiefs were not large, averaging an annual income of around 50,000 *koku* and mostly located in central Japan, making it possible for the régime to dominate Yedo and Kyoto as well as the *Tōkaidō*, the great highway which connected them. In contrast, the *tozama* (outside vassals) were originally those who had sworn fealty only after Ieyasu's victories in 1600 and 1615. Their lands had been reduced[2]— some confiscated—but their fiefs, lying usually in the south, west, and north-east, still accounted for forty per cent. of Japan's annual agricultural production. Always a possible source of subversive activity, the Tokugawa placed *fudai* on their borders to observe and report their movements. Among

---

[1] George H. Kerr, *Okinawa, The History of an Island People* (Tokyo, 1958), pp. 158–68. Robert K. Sakai, 'Satsuma–Ryūkyū Trade and Tokugawa Policy', *The Journal of Asian Studies*, xxiii (May 1964), 391–7.

[2] For example, those of Lord Shimazu, Daimyo of Satsuma, who had owned most of Kyūshū, were cut to two and a half provinces, and those of Lord Mori of Chōshū to a fourth of his previous domain. Albert M. Craig, *Chōshū in the Meiji Restoration* (Cambridge, Mass., 1961), pp. 11–12, 14.

the *tozama* were great daimyo: Maeda of Kaga, Shimazu of Satsuma, Date of Sendai, and several others, who were the wealthiest barons in Japan next to the Shogun. They took advantage of their remote, under-populated domains to bring new areas under cultivation, some more than doubling their tax yield by the nineteenth century, while at the same time they developed greater independence of Yedo—all contrary to the intentions of the early Tokugawa.[1]

In general, however, the policies of the Shoguns to weaken all daimyo financially and prevent disloyal activities were successful. All had to swear allegiance to each incoming Shogun who in turn confirmed them in their fiefs. All were forbidden to contract a marriage or military alliance, even with the Imperial Court, and to build or repair a castle without his consent. It is true they paid no regular taxes to Yedo but were constantly subject to levies for the construction and repair of *Bakufu* buildings and demands for labour and materials for flood control as well as the construction of roads and harbours. Most onerous of all was the *sankin-kōtai* (alternate attendance) system, which required each daimyo to spend four months of the year in Yedo, living in extravagant style under the eyes of the *Bakufu*, and leaving members of his family as hostages when he returned to run his own domain. Failures to comply or disloyalty could entail the transfer of the daimyo to another fief or the reduction or confiscation of his lands altogether.[2]

The daimyo were absolute masters in their own *han*. They had their own warriors and retainers, the samurai, who once followed them in battle but now administered the *han* governments and represented their lords in the numerous villages throughout the domains in return for a stipend paid in rice from the lords' granaries. Their number varied from fief to fief. During the era of peace under the Tokugawa, the samurai had become the governing classes and scholars of Japan, the top of the social structure beneath the daimyo. Their services differed according to their samurai rank, ranging from the formulation of *han* policy and control of finance or archives to those of attendants, scholars, guards, even messengers. All

[1] Sansom, *History*, iii. 19, 210–11. Beasley, *History*, pp. 7–8.

[2] Borton, *Japan's Modern Century*, pp. 18–19. Sansom, *History*, iii. 20–21, 27; *The Western World and Japan*, p. 170.

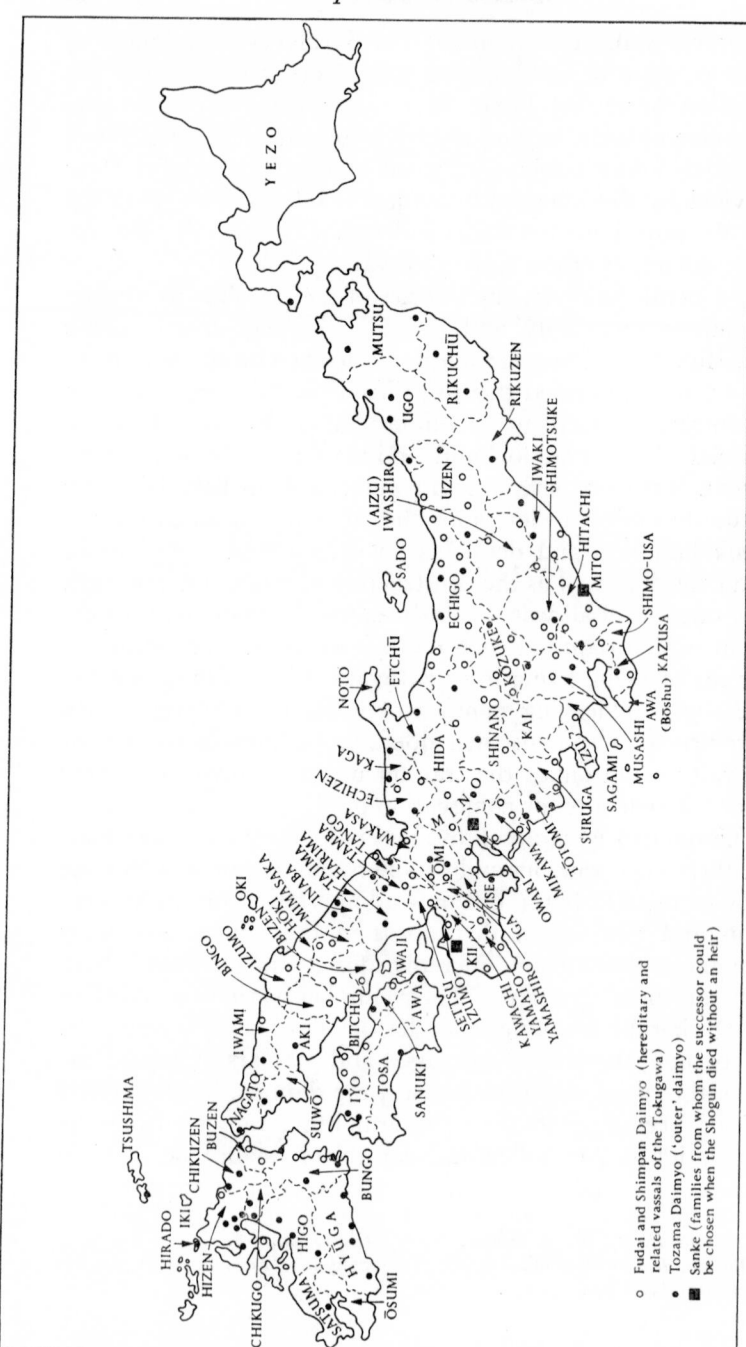

MAP I. PROVINCES OF JAPAN

Distribution of the *Han* of Daimyo assessed at 20,000 *Koku* or more, *circa* 1865

Sources: Shiba Katsumori, *Nihon Rekishi Chizu*, Plate 26 and *Johnson's New Illustrated Family Atlas*, Plate 29

were privileged to wear two swords but their hereditary class divisions were rigid and advance from one to another was rare. Nevertheless, by the late 1830s some daimyo such as Mōri Yoshichika of Chōshū, in search of able young men, were educating lower- and middle-class samurai with a view to advancing them to positions of major responsibility.[1] In all the official schools, those of both the government and the *han*, the Confucian and Buddhist values of loyalty, service, and obligation were instilled to produce men who would put the welfare of their group, whether family or domain, above their own, and who through diligence and economy in their administrative duties were expected to express such loyalty.[2]

Many samurai lost their masters and livelihood when their domains were confiscated or escheated to the Shogun. These were the *rōnin*—the ubiquitous trouble-makers of the Tokugawa régime. Unknown thousands of them roamed the countryside or took refuge in the cities, seeking adventure while nourishing their grievances. Varying in character from knights-errant to vulgar rowdies, their numbers and importance grew with the development of an anti-*Bakufu* sentiment in the mid nineteenth century. They became an unpredictable, often violent, element never to be ignored in the politics of the day.[3]

Beneath the samurai in Japan's descending social order were the farmers, the artisans, and the merchants (*chōnin*). Although recognized as the foundation of the nation because they produced her rice, the farmers were expected to live a frugal, often primitive existence, yielding at least fifty per cent. of their produce as taxes to their lord. They constituted four-fifths of the total population of 30 million, which had changed little since 1750. Living in more than 63,000 villages which their leaders governed under *han* supervision, they ranged from well-to-do landholders and minimal cultivators of the soil to serf-like labourers or servants who were not subject to tax. To keep society static early Tokugawa laws prohibited their selling their lands, dividing their property, and leaving their occupation.[4]

---

[1] Beasley, *History*, p. 34. Craig, op. cit., p. 60.
[2] Beasley, *History*, pp. 11–12.
[3] Sansom, *History*, iii. 32–34; *The Western World and Japan*, pp. 190–2.
[4] Ibid., pp. 224–5. Hugh Borton, *Peasant Uprisings in Japan of the Tokugawa Period* (*T.A.S.J.*, 1937), pp. 6–8. Irene B. Taeuber, *The Population of Japan* (Princeton, 1958), p. 37.

The lot of this class was frequently intolerable. In spite of the death penalty for those implicated there were over a thousand peasant uprisings owing to economic, financial, or administrative grievances during the Tokugawa period. Extra taxes to meet increasing demands of the *Bakufu* upon their *han*, monopoly prices for their produce, dishonest surveys of their land for tax purposes, harshness of the official representatives of their daimyo, the removal of their daimyo from one fief to another, as well as the ravages of famine resulting from floods, droughts, and pestilence, caused great suffering among them. With the deterioration of the *Bakufu* authority and because of a series of national calamities in the first half of the nineteenth century, uprisings became more widespread and involved great numbers of people. In 1823 in Kii, for example, 100,000 farmers rose in revolt in consequence of the corruption of the *bugyō* in co-operation with the rice merchants. Though seldom because of class lines, *rōnin* and townsmen sometimes allied themselves with the farmers, as in 1837 in Osaka, to rebel against official corruption and an unreasonable price of rice. All these revolts were local. None aimed at either the overthrow of the feudal system or the *Bakufu*. Occasionally, the rioters gained their ends. Even offending high officials were dismissed. But the persistence of disturbances and discontent made agricultural unrest a serious concern of the *Bakufu* when the Westerners demanded entrance to Japan.[1]

Farmers not only rioted. Some absconded to the castle towns or great cities, creating a new class of manual labourer and servant. If sufficiently skilled, they were absorbed into the third social class, the artisans. Here again the members varied in their importance and rewards, ranging from the sword-makers, gold- and silversmiths, and highly gifted artists who served the Shogun's court, to artisans living simply in the castle towns, the producers of luxuries and necessities for the samurai and neighbouring farms. Some artisans were part-time farmers; some farmers, part-time artisans who kept their families in the neighbouring villages.

Although industry remained in the handicraft stage until the 1850s, native skills had reached high levels in the production of

---

[1] Borton, *Peasant Uprisings*, pp. 17–30, 87–89, 93–97, 121–6.

porcelain ware, lacquer, paper, silks, and brocades.[1] Each trade had its own guild to protect its interests and a rigid system of apprenticeship. Different areas became known for different commodities which were sent to the great cities of Yedo, Osaka, and Kyoto for distribution. Thus the Kantō provinces east of Yedo were famous for lacquer and drapers, Aizu for candles, Kawachi for cotton cloths, etc.[2]

Merchants (*chōnin*), theoretically at the bottom of the Tokugawa social scale because they produced nothing and aimed for profit, rose to positions of power and influence as the creditors of the Shogunate and the warrior classes during the long period of peace. Their social stigma was not consistently a handicap, nor were they ever free from the possibility of injustice and exploitation in contempt for it.[3] The early Tokugawa Shoguns not only encouraged merchant activities by a nation-wide unification of currency,[4] weights, and measures, but employed several wealthy *chōnin* as fiscal and economic advisers to the government. Daimyo generally welcomed and utilized merchants in their domains as their source of goods and money through the sale of their tax rice or for advance credit on future crops.[5]

With the peace of the latter half of the seventeenth century came the building of good roads, improved methods of agriculture, the increase and diversification of crops, the growth of home industries—even small factories in the silk-producing areas—and a vast expansion of internal commerce.[6] The use of money rapidly invaded the rice economy of the feudal order. As the standard of living improved and Shogus, daimyo, warriors, and farmers all sought luxuries and urban entertainment, the tendency to evaluate everything in terms of money increased.

[1] Sansom, *History*, iii. 31. Borton, *Japan's Modern Century*, p. 18. Henry Rosovsky, *Capital Formation in Japan, 1868–1940* (New York, 1961), pp. 70, 86.

[2] Honjō Eijirō, *The Social and Economic History of Japan* (Kyoto, 1935), p. 74.

[3] Horie Yasuzō, 'The Feudal States and the Commercial Society in the Tokugawa Period', *Kyoto University Economic Review*, xxviii (Oct. 1958), 12. Charles David Sheldon, *The Rise of the Merchant Class in Tokugawa Japan 1600–1868* (Locust Valley, New York, 1958), pp. 101–30.

[4] The *ryō* was made the unit of gold currency. It weighed slightly more than six ounces avoirdupois and contained 67·7 per cent. of gold, 27·8 per cent. of silver, and 4·5 per cent. of copper. Sansom, *History*, iii. 5.

[5] Horie, *Kyoto University Economic Review*, xxviii, (Oct. 1958).

[6] Fairbank, Reischauer, and Craig, op. cit. ii. 189–90. Horie, *Kyoto University Economic Review*, xxviii, (Oct. 1958). 8. Crawcour, op. cit., p. 396.

The production of rice soon failed to meet the demand for the things money could buy. Prices rose. The population shifted. Castle towns grew into small cities while Yedo, Osaka, and Kyoto became populous metropolitan centres where great merchants and moneylenders bought the tax rice and local products of the *han*, made long-term loans at an annual interest of fifteen to twenty per cent., and mortgaged future crops. Organizations of wholesale merchants and shippers (*tonya*) developed a wholesale trade between the western provinces and Yedo, and secured exclusive privileges as government-licensed monopoly companies between the 1760s and 1841. The *han* had their own marketing boards which sought to market their local products and circumvent these government-sponsored organizations. By the 1820s or 1830s prosperous farmer-businessmen, the new leaders of the village communities in the economically advanced areas, developed local trade which challenged the established commercial channels. In 1859 Kyoto, which had once had almost a monopoly, supplied only ten per cent. of the silk fabric brought into Yedo. In Tosa businessmen became members of the lower-class samurai who like those in Chōshū promoted reform movements in the *han*, presaging a new national order.[1] In spite of Confucian tenets and *Bakufu* restraints, there is no doubt of a widespread commercial-mindedness in Japan by the mid nineteenth century.

Given the extensive development of a money economy and the power of the rising commercial classes, great changes in Japan's feudal order were inevitable. Financial distress became general as the money value of the rice revenues of both the *Bakufu* and the daimyo was seldom sufficient to meet the rising costs of living. The Shogunate's expenditures on luxuries, charity, music, and public works, and the huge sums required for the relief of victims of fires and earthquakes, soon depleted the great fortune Ieyasu had bequeathed to his successors. Further difficulties caused by decreasing outputs of gold and silver, the flight of specie abroad through the Dutch and China trade, and corruption among the administrators of finance had brought the Shogunate to the verge of bankruptcy by the end of the seventeenth century.[2]

[1] Crawcour, op. cit., pp. 392, 396–9.
[2] Honjō, *The Social and Economic History of Japan*, pp. 269–71.

Additional rice taxes could not be carried beyond production possibilities, and years of bad harvests had to be expected. Hence the *Bakufu* resorted to other methods to secure the extra cash which bad administration and national disasters periodically made necessary for the maintenance of solvency. Debasement of the coinage three times between 1696 and 1711 proved so successful that it became a regular way of raising funds. Soon afterwards the government began requiring annual cash payments from merchant associations in return for the grant of monopoly rights. The levying of forced loans on the rich merchants of Osaka began in 1761–2 and became frequent after 1800—a source which yielded 1·4 million *ryō* between 1853–60. Such loans (*goyō-kin*) were seldom repaid. Yearly cash deficits were the rule in the nineteenth century—amounting annually to at least 740,000 *ryō* between 1854 and 1856—while the measures to reduce them further jeopardized the stability of the feudal order. All caused commodity prices to rise, thus increasing the difficulty for retainers to make ends meet on a fixed stipend payable in rice.[1] And *Bakufu* efforts to ease their plight periodically by exhortation to frugality, the cancellation of samurai debts, or control of the interest thereon, availed little save to remind the merchants that they were not the governors of Japan.

The financial burdens of the daimyo were as great, sometimes greater, as those of the Shogunate. Most costly was their required residence in Yedo. The impressive processions to and fro and the maintenance of elaborate mansions (*yashiki*) in the capital had to be paid for in cash. To meet these demands the daimyo opened up new lands, secured monopolies of the sale of local products, issued provincial paper money, reduced the number of their retainers, or cut their stipends—as much as fifty per cent.—in the name of 'borrowing', and imposed heavier taxes on the peasantry. All with only limited success and at heavy social costs. Their expenditures usually exceeded their revenues and their indebtedness, plus interest, increased. The experience of the Toda family who borrowed 453 *kan* of silver (about 50,000 ounces troy) from an Osaka merchant between

[1] Beasley, *History*, pp. 24–25. Tsuchiya Takao, *An Economic History of Japan*, translation by Shidehara Michitaro, revised by Neil Skene Smith, *T.A.S.J.*, Second Series, xv (Tokyo, 1937), pp. 227–8.

1750 and 1772, and owed nearly 500,000 ounces in interest alone by 1836, shows what could and did happen. *Fudai* and *tozama* daimyo alike faced overwhelming debts. Those of Kanazawa, the richest of the latter class, approached three or four times its annual revenue in 1785. Satsuma owed about 5 million *ryō* in 1829, Chōshū more than 1·3 million in 1840.[1]

Both samurai and peasant registered discontent. The warrior class, impoverished and softened during years without war and eager for the urban luxuries of the day, stooped to unworthy practices. Many mortgaged their stipends or pawned their ceremonial attire. Others sacrificed moral integrity for small sums of money, adopted sons of more prosperous men as heirs, and sold the status of samurai to wealthy commoners. Purity of blood was surrendered for gain as commoners sought higher social station. Other warriors grew prosperous or earned a modest living by entering trade themselves. Some chose to be *rōnin*. Many, however, remaining in the service of the great daimyo held to the standards of the warrior-scholar class. Here a small number interested in economics and politics began to see the need of sweeping change—even the abolition of the exclusion policy—to improve Japan's economic condition.[2]

The break in the exclusion policy began in the early eighteenth century when Japanese scholars recognized the need for at least intellectural contacts with foreign countries. Reports of European developments in the arts and sciences from Dutch traders and the occasional learned men who accompanied the annual Dutch mission to Yedo led the enlightened Shogun, Yoshimuni, in 1720 to permit the importation of Chinese books which did not mention Christian teaching, thus making available Chinese translations of European works. He also ordered Japanese scholars to study the Dutch language. The first Japanese–Dutch dictionary, completed in 1758, facilitated the growing interest in Western ideas which then spread throughout the country with encouragement from the *Bakufu*.[3] Many scholars were attracted to Dutch studies (*rangaku*), especially

---

[1] Sansom, *History*, iii. 212–13. Beasley, *History*, p. 29. Tsuchiya, op. cit., pp. 228–233. *Kan* = 3·75 kilogrammes.

[2] Sansom, *The Western World and Japan*, pp. 233–5; *History*, iii. 128, 187–8. Honjō, Eijirō, *The Social and Economic History of Japan*, pp. 217–20.

[3] Sansom, *History*, iii. 168–70, 188–9.

to medicine and astronomy. By the end of the eighteenth century, however, accounts of British expansion in India and Russian activities in the North Pacific made military sciences and economic reforms the chief concern of the scholars. The subsequent appearance of Russian, British, and American ships at Japanese ports to return castaways, survey Japanese waters, or open trade in the early nineteenth century convinced many that Japan could not permanently escape the demands of the West and that neither her economy nor her defences were adequate to the encounter.[1] In general the leaders of Japanese thought agreed even before Perry that Japan must buy or build the powerful weapons used by the West in the interest of self-defence.[2] At least fifty *han* established schools for the study of Western medicine and military science with an emphasis on gunnery, which exerted great influence on public opinion as the foreign danger increased.[3]

At the risk of imprisonment and execution, individuals and groups circulated diverse proposals for political and economic reforms. To both the government and the Confucian scholars exponents of change were suspect. Intrigues against them became common, the penalties severe. Nevertheless, in the early decades of the nineteenth century thoughtful men advocated in unpublished works the abrogation of the exclusion policy and the expansion of foreign trade to remedy Japan's economic plight;[4] others openly accused the *Bakufu* of ignorance and incompetence and were executed.[5]

There had also been National Scholars from 1680 onwards whose interest in classical Japanese studies and a revival of the Shinto religion produced a loyalist school of thought. Here the emphasis on the belief in the Emperor as the direct descendant of the Sun Goddess fortified chauvinistic and anti-foreign propaganda in the nineteenth century and a renewed reverence

---

[1] Ibid. 202–5; *The Western World and Japan*, pp. 243–7.
[2] Beasley, *Documents*, p. 5. [3] Sansom, *History*, iii. 232.
[4] For example, Yamagata Banto (1789–1821), a merchant scholar, Honda Toshiaki (1744–1821), a great Dutch scholar, Satō Nobuhirō (Shun'en) (1769–1850), who pointed to England as a country of limited resources which attained wealth and power through foreign trade, and Takashima Shūhan (1798–1866), the specialist in Dutch military drill and ordnance who after imprisonment on false charges was released in 1853 to make ordnance for the *Bakufu* after Perry's demands had alarmed the government. Sheldon, op. cit., pp. 136–7. Sansom, *The Western World and Japan*, pp. 248–9. [5] Idem., *History*, iii. 230.

for the Emperor as the prestige of the *Bakufu* declined.[1] A great work, the *Dai Nihon Shi* (History of Japan), begun by Mito scholars in 1657 and published as a whole in 1851,[2] undergirded further a growing loyalist sentiment with the view that the dynasty was 'the institutional and personal embodiment of the unity and continuity of the Japanese nation' and supernatural in its origin. It proclaimed that no man or agency could govern the country without Imperial sanction. And if such authority were delegated, the same loyalty was exacted of the recipient as of any other Japanese subject. To some this appeared an indirect challenge to the legitimacy of the Tokugawa Shogunate.[3]

These loyalist ideas had much to do with the reform movement in Mito which differed radically in its goal from that of those who wanted to open the country. Here men sought to arouse Japan to the foreign danger and to unite the country in its own defence. They conceded that new weapons, including Western-style ships, financial reforms, and the promotion of men of ability were required but above all it was necessary to revive Japan's traditional spirit and overcome luxury and lethargy. This must involve, they declared, the government's fixed determination to defend the seclusion policy and reject all foreign demands for the opening of the country to foreign trade. Hence the slogan *jōi* (expel the barbarian) arose.

By 1853 Mito scholars in their desire to achieve national strength and international equality intimated doubts about the character of the *Bakufu* leadership. Some proposed that the Shogun seek the advice of great daimyo in addition to his usual Tokugawa advisers; others maintained the Emperor must again become a 'focus of national government creating unity by transcending other loyalties'. This in turn led to another cry, *son nō* (honour the Emperor) which after 1858 was united with that to expel the foreigners.[4]

The Daimyo of Mito, Tokugawa Nariaki (1800–60), was

---

[1] Sansom, *Western World and Japan*, pp. 210–11. Beasley, *History*, p. 51. For examples of Japanese chauvinistic literature, see writings of Motoori Norinaga (1730–1801) and Hirata Atsutane (1776–1843).

[2] See 1851 edition in 243 *kan* (books) in the Library of Congress.

[3] Herschel Webb, 'What is the Dai Nihon Shi', *The Journal of Asian Studies*, xix Feb. (1960), 146, 148. Borton, *Japan's Modern Century*, p. 21.

[4] Beasley, *History*, pp. 50–51.

himself the leader of the *jōi* adherents. Openly he advocated
expulsion, even if it involved war. A tempestuous man—not
always consistent—who as head of one of the *Sanke* had great
prestige, Nariaki was traditionally hostile to the Tokugawa in
spite of being a descendant of Ieyasu. He found in the *jōi* movement a means of attacking the *Bakufu*. He was also one of the
great daimyo who initiated reforms in his own fief, thus increasing its local strength and independence. He appointed
capable officials, reduced administrative expenses, established
village schools for the people and public granaries for famine
relief. Although hating foreign trade, he saw the necessity of
adopting Western industrialization and defence techniques in
order to repel the West. He recalled his samurai to their villages,
cancelled their debts, and instituted annual military manœuvres
and the casting of cannon without Yedo's consent. Such defiance
of the *Bakufu* regulations for internal security led to his home
arrest in 1844 for four years. Thereafter with Satsuma's help
he established an iron industry and was building Western-style
ships on a small scale by 1858.[1]

The *hans* of Hizen, Satsuma, Chōshū, and Tosa were also
distinguished for their industrial and military progress before
1858. Since the Daimyo of Hizen was responsible for the
defences of Nagasaki he had the benefit of *Bakufu* support in
the building of the reverberatory furnace for the production of
iron for *Bakufu* cannon and other weapons. Mito and Satsuma
men came to study these processes which began making cannon
in 1853. Hizen further experimented with shipbuilding and
ordered a complete shipbuilding plant from Holland in 1856.[2]

Both Satsuma and Chōshū began radical reforms in the
1840s or slightly earlier which made them financially solvent,
and initiated industrial and military programmes with an eye
to increasing their independence of the *Bakufu*. Satsuma produced guns by some Western techniques as early as 1846,
copied Hizen's reverberatory and blast furnaces for the production of its own modern weapons, and began to train
infantry, cavalry, and even a Western-style navy in the 1850s,
while purchasing European ships abroad. At the same time the
progressive Daimyo Shimazu Nariakira (1809–58) accumulated

[1] Ibid., p. 53; *Documents*, pp. 11–14. Borton, *Japan's Modern Century*, p. 24.
[2] Beasley, *History*, pp. 36, 53–54.

great profits from the Ryūkyū Island trade and sponsored the use of Western methods in non-military industries. By early 1858 a Dutch observer estimated that the domain employed over 1,200 men in the making of leather goods, paper, iron tools, glass, and porcelain.[1] Here as in Chōshū lay a traditional anti-*Bakufu* sentiment although neither fief at this time was planning the overthrow of the Shogunate. But in financial stability and industrial and military equipment they were fast approaching a position which might well alarm the Shogunate.

The daimyo were far more successful than the *Bakufu* in their domestic reforms. Yedo's legislation to control corruption, curtail extravagance, and increase production from 1786 to 1793 and again between 1841 and 1843 brought no lasting improvements as long as the government refused to recognize the economic penalties of its exclusion system.[2] Even after the early threats of foreign ships in Japanese waters the *Bakufu* tightened its isolation policy, ordering all coastal daimyo in 1825 to drive away by gunfire any foreign vessel approaching their shores and to kill members of the crew who landed in their territory. The summary execution of this order on the unarmed American ship *Morrison* in 1837, however, led thoughtful Japanese to fear retaliation by more powerful Western ships. In consequence the decree was modified in 1842 when coastal officials were told to furnish food and fuel to foreign ships while advising them to go away.[3] This order was carried out unevenly until 8 July 1853 when Commodore Perry arrived in Yedo Bay with four American gunboats and a letter from President Fillmore asking for trade with Japan, humane treatment of shipwrecked sailors, and the opening of a port for American steamers to obtain coal and provisions.[4]

Rapid changes in *Bakufu* policy on all fronts followed. Perry's promise to return to receive Japan's answer to America's requests made it necessary to act quickly. The now frightened dictatorship ordered all coastal defences to be strengthened, permitting individual daimyo—both *tozama* and *fudai*—to purchase cannon and ships directly from the Dutch or to build

[1] Beasley, *History*, pp. 33–35, 54–55.
[2] Sansom, *The Western World and Japan*, pp. 207–9.
[3] Idem., *History*, iii. 228.
[4] Beasley, *Documents*, pp. 99–101, Millard Fillmore, President of the United States of America, to His Imperial Majesty the Emperor of Japan, 13 Nov. 1852.

them in their own *han*.[1] Even the restrictions on the size of
vessels were removed in 1853 so that the daimyo could build
large ships.[2] The government itself founded a naval training
school with Dutch instructors in 1855, began shipbuilding at
Uraga and Shimoda in 1855–6, and started the construction of
an iron foundry at Nagasaki in 1857.[3]

At the same time the Shogun whose primary duty was the
protection of the realm notified the Imperial Court of Perry's
mission and the head of the *Rōjū*, Abe Masahiro, took an
ominous step. In the hope of uniting the nation in a common
programme Abe ordered a translation of Fillmore's letter sent
to all the daimyo—both *fudai* and *tozama*—the leading *Bakufu*
officials, the chief Confucian scholars, independent warriors,
and merchants, requesting their advice even if contrary to
established policy. This was an admission of weakness. The
fact that the *Bakufu* needed and sought counsel beyond that of
the councillors shocked the country. The replies brought into
the open sharp divisions of opinion throughout the nation which
paralleled those within the *Bakufu* itself. In general there was
an emphasis on defence and a dislike for trade. A powerful
minority of daimyo (including those of Hizen, Chōshū, and
Tosa) supported Nariaki of Mito who recommended an
adamant refusal to the American requests, the continuing of
seclusion, and the immediate strengthening of Japan's defences;
others, like Ii Naosuke, the rich *fudai* daimyo of Hikone, looked
upon trade as unavoidable, or even desirable as a means of
paying for Japan's armaments and were willing to make concessions to avoid a military defeat; about a third argued with
Shimazu Nariakira of Satsuma for a conciliatory reply to the
West without in fact making any concessions; and the Court
at Kyoto upheld those who wanted Perry sent home without
a treaty which seriously increased the difficulties of the policy
makers at Yedo.[4]

These conflicting opinions caused the *Rōjū* to compromise.
In a formal announcement to the daimyo on 1 December 1853
they promised to attempt to persuade Perry to leave without a

[1] Borton, *Japan's Modern Century*, pp. 31–32.

[2] Ishin Shiryō Hensan Kakari (Official Compiler of Restoration Materials),
Ed., *Ishin Shi* (History of the Restoration), 6 vols. (Tokyo, 1939), ii. 142–3.

[3] Beasley, *History*, p. 55.

[4] Borton, *Japan's Modern Century*, pp. 32–35. Beasley, *Documents*, p. 23.

definite answer to the American requests while making every reasonable effort for the maintenance of peace, but should they fail and Perry resort to force, all must meanwhile make preparations to defend the national honour loyally.[1] Thus they left themselves freedom to decide policy in the light of conditions they could not foresee. But Perry would take neither procrastination nor negation. His return in February 1854 with eight warships and the threat of still greater force made minimum concessions necessary, if war were to be avoided. And the preservation of peace had to be Japan's main concern.

Although these concessions[2] prevented war and postponed the opening of Japan to American trade, they intensified the divisions of opinion within the country, sharpened the personal animosity between leaders like Ii Naosuke and Tokugawa Nariaki, and heightened the growing criticism of the *Bakufu*, giving the *jōi* party greater determination to effect drastic reforms. Rival groups—those who saw the necessity of opening the country, *kaikoku*, and those who opposed the treaties with the West, *jōi*—were in conflict thereafter not only over foreign policy which became a major issue in domestic politics but over the control of the *Rōjū* and the choice of the Shogun's successor. As the Shogun who had come into power in the summer of 1853 was expected to die childless, intrigues in favour of either the first cousin of the incumbent and nearest in descent, Tokugawa Iemochi of Kii (1846–66), then a mere boy, or in support of the seventh son of Tokugawa Nariaki of Mito, Hitotsubashi Keiki, a young man of promise, lay in the background of all major political struggles until midsummer 1858.[3]

The *Rōjū* yielded to the demands of Britain and Russia for treaties modelled on that of the United States in 1854 and 1855 while Abe entrusted Nariaki with preparations for the defence of Japan, established a new office for the study of Western writings, particularly those dealing with military science and technology[4] and, at Nariaki's bidding, in the interest of more

---

[1] Beasley, *Documents*, p. 24.   [2] See p. 10.
[3] Borton, *Japan's Modern Century*, pp. 39–40.
[4] This was the *Bansho Torishirabe-, dokoro* established in Yedo in 1856 where to Dutch works the study of English, French, German, Russian, and a little chemistry were added in 1860. The name of the office was changed in 1862 to *Yoshō Shirabejo* when it began to send students abroad for study, and to *Kaiseijo* in 1863. It became part of Tokyo Imperial University in 1877. Beasley, *Documents*, p. 26. Sansom, *The Western World and Japan*, pp. 434, 451; *History*, iii. 234.

official competence dismissed some of the entrenched *fudai* officials from the government. Opposition to this last drastic action led to Abe's resignation as senior minister in November 1855, the exclusion of Nariaki from the inner councils, and in further proof of a reversal of policy, to Abe's appointment of Hotta Masayoshi as his successor.[1]

Hotta in common with Ii Naosuke had supported the conclusion of treaties with the West in 1853. With him at the helm efforts and pressures were soon directed towards extending Japan's arrangements for foreign trade. Donker Curtius, the Dutch Minister in Nagasaki, had succeeded in removing some restrictions on the trade at Deshima when in the summer of 1856 Townsend Harris took up residence at Shimoda as the first American consul bent on achieving a commercial treaty for the United States. Both Curtius and Harris then used their knowledge of British plans to send Sir John Bowring, the Superintendent of Trade at Hong Kong, to Japan to seek an agreement for trade, to persuade the Yedo government that making treaties amicably with them under no threat of force would be wiser than yielding to British demands backed by a powerful fleet. Such treaties, they argued, could then be used as a base for the inevitable concessions to Albion.

The outbreak of Britain's second war with China, it has been shown, prevented Bowring's arrival but Japan went ahead with preparations for an eventual deal with the British. The Shogun made Hotta responsible for the conduct of foreign affairs in November 1856, thus acknowledging the official decision to extend the foreign treaties, and a commission of 'able and experienced' Yedo officials was set up to study foreign trade. Further reports of British aggression in China in 1857 spurred their efforts to agree upon concessions both favourable to the *Bakufu* and sufficiently satisfying to the West to save Japan from a fate similar to China's. For this purpose the *Rōjū* sent two officials representing the right and left wings of the *kaikoku* adherents to Nagasaki in May 1857 to discuss with Donker Curtius the minimal provisions for a commercial treaty acceptable to the West. The draft of a treaty resulted which was sent to Yedo for approval in late August. In the absence of any reply by October and under sudden pressure for a treaty by

---

[1] Beasley, *History*, p. 61; *Documents*, pp. 25–26. Abe remained in *Rōjū* until 1857.

Russia, the *Bakufu* emissaries signed their treaty with the Dutch on 16 October 1857.[1] This gave private merchants the right to unlimited trade at Nagasaki and Hakodate under official supervision. Many restrictions, however, and a duty of thirty-five per cent. on goods sold at public sale or by private contract were imposed. The Russians were satisfied with a similar treaty a week later and the *Bakufu* accepted both agreements as the maximum to be granted the West.[2]

Harris, however, viewed these treaties with contempt. After attaining an audience with the Shogun that December, the American consul made clear his minimum requirements for a commercial treaty. He again exaggerated the imminence of Britain's armed demands when her struggle in China ended, urging peaceful negotiations on a basis of equality with himself. He insisted that the terms of the Dutch and Russian treaties be modified in the case of a treaty with the United States to permit 'the residence of an American minister in Yedo, trade without official interference, and an increase in the number of open ports'.[3]

The *Rōjū* then took another poll of feudal opinion which indicated great changes since 1853. Many daimyo now recognized that the time for seclusion had passed. Even Nariaki of Mito deserted his *jōi* extremists to the extent of suggesting that he himself be sent to America as Japan's emissary for trade and friendship although he continued to oppose the admission of foreigners to Yedo. Enough important officials backed Hotta in his belief that it was imperative for Japan to expand her trade, rearm, form alliances, and adopt the foreign ways necessary to fortify her against the West to make him agree to negotiate on the basis of Harris's requirements excepting that involving the opening of more ports. By patience equal to his determination the American won all his major points, including the opening of Nagasaki and Kanagawa in 1859 in addition to Shimoda and Hakodate, already open; Niigata in 1860, Hyogo in 1863, and the admission of merchants to Yedo in 1862 and Osaka in 1863.[4] But the text of the treaty ready for signature on 23 February 1858 met unexpected opposition.

---

[1] Beasley, *Documents*, pp. 27–31; *History*, pp. 64–65.
[2] Idem., *Documents*, pp. 149–55.   [3] Ibid., pp. 31–33, 159–65; *History*, pp. 65–66.
[4] Ibid., pp. 66–68; *Documents*, pp. 165–80.

The majority of daimyo then resident in Yedo opposed Hotta's concessions to Harris. They seemed dangerously beyond those which they had been willing to accept in the Dutch treaty. Hotta sought to silence this outcry by securing the Emperor's public sanction for his policy. Bribery and threats, his retainers believed, would accomplish this readily in Kyoto. But on this issue such methods proved inadequate. When Hotta arrived in the Emperor's capital he found he could count on the support of only two or three Court officials, the representatives of Nariaki and Ii, and a few great *fudai* daimyo. Kyoto had become the hotbed of all anti-*Bakufu* elements: those Mito men who without Nariaki's support were promoting the *jōi* arguments; the critics of the *Bakufu* weakness who favoured the choice of Hitotsubashi Keiki to strengthen its leadership; those who wanted domestic reform to precede the opening of the country; those who attributed to the *Bakufu* a spineless subservience to the hated foreigner; and those who believed in the future restoration of Imperial rule.[1]

To these men Hotta's request for Imperial approval of his treaty offered a great opportunity to challenge *Bakufu* policy as a whole and to register general disapproval by urging the rejection of the agreement with Harris. Influential *kuge* including Iwakura Tomomi and Sanjō Sanetsumu, and even the Emperor himself, resisted the treaty. An Imperial decree of 3 May ordered Hotta to reconsider his policy in consultation with the *Sanke* and other daimyo and report further to the Court.[2] This meant a complete rejection of the treaty. It was a deliberate affront to Yedo which indicated new strength and new tactics in the Emperor's Court.

This was a crisis—a turning-point—in *Bakufu* history. Before Hotta could get back to Yedo the *Bakufu* appointed a *Tairō* or Regent in an effort to recoup and strengthen its authority. Against the wishes of the Hitotsubashi party, the Shogun entrusted Ii Naosuke with this office on 4 June 1858, thus giving him the supreme power in the régime.[3] The great Daimyo of Hikone was by nature a dictator, decisive and ruthless in action, who had no interest in government reform or Western ideas as such. He had supported the foreign treaties

[1] Ibid., pp. 40–41; *History*, pp. 68–69.   [2] Idem., *Documents*, pp. 180–1.
[3] Ibid., pp. 41–42.

merely as the unavoidable expedients of the time, continuing to look upon foreign traders and foreign commerce with suspicion. His main purpose was to maintain traditional *Bakufu* power unchanged and to brook no outside interference with its policy. Almost immediately he cast the die in the selection of Tokugawa Iemochi for the next Shogun, and set about dismissing from office the men who had backed the candidacy of Hitotsubashi Keiki, including Hotta himself, and placing Nariaki of Mito under 'house arrest'.[1]

Near the end of July Ii had to make the great decision regarding the American treaty in light of reports from Harris that the Anglo-French victory in China had been complete and that British and French representatives would soon reach Japan to demand a commercial treaty. So convincing was Harris that the *Bakufu* should sign the American treaty at once to avoid national disgrace by yielding to the British under force that he persuaded Ii's advisers and Ii himself that this alone was the long-range patriotic policy. Although reluctant to act without the Emperor's assent, Ii took the responsibility upon himself and on 29 July 1858[2] ordered the treaty to be signed. Five days later Lord Elgin arrived at Nagasaki abroad the battleship *Furious*. And before the British negotiations were completed the *Bakufu* had signed treaties with both Russia and Holland similar to that negotiated by Harris.[3]

Ii's summary actions had consolidated the political alignments and strengthened anti-*Bakufu* factions. Thereafter the *Tairō's* only dependable supporters were the more conservative *fudai*. With his signing of the treaties the *jōi* party, soon united with the advocates of *son nō*, formed a confirmed opposition centring in Kyoto and demanding the abrogation of the treaties, while those who had advocated the opening of the country (*kaikoku*) gathered around the *Bakufu* in Yedo.

Between the two parties was a potentially powerful third group—the great *tozama* daimyo, Yamanouchi Toyoshige of Tosa, Date Muneki of Uwajima, the new leader of Satsuma, Shimazu Hisamitsu, and even the *fudai*, Matsudaira Keiei of

[1] Beasley, *History*, pp. 72–73.

[2] Idem., *Documents*, pp. 43 and 181–3, Journal of Utsuki Roku-no-jō, Secretary to Ii, entry 29 July 1858.

[3] Like terms were granted to France in negotiations with Baron Gros in Oct. 1858. Beasley, *History*, pp. 69–70.

Fukui (also known as Shungaku). All had supported Hitot-subashi for Shogun; all thought the concessions made in the treaties excessive but were not against opening the country. Their main concern was to reform the *Bakufu*, not overthrow it. And in so doing to gain for themselves and the Court a voice in the making of policy. Since their alignment with the Hitot-subashi party excluded them from influence at Yedo they turned to the senior nobles in Kyoto to make their wishes felt, hoping to effect a unified Japan at least in its dealings with the West. Thus they espoused a *kōbu-gattai* (Court-*Bakufu* unity) movement, urging *Bakufu* acceptance of the co-operation of the Court and great daimyo in the determination of policy and the Court's recognition of the necessity of limited agreements with the West.[1]

Each party had its followers in Kyoto or Yedo: ambitious young samurai seeking advancement, scholars concerned with changing or reaffirming the old order, and irresponsible hangers-on, *rōnin* or others bent on adventure. Each group had factions within itself and members sometimes moved from one to another as internal and external conditions changed. Allegiances could be temporary and issues confused in the inevitable struggle for power.

Japan was obviously heading towards a great political upheaval in the summer of 1858. Given the discontent of the peasantry and small townsmen living at subsistence levels, the bankruptcy of the government, and the incompetence of its officials, the Shogunate was already doomed when it signed the treaties. But the incoming Westerners had no immediate way to comprehend these facts. They could deal only with the *Bakufu* which had absolute control over the opened ports. And the *Bakufu* sought by duplicity, delays, and fake promises to both the Court and the treaty nations to hold on to its dictatorial power and feudal privileges regardless of the welfare of the Japanese people. With such tactics in mind, its ministers met Lord Elgin, the envoy of the most dreaded nation in the West.

[1] Idem., *Documents*, pp. 43–47.

II

BRITISH POLICIES AND PROBLEMS AT THE OPENING OF THE JAPANESE PORTS

The Treaty of Yedo

LORD Elgin was pressed for time. He hoped at least to explore the possibilities of a treaty with Japan and then return to China within a month. Contrary to Japanese expectations, his intentions were peaceful. He deeply regretted Britain's policy in China and did not wish to repeat it in Japan.[1] Moreover, his instruction from Lord Clarendon, Foreign Secretary, in 1857, had forbidden the use of force to obtain his ends.[2] Even his naval escort was small: a steam frigate, H.M.S. *Retribution*, a gunboat, *Lee*, and the *Emperor*, a steam yacht to be presented to the Shogun as a gift from Queen Victoria.[3] Elgin disregarded Japanese harbour regulations and laws at will and, against the protests of officials at Nagasaki and Shimoda, insisted upon going to Yedo to open treaty negotiations.[4] There he encountered skilful diplomats among the *Bakufu* and, yielding to

---

[1] Beasley, *Great Britain and the Opening of Japan*, pp. 184–7.

[2] Great Britain, House of Commons, *Sessional Papers* (hereafter cited as Parliamentary Papers, House of Commons, or P.P. H. of C.), 1859, xxxiii. 6–7, Clarendon to Elgin, 20 Apr. 1857.

[3] Ad. I/5693, Seymour to Adm., No. 272, 20 Aug. 1858. *North China Herald*, 21 Aug. 1858. A description of the yacht appeared in the *North China Herald* 12 June 1858 when the ship awaited Lord Elgin at Shanghai. The little vessel was 153 feet long, its beam 21½ feet, its burthen 318 tons. When loaded she drew 10½ feet of water. She was rigged as a three-masted schooner with topsail forward. She had 60-horsepower engines but her steam power was purely auxiliary. Her screw lifted up, making her a sailing vessel. She had a complement of 39 officers and men. She had two saloons. Both were panelled in bird's-eye maple with furniture of the same wood. The upholstery of the state saloon was maple green gold and velvet. The bedroom was furnished with pale green chintz and curtains to match. Its carpet was of velvet pile in a 'rich lively pattern'. Abaft the saloons there was a large cabin for the Imperial suite. The officers' quarters consisted of a mess room and two or three cabins located forward of the engine room. Her lower deck for the seamen was lofty and airy.

[4] Lawrence Oliphant, *Narrative of the Earl of Elgin's Mission to China and Japan*, 2 vols. (London, 1859), ii. 61, 87–88. Beasley, *Great Britain and the Opening of Japan*, p. 186.

their will, followed the pattern of the American treaty in the terms finally agreed upon between Japan and Great Britain. Reciprocal hospitality, punctuated by brief discussions, gave unique pleasure to both contracting parties. The British were free to travel, to observe, and to ask questions. Precautions taken by the *Bakufu* had prevented anti-foreign incidents but reports made it clear that Japan was divided and that powerful nobles still entertained exclusionist views.[1]

The treaty was signed at Yedo on 26 August 1858 by Elgin and seven of the Shogun's representatives—again without Imperial approval. The yacht was presented the same day amid a great celebration. Elgin returned to China with admiration for the Japanese nation but with no grasp of the political conflicts and economic difficulties which were besetting the Shogunate when its *Rōjū* reluctantly yielded to the treaties it had made with the West.[2] Although Lawrence Oliphant, his perceptive secretary, looked with concern upon the coming impact upon Japan of the 'overbearing and insolent behaviour' of many British subjects, neither he nor Elgin could foresee that, in order to gain Imperial sanction to the signing of the treaties, the *Bakufu* would within six months have to promise to try to obstruct their fulfilment and return to the seclusion policy as soon as possible.[3]

The Treaty of Yedo with its accompanying trade regulations provided that the opening of Nagasaki, Kanagawa, and Hakodate to British residents and trade would take place on 1 July 1859; that Niigata or another port on the Japan Sea would be opened from 1 January 1860 and Hyogo (Kobe) from January 1863. Foreigners would be granted residence in Yedo from 1 January 1862 and in Osaka from 1 January 1863. A British diplomatic agent was permitted to live at Yedo and consuls to reside at the open ports. The ranking representative could travel freely throughout Japan but other British subjects were

---

[1] Shiryō Hensanjo (Historiographical Institute, Tokyo University), Editor, *Dai Nihon Komonjo, Bakumatsu Gaikoku Kankei Monjo* (Old Japanese Documents— Documents relating to Foreign Affairs in the Last Days of the Shogunate, 1853–68 (hereafter cited as *B.G.K.M.*), 32 vols. (Tokyo, 1911–62), xx. 703, Doc. No. 299, *Rōjū to Machi-Bugyō*, Aug. 1858. Oliphant, op. cit. i. Preface, iii, ix; ii throughout.

[2] P.P. H. of C. 1859, xxxiii. 370–3, Elgin to Malmesbury, 30 Aug. 1858. Ad. I/5693, Seymour to Adm., 10 Sept. 1858 and enclosures. Oliphant, op. cit. ii. 239–42.

[3] Ibid. 244–6. Beasley, *Documents*, p. 159. The Emperor acknowledged, however, that under the circumstances the *Bakufu* had to sign the treaties. Ibid., pp. 193–4.

restricted to limited areas around the treaty cities. The British were granted extraterritorial rights and consular jurisdiction, freedom of worship, and most-favoured-nation treatment. The Japanese further agreed to freedom of trade between private individuals and to British employment of Japanese subjects in any capacity without government interference. Arms could be sold only to the Japanese government or to foreigners. The importation of opium was forbidden but the Japanese government was given entire responsibility for the control of smuggling. Export and import duties were fixed but could be revised after five years.[1]

The currency provisions require special notice. Here Lord Elgin followed exactly the terms of Article V of the American treaty made by Harris. Both negotiators, long in the East, must have known the unique workings of the Japanese currency when they exacted the following concessions from the aware but defenceless Japanese.[2] Article X of the British treaty required that: 'All foreign coin shall be current in Japan, and shall pass for its corresponding weight in Japanese coin of the same description.' This provision George Arbuthnot (a member of the Treasury and valued consultant on money and banking) later declared to be opposed to international principles and something that would have been considered preposterous between any two European nations.[3] But Lord Elgin considered it one of the principal advantages secured by the British government and its subjects.[4]

Article X further provided that British and Japanese subjects could 'freely use foreign or Japanese coin in making payments to each other', that coins of all descriptions (with the exception of Japanese copper coin), as well as foreign gold and silver uncoined could be exported from Japan; and that for one year after the opening of the ports, the Japanese government would 'furnish British subjects with Japanese coin in exchange for

[1] Gaimushō Jōyaku Kyoku (Foreign Office Treaty Bureau), *Kyu Jōyaku Isan* (Collection of Old Treaties), 3 vols. (Tokyo, 1930–6), i, pt. II, 3–38. P.P. H. of C. 1859, xxxiii. 375–81.

[2] Okada Shumpei, *Bakumatsu Ishin no Kahei Seisaku* (Currency Policy at End of the *Bakufu* and Early Meiji Periods) (Tokyo, 1955), pp. 18–19.

[3] P.P. H. of C. 1866, l. 3, George Arbuthnot, *Report on Japanese Currency to the Lords of the Treasury*, 24 Dec. 1862.

[4] P.P. H. of C. 1859, xxxiii. 374, Elgin to Malmesbury, H.M.S. *Furious*, 31 Aug. 1858.

theirs, equal weights being given, and no discount being taken for recoinage'.[1]

The Treaty of Yedo pleased the British people both at home and in China.[2] Lord Malmesbury expressed the 'satisfaction' of the Foreign Office and the 'approval' of the Queen and set about to establish three British consular offices in the Japanese empire.[3] The merchants of Hong Kong wrote enthusiastically to Lord Elgin when he left the Far East. They felt 'greatly indebted . . . for the opening of commercial relations with the rich and interesting Empire of Japan' and believed the Treaty of Yedo would eventually confer 'substantial advantages on the commerce of the world'.[4]

Anglo-Japanese Trade before July 1859

Although British businessmen in China and England could anticipate difficulties as well as profits in establishing trade with Japan, many were eager to undertake the risk. As early as October 1855 the Hong Kong press published accounts of Japan's complicated and debased currency, the devaluation of the dollar in relation to the silver *ichibu*, and of the established ratio of gold to silver at approximately one to five, as indications of the government's arbitrary control of coinage and trade in the long-isolated country.[5]

Captain Paul Bernard Whittingham, who accompanied the British Commodore, the Hon. Charles Elliot, in 1855 on the expedition against the Russian settlements in eastern Siberia and visited Hakodate, Shimoda, and Nagasaki en route, reported that the upper classes of Japan were already asking for 'watches, clocks, mechanical, nautical and mometrical instruments, telescopes and glasses of all descriptions'. He saw fine lacquer and porcelain for sale through a strictly government-controlled system which prohibited the people from trading directly and freely with foreigners. He noted the

[1] Ibid., p. 377.

[2] Beasley, *Great Britain and the Opening of Japan*, pp. 192–3. *North China Herald*, Editorial 4 Sept. 1858.

[3] P.P. H. of C. 1859, xxxiii. 382–3, F.O. to Elgin, 8 Nov. 1858.

[4] Ibid., p. 487, Jardine, Matheson & Co. *et al.* to Elgin, Hong Kong, 14 Mar. 1859.

[5] *China Mail*, Editorial 25 Oct. 1855. *Ichibu* was the Japanese silver coin most used by foreigners during the Shogunate. Its value varied from 10*d.* to 1*s.* 8*d.*, according to the rate of exchange. It was usually referred to as 'bu'.

debasement of the Japanese money, the great extent to which the depreciation of the national currency was carried, and the profits made by the government through the exchange forced on the people. No swords, sought for their excellently tempered steel, could be bought. Silks, satins, and crepes were inferior to, and dearer than, those of China. Pipes, tobacco cases, ink and penholders of Japanese metal, fans, toys, and grotesque pieces of china or metal were the chief articles for sale. He recognized the contempt in which merchants were held by the authorities, who kept them in subjection equal to that of petty shopkeepers, peasant farmers, and fishermen. The Japanese people, amiable, strong, and hardy in character, nevertheless won his affection. He foretold that their 'natural advantages of extensive sea coasts, mines, rich soil, fine climate, and well-situated position, would, under a tolerably enlightened government, render a flourishing commercial people'.[1]

Rear-Admiral Sir Michael Seymour reported equally important facts upon his visit to Nagasaki in September 1856. Arrangements for the transaction of business and the sale of goods and supplies in fulfilment of Stirling's treaty were 'carefully palisaded' so as to prevent all communication with the inhabitants. The Governor of Nagasaki had stressed the difference between 'Imperial' territory where Seymour could land under restrictions, and that of neighbouring princes, over which the Governor had no control. The Admiral was impressed, however, with the growing feelings of goodwill towards foreigners. He believed the authorities were honestly desirous of carrying out Stirling's treaty but warned 'that the fear of incurring the jealous suspicion of their Government acts as a check against the abrogation of long established customs'.[2]

British merchants themselves had some first-hand knowledge of the potentials of the Japan trade. Since 1846 they had exchanged British and Japanese products at Ryūkyū, and through Chinese intermediaries they trafficked at Nagasaki, encouraging

---

[1] Paul Bernard Whittingham, *Notes on the Late Expedition against the Russian Settlements in Eastern Siberia, and of a Visit to Japan and to the Shores of Tartary and of the Sea of Okhotsk* (London, 1856), pp. 31, 44, 56–59, 239–44.

[2] Ad. I/5672, Seymour to Adm., 22 Sept. 1856. Admiral Seymour was a great friend of the British merchants in Hong Kong, who so appreciated his services on the China station that they presented him with a large silver service at the close of his China command. Ad. I/5712, Seymour to Adm., 28 Mar. 1859.

the independent trade of the Daimyo of Satsuma.[1] Jardine, Matheson and Company, the most important British firm in Hong Kong, apparently carried on regular trade with these areas in the late forties.[2] At least their agent in Shanghai reported on 18 May 1853 that 'the usual shipment of chintzes and other goods will not be made to Japan in consequence of the American expedition'.[3] Japanese copper was purchased in small quantities for export to India. For example, forty boxes of ingots—a net of 9,655 pounds, at a cost of fourteen *carolus* dollars per picul—were acquired from Japan in February 1856 for reshipment from Shanghai to Hong Kong and thence to Calcutta.[4] Likewise, the *China Mail* of 25 December 1856

---

[1] The Ryūkyū Islands had been opened in 1846 to British and French trade with the tacit consent of the *Bakufu* under pressure from Satsuma. Both China and Satsuma still claimed sovereignty over the Ryūkyūans, who paid tribute to both. Iwata Masakazu, *Ōkubo Toshimichi, The Bismarck of Japan* (Berkeley, 1964), pp. 24, 186–8. Takekoshi, op. cit. iii. 277–9.

[2] 'Jardine, Matheson & Co. had its origin in a number of partnerships under other names, commencing with that of John Henry Cox, who was established as a private trader under licence from the East India Company in Canton in 1782. The firm established by Cox continued under a number of names until the early part of the nineteenth century when it was established as Magniac & Co. William Jardine was a Partner in Magniac & Co. and was subsequently joined by James Matheson. Jardine, Matheson & Co. came into being on the 30th June 1832. William Jardine and James Matheson were leading merchants in Canton at the time of the cessation of the East India Company's monopoly in 1834. They were established shipowners, merchants and agents in many connections and played a leading part in the negotiations with the British Government in connection with the opium trade.' Letter from Alan Reid of Matheson & Co., Ltd. to Grace Fox, London, 28 Aug. 1964.

Jardine, Matheson & Company, known as 'the Princely Hong', established its head office in Hong Kong in 1842, soon opened trading centres in Shanghai, Foochow, and Tientsin, and became leading importers of raw materials and manufactured goods from India and Britain, and exporters of teas and silk. When Jardine's nephew, William Keswick, went to Japan in 1859 the partners of the firm in Hong Kong were David Jardine, Joseph Jardine, Campbell Maclean, Robert Jardine, Alexander Perceval, and John Charles Bowring. J.M. MSS. (Hong Kong, Private), Co. to William Gaskell, 7 Apr. 1858. For early history of firm in China see Michael Greenberg, *British Trade and the Opening of China, 1800–1842* (Cambridge, 1951).

Extensive records of the early history of this firm have survived and with the reports of the British consuls form the base of our knowledge of the early Anglo-Chinese and Anglo-Japanese private trade. Fire, earthquakes, and war have destroyed most of the papers of their contemporaries. Hence much of the economic history in the following pages is taken from the Jardine, Matheson archives.

[3] J.M. MSS. (Shanghai, Private), A. G. Dallas to David Jardine at Hong Kong, 18 May 1853.

[4] Ibid. (Shanghai, 1853–6), Charles Wills to Joseph Jardine at Hong Kong, 2 Feb. 1856. A picul is 133⅓ lb. The *carolus* dollar, a silver coin, sometimes called the

reported the *Formosa* from Shanghai carrying 489 boxes of Japanese copper to Europe.[1]

Although these cargoes came from Shanghai, it was all but a year later that the *North China Herald* announced that the hongs which had the exclusive privilege of trading with Japan, but had been confined to Chapoo, were permitted to remove their establishments to Shanghai, from which a direct trade would then be carried on with Japan.[2]

Lord Elgin's treaty and experience in Japan received wide publicity in the English press of the China ports and in London. The attractions of Japan and her people were recounted at length and the 'go ahead' disposition of the latter was thought to indicate an important future market for British products. *The Times* correspondent admitted, however, that beyond camphor, wax, and copper, little was known about Japanese exports.[3] The *North China Herald* believed that the Japanese market for British goods would rival that made possible in China by the treaties of Tientsin and predicted silk, copper, gold, tea, paper, porcelain, bronzes, and lacquer ware as the principal exports. Rice would also be important, it said, when there was a scarcity in north China. In return, the Japanese would probably want sugar, woollens, patterns in Manchester cottons, machinery, and arms but her import market was still unknown.[4] Lawrence Oliphant was most cautious in his estimates. He recognized at once that the government's control of all commercial activities of the Japanese people would cause conflicts with the 'ideas of the English free trader'. He hoped the West would create a growing market for sugar and for cotton and woollen textiles at lower prices than those of native manufacture. He believed that Japan's minerals, copper and coal, both government monopolies, would be more profitable exports than her vegetable products. But he doubted that trade on 'an extensive and really profitable scale' could be carried on with Japan for many years.[5]

Spanish dollar, had been the only foreign coin accepted in China for over a century after its introduction in 1757 by the East India Company. Edward Kann, *Currencies of China* (Shanghai, 1926), pp. 295–7. Its intrinsic value was 4s. 2d., exchange varied from 3s. 11d. to 5s. Greenberg, op. cit., p. vii.

[1] *China Mail*, 25 Dec. 1856.   [2] *North China Herald*, 21 Nov. 1857.
[3] *The Times*, 2 Nov. 1858.
[4] *North China Herald*, 4, 11, and 18 Sept. 1858.   [5] Oliphant, op. cit. ii. 253–9.

How many British firms were influenced by such accounts cannot be estimated. Forty foreign ships were reported to have touched at Nagasaki between 29 June and 31 December 1858. Fourteen of these were British, but their purpose in stopping is not disclosed.[1]

Direct trade between Shanghai and Japan soon developed. Dent and Company, Jardine's chief British rival, dispatched the *Vindex* and the American firm of Russell and Company sent the *Florence* on exploring missions, each without cargo.[2] Both firms immediately began the purchase of vegetable wax which they sold in England. Jardine, Matheson, though sceptical of such ventures, determined to get first-hand information themselves. Upon the advice of their comprador, their Shanghai manager, James Whittall, decided upon sending a small cargo of such goods as the Chinese had usually taken over. In the meantime they looked to K. R. Mackenzie (who became their agent at Nagasaki) for reports on the prospects of trade when he took over a cargo of sundries on Chinese account, with the intention of settling there should they prove promising.[3] The Chinese were thought to be the principal movers in the trade and to confine themselves largely to native produce.[4] Oliphant's statistics for the last five weeks of 1858 show, however, that foreign textiles, printed and dyed cottons, camlets, handkerchiefs, grey long cloth, long ells, muslins, and Spanish stripes were also part of the cargoes from Shanghai to Japan.[5]

The dullness of the Shanghai market, the lack of reliable information from Japan because vessels engaged in the trade refused to carry letters, and the suspected success of Dent and other rival companies led James Whittall in January 1859 to dispatch Jardine's first ship to Japan. This was the *Troas* under Captain Henry Holmes. The cost of chartering the vessel— $2,000 Mexican per month—was shared by their Chinese comprador, Taku. He also shipped cargo valued at 9,000 taels, in addition to Jardine's 3,292 bags of sugar, 105 cases of velvet, and another 9,000 taels of Chinese cargo on joint account.

[1] 'Nagasaki Shipping List', *North China Herald*, 15 Jan. 1859.
[2] J.M. MSS. (Shanghai, Private), J. Whittall (J.M. agent in Shanghai) to J. Jardine, 6 Nov. 1858.
[3] Ibid., 27 Nov., 18, 21, and 30 Dec. 1858.
[4] Ibid., 3 Jan. 1859.
[5] Oliphant, op. cit. ii. 491.

William Keswick of the Shanghai office was sent along to stay a month and report his observations direct to Mr. Jardine in Hong Kong.[1] Whittall consigned the cargo to K. R. Mackenzie whom he advised to make as quick sales as possible. A yield of forty thousand taels was thought probable. Rice and coal were to be considered for return shipment.[2]

Letters from both Mackenzie and Keswick brought by a Russian gunboat convinced Whittall that the Japan trade was well worth looking after. Mackenzie had already attempted contracts with two rich individual shopkeepers for the delivery of several hundred piculs of two grades of silk and with the government's company of one thousand piculs of wax. He had acquired some godown room where he would store the Chinese produce from the *Troas* but feared the sugar and manufactures would have to be returned. Difficulties with payments were at once experienced. The Government Guild with which Mackenzie hoped to make extensive contracts for silk was averse to taking dollars in payment and their offers to barter silk for Chinese and other produce were too low to satisfy Mackenzie. Nevertheless, he was soon advising Whittall about sending dollars for silk and surmising that thirty to forty thousand Mexican dollars might be invested a month.[3] Evidently the shopkeepers found it difficult to resist foreign contracts in spite of their fear of trouble with the authorities.

[1] J.M. MSS. (Shanghai, Private), J. Whittall to J. Jardine, 6, 22, and 31 Jan. 1859. Capt. Henry Holmes, *My Adventures in Japan* (London, 1859), pp. 9, 29, 31, gives a slightly different account of this voyage.

The Mexican silver dollar, weighing $416\frac{1}{2}$ grains, $902\frac{7}{9}$ fine, was introduced into China in 1854 and rapidly succeeded the *carolus* dollar as the main foreign coin accepted in China and Japan for sixty years. W. P. Wei, *The Currency Problem in China* (New York, 1914), p. 44. Shinjo Hiroshi, *History of the Yen: 100 years of Japanese Money Economy* (Kobe, 1962), gives the Mexican dollar at 416 grains, 9/10 silver (374·4 grains or 24·2606 grams. fine). From 1861–5 its exchange value varied from 4s. to 6s. in Japan. M. Paske-Smith, *Western Barbarians in Japan and Formosa* (Kobe, 1930) (hereafter cited as *Western Barbarians*), p. 218. In 1876 its value was about fifty cents, U.S., or a little more than 2s. H. S. Williams, *Tales of the Foreign Settlements in Japan* (Tokyo, 1958), p. 154.

Tael: Chinese ounce weight as well as amount of money. One tael equals 10 mace, or $1·388, or 6s. 8d. One picul equals $133\frac{1}{3}$ pounds, or 10 catties, or 1,600 tael weights.

[2] J.M. MSS. (Japan Letter Book o/1), Shanghai Office to K. Mackenzie, 29 Jan. 1859. Here a more detailed invoice is given and two Chinese, Taku and Yuku, are listed as part owners of the cargo on whose account sales should be rendered separately.

[3] Ibid. (Nagasaki, Private), K. Mackenzie to J. Whittall, 23 Feb. 1859.

Keswick returned on 25 February with word that only one hundred piculs of silk had been secured by the time of his departure on the 21st. But the two qualities here represented at 'M. 9 and 15 Japanese per catty respectively' meant 'a very handsome margin'.[1] On the other hand, not a package of the cargo carried by the *Troas* had been disposed of when Keswick left. Whittall now thought silk would be important by another season and was also interested in wheat and wax. Keswick had instructed Mackenzie to secure all the silk possible, to land and store the sugar and other cargo of the *Troas* to await higher prices, if possible without too great expense, and to contract for ten thousand piculs of wax and a return cargo of wheat for the *Troas*.[2]

Whittall quickly decided to make terms with Mackenzie to the effect that Mackenzie receive one-third share in all raw silk shipments on condition that all his purchases be on Jardine, Matheson and Company's account. Whittall would specify no time limit, desiring to reserve for the firm the option of acting independently by giving due notice. Keswick should return promptly to Japan and work out the arrangements fairly for all parties. Whittall also wanted him 'to look after the silk market' jointly with Mackenzie until it was possible to act independently. The extensive monetary preparations of Adamson and Company, and other firms, which Whittall presumed were for entering the silk market, made him hasten Keswick's return to Nagasaki to secure Mackenzie's services.[3] He dispatched him on the *Hellespont* on 13 March with fifty thousand Mexican dollars to push ahead with the trade.[4] He anticipated even then the need of a schooner running regularly between Shanghai and Japan if Japan fulfilled its promises—a service he thought would pay well with Chinese freight.[5]

This trade with Nagasaki months before the date set by the Treaty of Yedo for the opening of the ports could be legally

---

[1] Catty: in China, 1⅓ pounds. M. Japanese: a *momme* = 57·9 gr. silver coin or weight.

[2] J.M. MSS. (Shanghai, Private), J. Whittall to J. Jardine, 27 Feb. 1859.

[3] Ibid. and Whittall to Jardine, 1 and 5 Mar. 1859. For Adamson see pp. 316–17.

[4] Ibid., J. Whittall to J. Jardine, 12 Mar. 1859, and (Japan Letter Book 1/2), Shanghai Office to K. Mackenzie, 13 Mar. 1859.

[5] Ibid. (Shanghai, Private), J. Whittall to J. Jardine, 5 Mar. 1859.

defended.[1] The most-favoured-nation clause in Admiral Stirling's Convention of 1854 made it possible for British merchants to profit by arrangements in the recent Dutch and Russian treaties which had already opened Nagasaki and Hakodate to trade under restricted conditions.[2] But Queen Victoria's government was determined to prohibit the smuggling and lawless behaviour in Japan which had accompanied the opening of the ports in China. Reports in the autumn of 1858 that certain British merchants in China had ready for immediate dispatch to Japan vessels partly laden with goods 'which even if the treaty were ratified and the trade duly opened, could not legally be imported into Japan' led at once to official action.[3] By Royal Proclamation, the Queen warned all her subjects who would violate the laws of Japan and attempt illegal traffic, that Her Majesty's Government would not protect them from fines or pecuniary penalties or the forfeiture of their goods and ships, and that commanders of British warships in Japanese ports and waters had been ordered 'to support by all lawful means the Tycoon of Japan and his Government in preventing any violation, evasion or contravention by British subjects of the laws of Japan, or of the provisions of the said Treaty'.[4] H.M.S. *Inflexible* was sent to Yedo in March to so inform the Shogun's government and to warn the masters of British vessels at Nagasaki against illegal trading with the Japanese.[5]

Japan's foreign trade between November 1858 and the opening of the ports plied largely between Nagasaki and Shanghai. The trade returns, even if not too trustworthy, indicate the general trends of the nascent commerce. Grey and white shirtings, dyed and printed cotton, handkerchiefs, chintz,

[1] 'The Nagasaki Shipping List' for Mar. 1859 recorded that 14 foreign ships, 5 of which were from Nagasaki, had come from Nagasaki, and 16 had gone there, 8 of the latter being British, *North China Herald*, 9 Apr. 1859.

[2] The Japanese Foreign Office, *Treaties and Conventions between the Empire of Japan and other Powers, together with Universal Conventions, Regulations, and Communications since March 1854* (Tokyo, 1884), p. 416, Art. V of Anglo-Japanese Convention of 1854; pp. 489–528, Netherlands Treaties with Japan, 16 Oct. 1857; and pp. 575–88, Russian Treaty with Japan, 24 Oct. 1857.

[3] Ad. R.O. (China 31), Malmesbury to Adm. F.O., 24 Nov. 1858.

[4] F.O. 262/1, Extract from *Supplement to London Gazette*, 1 Feb. 1859. Ad. 2/1616, Adm. to Seymour, 25 Nov. 1858. The official documents were also published in the *North China Herald*, 12 Feb. 1859 having been taken from the Hong Kong *Gazette*. 'Tycoon' was the title used by Westerners for the Shogun.

[5] Ad. I/5712, Seymour to Adm., 12 Mar. 1859 and encls.

alum, betel nut, 'carpenting' pieces, medicines, sapan wood, and sugar constituted the chief Japanese imports while coal, dried fish, rice, seaweed, shark skins, and wax constituted the bulk of her exports. Some manufactured goods, metals, and sundries had to be re-exported.[1]

Foremost among the early indications of future difficulties was currency. The Treasury authorities at Nagasaki at times refused to allow dollars to be received in payment for goods, sometimes issued paper money in exchange for dollars, and again required payment in goods for Japanese exports. They restricted the amount of foreign currency which they would exchange for local coins per head per day. Ten dollars was the limit in mid April, having been raised from four dollars. *Carolus* and Mexican dollars and five-franc pieces were received at the Treasury according to weight.[2] Barter, however, could be profitable as in the case of sugar against seaweed for which there was a promising market.[3] Trade was hampered by a lack of boats and coolies for loading ships. There were no efforts to stop pilfering. Smuggling was well understood.[4]

All foreigners were being placed in an unfavourable light with the Japanese people as well as the authorities because of the lawless behaviour of drunken foreign sailors who attacked the natives and broke into houses if they could not obtain drink.[5] To control these ruffians, the arrival of the consuls was timely. And it was obvious that men of experience, courage, and ability were required to represent English law in Japan and meet the problems of the ports.

The First British Consulates

Rutherford Alcock, then British consul at Canton, was appointed consul-general for Japan on 21 December 1858.[6] As Britain's first official representative in this little-understood

---

[1] P.P. H. of C. 1860, lxix (2648), 22–24, 'Trade Return of Japan with Shanghai from 1 Nov. 1858 to 23 May 1859'. Sapan wood: a red dyewood obtained from the East Indian Caesalpiniaceous tree.

[2] *North China Herald*, 16 Apr. 1859. J.M. MSS. (Nagasaki, 1859), K. Mackenzie to Hong Kong Office, 4 and 19 Apr. 1859; K. Mackenzie to Shanghai Office, 28 May 1859 (copy); (Shanghai, Private), J. Whittall to J. Jardine, 11 May 1859.

[3] Ibid., 26 Apr. 1859.

[4] Letter from Nagasaki, 24 Feb. 1859, published in the *China Mail*, 30 June 1859.

[5] *North China Herald*, 16 Apr. 1859.

[6] Great Britain, *Foreign Office List*, 1883, pp. 50–51.

country, his responsibilities were unique. Lord Malmesbury pointed out in his first instructions to him that the British government had to rely on his judgement to win the confidence of the Japanese people in British intentions towards them. He was to 'be content with gradual progress' instead of exercising pressure for their immediate compliance with his suggestions or demands. He should insist on the observance of the provisions of the Treaty of Yedo but not in a manner which would give offence to the Japanese government. And he should explain that he had full power and authority as well as determination to maintain order among British subjects, and to co-operate with the Japanese authorities in preserving a good understanding between their two peoples.

Official Britain's concern in Japan extended beyond the realm of trade. The country was to be a post for obtaining information regarding Russian activities in the Far East—in particular her activities on the Amur and in neighbouring countries. The Foreign Office wished all possible knowledge of such actions. Malmesbury instructed Alcock to try 'to dissuade the Japanese Government from making any cession of territory to Russia', but warned him against promising British support 'in resisting Russian efforts to obtain it'. Most of all Alcock was to play for friendly relations with the agents of the foreign powers in the area, and to avoid struggling with them for influence with the Japanese government. Malmesbury maintained that Her Majesty's Government did not aim at supremacy in the councils of Japan; it had no desire to interfere with the social institutions of the country; a faithful observance of the commercial treaty was its main interest.[1]

Alcock's original staff was small. At Yedo, a vice-consul, a man with the pay of a first assistant who studied Japanese, a Dutch interpreter, and two student interpreters, who were expected to be useful members of the consul-general's office while learning Japanese; at Nagasaki, a consul and a Dutch interpreter; at Hakodate, a consul and a Dutch interpreter. No British medical officers were appointed; the Foreign Office counted on the accessibility of Dutch physicians in the ports. The personnel regulations for the consular service then in use in China held also for Japan.

[1] F.O. 46/2 (copy), Malmesbury to Alcock, No. 1, 1 Mar. 1859.

Salaries were liberal for that day. The British government felt it necessary to offer financial inducements of some magnitude in order to attract competent men to the loneliness and personal hazards of official service in the Far East. At Yedo the consul-general received £1,800 a year; a vice-consul £750; an interpreter £500; an assistant interpreter £405; student interpreters £200. The salaries of all British civil servants at Nagasaki and Hakodate were somewhat lower. (Consuls received £800; an interpreter £500; an assistant interpreter £324.)[1] Funds for the maintenance of the establishment were issued from the commissarial chest at Hong Kong upon the requisition of the consul-general, until a better system could be devised in Japan.[2]

In its letters of appointment to the consuls, the vice-consul, and the interpreters, the Foreign Office made an obvious effort to avoid at the start in Japan some of the evils which the West had inflicted upon China. All were strictly forbidden to engage directly or indirectly in trade on their own account, or as agents for any other party. All were ordered to deal cautiously on all occasions with the Japanese people and authorities, to avoid controversy, and the giving of just causes for offence. The consuls were advised to abstain from stopping the payment of duties and from interfering in the collection of Japanese revenue—a policy then too often exercised in China. The British government further required from the consuls 'a firm administration of justice with temperate and considerate indulgence'. They should seek in their new communities to secure respect for the consular office and the personal goodwill of all classes: British subjects, other foreign citizens, and the Japanese themselves.[3]

The naval officers in the China Sea had equal responsibility for the promotion of peace and goodwill in British relations with Japan. When ordering Rear-Admiral Sir James Hope, Commander-in-Chief of the East Indies and China Station, to send a ship occasionally to visit Yedo and communicate with

[1] *Hansard's Parliamentary Debates*, 3rd Series, clii, col. 695, H. of C., 22 Feb. 1859.
[2] F.O. 46/2 (copy), Malmesbury to Alcock, No. 2, 1 Mar. 1859; 262/1 F.O. to Capt. Vyse, 7 Feb. 1859; F.O. to Interpreters Eusden, Myburg, and Cowan, 25 Feb. 1859; F.O. to Student Interpreters, Fletcher and MacDonald, 4 Jan. 1859.   [3] Ibid. and draft, F.O. to Morrison and Hodgson, 23 Feb. 1859.

Her Majesty's Consul-General, the Lords of the Admiralty urged upon their officers and men great caution and consideration in their dealings with the Japanese people. In Japan as in China, they said, 'actions indifferent in themselves and which among European nations would lead to little or no inconvenience, might produce an impression highly unfavourable to the British character'.[1] They, too, had learned from the injustices committed in China.

Since the Treaty of Yedo (Art. IV) had provided that all questions of personal or property rights between British subjects in Japan, and all British citizens who committed crimes against Japanese subjects or those of any other country, were to be tried by the consuls or other appointed authority according to the laws of Great Britain, it was necessary for Her Majesty's Government to confer jurisdiction upon the consul-general and the consuls before they arrived at their posts, in order that as soon as the treaty came into effect, British subjects in the Japanese ports would be under consular control. This was done on 3 March 1859 by an Order-in-Council, closely resembling that for China and Siam.[2] Hereby Great Britain granted to her consuls in Japan the power to enforce all Anglo-Japanese treaties and to make rules for their observance as well as for the government of all British subjects in Japan. The Order also defined the limits of consular jurisdiction and the procedures and penalties in consular courts.[3]

To carry out these responsibilities the British government tried to choose its officers with great care. Even Parliament took an interest in the calibre of the men about to be sent to Japan, insisting upon special training in the Japanese and Dutch languages for the appointees to the consular service. Merchants were not selected as consuls—a deviation from a common and much-abused practice in that day. Usually men of integrity with experience in commercial affairs and preferably with knowledge of the East were appointed.[4]

Rutherford Alcock, at the age of fifty, brought to the consul-

[1] Ad. 13/4, Adm. to Hope, 28 Feb. 1859.
[2] F.O. 46/2 (copy), Malmesbury to Alcock, No. 1, 1 Mar. 1859.
[3] *British and Foreign State Papers* (London, 1867), xlix. 554–69.
[4] F. C. Jones, *Extraterritoriality in Japan* (New Haven, 1931), pp. 49–50. *Hansard's Parliamentary Debates*, 3rd Series, clii, col. 1056, H. of C., 1 Mar. 1859.

generalship in Japan a knowledge of medicine, an interest in art, and practical wisdom gained from fifteen years as consul in Amoy, Foochow, Shanghai, and Canton. He was a graduate of the Royal College of Surgeons, but his distinguished medical career had been terminated prematurely by rheumatic fever which had limited the use of his hands. He had demonstrated courage, powers of decision, and self-detachment. His sympathies were broad, his insight keen, his manner dignified and courteous.[1]

During his stay in China Alcock had developed views which would inevitably influence his interpretation of coming events in Japan. He looked criticially upon British policy in China—the forced conditions under which the treaties had been concluded, not to mention the temporizing and the concessions which followed. He hated the opium trade, which he believed was the sole cause of Chinese distrust and hostility. At the same time he had seen through China's calculated resistance to the treaty stipulations and determined to prevent it in Japan. In his view treaties once signed must be fulfilled.[2] Hesitation and compliance by the British, he thought, had led only to further humiliation and arrogance on the part of the Chinese. He had advocated coercive measures. Economic sanctions and a threat of force, he thought, were justifiable.[3] The Chinese, he believed, should be taught fear and respect. Alcock came to Japan thinking that he knew what to expect of all Far Eastern peoples. He seemed strangely unfamiliar, however, with the information which Whittingham, Seymour, and the English press had circulated about Japan.

George Stanton Morrison and C. Pemberton Hodgson were the consuls assigned respectively to Nagasaki and Hakodate, the former having had experience in China.[4] The interpreters were young men, often in training for more advanced service, lured to the East by high salaries.

---

[1] Great Britain, *Foreign Office List*, 1883, pp. 50–51. A. Michie, *The Englishman in China*, 2 vols. (Edinburgh, 1900), i. 1–28, 116–19, 129–35. Baron Algernon Redesdale, B.F.M., *Memories*, 2 vols. (London, 1915), i. 355–8.

[2] Michie, op. cit., pp. 194–8, Appendix I, pp. 411–19, 'Note on Our Present Position and the State of Our Relations with China', 19 Jan. 1849.

[3] Ibid., p. 424 and Appendices II and III, Alcock to Sir George Bonham, 13 Jan. and 17 June 1852.

[4] Great Britain, *Foreign Office List*, 1883, p. 152; 1861, p. 97.

The Opening of the Ports

As the time for the opening of the ports approached Alcock arranged with Admiral Sir James Hope to take him and the other members of the consular staffs to Japan in H.M.S. *Sampson*.[1] The party left Hong Kong on 17 May 1859, stopping at Shanghai and Nagasaki en route to Yedo. From Townsend Harris, then visiting Shanghai, Alcock learned something of the isolation which he must face at his new post. The requirements of trade between Nagasaki and Shanghai made possible several mails each month between those two ports, but there was no such communication between Nagasaki and the seat of the Shogun at Yedo where the consul-general must reside. A powerful steamer could make the trip from the capital to Nagasaki in four or five days. Alcock, therefore, asked Hope to provide a ship for such service, but he had to wait many months before it was established. A letter sent overland required thirty days to reach Nagasaki and three months more to reach London. This meant that eight months would elapse before Alcock could receive an answer to any communication with the Foreign Office. Harris encouraged Alcock to believe that a consulate would be welcomed at Nagasaki and at other ports since the Japanese were having to deal with adventurous foreigners who were under no local control by their own governments. This proved true.[2]

When the *Sampson* entered the beautiful harbour of Nagasaki on that rainy morning of 4 June fifteen square-rigged vessels awaited her, men-of-war and merchantmen under British, Dutch, American, and Russian flags. At least fifteen British nationals were already established on shore, carrying on an active trade by means of contracts with the Japanese government or its officers. Fifteen thousand tons of foreign shipping had apparently passed through this port alone during the first six months of 1859, all sanctioned by the Governor of Nagasaki. Having helped the merchants acquire houses and business offices, he earnestly requested Alcock to establish a consular office at his port.[3]

[1] Ad. I/5712, Hope to Adm., 5 May 1859.

[2] F.O. 46/3, Alcock to Malmesbury, Nos. 1 and 6, 29 May 1859. Sir Rutherford Alcock, *The Capital of the Tycoon*, 2 vols. (London, 1863), i. 27.

[3] P.P. H. of C., 1860, lxix (2648), 1–4, Alcock to Malmesbury, 16 June 1859 and enclosure 1. J.M. MSS., Letters from Nagasaki, 1859.

It was Pemberton Hodgson's good fortune to be with Alcock on the *Sampson*. Although he had been designated for the consulship at Hakodate, Alcock placed him in charge of British subjects at Nagasaki until Morrison could arrive from England. A temple renting at thirty-nine dollars per month became his headquarters. There the British consular flag was first raised and Hodgson and his family took possession on 14 June. An official circular notified the British community of their obligations to the consul and informed them of the *Regulations for Trade* which, along with the treaty, would come into force on 1 July.[1]

Selecting a site for a more adequate and permanent consular establishment and making arrangements for the administration of those affairs in which British interests were involved proved more difficult. Months of irksome negotiations were to pass before a satisfactory foreign habitation was granted. The Governor of Nagasaki, although courteous and expressing friendly assurances, was obviously determined to 'take as little responsibility upon himself as possible'. Alcock was sympathetic. To him it seemed natural that on the eve of the enforcement of the treaties the Japanese would be hesitant since they had everything to learn about Western methods and habits and about the ultimate consequences of the measures that had been pressed upon them.

Alcock was also acutely aware of the dangers inherent in British ignorance of the Japanese language. Whatever the representatives of either nation had to say to each other on a wide variety of topics, involving even the technicalities of trade, had to be put into Dutch and there was no guarantee that what either nation said would be understood or faithfully rendered by the intermediaries. On many issues the Consul-General was pessimistic as he attempted to arrive at an understanding with the Governor.

At the conclusion of his visit to Nagasaki Alcock felt that some progress had been made. He had contracted for a temporary and modest consular establishment which when fitted up would cost approximately £150 per year. The Governor had assured him that by the time trade was to open on 1 July the

[1] P.P. H. of C. 1860, lxix (2648), 1–2, 4–7, Alcock to Malmesbury, 16 June 1859.

preliminaries would be completed. These included the organization of a customs house, provision of sufficient Japanese coin to
exchange against foreign gold and silver, and a public notification, declaring the end of all government interference in the
hire of boats or coolies and in the purchase or payment of
goods. Moreover, all articles hitherto monopolized by the
Chinese Guild, in particular dried oysters, sea slugs, and
ginseng, were to be open to competition with foreign merchants
—all to prove false promises within weeks.[1]

Knowing that the *Bakufu* had stalled on granting diplomatic
residence at Yedo before the year 1861, Alcock arranged to
arrive at his post unexpectedly before objections to his coming
could be reiterated. The *Sampson* cast anchor in Yedo Bay on
26 June. Alcock at once sent a letter to the Commissioners of
Foreign Affairs, saying that he had come to take up residence
and was the bearer of the ratified treaty with full power to
exchange ratifications. To his great surprise he was welcomed
the next day by the five commissioners who called on him on
board the *Sampson* bringing with them plans of four temples
from which he might select a temporary residence.

Alcock decided to go ashore and choose the quarters himself.
He found nothing imposing about Yedo from the bay. Timber
everywhere concealed the low, often single-storied houses, and
high land rose between the shore and the larger part of the city.
There were shoals all along the banks so that at low water not
even a ship's boat could approach within a mile. This natural
defence was strengthened by solid granite batteries with guns
on every side. The Consul-General selected the temple of
Tōzenji, one of the largest and best endowed in Yedo, which
his guides said had been especially designated for British
occupation. A fine suite of apartments standing in spacious
grounds shaded by a great variety of trees faced a delightful
garden.[2]

While these quarters were made ready for housing half a
dozen Europeans and their servants with the necessary kitchens,
stables, storerooms, and outhouses, Alcock turned his attention

---

[1] P.P. H. of C. 1860, lxix (2648), 1–7 Conversation with Governor of Nagasaki,
14 June 1859. Paske-Smith, *Western Barbarians*, pp. 229–30.

[2] P.P. H. of C. 1860, lxix (2648), 7–9, Alcock to Malmesbury, 9 July 1859.
Alcock, *The Capital of the Tycoon*, i. 93–94, 102–4.

to Kanagawa. This was the port of Yedo and had been designated to open for trade on 1 July. Sixteen miles from the capital, it consisted mainly of a line of houses on each side of the *Tōkaidō*, the great eastern circuit highway linking Yedo with every part of the empire. Here Alcock intended to install a consular officer, Captain F. Howard Vyse, in charge of opening the port. But the Japanese government had willed otherwise.

According to Japanese sources, it was Lord Ii himself who, fearing conflicts between foreigners and Japanese in Kanagawa, the usual stopping-place for the daimyo en route to Yedo, had appointed officials to investigate and suggest another location. On the recommendation of Katsu Kaishu, a naval authority, Lord Ii and subsequently the cabinet, decided to open Yokohama instead of Kanagawa to foreign trade.[1] This did not seem to them a serious violation of the treaties, since Yokohama lay in the Kanagawa district, and 'Kanagawa' could mean somewhere in the area as well as the port itself. The Japanese could also point to the United States Treaty of 1854 which was signed at Yokohama but was called the Treaty of Kanagawa. They argued that Kanagawa was overcrowded, lacked space for new houses and shops as well as the necessary port accommodations. Its harbour was shallow while that of Yokohama was suitable for large ships. The *Bakufu* therefore began preparatory building operations at Yokohama.[2]

The area selected for the new port measured about one mile (15 *chō*) from east to west and one and two-tenths miles (18 *chō*) from north to south. It included the old villages of Yokohama and Tobe and parts of Nakamura and Ohta. By cutting a canal through the salt water swamp to the rear of this territory, which united the creek on its west and the estuary on the east, the *Bakufu* transformed the settlement into an island where they hoped to restrict the activities of the foreigners. There were only

[1] For Katsu Kaishu see p. 231.
[2] *Yokohama Shiyakusho* (Yokohama Municipal Office), *Yokohama-shi Shi Kō* (History of Yokohama City), 11 vols. (Yokohama, 1931–3), ii. 327. Fujimoto S., *Kaikō to Kiito Bōeki* (The Opening of the Ports and the Raw Silk Trade), 3 vols. (Tokyo, 1939), i. 211. Koizuka Ryū, *Yokohama Kaikō Gojūnen Shi* (Fifty-Year History of the Opening of Yokohama), 2 vols. (Yokohama, 1909), ii. 80–87. Kimura Ki, 'Yokohama, One Hundred Years Ago', *Contemporary Japan*, xxii. 636. Joseph Heco, *The Narrative of a Japanese*, 2 vols. (Yokohama, 1892), i. 214.

two exits: one across a bridge to the village of Homura, and another by a bridge over the eastern estuary to a new viaduct three miles long, which led to Kanagawa. Guard houses and a gate which was to be shut at sunset protected the western entrance of each bridge. After clearing the land and reclaiming paddies, broad streets were laid out and houses and facilities needed for overseas trade were built. The Shogunate placed this new Yokohama under its direct jurisdiction and in the spring of 1859 encouraged the merchants of Kanagawa, Yedo, and Shimoda to open shops. To them it offered such profitable inducements as tax-free land for three years. However, mostly adventurers and speculators responded. More respectable traders, it was reported, 'were afraid to come in contact with the foreign "barbarians" with their strange speech and uncouth, outlandish ways'.[1]

Alcock had been warned in Nagasaki of this development at Yokohama.[2] Upon arrival he found the town to be still in course of construction. It consisted of streets of wood huts with shops extending three-quarters of a mile and a large customs house. The approach from the water was marked by two imposing and beautifully built landing-places with flights of well-laid granite steps. A few Japanese merchants had arrived and were unpacking lacquer, porcelain, silks, fancy articles, birds, and other items. The Governor of Kanagawa, in spite of promises to the contrary, refused to allow Captain Vyse and British merchants even a temporary residence at Kanagawa.[3]

Alcock considered such cunning circumventions of the treaty provisions intolerable. They aimed at repeating too closely the humiliating restrictions which the Japanese had imposed on the Dutch at Deshima two centuries earlier. Nevertheless he had to admit the validity of the Japanese arguments. Yokohama was superior to Kanagawa in such important respects as access

---

[1] J. R. Black, *Young Japan*, 2 vols. (London, New York, and Yokohama, 1880–3), i. 28. *Yokohama-shi Shi Kō*, ii. 333. Koizuka, op. cit. ii. 83–91. Kimura, op. cit., p. 636. Otsuka Takematsu, *Bakumatsu Gaikō Shi no Kenkyū* (Diplomatic History in Latter Days of Tokugawa Shogunate), (Tokyo, 1952), p. 22. Heco, op. cit. i. 249. Tanabe Taichi, *Bakumatsu Gaikō Dan* (Tales of Foreign Relations in the Late *Bakufu* Period), (Tokyo, 1898), pp. 109–11. Chō: 2·45 acres.

[2] P.P. H. of C. 1860, lxix (2648), 10, Alcock to Malmesbury, 13 July 1859.

[3] F.O. 46/3, Alcock to Malmesbury, Nos. 8 and 14, 9 and 13 July 1859; Vyse to Alcock, 2 July 1859. See also P.P. H. of C. 1860, lxix (2648), 7–12.

from the bay with the aid of the fine jetties, depth of water, and free and open space on shore. But these advantages were too costly, he thought, when purchased at the price of removal from the great lines of traffic, and isolation from the centre of population. Harris and others on the spot agreed that if this location were accepted, any hope of establishing a mutually advantageous trade at the port of Yedo must be abandoned. Alcock, therefore, demanded that a site in Kanagawa for the permanent settlement of British subjects be mutually agreed upon by Japanese and British officials.

But Western traders complicated the problem. Several ships had already arrived with merchants from Nagasaki and China clamouring for immediate accommodations and facilities. They had little regard for long-range national interests or policy. Some in urgent need of quarters were lured into Yokohama by the Japanese who delighted in setting the merchants and their official representatives at cross purposes.[1]

William Keswick was the first to take a house in the new settlement. Dutch and American merchants followed his lead, while Alcock's *Notification* that such behaviour defeated efforts for a more desirable location and 'better understanding with the Japanese authorities' accomplished nothing. The Consul-General found 'it too provoking that the ill advised proceedings' of his own people created 'the greatest obstacles'.[2] Though sympathetic to Alcock's firm stand on the treaty provision, Keswick saw little prospect of success unless the latter adopted the piece of ground for the foreign settlement which had already been appropriated to that purpose by the Japanese government. What is more, the houses on it were by now all inhabited by foreigners.[3] Thus the cleavage between the representatives of the British Foreign Office and the merchant community had begun.[4]

Two months of tedious discussion passed before Alcock accomplished his purpose. The site which he and Harris originally proposed—the land on either side of the old fort at Kanagawa—was finally designated as the place for the

---

[1] Alcock, *The Capital of the Tycoon*, i. 138–40. Otsuka, op. cit., p. 24.
[2] P.P. H. of C. 1860, lxix (2648), 24–25, Alcock to Malmesbury, 14 July 1859.
[3] J.M. MSS. (Kanagawa, 1859), W. Keswick to J. Whittall, 21 July 1859.
[4] *Japan Times*, Editorial 5 Jan. 1866.

consulate and also where foreigners could build. But Jardine, Matheson and Company were already established in Yokohama, deeply involved in evaluating the Japanese trade.[1] This meant that the Japanese had won, Yokohama would be the real port. The Foreign Office, though applauding Alcock's efforts, recognized that 'The house of Jardine, Matheson, and Co. have so established a reputation in the East that where they settle other merchants are likely to follow'. Alcock could not prevent this. He could only warn those who did so that 'they ought not to admit any right of the Japanese to confine them to that spot'.[2]

While this and other issues were in ferment, Alcock exchanged the ratified texts of the Treaty of Yedo with the Shogun's commissioners of foreign affairs (*gaikoku–bugyō*) on 11 July 1859. Before the ceremony a formal procession of Englishmen for the first time passed through the streets of Yedo from the British consulate to the residence of the senior commissioner of foreign affairs. It was a march of about four miles through both the commercial quarter and the walled enclosures of the official area. Four petty officers carried the treaty on a silk cushion under a canopy draped with flags and evergreens. They were preceded by the flag of Great Britain, and surrounded by a guard of marines. Immediately behind rode Alcock with four attendants. Mounted officers of the consulate and the *Sampson* and fifty armed seamen on foot completed the parade.

The guard formed outside the commissioner's official residence as Alcock entered and the treaty was borne inside. The full powers of the plenipotentiaries were produced. The copies of the treaty were written in English, Japanese, and Dutch and signed by Lord Elgin and the Japanese plenipotentiaries. To Alcock's copy the sign manual and great seal were attached; to the Japanese copy, the Shogun's ratification and seal were appended. The two Dutch versions being understandable to both countries were compared as part of the formalities. Signals arranged in advance by the Japanese conveyed the news of the exchange in a minute and a half to the *Sampson* six miles away. A royal salute of twenty-one guns and the raising of the British and Japanese flags at the main mast concluded the

[1] J.M. MSS. (Kanagawa Correspondence), July–Nov. 1859.
[2] P.P. H. of C. 1860, lxix (2648), 26, Russell to Alcock, 7 Oct. 1859.

PLATE 1

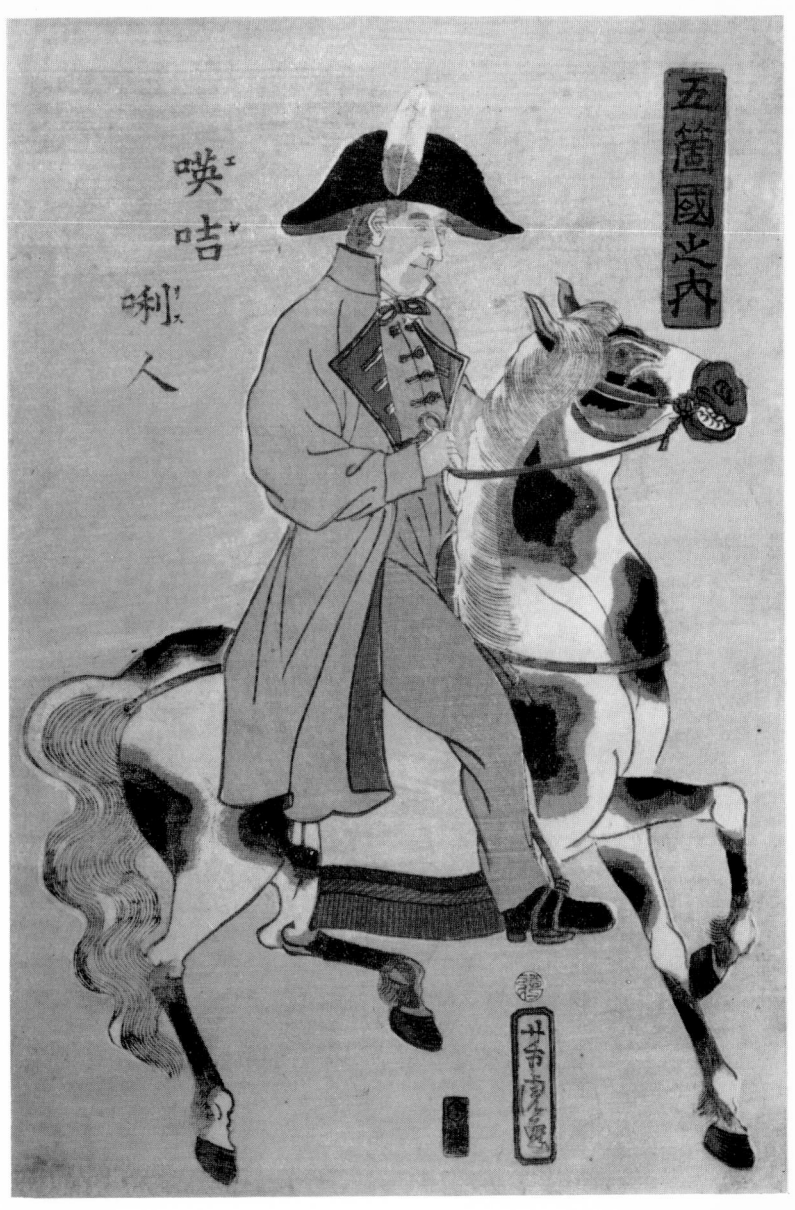

五箇國此内

嘆咭唎人

An English Naval Officer on Horseback, 1861
By Utagawa Yoshitora

celebration. Alcock dared to think that these events had demon-strated to the Japanese that their relations with foreigners were now based on equality and mutual respect.[1]

Shortly afterwards the *Sampson* returned to southern waters leaving the Consul-General to struggle, unsupported by war-ships, against the efforts of the *Bakufu* to nullify the treaties. To further his work he pleaded with London for stationery, letter books, registers, and essential office supplies. He asked for Smith's *Mercantile Law*, McCulloch's *Commercial Dictionary*, Best's one volume on the law of evidence, and a standard work on criminal law.[2] He looked to the Commander-in-Chief of the China Station for the assignment of British warships to Japanese waters and for postal communication between the open ports.

Delay in the Admiral's response meant that the British flag was not raised over a consulate at Hakodate until 15 October. Since Morrison had taken up the duties in Nagasaki in August, Hodgson was then free to leave for his northern assignment. With the arrival of H.M.S. *Highflyer* in September Alcock determined to accompany him and his family to Hakodate in order to judge the potentialities of the port. It was a journey of nine windy days from Kanagawa. The party arrived 5 October, bringing with it forty thousand Japanese *ichibu* for the Governor of Hakodate, the first Western bearers of such an official trust.[3]

Hakodate proved to be a large, bleak, fishing village, con-taining about a thousand houses and six thousand inhabitants of the poorest class. The main street, extending approximately a mile along the edge of the bay at the base of a high promon-tory, was little more than a collection of huts and shops, mostly one-storey buildings with roofs of thin shingle held down by pebbles and boulders.

There were only four temples—the accommodation usually offered to foreign officials. Three were already occupied by the Russian consul and three Russian officers, the American commercial agent, and an American merchant. The fourth and

---

[1] F.O. 46/3, Alcock to Malmesbury, No. 11, 14 July 1859. Also, P.P. H. of C. lxix (2648), 16–20. Alcock, *The Capital of the Tycoon*, i. 152–8.

[2] F.O. 46/3, Alcock to Malmesbury, No. 14, 14 July 1859.

[3] *B.G.K.M.* xxvii. 133, Doc. No. 62, Report of Hakodate *Bugyō* to *Rōjū*, 8 Oct. 1859. C. P. Hodgson, *A Residence at Nagasaki and Hakodate, 1859–60* (London, 1860), pp. 90–94. P.P. H. of C. 1860, lxix (2648), 63, 69, Alcock to Russell, Yedo, 24 Sept. 1859.

most desirable was being prepared for the new governor of the island. The house offered to the British contained four small rooms, the largest being about eight or ten feet square. With little space for expansion this accommodation was wholly inadequate for the first British consul, his family, and his office. The setting was so grim that Hodgson considered claiming three months' leave of absence and retiring to Shanghai until something better could be built. A cold winter lay ahead. Not even the better temples that housed the Russians and the Americans were rainproof.[1]

William Keswick, who had proceeded to Hakodate in the *Troas* in midsummer, had found Hakodate 'the most miserable of the three ports opened to trade in Japan', and 'was quite certain there would be no business worth looking after'. The people appeared extremely poor and except for a limited amount of seaweed he thought they had nothing to export. He could not within a reasonable period of time buy a cargo of seaweed or peas, and had to depart with only five hundred piculs of chintai on which he had to pay both duty and commission.[2]

Alcock was glad to be in Hakodate at this time. It seemed to him that his presence, in addition to the fine corvette, H.M.S. *Highflyer*, and the unexpected arrival of two more British warships, *Actaeon* and *Dove*, all gave evidence to the Japanese of the interest and importance attached to the installation of the British consul. To their presence he attributed in part his success in negotiating for the one building suitable for Hodgson, namely the temple designated for the new governor, and for a small house for the interpreter at a joint rental of less than £100 per annum.[3] The people occupying the small house were turned out 'by order and at a day's notice'.[4] The incoming governor was forced to share the quarters of his predecessor, who made it clear to the *Bakufu* in Yedo that he considered the arrangements for the British officials both unavoidable and temporary.[5]

[1] P.P. H. of C. 1860, lxix (2648), 70–71, Alcock to Russell, Yedo, 20 Oct. 1859. *B.G.K.M.* xxvii. 221, Doc. No. 111, Report of Hakodate *Bugyō* to *Rōjū*, 17 Oct. 1859.

[2] J.M. MSS. (Hakodate, 1859), W. Keswick to J. Whittall, Hakodate, 9 and 12 Aug. 1859. Chintai is a type of good quality seaweed.

[3] P.P. H. of C. 1860, lxix (2648), 70–72, Alcock to Russell, 20 Oct. 1859.

[4] Ibid., p. 72, Alcock to Hodgson, 15 Oct. 1859.

[5] *B.G.K.M.* xxvii. 221–22, 222, Doc. No. 111, Report of Hakodate *Bugyō* to *Rōjū*, 17 Oct. 1859.

Alcock's views on the commercial future of Hakodate were more optimistic than those of Keswick. The town had a secure, accessible harbour and a good anchorage. The people were friendly and quiet. No previous relations with the Dutch and no long-established monopolies or exactions had jeopardized their relations with foreigners. Salted and dried salmon were abundant and cheap; Irish potatoes, small but good, were plentiful. Bear, sea otter, and deer skins were more likely articles for European markets; and though badly dressed, were cheap enough to allow for redressing and some risk. Pheasants and wild duck were also available in quantities. In addition to these perishables there appeared to be large quantities of sulphur and lead, but these the Governor said were reserved for Japanese use.

The new order at Hakodate was yet to begin. Only three merchants had arrived, one British and two American. Certainly the immediate duties of Consul Hodgson were not onerous. As Alcock left him to the rigours and loneliness of Japan's northern winter—twenty-five days by the Japanese tri-monthly land post from Yedo—he stressed the following in his government's instructions regarding British relations with the Japanese.[1]

Firmness tempered with moderation, and great patience are essential conditions to success with the Japanese officials. . . . Rights secured by Treaty are never lightly to be abandoned, even when they appear to be of secondary importance; and when they bear directly upon material interests the faithful observance of its conditions must be steadily insisted upon. There are many modes, however, of insisting, and firmness is quite compatible with courtesy. Neither are all rights of equal importance, nor all times equally fitting for their assertion.

He further pointed out that

a collision with the authorities, or a resort to force . . . [was] the last thing Her Majesty's Government would desire. [It was] to be avoided by all means consistent with the safety of life and property, and the position it was the object of the Treaty to secure.[2]

Obstructions to Trade and Exchange

To live up to their government's instructions proved increasingly difficult for the British representatives during the

[1] P.P. H. of C. 1860, lxix (2648), 75–76, Alcock to Russell, Yedo 20 Oct. 1859.
[2] Ibid., p. 74, Alcock to Hodgson, H.M.S. *Highflyer*, 12 Oct. 1859.

summer and autumn of 1859. Britain's reverses in China seemed
to make the Japanese more indifferent to their treaty obligations. Alcock struggled patiently to fathom the internal political
conflicts which he thought might explain Japanese duplicity.
At the same time he sought to uphold the treaty rights of
British subjects.[1]

The *Bakufu* interposed more obstacles to the initiation of
unrestricted trade than to the opening of the ports. They were
not prepared to meet the extensive demands of the West for
Japanese products and were alarmed by the early drain on
the domestic market. They restricted direct dealing of Japanese
merchants with foreigners in most of the sought-after foods, as
well as in coal, raw silk, rapeseed oil, and vegetable wax. They
persisted in examining the contracts made with Japanese
merchants and raised objections to them. They permitted the
special privileges of the Chinese Guild at Nagasaki to continue,
in particular its control of the export market and monopoly on
copper and other products.[2]

The policies of the Japanese Treasury (*Kanjōkata*) which
handled the foreign exchange banking business at the customs
offices were even more frustrating to active free trade.[3] In
accordance with the 'weight for weight' provision of the
treaties, incoming foreign merchants could demand three
Japanese silver *ichibu* for one Mexican dollar. They anticipated
that the Japanese coin would continue to circulate not in
accordance with the prevailing market value of its metallic
content, but at three times that value—a precedent that had
brought profits to the Shogunate which had power to regulate
the supply of gold and silver and 'to adjust the balance between
these token silver coins and the two current measures of value,
gold and copper'. The Tokugawa had long kept the ratio of
gold to silver at about one to five and made four *ichibu* the
current equivalent of one gold cobang (*koban*), the chief gold
coin of the Empire. It was evident, however, that the fulfilment
of the treaty requirements would mean, if these national
regulations persisted, that the foreigners could demand twelve

[1] P.P. H. of C. 1860, lxix (2648), 27, 31–33, and F.O. 46/3, Alcock to
Malmesbury, No. 18, Yedo 28 July and No. 25, Yedo, 11 Aug. 1859.

[2] Paske-Smith, *Western Barbarians*, pp. 199–200. *Yokohama-shi Shi Kō*, vii. 89–91.
Otsuka, op. cit., p. 25.

[3] Paske-Smith, *Western Barbarians*, p. 219.

ichibu for four dollars and then purchase three gold cobangs which could be exported freely and sold in China for silver at the world rate of one to sixteen. The disappearance of Japan's gold seemed inevitable since it could thus be purchased at one-third of its current value.[1] The *Bakufu* having opposed the foreigners' currency demands from its first discussions with Perry, prepared to counteract them as soon as the ports were opened and prevent the loss of its gold.[2]

The Treasury therefore had several new coins ready for use in foreign trade. The most important was the half *ichibu* (*nishugin*) which contained as much silver as one and a half *ichibu* of the old currency. Two of these therefore equalled in weight one Mexican dollar. As the gold cobang still passed as four *ichibu* the foreigners using these new coins would have to pay four dollars for one cobang which was about its correct value.[3] Orders from the *Rōjū* on 24, 25, and 29 June 1859 announced that foreign gold and silver coins could be used in Japan and exchanged according to weight with this newly created Japanese currency beginning 30 June.[4] A commissioner of foreign affairs so notified the foreign consuls.[5] The Treasury continued to limit the number of dollars its officers could exchange for Japanese silver for any one person, thus thwarting, for example, Mackenzie's efforts in Nagasaki to invest his dollars on hand in gold upon satisfactory terms and leading Keswick to conclude that the only profitable trade at Yokohama would for some time be through barter.[6]

The effects of the new currency were drastic. To foreigners the prices of Japanese goods rose two hundred per cent. Trade

---

[1] P.P. H. of C. 1866, 1. 3–4. Ibid. 1867, lxix. 627, Sidney Locock, Secretary of the British Legation, *Report on the Weights, Measures and Currency of Japan* (Yokohama), 10 Jan. 1867.

[2] *B.G.K.M.* xxiv. 135–9, Doc. No. 82, Letter from three *gaikoku-bugyō*, 20 July 1859, shows clearly the *Bakufu* intentions in the issue of the new currency. The British called these *gaikoku-bugyō* governors, commissioners, and ministers of foreign affairs. As 'ministers' was generally used in the F.O. correspondence, it appears sometimes in this text. This office, however, should be understood as that of an under-secretary of foreign affairs.

[3] Locock, op. cit., p. 628. An assay in England showed that the gold cobang was worth about four silver dollars. P.P. H. of C. 1866, 1. 3–4.

[4] *B.G.K.M.* xxiii. 288, 295–6, 350–2, Docs. nos. 143, 148, and 180.

[5] P.P. H. of C. 1860, lxix (2648), 34–35.

[6] J.M. MSS. (Nagasaki, 1859), K. Mackenzie to Hong Kong Office, 5 July 1859; (Kanagawa, 1859), W. Keswick to J. Whittall, 21 July 1859.

stopped in protest at Yokohama. Although cobangs and silk were cheap in terms of prices outside Japan, the new value of the dollar precluded purchases. Keswick considered the situation so serious that unless changed, it were better not to have made the treaty. Old and new issues of paper notes in Nagasaki and the contracts between British and Japanese merchants made prior to 1 July caused additional complications in this city of the south. Consuls and merchants united in protest. The former demanded that proper notice and time be given for such a change and held the Japanese government responsible for damages and losses resulting from the new coinage.[1] By 14 July Mackenzie reported that the changes in the value of the dollar had stopped all transactions in produce.[2]

The *Bakufu* soon realized it was impossible either to mint enough of the new coins at the rate needed or to distribute them promptly enough to command their general use in foreign trade. For example, samples of the new money did not reach Hakodate until the end of July.[3] In consequence there is evidence that the government issued several general orders permitting the use of the old money under various circumstances and restrictions until enough new coins became available, advising the use of barter in foreign trade whenever possible.[4]

About the same time Alcock threatened the *Bakufu* with the consequences of the unexpected issue of their new currency. Although the British Consul-General had protested on 3 July that the new coinage was an obstacle to trade and had requested a meeting with the Japanese Commissioner of Foreign Affairs, he and Consul Hodgson openly admitted Japan's sovereign right to change her currency and sympathized with her desire to prevent a loss of gold.[5] The method adopted and its effect on the nascent foreign commerce, however, caused Alcock to take a firm stand in the interest of British subjects.

---

[1] J.M. MSS. (Kanaqawce, 1859), W. Keswick to J. Whittall, 21 July, 1859. P.P. H. of C. 1860, lxix (2648), 15, 34–35, 37. Alcock supported this in a letter to a Japanese commissioner of foreign affairs, 9 Aug. 1859. *B.G.K.M.* xxv. 6 (Eng. Docs.).

[2] J.M. MSS. (Nagasaki, 1859), K. Mackenzie to Shanghai Office, 14 July 1859.

[3] *B.G.K.M.* xxiii. 374–5, Doc. no. 194.

[4] Ibid., 295–96, 356–52, Docs. nos. 148 (24 June), 180 (29 July) and xxiv. 199–201, Doc. no. 117 (24 July 1859).

[5] Ibid. xxiii. 9–10 (Eng. Docs.). P. P. H. of C. 1860, lxix (2648), 15, 34, Alcock to Malmesbury, Yedo, 13 July 1859; Hodgson to Alcock, Nagasaki, 12 July 1859.

He asked that funds needed for the maintenance of his consulate be supplied by the Treasury at the rate in use when the treaty was signed—specifically, three *ichibu* to the dollar—and declared that the introduction of any new coin in exchange for foreign money must have the concurrence of the treaty powers that it conformed with the treaty and was equitable to the foreign merchant.[1] He recognized that the new currency accorded with the letter of the treaty by giving the British weight for weight in silver coins. The Japanese government had, however, arbitrarily and singly called into question the whole sense and object of Article X by decreeing that 'the money of the foreigner shall be depreciated by two-thirds of the value he has hitherto been led to consider it in the Japanese market, to his loss and the corresponding profit of the Japanese'. The right of the Japanese government to bring their currency into accord with that of other nations recently associated with it by 'Treaties of Amity and Friendship' was undoubted. Since these treaties guaranteed from wrong and injury all signatory powers, however, any measure affecting the currency as it existed when the treaties were concluded must not be designed to tax foreign trade or mulct the foreigner for the profit of the Japanese government or native dealers. Efforts to do so would cause 'heavy claims for indemnity in the shape of compensation for loss inflicted'.[2]

Much to Alcock's surprise and without further pressure the *Bakufu* capitulated. The Japanese Commissioners of Foreign Affairs feared war and hoped the currency issue could be reasonably settled in amicable discussion.[3] Upon their recommendation the *Rōjū* notified Alcock and Harris that the new coins would be withdrawn until negotiations on the currency were completed and announced that the exchange rate of one dollar to three *ichibu* would be resumed for a while.[4] The Shogunate regarded the treaties at best as temporary, and this

[1] *B.G.K.M.* xxiv. 9–10 (Eng. Docs.), Alcock to Japanese Commissioner of Foreign Affairs, Yedo, 17 July 1859.

[2] Ibid. 11–16, Alcock to Japanese Commissioner of Foreign Affairs, Yedo, 19 July 1859.

[3] Ibid. 135–9, Doc. No. 82, *Gaikoku-bugyō* probably to *Rōjū*, 20 July 1859.

[4] Ibid. 150–1, Doc. No. 92, Two *Rōjū* members to Alcock and Harris, 21 July 1859; 166, Doc. No. 102, notification—*Rōjū* to town officials (*machi-bugyō*), about 22 July 1859.

concession an expedient of brief duration. But on 8 August the *Rōjū* led Alcock to think the order was not provisional, but definite.[1]

Alcock's hope that the currency issue was thus settled was far from fulfilled. The import trade now suffered.[2] Japanese tradesmen still refused to receive dollars in spite of the government's order to do so. The Treasury strictly limited the supply of Japanese coins in exchange for dollars. Alcock had difficulty getting *ichibu* to run the consulate, British merchants protested and demanded compensation for losses arising from non-exchange of dollars and the detention of ships with unemployed capital. By 27 August Alcock calculated that 100,000 dollars would not liquidate the losses suffered by British merchants in Kanagawa alone. Again he held the Japanese government responsible for these damages resulting from its violation of Article X.

To limit the growing burden of such claims and to meet the demands of foreign trade, he persuaded the Commissioners of Foreign Affairs to increase their silver currency by recoining into *ichibu* any dollars which the foreign merchants might desire to exchange. They promised in ten days to have dies ready to coin sixteen thousand *ichibu* a day. And it was agreed that the Treasury would receive not less than one thousand dollars nor more than five thousand dollars from one individual. Alcock hoped by this policy to check the current export of gold and silver coin, the former then yielding a profit of one hundred per cent. and the latter between six and seven per cent. Alcock advised specific care against the counterfeit dollars and *ichibu* already in circulation. And he urged the Japanese to increase the value of their gold coinage in relation to silver.[3]

The *Bakufu* failed to follow this last advice and its decree of early July declaring gold and silver contraband soon went unheeded.[4] With an increase in the supply of silver *ichibu*, trade

[1] P.P. H. of C. 1860, lxix (2648), 42, Alcock to Malmesbury, Yedo, 13 Aug. 1859.

[2] Ibid., p. 48, Alcock to Russell, Yedo, 3 Sept. 1859. *B.G.K.M.* xxv. 7, 25, 33–34, 40 (Eng. Docs.), Alcock to Japanese Commissioner of Foreign Affairs, 9, 17, 27, and 30 Aug. 1859. J.M. MSS. (Kanagawa, 1859), W. Keswick to J. Whittall, 25, 27 July 1859.

[3] *B.G.K.M.* xxvi. 4 (Eng. Docs.), Alcock to Japanese Commissioners of Foreign Affairs, 9 Sept. 1859. P.P. H. of C. 1860, lxix (2648), 53, Alcock to Russell, Yedo, 7 Sept. 1859.   [4] Takekoshi, op. cit. iii. 336.

was resumed at a moderate rate and barter continued.[1] A great traffic in gold began in October. Knowing that their government dared not violate the treaties, Japanese hoarders of the coins willingly offered them to foreigners who could now pay in negotiable Japanese silver. Old gold coins, held back in violation of laws requiring their being turned in for new and debased currency, brought relatively higher prices. British traders contemptuously disregarded the consular *Notification* which limited British subjects to five thousand dollars in exchange at one time.[2] Even Keswick and Barber of Jardine, Matheson & Company took part, sending in to the Government Exchange Bank in the customs house on 3 November requisitions for 5,400,000 dollars for which, however, they received 746 dollars in *ichibu*. False names were used to increase individual funds and to mock the Japanese. For instance, about the same time, 'Mr. Doodle-doo', 'Mr. Is-it-not', 'Mr. Hookit', and many other fakes applied for *ichibu* equivalent to sums ranging from 250 million dollars to one sextillion dollars.[3]

This frenzy for *ichibu* to buy Japanese gold coins lasted about six weeks. It aroused animosity between Alcock and the British merchants and led to exaggerated accounts of the gold export and the profits realized. Recent research in the Jardine, Matheson Archive points out that the gold drain at its height in 1859 amounted to 'some three large shipments salable at roughly $200,000': and that Jardine's profits on gold coins averaged about fifty per cent.—much below those usually reported as possible at the official rate of exchange, and much less than the current profits in silk, seaweed, and fish oil.[4]

An alarming amount of gold, nevertheless, left the country in 1859 and early 1860. Both Japanese and foreign merchants made money rapidly. Trade expanded in consequence. The government failed to maintain strict control. But the quicker

[1] J.M. MSS. (Kanagawa, 1859), J. S. Barber to J. Whittall, 16 Sept. 1859; (Nagasaki, 1859), K. Mackenzie to Hong Kong Office, 3 Oct.; to J. Whittall, 5 Oct. 1859.

[2] P.P. H. of C. 1860, lxix (2617), 1, 4–6, Alcock to Russell, Yedo, 23 Nov. 1859. Alcock, *The Capital of the Tycoon*, i. 281–3. John McMaster, 'The Japanese Gold Rush of 1859', *The Journal of Asian Studies*, xix. (May, 1960), 278–9.

[3] P.P. H. of C. 1860, lxix (2617), 8–9, *Requisitions on the Japanese Treasury Dept.*, 2, 4, 6 Nov. 1859.

[4] McMaster, op. cit., pp. 279–84.

readjustment of the relative value of gold to silver may have resulted.[1] Anglo-Japanese relations, however, were seriously jeopardized. Alcock's orders to the consuls to punish the culprits with fines and imprisonment in accordance with the Queen's Order-in-Council, and to send incorrigibles out of the country, had little effect and Russell's repudiation of the traders' behaviour came too late.[2]

Terrified at the disappearance of its gold, the *Bakufu* in desperation stopped the issue of silver *ichibu*, indicted the sale of copper, and further restricted for an indefinite period the sale of Japanese goods in foreign demand.[3] Keswick reported calmly that the inadequate issue of *ichibu* was a serious obstacle to trade, that the dollar had declined fifteen per cent. in its circulation among natives, and that, seaweed excepted, all produce was limited to the sale of only a picul or two per person a day.[4] In Nagasaki the daily allowance of exchange at the Treasury—three dollars for residents and one dollar for servants and seamen—was cut in half for forty-five days because no money came from Yedo. And, of course, no attempt was made to redeem the paper money held by merchants.[5] In Hakodate the customs house was closed.[6]

Alcock protested on 3 December that no *ichibu* had been issued in exchange for dollars for more than two weeks. He demanded resumption of the Treasury service to meet the requirements of trade. He admitted the guilt of foreigners in their excessive demands for *ichibu* but also attributed blame to the Japanese— their inadequate provision of coin in relation to their promises in August, as well as their faulty and not impartial system of distribution.[7]

British grievances intensified as the first six months of the treaties drew to a close. On 6 December Alcock wrote Russell

[1] Paske-Smith, *Western Barbarians*, pp. 212–13. Shinjo, op. cit., p. 10.

[2] P.P. H. of C. 1860, lxix (2617), 2–8, Alcock to Vyse, Yedo, 21 Nov. 1859; (2648), 88, Russell to Alcock, 25 Feb. 1860.

[3] Ibid. (2617), 1, Alcock to Russell, Yedo, 23 Nov. 1859. *B.G.K.M.* xxviii. 37 (Eng. Docs.), Eusden to commissioners of Foreign Affairs, Yedo, 17 Nov. 1859.

[4] J.M. MSS. (Kanagawa, 1859), W. Keswick to J. Whittall, 25 Nov. 1859.

[5] P.P. H. of C. 1860, lxix (2648), 98, Consul Morrison to Alcock, Nagasaki, 28 Nov. 1859.

[6] Ibid., p. 97, Consul Hodgson to Alcock, Hakodate, 4 Nov. 1859.

[7] *B.G.K.M.* xxix. 11–13 (Eng. Docs.), Alcock to Japanese Comms oners of Foreign Affairs, Yedo, 3 Dec. 1859.

that the treaties with Japan were 'virtually annulled'.[1] Responsible Japanese ministers refused to receive Alcock, delegating to subordinates the discussion of all matters with foreign representatives. Alcock's intimation that such action could lead to war with England gave him access to the Commissioners of Foreign Affairs the next day. He confronted them with their continued violations of the treaty: (1) their prohibition of trade in iriko, awabi, lead, and sulphur at Hakodate and Nagasaki; their illegal interference with the export of silk and other articles; and the intervention of officials, interested in trade, in the free transaction of business between foreigners and Japanese dealers; (2) their failure to provide facilities required by trade for the exchange of foreign money with Japanese currency and to permit the dollar to pass current thoughout Japan for corresponding values in native currency; (3) their lack of protection to foreign life and property—foreigners were attacked, insulted, and stoned. In November a British subject was killed and Alcock himself was threatened by a samurai. Pilfering, robberies, and incendiarism were frequent in Nagasaki; (4) their denial or delays in granting the needed facilities for the choice or occupation of foreign locations at the ports. He asked for immediate redress of these continuing violations, and concluded with a threat. War, he said, was the alternative when reason failed to settle affairs between nations. The armies of England and France were already en route to China to enforce their treaties with that country and would soon be within five days of Yedo.[2]

Here, to Lord Russell's dismay, Alcock distinctly exceeded his instructions. The British government did not want war, nor loss of face if the grievances were not redressed. The British Foreign Minister advised Alcock 'to soothe differences' rather than 'insist upon peremptory demands'.[3] Alcock had lost his patience. He felt responsibility for enforcing the treaty, exaggerated the seriousness of the situation, and always suspected oriental tactics. He and the consuls complained more about the

[1] P.P. H. of C. 1860, lxix (2648), 89.

[2] Ibid. 92–96, Alcock to Russell, Yedo, 10 Dec. 1859 and encls. *B.G.K.M.* xxx. 7–15 (Eng. Docs.), Alcock to Japanese Commissioners of Foreign Affairs, Yedo, 14, 19, and 21 Dec. 1859; xxxi. 1–4 (Eng. Docs.), Alcock to same, Yedo, 24 and 28 Dec. 1859.

[3] P.P. H. of C. 1860, lxix (2648), 98, Russell to Alcock, 28 Feb. 1860.

hindrances to trade than the British merchants themselves who, either legally or illegally, had done well. Nevertheless, Alcock found encouragement in the extent of trade carried on in spite of the handicaps. For the first six months Japan's foreign trade was approximated at £1,000,000 and the British controlled more than half of it. Tea and silk promised to be the great staples of the future. Two thousand piculs of raw silk at from 450 to 500 dollars per picul had been shipped at a reported profit of forty per cent., and tea of excellent quality was sent in quantity to the American market.[1]

In conjunction with the threat of war Alcock had offered more remedies for the currency problem in an effort to make the legitimate dollar pass current and to effect a more equitable distribution of whatever native coins were supplied. These suggestions and his frequent advice on changing the relative value of gold and silver bore fruit with the coming of the new year. The *Bakufu* did agree to stamp the dollar at the value of three *ichibu* to ensure its acceptance by native dealers and to require all requisitions on the Treasury for the still limited number of *ichibu* which could be minted daily, to be counter-signed by the consuls.[2] Changing the value of gold in relation to silver proved more difficult. The *Bakufu* wished to fix the value of the gold cobang at fifteen *ichibu*. Alcock recommended that it be twelve in order to establish the equilibrium existing else-where in the world. The Japanese compromised at thirteen and a half *ichibu* as an experiment, a rate Alcock believed too high to prevent the use of foreign gold to purchase silver *ichibu* for export. At the same time the Shogunate redeemed the old paper money issued by them at Nagasaki, much to Alcock's satisfaction.[3]

These efforts to correct the currency situation combined with the growth of trade, regardless of *Bakufu* interference, tempered Alcock's outlook at the beginning of 1860. But the past six months had been exasperating for the officials of both Britain and Japan. Suspicion and fear were mutual. Neither government could control factions among its own nationals.

[1] P.P. H. of C. 1860, lxix (2673), 8, Alcock to Russell, Yedo, 6 Mar. 1860.

[2] *B.G.K.M.* xxxii. 20–23 (Eng. Docs.), Alcock to Japanese Commissioner of Foreign Affairs, Yedo, 18 Jan. 1860.

[3] P.P. H. of C. 1860, lxix (2673), 1–3, Alcock to Russell, Yedo, 20 Feb. 1860 and encls. This letter was written more than a month after the good work began.

Rōnin and samurai attacked foreigners. Drunken and disorderly sailors from Western ships repeatedly outraged the peaceful native population. Responsible Englishmen in London and Japan demanded that Alcock enforce the treaty. The Japanese at the same time hated what many British and other foreigners were doing to their country. By direct and indirect means they hoped to drive them away.[1] In appraising the situation at the close of 1859, Alcock could not be confident of the future. Both trade and diplomatic relations with Japan would depend, he thought, upon the real intentions of the Japanese government, on the conduct of foreigners and daimyo, and on the progress of British affairs in China.[2]

[1] Tokyo University MSS., *Dai Nippon Ishin Shiryō Kohon* (Manuscripts of Historical Data of the Restoration), 3,000 vols., mlxxvi. Report on Foreign Attitudes and Sentiments Toward Japan, Dec. 1859. P.P. H. of C. 1860, lxix (2617), 2–3, Alcock to Vyse, Yedo, 21 Nov. 1859.

[2] Ibid. (2648), 98–100, Alcock to Russell, 7 Jan. 1860.

III

CONTENTION AND COMPROMISE
1860–JUNE 1862

British Insecurity and Isolation

WHILE British trade prospered during the first half of 1860, anti-foreign activities multiplied. Alcock began to realize they had wide implications for the *Bakufu* as well as the West. His native linguist, Denkichi, hated by Japanese officials because of the information he gave Alcock, was murdered on 29 January at the gateway of the legation.[1] The assassination of two Dutch sea captains in February further emphasized the insecurity of life in the foreign community. Alcock's protests to the Japanese authorities accomplished nothing. No efforts were made to apprehend or punish the criminals. Was it weakness or complicity on the part of the Shogunate?[2] The British minister could not determine.

The assassination of the *Tairō*, Ii Naosuke, on 24 March by the followers of the disgruntled Prince of Mito not only proved the extent of the hatred of the Shogun's government but also seemed to cast light on the anti-foreign movement. In his letter to Russell recounting the event, Alcock speculated that the anti-foreign actions of the Shogun's enemies might in the end lead to a broader policy towards the West. Mito, he said, was alleged to have promoted the second American treaty negotiated by Harris.[3] His violence and the hostility of other daimyo might well be a deliberate strategy to cause confusion in which the discontented—perhaps the best friends of the West—could seize the reins of power and inaugurate a more liberal and enlightened national policy. Sensing the growing political

---

[1] P.P. H. of C. 1860, lxix (2694), 1–2, Alcock to Russell, Yedo, 21 Feb. 1860. Alcock, *Capital of the Tycoon*, i. 331–7. [2] Ibid., pp. 340–1.

[3] For Mito, see for consistency, pp. 32–33, 35–40. Actually Nariaki had only conceded that the *Bakufu* might not be able to refuse the treaty and suggested as an alternative that he be sent on a friendship mission to America. Beasley, *Documents*, pp. 168–9.

antagonisms in Japan, Alcock concluded that foreigners were likely to be attacked or defended on much the same principle, that of indifference to anything but the probable effect of the consequence on the current political contest.[1]

The need for greater protection for the foreigners in both Yedo and Yokohama (no matter who their assailants) was obvious to Alcock and the *Bakufu* alike. Although aware that the murders of foreigners had always occurred when Western warships were in Japanese waters, the British minister appealed to Vice-Admiral Hope to allocate permanently more than one British man-of-war to the treaty ports, believing that the absence of such protection emboldened the government and the anti-foreign factions to violate the treaty and neglect their obligations for the safety of foreigners.[2] The Foreign Secretary and the Admiralty Board supported Alcock's request. More ships could be released for Japan now that the war with China had ended. Lord Russell made clear, however, the purpose of these additional British ships in Japan. They were to impress on the authorities and people of Japan the power of Britain and threaten them with serious difficulties should they disregard or obstruct Britain's treaty rights. He prohibited any recourse to violence, except as a means of protecting the lives and properties of British subjects and those of all nations in Japan then friendly to Britain.[3]

The *Bakufu*, on their part, used the need for protection as a cause for further restrictions on the liberties of the foreign officials and the *Rōjū* continued to withhold all information regarding current political developments. Troops from certain daimyo and the Shogun's own bodyguard filled the legation. A few mounted native guards of doubtful loyalty in case of danger accompanied Alcock whenever he rode out of the grounds of his residence in defiance of the government's request that all ministers remain within their gates. Alcock considered himself and his diplomatic colleagues virtual prisoners in their own legations. They were surrounded by spies and systematically isolated from all contacts with Japanese of the educated

[1] F.O. 46/7, Alcock to Russell, No. 24, Yedo, 26 Apr. 1860.
[2] Ad. I/5735, Alcock to Hope, Yedo, 4 Feb. 1860, encl. in Hope to Adm., 8 Mar. 1860.
[3] Ad. I/5745, Russell to Adm., 25 Apr. 1860. Ad. 13/29, Adm. to Hope, 26 Apr. 1860.

and higher social classes. No one could approach them without permission from the government. They had no reliable sources of information. When reviewing conditions as the first year of the Treaty of Yedo came to its close, Alcock felt that the foreign communities, defenceless and ignorant, were at the mercy of the government of the day and could be massacred at any moment.[1]

Although he could understand Japan's adverse reactions to the intrusions of the West in the light of England's own resentments to great innovations, the British minister felt alone and weary and saw no relief from his difficulties. Up to six months were still required for an answer to his letters to the Foreign Office, a fact often detrimental to the public service and to the position of the minister himself. He asked London to consider the offer of the Peninsular and Oriental Steam Navigation Company to establish a monthly or bi-monthly communication between Yedo, Nagasaki, and Shanghai upon the grant of a moderate subsidy.[2]

Commercial Prosperity

The British merchants' view of their first year in Japan was more favourable. The residences of foreign consuls and merchants in Nagasaki and Kanagawa were now established. Transit on the high road between Yokohama and Yedo was open to consuls and their couriers. The Japanese ratio of gold to silver had been altered to approximate that in Europe—one cobang equalled twelve *ichibu* or four Mexican dollars. Thus the temptation to export gold was curtailed; and the termination in July 1860 of the treaty stipulation that the Japanese government should furnish British subjects with Japanese coin in exchange for theirs removed another cause of difficulty. The nature and extent of trading operations at any given time could now determine the exchange value of the dollar.

Britain's share in Japan's foreign trade had amounted to a million sterling, and profits were large. The year had proved conclusively that Japanese tea and silk could compete in the

---

[1] Alcock, *Capital of the Tycoon*, i. 354–6, 376–8. F.O. 46/8, Alcock to Russell, No. 40, Yedo, 11 July 1860.

[2] F.O. 46/8, Alcock to Russell, No. 53, Yedo, 29 July 1860.

home market in quality and price with that of China and there was promise of an ample increase in the quantity for export. The Jardine, Matheson firm was counting on 30,000 bales of silk from Japan in 1860 which combined with at least 70,000 bales from China would be 'the largest export ever known from the East by about 20,000 bales'.[1] Numerous other commodities —vegetable wax and oils, mother-of-pearl shells, camphor, gall-nuts—had been discovered and were calculated to yield large profits.[2] It was known that minerals existed in abundance but the Japanese prohibited their export. The local coal had proved acceptable to the British Navy. In March Admiral Hope had ordered a depot of 10,000 tons established at Nagasaki.[3] An import trade, however, had yet to be developed by creating wants for British manufactures.

British merchants in England and China were also well satisfied with the results of the past twelve months' trade—even surprised that so much had been accomplished.[4] Edmund Hammond, then Permanent Under-Secretary of Foreign Affairs, was so impressed with these prospects for trade with Japan that he recommended 'official support without any consideration of expense' for Alcock's request for an increase in personnel in Britain's consular and diplomatic establishments in the Japanese ports.[5]

Bakufu *Duplicity*

In spite of this prosperity no peace lay ahead for the frightened and frustrated British minister in his struggle with the double-dealing *Bakufu*. It, too, was harassed and disturbed, being pressed by the Court for the abrogation of the treaties and by the foreigners for treaty enforcement. Hoping to gain time, the

[1] J.M. MSS. (Shanghai, Private), J. Whittall to W. Keswick, who was at Kanagawa, Shanghai, 23 July 1860.

[2] F.O. 46/8, Alcock to Russell, Nos. 40 and 46, Yedo, 11 and 24 July 1860.

[3] Ad. I/5735, Hope to Adm., 14 Mar. 1860.

[4] Alcock, *Capital of the Tycoon*, i. 374. P.R.O. 30/22/49, Elgin to Russell, 6 Dec. 1860.

[5] F.O. 46/8, Hammond's comment on back of Alcock to Russell, No. 41, Yedo, 13 July 1860. Consequent arrangements with H.M. Treasury provided for a resident consul at Kanagawa, a secretary at Yedo, a secretary and interpreter in charge of student interpreters, two assistants, an assistant and medical attendant at Hakodate, a medical attendant at Yedo, two further interpreters, and a junior assistant as a supernumerary interpreter; 262/14, Russell to Alcock, 7 Dec. 1860.

Rōjū blamed their ineffective action in both cases on the disunity of the country. In September 1860, however, they committed themselves to the Court's demands. In their memorandum requesting the marriage of the Emperor's sister with the Shogun to demonstrate the unity of Kyoto and Yedo, the *Rōjū* promised to 'cancel the treaties by negotiation or expel the foreigners by force' within a period of seven to ten years. They planned to use the intervening time to develop the required naval and military forces. But should the foreigners initiate hostilities earlier the Yedo ministers promised immediate action. A few months later they admitted the need for limited concessions to foreigners during this interim period to ward off a hasty conflict. Thus they justified their commercial treaties with Prussia, Switzerland, and Belgium which, however, did not extend trade beyond the already opened ports.[1]

That this lay behind the exasperating delays, unfulfilled promises, and increasingly apparent weakness of the *Bakufu*, Alcock had no way of knowing. Completely cut off from Kyoto, denied all contacts with *Bakufu* ministers except in the presence of numerous Japanese of lower rank, and surrounded by spies in his own legation, the British minister had to grope his way to an understanding of the realities of Japanese intentions. His audience with the Shogun and presentation of his credentials in August 1860 added to his knowledge of Japanese ceremonials, but opened up no better relation with the Japanese ministers.[2] A trip into the country beyond the treaty ports, however, soon gave him faith in the friendliness and intelligence of the Japanese people while he grappled with the two major issues of the period:[3] the security of foreign lives and the Japanese efforts to postpone the opening of Hyogo and Niigata to trade and Yedo and Osaka to foreign residents, issues which soon became involved with each other.[4]

---

[1] Beasley, *Documents*, pp. 52, 54, 203–8.

[2] Alcock, *Capital of the Tycoon*, i. 377–94.

[3] F.O. 46/8, Alcock to Russell, No. 59, Yedo, 10 Oct. 1860. This friendliness of the common people, frequently noted by Alcock and other Westerners, had no political significance, as these people had little knowledge of and no part in the current political issues which were dividing the upper classes in the feudal hierarchy. Oka Yoshitake, *Kindai Nihon Seiji Shi* (Political History of Modern Japan) I (Tokyo, 1962–), i. 36–37.

[4] Treaty of Yedo, Art. III provided that Niigata, or another convenient port on the west coast of Japan should be opened to trade on 1 Jan. 1860 and Hyogo on 1 Jan.

The Removal of the Legation to Yokohama

The *Bakufu* put forth its request to defer the opening of the ports and cities in August 1860. At a conference with Alcock its Commissioners of Foreign Affairs argued the need for this concession because of the ill feeling towards foreigners arising from the increasing prices and outflow of native produce. Alcock yielded regarding Yedo. As the seat of government not directly connected with trade, he conceded that its opening might be temporarily postponed. No other change in the treaty stipulations, he said, could be considered.[1] He then turned his attention to matters of security.

The arrival of four British warships in December, professing a friendly visit, reinforced Alcock's stand on Britain's interest in the fulfilment of the treaties. At Nagasaki they seemed to bring the Japanese authorities to terms with the British merchants over the latter's long-standing grievances.[2] Such a squadron, however, had no effect on the periodic alarms of a general massacre of the foreign communities. A warning by a Japanese Commissioner of Foreign Affairs and a display of government anxiety about a rumoured attack by a mob of several hundred *rōnin* made Alcock question the gravity of the danger. He already doubted the alleged popular discontent and saw no signs of ill feeling towards foreigners among the common people. He knew, however, that the *Bakufu* was determined to defer the opening of more ports and further restrict foreign intercourse. He suspected that among both daimyo and officials men existed who saw in foreign trade the seeds of revolution and who might risk a rupture with all Western powers at once to prevent its development.[3] He asked Rear-Admiral Lewis T. Jones to leave two ships in the bay of Yedo to protect Yoko-hama until he verified the situation.[4]

1863. British subjects were promised residence in Yedo from 1 Jan. 1862 and in Osaka from 1 Jan. 1863 'for purposes of trade only'.

[1] F.O. 46/8, encl. in Alcock to Russell, No. 56, 28 Aug. 1860. Japan Gaimushō (Japanese Ministry of Foreign Affairs), *Nichi-Ei Gaikō Shi* (History of Japanese-British Relations), Secret, 3 vols. (Tokyo, 1937–8), i. 75. Among microfilms of the Archives of Japanese Ministry of Foreign Affairs 1868–1945 in the Library of Congress and listed as SP 2.

[2] F.O. 46/8, Alcock to Russell, No. 82, Yedo, 31 Dec. 1860 and encl., Morrison to Jones, 19 Dec. 1860.

[3] P.P. H. of C. 1861, lxvi (2829), 1–3, Alcock to Russell, Yedo, 1 Jan. 1861.

[4] Ad. I/5762, Alcock to Jones, 1 Jan. 1861, encl. in Jones to Hope, 2 Jan. 1861.

Another murder on 15 January justified this request. Hendrik Heusken, the secretary of the American legation, was the victim. The desertion of his Japanese protectors, and the subsequent indifference of the officials convinced Alcock that the *Bakufu* could neither be trusted to prevent such crimes nor to punish the guilty. He and his colleagues from France, Holland, and Prussia moved their legations to Yokohama where the British fleet could defend them.[1] Although approved by Russell on Alcock's grounds that the move avoided a rupture with the Japanese government while Alcock demanded more effective protection, this was a foolish act.[2] Harris refused to leave Yedo, claiming full confidence in the guards of the *Bakufu*—thus beginning his cleavage with Alcock.[3] The Japanese government was relieved of responsibility and, as Alcock soon realized, would have been glad to let the foreign envoys remain indefinitely in Yokohama.[4] And the British merchants, although given a chance to air their grievances and learn about the difficulties of the British minister in securing the enforcement of the treaty, did not relish the presence of the legation in their midst.[5] Keswick had already written that the recent alarm seemed groundless and that he hoped Alcock would soon re-establish his residence in the capital.[6]

Alcock forced the *Bakufu* to hasten its arrangements for his return to Yedo by threatening to use the intervening time to travel through the country and visit the ports, the opening of which the Japanese had asked to postpone. During three conferences with an accredited Japanese minister on 21, 22, and 27 February, the French minister, M. de Bellecourt, and Alcock exacted the following: a formal invitation in the name of the Shogun for their return to Yedo; the promise of the Shogun and the *Rōjū* to provide thereafter for the safety of the legations; the alleviation of some of the grievances of the Yokohama merchants; and arrangements for a public recep-

[1] P.P. H. of C. 1861, lxvi (2829), 6–10, Alcock to Russell, Yedo, 26 Jan. 1861 and encls. 1 and 2.
[2] F.O. 262/21, Russell to Alcock, No. 36, Apr. 1861 (no day given).
[3] Alcock, *Capital of the Tycoon*, ii. 55.
[4] Ibid. 61.
[5] P.P. H. of C. 1861, lxvi (2829), 57–69, Minutes of Meeting, 7 and 19 Feb. 1861.
[6] J.M. MSS. (Kanagawa, 1861), W. Keswick to Shanghai Office, 17 Feb. 1861, and to Hong Kong Office, 13 Feb. 1861.

tion of the foreign representatives upon their arrival in the capital with a royal salute to the national flags when they were again raised over the legations. Yedo's unusually prompt acceptance of these conditions made possible the return of the foreign representatives on 2 March. Alcock foolishly believed they had achieved a more open, respected, and secure position in relation to the Shogunate.[1]

Alcock's Growing Awareness of Bakufu Motives

Such optimism was short-lived. Thwarted continuously in his efforts to get reliable information about political and commerical developments from the Japanese authorities, Alcock determined to see more of the country and the people for himself.[2] During June despite warnings of danger and opposition from the local officials, the British minister travelled overland from Nagasaki across Kyūshū through the Inland Sea to Hyogo and Osaka, and thence overland to Yedo. The Netherlands minister, J. K. de Wit, Consul Morrison, Charles Wirgman of the *London Illustrated News*, and A. J. Gower of the consular service went with him. Their journey was arduous and enlightening. Formidable restrictions on their route through the territories of some daimyo and strenuous efforts to keep them away from Kyoto in violation of the treaty, made Alcock recognize for the first time the limits of the Shogun's power and of the treaties made with him. Since the Mikado had not ratified these treaties, the daimyo outside the Shogun's domains could not be compelled to observe them. He now understood the government's need to consider public opinion and its recent petition to be released from the opening of the two cities and the two ports.[3] What he saw of Hyogo and Osaka, however, convinced him that the free development of foreign commerce with Japan would be dependent on the right of free access to those cities. He perceived clearly why the *Bakufu*, in its hostility to any extension of Western trade, was striving to keep the foreigners from these great commercial centres and the Inland Sea and to gain time for military preparations 'before a final

---

[1] P.P. H. of C. 1861, lxvi (2829), 81–82, Alcock to Russell, Yedo, 2 Mar. 1861. Alcock, *Capital of the Tycoon*, ii. 61–63. *Nichi-Ei Gaikō Shi*, i. 56.

[2] F.O. 46/12, Alcock to Russell, Nos. 38 and 48, 18 Apr., 28 May 1861.

[3] Alcock, *Capital of the Tycoon*, x., ii. 68–70, 77–81, 103–6, 135–8.

rupture and chances of collision'.[1] Thus after two years Alcock was sensing some of the actualities of *Bakufu* policy.

With such judgements in mind Alcock returned to his residence at Tōzenji on 4 July to welcome the newly appointed secretary of the legation, Lawrence Oliphant. Two important letters awaited him—one from the Shogun to Queen Victoria, the other to him from the Japanese Commissioners of Foreign Affairs. Both asked that the opening of the two ports and the two cities be postponed for seven years in order to mollify and enlighten the hostile Japanese public regarding the extension of foreign trade.[2] Similar notes were sent to the other foreign representatives. No action could be taken, however, before the question of the security of life at the legation became uppermost.

The First Attack on the British Legation

Near midnight the next day, 5 July, a band of assassins broke into the British residence determined to kill the entire staff. Owing to their ignorance of the building they failed. Oliphant, Morrison, and two servants of the legation were wounded. Seventeen of the *Bakufu* guards were killed or wounded in the surprise attack. And of the fourteen assailants, the guards killed three and arrested one. Three others committed suicide. Seven fled.[3] Alcock immediately asked Captain Craigie of H.M. dispatch boat *Ringdove* then at Kanagawa for a guard of marines to protect the legation.[4] And he appealed to Admiral Hope for the adequate naval protection long sanctioned by London but never provided by the commander of the China Station.[5] He had no intention of leaving Yedo at this time. It was more than a month later that he decided to have a temporary residence in Yokohama while keeping his official headquarters in Yedo.[6]

[1] F.O. 46/12, Alcock to Russell, No. 55, Yedo, 10 July 1861.

[2] P.P. H. of C. 1862, lxiv. 33–35, letters from the Shogun enclosed in Alcock to Russell, Yedo, 16 Aug. 1861.

[3] Ibid. 1–4, 18–19, Alcock to Russell, Yedo, 6 July 1861 and encl. 2; encls. 3 and 4 in 25 July 1861. *Nichi-Ei Gaikō Shi*, i. 58.

[4] Ad. I/5762, Alcock to Craigie, Yedo, 6 July 1861, 2 a.m., encl. in Hope to Adm., Yedo, 10 Aug. 1861.

[5] F.O. 46/12, Alcock to Hope, No. 39, Yedo, 8 July 1861; encl. in No. 54 to Russell.

[6] F.O. 46/13, Alcock to Russell, No. 66, Yedo, 18 Aug. 1861.

The attack on Tōzenji was attributed to the disbanded followers of Mito at the instigation of an emissary from the Prince of Tsushima.[1] It established the impotence of the *Bakufu* to protect the lives of the foreign representatives and led to Britain's assignment of a mounted escort from her forces in China to defend her legation in Yedo.[2]

Japanese Efforts to Postpone the Opening of Additional Ports

The recent requests of the *Bakufu* for the postponement of the opening of the two ports and the two cities came up for discussion in conferences in August. By this time Admiral Hope had arrived with the squadron and the wounded Oliphant was about to be dispatched to London with the Shogun's letter to the Queen, together with Alcock's recommendations on its proposal. The naval commander and Oliphant both accompanied Alcock to these conferences when for the first time the British envoy talked in confidence with the Japanese Commissioners of Foreign Affairs without the presence of all the governors, the *ōmetsuke* (chief censor), and a retinue of subordinates.[3] Several developments made Alcock conciliatory. It now seemed probable that the *Bakufu* had neither foreknowledge nor connexion with the attack at Tōzenji. The trade reports for the first six months of 1861 were so encouraging that Alcock wished to avoid a political crisis which might check Britain's expanding commerce.[4] A recent letter from Russell had sanctioned some concession in that it empowered Alcock, should he decide on postponement, to make a rule under his Order in Council, which would prohibit British citizens under penalty to take up residence in Yedo on 1 January 1862 in accordance with the treaty.[5] Furthermore recent Russian activities in

---

[1] The Daimyo of Tsushima, the victim of Russian hostilities in his territory because of his opposition to the erection of permanent buildings by a Russian naval officer, alleged to be for the repair of Russian ships in the harbour at Tsushima, was reported to have wished to destroy the great 'foreign chief' in revenge against all foreigners. F.O. 46/12, Alcock to Russell, No. 59, Yedo, 26 July 1861; 46/13, Alcock to Russell, Conf'l., Yedo, 2 Aug. 1861.

[2] Ibid., No. 63, Yedo, 14 Aug. 1861; 46/15, Alcock to Russell, No. 96, Yedo, 15 Nov. 1861.

[3] F.O. 46/13, Alcock to Russell, Yedo, 16 Aug. 1861. Alcock, *Capital of the Tycoon*, i. 187–90.

[4] P.P. H. of C. 1862, lxiv. 29–31, 36–64, Alcock to Russell, Yedo, 16 Aug. 1861 and encls. 3–10.   [5] F.O. 262/21, Russell to Alcock, 10 Apr. 1881.

Yezo and Tsushima had alarmed both the British and the Japanese and given them a common cause in which the *Bakufu* solicited help.[1]

Desperately in need of success in appeasing the Court by an agreement for postponement, the uneasy *Bakufu* sought Alcock's sympathy by openly stressing its political difficulties: the hostility of the powerful daimyo and the Court party to the treaties, and the historically justified anti-foreign sentiment of the Japanese people, now aroused by the shortage of goods and high prices attributed to foreign trade. The Japanese ministers explained the supremacy of the Emperor and tried to make Alcock believe that he had sanctioned the treaties, admitting, however, that this had not been made public.[2] With dubious sincerity they argued again that the passage of seven years before more markets were opened would provide a necessary concession to their enemies and grant time to increase production, propitiate those suffering from high prices, and thus ensure a greater future for foreign trade. They were frank to acknowledge, however, that they could not guarantee that attacks on foreigners would not be repeated, even if the opening of the cities were postponed.

Alcock with Hope's support yielded to their entreaties. He recommended to Russell that he trust the Japanese government and strengthen its hands by lessening the danger of civil war through his consent to defer the treaty rights for the opening of more ports. But not without conditions. These should include: the opening of the port of Tsushima for all treaty powers during the deferred period; the payment of an indemnity for Oliphant's injury in the attack on Tōzenji; the Shogun's assurance that trade would develop without obstruction, and efforts would be made to allay the ever dangerous public discontent.[3] Thus Alcock began a temporary *rapprochement* with the *Bakufu*.

---

[1] F.O. 46/12, Alcock to Russell, No. 37, Conf'l., Yedo, 3 Apr. 1861. *Nichi-Ei Gaikō Shi*, i. 56. Ad. I/5762, Ward to Hope, *Acteon*, Albo Bay, 17 July 1861, encl. in Hope to Adm., 16 Aug. 1861.

[2] Alcock does not report that they admitted the Imperial sanction of the treaties had not been made public until his *Memorandum* of 14 Feb. 1862. See p. 91. Exactly when this admission was made is not clear.

[3] P.P. H. of C. 1862, lxiv. 28–29, 31–35, 71–72, Alcock to Russell, Yedo, 16 Aug. 1861. and encl. 2; Report of Hope, 20 Aug. 1861. Ad. R.O. (Japan 26), Hope's Notes on Conferences of 15 and 16 Aug. 1861, encl. in Hope to Adm., 20 Aug. 1861. According to Alcock the conferences were held 14 and 15 Aug.

He realized his 'grievous want' of full and reliable information as to the actual government of Japan but the immediate efforts of the *Bakufu* to remove the grievances of the Yokohama merchants, to build a prison, and a fine bund reinforced his growing trust in them.[1]

The Japanese also gained at these discussions the promise of Admiral Hope to order the Russians away from Tsushima since their own protests to the Russian officials had failed.[2] And the prompt dispatch of H.M.S. *Actaeon* to Tsushima resulted in the peaceful departure of the Russians by late September, leaving their whole establishment, pending orders from their naval commander, in the hands of Japanese officials who did not impinge on the authority of the established daimyo.[3]

Before Russell's instructions on the 'postponement' question could reach Alcock a Japanese mission of thirty-six men led by Takeuchi Yasunori and Matsudaira Yasunao, both Commissioners of Foreign Affairs, sailed for Europe on 30 January 1862. They went as a result of a proposal by Alcock and de Bellecourt the previous spring supported by the offer of British and French transportation. They wanted primarily to put their case for deferring the opening of the four cities before the governments concerned and to observe Western power and ways of life. Alcock expected to meet them in London on his home leave during the coming spring.[4] Their sojourn in France *en route* to England was unrewarding. The Minister of Foreign Affairs, E. Antoine Thouvenal, convinced them that since Britain was the undoubted leader of foreign interests in Japan, their negotiations should begin in London. Lord Russell, however, proved to be in no mood to listen to them before the settlement of the Tozenji affair. He insisted upon having Alcock's advice and postponed negotiations until his envoy's arrival.[5]

[1] F.O. 46/13, Alcock to Russell, Conf'l., Yedo, 25 Aug. 1861.

[2] Ad. R.O. (Japan 26), Hope's Notes on the Conferences 15 and 16 Aug. 1861.

[3] *Nichi-Ei Gaikō Shi*, i. 56. F.O. 46/14, Alcock to Russell, No. 94, Yedo, 19 Oct. 1861; 46/15, Hope to Alcock, at Sea, 13 Nov. 1861, encl. in Alcock to Russell, No. 105, Yokohama, 25 Nov. 1861.

[4] F.O. 46/11, Alcock to Russell, No. 18, Yedo, 18 Mar. 1861; No. 29, Yedo, 1 Apr. 1861; 46/12, same to same, No. 30, Yedo, 2 Apr. 1861; 262/22, F.O. to Alcock, 24 May 1861.

[5] *Nichi-Ei Gaikō Shi*, i. 75–76. Beasley, *Documents*, p. 55.

Negotiations in Japan

Alcock had already issued a notification prohibiting British citizens from residing in Yedo after 1 January 1862 when he received Russell's full instructions.[1] In general the Foreign Secretary now ordered him to make no 'concessions without equivalents' and to maintain and if possible to enlarge British trade with Japan, preserving 'undiminished the reputation of the British name'. Russell considered the postponement of the opening of the ports reasonable as a probable deterrent to civil war in Japan. For this concession he required the following:

1. The opening to trade with the treaty powers of the ports of Tsushima and those under Japanese authority on the Korean coast.
2. The grant of land at Yedo for the British minister's residence, the fortification of the area by walls and palisades and the maintenance of a British guard therein to protect the envoy and his staff.
3. The payment of an indemnity to Oliphant and Morrison for their injuries on 5 July.
4. The trial and execution, if convicted, of the assassins who escaped after the attack at Tōzenji.[2]

Adverse circumstances delayed and overshadowed Alcock's negotiations with the Japanese. Admiral Hope had withdrawn H.M. battleships and marines at the alarm of war between England and the United States, leaving the British minister 'without material or moral support'. The wounding of Ando Nobumasa by native assassins in mid February had caused Alcock to postpone the conferences with the Japanese in the futile hope that the pro-Western *Rōjū* would be able to participate. And Townsend Harris after an initial opposition had already conceded everything the Japanese asked.[3]

In contrast to the leniency of the American minister, Alcock determined upon a stern interpretation of his orders from

---

[1] F.O. 46/15, *Notification* encl. in No. 110, 28 Dec. 1861.

[2] F.O. 262/23, Russell to Alcock, No. 120, 23 Nov. 1861. (*Author's Digest.*)

[3] F.O. 46/21, Alcock to Hope, encl. in Alcock to Russell, No. 17, Yokohama, 18 Feb. 1862; Alcock to Russell, No. 23, Conf'l., Yedo, 17 Mar. 1862; 46/15, same to same, No. 108, Yokohama, 28 Nov. 1861.

London. He wrote his French and Dutch colleagues in confidence that:

1. Any negotiations affecting treaty rights must be based upon redress and satisfaction for the attack on Tōzenji;
2. since his government would not abandon any right which would involve the restriction of trade, the postponement of the opening of Hyogo and Osaka was well nigh impossible;
3. as neither Yedo nor Niigata was important for trade, however, and Yedo was a focus of anti-foreign hostility, and as Her Majesty's Government recognized Japan's internal difficulties precipitated by the treaties and wanted to avoid civil war, he could agree to the Shogun's petition regarding Yedo and Niigata in return for the opening of Tsushima and a port on the Korean coast.

At the same time he pointed out to his colleagues that their treaties with the Shogun were not valid throughout Japan, that the public assent of the Emperor must be obtained or that of the daimyo hostile to the Shogunate, in order to give the treaties legal force beyond the territory subject to Yedo. Equally the law of *Gongen-sama* (Tokugawa Ieyasu) legally justifying the killing of foreigners by any Japanese must be publicly abrogated before foreign relations could be stabilized and foreign life and property be secure. The eventual alternative, Alcock suggested, would be 'determined action' by one or more of the treaty powers on the authority of their central governments.[1] Here Alcock shows he understood the supremacy of the Mikado's position and the necessity of his public sanction of the Shogun's treaties. Furthermore he was aware of the power of the daimyo who opposed the *Bakufu* and regarded its treaties as waste paper. He saw no value, however, in fully appeasing the *Bakufu* at this time, and thus postponing the issue of treaty enforcement throughout the country until Japan grew strong enough to resist the West. The French and Dutch representatives agreed with Alcock on much of this, although their views on the reasons for Japanese policy differed slightly.[2]

The Japanese ministers led by *Rōjū* Kuze Hirochika finally

[1] F.O. 46/21, Conf'l. Memo, 14 Feb. 1862, encl. in Alcock to Russell, No. 23, Yedo, 17 Mar. 1862. Beasley, *Documents*, pp. 211–16.

[2] Ibid., p. 56.

met Alcock for two confidential interviews on 12 and 16 March. They readily agreed to Britain's requirements for reparations for the Tōzenji affair and promised future protection. In fact they had already given evidence of their good faith in these respects. Some of the assassins had been executed, the remaining six were soon to meet the same fate, the first instances of the punishment of Japanese criminals for attacking foreigners.[1] The concession for a site for a new legation with ample defences at Japanese expense was also in progress and an indemnity of $10,000 for compensation for the wounding of Oliphant and Morrison had been agreed upon.[2]

Alcock made no headway, however, with the policy regarding the two cities and the two ports which he had recently put forward in the light of Russell's instructions. The Japanese were adamant in their opposition. Insistence upon the opening of Hyogo and Osaka, in fact any further extension of foreign trade, they said, would precipitate civil war. Alcock's proposal that the public proclamation of the Mikado's ratification of the treaties and the repeal of the law of *Gongen-sama* be considered as equivalents for full concessions regarding Yedo and Niigata, was declared impossible as well as the opening of Tsushima and a Korean port. In the light of the opposition of both the Emperor and the daimyo, the Japanese refused all equivalents for deferring the opening of Yedo and Niigata except the vague hope that within six or seven years they could convert the current opposition to the extension of foreign trade to an appreciation of its benefits, and the treaty obligations could be fulfilled without danger. Although Alcock was at first equally firm in demanding Britain's treaty rights or specific compensations for any concessions, Kuze was able to convince him of the difficulties of the Shogun's government threatened by civil war within or hostilities from without, and that British trade itself would suffer in consequence of increased anti-foreign activities if Britain did not yield to the request of the *Bakufu*. His frank

[1] P.P. H. of C. 1863, lxxiv. 4, Alcock to Russell, Yokohama, 11 Feb. 1862. F.O. 46/21, Alcock to Russell No. 14 Conf'l., Yokohama, 18 Feb. 1862.

[2] Ibid., Alcock to Russell, No. 26, Yedo, 3 Mar. 1862. Although the indemnity is reported settled in this letter, it was brought up again, sanctioned by the Japanese minister, referred to Ando Nobumasa, and acceded to on 16 Mar. Minutes of Conferences with Japanese Ministers 12 and 16 Mar. 1862 encl. in Alcock to Russell, No. 23, Conf'l., Yedo, 17 Mar. 1862.

admission that there was no certainty that Japan's internal conditions would improve if the concession were granted, further won Alcock's sympathy.[1]

In his subsequent letter to Russell, Alcock said: 'their unwillingness to guarantee anything, I think is the best trait in the character of those at the helm I have known, for I am certain it arises from utter powerlessness to answer for the future'. He then left it to Her Majesty's Government to decide whether under existing conditions it would be better to yield unconditionally to the Japanese petition, trusting to some improvement in trade both during and at the end of the period, or to insist upon the execution of the treaty. The latter would involve the use of military force and it seemed probable that none of the other treaty powers would resort to this if Britain refrained. Alcock promised Kuze to recommend to Lord Russell upon his return to London that a delay of five years in the opening of the two cities and the two ports be granted in return for specific equivalents.[2] The Japanese on their part resolved to send their most trusted and best-informed interpreter, Moriyama Takichiro, to London with Alcock to bring fresh instructions to their mission. These men left Yedo for Shanghai 23 March.[3]

The Japanese Mission in England

While awaiting Alcock's arrival in England, Takeuchi Yasunori and his associates learned much about the power and resources of Britain. They inspected all departments of the Woolwich Arsenal and with the Duke of Cambridge witnessed the garrison in a series of field-day drills. They visited the Stock Exchange, the docks, the Thames tunnel, the Tower, the Bank of England, parts of Greenwich Hospital and the Royal Observatory, the International Exhibition, and the Mint. They were astounded by the grandeur of the House of Lords and found special pleasure in the zoo. Here their draughtsman sketched skilfully the birds and beasts which attracted him while another retainer 'took copious notes on all he saw'. They were disappointed that owing to her bereavement Queen Victoria could not receive them; but a half-hour interview with Lord Russell,

---

[1] Ibid., Minutes of Conferences with Japanese Ministers 12 and 16 Mar. 1862, encl. in Alcock to Russell, No. 23, Conf'l., Yedo, 17 Mar. 1862.

[2] Ibid., Alcock to Russell, No. 23, Conf'l., Yedo, 17 Mar. 1862, and Minutes of Conference, 16 Mar. 1862.   [3] Alcock, *Capital of the Tycoon*, ii. 400–2.

when they delivered the Shogun's letter to Victoria, gave them a lesson in British diplomatic procedures. Socially they became popular, enjoying receptions, assemblies, and balls in the great homes of London.[1] Fukuzawa Yūkichi, their official interpreter, made strenuous efforts to understand current politics in Europe. A member of Parliament showed him a Bill about to be introduced which criticized Alcock for his high-handed attitude towards the Japanese and callous indifference to Japanese sensibilities and customs, as if Japan were a nation conquered by military force. Fukuzawa rejoiced to learn that foreigners were not all 'devils' and to find 'truly impartial and warm-hearted human beings among them'. As a result he grew even more determined in his 'doctrine of free intercourse with the rest of the world'.[2]

The London Protocol

Russell put Alcock in charge of the meetings with the Japanese envoys as soon as he reached London. Since the Japanese had met all of Britain's demands resulting from the attack on Tōzenji, agreement was reached quickly on the question of the ports. On 6 June Russell and the three Japanese envoys[3] signed a *Memorandum*, known as the London Protocol. Here Britain agreed to defer until 1 January 1868 the opening of the two ports and the two cities provided for in Article III of the Treaty of Yedo in order to give the Japanese ministers time to overcome the opposition to intercourse with foreigners in Japan. For this concession, the British government required the Shogunate to execute strictly all other stipulations of the treaty at the three open ports; to publicly revoke the old law outlawing foreigners; and to remove all restrictions on foreign trade and free social intercourse between foreigners and the Japanese people, hitherto imposed at Nagasaki, Hakodate, and Kanagawa in defiance of the treaty.

Should the Japanese government default in the strict fulfilment of these conditions at any time during the five-year period

---

[1] *Illustrated London News*, 10 and 17 May 1862. P.P. H. of C. 1863, lxxiv. 4–5, Russell to Alcock, F.O., 10 May 1862. The Prince Consort had died 14 Dec. 1861.

[2] *The Autobiography of Fukuzawa Yūkichi*, translated by Kiyooka Eiichi (Tokyo, 1940), pp. 138–9.

[3] The gaikoku-bugyō, Takeuchi Yasunori and Matsudaira Yasunao, and the metsuke, Kyōgoku Kōrō. Beasley, *Documents*, p. 216.

it was agreed that the British government would withdraw the concessions here granted and ask the Japanese ministers to open without delay the aforesaid ports and cities for the trade and residence of British subjects.[1]

The Shogun's envoys promised to recommend to their government the opening to foreign commerce of the port of Tsushima, the reduction of some duties, and the building of bonded warehouses at Yokohama and Nagasaki for the storage of foreign goods without payment of duty, until sold. At the same time they submitted three additional requests from their government; the exclusion of British warships from Japanese ports, permission to prohibit the export of food products in case of scarcity, and some changes in the state of the currency in Japan. Russell refused the first, consented to the second, and postponed the currency question for a fair settlement in Japan in accordance with instructions he would send to the British minister in Yedo.[2]

Russell and Alcock both thought they had acted in the enlightened self-interest of England. Britain's main purpose was to expand her market in Japan. The Tōzenji incident had finally convinced Alcock of the political plight of the Shogunate. By granting its request to postpone the opening of the two ports and the two cities he hoped to strengthen it, to destroy its anti-foreign adversaries, and thus to remove the hindrance to trade. He also believed it was better to give the *Bakufu* the 'benefit of any doubt' regarding its ability and desire to overcome its opposition, before risking the high cost and uncertain outcome of hostilities to enforce the rights of the treaty. Perhaps more important still was the maintenance of British prestige in the East. Alcock wanted to avoid a break with Japan and possible

[1] P.P. H. of C. 1863, lxxiv. 8 for text of *Memorandum*; 6–7, Russell to Winchester, F.O., 9 June 1862.

[2] Ibid., p. 12, Russell to Cowley, F.O., 7 June 1862. The Foreign Office requested an investigation of all currency problems in Japan which the Treasury assigned to George Arbuthnot, its economic adviser. Arbuthnot warned Gladstone at once that he 'could not stir a step in the business without denouncing the Treaties'. B.M. (Add. MS. 44096), Gladstone Papers xi, Arbuthnot to Gladstone, Treasury, 20 Dec. 1862. His four reports during the following year led to a better understanding in London of Japan's currency difficulties but the Japanese requests in 1862 and 1863 to issue new silver coins of different value in relation to the dollar instead of the current *ichibu* were not granted. P.P. H. of C. 1866, l. for texts of these reports. Japanese sources on this period of Tokugawa financial history are not available.

British withdrawal in order to prevent the acquisition of Japan as part of Russia's current advance in eastern Asia. But he was not optimistic about the results of the Protocol. His long experience in the Far East gave him little confidence in 'the solemn engagements' of Asiatics.[1] His doubts were fortified by the list of nine other restrictions which the Japanese envoys had been charged to impose on the European governments. Although the British Foreign Secretary referred these requests to Yedo for consideration and they were generally disregarded, they indicated again the exclusionist efforts of the *Bakufu*.[2] Equally sceptical was Charles W. Winchester, British consul at Yokohama. Anticipating the British concessions in London, he expressed no confidence in the sincerity of the *Bakufu* to use the time gained before the opening of the ports to eliminate the obstacles to the full enforcement of the treaty.[3]

To the Japanese envoys their promises, though dubious, seemed minor in comparison with their apparent success in postponing a crisis. Takeuchi and Matsudaira even considered that later Tsushima might be offered as a substitute for Hyogo or Osaka, as they had made no formal commitment about it. During the early autumn of 1862 they made similar agreements with the other treaty powers and returned to Japan to find that neither harmony between Yedo and Kyoto, nor a respite from difficulties with foreigners, had been achieved.[4]

---

[1] Alcock, *Capital of the Tycoon*, ii. 217–20, 403–9. For an interesting leftist Japanese interpretation of this Protocol, see Ishii Takashi, *Meiji Ishin no Kokusaiteki Kankyō* (International Surroundings of the Meiji Restoration) (Tokyo, 1957), pp. 59–65, 131–40.

[2] P.P. H. of C. 1863, lxxiv. 13–14, Russell to Winchester, F.O., 9 June 1862 and encls.

[3] F.O. 46/22, Winchester to Russell, No. 5, Yokohama, 2 Apr. 1862.

[4] Beasley, *Documents*, pp. 57 ff.

IV

BRITISH RESPONSE TO JAPANESE
HOSTILITIES

JUNE 1862 – DECEMBER 1863

The Second Attack on the British Legation and the Murder of Richardson

BEFORE news of the Protocol could reach Japan, British relations with the Shogun's government had rapidly deteriorated. On 26 June a member of the guard assigned by the Daimyo, Matsudaira Tamba, to protect the British headquarters, instigated an attack on the legation at Yedo. Two British sentries were fatally wounded while five hundred Japanese failed to prevent the assault. Edward St. John Neale, chargé d'affaires in Alcock's absence, protested firmly and demanded more assured protection from the *Bakufu*. He increased the detachment from H.M.S. *Renard* to fifty-one men to guard the legation and soon moved to Yokohama to await instructions from Lord Russell as well as the completion of the new British legation in Yedo.[1]

When the Japanese authorities did nothing to investigate the crime nor to punish those implicated, Admiral Hope advised London that demands supported by the fleet be made upon their government. Should these be refused, he proposed direct communication with the Mikado from the fleet at Osaka, to be followed if necessary by a blockade of all the ports of Japan's southern coast until the receipt of further instructions from London. His final method of coercion was to be the destruction of the forts in front of Yedo and those at other ports on the coast.[2] He lamented the use of force but thought the time had come for Britain to act.

[1] P.P. H. of C. 1863, lxxiv. 30–32, Neale to Russell, Yedo, 3 July 1862; p. 39, Neale to Japanese Ministers of Foreign Affairs, Yedo, 27 June 1862. Neale, a former member of the Spanish Legion who had had consular experience in Europe, was then about fifty-five, a man of 'sour and suspicious temper' who, according to Ernest Satow, then an observant young interpreter, did not understand the circumstances into which he was thrown. Sir Ernest Satow, *A Diplomat in Japan* (London, 1921), pp. 29–30 (hereafter cited to as *Diplomat*).

[2] P.P. H. of C. 1863, lxxiv. 52, Neale to Russell, Yokohama, 1 Aug. 1862. Ad.

Lord Russell still knew nothing of the attack on the legation when another anti-foreign assault caused greater consternation in the Yokohama foreign community. On 14 September 1862 a British merchant, C. Lennox Richardson, was killed and two British merchants were wounded at Namamugi when riding with Mrs. Borrodaile, an English visitor from Hong Kong, along the *Tōkaidō* within the area specified by the treaty. They had encountered the escort of the Daimyo of Satsuma, Shimazu Hisamitsu, who was returning from Yedo to Kyoto. Some of its members took umbrage when the British did not dismount in respect to the Daimyo as they moved to the side of the road to let the cortège pass.[1] Nothing before had so disturbed the Yokohama community as this attack in broad daylight on unarmed fellow merchants riding within their assigned quarter. A near panic took place. The foreign residents demanded the immediate arrest of the Daimyo by the military and naval forces then in their midst.[2] Five British warships were now at Yokohama as Rear-Admiral Augustus Kuper had arrived on the fourteenth with his flagship *Euryalus* and H.M.S. *Ringdove*. Neale and Kuper both opposed such precipitate action, realizing it could lead to war with Japan which the British government did not want.[3] The chargé insisted upon awaiting instructions from London without tying Russell's hands by 'premature acts of reprisal' against the Japanese government, a stand which brought the criticism of the community upon him.[4] He left the Shogun's government in no uncertainty, however, that London would require reparations. In the meantime he demanded the arrest of the assassins and their safe custody in the hands of the Shogun's government, the summoning of Shimazu Hisamitsu for investigation, and the increase of the guards on the road from Yokohama then open to foreigners.[5]

I/5790, Hope to Adm., 28 Aug. 1862. F. O. Adams, *The History of Japan*, 2 vols. (London, 1875), i. 155–73.

[1] *Nichi-Ei Gaikō Shi*, i. 62–64. P.P. H. of C. 1863, lxxiv. 73–74, Neale to Russell, Yokohama, 15 Sept. 1862.

[2] Ibid., pp. 86–92, Minutes of meeting of merchants resident in Yokohama, held 15 Sept. 1862.

[3] Ibid., p. 81, Neale to Russell, Yokohama, 16 Sept. 1862; p. 93, Kuper to Hope, Yokohama, 20 Sept. 1862.

[4] Ibid., p. 86, Messrs. Bell, Bailey, and Gower to Russell, 16 Sept. 1862.

[5] Ibid., pp. 74–75, Neale to Japanese Commissioners of Foreign Affairs, Yokohama, 15 Sept. 1862.

Men from British, French, and Dutch ships were at once detailed to increase the protection of the foreign settlement.[1]

Neale and Kuper, believing that the display of force would hasten Japanese compliance with British demands, decided to move the *Euryalus*, *Ringdove*, and *Kestrel* to Yedo for a few days. On 23 September at a conference with the Japanese Commissioners of Foreign Affairs, Neale was persuaded of their desire to arrest and punish the assassins, but aware that probably they could not accomplish it.[2]

The *Bakufu*, however, knew that it was impossible. The Daimyo of Satsuma was not in favour with the Tokugawa government, and had further vexed them by this incident. When asked by the Kanagawa officials to search for the criminals and to remain in Kanagawa until the settlement of the issue, he had refused. Likewise the government's orders to the counsellor of Satsuma in Yedo, to produce the criminal led only to a statement that his whereabouts were unknown and that it was an old custom of Satsuma to kill anyone who disturbs the escort of the Lord. He even seemed to dare foreign warships to appear at Satsuma's harbour.[3] The Japanese Commissioners of Foreign Affairs finally admitted to Neale that their government could not take action against Satsuma in his own domain.[4]

While stalling on the round-up of Richardson's murderers, the *Bakufu* erected fifteen guard houses, each containing five armed men along the portion of the highway open to foreigners. This measure of protection was amplified by a major change in Tokugawa policy. Daimyo were no longer required annually to attend the court at Yedo. This meant the evacuation from the capital of between two and three hundred thousand of their two-sworded retainers, the class from which the foreigners had suffered most. Even a new road was begun whereby the daimyo processions could circumvent that used by the treaty powers. Neale thought the Japanese were doing their best under difficult conditions.[5]

Neale's inclination to have faith in the *Bakufu* differed

[1] Ibid., p. 84, meeting of British, French, and Dutch naval officers at Yokohama, 15 Sept. 1862.

[2] Ibid., pp. 96–100, Neale to Russell, Yokohama, 1 Oct. 1862 and encl.

[3] *Nichi-Ei Gaikō Shi*, i. 64–66.

[4] P.P. H. of C. 1863, lxxiv. 95, Neale to Russell, Yokohama, 30 Sept. 1862.

[5] Ibid., p. 106, Neale to Russell, Yokohama, 29 Oct. 1862.

greatly from the attitude of the merchants who were disturbed by the Shogunate's continuing interference with trade at Kanagawa.[1] One merchant at least was already aware of the relation of these restrictions to Japan's internal political conflict and of the government's misrepresentation of the antiforeign movement among the daimyo. S. J. Gower, the agent of Jardine, Matheson, and Company at Yokohama, was convinced by the late summer of 1862 that

many of the reports spread about the generality of Daimyo being inveterately opposed to foreigners, are utterly false, and are set on foot by the Government for the express purpose of preventing any possible intercourse with them, and guarding more jealously the monopoly of foreign trade which the Tycoon enjoys, to the detriment of those independent Princes who are most anxious to share in it, and naturally to the great prejudice of trade, which would be immeasurably increased were it thrown open to all alike.

Gower himself had already met with the agents of a great daimyo who wanted to purchase ships but being prevented by the *Bakufu* from examining the vessels went on board disguised as coolies or carpenters to accomplish their purpose. Gower had also learned that a most powerful daimyo reputed to be a great enemy of foreigners, was on the contrary eager for commercial relations with them. His agent invited Gower to begin business with him at Osaka and other ports not open to foreigners. When told that this was contrary to the existing treaty, the agent proposed a separate treaty to enable his master to trade with foreigners. He assured Gower that there was nothing to fear, as none of the Shogun's officials were permitted to enter the domains of this daimyo. Gower took this to mean 'that the Tycoon has made a treaty merely for his own benefit, and in order to monopolize the enormous harvest which he reaps from it, and was only too glad to find any pretext or excuse for preventing any more ports from being opened, whereby much of the profit which now flows into his coffers would have to be shared by some of his powerful neighbours'. It was clear to Gower that the Shogun's system—with its monopoly of much-needed coolies, cargo boats, and boatmen, its squeeze on the proceeds of native traders, and on the wages of natives employed by foreigners, its

[1] P.P. H. of C. 1863, lxxiv. 61–73, Neale to Russell, Yokohama, 14 Sept. 1862 and encls.

regulations of the value of dollars through keeping back the requisite supply of *ichibu*, and its constant evasion of Japan's responsibilities under the treaties—was bad and could never benefit commerce.[1] Such views were at hand when Her Majesty's Government was deciding how it should deal with the Japanese attacks on its citizens.

Policy Revision in London

News of the attack on the legation led Russell to act promptly. He ordered Neale to demand £10,000 in gold as compensation for the families of the murdered marines—a sum to be levied on the estate of the daimyo in charge of the legation at the time of the assault. He required that the daimyo be publicly degraded if found guilty of complicity in the outrage. And he asked Neale to inform the *Bakufu* that murders and insecurity would never induce the British to abandon Yedo and permit the prohibition of trade to be re-established. He said, 'It would be better that the Tycoon's palace should be destroyed than that our rightful position by Treaty should be weakened or impaired.' Meanwhile he expected Admiral Hope to provide the legation with the necessary protection.[2]

Reports of Richardson's murder caused longer deliberations in England before Russell finally defined the policy he wished Neale to enforce. Many minds worked upon the instructions. Alcock, who was still in England, saw in the second attack on the legation and Richardson's murder reasons for the complete nullification of all concessions granted the Shogunate in the London Protocol. He realized that his policy of appeasing the *Bakufu* in the light of its difficulties had failed. His analysis of Japan's political confusions made him advocate decisive action. But his knowledge of the Japanese people and their terrain made him oppose Admiral Hope's coercive recommendations for fear of arousing the hostility of the friendly

[1] Ibid., pp. 71–73, encl. 14, S. J. Gower to Consul Vyse, Yokohama, 5 Sept. 1862. The daimyo was none other than Shimazu Hisamitsu himself, but Gower did not reveal the fact, if he knew it, at this time. Kagoshima Ken (Kagoshima Prefecture) Compiler, *Kagoshima Ken Shi* (*History of Kagoshima Prefecture*), 5 vols. (Kagoshima, 1939–43), iii. 240–1.

[2] P.P. H. of C. 1863, lxxiv. 49–51, Russell to Neale, 22 Sept. 1862. The Duke of Somerset protested the size of this indemnity, believing £1,000 for the family of each Marine sufficient. P.R.O. 30/22/24, Somerset to Russell, Adm., 29 Sept. 1862.

daimyo and the common people. Alcock himself proposed that if the Shogun failed to produce the chief criminal in a given time, Britain in conjunction with the other treaty powers should move against the Daimyo of Satsuma himself. He argued that the territory of this daimyo lay within their grasp being exposed to attack and blockade from the sea. A hostile move by the *Bakufu* could be met by the blockade of Yedo which could be reduced to famine in three weeks. He saw by this time that Britain's position was 'untenable'. Any satisfactory arrangement with Japan must include the ratification of the treaty by the Mikado, the abolition of the Shogun's monopoly of foreign trade, and the opening of other ports with the concurrence of their presiding daimyo.[1]

Queen Victoria, herself, fully aware that war with Japan could result from British action, insisted that 'the opinion of the whole cabinet be ascertained before the country is committed to demand a reparation which the Government of Japan may have no power to enforce'.[2] The resulting consensus seems to have followed Alcock's advice and the opinion of the Duke of Somerset, then First Lord of the Admiralty: Britain should punish the daimyo who were hostile to foreigners, especially Satsuma to whom Richardson's assassins belonged; his port should be blockaded and his capital probably shelled. Thus he and his people could be embarrassed without any general interference with British–Japanese trade. If the central government was weak and unable to afford Britain redress, it was Britain's responsibility to convince these daimyo that they must suffer personally for their misdeeds.[3] The Cabinet advised a short operation which would concentrate the attack on Satsuma, 'disclaiming any hostility to the nation, but even, all things considered, to the State'.[4] Satsuma's position was well understood: his overlordship of the Ryūkyū Islands, his purchase of some fine English merchant ships, the belief that he favoured trade with foreigners and 'was anxious to embroil the Government with the Europeans' in order to have a port

---

[1] F.O. 46/25, Alcock to Russell, Belvedere, 29 Nov. 1862.

[2] George Earle Buckle, *The Letters of Queen Victoria*, 2nd Series, 2 vols. (London, 1926), i. 51, Sir Charles Phipps to Russell, Dec. 1862.

[3] P.R.O. 30/22/24, Somerset to Russell, Adm., 5 Dec. 1862. Rough note signed P., probably Palmerston, 5 Dec. 1862.

[4] Ibid., rough note signed W. G., 9 Dec. 1862.

opened in his territory.[1] Everyone, including Hope, wanted to avoid war with the Japanese people.[2]

Britain's demands for reparations sent out 24 and 27 December 1862 reached Japan in late March 1863. Russell instructed Neale to ask of the Japanese government:

1. An ample and formal apology for the offence of permitting a murderous attack on British subjects passing on a road open to them by treaty.
2. The payment of £100,000 as penalty on Japan for this offence.

From the Daimyo of Satsuma, he was to demand:

1. The immediate trial and execution, in the presence of one or more British naval officers, of the chief perpetrators of the attack on Richardson and his companions.
2. The payment of £25,000, to be distributed to the relatives of the murdered man, and to those who escaped with their lives the swords of the assassins.

Should the *Bakufu* refuse this redress Neale should call upon the admiral or senior naval officer on the China Station to adopt such measures of reprisal or blockade, or both, as he might judge best calculated to attain the end proposed. Russell emphasized that the distinction between the government and the daimyo must be kept clear. And if the daimyo could not be coerced by the *Bakufu*, they must nevertheless be made to pay for their misdeeds.[3] Thus final action was left in the hands of the newly appointed commander of the China Station, Vice-Admiral Augustus Kuper, who it was said had never seen a gun fired in action.[4]

The Mikado's Expulsion Order

Events preceding the arrival of these instructions in Japan presaged increasing difficulties in Anglo-Japanese relations. Britain's demand of 22 September for an indemnity of £10,000 paid in gold to the families of the murdered guards in the attack on the legation of 26 June had been refused. Both the *Rōjū* and the daimyo denied any foreknowledge of the attack.

---

[1] Ibid., extract of letter from General Hanley (sp. ?), Dec. 1862.
[2] Ad. I/5790, Hope to Adm., *Imperiuse*, Woosing, 18 Oct. 1862.
[3] P.P. H. of C. 1864, lxvi (3242), 1–2, Russell to Neale, 24 and 27 Dec. 1862.
[4] Satow, *Diplomat*, p. 79.

The latter, Matsudaira Tamba, was punished according to Japanese law and $3,000 in silver was offered for the relatives of the dead.[1]

While Neale awaited further orders from London alarming news and explanations of the anti-*Bakufu* and anti-foreign activities of leading daimyo had come from Hakodate. Official Japanese documents translated by acting consul James J. Enslie and sent to Neale showed that the Daimyo of Kyūshū and Shikoku followed by other daimyo of the south-west, having for centuries resented the demands and encroachments of the Shogun's government and desiring to avenge their personal grievances, were making the opening of Japan to foreigners a pretext to demand the deposition of the Shogun.

Another document thought to be authentic instructions from the Mikado to the *Chokushi* (*Ontsukai*), his envoy to the Shogun, contained the demands of these daimyo. They called for the restriction of the foreigners to Nagasaki. Kanagawa was to be closed owing to high prices and the discontent of the people arising from the presence of foreigners. But it was recognized that Japan was too weak to enforce this and that the treaty powers would not readily consent. Hence they should be allowed to remain in Hakodate, and Shimoda could be offered as a substitute for Kanagawa. The Mikado's envoy, however, was not to leave Yedo until the Shogun had promised to do his utmost to return Japan to the position it occupied when the Dutch were at Deshima.[2]

Enslie's report was a warning of what Neale might expect from Yedo. The Imperial Court's emissary, Sanjō Sanetomi, arrived in the Shogun's capital in December with orders for the expulsion of foreigners, but so modified as to leave the methods and timing of the expulsion to the discretion of the *Bakufu*. This gave the *Rōjū* some chance to evade the command. The Great Council, however, formally agreed to the policy of expulsion on 24 January 1863. Although Hitotsubashi Keiki, who had been appointed 'Guardian of the Shogun' in August 1862 with powers of a *tairō*, had supported this decision reluc-

---

[1] P.P. H. of C. 1864, lxvi (3242), 14–16, Japanese Commissioners of Foreign Affairs to Neale, 20 Dec. 1862.

[2] Paske-Smith, *Western Barbarians*, pp. 144–6, Enslie to Neale, Hakodate, 17 Oct. 1862. The British called the *Chokushi* 'Gioshee'.

tantly, he pledged the Shogunate's allegiance to it when in February he went to Kyoto to arrange for the approaching visit of the Shogun. By the end of March the pressure of the extremist anti-foreign faction forced him and his colleagues to consent to effect without fail the withdrawal of foreigners twenty days after the Shogun's return to Yedo. Further pressure made the *Bakufu* set the date for 25 June. The Court notified the *han* of this decision on 7 June. Keiki and the *Rōjū*, however, still hoped to negotiate some compromise and in their statement to the daimyo about the date implied that force was only to be used 'in the event of invasion'.[1]

Hostility between the Shogunate and the anti-foreign party of the Mikado became increasingly obvious to the British. On 1 February the splendid new British legation, built at *Bakufu* expense at Goten-yama in Yedo, and still unoccupied, was burned to the ground by political incendiaries, later known to be Chōshū leaders. Daimyo in numbers left the Shogun's court at Yedo for that of the Mikado. Others were degraded and had their lands confiscated, having been denounced as pro-foreign by the Mikado's envoy.[2]

Neale also knew that the Shogun, contrary to all precedent, was going to Kyoto in March to report affairs in person to the Mikado, an event which marked his dependence on the Emperor's authority. The chief censor of the *Bakufu* (*ōmetsuke*) had asked the British chargé on 28 January whether Britain would come to the Shogun's assistance should the *Bakufu* fail in settling matters with the Mikado in respect to foreigners. This would mean British intervention in the event of civil war which Neale knew London would oppose. As an alternative, he suggested to Russell that, backed by an imposing force, the British insist upon direct communication with the Mikado at Hyogo or Osaka, with the request that His Majesty support the Shogun's foreign treaties by public proclamation or prepare for the immediate opening of Osaka.[3]

Although the Japanese had maintained an ominous silence regarding the demands for reparations expected from London,

---

[1] Beasley, *Documents*, pp. 60–66, 234. Craig, op. cit., p. 199.
[2] P.P. H. of C. 1864, lxvi (3242), 21–22, Neale to Russell, Yokohama, 3 Feb. 1863. Satow, *Diplomat*, p. 71.
[3] F.O. 46/32, Neale to Russell, No. 20, Yokohama, 10 Feb. 1863.

the *Bakufu* obviously were preparing for hostilities. Volunteers were enlisted. Forts were erected at points on the Inland Sea and along the coast. A new group of daimyo was ordered to prepare for resistance. And with deliberate forethought the *Rōjū* saw to it that the Shogun and his entourage had left for Kyoto before Neale made known his demands, a manœuvre Neale recognized at once as a measure to gain time.[1]

In spite of the threatening political uncertainties for the details of which Neale had no reliable source of information, Neale and Winchester found no basic cause for discouragement.[2] In three years Britain's trade with Japan, the sole object of her establishment, had tripled. Her exports from Japan in 1862 exceeded a million sterling. Winchester rejoiced in the rapid development of commerce at Nagasaki and in the excellent relations being cultivated by the agents of the Daimyo of Kyūshū with the foreign merchants. He was not blind, however, to the great changes and apprehension which the contacts with foreigners were causing among the people. Like Neale, he thought that future peace and security for the West lay in Japan's recognition of the powerful 'forces' which the Europeans controlled.[3]

Britain's Demands and War Preparations

The belief in an impressive show of force caused Neale to wait for the arrival of Vice-Admiral Kuper with nine ships of Britain's China fleet, before he confronted the Yedo government with Russell's demands resulting from the Namamugi incident.[4] On 6 April 1863 he exacted from the 'men of straw' left in charge at the Shogun's capital not only the reparations for Richardson's murder but also the £10,000 formerly demanded for the families of the marines who were killed at the British legation in June 1862. He gave the *Bakufu* twenty days

[1] P.P. H. of C. 1864, lxvi (3242), 35, 38–39, Neale to Russell, Yokohama, 14 and 30 Mar. 1863 and encls.

[2] For details of Japan's internal political struggle, see Beasley, *Documents*, pp. 58–77.

[3] P.P. H. of C. 1864, lxvi (3242), 24–25, Neale to Russell, Yokohama, 10 Feb. 1863. F.O. 46/33, Winchester to Hammond, Nagasaki, 11 Mar. 1863. Here the estimate of Japanese exports in 1862 is about twice the figure given for that year in the *Statistical Abstract of the United Kingdom*, No. 17, p. 22. See Table I, Chapter XII, p. 368.

[4] P.P. H. of C. 1864, lxvi (3242), 36–37, Neale to Russell, Yokohama, 29 Mar. 1863. Kuper and his successors when commanding the China and Japan Station were made vice-admirals to give them equal authority with the French naval commander. Ad. 13/33, Adm. to Kuper 31 March 1863.

to accept these requirements. Their refusal or evasion at the close of that period would be met within twenty-four hours by such measures as the British admiral thought necessary. Any violence to British subjects or property in Japanese ports during the period of 'preliminary measures', would cause the immediate outbreak of hostilities of unpredictable extent. He announced that a British naval force would proceed to a port in Satsuma's territory and present Russell's demands to the Daimyo, whose refusal would prompt immediate coercive measures. He suggested that to avert any obstinate action by the Prince, the *Bakufu* might send a high officer to Satsuma with the British squadron to explain Britain's power and determination 'to enforce redress for unprovoked injuries'.[1]

Opposing at once the British expedition to Satsuma, the Japanese Commissioners of Foreign Affairs asked that the settlement of British grievances be left for some time in their hands. They promised that Neale's letter would reach the Shogun by special messenger on 12 or 13 April.[2] Thereafter these officials, devoid of all power to act, maintained silence, leaving Neale to expect to resort to force on 26 April. On the twenty-first, however, a letter from the acting authorities requested an extension of thirty days for the Shogun's reply in order to enable him to return to Yedo and make his decision in conference with Keiki and the *Rōjū*.[3] Urged to do this by the American minister, Neale conceded by granting them fifteen more days beginning with 27 April, a period he thought sufficient for them to communicate and receive instructions from the Shogun's ministers at Kyoto. He had no faith whatever in the return of the Shogun within thirty days and recognized the Japanese efforts to gain time by any excuse.[4] He saw clearly that the British demands were but an incident in Japan's current revolutionary crisis. He wrote to London that the continued residence of foreigners in Japan was now at stake. Prevailing reports held that the Shogun, 'overpowered by the

---

[1] Ibid., pp. 40–44, two letters, Neale to Japanese Commissioners of Foreign Affairs, Yokohama, 6 Apr. 1863. For demands, see p. 103. The British often called a daimyo a prince.

[2] P.P. H of C. 1864, lxvi (3242), 45, letters of Japanese Commissioners of Foreign Affairs, 8 and 12 Apr. 1863.

[3] Ibid., pp. 52–53, Neale to Russell, Yokohama, 30 Apr. 1863, encl. letter from Japanese ministers of 21 Apr. 1863.

[4] Ibid., pp. 53–54, Neale to Japanese ministers, 24 Apr. 1863.

Mikado and the more powerful Daimyo', had renounced his foreign policy and thus saved his own life, 'while some of the more powerful Daimyo' had 'undertaken to urge a war of expulsion or extermination against foreigners'.[1] As noted above, Hitotsubashi Keiki had already agreed in Kyoto to expulsion, and the date had been fixed.[2]

Neale himself and the mercantile community also welcomed more time to prepare for the expected hostilities.[3] Neale and Kuper saw at once that British coercion against Japan would endanger British residents in the open ports. No land force was at hand to protect them in their homes and General Brown in China refused Neale's request for such assistance.[4] Evacuation to Shanghai or to hired transports for residence afloat seemed the only solution for their safety.[5] On 22 April Kuper issued a memorandum for the squadron detailing arrangements for the safety of the foreign community at Yokohama, a group of 228 persons of whom ninety-one were British.[6] The unqualified offer by both the French chargé, M. de Bellecourt, and Admiral Jaures to co-operate in support of the British demands strengthened Neale's morale although their naval force was limited to two or three vessels.[7] Dutch concurrence in the British policy was also a source of help.[8]

The first public announcement of possible Anglo-Japanese hostilities came through the *Japan Herald* on 24 April 1863. Disturbing rumours and reports of war preparations abounded. Japanese sources stated trade had stopped at Yedo. Rice was dearer. The rich were sending their property to the interior. Dollars were going up. Bridges were barricaded. Amusement

[1] P.P. H. of C. 1864, lxvi (3242), 52–53, Neale to Russell, Yokohama, 30 Apr. 1863.

[2] See pp. 104–5.

[3] F.O. 46/34, Neale to Russell, No. 64, Yokohama, 30 Apr. 1863.

[4] F.O. 46/35, Brown to Neale, Shanghai, 22 Apr. 1863 and encl. in No. 92, Neale to Russell, Yokohama, 14 June 1863.

[5] Ad. I/5824, Kuper to Adm., 14 Apr. 1863 and encls. F.O. 46/33, Neale to Russell, No. 46, Yokohama, 14 Apr. 1863.

[6] Ad. I/5824, Kuper to Adm., 27 Apr. 1863 and encl. *Memorandum* of 22 Apr. F.O. 46/33, Winchester to Neale, Kanagawa, 27 Apr. 1863, encl. in Neale to Russell, Yokohama, same date.

[7] P.P. H. of C. 1864, lxvi (3242), 50, Neale to Russell, Yokohama, 14 Apr. 1863. F.O. 46/34, Neale to Russell, Conf'l., Yokohama 29 Apr. 1863. Napoleon III proposed to co-operate with the British in China and Japan in return for similar services from the British to the French nearer home.

[8] Ad. I/5824, Kuper to Adm., Yokohama, 13 May 1863.

places closed. Women and old people were leaving the Shogun's capital. Americans were selling fire-arms in coffins to the Japanese. Americans in Yokohama and Russians in Hakodate spread unfounded reports of British intentions, the former also seeking letters of marque to use when war should begin.[1]

In Nagasaki Consul Morrison feared the consequences of the proximity of the city to the domains of the Daimyo of Satsuma in the event of hostilities.[2] Great excitement and sinister rumours already prevailed. Princes and their agents came and went. Large forces were quietly assembled. The anxiety of the Governor of Nagasaki could not be over-estimated. 'The train is laid for civil war', Morrison wrote, 'and the foreign question is the match to light it'. With some understanding of the Shogun's embattled position at Kyoto over the question of the forcible expulsion of foreigners, Morrison expressed his hope that 'the difficulties of the Tycoon may be weighed in determining the direction in which our arms are to be employed; that we may not be blindly made the instruments of furthering the success of our real enemies by breaking down the power of our friends in Japan, simply because they are technically responsible (according to European diplomacy) for the actions of those over whom they have no real control'.[3] Here was the first intimation by a man on the spot that British demands might be neither reasonable nor expedient.

Neale himself had sympathy for the Shogun's political weakness without ever questioning the enormity of his own government's orders. He therefore yielded to the *Bakufu* request of 1 May to extend the time required for its answer to Britain's demands until 23 May when the Shogun's return was expected. And he offered in conjunction with the French to assist the Shogun in subduing the resistance of the anti-foreign party. Thus he gave an unauthorized affirmative answer to the Shogun's indirect request of 28 January for aid.[4]

[1] F.O. 46/34, Neale to Russell, Nos. 61 and 67, 29 and 30 Apr. 1863 and encl. *Memorandum*, Winchester to Neale, Yokohama, 21 Apr. 1863; 46/33, Neale to Russell, Conf'l., Yokohama, (no day) Apr. 1863 and encl.; 262/54, British consul in Boston, Mass. to Russell, 28 July, encl. in F.O. to Neale, 10 Aug. 1863. Ad. I/5851, F.O. to Adm., 13 Aug. 1863.

[2] Paske-Smith, *Western Barbarians*, p.156, Morrison to Neale, Nagasaki, 14 Apr. 1863.

[3] Ibid., p. 157, Morrison to Neale, Nagasaki, 10 May 1863. Also in F.O. 46/34, encl. in Neale's No. 77, 26 May 1863.

[4] Ibid., Neale to Russell, No. 68, Yokohama 11 May 1863. P.R.O. 30/33,

Neale's leniency and patience, however, did not retard the Japanese preparations for war. The outbreak of hostilities grew more probable not only because of Japan's reactions to British demands, but because of the Mikado's expulsion order, of which Neale now had proof.[1] The *Bakufu* alerted the daimyo for war in the eight neighbouring feudatories and issued orders concerning arrangements for refugees, food supply, and defence. The Governor of Kanagawa ordered Japanese citizens at the open ports to evacuate. At Nagasaki and Hakodate foreign consuls notified their citizens to prepare for evacuation on twenty-four-hour notice. Japanese employed by or having commercial dealings with foreigners demanded dismissal and immediate payment. Villainies and threats of violence aggravated the situation. Seventeen foreign warships and six merchantmen assembled in readiness to protect foreigners and their property.[2]

The Payment of the Indemnity

Word on 15 May that the Shogun's return to Yedo was indefinitely delayed—actually the Emperor refused to let him leave Kyoto—made Neale adamant in exacting the Shogun's answer to the British demands as soon as the Shogun could send it to the government at Yedo.[3] The destruction of the American legation on 24 May brought further evidence of anti-foreign activities which the *Bakufu* could not prevent.[4] On 25 May Neale and the French consul met the acting Commissioner of Foreign Affairs, who refused their offer of help against the anti-foreign daimyo at that time on the ground that even the mention of foreign aid for the *Bakufu* would precipitate great disturbances in the country. He assured Neale at the same time that the money demand of the British would be paid but asked

Satow MSS. *Diary*, i. 169; Satow, *Diplomat*, p. 74. Ad., I/5824, Kuper to Adm., 13 May 1863. Neale's initiative in this matter received Russell's support. F.O. 262/54, Russell to Neale, No. 85, 22 Sept. 1863.

[1] F.O. 46/34, Neale to Russell, No. 68, Yokohama, 11 May 1863. P.P. H. of C. 1864, lxvi (3242), 57–58, Neale to Russell, 12 May 1863 and encls.

[2] *Nichi-Ei Gaikō Shi*, i. 70–71. For details of conditions in Nagasaki where war was anticipated as soon as the rupture between Yedo and the English was announced, see Paske-Smith, *Western Barbarians*, pp. 158–9.

[3] P.P. H. of C. 1864, lxvi (3242), 60–61, Neale to Russell, Yokohama, 27 May 1863, two letters and encls.

[4] Ibid., pp. 61–62, Neale to Russell, Yokohama, 11 June 1863 and encl.

that this not be made public and that the demands on Satsuma be deferred until the Shogun's return.[1] A plea on 7 June for further delay in paying the two indemnities caused Neale to lay before the Japanese his knowledge of the expulsion order and to win an agreement that the first instalment of the money would be delivered in ten days.[2] On 14 June the harassed Japanese authorities promised in writing to pay the £110,000 covering the two indemnities in seven instalments beginning 18 June.[3] The *Bakufu* further conceded the justice of England's demands on Satsuma and even offered to pay the £25,000 indemnity if England would be patient about the immediate execution of Richardson's murderer, a proposition Neale refused to countenance. Although it was known that the Samurai Nakabara was the culprit and that the Daimyo of Satsuma had declared he would resist to the last the British demands, the *Bakufu* maintained Shimazu was willing to arrest the murderers and though at present it was impossible to find them, he and Yedo would not relax in the quest.[4]

Ogasawara Nagamichi, a member of the *Rōjū* who favoured the payment of the indemnity as a prelude to the opening of negotiations with foreigners on the expulsion issue, was in charge of these arrangements. His confusion was scarcely less than Neale's when a letter from Keiki, then *en route* to Yedo with the edict for expulsion on 25 June, ordered that the indemnity should not be paid.[5] Ogasawara softened the meaning of this in a note to Neale by stating that the money could not be paid on the eighteenth, 'owing to unforeseen circumstances' and that he would discuss the matter with Neale in Kanagawa on the twenty-second. This reached the chargé a few hours before the first instalment was due. Neale's patience gave way. He refused further discussions with the Japanese ministers unless the whole indemnity, not an instalment, was paid at the end of the twelve hours needed for another communication from

---

[1] F.O. 46/34, Summary of Conference at British Legation, 25 May 1863, encl. in Neale to Russell, No. 82, Yokohama 27 May 1863. *Nichi-Ei Gaikō Shi*, i. 71.

[2] F.O. 46/34, Summary of Conference, 7 June 1863, encl. in Neale to Russell No. 85, Yokohama, 10 June 1863.

[3] P.P. H. of C. 1864, lxvi (3242), 68–69, Neale to Russell, Yokohama, 14 June 1863 and encl.

[4] Ibid., p. 70, Neale to Russell, Yokohama, 20 June 1863 and encl. Murdoch, op. cit. iii. 733.

[5] Beasley, *Documents*, pp. 66–68. *Nichi-Ei Gaikō Shi*, i. 72.

Yedo. No money arrived. And a report from the Governor of Kanagawa stated that the Shogun could not pay the indemnity on penalty of his life. Neale therefore requested Admiral Kuper 'to adopt prompt coercive measures to punish the Japanese government for its breach of faith and to bring them to a sense of their engagements'.[1]

Efforts of the *Bakufu* at this moment to induce the French to intervene on their behalf naturally failed in the light of the current expulsion order. Both the chargé and Admiral Jaures insisted the *Bakufu* must satisfy Britain's demands and arranged to undertake the defence of Yokohama. Neale at the same time became more suspicious of the secret workings of the Shogun's government and its duplicity in relation to the treaty powers.[2]

The appearance of a messenger at one o'clock in the morning of 24 June telling Neale that the money would be paid and asking at what hour he would receive it, came as a surprise. The chargé's demand for the immediate delivery of the entire amount led to the arrival at five a.m. of a procession of carts laden with boxes each containing two thousand dollars. As Chinese shroffs counted and tested the money—a total of 440,000 Mexican dollars—it was put on board Her Majesty's ships then in Yokohama harbour, a process requiring three days.[3]

The Expulsion Issue

Neale had relieved Kuper of his coercive responsibilities at once but was confronted the same day with the still graver expulsion issue. Ogasawara, who claimed the responsibility for paying the indemnity, now presented all the foreign representatives with the Mikado's order to close the ports and drive out foreigners 'because the people of the country do not desire intercourse with foreign countries'. That the *Bakufu* had had part in the decision and had set the date was of course not intimated.[4] Neale had long been prepared for the now official

---

[1] P.P. H. of C. 1864, lxvi (3242), 70–71, Neale to Russell, Yokohama, 20 June 1863. Ad. I/5824, Kuper to Adm., Yokohama, 26 June 1863.

[2] F.O. 46/35, Neale to Russell, No. 95, Yokohama, 24 June 1863. Satow, *Diplomat*, p. 80. Ad. I/5824, Kuper to Adm., 26 June 1863.

[3] P.P. H. of C. 1864, lxvi (3242), 75–76, Neale to Kuper, Yokohama, 24 June 1863 and Neale to Russell, Yokohama, 26 June 1863. Satow, *Diplomat*, p. 80.

[4] P.P.H. of C. 1864, lxvi (3242), 73–74, Neale to Russell, Yokohama, 24 June 1863 and encls. Beasley, *Documents*, p. 68. *Nichi-Ei Gaikō Shi*, i. 72–73. Craig, op. cit., p. 199.

announcement. He neither fully accepted nor rejected it, knowing from the recent French conferences with the *Bakufu* that the Shogun's ministers had secret plans to palliate the hostile character of the Imperial order, but aware that such plans might be part of a 'series of frauds' devised by the Yedo government to gain time until it could carry out the edict with better chance of success.[1] Fortified by the presence of their warships he and his French colleagues determined to remain in Yokohama and assume an attitude of 'defensive expectancy'. To the Japanese he called the edict 'a declaration of war by Japan itself against the whole of the Treaty Powers' and threatened them with severe chastisement.[2]

No immediate action demanding expulsion came from Yedo. The retainers of the Daimyo of Chōshū, a leader of the 'expulsion' policy and anti-*Bakufu* faction in Kyoto, however, took matters into their own hands and further complicated Japan's relations with the West. Eager to act on the orders from both the Court and Yedo, two Chōshū steamers fired on the American ship *Pembroke* en route through the Shimonoseki Straits on 25 June 1863, the day fixed for the expulsion of foreigners by Keiki and the Court party in Kyoto. Similar attacks on French and Dutch ships in the succeeding weeks were all a part of Chōshū's deliberate effort 'to force the *Bakufu*'s hand'.[3]

When the Governor of Kanagawa asked the French for transports to send troops to Osaka to defend the Shogun against the daimyo who opposed his disregard of the Mikado's expulsion edict as impracticable, Neale summoned a conference on board H.M.S. *Semiramis*. Here Sakai Tadayasu, a junior councillor at Yedo, and the Governor told the British and French chargés and their naval commanders that the edict of expulsion could be considered null and void. It would not be acted upon as Yedo had sent orders to this effect to Yokohama and Nagasaki with the Imperial mandate. They now determined to send an expedition to Osaka to urge the Mikado to

---

[1] F.O. 46/35, Neale to Russell, No. 95, Yokohama, 24 June 1863.

[2] P.P. H. of C. 1864, lxvi (3242) 73–75, Neale to Russell, Yokohama, 24 June 1863 and encl. 2

[3] Ibid., pp. 79–80, 83–84, Neale to Russell, Yokohama, 12 and 29 July 1863. Beasley, *Documents*, p. 69. 'Chōshū' and 'Nagato' were used at this time interchangeably as names of this province which borders on the Inland Sea and controls the Straits of Shimonoseki.

give his support to the full execution of the treaties. Denying that the Mikado was hostile to the Shogun, they admitted the animosity of certain daimyo. If the Shogun were successful in controlling the hostile party at Osaka, the city would probably be opened at once. In the meantime the *Bakufu* voluntarily confided the defence of Yokohama to the British and the French. Neale, never averse to a bargain, made the arrangements for British steamers to transport the Shogun's troops dependent upon his receipt of the Shogun's letter of apology for the Richardson murder.[1]

The letter arrived promptly on 3 July and the steamers were chartered at rates advantageous to their British owners.[2] Neale rejoiced in the fact that the foreign trade of Japan, then amounting to at least £7,000,000 sterling, of which one-half was in the hands of British merchants, had been only slightly interrupted by the recent political uncertainties.[3]

Hostilities at Kagoshima

With his demands on the Yedo government satisfied and the fear of expulsion allayed, Neale turned his attention to Satsuma.[4] The British expedition left Yokohama on 6 August. Neale and the entire legation staff accompanied Vice-Admiral Kuper, who commanded seven British ships. Six days later the squadron anchored off Kagoshima, which was well fortified by batteries with guns trained on the harbour. The Japanese steamer with a high official on board, promised by the *Bakufu* on 6 August, never appeared. Neale presented a letter containing the British demands—already known in Satsuma—to four men who came

---

[1] F.O. 46/35, Minutes of Conference 2 July, encl. in Neale to Russell, No. 111, Yokohama, 12 July 1863. Ad. I/5825, Kuper to Adm., 13 July 1863. For Keiki's account of the refusal of the *Bakufu* to carry out the expulsion order as impracticable and his offer of resignation in consequence on 9 July 1863, see Beasley, *Documents*, pp. 250–3.

[2] P.P. H. of C. 1864, lxvi (3242), 80–81, Neale to Russell, Yokohama, 13 July 1863 and encls. J.M. MSS. (Yokohama, 1863), S. J. Gower to W. Keswick, 13 July 1863. *S.S. Rajah* was rented at $12,000 per month to move Japanese troops.

[3] P.P. H. of C. 1864, lxvi (3242), 77, Neale to Russell, Yokohama, 27 June 1863. Paske-Smith, *Western Barbarians*, pp. 205–6 gives the consular estimates of the true value of Japan's foreign trade for 1863 as £4,702,971 which makes Neale's figures seem extremely optimistic. The total given out by the Japanese customs, thought to be undervalued by at least 50 per cent., was only $8,256,000. Ibid., pp. 203–4, 303.

[4] P.P. H. of C. 1864, lxvi (3242), 81, Neale to Russell, Yokohama, 13 July 1863.

to the flagship to receive it. He and Kuper refused to go ashore to discuss the issues. A plan to assassinate them by a contingent of Japanese the next day failed through the vigilance of the British marines. Satsuma's answer that evening, 13 August, was evasive and non-committal. He blamed the Shogun for gaps in the treaty which permitted Richardson's murder. He said the murderers could not be found and postponed any payment of the indemnity until it was decided whether Yedo or Satsuma was to blame for the murder. To Neale this was 'utterly unsatisfactory'. He asked Admiral Kuper to take coercive measures.[1]

Britain's seven ships carrying one hundred and one guns, some revolving Armstrong models, now faced Satsuma's ten batteries armed with eighty-three guns. The young admiral ordered the seizure of three Western-built ships belonging to Satsuma as reprisals. Their capture on the fifteenth at dawn led the Japanese to open fire on the British squadron. The British burned the Satsuma vessels in order to free their forces for operation, a total loss of more than $300,000 as prize. Kuper then ordered his ships to engage the batteries in the midst of a stiff gale. During three and a half hours of exchange of fire Captain Josling and Commander Wilmot of the flagship *Euryalus* and nine men were killed; fifty were wounded; and several British ships were damaged. Japanese and British sources differ as to the extent of the destruction of Kagoshima—the former claimed ten per cent.; the latter, Kuper himself, reported the entire town in ruins, including an arsenal and gun factory, in addition to the burning of five ships in Satsuma's Ryūkyū fleet. On 16 August while the Japanese batteries continued their fire, Kuper withdrew his ships for repairs to the entrance of Kagoshima Bay, much to the disgust of the younger members of the legation who would have continued the bombardment until every Japanese gun was silenced. The British shelled the island fort, Sakurashima, *en route* and left for Yokohama the next day.[2] Both sides claimed success; the Japanese on account of driving

---

[1] Ibid., pp. 90–92, Neale to Russell, Yokohama, 26 Aug. 1863.
[2] Ibid., pp. 96–97, Kuper to Neale, 17 Aug. 1863. Ad. I/5825, Kuper to Adm., 22 Aug. 1863. Satow, *Diplomat*, pp. 84–92. *Nichi-Ei Gaikō Shi*, i. 73–74. *London Gazette*, 30 Oct. 1863. The prize value of the ships seems exaggerated. According to Black, op. cit. i. 231, Satsuma paid $245,000 for his British-built ships. Neale, in contrast to *Nichi-Ei Gaikō Shi*, says Satsuma had 81 guns.

off the British squadron; Kuper in the light of his destruction of Satsuma's ships and devastation of Kagoshima.[1] Neale estimated Satsuma's property loss at £1,000,000, his men killed or wounded at fifteen hundred.[2]

Although the British promised to return and Satsuma repaired and strengthened his defences, this was the end of hostilities between them. The development of pro-British sentiment in Satsuma led in November to the opening of direct negotiations between envoys of the Prince and the British chargé. In their subsequent agreement Satsuma promised the immediate payment of the indemnity and a constant search for Richardson's murderers. When arrested, he agreed to execute them in the presence of British officers. Neale received 100,000 Mexican dollars (the equivalent of £25,000) on 9 December, the Daimyo having borrowed the entire sum from the impoverished *Bakufu* government. So cordial were the negotiations that Neale promised at Satsuma's request to help him purchase a warship in England if British relations with the Shogun and Satsuma continued to be satisfactory.[3] Satsuma's agents now acknowledged before representatives of the Shogun and the British legation 'the irresistible superiority' of British power, expressed their desire for friendly relations, and presented gifts of fruit in mark of their goodwill.[4]

The Reaction in England

While Neale gloated over his military success as a salutary influence on hostile daimyo, and Russell approved the fulfilment of his instructions by awarding Neale the Companionship of the Order of the Bath, important voices in England attacked with vehemence British actions in Japan.[5] Neale's and Kuper's

---

[1] Beasley, *Documents*, p. 69.

[2] P.P. H. of C. 1864, lxvi (3242), 116–17, Neale to Russell, Yokohama, 17 Nov. 1863.

[3] *Nichi-Ei Gaikō Shi*, i. 74. P.P. H. of C. 1864, lxvi (3242), 116–17, Neale to Russell, 17 Nov. 1863; (3303), 1–3, Neale to Russell, Yokohama, 17 Dec. 1863 and encls. Soon afterwards Satsuma's agents asked Neale to assist them in arranging for a warship similar to H.M.S. *Perseus* to be built for them in England for about £30,000, and expressed their friendship for England and desire for opening the whole of Japan. Ad. I/5902, F.O. to Adm., 26 Apr. 1864, and encl. Neale to Russell, Yokohama, 9 Feb. 1864.

[4] P.P. H. of C. 1864, lxvi (3303), 4, Neale to Russell, Yokohama, 30 Dec. 1863.

[5] P.P. H. of C. 1864, lxvi (3242), 100 and 117, Russell to Neale, 10 Nov. 1863 and 11 Jan. 1864, for Russell's approval of Neale's 'patience, good temper and firmness' in conducting the negotiations.

correspondence with London on the exaction of reparations for the murder of Richardson had been promptly published in *The London Gazette* and in *Papers for the Consideration of Parliament.* Hence the public had most of the facts.[1] British humanitarianism went on a rampage, using the burning of Kagoshima, greatly exaggerated in detail, to attack the policy of Palmerston's Whig-Liberal coalition ministry. Although Neale had expressed his regrets over the destruction of Satsuma's capital and the Lords Commissioners' speech at the opening of Parliament on 4 February 1864 reported the Queen's 'regret' that the coercive measures needed to bring Satsuma to terms had 'led incidentally to the Destruction of a considerable Portion of the Town of Kagoshima',[2] Kuper's action was hotly debated in the House of Commons. Charles Buxton, the member for Maidstone 1859–65, introduced a motion, 'That this House, while only imputing to Admiral Kuper a misconception of the duty imposed upon him, regrets the burning of the town of Kagoshima, as being contrary to those usages of war which prevail among civilized nations, and to which it is the duty and policy of this country to adhere'.[3] The author found it 'mournful to think that the flag of Christian England should be the herald, not as it should be, of peace and good will toward men, but of anarchy, of tumult, of fire, and sword'. In tearful tones he pictured the seven British men-of-war throwing shells broadcast into a city of 180,000 people and the consequent suffering of women and children, the aged and the infirm.[4]

Lengthy indictments of all British policy in Japan followed: the condemnation of the treaty of 1858 as a hasty and inconsiderate piece of diplomacy entered into without knowledge of the manners, custom, and laws of Japan, a treaty which should have been negotiated with the Mikado, not the Shogun, and which should now be revised; a criticism of British interference with Japanese sovereignty illustrated in Kuper's opposition to the *Bakufu* erection of batteries at Yokohama; revulsion at the arrogance and predatory behaviour of British merchants; an outcry against the rashness and ignorance of Russell's instructions to Neale which claimed that British demands on both the

---

[1] *London Gazette*, 30 Oct. 1863. P.P. H. of C. 1864, lxvi (3242), 81–83, 90–101.
[2] *Hansard's Parliamentary Debates*, 3rd series, clxxiii, col. 4, H. of L. 4 Feb. 1864.
[3] Ibid., col. 335, H. of C. 9 Feb. 1864.   [4] Ibid., cols. 347–8.

Shogun and Satsuma were unjust. Here the honourable member believed the sums required from the Japanese were exorbitant since one-tenth the amount would have been thought sufficient for a similar offence by a European country. There was also evidence of sympathy for the Shogun's government, torn between the pressures of the great daimyo and the foreign merchants. It was argued that Britain should deal moderately with the Japanese ministers and try to undermine the influence of the daimyo on the people.

Other members maintained that the slaughter of Englishmen could not be ignored. Britain had to prove her power to exact reparation for injustice in order that Japan should treat her with justice. The Under-Secretary for Foreign Affairs, Austin Henry Layard, and Palmerston himself, rose in defence of their government justifying both the treaty and the double demand on the Shogun and Satsuma since the former could not control the latter. The entire government they said approved Russell's instructions and Kuper's fulfilment of them. The destruction of the town was incidental to the action of the Japanese batteries in a violent gale. Regrets had been expressed. Lamentable as it was, the burning of a town could not be called inconsistent with the practice of civilized warfare as several instances in the last ten years proved. Russell's policy was the 'only course consistent with his duty as a minister of the Crown and as representing the interests of this country abroad', a country which it had already been stated controlled more than one-half of a growing annual trade with Japan then equal to £7,000,000. The motion was withdrawn. The discussion had satisfied its author that burning of towns was not an approved precedent.[1]

To *The Quarterly Review* the attack on Kagoshima provided a good example

of English foreign policy towards the weakest powers. In principle it is overbearing, exacting, pushing every right to the extremest limit, and where the very existence of a right is doubtful, cynically throwing the sword in the balance. In execution these principles are carried out with no diplomatic courtesy; and with no consideration of the feelings or the wounded honour of those to whom they are applied, but rather with an ostentatious insolence.

[1] *Hansard's Parliamentary Debates*, 3rd series, clxxiii, cols. 335–423, H. of C. 9 Feb. 1864.

The *Review* maintained that Kuper's boast of British superiority to the Japanese ambassadors expressed admirably the general attitude of the English Foreign Office to every weaker power.[1]

Richard Cobden, an unsparing critic of foreign secretaries, foreign representatives, and of British sword-rattling under Palmerston, burst out against the destruction of Kagoshima on 4 November 1863 in a public letter to the Mayor of Rochdale which was widely quoted and at least once repudiated.[2] Booklets and pamphlets burned with indignation based on ill-founded facts. Neale, disturbed by this uproar, attempted to correct its misconceptions in a letter read to the Commons on 14 March 1864. He explained that the population of Kagoshima had never exceeded 40,000, 'far less 180,000, as has been strangely imagined'—and that these men, women, and children had withdrawn from the city during the justified attack by the British. Satsuma's voluntary payment of the indemnity and the expression of his envoys of their desire for friendly and social intercourse with the British implied, Neale believed, that 'the agents of Her Majesty displayed a degree of caution and moderation duly appreciated by those most deeply interested'.[3]

Persistent Anti-foreign Activity; the Proposal to Close Yokohama

The settlement with Satsuma was merely a localized step toward better relations between Britain and Japan. Chōshū's continuing anti-foreign activities during the summer of 1863 soon injured Japan's rapidly growing trade with the West. Neither the united protests of the treaty powers nor the threat of a forced opening of the Shimonoseki Straits, nor the French and American destruction of the forts at Shimonoseki in July discouraged the belligerent *han* which had fired on American, French, and Dutch ships during the previous weeks. It hastily rebuilt its batteries and set about reforming its military organization along Western lines while stopping all vessels bound for

[1] *Quarterly Review*, lxv. Apr. 1864, 499–500.

[2] W. H. Dawson, *Richard Cobden and Foreign Policy* (London, 1926), pp. 103, 181, 256–7. F.O. 46/38, printed letter repudiating Cobden's letter (Brighton, 16 Nov. 1863) signed 'F'. Booklet, Henry Richard, *The Destruction of Kagoshima, Our Intercourse with Japan* (London, 1863).

[3] *Hansard's Parliamentary Debates*, 3rd series, clxxiii, cols. 1910–11, H. of C. 14 March 1864.

Nagasaki and Shanghai by the Shimonoseki route and effectively closing the Straits to foreign commerce for months.[1]

Little produce reached the southern treaty port. The Governor of Nagasaki notified the consuls that it was no longer safe for foreign vessels to pass through the Shimonoseki Straits.[2] A band of *rōnin* sent by Chōshū to Nagasaki caused great excitement among the native population. Warnings to the leading native merchants to have no further dealings with foreigners meant they could expect no protection from the local government and caused them to discontinue business. The Governor declared his inability to protect foreigners as well and advised the consuls and senior officers to take measures for the defence of the settlement.[3] A *Bakufu* order forbidding daimyo to purchase steamers meant that many vessels offered for sale at Yokohama were lying idle.[4] Native traders were leaving Yokohama. Some were persecuted in Kyoto, Osaka, and Yedo for having dealings with foreigners. Aggressive actions against the *Bakufu* as well as against foreigners multiplied.[5] On 14 October a French lieutenant was murdered by Japanese assassins while riding unarmed on a country road.[6]

War preparations had become more general. Both the Yedo authorities and agents of hostile daimyo were buying cannon, rifles, and munitions. Able-bodied men were widely conscripted and drilled even at night. Batteries not only at the Shimonoseki Straits, but at Uraga, Yedo, and elsewhere were rapidly built. In spite of the promise of the *Bakufu* to annul the expulsion order in July, an attempt at its enforcement now seemed imminent. Neale warned the *Bakufu*, now mysteriously uncommunicative about its policy towards foreigners, that the treaty powers would 'insist at any cost upon the execution of their

[1] P.P. H. of C. 1864, lxvi (3242), 83–89, Neale to Russell, Yokohama, 29 July 1863 and encls. Beasley, *Documents*, pp. 69–70. Craig, op. cit., pp. 200–1. Satow, *Diplomat*, pp. 95–96.

[2] J.M. MSS. (Nagasaki 1863), Glover and Company to Jardine, Matheson, Shanghai Office, Nagasaki, 28 Aug. 1863.

[3] Ibid., same to same, 28 Sept. 1863. F.O. 46/37, encls. in Neale to Russell, No. 150, Yokohama, 14 Oct. 1863. Ad. I/5825, Kuper to Adm., 14 Oct. 1863.

[4] J.M. MSS. (Yokohama, 1863), S. J. Gower to W. Keswick, 26 Aug. 1863.

[5] Ibid., Yokohama, 19 Sept. and 31 Oct. 1863. F.O. 46/37, Neale to Russell, No. 107, Yokohama, 29 Oct. 1863. Ad. I/5825, Kuper to Adm., 14 Oct. 1863.

[6] P.P. H. of C. 1864, lxvi (3242), 110, Neale to Russell, Yokohama, 14 Oct. 1863.

treaty rights'. Should large-scale defensive measures become necessary, Japan must pay for them.[1]

The *Bakufu* broke its silence with a proposal to close the port of Yokohama, an alternative devised during the summer to meet the continued demands of the Court for the complete expulsion of the foreigners, already recognized as an impossibility. The *Rōjū* admitted the Shogun's inability to control the anti-foreign forces and stressed the imminent danger of revolution. It blamed the opening of Yokohama, which then controlled eighty per cent. of the foreign trade, for the current disturbances. With the restriction of trade to Nagasaki and Hakodate, Yedo hoped to appease the Court and reduce the strain on the national economy while winning the consent of the treaty powers through negotiations by another embassy to Europe. At least it would not be compelled to take action until their envoys returned. The Commissioners of Foreign Affairs requested the return of the *Rōjū*'s letter concerning expulsion as the government had changed its policy.[2]

Neale, though sceptical of the outcome of their proceedings, also welcomed the time thus gained as a possible respite from 'extreme anxiety and overwhelming danger'.[3] He argued, however, that in all events, given the intrigues and disorders prevailing in Japan, a moderate British military force should be available for precautionary purposes. This time Major-General Brown, on instructions from the War Office, promised to grant his request for troops.[4] Neale had reason to hope that Alcock would be back at his post before the next great decision.

Military Enforcement of Britain's Treaty Rights

In London Lord Russell was obviously confused and uncertain about the policy Britain should adopt in Japan. His objectives continued to be the maintenance of peace and the expansion of trade. The recently published correspondence between Neale and Satsuma renewed his conviction that the

[1] Ibid., pp. 107–8, Neale to Japanese Commissioners of Foreign Affairs, Yokohama, 30 Sept. 1863.

[2] Ibid., pp. 112–13, Neale to Russell, Yokohama, 31 Oct. 1863. Beasley, *Documents*, p. 71. *Nichi-Ei Gaikō Shi*, i. 81.

[3] P.P. H. of C.¹1864, lxvi (3242), 115, Neale to Russell, Yokohama, 16 Nov. 1863.

[4] F.O. 46/37, Neale to Russell, Nos. 166 and 174, Yokohama, 31 Oct. and 16 Nov. 1863.

power and right of treaty-making resided with the Shogun. On these grounds he postponed, until the situation clarified, Britain's acceptance of an American offer to co-operate in demanding the ratification of the treaties by the Mikado by a joint naval demonstration at Osaka, to be followed, if unsuccessful, by the march of a land force on Kyoto.[1] At the same time, acting apparently on advice from Alcock, he sought to treat with the friendly daimyo who would like a share of the profits of trade. By separating these princes from the violently anti-foreign minority faction and holding a balance between them and the Shogun through the exaction of concessions from both, he aimed to avert civil war.[2] He empowered Neale to make temporary arrangements, in accordance with terms applicable to the treaty ports, and in concert with the ministers of other treaty powers, with any daimyo who had separate seaports under their control and expressed a willingness to open them to foreign trade. To the *Bakufu* Neale was to explain that nothing in the Anglo-Japanese treaties excluded the extension of such benefits.[3] Before such orders were carried out, Alcock had returned with still greater powers.

Both Alcock and Morrison, also in England on home leave, aided Russell in defining this policy. They both believed in the friendliness of the Japanese people and their sanction of foreign trade when exposed to its benefits. They agreed that the chief enemies of the treaty powers were a small group of highly privileged daimyo who feared the break-up of their feudal organization by the intrusion of Western ideas among their subservient people, who resented the Shogun's monopoly of foreign trade, and who were the strength behind the Mikado's exclusion policy. They recommended that this group be defeated decisively and promptly in the field for which a large squadron, artillery, and a land force would be required. Morrison proposed that the British support the Shogun against the Mikado and anti-foreign daimyo in an overwhelming demonstration of power as a first step to peace, and as a basis for a new treaty to be negotiated with the Mikado, the real

---

[1] F.O. 262/54, F.O. to Neale, 10 Nov. 1863 and encls., Adams to Russell, 30 Sept. 1863, and Pruyn (U.S. Minister in Yedo; to Seward (U.S. Sec. of State) Yokohama, 27 June 1863.

[2] F.O. 46/37, Alcock to Russell, London, 5 Nov. 1863.

[3] F.O. 262/54, Russell to Neale, 14 Nov. 1863.

head of the nation.[1] Alcock, on the other hand, saw the need of imposing on the Shogun, whom he considered scarcely less hostile and mischievous than the anti-foreign daimyo, the sacrifice of his trading profits and exclusive privileges for some reasonable arrangement with his and Britain's enemies, the anti-foreign daimyo, to make possible peaceful relations with all ruling classes. Considering a conflict between the ancient feudal organization of Japan's ruling classes and the social and political institutions of the West inevitable, he thought Britain's long-range objectives in Japan should be to bring about a gradual transformation from the medieval practices to the modern concept of equal rights and freedom for all, through the influence of commerce and European thought—even if it involved an armed truce to keep the peace during the transitional period.[2]

Russell's instructions to Alcock as he returned to his post made this policy more definite but took into consideration the public outcry over British action at Kagoshima. The Foreign Secretary anticipated the need for force to maintain Britain's treaty rights but strictly prescribed its use. Alcock was to require the Shogun and the daimyo to execute the treaty as modified by the London Protocol. He was to consult the Admiral and any military officers dispatched to Japan regarding the best means of strengthening and holding the British position in Yokohama or 'if any other position should be found more advantageous' the British forces might occupy it with Alcock's concurrence. A regiment of infantry could be requested from Hong Kong for the defence of Yokohama. In case of an attack on Nagasaki, however, British action should depend on whether it was believed that British commerce could be maintained there with any hope of success. Should batteries, erected for the purpose of interrupting the passage of British merchant ships, resort to clearly proved hostile action, the Admiral would be empowered, if approved by Alcock, to land marines, to destroy the batteries, and spike the guns. No unarmed and peaceful town should be bombarded. But British warships if fired upon

---

[1] F.O. 46/37, *Memorandum on Japanese Affairs*, Alcock to Russell, London, 5 Nov. 1863; 46/38, Morrison to Alcock, Brighton, 4 Dec. 1863. G. S. Morrison, *Our Position and Policy in Japan* (Brighton, 24 Nov. 1863).

[2] F.O. 46/37, Alcock to Hammond, St. Leonards, 14 Nov. 1863.

must return that fire.[1] Correspondingly, the Admiralty's instructions to Kuper urged his unreserved communication with Alcock and cautioned him against any attack on the Japanese batteries unless success and some ultimate advantage seemed assured. Her Majesty's Government hoped to maintain its position in Japan and extend trade without resort to hostilities.[2] Even so, it did not hesitate to permit British occupation of more territory for military purposes, in spite of earlier professions that Britain had no interest in the acquisition of land.

To lessen the chance of conflict, an Order in Council passed in early January after Alcock's departure empowered the British consul-general to restrict or prohibit altogether the entrance of British vessels other than warships into the inland waters of Japan.[3]

[1] F.O. 262/54, Russell to Alcock, nos. 1 and 2, 17 and 19 Dec. 1863.
[2] Ad. 13/34, Adm. to Kuper, 26 Dec. 1863.
[3] P.P. H. of C. 1865, lxvii (3428), 3–4, Order-in-Council, 7 Jan. 1864.

V

THE GENESIS OF A NEW ORDER

British Reaction to the Shogun's Second Diplomatic Mission

EVENTS during the two months preceding Alcock's arrival in Japan and the journey of the Japanese ministers to Europe deserve notice. Two companies of the 20th British regiment arrived from Hong Kong and were quartered in barracks in the centre of Yokohama, much to the satisfaction of Neale.[1] The Shogun's government reduced the duties to five per cent. upon most articles bearing a duty of twenty per cent. in accordance with its promises to England and France in 1862 and later to the United States.[2] Trade flourished in spite of Chōshū's blockade of the Inland Sea and government interference with the export of silk.[3] Yokohama grew rapidly, causing the value of land to soar. The Yedo government extended the areas to be settled by both the Americans and British.[4] This in particular made the Shogun's declared intention of evacuating the foreigners from that area seem false. Still another evidence of *Bakufu* inconsistency was its ratification of commercial treaties with Prussia and Switzerland in January and February 1864.[5]

The *Bakufu* nevertheless had dispatched its second mission to Europe—thirty-four men led by Ikeda Chōhatsu Chikugo-no-kami, to report on the anti-foreign agitation in Japan and to negotiate, as its only remedy, the closing of Yokohama. Furthermore, the envoys deposited £100,000 at a British branch bank in Yokohama with the promise of the addition of a similar amount, and opened a like credit in Europe—all to be used, it was believed, for the purchase of cannon, rifles, and

[1] P.P. H. of C. 1865, lvii (3428), 8, Neale to Russell, Yokohama, 30 Jan. 1864.
[2] Ibid., p. 9, same to same, Yokohama, 6 Feb. 1864. *London Gazette*, 22 Apr. 1864 for new scale of import duties.
[3] P.P. H. of C. 1865, lvii (3428), 12, Neale to Russell, Yokohama, 1 Mar. 1864.
[4] F.O. 46/43, Neale to Russell, Yokohama, No. 6, 28 Jan. 1864.
[5] Ibid., No. 16, 10 Feb. 1864.

one or two warships.[1] The secret agents of Satsuma confirmed the Shogun's sincerity in desiring to close Yokohama to trade in order to stop the constant danger of clashes between the foreigners and the many disaffected Japanese in the city. The agent could say this while discussing the building of a warship for his master in England and expressing his desire for foreign trade in his own territories. He even claimed that within the rights of the Anglo-Japanese treaties temporary agreements were possible with daimyo having quasi-independent territories and seaports[2]—a clear indication of his dubious relation to the Shogunate and an echo of British opinion.

The Japanese ambassadors left Japan with little hope of attaining their purpose. Neale had made it abundantly clear to their government that their reception in England was uncertain and that in case of the stoppage of trade or aggressive acts in Japan by the Shogun's government he would retaliate with Her Majesty's forces near at hand.[3] Alcock, who met the envoys *en route*, realized that although they expected to fail in the closing of Yokohama, they would gain in being able on their return home to prove to the anti-foreign party that it would have all Europe to face if it persisted in its attempts at expulsion. Russell, who was now taking a close personal interest in the Japanese situation, saw to it that all the courts where the previous Japanese mission had visited were informed that Her Majesty's Government had no desire to see the envoys in London and if they came, the British would not give up Yokohama as a port of trade.[4] France, Holland, Prussia, and the United States agreed to do likewise, the French further promising to try to prevent the Japanese purchase of vessels and munitions of war in France and hoping that the same would be done in England. Russell naïvely believed that the unanimous refusal of the treaty powers to close the ports would mean the strengthening

---

[1] F.O., 46/43, Neale to Russell, Yokohama, Nos. 8 and 9, 29 Jan.; No. 11, 30 Jan.; No. 14, 7 Feb.; and No. 19, 15 Feb. 1864. P.P. H. of C. 1865, lvii (3428), 9, same to same, 6 Feb. 1864. *Nichi-Ei Gaikō Shi*, i. 81.

[2] F.O. 46/43, Neale to Russell, Yokohama, No. 15, 9 Feb. and No. 21, 16 Feb. 1864.

[3] P.P. H. of C. 1865, lvii (3428), 5–7, Minutes of interview with the Shogun's Ministers, 4 Jan. 1864.

[4] F.O. 46/43, Alcock to Russell, Private, Shanghai, 21 Feb. 1864 and Russell's note at end.

of the Shogun's hands in his endeavours to keep faith with the West.[1]

Alcock's Decision for Military Action

Alcock resumed his duties in Yokohama the second of March. He learned that the Shogun and most of his ministers were attending a council with the great daimyo in Kyoto where the expulsion of foreigners was being debated. Here, against the realistic arguments of the Daimyo of Satsuma that expulsion and even the closing of Yokohama should be abandoned as impossibilities, the *Bakufu* reasserted on 26 March their determination to close Yokohama, hoping thereby to maintain their ancient prerogatives and negotiate the issue, if necessary, with the treaty powers.[2] Alcock had no access to these facts. From uncertain reports or rumours, however, he concluded that the Shogun's government was threatened, that the Mikado might be restored to his legitimate position as sovereign, and that peace or war, civil or foreign, hung in the balance. He observed many preparations for war; the Yedo government was calling in recently issued copper coin and melting the bells of the temples of the capital in order to cast numerous cannon on European models. The daimyo generally were active in buying steamers and drilling men with capped muskets and bayonets—arms usually imported from Macao, often by American firms. Civil war on a small scale seemed to have commenced in that Chōshū, the anti-foreign leader, had fired upon one of the Shogun's steamers lent to Satsuma for purposes of trade. A British seaman had been assaulted in Nagasaki. Alcock feared a sudden attack on the foreign community from the hostile daimyo, 'with or without the concurrence of the Tycoon or less open aggression but no less seriously obstructive acts on the part of either'.[3]

Clear evidence of the Shogun's continued interference with foreign trade had come from Hakodate. There Western merchants were handicapped by Yedo's regulations which made it impossible for any Japanese to trade with any foreigner without

[1] P.P. H. of C. 1865, lvii (3428), 11–12, Nos. 13, 14, 16, 17 for correspondence about concerted policy of Britain, France, Holland, and Prussia, Apr. and May 1864.   [2] Beasley, *Documents*, pp. 73–74.

[3] P.P. H. of C. 1865, lvii (3428), 14–16, Alcock to Russell, Yokohama, 31 Mar. 1864. F.O. 46/43, Alcock to Russell, No. 5, Yokohama, 28 Mar. 1864.

permission from the officials, who took note of his trade and claimed an exorbitant percentage of his income. The lower classes were kept in great fear of the officials, never daring to witness against them. And these officials spread erroneous reports about the opposition of local daimyo to foreign trade in order to guard the Shogun's monopoly of it. One prince especially had expressed his desire for trade but did not know how to keep it secret from the government. Dent and Company's agent reported that ports on the west coast belonging to independent daimyo could be opened to trade with the willing assent of the daimyo if the Shogun would permit their friendliness to foreigners, often shown by their generosity in shipwrecked cases.[1]

In Nagasaki Consul Myburgh was reporting difficulties resulting from the blockade of the Straits. Chōshū had entire command of the channel and had stopped the trade between the Inland Sea and Nagasaki. Traders refused to risk the destruction of their property by attempting the passage beneath his batteries. Foreigners and Japanese alike were said to welcome the forced opening of the waterway by foreign men-of-war.[2]

Alcock concluded that the time for concession had passed. Indiscriminate aggression and 'increased insecurity' had followed British efforts at conciliation. He determined to be prepared to meet sudden hostilities. He would make it clear to all Japanese authorities that Britain intended to enforce respect for her treaty rights and would resist with force all attacks. The growth of trade in spite of all adverse conditions was his great source of encouragement. He believed that could he get timely information, the weight of the treaty powers or even Britain's alone, if thrown into the present situation, could avert both civil war and hostilities with the foreign powers and so strengthen and stimulate the pro-foreign forces that no serious effort would be made to disturb them.[3]

[1] F.O. 46/43, Alcock to Russell, encl. letters from Hakodate in Nos. 5 and 6, 28 and 30 Mar. 1864. For Dent and Company, see p. 314.

[2] P.P. H. of C. 1865, lvii (3428), 41–42, Myburgh to Alcock, Nagasaki, 26 Mar. 1864.

[3] Ibid., pp. 14, 16, Alcock to Russell, Yokohama, 31 Mar. 1864. Japanese imports to the United Kingdom had grown from £538,687 in 1861 to £1,283,631 in 1863; exports from the United Kingdom from £43,100 in 1861 to £108,897 in 1863; 1866, lxviii. 316. The figures vary, however, in different sources.

The *Bakufu* as usual appeared to be delaying a showdown by freeing itself from foreign pressures during a prolonged stay in Kyoto. The Shogunate counted on Britain's repugnance to national war as witnessed by the Parliamentary outburst over the attack on Kagoshima, and rejoiced over the rumoured possibility of war between the treaty powers in Europe and the unsettled conditions in America as likely preventives to a war against Japan. Alcock recognized all this, almost admiring the Japanese ingenuity in removing their treaty-making government beyond the reach of the treaty powers while it planned to expel them. Alcock continued to think in terms of coercive measures, however, and outlined for Russell the requirements for their success in terms of ships, infantry, the protection of Yokohama, and the embarkation of the smaller foreign communities from Nagasaki and Hakodate.[1]

Letters between the Mikado and the Shogun containing the Imperial orders for the closing of Yokohama and the Shogun's promise to carry them out as soon as he completed the needed military preparations soon fell into Alcock's hands.[2] They seemed legitimate evidence of the Shogun's intentions. Alcock determined to act before the Japanese were ready, to stop their underhanded plotting for the expulsion of foreigners. He wished to localize the conflict by making a direct attack on the batteries of Chōshū whose original hostility to the foreign treaties was now known and whose unprovoked attack on foreign commerce was a clear-cut violation of treaty rights. Alcock hoped thereby to teach the whole body of hostile daimyo a lesson by destroying Chōshū's batteries and thus proving to them all the 'utter futility of their most formidable preparations either for attack or defence'. Adequate force would soon be at hand. The marines were expected on H.M.S. *Conqueror* and the major portion of the 20th Infantry was coming from Hong Kong.

The treaty powers were free to act since both the Mikado and Shogun were said to have disavowed Chōshū's action but had as yet taken no measures against him. Although Alcock doubted this disavowal, he believed that the Shogun could neither dispute 'the right of the Treaty Powers to take the law into their own

---

[1] F.O. 46/44, Alcock to Russell, No. 20, Yokohama, 14 Apr. 1864.
[2] P.P. H. of C. 1865, lvii (3428), 27–32, Alcock to Russell, 1 May 1864, encl. the Shogun's correspondence with the Mikado.

hands', nor consider their assault on Chōshū an act of war against his government or the nation. Furthermore the open ports and great centres of population were not likely to be endangered since the proposed hostilities would take place at some distance from them.[1]

Thus the British minister argued for the decisive and prompt use of force. He hoped it was not too late to recover the ground lost since July when after Chōshū's first provocation the treaty powers made a formal agreement to reopen the passage to the Inland Sea if the *Bakufu* did not do so, and then did nothing effective about it.[2] The Shogun neither took notice of their protocol nor took redress on Chōshū himself. The powers now recognized 'that they had been in a false position ever since'. But how much co-operation from them could now be expected, Alcock did not know. He was determined, however, on seizing the initiative as quickly as possible believing that Britain was not only at the mercy of the *Bakufu* because of its extensive control of her trade but also because Yokohama could not be defended without the building of specific fortifications to which there were insuperable obstacles.[3]

International Action against Chōshū

Alcock was soon encouraged by the promise of military co-operation from the American minister, Robert H. Pruyn, as well as support in the belief that an attack on Chōshū was essential to the maintenance of treaty rights. Pruyn agreed that it could be carried out without war with the Yedo government, even strengthening the Shogunate and averting civil war.[4] A common understanding regarding united action in all contingencies was also reached with Holland and France while the *Bakufu* request to be allowed to punish Chōshū without foreign interference was regarded as another ruse to keep the treaty powers passive while Shogun and daimyo armed frantically to expel them. Yedo now appeared impregnable from the sea with from six to eight hundred guns trained on the

---

[1] P.P. H. of C. 1865, lvii (3428), 32–36, Alcock to Russell, Yokohama, 6 May 1864.   [2] See p. 119.

[3] F.O. 46/44, Alcock to Russell, Nos. 25 and 27, Yokohama, 6 May 1864 and encl. on defence of Yokohama.

[4] Ibid., Pruyn to Alcock, Kanagawa, 13 May 1864, encl. in Alcock to Russell, No. 29, 14 May 1864.

only approach to the bay. New batteries bearing on Kanagawa and the entrance to Nagasaki also could put these foreign settlements at their mercy. And in a recent conference between the Shogun's ministers and the newly arrived French minister, M. Léon Roches, the closing of Yokohama had again been declared a necessity. Alcock put three choices before the treaty powers: acceptance of Japan's violations of the treaties, withdrawal altogether from Japan, or the maintenance of their treaty rights with effective force.[1] All chose the last.

The four powers moved forward by stages. On 30 May they sent identical letters to the Japanese Commissioners of Foreign Affairs, complaining that their demand of 25 July 1863 for the opening of the Inland Sea had been ignored, and that the Shogun had shown sympathy with the anti-foreign parties by requesting the closing of Kanagawa. They firmly refused this concession, asking that the request be withdrawn. And they declared their intention to remove 'the continuing obstruction to commerce' and put an end to the hostile acts of Chōshū themselves.[2] A month later the Japanese reply merely repeated the Shogun's plea that the Chōshū affair be left in his hands, and declared again that Yokohama must be closed as the only means of calming national feelings and improving relations between Japan and the treaty powers.[3]

To the four foreign representatives this seemed a formal denial of their treaty rights. At the same time their position in Japan was strengthened by the arrival of fifteen hundred British marines. And the return of the Shogun to Yedo on 23 June gave them a government with which to deal. They met again on 22 July. In a long memorandum they agreed to chastise Chōshū, believing that the destruction of his batteries and the opening of the Inland Sea would ruin Chōshū's prestige and prove to the other hostile daimyo their inability to resist the science and military resources of the West. They established the following principles as the basis of their undertaking: the

[1] Ibid., Alcock to Russell, No. 30, Yokohama, 21 May 1864. For Holland's support of the attack on Chōshū, see ibid., Van Polsbroek to Alcock, Kanagawa, 30 May 1864, encl. in Alcock to Russell, No. 34, 9 June 1864.

[2] P.P. H. of C. 1865, lvii (3482), 49–54, Alcock to Russell, Yokohama, 25 May 1864 and encls. *Nichi-Ei Gaikō Shi*, i. 83–84.

[3] Ibid., p. 84. P.P. H. of C. 1865, lvii (3428), 67, Japanese Commissioners of Foreign Affairs to Alcock, 30 June 1864. For the domestic conflict and *Bakufu* duplicity lying back of this letter, see Beasley, *Documents*, pp. 72–75.

neutralization of Japan; and while awaiting ratification by their home governments, they pledged that this principle should apply at the open ports; common agreement on measures to be taken to maintain the treaty rights intact; common efforts to protect Yokohama; 'neither to ask for nor to accept any concession of territory, nor any exclusive advantage whatever either in the open ports or elsewhere in Japan'; and to 'abstain from all interference in the jurisdiction of the Japanese authorities over their people, as well as from all intervention between the contending parties in the country'. In identical ultimatums to the *Rōjū* they rejected its letter of 30 June and declared they would take military and naval action themselves against Chōshū without further notice, if within twenty days the *Bakufu* had failed to give them a satisfactory guarantee for future security. Regarding the continuing demand for abandoning Yokohama, the powers would answer by withdrawing the concessions of 1862 and requiring the opening of Yedo, Osaka, Hyogo, and Niigata in accordance with the treaties.[1]

The unexpected appearance of two Chōshū youths, Itō Hirobumi and Inoue Kaoru, who had hastened home from their studies in England to tell their daimyo of the power and resources of Britain and to persuade the Chōshū government to renounce its anti-foreign activities, gave Alcock an opportunity, he hoped, to avert hostilities.[2] He ordered Admiral Kuper to provide transportation to take these young samurai to their *han*, rejoicing in this chance for direct communication with their daimyo and for a British naval officer to observe Chōshū's fortifications in the Straits. He assigned Ernest Satow and James Enslie, his most competent interpreters who had also served at Kagoshima, to accompany the expedition. And he allowed twelve days for the youths to visit and return an answer from their Prince.[3]

Alcock's letter to the Daimyo of Nagato stated clearly the Allies' policy: their determination to maintain their treaties with Japan and to destroy his forts if he persisted in his

[1] P.P. H. of C. 1865, lvii (3428), 62–66, *Memorandum*, 22 July 1864. *Nichi-Ei Gaikō Shi*, i. 84–85.

[2] J.M. MSS. (Yokohama, Private), C. S. Hope to J. Whittall, 26 July 1864. Here Hope reports that he introduced the two Japanese to Alcock, who received them most kindly.

[3] P.P. H. of C. 1865, lvii (3428), 71, Alcock to Kuper, Yokohama, 19 July 1864.

hostilities. It admitted a willingness, however, to adjust the treaties to the political conditions as they were now understood especially the desire for a freer trade which would benefit all the Japanese people, low and high alike. He wrote:

If the Treaties, as some Daimios contend, require the formal assent of the Mikado to make them legal and binding on the whole nation, let it be obtained, and if certain modifications are in their opinion imperatively required to put an end to the monopoly, secured by the Tycoon, in his own interest exclusively, of all trade, which he has carefully restricted to his own ports, let some direct means of communication be established with the foreign Representatives on the part of the Mikado and these Daimios. A good understanding might then be come to, and the end desired happily accomplished. Whereas a persistent attempt to expel foreigners from Japan, or even from Yokohama, instead of peaceful envoys, may bring armies to Kioto as similar conduct led the armies of Great Britain and France victoriously to Peking not five years ago.

But some sovereign authority must be recognized, whether as vested in a Mikado, or a Tycoon, or a Gorogio, with whom national compacts can be made, and by whom formal Treaties can be duly executed. . . . Whether this sovereign authority be vested in one or many hands it is for the Japanese themselves to settle, and is a matter of perfect indifference to foreigners. There is no desire in Europe to interfere in such questions. Neither is there any wish to uphold the Tycoon as the rightful or sole possessor of sovereign power. Still less is there any desire to uphold the Tycoon in his present monopoly of trade, restricting it to his own ports and officials. On the contrary, this is directly opposed to the spirit and object of all the Treaties. Foreign Powers desire to see all the Daimios who are lords of the soil, and the Japanese equally, who assist in its cultivation, participate in the advantages, the movement, and the profits of trade. Then all ill-will and distrust would soon disappear. A freer intercourse would greatly tend to remove all prejudices, and prevent all such restrictions and monopolies as now exist by the Tycoon's policy, for the advantage of the few at the expense of the many. Foreign Powers only desire to see these removed. They have no wish for territorial possessions in Japan. and [*sic*] no desire to call into question the rights and privileges of the ruling classes, so long as their existence is compatible with intercourse and trade. They desire only to enter into peaceful relations, and for their subjects to trade without vexations, interruptions or molestation, within such limits and under such conditions as Treaties may provide.

If some change should be required, either in the existing form of government, or the exact wording and provisions of Treaties, in order to secure such a desirable end as peaceable and mutually profitable intercourse, the Treaty Powers, are not likely to interpose any insuperable obstacle, if they are properly addressed. Nor, these ends secured, have they the slightest wish to interfere with the forms of government, the distribution of power, or the internal administration of the country.

But if any Daimio, or combination of hostile parties, should seek to make changes in the Government and Administration, as a means of destroying Treaties, and expelling foreigners; or begin hostilities with them, and the repudiation of Treaties, as a means of effecting either the destruction of the Tycoon, or other changes in Government, in that case the Treaty Powers will treat them as common enemies, and combine their forces for their destruction.

On the other hand, they are ready to aid and support whoever may stand forward for the good of their country to maintain peace and order, recognizing existing Treaties as the basis of all future relations of amity and commerce with foreign Powers.[1]

Thus the Daimyo of Chōshū had the chance to recant, even to step forward as the leader of a new order. He chose, however, to refuse to change his policy on the ground that he was obeying orders from the Mikado and the Shogun. He admitted he was powerless in the face of European strength, and asked for three months' delay to try to get an annulment of the Imperial command.[2] To the dismay of the British, Itō and Inoue brought back merely this verbal reply to Alcock's note, not even a receipt for the dispatches they had delivered to their Daimyo. Although they promised to secure the authorized documents within two or three days, they were told to send them to Yokohama or Nagasaki, as the British ships would return the next day. In a private conversation with Satow the young samurai admitted that the matter could be settled only by war. They further suggested 'that the foreign Representatives should throw the Tycoon overboard, and going to Osaka, demand an interview with the Mikado's Ministers, and conclude a Treaty with him'. They spoke with great bitterness of the Tycoon's dynasty. They complained it kept all trade, not only foreign, but native also, to itself by seizing all places where trade was likely to develop, such as Nagasaki and Niigata. And they said

---

[1] P.P. H. of C. 1865, lvii (3428), 72–73, *Memorandum* of Alcock, delivered to Officers of the Prince of Chōshū, 21 July 1864.

[2] Ibid., p. 74, extract from Enslie's Report.

that 'these feelings were shared by most of the people of the country'. This made a lasting impression on the keen and gifted young interpreter.[1]

Chōshū's message caused the treaty powers to order military and naval operations against his batteries in accordance with their *Memorandum* of 22 July. Even if the Daimyo, awed by the great flotilla, should not fire, the allied commanders were required to destroy the batteries and take necessary measures to prevent future hostilities from the same quarter. They were urged to avoid any demonstration of force in the Osaka area, however, in order to limit the expedition exclusively to the chastisement of Nagato.[2]

Again the expedition was delayed, not only by another plea from the *Bakufu* that the foreign powers should leave in its hands the punishment of Chōshū, but by the unexpected return of the Shogun's envoys directly from France. Having failed to negotiate the closing of Yokohama, the Japanese ambassadors had agreed to a convention with the French which pledged the Shogun's government to open the Straits of Shimonoseki within three months, assisted if necessary by the French navy.[3] This could have altered the entire situation had not the *Bakufu* promptly annulled the Convention, on the grounds that it would precipitate civil war and destroy Japan's friendship with France.[4] In the light of this decision and the admission of the Shogun's government that it could not open the Straits by its own efforts, the foreign representatives commanded their naval forces to proceed against Chōshū.[5]

The allied powers sought, however, to secure more by the use of force than the opening of the Straits and the chastisement of Chōshū. They hoped to stop the activities of the anti-foreign

---

[1] Ibid., p. 75, extract from Satow's Report. Satow, MSS. *Diary*, i. opp. p. 155.

[2] P.P. H. of C. 1865, lvii (3428), 79–80, Alcock to Kuper, Yokohama, 16 Aug. 1864 and encl.

[3] Ibid., pp. 81–82, Interview of Treaty Powers with Bakufu Officials, 19 Aug. 1864; 82–83, Alcock to Kuper, 20 Aug. 1864 and encl.; pp. 25–27, Text of Convention, 20 June 1864. Beasley, *Documents*, pp. 75–76. For the negotiations in France, see Meron Medzini, 'Léon Roches in Japan (1864–1868)' in Harvard University, East Asian Research Center, *Papers on Japan* (Cambridge, Mass., 1963), ii. 192–5.

[4] *Nichi-Ei Gaikō Shi*, i. 85. P.P. H. of C. 1865, lvii (3428), 84, Japanese Ministers to Alcock, 25 Aug. 1864.

[5] Ibid., pp. 84–85, *Memorandum* of Treaty Powers, 25 Aug. 1864; Alcock to Kuper, Yokohama, 25 Aug. 1864.

factions who were urging violent measures for the closing of Yokohama and to win permanent advantages for the expansion of trade. All foreign representatives considered it most important that once the Straits were within their grasp there should be no relaxation until the ulterior political aims were secured. Alcock wrote to Kuper in confidence:

The imperialization of a large portion of the territories of Nagato (all those bordering on the Straits from Shimonoseki westward) the conversion of the latter into an open port for Foreign trade, as the penalty on its Prince for his high handed violence and open repudiation of the Treaties, and as a compensation to Foreign powers from the Tycoon, for the valuable service rendered in putting down a rebellious vassal too strong for him, and an enemy openly plotting against the stability of his Government, would be only a fitting return.

The British minister believed that with Shimonoseki as a trade centre at one end of the Inland Sea and Hyogo and Osaka at the other, the Western powers would be in the heart of Japan. Their expulsion would then become impossible and they could compel the government of Japan to adhere to the treaty as a condition of its own safety.

The allies had no objection to the squadron going into the Inland Sea to gain knowledge of the nature and extent of any military preparations at the upper end and near Hyogo. Should there be an exchange of shots, their ships should go no further. Any resistance, however, would prove that the hostility was not limited to Chōshū but that he was acting under the authority of the Mikado or the Shogun or both. The allies could then demand an unequivocal disavowal of the proceedings of the Daimyo or adopt such measures as might compel the Court to reconsider its own position and policy.[1]

To Russell, Alcock not only forwarded a copy of this *Memorandum*, but in another letter pointed out that the time had come to put an end to the Japanese movement for the expulsion of foreigners. He now recognized that both the intrusion of foreigners and their final expulsion were 'little more than an ostensible gage of battle between rival factions' involved in an 'internecine struggle for a transfer of political power and

---

[1] F.O. 46/45, Alcock's confidential *Memorandum* for Kuper, Yokohama, 18 Aug. 1864, encl. in Alcock to Russell, No. 50, Yokohama, 23 Aug. 1864.

supremacy'. The real motives for the effort were 'the disposition of the Tycoon for the benefit of some other candidate . . . the emancipation of the Daimyo class from the government, and control of the Tycoon—and the more or less complete restoration of the authority of the Mikado to the prejudice of the Tycoon who is only *de jure* his Lieutenant'.

He argued that the expedition which he advocated against Chōshū was a defensive measure. Yokohama was not tenable from a military point of view. To wait to be attacked would invite 'certain defeat and expulsion'. His ulterior aim was to establish relations on a better basis. He felt confidence in the combined forces of Britain and her allies for this expedition, their ships, marines, and drilled soldiers. He had made the *Bakufu* responsible for the protection of all the open ports on pain of reprisals not only at Yedo but also at Osaka and Kyoto. And in the absence of the fleet from Yokohama, one thousand bayonets and a whole artillery battery had arrived from China to give more security to that port.

Finally Alcock told Russell that the allies had required their senior naval officers to retain 'possession of the Straits or some position commanding them, until negotiations could be concluded between the Representatives of the four Powers in concert with the Tycoon's Government, for the imperialization of the adjacent coasts and the repayment of the costs of the expedition, as an indemnity to be exacted at the Prince of Chōshū's expense, should this be approved by their respective Governments'.[1]

By 1 September the allied forces, consisting of seventeen sail—eight of which were British—and about four hundred men of the British marine battalion over and above the complements of the ships, presented a formidable appearance off the coast of Chōshū. The *han* authorities had recently learned that their extremist anti-foreign forces had been defeated and disgraced in Kyoto in their attempt to regain their position at the Court in opposition to the then ascendant influence of the *Bakufu*–Satsuma coalition. Their panic at the report about the arrival of the foreign flotilla led them to hurried efforts to avoid

---

[1] F.O. 46/45, Alcock to Russell, No. 51, Yokohama, 25 Aug. 1864. P.P. H. of C. 1865, lvii (3428), 90, Alcock to Japanese Commissioners of Foreign Affairs, 29 Aug. 1864.

a conflict. They ordered their officers stationed at Shimonoseki not to fire on foreign ships and they made two attempts to negotiate for the withdrawal of the foreign fleet, instructing emissaries to both Himeshima where the ships were first anchored, and later to Shimonoseki, to say again that the Daimyo of Chōshū himself had no objection to the passage of foreign vessels through the Straits and that his action against them had been ordered from Kyoto and Yedo. Both pairs of messengers arrived too late. Itō and his companion got to Himeshima after the fleet had left. And Inoue and Maeda, delayed by the Chōshū militia, reached the fleet at Shimonoseki on 5 September just as it began the bombardment of the Chōshū forts.[1]

When the Japanese returned the fire, a brief struggle started. Gower's belief that the Straits would be opened easily, in spite of current Japanese opinion to the contrary, was confirmed.[2] Five batteries were silenced that first afternoon. By 8 September all ten batteries had been destroyed. On the tenth landing parties of marines and seamen completed under many difficulties the embarkation of Chōshū's guns, a total of sixty-five pieces of ordnance of various sizes. The Japanese defenders—somewhere between three and six hundred men—had been completely outnumbered by the allied landing force, perhaps nineteen hundred men, of whom fourteen hundred were British.[3] Among the latter eight were killed, and forty-eight wounded, out of a total of twelve killed and sixty wounded in the entire allied force.[4]

A peace mission from Chōshū had arrived on the eighth with Itō and Inoue as interpreters. The delegates asked to negotiate for the cessation of hostilities in accordance with instructions from Nagato and stated that no further opposition would be made to the free passage of the Straits. They produced documents to prove that their Prince's hostile acts had been ordered by the Mikado and the Shogun. The French and British commanders insisted upon an admission to this effect signed by the Daimyo himself. Two days were required to obtain this document

[1] Craig, op. cit., pp. 223–33. Satow, *Diplomat*, p. 105.

[2] J.M. MSS. (Yokohama, Private), S. J. Gower to J. Whittall, 1 Sept. 1864.

[3] Ad. I/5876, Kuper to Adm., 10 and 15 Sept. 1864. Satow, *Diplomat*, pp. 105–15. *Nichi-Ei Gaikō Shi*, i. 87.

[4] *London Gazette*, 18 Nov. 1864, p. 5473.

while the squadron flew flags of truce and the embarkation of the guns was completed. Kuper's personal inspection of the Straits led him to decide not to hold any position on either an island or the mainland, but merely to leave an English, a French, and a Dutch ship in possession of the Straits until satisfactory negotiations regarding that territory had been arrived at by the Shogun and the treaty powers. The sudden friendliness of the nearby Japanese people and the arrival of fowls and vegetables as presents to the flagship during this truce seemed to prove a general interest in peace.

On the fourteenth a certified minister of Nagato agreed to Kuper's terms of peace: (1) the free navigation of the Straits with permission for all ships to coal, to purchase provisions, wood, and water and all necessities, and to land without opposition in bad weather; (2) no batteries to be repaired or rearmed, or newly constructed; (3) the payment of a ransom for sparing the town of Shimonoseki, and reimbursement for the cost of the expedition by the Daimyo as agreed upon by the foreign representatives at Yedo. On 16 September the envoys of Chōshū brought their Prince's ratification of this agreement to the British flagship.[1]

Admiral Kuper returned to Yokohama through the Inland Sea fully prepared to resist further hostilities but found no evidence of animosity anywhere. Satow stayed with H.M.S. *Barrosa* and the Dutch and French ships at the Straits for several weeks.[2] He explored the surrounding country and talked with the Chōshū people. He liked and respected them, while beginning to dislike the Shogun's adherents because of 'their weakness and double dealing'. Henceforth his sympathy was with the daimyo party from whom the *Bakufu* had always tried to separate the treaty powers. Chōshū, like Satsuma, appeared to cherish no resentment against them because of their proven military superiority. But Satow did not know that most of the politically active Chōshū samurai continued to believe in the expulsion of foreigners and constantly threatened their negotiators with assassination.[3]

[1] Ad. I/5876, Kuper to Adm., 17 Sept. 1864 and encl. P.P. H. of C. 1865, lvii (3428), 117–19, Minutes of Conference between Admirals Kuper and Jaurés and Chōshū's representatives on British flagship, *Euryalus*, 14 Sept. 1864.

[2] Ad. I/5876, Kuper to Adm., 30 Sept. 1864.

[3] Satow, *Diplomat*, pp. 127–32. Craig, op. cit., p. 234.

New Instructions from Russell

Before the peace conference with the *Bakufu* could be convened, and while Alcock was rejoicing in the success of the expedition—its limited cost, and the fact that the non-combatants among Chōshū's subjects had escaped without loss of life or property—new orders from Russell quickly blighted his enthusiasm. In two letters of 26 July the Foreign Secretary made a forthright statement of British policy for Japan. Replying to Alcock's report of the expulsion order, and his consequent recommendation for an allied attack on Chōshū in defence of the treaty rights, Russell approved neither the precipitation of hostilities nor the abandonment of treaty rights. He set forth that British policy should consist in:

1. 'Giving every encouragement and support to such of the Tycoon's Ministers and to such of the Daimios as are favourable to foreign trade, and thus to lead to the ultimate weakening of the feudal system, and of the protectionist theory of Japan.'
2. Making 'arrangements with the Japanese Government for the protection of the foreign settlement at Yokohama.'
3. Keeping 'for the present a strong squadron in the Japanese seas.'
4. Endeavouring 'to establish an understanding with the Governments of France, the Netherlands, and the United States, with a view to our common interests in Japan'.[1]

Her Majesty's Government ordered Alcock positively 'not to undertake any military operations whatever in the interior of Japan'. There should be no 'measures of hostility against the Japanese Government or Princes, even though limited to naval operations, unless absolutely required by self-defence'. The action of British naval and military forces in Japan, he said, 'should be limited to the defence and protection of H.M.'s subjects resident in Japan, and of their property, and to the maintenance of our Treaty rights'. He hoped that the Order-in-Council of January last would enable Alcock to prevent occurrences in the Inland Sea which would necessitate hostilities to redress injuries to British vessels.[2]

---

[1] P.P. H. of C. 1865, lvii (3428), 44–45, Russell to Alcock, F.O., 26 July 1864.
[2] Ibid., p. 45. For Order-in-Council, see p. 124.

Before Alcock was able to justify the allied attack on Chōshū as consistent with these instructions, the Foreign Secretary ordered Alcock home in a letter of 8 August, to explain the actual condition of affairs, and confer with Her Majesty's Government as to the measures to be taken. Russell could not understand from Alcock's accounts why he feared any immediate attempt to expel foreigners from Japan or why the Inland Sea was necessary for foreign commerce so long as Osaka was not open, and the Mikado remained in Kyoto.[1]

Alcock's Initiation of a New Order

Alcock had the satisfaction of laying the foundation of a new policy before he left his post. The representatives of the four treaty powers met the Shogun's Commissioners of Foreign Affairs at Yokohama on 18 September to report their victory at Shimonoseki. They confronted the Japanese with the proofs of their government's duplicity in its relations with the powers as well as with the Mikado over the expulsion order; its stoppage of the silk trade as preliminary to the execution of that order, and its proven inability to uphold its treaty obligations against the opposition of the Mikado and hostile daimyo. Alcock threatened that if the Shogun, now strengthened by the powers' decisive defeat of his arch enemy, Chōshū, was unable to reconcile the Mikado and anti-foreign daimyo to the maintenance of the treaties, the Western powers might be compelled in self-defence to go beyond the Shogun and enter into 'more or less direct relation with the Mikado and those Daimios who had hitherto supported him in a hostile course of action'.[2]

This drove the *Bakufu* to concessions. In separate conferences between Alcock and the Japanese officials and Roches and the Japanese on 23 September, the *Bakufu* declared: (1) that the Shogun had renounced his double-faced policy and the pretence of closing Yokohama; (2) that a member of the *Rōjū* would proceed at once to Kyoto to obtain the Mikado's revocation of this order and, if possible, his public ratification of the treaties. In return the *Bakufu* asked that all foreign warships be withdrawn from the Straits immediately so that the Shogun and daimyo could operate unhindered against Chōshū. The British

---

[1] P.P.H. of C. 1865, lvii (3428), p. 54, Russell to Alcock, 8 Aug. 1864.
[2] Ibid., pp. 122–5, *Memorandum of Conference*, Yokohama, 18 Sept. 1864.

made the granting of this request dependent on the Shogun's agreement to pay the Shimonoseki indemnity, or, in lieu of that, to make arrangements for the opening of the port of Shimonoseki.[1]

Alcock actually had no desire to extort an indemnity for its own sake. His entire interest was in obtaining the Mikado's approval of the treaties. The demand for the indemnity gave him the means of pressure upon the Yedo government needed for procuring the Emperor's ratification and 'the consequent extension of commercial relations'. The *Bakufu* quickly accepted the obligation of the indemnity and Alcock awaited instructions from London as to the arrangements for payment.[2] Kuper independently ordered the ships remaining in the Straits to return to Yokohama after 5 October as he saw no reason for maintaining a naval station in those waters under existing circumstances.[3]

Escorted by twelve ships from the allied squadron—seven of which were British—the four foreign representatives sought to confirm the fruits of their victory in a conference with the leaders of the Shogun's government on 6 October at Yedo. Alcock spoke for all his allies, emphasizing without mercy that recent events had proved that no hostile policy toward foreigners could be carried out with impunity by any party within Japan nor could Japan hope to be the victor in any conflict with the West. He asked for confirmation of the Shogun's promise to pay the indemnity. This was agreed to, but an answer to the alternative, the opening of Shimonoseki, was postponed until the return of a member of the *Rōjū* from Kyoto. Alcock then asserted that the ratification of the treaties by the Mikado could be deferred no longer. He presented letters from each envoy to the Shogun insisting upon this as the only measure guaranteeing peace and security which the treaty powers would accept.[4]

A second interview with the Japanese authorities, held in

[1] F.O. 46/46, Confidential Conference at British Legation, 23 Sept. 1864, encl. in Alcock to Russell, No. 62, Yokohama, 28 Sept. 1864.

[2] Ibid., Alcock to Russell, No. 63, 28 Sept. 1864. Satow, *Diplomat*, p. 132.

[3] P.P. H. of C. 1865, lvii (3428), 126–7, Kuper to Adm., 30 Sept. 1864.

[4] Ibid., pp. 129–31, *Memorandum of Conference* on 6 Oct. 1864 and Alcock to Shogun, Yedo, 5 Oct. 1864. *Nichi-Ei Gaikō Shi*, i. 88. Ad. I/5877, Kuper to Adm., 17 Oct. 1864.

confidence the day after the Shogun had seen the letters, gave Alcock the assurance of many long-sought changes. Again the Japanese ministers promised to obtain the Mikado's public acceptance of the treaties and reported that a member of the *Rōjū* was already on his way to Kyoto for this purpose. They even professed to be willing to let other daimyo trade with the West in their own or the Shogun's ports, and they agreed to remove all obstructions to trade, particularly the partial closing of Yokohama which had resulted from the recent stoppage of the silk trade. In return the allies promised the withdrawal of their ships from the Straits—not knowing that was already in progress.[1]

Although these promises of the *Bakufu* were satisfactory, long experience of their promises left Alcock still sceptical of their fulfilment. This was amply justified in the matter of the silk trade which, in spite of the Japanese assurances at the Yedo conferences, was not resumed without further vigorous efforts by Alcock and his colleagues. Before silk began to come in freely they had to break up a government scheme to establish a giant monopoly which would operate through certain licensed guilds in Yedo and aimed to control the whole foreign trade.[2]

The *Bakufu*, however, did agree on 22 October to a convention with the powers fixing the indemnity for the operations at Shimonoseki at three million dollars to be paid quarterly in instalments of $500,000. If the Shogun preferred the opening of Shimonoseki or some other port on the Inland Sea in lieu of the payment of this fixed sum, the powers were granted the right to choose one or the other. The Shogun was required to ratify the convention within fifteen days. A *Memorandum* signed by the four representatives at the same time provided for the apportionment of the money among them. As Great Britain had furnished the largest number of ships, men, and guns for the operation, her share of the remaining money would be the greatest after the other powers had been reimbursed for their losses in July 1863.[3]

In accordance with Russell's orders, Alcock now planned

[1] F.O. 46/46, Alcock to Russell, No. 75, Yokohama, 15 Oct. 1864.
[2] P.P. H. of C. 1865, lvii (3428), 131–3, Alcock to Russell, Yokohama, 15 Oct. 1864 and encls.
[3] F.O. 46/46, Alcock to Russell, No. 79, Yokohama, 28 Oct. 1864, encl. text of Convention. *Nichi-Ei Gaikō Shi*, i. 89.

to return to England in early December, hoping by that time to know the results of the negotiations in Kyoto for the Mikado's ratification of the treaties. Meanwhile he would push ahead on the large improvements in Yokohama—the extension of the land to be used by foreigners, the filling up of a great swamp, the building of a hospital, etc.—to which the Japanese officials had also consented.[1]

Many voices were raised in praise of Alcock's recent policy. Mizuno Tadakiyo Izumi-no-kami, senior Commissioner for Foreign Affairs, wrote to Earl Russell commending Alcock's knowledge of Japan since the opening of the ports, his skill in bringing the difficulties between Japan and the treaty powers to a 'satisfactory settlement', and his helpful advice during the current political conflict. He requested in the name of the Shogun that Alcock return to Japan at the close of his duties in England.[2] Admiral Kuper urged Alcock not to hurry home as the Japanese might consider his recall a sign of the British government's disapproval of his policy which could have disastrous consequences in Japan.[3] Gower, other merchants, and Charles Rickerby of the Yokohama branch of the Central Bank of Western India all regretted Alcock's departure. The former applauded his measures which in co-operation with the other resident Western ministers had increased the security of the lives and property of foreigners and restored a vanishing trade to its usual channels without causing a collision between the British and Japanese governments.[4]

Rickerby, after trips to Nagasaki, wrote enthusiastically about the resumption of trade in the Inland Sea and the friendliness of the authorities and people at Shimonoseki in addition to the resumption of the silk trade on a larger scale than ever before at Yokohama—all results of Alcock's policy. Like Gower, he feared the recall of Alcock would have a detrimental effect upon the improved relations between Britain and Japan which he attributed to Alcock's firm policy.[5]

[1] P.P. H. of C. 1865, lvii (3428), 139–42, Alcock to Russell, Yokohama, 29 Oct. 1864 and encls.

[2] Ibid., p. 140, Mizuno Izumi-no-kami to Russell, 27 Oct. 1864.

[3] F.O. 46/46, Kuper to Alcock, Conf'l., 20 Oct. 1864, encl. in Alcock to Russell, No. 81, 29 Oct. 1864.

[4] P.P. H. of C. 1865, lvii (3428), 143, Gower, Kingdon, etc., to Alcock, Yokohama, 20 Oct. 1864.

[5] Ibid., pp. 145–6, 154–5, Rickerby to Alcock, 14 Nov. 1864; British residents to

The foreign envoys joined the chorus urging Alcock to stay. Alcock believed, however, that he must obey orders, and justify his action in London. Furthermore, he doubted whether his services were now so essential in Japan, since his recent instructions would not permit him to carry out the policy he considered necessary should the Mikado not ratify the treaties promptly.[1]

Alcock's Valedictory

On 19 November Alcock wrote what he hoped would be his final letter from Japan to London. He saw in his recall 'something of censure and condemnation' but believed that Russell would approve his action in the light of further information. This he gave in voluminous detail, covering the Shogun's involuntary acceptance of the expulsion policy, his consequent stoppage of the silk trade at Yokohama, and his inability to take action against Chōshū, who had paralysed trade at Nagasaki by the blockade of the Straits.

He pointed out that the growing hostility of the daimyo party towards the Shogun and his foreign policy in addition to the divisions within the Shogun's own councils threatened the existence of the Shogunate and all foreigners. The dissolution of this government would mean, aside from immediate dangers, the destruction of the treaty-making power, and deprive the Western nations of their 'only solid foundation for the assertion of treaty rights'. Seeking a better basis from the Mikado at Kyoto would be costly and fraught with unpredictable difficulty. Therefore he had aimed to unite the treaty powers in a common interest and 'to rescue the Tycoon's Government from its helpless condition so pregnant with danger to us as well as to them'.

Alcock took issue with Russell on two counts. First, obvious preparations for war, he said, had made the attack on Yokohama imminent, and the city could not be defended with the Western forces at hand. What he had done was necessary to avert the expulsion of foreigners from the port and 'war as a certain consequence'. Secondly, he declared the development of foreign trade depended on the opening of the Straits, even

Alcock, Nagasaki, 11 Nov. 1864; Glover to Alcock, Nagasaki, 12 Nov. 1864. J.M. MSS. (Yokohama, 1864), S. J. Gower to J.M., Hong Kong Office, Yokohama, 31 Oct. 1864.

[1] F.O. 46/46, Alcock to Kuper, Conf'l., Yokohama, 30 Oct. 1864.

if Osaka was closed, because of the importance of Shimonoseki as a depot for the import and export trade of Nagasaki and of the connexion with the native traffic in the Inland Sea.

In spite of his respect for Her Majesty's Government's desire to avert war, he doubted whether the government or the people of England would accept the destruction of trade, the loss of their position, and the rupture of all relations with Japan as the price of abstaining from the use of force in their defence. He maintained that his instructions from Russell upon his return to Japan justified his action against Nagato in concert with the other treaty powers. His recent orders were not applicable to the situation on the spot.

With pride but lack of understanding he enumerated the results of his policy. The danger of war was indefinitely deferred; the foreign position at Yokohama was secured from immediate risk; trade had 'been restored with increased vigour'; the Shogun had formally renounced his 'obstructive and disingenuous policy so long pursued under intimidation from hostile Daimios' who had determined to expel foreigners. His power with that of the moderate party had been so strengthened that for the first time there appeared a 'fair prospect of obtaining the Mikado's formal adhesion to existing treaties and thus putting an end to a conflict of authority between Yedo and Kyoto which had been a constant source of danger alike to the empire and to foreign Powers'. The Straits had been opened permanently. The whole Sakō (anti-foreign party), of which Chōshū was the head, 'had been discouraged and paralysed'. All this had been achieved, he said, in the only way possible, by creating 'respect for our prowess, and a consciousness of our superiority in the art of war'.

In conclusion Alcock not only re-emphasized the need for diplomacy in the East 'to rest on a solid substratum of force' but asked that his successor in Japan be given 'a large discretionary power, to speak with firmness and decision, in defence of important Treaty rights, and on occasions where delay and vacillation would be obviously fatal, to act in keeping with such language, and according to circumstances, which no Government on the other side of the globe, not gifted with omniscience, can always foresee or make adequate provision for by precise instructions'.[1]

[1] F.O. 46/47, Alcock to Russell, Separate, No. 97, Yokohama, 19 Nov. 1864.

The Murder of Baldwin and Bird

Alcock's last letter, however, was yet to be written. The murder of two officers of Britain's 20th Regiment, Major George Walter Baldwin and Lieutenant Robert Nicholas Bird, by two samurai on 20 November at Kamakura within twelve miles of Yokohama detained Alcock until 24 December, and gave him further proof of changes in Japan's relations with foreigners as a result of the latter's victory at Shimonoseki. This was the thirteenth fatal assault upon foreigners since July 1859. Only once, at the time of the first attack on the legation at Tōzenji, had the *Bakufu* acted to Alcock's satisfaction to punish the assassins. He now believed that the Shogun's government had never dared, in the face of the widespread anti-foreign feeling, to punish men publicly who had killed foreigners. In this last incident, however, the Shogun's representative seemed deeply affected by the tragedy and promised to track down the assassins and execute them before Alcock's departure. Alcock demanded immediate action and the Japanese gave it at all levels of authority.[1] For the first time in the history of Japan the murder of foreigners was publicly declared a crime. A government proclamation denounced the assassins and called upon all Japanese people to arrest, and if necessary, kill any future offenders who killed or molested foreigners. On 16 December two *rōnin* held to have been accomplices in the murder of Baldwin and Bird were executed publicly by decapitation and placards recording their sentence were posted in four central places so that all could know the new stand of the *Bakufu* authorities. The next day one of the actual murderers was arrested. He confessed his crime, and was decapitated a few days later in the presence of a detachment of the 20th Regiment and several British officials. His head was exposed on a gibbet for three days at the northern entrance to Yokohama.[2] Ten months later his accomplice suffered the same humiliating punishment with British officials as witnesses.[3]

Alcock left Japan on 24 December 1864 feeling that his

[1] P.P. H. of C. 1865, lvii (3429), 3–32, Alcock to Russell, Yokohama, 29 Nov. 1864 and encls. Hart's *Army List*, 1865, p. 265, gives the full names of the murdered Englishmen.

[2] P.P. H. of C. 1865, lvii (3459), 2–15, Alcock to Russell, Yokohama, 23 Dec. 1864 and encls.; Winchester to Russell, Yokohama, 29 Dec. and encls. Satow, *Diplomat*, pp. 137–40. [3] Ibid., p. 142.

policy regarding Chōshū had brought nation-wide rewards. He not only knew that the *Bakufu* had fulfilled its promises regarding one assassin and expected to capture the other, but a secret communication from a Commissioner of Foreign Affairs at Yedo stated that existing relations with the foreign powers were now 'well understood and approved' at Kyoto. All negotiations regarding the closing of Yokohama had consequently been given up. This was the most Alcock could hope for and convinced him that the moderate party was now in the ascendancy in Japan.[1]

In appreciative response, Alcock approved on 23 December 1865 the request of the Japanese Commissioners of Foreign Affairs for British military instructors to train the chief of the Japanese garrison and some of his officers. And he accepted the presents for the Queen which the Shogun had offered months before in gratitude for Britain's cordiality to the Japanese envoys in 1862 but which Alcock had refused until this recent proof that the Shogun intended to fulfil the treaties.[2]

The minister left his post, however, before he knew that his action at Shimonoseki in conjunction with the other treaty powers had received the 'full approbation' of his government and his Queen.[3] A telegram sent via Alexandria reaffirmed this approval, stating that Alcock would probably return to Japan soon after he reached London.[4]

An Appraisal of Alcock

The administration of Britain's first minister to Japan ended on a note of hope. Rutherford Alcock and the British admirals had managed to keep peace with the Shogun's government, had defeated the leading anti-foreign daimyo and won their professed friendship, and had required the Mikado's public ratification of the treaties as the *sine qua non* of future peace with the West. Trade had developed and gave promise of increasing

[1] F.O. 46/47, Alcock to Russell, No. 102, Yokohama, 15 Dec. 1864.
[2] Ibid., Nos. 113, 115, Yokohama, 23 Dec. 1864; 46/46, Alcock to Japanese Commissioners of Foreign Affairs, Yokohama, 4 Oct. 1864, encl. in Alcock to Russell, No. 68, Yokohama, 10 Oct. 1864. H.M. Government decided that British troops should not train Japanese troops in European drill but the *Bakufu* were not notified of this decision which was later reversed; 262/86, Russell to Winchester, 25 Mar. 1865. See p. 253.
[3] F.O. 262/72, Russell to Alcock, 2 Dec. 1864.
[4] Ibid., F.O. to Winchester, 28 Dec. 1864.

value, especially in silk and cotton. All this had been accomplished in spite of constant danger to life and property, bewildering duplicity on the part of the *Bakufu*, and many obstructions to the fulfilment of the treaty rights.

Although denied communication with the Court and the daimyo, Alcock had come to a partial understanding of the issues between them and the Shogunate and the relation of the foreign treaties to the internal political struggle. He exhibited political insight early; having surmised in April 1860 that the enemies of the Shogunate might be the best friends of the West. He suspected the anti-foreign daimyo of double motives in resisting the treaties, both fear of disruption of their feudal privileges and a method of opposing the Shogun. He recognized the limitations of the Shogun's authority in the domains of the southern daimyo during his travels in 1861 and made clear the necessity of the Mikado's public ratification of the treaties in early 1862 when discussing the equivalents for the postponement of the opening of the ports.

But he was deeply aware that he still knew 'little of the Japanese Government and its mode of working', that 'much must be a matter of surmise and inference'.[1] The limits of his grasp of the anti-*Bakufu* movement and the growing sentiment for the restoration of the Emperor are evident in his belief that the allied action at Shimonoseki had so strengthened the Shogunate that he could look forward to the end of its conflict with the Court. Although he recognized the supreme authority of the Emperor and the legitimate grievances of the *tozamo* daimyo, he considered the Shogunate the *de facto* government, and wanted to reform and support it.

Alcock's admiration and sympathy for the Japanese people was great. He appreciated their friendliness, their industry, and their cultural achievements. He lamented their feudal bondage and saw as the great goal of British influence, operating through free trade in fulfilment of the treaties, the gradual destruction of Japan's feudal organization and the enrichment and emancipation of all her people. He admitted, however, that unarmed Japan had yielded to the treaties in fear of Western military power and held to his belief, developed in China, that the presence and threat of force were essential to

[1] F.O. 46/47, Alcock to Russell, Separate, No. 97, Yokohama, 19 Nov. 1864.

the maintenance of agreements with the Japanese government. His experience with the *Bakufu* had merely confirmed his suspicion of oriental character and his expectation of bad faith. The British minister's long-range idealism was always tempered by efforts at hard realism in appraising any immediate situation.

Alcock's personal integrity and desire for the honourable execution of Britain's treaty meant that he had no sympathy for the predatory practices of the foreign merchant community in Kanagawa and that he early estranged himself from it. He deplored the evil effects which the drain of gold had on the Japanese economy and sought to correct the abuse, never hesitating to criticize the involvement of his own nationals. The *Japan Times* judged him 'unequal to dealing' with these 'young, ardent, active spirits impatient of control and especially impatient of dictation on technical points of which they considered themselves competent judges'. The editors commended, however, the results of his action at Shimonoseki, in a belated recognition of his efforts to protect and expand British trade.[1]

Alcock's relations with his home government were a different matter. The Foreign Office relied on his judgement when defining its policy, yielding to conciliation and concession in the London Protocol, assenting to the punishment of daimyo guilty of attacks on foreigners, agreeing to trade with the independent princes, supporting his belief in strengthening the Shogunate, and finally, approving his decision to use force in defence of treaty rights. In five years Her Majesty's Government had changed from strict orders to resort to force only in self-defence and the protection of property, to sanctioning its use to end obstructions to its growing trade. In recognition of Alcock's service, Queen Victoria made him Envoy Extraordinary and Minister Plenipotentiary to China, 7 April 1865.[2]

---

[1] *Japan Times*, 6 Jan. 1866.
[2] Great Britain, *Foreign Office List*, 1883, p. 51.

VI

THE WINCHESTER INTERLUDE

Japanese Politics

CHARLES WINCHESTER, Britain's consul at Yokohama, became chargé d'affaires in Alcock's absence. Like Alcock and soon Russell himself, he believed a new order had begun, not only in Japan's relations with foreigners but in Japan herself. This they all attributed to the strengthening of the Shogun's hands through their chastisement of Chōshū to the extent that the *Bakufu* could execute assassins of foreigners and keep faith with the treaty powers. Winchester, however, recommended that British troops be kept in Japan for two years and be in a state of 'readiness' as Japanese actions were unpredictable from day to day.[1]

Great changes were indeed in the making in the Mikado's empire, but the foreigners recognized only little of their significance. The Shogun's long-promised expedition against the politically divided Chōshū *Han* ended in January 1865. Surrounded by the *Bakufu* armies, the *han* yielded to the united demands of the representatives of the Court and Yedo. Military action was avoided and the *Bakufu* forces promptly disbanded.[2] Civil war in Chōshū followed from which Chōshū again emerged as a leader of the anti-*Bakufu* movement. Nagato men determined to resist to the end the Shogun's second expedition against their *han*, which was announced in May 1865 on the grounds of the *han*'s continued hostility and a 'grave plot'. Meanwhile the high-handed efforts of the *Bakufu* to restore its power over the Court and daimyo met with no success. Its own supporters, the *shimpan* and *fudai* factions, were divided among themselves. Many daimyo in Kyoto opposed the renewed attack on Chōshū. Even Satsuma, Chōshū's great

---

[1] P.P. H. of C. 1865, lvii (3428), 152, Alcock to Russell, Yokohama, 19 Nov. 1864; (3459), 2, same to same, Yokohama, 23 Dec. 1864; 9, Winchester to Russell, Yokohama, 29 Dec. 1864. F.O. 46/47, Winchester to Hammond, Yokohama, 31 Dec. 1864, with Russell's comment on back.   [2] Craig, op. cit., pp. 236–50.

antagonist, who had opposed expulsion, was by the spring of 1865 not only openly against the Shogun's second expedition but the Daimyo, Shimazu Hisamitsu, joined the movement to restore the Emperor's administrative power, based on the union of the great *han*.[1] An alliance with Chōshū was already in embryo.[2]

British Relations with Daimyo and Efforts to Control Smuggling

The treaty powers were bound to be connected with the forthcoming struggle. British trade with individual daimyo had begun. As early as January 1865 S. J. Gower, agent for Jardine, Matheson, contracted with the officers of Lord Nambu of the Morioka *Han* to take all of his silk at market rates for three years and hoped that this was the beginning of similar business with more of the daimyo who, he understood, wanted to sell the produce of their lands to good foreign houses.[3]

An interpreter, A. von Siebold, confirmed this opinion after a visit to Nagasaki. In conversation there with agents of the daimyo of Hizen and Chikuzen and with the *karō* of Iyo, he learned of the desire of the daimyo to trade with foreigners in order to repair their financial position, depleted by the current high prices and the Shogun's restrictions on their trade at the open ports. They hoped for the opening of Shimonoseki as a boon to their fortunes.[4]

The efforts of the Chōshū *Han* to buy arms at points outside the treaty ports to equip its men against the *Bakufu* brought opposition from both the government and the British chargé. The government's protest against the arming of the 'rebellious Prince' by foreigners arose from the action of an American vessel in the territory of the Daimyo of Bizen but Winchester feared that British traders might attempt the same thing—thus prolonging rebellion in Japan and being detrimental to the legitimate interests of foreign commerce. In a circular to all British consuls directing them to discourage all British subjects from entering into such commerce, he pointed out that legiti-

---

[1] Craig, op. cit., pp. 302–11, 313–14. Murdoch, op. cit. iii. 748–50.

[2] Craig, op. cit., pp. 314–16. Murdoch, op. cit. iii. 751–3.

[3] J.M. MSS. (Yokohama, 1865), S. J. Gower to J. Whittall, 17 Jan. 1865.

[4] P.P. H. of C. 1866, lxxvi. 12, Winchester to Russell, Yokohama, 30 Mar. 1865. A *karō* was the intendant of a daimyo.

mate trade could be conducted only at the recognized ports: that even there sales of munitions of war were restricted to the Japanese government by the treaty regulations. British ships and subjects engaging in any illegitimate traffic would forfeit, *ipso facto*, for the time being any claim to protection and should be dealt with as the consul saw fit.[1]

British merchants, nevertheless, found ways of arming the Chōshū *Han* which was then effectively reorganizing its military forces, for its second encounter with the *Bakufu*. For example in the autumn of 1865 Itō and Inoue arranged in the name and with the permission of Satsuma to buy a warship and 7,300 rifles from Thomas Glover, Jardine, Matheson's agent, and a rebel sympathizer at Nagasaki.[2]

Reports of the desire of the southern daimyo to open their ports to foreign trade and Chōshū's expressed determination to open Shimonoseki encouraged the smuggling trade.[3] Chōshū's men proposed to Consul Gower the sending of a mission to England to conclude a commercial convention for the opening of direct trade relations with foreigners from the shores of the Inland Sea without the exactions of the Yedo government. Satsuma already had a secret mission in London which asked that its presence be kept from the press. Russell apparently was not averse to these emissaries, but, of course, could not recognize them officially.[4]

In Japan Winchester took a firm stand. British subjects who violated the treaty in supplying war materials to private buyers or traded beyond the open ports were to be punished.[5] He realized, however, that according to the Treaty of Yedo, the prevention of smuggling must depend locally on the effectiveness of the Shogun's measures, which were not likely to be substantial in the south. At the same time Gower saw that

---

[1] F.O. 46/53, Winchester to Russell, No. 8, Yokohama, 30 Jan. 1865 and encls.

[2] Craig, op. cit., p. 316. Ishii, *Meiji Ishin no Kokusaiteki Kankyō*, pp. 410–12.

[3] P.P. H. of C. 1866, lxxvi. 26–27, *Memorandum of Conference* between Winchester and Japanese Ministers, 2 May 1865. Ishii in *Meijii Ishin no Kokusaiteki Kankyō*, pp. 395–6, argues that the trade between Shimonoseki and Shanghai was so great in May 1865 that Shimonoseki had been *de facto* opened.

[4] F.O. 46/54, Winchester to Russell, Conf'l., Yokohama, 27 Apr. 1865 and encl., A. J. Gower to Winchester, Nagasaki, 17 Apr. 1865 with Russell's and other F.O. notes added.

[5] F.O. 46/55, Winchester to A.J. Gower, Conf'l., Yokohama, 29 Apr. 1865, encl. in No. 84 to Russell, 11 May 1865.

Britain's prohibitions merely threw the trade into the hands of the Americans, already engaged in contraband for Chōshū with the silent acquiescence of both American and Japanese officials.[1]

The *Bakufu* were considerably disturbed by Chōshū's proposals for an independent commercial treaty. In an interview with a vice-minister Winchester pointed out Britain's stand on the matter. His government, he said, saw no advantage in 'multiplying relations with various princes' and would prefer to have the direction of foreign relations 'remain vested in one Power'. Britain would fulfil her obligations under her treaty with the Shogun. Nevertheless he thought the movement of the Prince towards trade should not be crushed. He hoped that some compromise might be reached embodying a liberal policy in that respect, which the Mikado would fully sanction, and which would save Japan from civil war. He expressed sympathy with the Shogun's government and offered his help within the limits of his instructions from London.[2]

Preparations for the Shogun's second expedition against Chōshū went forward, emptying in their course the 'godowns and shops of Yokohama of every gun, rifle, pistol, and keg of powder which was for sale'. Even all the disposable canvas was bought up for tents. Sixteen cannon and guns which Roches had ordered from France in January at the request of the *Bakufu* arrived via a French transport at the last minute. The expedition was reported to consist of sixty thousand men. The Shogun left Yedo on 9 June to take charge of his forces assembled near Kyoto with the avowed purpose of defeating Nagato and his ally Suwō.[3]

Winchester was aware that the impending hostilities might well disturb the foreign trade passing through the Inland Sea, and initiated a conference with the other foreign representatives to decide on a common policy. All agreed to the maintenance of free navigation of the Straits; absolute non-intervention in the approaching civil hostilities, and 'support as required by the

---

[1] F.O. 46/54, A. J. Gower to Winchester, Private, Nagasaki, 17 Apr. 1865.

[2] P.P. H. of C. 1866, lxxvi. 32–33, Winchester to Russell, Yokohama, 26 May 1865. It will be remembered that Russell had empowered Neale 14 Nov. 1863 to deal directly with friendly daimyo who wanted to trade.

[3] Ibid., pp. 33–36. F.O. 46/55, Winchester to Russell, No. 98, Yokohama, 10 June 1865. Medzini, op. cit., p. 203.

Treaty, of measures employed by the Tycoon for the suppression of illicit trade, and especially of contraband of war.'[1]

The British chargé, knowing that one or more English firms in Nagasaki were engaged in trade at Shimonoseki, issued a public warning to 'all British merchants, traders and shipmasters resident in or frequenting Japan' reminding them of the penalties of illegal trade as laid down in the Treaty of Yedo, the Trade Regulations, and the Order-in-Council of 23 January 1860. He pointed out again that Her Majesty's warships would support the officers of the Shogun in their measures for its suppression.[2] He asked Captain Luard, R.N., to reinforce the British naval commander at Nagasaki with an additional warship so that the senior officer there might give the promised support to the Shogun's measures suppressing unauthorized commerce. He made it clear, however, that although the initiative should come from the Yedo government and not from independent action by British ships, it was *not* desirable that the anticipated hostilities should 'be fed under cover of the British flag by delivery of arms and ammunition'. Hence he authorized the naval commander to adopt at his discretion 'a wider scope of repressive action than would be necessary under ordinary smuggling'.[3] In spite of these official warnings, there is no evidence among the archives here consulted that the British authorities checked the smuggling or penalized any smugglers.

French Policy and the Shimonoseki Indemnity

From the time of her decision to support the Shogunate in the unauthorized treaty of 1864, France sought to strengthen the Yedo government for her own commercial and political advantage. The new French minister, Léon Roches, committed his support most generously to the Tokugawa government as early as the winter of 1865 when he worked out with the *Bakufu* an arrangement whereby in return for large quantities of silk delivered by the *Bakufu* on its own account, France promised to provide the engineers, machinery, and instructors to build a naval dockyard at Yokosuka. The guns and cannon

---

[1] P. P. H. of C. 1866, lxxvi. 38, Winchester to Russell, Yokohama, 23 June 1865.
[2] Ibid., pp. 43–44, *Official Notification*, 22 June 1865.
[3] Ibid., p. 41, Winchester to Capt. Luard, Yokohama, 21 June 1865.

also ordered by Roches through his government at that time
which arrived in June 1865 to assist the *Bakufu* against Chōshū
were accompanied by five or six officers to give military instruction to the Japanese. Although Roches claimed that this ordnance had been privately purchased by the Ikeda mission at
Toulon or Havre in 1864 rather than through French arsenals,
Winchester had reliable evidence of the French legation's
responsibility for it. Such misrepresentation on Roches's part
in addition to his growing intimacy with the *Bakufu* leaders and
rumours of the Shogun's grant of a monopoly on silk to French
merchants in return for arms made French policy a subject of
concern to the British. These rumours are now held to have
been unfounded, but they had wide credence at the time, and
combined with the building of an impressive French residence,
huge barracks, and stores at Yokohama, as well as the establishing of a school there, where history, geography, mathematics,
and French were taught, made French influence seem paramount.[1]

An ever-widening political cleavage between British and
French policy also began during the first year of Roches's
ministry. Britain favoured opening the port of Shimonoseki in
lieu of Japan's payment of an indemnity in order to begin
legal commercial relations with the southern daimyo, but
Roches maintained that France wished to claim the money
even before the Shogun's choice of the alternatives was known,
on the grounds that France needed reimbursement for her
civil and military expenses in Japan.[2] Since Roches had
several conferences with the *Rōjū* in Yedo and reports were
current of French entreaties that Japan elect to pay the
indemnity, it is probable that the *Rōjū* yielded to French advice
in their decision of 6 April.[3] Their dispatch said they preferred
to pay the indemnity and asked for a longer time to pay it than
had been agreed upon in the Convention of October 1864.

[1] Beasley, *Documents*, pp. 78–79. F.O. 46/53, Winchester to Hammond, Private,
Kanagawa, 17 Jan., and Yokohama, 31 Jan. 1865; 46/55, Winchester to
Russell, No. 96, Yokohama, 7 June and encl.; No. 108, same to same, Conf'l.,
Yokohama, 23 June 1865. Medzini, op. cit., pp. 203–4.

[2] F.O. 46/54, Winchester to Russell, No. 49, Yokohama, 27 Mar. 1865. P.P.
H. of C. 1866, lxxvi. 26–27, Conference of 2 May 1865 for Winchester's argument
for daimyo trade.

[3] F.O. 46/55, Winchester to Russell, No. 83, Yokohama, 11 May 1865; 262/87,
Milbank to Russell, 17 July 1865.

They argued that the opening of a port on the Inland Sea would affect adversely both the internal and external affairs of Japan. They promised to pay the first instalment of the indemnity as agreed in the summer of 1865 and asked, since the difficulties with Chōshū were not settled, to defer the second payment until the summer of 1866.[1]

Aware of the limited resources of the *Bakufu*, Winchester and others realized that this was probably the beginning of a series of requests for the postponement of the payment of other instalments. Furthermore, the best-informed foreign residents presumed that the indemnities would be met by the levy of an additional duty on foreign commerce. To Winchester the protracted payment of this indemnity looked like 'the hanging of a millstone for five or six years round the neck of our own trade'. He humbly suggested that the four powers might use the long interval between the first and second instalments to secure some general advantages, such as the opening of Hyogo or a revision of the tariff, in return for a reduction of the total amount of the indemnity. He believed that France's demand 'for the whole money and nothing but the money' was generally harmful to foreign commerce. She had no interest in trade beyond Yedo, the emporium for silk hence was not concerned with the opening of a port on the Inland Sea which would be so valuable to the other more commercial powers. Neither was she concerned with the exaction of duties on the over-all trade.[2] All four representatives agreed to await instructions from their home governments before acting on the *Bakufu* proposal. In the meantime they would accept under reservation the payment of the first instalment of the indemnity in July 1865.[3]

The British government proposed to the three powers that Japan's payment of the first instalment be accepted but that two-thirds of the whole indemnity should be waived—leaving only $500,000 beyond the present payment, which balance should be paid before the end of 1865—in return for the Shogun's agreement that: (1) Hyogo and Osaka be opened to the

[1] P.P. H. of C. 1866, lxxvi. 16, Japanese Commissioners of Foreign Affairs to Winchester, 6 Apr. 1865.

[2] F.O. 46/54, Winchester to Russell, No. 59, Yokohama, 12 Apr. 1865; Winchester to F.O., Private, Yokohama, 13 Apr. 1865.

[3] P.P. H. of C. 1866, lxxvi. 19–20, Winchester to Japanese Commissioners of Foreign Affairs, Yokohama, 19 Apr. 1865.

trade and residence of foreigners on 1 January 1866; (2) that the Mikado formally sanction the treaties existing between the Shogun and the four powers; (3) that the duties on imports into Japan be generally reduced to five per cent. and should in no case exceed ten per cent. Her Majesty's Government believed this arrangement would best serve the interests of trade and foreign relations with Japan. Should the *Bakufu* not agree to these terms, Britain would demand the literal fulfilment of the second article of the Convention of 22 October 1864— which meant the payment of the entire indemnity by October 1866 in quarterly instalments of $500,000 each. If the *Bakufu* refused both alternatives Britain would consider the London Protocol of 1862 withdrawn and would demand the opening of Hyogo and Osaka from 1 January 1866.[1] Both France and the Netherlands had already agreed with Britain that since the *Bakufu* had chosen to pay the indemnity it must all be paid by 1866.[2] Russell hoped that all three powers could still be induced to forgo the major portion of the indemnity in the interest of the extension of trade. With questionable altruism he wrote: 'It is but just that the great Daimyo should partake of the benefits of commerce which is so beneficial to Japan and so profitable to the Tycoon.'[3] The matter, however, was not settled until after a new minister, Sir Harry Parkes, had taken up his residence in Japan.

Before his departure to become consul in Shanghai, Winchester reviewed the positions of the several treaty powers in Japan. He noted Russia's opposition to the extension of all Western trade with Japan. Her interest lay in expanding her territory to include all Sakhalin, then held in common with Japan, because of its coal and minerals; the possession of Tsushima to create another Malta; and the annexation of Yezo. Although the United States agent in Hakodate was influenced by the Russians, the representatives of the United States were generally considered to have sound commercial views. They, too, were concerned about the increasing influence of France in Japan, her extensive building and military assistance programme, believing that France intended to make

---

[1] P.P. H. of C. 1866, lxxvi. 20–21, Russell to Sir Frederick Bruce, 12 July 1865.
[2] Ibid., pp. 21–22, Russell to Cowley, 13 July 1865.
[3] Ibid., pp. 29–30, Russell to Winchester, 24 July 1865.

Japan do her work in the guise of neutrality, should Emperor Napoleon's Mexican venture lead to a crisis. France's new policy in China and Japan as a result of her recent adoption of free trade was also suspect to Winchester. He believed that Roches aimed to divert directly to France the silk then going to London and to make the Shogunate France's special customer. Roches's over-riding ambition for political ascendancy brought him little sympathy from the foreign community. The Dutch agents, in contrast, were usually fair and open in their dealings with the other treaty powers. They were influenced at times by traditions from the pre-treaty period, and jealous of privileges considered due to old friends. Their long political connexion with Japan and the knowledge of the language gave them a better understanding of current developments, but they did not seek special influence from political greatness nor the extent of their commerce.

Finally, Winchester advised Russell that the British would do well to follow the example of both the French and the Dutch in encouraging the desire of the Japanese to improve themselves in the arts of both peace and war by supplying them with competent teachers. He feared that the refusal to do so made them think that Britain 'expected their increased knowledge to be turned against' her. Distrust of Britain resulted, not because of the commercial and pacific character of British aims, but because of her apparent and constant anticipation of a contest.[1]

---

[1] F.O. 46/55, Winchester to Russell, No. 108, Conf'l., Yokohama, 23 June 1865.

VII

BRITAIN'S EFFORTS AT NEUTRALITY

Russell's Instructions for Parkes

IN March 1865 Queen Victoria appointed Sir Harry S. Parkes Britain's Minister Plenipotentiary to Japan. Although only thirty-seven years old, he had already done distinguished work in the consular service in China and had demonstrated his diplomatic skill in the negotiations of Britain's treaty with Siam in 1855 and the peace with China in 1861. A large head, impressive brow, and alert blue eyes dominated his slight, short stature. He was fearless in danger, tireless in the fulfilment of duty, strict and severe with his staff but loyal and gracious in his private relationships. His determination to get at the facts in every situation led him to require from his subordinates careful research in many areas of Japanese life which resulted in important reports on the period and gave Parkes a better understanding of the new Japan than any other Western representative. Parkes's easily aroused anger and blustering, noisy language when provoked, were handicaps, however, in his relations with the Japanese which embarrassed his sub-ordinates and which he never overcame. He had definite con-cepts of Britain's interests and imperial responsibilities and adhered to them with zeal, so much so that the Japanese often considered him arrogant and domineering, but they knew they could not trifle with him. By European residents in the Far East he was regarded as the outstanding member of the British Civil Service.[1] His salary was £3,000 a year, another £1,000 being allowed for his outfit.[2]

[1] S. Lane-Poole and F. V. Dickins, *The Life of Sir Harry Parkes*, 2 vols. (London, 1891-4), (hereafter cited as Dickins, since he wrote the second volume which deals with Parkes in Japan) i. 509. The Parkes Papers on which this book is based are in the University Library at Cambridge but are not yet open to scholars. Satow, *Diplomat*, pp. 141-2. Murdoch, op. cit. iii. 757. Redesdale, op. cit. i. 376. Shinobu Zumpei, 'Meiji no Gaikōshijo Parkes-no Ichi' (The Position of Parkes in Meiji Diplomatic Affairs), *Kokusaiho Gaikō Zasshi* (Journal of International Law and Diplomacy), xxvii. 675-9; xxviii. 174-6.   [2] F.O. 262/88, Russell to Parkes, 7 Apr. 1865.

PLATE 2

SIR HARRY S. PARKES

Russell's instructions to Parkes, patterned after Alcock's advice, gave him freedom to act as the state of affairs in Japan seemed to warrant.[1] Russell anticipated that the advantages gained by Alcock and Kuper at Shimonoseki would, upon Parkes's arrival, still bear fruit in peaceable intercourse and continued tranquillity. These advantages he defined as:

1. The abandonment of any pretence on the part of the Mikado or the Tycoon to violate treaties, and banish foreigners from Japan.

2. The faithful execution of these Treaties, with the modifications and delays allowed by the Treaty Powers when the Japanese Envoys came to Europe in 1862.

3. Either the confirmation of the Treaties by the Mikado, or the formal admission that the Tycoon having, as the Prince of Satsuma said, the Treaty-making power, required no sanction from the Mikado for the conclusion and execution of the Treaties with European Powers and the United States of America.

4. The trial of all persons accused of murdering British subjects and their execution, if convicted.

5. The assignment of a fit residence or site for a residence, at Yedo, for Her Majesty's Envoy and fit barracks and hospitals at Yokohama, to be maintained in repair by the Tycoon's Government.

Russell observed that it would be easier to maintain these 'advantages' as then established by Britain, than to restore them if once lost. He instructed Parkes to cultivate cordial relations with the ministers of France, Holland, and the United States, to act in concert with British naval and army commanders, and to pursue 'a firm but conciliatory policy' towards the Shogun and his ministers.[2]

Parkes came to Japan at the time when a Supreme Court for China and Japan was being established. Although its ordinary sittings were held at Shanghai it had authority to hold them at any open port in China and Japan. The British legation at Yedo was thus relieved of all judicial and magisterial duties, appellate and otherwise. The judge, Sir Edmund Hornby, had instructions to advise Parkes on questions of law.[3]

Ernest Satow, a brilliant young interpreter, assisted Parkes at first in the Yokohama consulate and after 1866 in the legation

[1] See Alcock's advice, 19 Nov. 1864, p. 146.
[2] P.P. H. of C. 1866, lxxvi. 8–9, Russell to Parkes, 8 Apr. 1865.
[3] F.O. 262/86, Russell to Parkes, 10 May 1865, enclosing Order-in-Council, 9 Mar. 1865.

at Yedo. His increasing ability to communicate at all levels with the Japanese people brought Parkes first-hand knowledge of Japan's internal developments and influenced his policy.

Parkes's First Policies

Sir Harry Parkes arrived on 27 June 1865 at Nagasaki. His sympathy in favour of the local daimyo was soon aroused. He found the monopolies enjoyed by the Chinese still hampering trade. The Governor awaited orders from Yedo to remove them. These and other restrictions enforced by the Shogun brought protests from foreign traders as well as those daimyo who sought an extension of foreign commerce. Officers of these feudal lords asked Parkes to receive them and told him of the opposition to the Shogunate among some of the governing classes and predicted a civil struggle soon.[1] During the trip through the Inland Sea Parkes found the Japanese people friendly. The Chōshū *Han* was prepared to resist the Shogun's forces a second time but the expedition was delayed owing to the Mikado's order for the Shogun to come to Kyoto for a meeting of daimyo.[2]

Parkes faced at once many of the problems which had plagued his predecessors. With the Shogun and most of his advisers in Kyoto, he found it difficult to get reliable information from Yedo regarding internal political developments. And private sources in Yokohama also yielded little because of the *Bakufu* system of surveillance. The Governor of Nagasaki, under orders from the Shogun, arrested the Japanese teacher and a servant of the British consul, F. Lowder, because they had given the British information concerning local political developments. The country obviously suffered from the unsettled conditions. Trade was interrupted and native dealers bought very few imports.[3]

[1] P.P. H. of C. 1866, lxxvi. 47–48, Parkes to Russell, Nagasaki, 30 June 1865. That the *Bakufu* were aware of this and recognized the duplicity of the daimyo in professing to the treaty powers their desire for trade while representing to the Mikado their opposition to all foreign intercourse, as a part of their strategy to weaken the Shogunate, was made clear to Winchester when arguing with a Commissioner of Foreign Affairs for the extension of trade to the daimyo, shortly before Parkes arrived. F.O. 46/55, Précis of Interview, 22 June 1865, encl. in Winchester to Russell, No. 107, Yokohama, 23 June 1865.

[2] P.P. H. of C. 1866, lxxvi. 48–49, Parkes to Russell, Yokohama, 12 July 1865.

[3] Ibid., pp. 56–57, Parkes to Russell, Yokohama, 26 Aug. 1865. F.O. 46/56, Parkes to Russell, No. 41, Yokohama, 11 Sept. 1865.

The protests of the *Bakufu* against the continuing contraband trade in the Chōshū territory forced Parkes into immediate action. The Japanese announced the dispatch of two warships to the Inland Sea to seize any vessels proven to be engaged in illicit trade and asked Parkes to so inform all British ships passing through that area. The new minister immediately issued another *Notification* to all British subjects announcing the Japanese project and secured the co-operation of the new commander of the China squadron, Vice-Admiral George St. V. King, in assisting the government's ships to suppress the 'illegal trade'. At the same time he suggested that the removal of all existing obstacles to the free trade of the daimyo was long due for the Shogun's attention.[1]

The *Bakufu* itself made efforts to improve its relations with foreigners on several fronts. Although the ratifications of the Convention of 22 October 1864 had not yet reached the foreign representatives, the *Bakufu* fulfilled its offer to pay the first instalment of the Shimonoseki indemnity on schedule between 22 August and 1 September. The money in two equal sums of $250,000 was deposited in the Oriental Bank and the Chartered Mercantile Bank at Yokohama. Later it was deposited in the British Commissariat Chest at Yokohama, and an equivalent amount in sterling made available in England for distribution among the powers. The foreign representatives stated on the receipt of the money that its payment in no way affected the right of the powers to require the punctual payment of the whole indemnity in quarterly instalments in accordance with the Convention.[2]

The treaty powers recovered the right of residence in Yedo which had been in abeyance since 1862. Parkes, however, preferred to live in Yokohama with frequent visits to Yedo while the unsettled conditions continued in the country and the seat of administrative power remained uncertain.[3] The *Bakufu* promised to relinquish on 8 November its monopolies on *bêche-de-mer*, shell fish, and sharks' fins, which, contrary to the treaty and the London Protocol, it had maintained, and

[1] P.P. H. of C. 1866, lxxvi. 49–51, Parkes to Russell, Yokohama, 10 Aug. 1865 and encls.

[2] Ibid., pp. 54–56, 58, Parkes to Russell, Yokohama, 25 Aug. and 12 Sept. 1865 and encls.; 63, Clarendon to Grey, F.O., 12 Dec. 1865.

[3] Ibid., p. 58, Parkes to Russell, Yokohama, 12 Sept. 1865.

which caused hardship for both the native fishermen and foreign traders at Hakodate and Nagasaki.[1] Restrictions on the sale of silkworm eggs, suddenly demanded in great quantities in France and Italy because of the ravages of a fatal disease in silk culture, were also removed and an enormous export trade in the seed developed.[2] A *rōnin* who had killed the Chinese servant of a French consul in 1859 was finally apprehended and executed for this and other crimes, but the Japanese who had attacked several foreigners in Nagasaki in June 1865 was still at large in spite of the government's efforts to the contrary.[3]

The Mikado's Ratification of the Treaties

The great event of Parkes's early months in Japan, however, was the Mikado's ratification of the treaties of 1858. Complying with the wishes of the French Foreign Minister, Drouyn de Lhuys, Russell instructed Parkes to submit for the decision of the French, Dutch, and United States envoys in Japan Britain's proposal to remit two-thirds of the Shimonoseki indemnity in return for the prompt opening of Hyogo and Osaka, the ratification of the treaties by the Mikado, and the regularization of the tariff on the basis of five per cent.[4] In a conference on 26 October Roches joined the other representatives in support of the British proposal, explaining that these alternatives to the payment of the indemnity were superior to the opening of a single port as stipulated in the Convention. The choice of accepting these new proposals or paying the indemnity, however, still lay with the Shogun. And should his preference be for the indemnity, Roches also agreed that quarterly instalments should be exacted quickly.[5]

Such unanimity led to rapid action. Since the Shogun was having difficulties in carrying forward his operations against Chōshū and his return to Yedo was unpredictable, Parkes suggested that he and his colleagues undertake their negotiations at Osaka accompanied by ships from their respective fleets. Four of the *Rōjū* were now in that area while only one

[1] P.P. H. of C. 1866, lxxvi. 60–61, Parkes to Russell, Yokohama, 30 Sept. 1865.
[2] F.O. 46/57, Parkes to Russell, No. 42, Yokohama, 12 Sept. 1865.
[3] P.P. H. of C. 1866, lxxvi. 61–62, Parkes to Russell, Yokohama, 30 Sept. 1865.
[4] Ibid., pp. 20–22, Russell to Bruce and Russell to Cowley, 12 and 13 July 1865. See pp. 157–8.
[5] P.P. H. of C. 1866, lxxvi. 63–65, Parkes to Russell, Yokohama, 30 Oct. 1865.

remained in Yedo. Furthermore, Parkes thought he could best ascertain in Osaka whether the opening of Hyogo to foreign trade would endanger the Shogun's government—a question Russell wished answered. Again Roches co-operated, believing that the appearance of the representatives at Osaka would give the Shogun another excuse for again postponing his expedition against Chōshū and avoiding civil war. As the Dutch and United States representatives also agreed, the four envoys prepared a *Memorandum* in which they offered their terms for the settlement of the Shimonoseki indemnity and informed the remaining *Rōjū* in Yedo of their departure for Osaka.[1]

A squadron of nine ships, five British, three French, and one Dutch, left Yokohama on 1 November in spite of the opposition of the remaining member of the *Rōjū* and a vice-minister at Yedo who called on Parkes at his residence in Yokohama to attempt to halt the proceedings—the first visit of a member of the *Rōjū* to the home of a foreign representative. Admiral King accompanied Parkes and his staff, John MacDonald, Alexander von Siebold, and Ernest Satow, aboard his flagship, the *Princess Royal*, and provided accommodation for the American chargé d'affaires as there was no United States warship in Japan.[2]

Sir Harry approached the negotiations with fresh insight into Japan's political troubles. The complaints of the *Bakufu* about the foreign policies of the hostile daimyo of Satsuma and Chōshū had convinced him that it was opposition to the Shogun's supremacy, not the foreign treaties, which was the primary object of the alleged hostility.[3] He determined to remain neutral in the civil struggle and in consequence had recently refused the request of Chōshū's officers to rearm the batteries at Shimonoseki in defence against the Shogun's anticipated attack.[4] He was equally determined to ascertain the real position of the Shogun in the government of Japan while he demanded the fulfilment of the treaties in the forthcoming interviews with the Shogun's ministers at Osaka.

The allied squadron spent three weeks in the waters of

[1] Ibid., pp. 64–67, Parkes to Russell, Yokohama, 30 Oct. 1865 and *Memorandum* of same date.

[2] Ad. I/5963, King to Adm., 31 Oct. 1865. Satow, *Diplomat*, pp. 143–4. Satow gives one less ship than King.

[3] F.O. 46/57, Parkes to Russell, No. 59, Yokohama, 30 Oct. 1865.

[4] Ibid., No. 51, 30 Sept. 1865 and encls.

Hyogo harbour. Crisis succeeded crisis in the Shogun's councils as the negotiations progressed under the menacing shadow of Western power. Parkes knew he was forcing a showdown between the Mikado and the Shogun on the long-unsettled question of foreign policy at a moment when even the existence of the Shogun's government hung in balance. He felt secure in the presence of the fleet. What he called a 'friendly' but firm policy seemed to the Japanese a threat to their national existence.[1] Roches, who had recently professed his devotion to the Shogun as equal to that of his own subjects, maintained a detachment from his colleagues and attempted to mediate between Britain and Japan.[2]

On 5 November the British and French interpreters presented a letter to the *Rōjū* Ogasawara Nagamichi at Osaka, stating the demands of the foreign envoys for the prompt settlement of the indemnity question. Should they not reply within seven days, the *Bakufu* were soon led to fear that the representatives would go to Kyoto and demand an interview with the Mikado—a threat made by Roches in a secret memorandum of 7 November to the *Rōjū* which also urged for the sake of unity and the strengthening of Japan, the Mikado's ratification of the treaties and the opening of Hyogo.[3]

Rōjū Abe Masatō promised to meet the foreign delegates on the ninth on board their ships, a meeting which was postponed until the eleventh. The Japanese minister then held two similar interviews, the first with the British, Dutch, and American representatives aboard the *Princess Royal*, the second with Roches on his frigate. Abe admitted that the *Bakufu* promise of October 1864 to secure the Mikado's sanction of the treaties had not been fulfilled. He reported that the Shogun

---

[1] P.P. H. of C. 1866, lxxvi. 74–75, Parkes to Clarendon, *Princess Royal* off Hyogo, 14 Nov. 1865. Murdoch, op. cit. iii. 760.

[2] P.R.O. 30/33, 1/2, Secret Communication of Roches, 14 May 1865. Beasley, *Documents*, p. 81. Medzini, op. cit., p. 207.

[3] P.P. H. of C. 1866, lxxvi. 76 and 78, Parkes to Russell, *Princess Royal* off Hyogo, 17 Nov. 1865 and encl. 1. Beasley, *Documents*, p. 80. Beasley gives 7 Nov. as date for delivery of letter. P.R.O. 33/30, 1/2, Roches's *Memorandum*, 7 Nov. 1865. None of the F.O. Papers for 1865 here examined mentioned the seven-day time limit required for the Shogun's reply. Parkes did not know of Roches's memorandum as he says the Shogun had no authority from the foreign representatives to tell the Mikado that they would go to Kyoto and demand to see His Majesty. F.O. 46/48, Parkes to Russell, No. 65, 28 Nov. 1865.

considered the opposition to foreign intercourse still too strong
to permit its extension by the opening of Osaka and Hyogo.
He conceded that the hostile daimyo had given up their active
opposition, however, and if the Mikado ratified the treaties
'all obstructions to foreign intercourse would disappear'.

Parkes yielded nothing, pointing out that since the *Bakufu*
had not removed the illegal restrictions on trade as it had
promised in the London Protocol, Her Majesty's Government
could at any time insist upon the opening of all the cities named
in the Convention and mercilessly stated that the Shogun must
prove himself equal to the discharge of all the obligations of the
treaties if he wished to be regarded as the ruler of Japan. The
foreign powers would judge him by his acts, not by the professions of his ministers. The treaties must be fulfilled. Abe was
convinced of Western determination. Further conflicts with
the opposition in Kyoto and Osaka, however, led to another
request for the postponement of Japan's answer, and Parkes
ungraciously extended the time until 24 November.[1]

The *Bakufu* was in great difficulty. Its decision in council
before the Shogun on 13 November to accept all the foreign
terms was overridden the next day by Hitotsubashi Keiki, who
maintained this would end the recently developed co-operation
between Kyoto and Yedo. The opening of Osaka and Hyogo
caused the main dissension. For advocating this Abe and his
colleague on the *Rōjū*, Matsumae Takahiro, were deprived of
rank and office by Imperial decree—an unprecedented act of
the Court towards Tokugawa councillors. The Shogun therefore
offered his resignation to the Mikado, and recommended
Keiki as his successor. In an accompanying *Memorandum* he
reviewed Japan's relations with the West since Perry and,
stressing the inevitability of intercourse with the West in the
light of Japan's military weakness, he requested the Emperor's
prompt ratification of the treaties.[2]

Kyoto was not yet ready for such a change. Consternation
reigned. Ōkubo Toshimichi, Satsuma's representative, acting
through a leading court noble, urged the acceptance of the

---

[1] Beasley, *Documents*, pp. 81, 300 n. P.P. H. of C. 1866, lxxvi. 76–78, Parkes
to Russell, off Hyogo, 17 Nov. 1865.
[2] Beasley, *Documents*, pp. 297–9, Shogun Iemochi to Emperor Kōmei, Osaka,
18 Nov. 1865.

resignation and the Court's assumption of the direction of affairs. He also repeated his recent proposal for the immediate convocation of a council of great daimyo to deal with national affairs. But the Shogun was not permitted to abdicate. A threatening note of 21 November from Parkes held the dismissal of Abe to be an unfriendly act and demanded with characteristic firmness that the Shogun find peaceful means of securing the execution of the treaties. In the absence of a written reply to the proposals of the powers by the 24th, he warned, the representatives would be 'free to act as we may judge convenient'.[1] Keiki and three important *Bakufu* officials wrote the Court pleading for the Mikado's ratification to avoid national disaster. The Imperial Prince Asahiko supported their request.[2] The great majority of the representatives of the fiefs, summoned to express their views, agreed that the Imperial sanction should be granted. Under such pressures the Mikado's ratification was declared unavoidable.

The Imperial Decree on 22 November marks a turning-point in Japan's relations with the West. It read:

The Imperial consent is given to the treaties and appropriate action is to be taken accordingly.

Separate [intended for the *Bakufu* only]

With reference to the instructions given in the enclosed announcement, there are various unsatisfactory provisions in the treaties previously concluded. They do not conform to the Emperor's wishes. They are therefore to be re-examined and fresh arrangements are to be made after consultation with the fiefs.

With regard to Hyogo no action is to be taken.[3]

In the afternoon of 24 November a member of the *Rōjū*, Matsudaira (Honjō) Munehide, Hōki-no-kami, and lesser Japanese officials brought the news to the foreign envoys. After announcing that the Shogun's efforts had secured the Imperial consent to the treaties they reported on the two remaining

[1] P.P. H. of C. 1866, lxxvi. 82–85, Parkes to Russell, H.M.S. *Perseus*, 28 Nov. encl. Parkes to the Tycoon, *Princess Royal* off Hyogo, 21 Nov. 1865. Parkes and Beasley differ as to date this reached the Shogun. Parkes gives 23 Nov. after the Emperor's decision while Beasley considers it influential in making his decision. *Documents*, p. 292.

[2] Ibid., pp. 301–3, *Bakufu* officials to Imperial Court, Kyoto, 22 Nov. 1865; Ōkubo Toshimichi to Saigō Takamori and Minoda Dembei, Kyoto, 24 Nov. 1865.

[3] Ibid., p. 304, Imperial Court to the *Bakufu*, 22 Nov. 1865.

foreign proposals and a compromise, attributed to Roches, was reached. The opening of Hyogo could not be immediate. The Shogun's government planned to open Hyogo in accordance with the London Protocol in 1868 and earlier if possible. Instead the *Bakufu* promised to pay the second instalment of the indemnity upon the return of the representatives to Yedo and to make the remaining four payments promptly. It consented to the revision of the tariff on a general five per cent. basis and had arranged for early negotiations at Yedo. Identical notes signed by three *Rōjū* were sent to each of the representatives on the twenty-fifth confirming these promises and enclosing the Mikado's decree approving the treaties. In the copy given to the representatives, however, no mention was made of Hyogo or the revision of the treaties.[1]

There was general rejoicing over the results of the negotiations among the foreign representatives and the government in London. Parkes hoped that the Mikado's formal sanction of the treaties would unify Japan on the question of foreign intercourse and deprive the daimyo of their principal pretext for attacking the Shogunate. As Alcock and others had realized earlier, he also believed this was not only essential for the security of Western relations established by the treaties but the main prerequisite for any extension of the existing privileges of the West. The Japanese records show that despite Parkes's and Clarendon's claims to the contrary, the Mikado's ratification was yielded as were the previous treaties, because Japan feared the use of overpowering force by the West. And Parkes himself attributes the success of the negotiations to the presence of the fleet although used for a 'purely peaceful object'. To his credit, however, Parkes admits that his predecessors had patiently prepared the way for Imperial sanction and that his main contribution lay in seizing the time of the Shogun's stay at Kyoto to force the issue.[2]

The *Bakufu*'s consent to a revision of the tariff in the near future and promise to pay the remaining instalments of the

---

[1] Ibid., pp. 82–83, 304–5. P.P. H. of C. 1866, lxxvi. 83–84, 86, Parkes to Russell, H.M.S. *Perseus*, 28 Nov. 1865 and encls. 2 and 3. Here Parkes speaks of the next payment of the indemnity as the 'second' while the *Bakufu* call it the 'third'.

[2] Ibid., pp. 84, 87, Clarendon to Parkes, 5 Feb. 1866. Beasley, *Documents*, pp. 297–9, 301. Clarendon succeeded Russell as Foreign Secretary on 3 Nov. 1865 when Russell, following Palmerston's death, became Prime Minister.

indemnity promptly satisfied the powers.[1] Few people had expected agreement on the opening of Hyogo and Osaka on 1 January 1866 and the fresh guarantee of the fufilment in January 1868 of the London agreement seemed acceptable.[2] Parkes himself was led to think that under the existing political dissension and the constant movement of troops in the vicinity of Osaka and Hyogo, the entrance of foreign merchants in the area might be a cause of conflict and make the Shogun liable for still more heavy indemnities.[3] The merchants themselves in Yokohama were pleased with the outcome as they were not prepared at that time to start branch houses in other Japanese cities.[4]

Parkes's Views on the Position of the Daimyo and the Shogun

The year 1865 ended with some clarification of the position of the anti-*Bakufu* daimyo regarding the opening of more ports. Parkes visited Shimonoseki and Nagasaki before returning to Yokohama, wanting to determine that the Shogun had made no improper use of the presence of the allied squadron at Osaka in his proceedings against Chōshū. In conversation with Chōshū's officers he stressed Britain's neutrality in the *han*'s dispute with the *Bakufu* and urged a policy of accommodation as he had done with the *Rōjū*. He found that the Emperor's decree sanctioning the treaties was well received in both Chōshū and Nagasaki by agents of daimyo and officers of the Shogunate. And there was no regret that Hyogo remained closed. Chōshū men further admitted, in contradiction to earlier reports, that as long as difficulties with the Shogun continued they could not advocate the opening of Shimonoseki nor would they ever consent to its being placed under the Shogun's control as were the other open ports. Although they themselves favoured the extension of foreign commerce, they knew that many daimyo continued to oppose it. Fear of alienating these daimyo who might assist Chōshū against the Shogunate explained, in Parkes's opinion, Chōshū's refusal to open Shimonoseki. In contrast Satsuma's officers reported a general desire in Kyūshū for the extension of foreign trade and hope for the

---

[1] Beasley, *Documents*, pp. 82–83.   [2] Satow, *Diplomat*, p. 154.
[3] F.O. 46/58, Parkes to Russell, No. 69, H.M.S. *Perseus*, 28 Nov. 1865.
[4] J.M. MSS. (Yokohama, Private), C. S. Hope to J. Whittall, Yokohama, 1 Dec. 1865.

eventual opening of Kagoshima. Nevertheless, it was soon known that Satsuma's agents in Kyoto and in Yedo were opposing the opening of Hyogo which was thought to be part of their anti-*Bakufu* tactics.

Parkes believed that the daimyo were mainly activated by jealousy of the Shogun's adding to his resources and increasing his military strength. At the same time he questioned the wisdom of allowing foreigners to settle as individuals in daimyo ports. To protect them and to prevent them from intriguing with individual daimyo and influencing them against other powers would be difficult. Commerce would suffer in consequence. He now realized that the daimyo wanted to reserve all commercial privileges within their territories exclusively to themselves and prohibit their subjects from trade, while on the other hand the Shogun was beginning to recognize that a middle class developed through an extended commerce would strengthen his own position.[1] Such views prompted instructions from London which favoured the Shogunate.[2]

The Shogun's weakness was evident, however, on many fronts. Not only had he been unable to prevent the Mikado's dismissal of his two councillors but it was soon known that his return to Yedo, his seat of power, was indefinitely postponed. Even before the year ended—within weeks after its promises at Osaka—the *Bakufu* was pleading lack of funds for the payment of the indemnity. The second instalment so glibly pledged immediately in Yedo was arriving only in driblets and in copper cash. Parkes now understood that the Shogun was not even in a position at Osaka where he could have accepted the alternative to paying the indemnity. He could not open Shimonoseki without seizing it first from Chōshū and he could not open Hyogo without violent opposition from the daimyo supported by the anti-foreign court. The *Rōjū* further admitted that foreigners were still in danger from attack by savage and fanatical opponents—implying their inability to afford adequate protection for which Parkes held them responsible. Yet foreign trade during the previous six months prospered more than ever

[1] F.O. 46/58, Parkes to Russell, Nos. 70, 72, and 80, Shanghai, 8, 15, and 29 Dec. 1865. For Chōshū's earlier efforts to effect the opening of Shimonoseki, see Ishii, *Meiji Ishin no Kokusaiteki Kankyō*, p. 397.

[2] F.O. 46/58, F.O. note at end of Parkes to Russell, No. 72, 15 Dec. 1865; 262/104, Clarendon to Parkes, No. 30, 20 Feb. 1866.

before, and imports almost balanced exports.[1] All these factors were to influence British policy.

British and French Policies towards Japan's Domestic Conflict

British policy for some time was marked by contradictions, while the *Bakufu* progressively lost face and power and its chief enemies in the Chōshū and Satsuma clans, united in March 1866 by a secret agreement to overthrow the Tokugawa, moved deliberately to cause its downfall.[2] Although it was almost impossible for Parkes to get accurate current information from Yedo or Kyoto on the developments in this civil conflict, his view of what was best for the peace and prosperity of the Japanese nation differed drastically from that of Roches. While both ministers professed neutrality, each gave encouragement to the side he favoured. It has been noted that Roches as well as Parkes insisted upon the Imperial ratification of the treaties, but for different reasons. Roches thought this would strengthen the Shogun who had signed the treaties and deserved foreign support as the legitimate guardian of foreign interests in Japan. He also upheld the *Bakufu* monopoly of foreign trade hoping thereby to strengthen France's commerce with Japan. He suspected and opposed the liberal Western clans as self-seeking revolutionaries not to be trifled with. His home government concurred in this and willingly provided financial and military aid.[3]

British policy moved towards the opposite direction. Both at home and in Japan, British officials and merchants became increasingly sympathetic with the anti-*Bakufu* sentiment of the daimyo of the south-west and their desire for a greater part in Japan's foreign trade. Through the hostilities at Kagoshima and Shimonoseki Satow and others had seen the weakness and duplicity of the Shogunate. In subsequent negotiations with officials of the two *han* the British had learned of their demand for a share of the foreign trade which the Shogun monopolized in violation of the treaties.[4] Hence as the *Bakufu* had admitted

[1] F.O. 46/58, Parkes to Russell, No. 80, Yokohama, 29 Dec. 1865; No. 81 and Private, 30 Dec. 1865.

[2] Beasley, *Documents*, pp. 84–90. For Satsuma–Chōshū Agreement see Craig, op. cit., p. 318.

[3] Ishii, *Meiji Ishin no Kokusaiteki Kankyō*, pp. 568–72. Beasley, *Documents*, pp. 78–79.

[4] Satow, *Diplomat*, pp. 128–9. P.P. H. of C. 1866, lxxvi. 23–30, Winchester to Russell, Yokohama, 11 May 1865 and encls.; Russell to Winchester, 24 July 1865.

to Winchester on 22 June, it became generally clear that the
early anti-treaty agitation of these daimyo and their continued
opposition to the opening of Hyogo and Osaka were merely a
way of attacking the *Bakufu* and undermining its authority in
order that the daimyo themselves might participate in the
government and foreign commerce of all Japan. Contacts with
the Japanese people at Hyogo during the negotiations for the
Imperial sanction of the treaties disproved their reputed hostility
to foreigners. Parkes, his staff, and the officers and crews of the
squadron experienced only goodwill and friendliness from all
classes of residents. It was obvious that the *Bakufu* warning of
fear and malevolence in this area was merely a device for
preventing contacts between foreigners and the Japanese outside their jurisdiction. Satow now doubted the desirability of
Britain's trying 'to bolster up' the obviously decaying Shogunate.[1]

Merchants, especially Thomas Glover at Nagasaki, supported
this point of view.[2] Glover had developed a flourishing trade
with Satsuma and through Satsuma with Chōshū. Up until
February 1866 Satsuma had already purchased fifteen steamers
and one sailing vessel and had ordered two more sailing vessels
and two steamers. He had also bought six steam saw factories and
machinery for a dock and engine shop. Glover looked forward
to developing trade with the Ryūkyū Islands, a tributary of
Satsuma and a source for sugar. He had found Satsuma honourable in all his dealings and considered him a potentially great
source of business as Japan opened more to trade. He had a
sufficiently personal friendship with the Prince to be invited
to visit him in Kagoshima.[3]

Although not averse to trading with members of the Shogunate, Glover found them less reliable. The Shogun's brother,
also a purchaser of ships, had broken his contract four or five
times as to the time of payment. The British merchant considered him a safe customer in the long run, however, as he was
secured under the Customs House official stamp and made no
objection to paying a high rate of interest—upon occasion as

[1] Satow, *Diplomat*, p. 147.
[2] For Glover see pp. 330–1.
[3] J.M. MSS. (Nagasaki, 1866), T. Glover to W. Keswick now in Shanghai, Nagasaki, 1 and 12 Feb. 1866. p. 186.

much as five per cent. a month, with the seal of the government as security.[1]

Representatives of the Shogunate and those of Satsuma were also competing for the favour of the government in London. Shibata Gōchū (Masanaka), a Commissioner of Foreign Affairs, and a suite of ten officials had left Japan in the early summer of 1865 for France and England, to learn about the military and industrial developments in the West and to discuss with the authorities Japan's objection to receiving as consuls private merchants and traders and to treating and communicating with consuls as diplomatic agents.[2] Major F. Brine of the Royal Engineers took charge of the envoys upon their arrival in London in December. Under his tutelage they visited battleships, docks, dockyards, and barracks, *The Times* office, 'The City', the Bank of England, the Royal Mint, the Royal Exchange, Lloyd's, Chelsea Hospital, the London underground, the Grosvenor Hotel, railway stations, Westminster Abbey, Parliament, the Millbank prison, a sword factory, and other unrelated centres of British military, business, social, and official life.[3] They were so impressed with the kindness everywhere that Shibata gave a dinner to show his appreciation, the first dinner given by a Japanese to British officials in England.[4] Nothing has been found, however, to show that they held interviews of political importance with the British. With the French, on the contrary, they made arrangements for military and naval training missions.[5]

Near the same time and in contravention of Tokugawa law, Satsuma had sent his officials to England primarily to purchase war materials. They not only arranged for a very large loan for the daimyo to pay off his debts but made an impression on Clarendon's thinking about Japan.[6] The Foreign Secretary as late as 20 February 1866 had instructed Parkes that the time had not yet arrived to enter into separate trade engagements

[1] J.M. MSS. (Nagasaki, 1865), T. B. Glover and Co. to Armstrong Co., Nagasaki, 30 Dec. 1865; (Nagasaki, 1866), T. Glover to W. Keswick (copy), Nagasaki, 10 Mar. 1866.

[2] F.O. 46/55, Winchester to Russell, No. 110, Yokohama, 26 June 1865.

[3] F.O. 262/104, visits paid by Japanese commander and suite, 18–30 Dec. 1865.

[4] Ibid., Brine to F.O., 3 Jan. 1866, encl. in Clarendon to Parkes, 9 Jan. 1866.

[5] For their arrangements in France, see p. 253.

[6] J.M. MSS. (Nagasaki, 1866), T. Glover to W. Keswick, Nagasaki, 21 Feb. 1866.

with individual daimyo. Influenced by Parkes's letter of 15 December 1865, he had directed him to impress upon the Shogun the expediency of strengthening his position by the creation of a 'prosperous and enlightened middle class throughout the whole country' through the agency of commerce.[1]

Shortly before 25 March, however, Clarendon had three meetings with Satsuma's chief envoy, Matsuki Kōan (Hiroyasu), whose explanation of his daimyo's point of view and proposal for the extension of foreign trade in Japan coincided with Britain's own desire for an expanding commerce. Matsuki, a close friend of Lawrence Oliphant, restated what Glover, Satow, and others knew and Parkes suspected, that Satsuma and most of the other daimyo felt no hostility to foreigners as such but resented the Shogun's monopoly of foreign trade and would continue to oppose the opening of Osaka and Hyogo as long as the *Bakufu* alone would gain by it. He said the great daimyo asked for their share in the advantages of foreign commerce. They proposed that the means of changing the present system to include the Mikado, daimyo, and Shogun in an expanding international commerce, should be discussed freely in an assembly convoked by the Mikado for that purpose. Since the Mikado's ratification of the treaties had made direct communication possible between the powers and His Majesty, the daimyo wanted the powers to request the Mikado to call into conference in Kyoto the three branches of the Tokugawa House (*Sanke*), the eighteen great daimyo (*Kokushu*), and any other daimyo the Mikado might wish. No foreign minister should be present. All the daimyo should ratify the treaties. After at least three months to permit the introduction of new arrangements to meet the new conditions, the commissioners of the daimyo should exchange ratifications with the foreign ministers at Osaka. Thus the daimyo hoped to bring about a needed reform peaceably. They threatened civil war upon the opening of another port in the Shogun's territory, however, should some arrangement similar to this be rejected.[2]

---

[1] F.O. 262/104, Clarendon to Parkes, No. 30, 20 Feb. 1866.
[2] Ishii, *Meiji Ishin no Kokusaiteki Kankyō*, pp. 427–32. Dickins, op. cit. ii. 61–63, Hammond to Parkes, 26 Apr. 1866; Oliphant to Clarendon, 25 Mar. 1866.

Before Parkes could comment on this, Clarendon gave him further cautious instructions which show the influence of Matsuki. The British representative was not to take sides or express an opinion for or against either party in the approaching contest. Britain's aim in Japan was not to seek political influence but to develop commerce. Although he ruled out separate arrangements with any daimyo, Clarendon suggested that Parkes encourage the daimyo 'to adopt some general measure in concert with the Mikado and the Tycoon to remove causes of internal dissension and foreign quarrel by putting an end throughout Japan to the restrictive and exclusive system which has been productive of so much mischief already and which if persevered in will probably end in civil and possibly foreign war'. He emphasized that 'In any civil contest the policy of the British Government is to remain neutral while exacting from all parties who may be in the ascendant in any quarter, a strict observance of the Treaties with the Government and protection and good usage for British subjects and their property.'[1]

French policy professed a similar neutrality in the internal affairs of Japan but at the same time wanted nothing done to undermine the authority of the Shogun which Clarendon claimed that England, equally with France, wished to uphold. Roches's reports of combating the tendency of his (British) colleagues, influenced by merchants, to enter into direct relations with the daimyo and thus violate the treaties had alarmed Napoleon's government, causing Clarendon to promise France that Parkes would do nothing 'to encourage the Daimio to subvert the authority of the Tycoon'.[2] France and Britain were further united at this time in their distrust of Russia's aloofness in relation to the other treaty powers. They suspected her activities in the north where they thought Russia was anxious to extend her frontier in Sakhalin and to obtain other advantages from the weakness of the Japanese government. In consequence Clarendon ordered Parkes to watch Russian proceedings and warn the Japanese about them.[3]

[1] F.O. 262/105, Clarendon to Parkes, 9 Apr. 1866.
[2] Ibid., 7 May 1866.
[3] Ibid., 19 Apr. 1866.

Parkes's Policy of Neutrality

While these instructions took their two months' course to
Japan they crossed letters from Parkes who was attempting to
work out independently a policy of neutrality in Japan's
domestic conflict. The British minister was now well informed
of Satsuma's opposition to the opening of Hyogo and his use of
this tactic as an attack on the Shogun and not as an anti-foreign
measure. He determined 'to try to tell Satsuma or his officers that
they pursue a dangerous game assailing the Tycoon through
Foreign Powers as the latter must repel attacks on the Treaties
regardless of where they come from or on what motives'. He
said: 'I will support the Tycoon if he really endeavours to give
effect to the Treaties but at the same time urge him to remove
restrictions to free intercourse between Daimios and Foreigners
and give the former full advantage of foreign trade.' He knew,
however, that both parties were undependable in their relations with foreigners. For example, the *Bakufu* had failed until
pressured by Parkes to publish in Nagasaki the Mikado's decree
sanctioning the treaties.[1]

At the same time Parkes believed that Satsuma's efforts to
force the resignation of the Shogun might be disastrous for
foreign trade as the successor might prove even less liberal
towards the West. He was led by Consul Gower to believe that
neither Satsuma nor Chōshū wished to open their ports on a
treaty basis to all foreigners indiscriminately—but wished for
freedom to arrange for themselves such communications with
foreigners as they found convenient for promoting their own
views and monopolies. He knew now that the daimyo were
always divided among themselves, that the people of both
Chōshū and Satsuma were divided on foreign policy, and that
their power was great only when they could unite. Hence he
believed that he could accomplish more through the Shogun
who at last seemed to be acting in good faith because he could
not afford the enmity of foreigners while contesting the daimyo.
The progress of the promised tariff negotiations between a commission appointed by the *Rōjū* and the foreign representatives

[1] F.O. 46/67, Parkes to Clarendon, No. 38, Conf'l., Yokohama, 28 Feb.;
and 46/68, No. 82, 16 May 1866. Beasley says that the *Bakufu* had also tried
without success to repudiate its promises of 24 Nov. 1865 on the ground that they
were signed privately by three *Rōjū* rather than by the government. *Documents*,
pp. 83 and 304. See p. 169.

as well as increasing opportunities for direct intercourse with the *Rōjū* themselves, and an invitation to visit the daimyo of Satsuma, encouraged Parkes to feel he was getting closer to understanding the political situation as a whole.[1]

While lacking information from Kyoto he was aware that the Shogun's continued residence at the Emperor's city when he was needed at Yedo, indicated the importance of the discussions in progress there. He forecast that a constitutional change would come and make for greater stability. He envisaged a central power emerging which would supersede the 'dislocated control of feudality', but not without a struggle. He recognized the difficulties in organizing a chamber of daimyo because he thought the daimyo were as distrustful of each other as they were of the Shogun.[2] By 29 May Parkes not only had received Oliphant's report on the proposal of Satsuma's envoy, Matsuki, in London, but was able to report many progressive measures accepted by the Shogunate during the tariff negotiations,[3] which he thought would benefit foreign trade and help to silence the criticism of the daimyo.

Sir Harry's sympathies were clearly not yet with the opposition daimyo, although he had made it known to the *Rōjū* that the Shogun's demands on Chōshū were vindictive and that he would gain esteem from his own people and from foreigners by being generous.[4] Shortly afterwards Parkes advised the Foreign Office to exercise great caution in acting on Matsuki's proposal in London. He was uncertain about the number of daimyo who would support Satsuma's views or trust his agent to represent them. He refuted the idea that the Mikado's sanction of the treaties had given the foreign representatives direct access to him. In fact he and his colleagues had had no communication with the Emperor or his

[1] F.O. 46/67, Parkes to Clarendon, No. 55, Yokohama, 31 Mar. 1866; 46/68, Parkes to Hammond, Private, Yedo, 28 Apr. 1866.

[2] Ibid., Parkes to Hammond, Private, Yokohama, 16 May 1866.

[3] Ibid., Parkes to F.O. (probably Hammond), Private, Yokohama, 29 May 1866; Parkes to Clarendon, No. 87, Yokohama, 29 May 1866 and encls.

[4] Ibid., Parkes to Clarendon, No. 74, Yedo, 28 Apr. 1866. The *Bakufu* demands on Chōshū had already been modified because of the opposition of the most powerful *han* supported by the Court. Its final demands on the *han* were that the daimyo and his son should retire in favour of the grandson and that 'their domains should be reduced by 100,000 *koku*', in the hope that the *han* would submit to such leniency and war could be averted. Craig, op. cit., pp. 307–10.

Court when at Osaka. The British minister doubted whether an appeal from the representatives to the Mikado to convene a council of daimyo would be noticed but the daimyo themselves could effect it if they wished. Although Parkes believed that such an assembly, if convened, should consider measures for executing the treaties effectively, he warned against letting the daimyo suppose their approval essential to the validity of the treaties as that was never considered in connexion with the Mikado's ratification. He recognized in Matsuki's proposal Satsuma's desire to depress the power of the Shogun whom he considered a rival and to raise the power of the Emperor over whom Satsuma expected to wield a predominating influence. Foreign intervention and support for this would offend the Shogun. Parkes preferred that the Mikado, the Shogun, and the daimyo should determine their respective duties themselves. He knew foreign intervention would be unwelcome. Nevertheless he was convinced of the desirability of opening communication with the daimyo if they wanted it. He wanted to explain to them that Britain had no desire to interfere with their form of government. She was merely determined to insist upon the universal observation of the treaties in Japan and her sympathy would be with whichever party was ready to fulfil these obligations. His uncertainty about the feelings and wishes of the various daimyo made him decide to visit Satsuma and others in their own territories at the conclusion of the tariff negotiations.[1]

Satow's Articles on English Policy

There is nothing in these letters of Parkes—either official or private—that indicates his support or knowledge of the three articles which Ernest Satow had published in the *Japan Times* between 16 March and 19 May 1866 and which recommended a new basis for Japan's relations with the West. Parkes neither sent copies of the articles home nor mentioned them in his letters and Satow himself believed that his chief had no knowledge of them. The three articles were translated into Japanese and presented as a pamphlet for the consideration of the Daimyo of Awa, the feudal lord of Satow's native teacher. Copies circulated among the retainers of other daimyo brought

[1] F.O. 46/68, Parkes to F.O. (undoubtedly to Hammond), Private, Yokohama, 29 May 1866, encl. *Memorandum* on Oliphant's letter to Clarendon of 25 Mar. 1866.

Satow favourable recognition during his subsequent travels. The translation was soon printed under the title *Eikoku Sakuron* (English Policy by the Englishman Satow), and sold widely in Kyoto and Osaka. In consequence both the *Bakufu* and the Court party assumed that this completely unofficial work by Satow represented the views of the British legation. As such its influence on the policies of both can be neither measured nor denied.[1]

Satow's solution for Japan's political ills developed from his many conversations with the retainers of daimyo and two-sworded men and from the state papers they gave him. From the latter he learned that the Shogun considered himself merely the Mikado's principal vassal, a fact which convinced Satow that foreigners should not continue to regard the Shogun as the sovereign of Japan but should enter into direct relations with the Mikado.[2] Satow was also made aware of the weakness of the Shogun in relation to Chōshū, and learned that the former would lack support from the daimyo in the approaching conflict. His first article on 16 March 1866 came out forcibly for giving up 'the worn-out pretence of acknowledging the Tycoon to be sole ruler of Japan, and take into consideration the existence of other co-ordinate powers'. He urged 'we must supplement or replace our present treaties by treaties with the Confederate Daimios of Japan'. He wanted 'not a treaty with a single potentate, but one binding on and advantageous to everyone in the country'. He believed that the Shogun as well as the daimyo would welcome a proposal to discuss such a plan, since the *Bakufu* would thus be relieved from many current 'embarrassments by the participation of the Daimios in the advantages of trade'. He argued that such a new treaty would not be a 'political revolution, deposing the Tycoon from the position which he arrogated as head of the Government, for that has already taken place. It would be merely recognizing the actual state of affairs.' There was ample time between then and the promised opening of Hyogo on 1 January 1868 for negotiating with the daimyo every point in dispute, for deter-

[1] Satow, *Diplomat*, pp. 159–60. I have found no copy of the pamphlet in London or Japan. The broken files of the *Japan Times* in the Ueno Library in Tokyo contain the whole of the article of 16 Mar. and the first part of that of 19 May. A complete copy of the latter exists in the Satow MSS., P.R.O. 30/33/1/4. For texts see Appendix II, pp. 565–74.　　　　　[2] Satow, *Diplomat*, p. 157.

mining 'what new ports shall be opened and in which Daimio's territories, and for establishing our relations generally on a secure and permanent footing'. To avoid undoubted bloodshed and coercion at the entry of foreign residents in Hyogo, Satow appealed to the representatives of the treaty powers, 'to treat with the Daimios, for they are responsible rulers of the country equally with the Tycoon'. He was convinced such a measure would not only be of 'immense benefit to the country' but a great stimulus 'to our own rising trade with Japan'. He believed that the Shogun's cabinet with slight pressure would acknowledge that Article XIV of the treaty, which gave all Japanese the right to trade with the British, could no longer be treated as a dead letter. He commended the matter to the consideration of the representatives of the treaty powers.[1]

Satow's third article implies that in the second he developed the idea of substituting for the treaties of 1858 'a more equitable and comprehensive convention with the Mikado and the Confederated Daimios of Japan'.[2] In article one he had merely said that to a treaty made with the daimyo, 'the sanction of the titular Emperor would be necessary, or at least desirable, but he could not enter into a treaty himself, for he would be unable to enforce its observance'. In article three Satow sought to explain in detail the inadequacies of the existing treaties, in an effort to strengthen his position against a continuance of their operation. He wanted to make clear again 'how completely wrong was the Tycoon in taking the first step of signing the treaties in a character which did not belong to him—how utterly incapable he has since proved himself to be of carrying out his own engagements—and finally, how generally insufficient are the Treaty and Trade Regulations for commercial as well as international purposes'. He maintained that the Mikado alone could claim the title 'Tycoon' which the Shogun had usurped in the treaties. Thus the Shogun 'had signed a contract to which the letter of the law makes him no party'. He was never the bona fide sovereign of the whole country as he led Lord Elgin to believe—a fact which Satow considered reason enough 'to absolve the Western Powers from the observance of the existing Treaty'. Actually, Satow said, they had only 'a treaty with the master of

[1] *Japan Times*, 16 Mar. 1866.
[2] No copy of this second article has been located.

Yedo and the eight provinces round it and with a few outlying spots scattered through the islands of Dai Nippon—but with Sendai, Chōshū, Satsuma, and the other great Daimios, we can claim no more than what they may choose to consider the general duties of man to man may require'. He foresaw that this difficult position would become even more complicated when Osaka was opened and the powers entered the neighbourhood of the Mikado where several powerful daimios were 'busily intriguing against the Yedo usurper'.

Satow's analysis of the major articles of the treaties consistently showed that the Shogun was powerless to carry out many of them beyond the boundaries of his own limited domain and that he had persistently *violated* those he had the power to observe. The continuance of such arrangements Satow predicted would 'lead to a political crisis in Japan' and a serious disturbance of British trade which could never 'under present regulations, acquire the importance and value which is its due'. He appealed to those in power to find the solution, hoping that the present treaty might be promptly abrogated 'in favour of a more comprehensive and satisfactory one—a fair and equitable Convention with the Mikado and the Confederate Daimios—the real rulers of Japan'.[1]

The Tariff Convention of 1866

The demand of the foreign representatives to proceed with the promised amendments of the tariff upon their return from Hyogo led the *Bakufu* to appoint the Commissioner of Finance (*Kanjō-bugyō*), Oguri Tadamasa, to take charge of the negotiations at Yokohama.[2] Parkes is given the major credit for both the conception and the execution of the work which followed.[3] The admitted depletion of the Shogun's treasury and the *Bakufu* request for postponing the remaining payments of the Shimonoseki indemnity obviously gave the Western powers the upper hand. Parkes made it clear in January that compensation would be required for any concession regarding the indemnity. His renewed proposal for the immediate opening of Hyogo in return for postponement—a recognized impossiblity for the *Bakufu* and not even desired by the powers—probably made

[1] *Japan Times*, 19 May 1866.
[2] *Nichi-Ei Gaikō Shi*, i. 93. F.O. 46/65, Parkes to Clarendon, Nos. 6 and 9, Yokohama, 17 Jan. 1866. [3] Dickins, op. cit. ii. 65.

the Japanese amenable to the alternatives he suggested two weeks later.[1] These included liberal arrangements for the tariff; the establishment of a mint where foreign merchants could obtain Japanese currency in return for bullion or foreign money of the same intrinsic value on the payment of a fair seignorage; the lighting of the Japanese coasts and approaches to the ports; and the complete removal of all the restrictions to trade mentioned in the London Protocol.[2] He soon elaborated the last to mean: the removal of restrictions on the trade of daimyo agents at the open ports; the permission for all Japanese to buy foreign ships, to visit foreign countries, and to employ foreign engineers, mechanics, etc.; and the prohibition of transit duties on Japanese products and any other charges other than the duties stipulated in the tariff under negotiation. Although Parkes inclined towards leniency regarding the indemnity because he hesitated to weaken the Shogun further by making him pay and in return hoped for better terms in the forthcoming convention, he and his colleagues refused to submit to their home governments the April application of the *Rōjū* for a delay in the payment of the last three instalments until the Japanese attitude towards these proposals was known.[3]

Gradually, and not without opposition, the Japanese yielded on every major point.[4] Oguri's efforts to abolish the export tax as a whole while maintaining the current rates on imports were defeated by the foreigners' demand for a five per cent. duty on the value of all imports and exports in accordance with the general basis for tariff revision accepted by the Japanese at Osaka.

On 25 June 1866 the envoys of Britain, France, the United States, and Holland signed the Convention and the accompanying tariff revisions with a member of the *Rōjū*, Mizuno

---

[1] F.O. 46/65, Parkes to Hammond, Private, Yokohama, 17 Jan. 1866; Parkes to Clarendon, No. 9, same date.

[2] Ibid., No. 18, 31 Jan. 1866.

[3] F.O. 46/67, Parkes to (?) Hammond, Private, Yokohama, 28 Feb. 1866; 46/68, Parkes to Clarendon, No. 73, Yedo, 28 Apr. 1866. In February the foreign representatives had granted a three months' delay on the third instalment and the *Bakufu* met this payment in May; 46/65, No. 31, Yokohama, 15 Feb. 1866; 46/68, No. 88, Yokohama, 29 May 1866.

[4] Ibid., Parkes to Clarendon, No. 81, 14 May; Parkes to F.O., Private, Yokohama, 29 May, and Yedo, 14 June 1866; Parkes to Clarendon, No. 99, Yokohama, 27 June 1866.

Tadakiyo, Izumi-no-kami. The new tariff regulations replaced all previous tariff schedules between Japan and the powers but were subject to revision in July 1872 and special arrangements made possible earlier changes in the duties on silk, tea, and timber. In addition to the imports and exports listed as having the *ad valorem* duty of five per cent., prohibited goods and duty-free goods were defined, and specific rates were fixed according to quantity for eighty-nine imports and fifty-three exports.[1]

The Convention also provided for: the establishment of bonded warehouses, making it possible for foreign merchants to re-export unsalable goods without the payment of duty; the abolition of transit duties and any tax on Japanese produce *en route* to market other than the general road and navigation tolls; the establishment of a free mint; permission for any Japanese to buy all types of cargo or passenger ships at home or abroad; the abolition of all the irksome restrictions on trade and intercourse between foreigners and the Japanese, promised by the *Bakufu* in the Protocol of 1862 but not carried out; and the erection of lighthouses, buoys, or beacons in the open ports.

Most important of all, in Parkes's opinion, were Articles IX and X. Here the *Bakufu* completely abandoned their exclusion policy and the Shogun's monopoly of trade. They granted freedom to all Japanese merchants, daimyo, and daimyo retainers—to trade or associate with foreigners without government interference at the treaty ports; to employ foreign shipping in trade with the open ports or abroad; and being provided with passports, according to the Proclamation of 23 May 1866, to travel abroad for study or trade, and to be employed on foreign ships. Parkes thought travel for foreigners in the interior of Japan would follow in time and accepted the fact that it was not yet safe for them to do so. He had been willing to make a few concessions in order to accomplish this much, and he had the promised co-operation of the ruling powers at Osaka in the fulfilment of the Convention.[2]

The Convention came into operation at Yokohama on

---

[1] P.P. H. of C. 1867, lxxiv (3758), 2, 5–6. The import of opium and the export of grains, flour, and saltpetre were forbidden.

[2] Ibid. 1–10. Here the text of the Convention, the Tariff Schedules, and Parkes's comments of 16 July 1866 are printed. F.O. 46/68, Parkes to Clarendon, and Private, Yedo, 14 June 1866.

PLATE 3

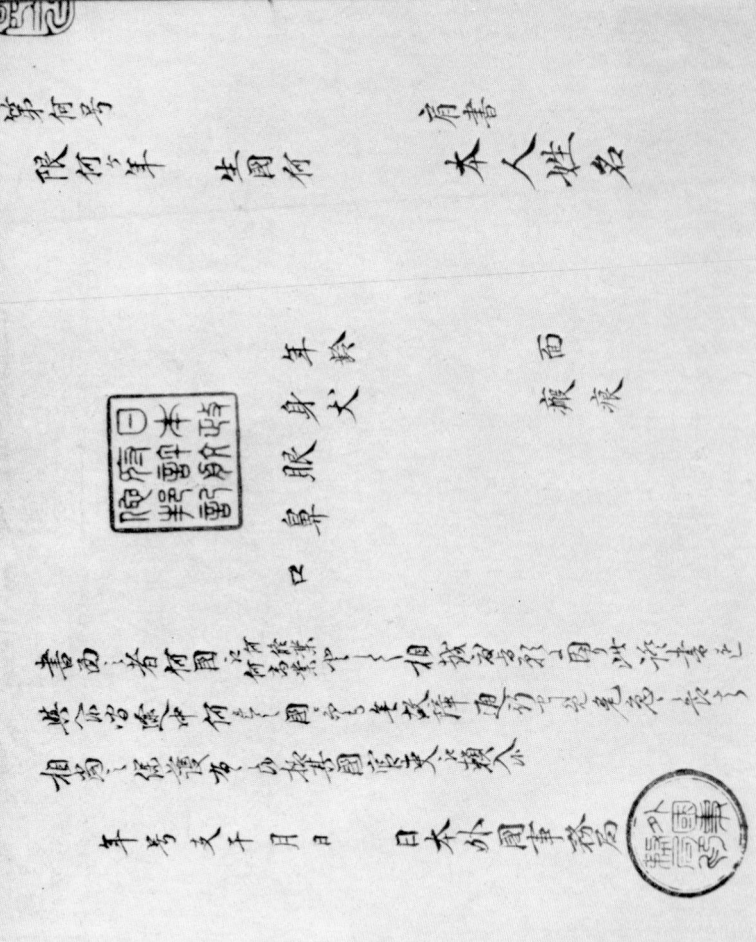

N°

limited years   Birthplace   Name of the person

et. etc. etc.

Age   Face
Stature   Scar
Eyes
Nose
Mouth

This passport is supplied to the above mentioned person
upon his request to go to   country for the purpose
of study of   . It is requested to the Authorities of
  trade of
every Government to permit safely & freely to pass
him on any country which he will travel, & in case of
need to give him the lawfull aid and Protection.
  day of month of the   year   the Foreign Office
                                           Japan.

1 July 1866, and a month later at Hakodate and Nagasaki. Many innovations favourable to the extension of foreign trade now became law and in the turbulent years ahead the foreign powers were to hold Japan's new government to the agreements here made by the Shogunate. To the Japanese the new tariff meant a great reduction in the revenues from their customs and prevented the enactment of appropriate measures to protect the development of their own industry against the competition of foreign products. As a result the restoration of customs autonomy became a major goal in their future dealings with the West.[1] In 1866 the Japanese officials knew nothing of the theories of free trade and protectionism, nor of the relative merits of the two systems. They adopted the free-trade policy because of the pressure of the West—not because they understood and desired it.[2]

Parkes's Visits to Satsuma and Uwajima

The British minister was now free to accept Satsuma's invitation to visit him at his residence in Kagoshima, the first instance of such an overture by a *tozama* daimyo since the conclusion of the treaties of 1858.[3] Vice-Admiral King, commander of the British naval forces in the China Station, was also invited. He provided his flagship and H.M.S. *Serpent* and *Salamis* for the expedition which arrived in Nagasaki on 9 July. Lady Parkes, with Dr. Willis, A. Siebold, and Captain Applin as interpreters, made up the party. Parkes carried dispatches from the *Rōjū* to the Governor of Nagasaki reporting the conclusion of the recent Convention, which the Governor and the agents of the daimyo received with satisfaction. The Governor not only promised co-operation in carrying out the new arrangements but approved Parkes's visit to Satsuma and offered him letters to another daimyo, the Prince of Uwajima, who, pending the Governor's approval, had asked the British minister to visit him. Parkes felt, therefore, that his visit to the palace of Kagoshima could not arouse the mistrust of the Yedo authorities. He hoped to persuade this once hostile daimyo of the importance

---

[1] *Nichi-Ei Gaikō Shi*, i. 95.
[2] Ōkuma Shigenobu, 'The Industrial Revolution in Japan', *North American Review* clxxi (Nov. 1900), 677.
[3] For treaties, see pp. 38–40, 42–45.

of the preservation of a good understanding among the Mikado, the Shogun, and the daimyo, and to use the influence of the daimyo to correct 'the unenlightened opposition to foreign intercourse still prevailing in parts of Japan'.[1]

The Nagasaki merchant Thomas Glover, said to be the go-between for the host clans and the British minister, accompanied Parkes's party to Kagoshima and Uwajima.[2] All classes of people in both clans welcomed the British most heartily and evinced great interest in their ships, their artillery, target firing, and the drills put on by the marines. Thousands visited the ships while Parkes and his party enjoyed six days of royal entertainment by Satsuma's young prince, Shimazu Tadayoshi Shūri-daibu, and his father, the famous Shimazu Hisamitsu.[3] Outstanding festivities included a dinner at the palace lasting five hours 'when forty different dishes were served with English beer and Japanese and foreign wines', and a hunt in a forest abounding in deer, wild boar, and monkeys. The British were astounded to find a foundry adjoining the palace grounds where Japanese 'without European aid, cast great cannon, shot and shell and work a steam turning lathe'. There was also a glass foundry nearby where Japanese blew and cut bottles and ornaments with great skill.[4]

Uwajima's prince, Date Muneki, Iyo-no-kami, was an equally generous host, whose palace overlooked a more beautiful harbour than that of Nagasaki. He and his officers proved to be not only well-read in their own literature but knew that of the West and could discuss such subjects as the battle of Waterloo. Equally surprising was the precision and steadiness with which the clansmen went through their own drill after the British marines had been reviewed by this daimyo. A dinner in native style where the princesses and ladies of the household were introduced also delighted the foreign guests.[5]

Parkes considered these visits politically revealing. Both

[1] F.O. 46/69, Parkes to Clarendon, No. 106, Nagasaki, 18 July 1866. Ad. I/5992, F.O. to Adm., 17 Sept. 1866, encl. two of Parkes's letters of 18 July 1866.

[2] Ishii, *Meiji Ishin no Kokusaiteki Kankyō*, p. 457.

[3] Shimazu Hisamitsu was also called Shimazu Saburō.

[4] Account by Officer of H.M.S. *Princess Royal* given in Black, op. cit. ii. 2–5. Dickins, op. cit. ii. 65. F.O. 46/69, Parkes to Clarendon, No. 121, Nagasaki, 2 Aug. 1866. Ad. I/5966, King to Adm., 10 Aug. 1866.

[5] F.O. 46/70, Parkes to Clarendon, No. 130, Yokohama, 13 Aug. 1866. Black, op. cit. ii. 5–7.

daimyo expressed their desire to share in planning the opening of Hyogo and Osaka, fearing they might otherwise lose the advantages which they then enjoyed because of Osaka being to them a free port. They reported that the Mikado had ratified the treaties on the Shogun's assurance that only the three ports would be opened, and that the Shogun was preventing the longed-for assembly of daimyo. Parkes urged the necessity for amicable negotiations in bringing about changes in their government. His hosts declared they held no ill will towards the Shogun—that they wanted 'a change of system only'—a voice in the management of affairs or at least in legislation, 'not a change of dynasty'.[1] In no way did Satsuma imply that he had already in March 1866 formed a secret alliance with Chōshū to support the clan in the event of *Bakufu* military action and to work with Chōshū for the overthrow of the Tokugawa régime.[2]

Parkes was convinced that such visits as this gave Japanese people, unacquainted with Westerners, opportunities to become aware of their 'good feeling' and their power. The daimyo themselves had assured him that the presence of the British ships would aid them in convincing their followers, apparently divided among themselves, of the true character and strength of foreigners, and urged Parkes to make similar visits to other diamyo.[3] Upon his return to Yedo, Parkes not only received Yedo's sanction of his visits but the *Bakufu* promised to tell the daimyo that their reception of Parkes had government approval.[4]

Parkes's predominantly neutral reports of his findings are in great contrast to those of the *Japan Times (Nihon Shimbun)* and the *Yokohama News Letter (Yokohama Shimpo)* which exulted in Parkes's and King's visits to Satsuma and Uwajima as a first step towards the fulfilment of Satow's *English Policy* and predicted further visits of the British authorities to other daimyo of the south. It is significant, however, that Thomas Glover, suspected as the author of one of these reports,[5] is not mentioned by Parkes or King in their official correspondence, nor does

[1] F.O. 46/69, Parkes to Hammond, Private, Nagasaki, 2 Aug. 1866.

[2] Craig, op. cit., p. 318. Beasley, *Documents*, pp. 85–86.

[3] Ad. I/5966, Parkes to King, Uwajima, 10 Aug. 1866, encl. in King to Adm., 10 Aug. 1866.

[4] F.O. 46/70, Parkes to Stanley (now Foreign Secretary), No. 137, 2 Sept. 1866.

[5] Ishii, *Meiji Ishin no Kokusaiteki Kankyō*, pp. 453–7.

Glover report the visit in his now available letters to the Jardine, Matheson firm.

British Policy during the Shogun's Second Campaign against Chōshū

During the British minister's absence from Yokohama the Shogun launched his second campaign against Chōshū.[1] Neither party responded to French and British overtures for mediation while Parkes was still in the area of the Straits. Parkes assured them both that while regretting the strife, Britain would remain neutral and friends of those who respected the treaties. He also held a conference with a member of the *Rōjū* concerning the report by the governor of Nagasaki that owing to the hostilities the Straits were to be closed to foreign ships. Parkes interpreted this as a violation of the Osaka agreement of 1865. The *Rōjū* had not understood it as such. The councillors said they meant only to warn the foreign powers of grave danger during hostilities. Foreign navigation would not be suspended. But the Shogun could not be responsible for the safety of foreign ships.[2]

Parkes soon won the support of his colleagues at Yokohama in refusing to close the Straits. They all agreed, however, to prohibit their vessels from anchoring, stopping in, or passing through those waters during hostilities. Parkes issued such regulations to British ships and asked Admiral King to station in the Straits one or two ships to ensure their observation. British subjects were further notified of penalties to be imposed for aiding the war against the Shogun and for trading at ports not opened by treaty. These efforts satisfied the *Rōjū* at Yedo who in turn promised to supply coal for foreign ships at Kokura.[3]

The accusation that Parkes aided Chōshū during the struggle is not without some evidence. In the guise of protecting foreign trade, the British minister successfully opposed the *Bakufu* invasion of Chōshū by crossing the Straits from Kyūshū to Shimo-

[1] Craig, op. cit., pp. 329–33, for details of the campaign.

[2] F.O. 46/70, Parkes to Clarendon, No. 131, Yokohama, 13 Aug. 1866 and encl. *Memorandum* on interview with a member of the *Rōjū*. Parkes believed that the *Bakufu* had later refused offers of both mediation and military assistance from Roches which showed that the employment of foreign forces in settling native dissension was generally unpopular. Parkes to Stanley, No. 141, Conf'l., Yokohama, 2 Sept. 1866.

[3] Ibid., Parkes to Stanley, No. 135, Yokohama, 1 Sept. 1866. Ad. 13/57, Adm. to F.O., 31 Oct. 1866, encl. King's letter of 3 Sept. 1866.

noseki and hence cut the supply route from Nagasaki.[1] He also chose 'to ignore but observe' Chōshū's temporary rearmament of the northern side of the Straits in contravention of the agreement in 1864 on the ground that Nagato would never again close the Straits to foreign trade and that to interfere would be a breach of neutrality.[2]

These and perhaps other British deviations from strict neutrality could not have swayed the victory from Chōshū. The *han* not only possessed well-drilled troops efficiently armed with Western weapons but was confident in its cause and in the secret assurance of any necessary help from its former rival, Satsuma. The Shogun's forces were doomed from the start. Even their daimyo supporters were half-hearted. When the Shogun Iemochi died in Osaka on 19 September 1866 his troops were retreating on all fronts. Not even his provisional successor, Tokugawa Keiki, could rally them or the forces of the supporting *han* to another advance against Chōshū. In the peace negotiations of October, the *Bakufu* envoy, its naval commander, Katsu Kaishu, achieved nothing more than the promise of Chōshū not to attack the *Bakufu* troops as they retreated to Hiroshima, even though he told them of Keiki's plans for the reform of *Bakufu* politics and for convening a council of daimyo to settle the Chōshū question. It was the death of the Emperor Kōmei in late January 1867 that provided the final pretext for the *Bakufu* to end their expedition officially.[3]

As early as October 1866 Parkes diagnosed the political developments as he then understood them. He looked forward to a new government in Japan which would benefit Japan, believing—as did Satow—that the Mikado was undoubtedly

[1] Craig, op. cit., p. 330. Beasley, *Documents*, p. 86.
[2] F.O. 46/72, Parkes to Stanley, Nos. 199 and Conf'l. 207, 1 and 15 Dec. 1866. Prof. Ishii Takashi maintains that Parkes carried out his neutrality policy as favourably as possible to Chōshū because he saw in the Shogun's expedition to Chōshū a prolongation of the civil war and an obstruction to the expected adjustment between different internal forces. His interest lay not in assisting the anti-*Bakufu* party to supreme power but in promoting the reorganization of the central power on the basis of co-operation between the Shogunate and the leading clans with an alteration in the former's policy towards the latter. This seems consistent with Parkes's general idea of what was good for Japan was also good for foreign trade. Ishii Takashi, 'Bakuchō Kōsenki ni Okeru Eikoku Kōshi Pakusu no Tainichi Seisaku' (The Policy of British Minister Parkes for Japan during the *Bakufu–Chōshū* War), *Bunka* (Culture), xxvi, No. 3.   [3] Craig, op. cit., pp. 332–3.

now the sovereign of Japan and the Shogun 'one of his principal and most intelligent ministers and advisers'. He looked forward to the long-talked-of assembly of daimyo, knowing that Keiki would not accept the investiture of Shogun until he knew its powers and whether he could count on daimyo support. Parkes recognized that the main issues confronting the assembly were the determination of the relative powers of the Mikado and Shogun, 'the representation of the Daimios, and the management of foreign affairs, the opening of Osaka being the real test of the question'.[1]

The year closed with no definite solution for the Japanese conflict. The assembly of daimyo failed as the majority refused to accept the Court's invitation to take part in a council on national affairs. The anti-*Bakufu* factions quietly consolidated their strategy. Satsuma and Chōshū united the discontented samurai and the military resources of the great fiefs in the cause of the Imperial Restoration. The *Bakufu* gained temporary strength in the light of Keiki's effective reforms in administration.[2] Satsuma was the first to send an envoy openly to Europe in accordance with the June Convention.[3] In November the British legation moved from Yokohama to Yedo.[4] In December great fires ravaged Yokohama and Yedo.[5]

---

[1] Parkes to Consul Flowers, 14 Oct., and to C. A. Winchester, 31 Oct. 1866, given in Dickins, op. cit. ii. 69–70.

[2] Craig, op. cit., pp. 334–6. Beasley, *Documents*, p. 86.

[3] F.O. 46/71, Parkes to Stanley, No. 181, Conf'l., Yokohama, 31 Oct. 1866.

[4] F.O. 46/72, Parkes to Stanley, No. 185, Yedo, 15 Nov. 1866.

[5] Ibid., Parkes to Stanley, No. 202, Yokohama, 1 Dec. 1867. Dickins, op. cit. ii. 71–72.

VIII

BRITISH ATTITUDES DURING THE LAST YEAR OF THE SHOGUNATE

The British Quest for Political Information

THE need to understand current developments in Japan's political conflict and the impossiblity of getting reliable or impartial knowledge at Yedo caused Parkes to seek it nearer the centre of the struggle. In December 1866 he sent Admiral King on H.M.S. *Princess Royal* accompanied by Ernest Satow to Nagasaki, Kagoshima, Uwajima, and Hyogo to collect information and to make Britain's position clear. Not aware that the first effort at a council of daimyo had already failed, Parkes was concerned about a possible negative vote on the opening of Hyogo and the three other cities. He encouraged King to accept the recent invitations of the daimyo near Nagasaki and to secure information from daimyo and other Japanese who were considered favourable to Britain, among whom he now included Tosa. He also sought contacts with those on the West coast to ascertain which port on that coast, in place of Niigata, should be opened on 1 January 1868.[1] In all interviews with daimyo or their agents, Parkes told Satow: '1. To assure them the British Government would uphold the treaties in general and insist upon the opening of Hyogo in particular.' 2. To declare that in all 'internal disputes as to the possession of supreme authority (in Japan) Her Majesty's Government would afford no assistance of any kind to either party.' '3. To seek for information concerning the proposed meeting of the daimios, the adjustment of the Chōshū difficulty, the opening of Hyogo to foreign trade, the position of Shitotsubashi, and parties in general.'[2] This scouting expedition reached Nagasaki on 23 December 1866.

[1] F.O. 46/72, Parkes to King, Conf'l., Yokohama, 10 Dec. 1866, encl. in Parkes to Stanley, No. 208. Conf'l., Yedo, 15 Dec. 1866.

[2] F.O. 46/78, Satow's *Memorandum*, 17 Jan. 1867, encl. in Parkes to Stanley, No. 8. Conf'l., Yedo, 18 Jan. 1867. 'Shitotsubashi' was the generally used pronunciation in the region around Tokyo for 'Hitotsubashi' which was another name for Tokugawa Keiki.

Shortly afterwards, on 10 January 1867, Keiki reluctantly accepted investiture with the traditional powers of the Shogunate[1] and Satow interpreted Parkes's instructions liberally in conversations with leading daimyo and gathered facts for his chief. His *Memorandum* for Parkes and his memoirs indicate what he considered important for Britain and the Japanese to know about each other. He reported the following: the Mikado had ratified the treaties on condition that the opening of Hyogo and Osaka be prevented through *Bakufu* negotiation with the powers.[2] The council of daimyo at Kyoto was postponed. Its leaders refused to assemble in protest against their exclusion from any voice in the government by the powers with which Keiki had been invested as Shogun.[3] The close association of Satsuma and Chōshū officials in Kagoshima made it obvious—but not admitted—that the two great *han* would henceforth be united against the Shogunate. Although the Chōshū question was still unsettled, a Satsuma official stated that the Shogun had now lost the support of the daimyo and all chance of victory.[4] Keiki, Satsuma, and others originally opposed for different reasons to the opening of Hyogo, now recognized its inevitability. But Saigō Takamori, who in conjunction with Ōkubo Toshimichi was leading the anti-*Bakufu* movement in Satsuma, insisted that it must be opened for the benefit of all Japan, not for the exclusive interests of the *Bakufu*. Hyogo and Osaka, he said, were important financial centres for most of the daimyo, whose business affairs would be seriously disturbed if these cities were opened on the same plan as Yokohama. All questions concerning Hyogo, Saigō said, should be handled by a committee of five or six daimyo who could prevent the *Bakufu* from exercising exclusive and selfish control.[5]

In his conversations with the influential retired Daimyo of Uwajima, Date Muneki (Munenari) Iyo-no-kami, as well as

[1] Marius B. Jansen, *Sakamoto Ryōma and the Meiji Restoration* (Princeton, 1961), pp. 278–9. Tokugawa Yoshinobu (Keiki) was an able young man of thirty, fully aware of the hazards of his position and already working in a close, confidential relationship with Roches. Medzini, op. cit., pp. 213–14.

[2] Satow, *Diplomat*, p. 169.

[3] Ibid., p. 178. F.O. 46/78, Parkes to Stanley, No. 8, Conf'l., Yedo, 18 Jan. 1867.

[4] Satow MSS. *Diary*, i, opp. p. 37, 3 Jan. 1867; *Diplomat*, pp. 172–3.

[5] Ibid., pp. 183–4. F.O. 46/78, Parkes to Stanley, No. 8, Conf'l., Yedo, 18 Jan. 1867.

with Saigō, Satow learned not only of their mistrust of the growing intimacy of the French with the Shogunate, but of different points of view within the anti-*Bakufu* movement. He seized such opportunities to stress the difference between French and British policy in Japan and to push forward his own ideas. The French, he believed, thought it necessary to have 'a recognized head in the country and that as they had a treaty with the Shogun, and he had the greatest apparent power, they wished to exalt him and give him all the assistance in their power'. English policy was different. The British had a treaty with Japan, not the Shogun in particular. If they had, the treaty would be in abeyance, since the Shogun had died. Britain did not wish to interfere in Japan's internal affairs. The Japanese must settle their internal disputes among themselves.[1] With Saigō, Satow went further. Admitting British doubts about the supremacy of the *Bakufu* in the light of its request for the London Protocol, and its weakness at the time of the Richardson murder, as well as in relation to Chōshū, he said, his people would like to know 'who is the real head' of the nation. Britain did not care, however, whether Japan was governed by the Mikado, the *Bakufu*, or became a confederation. She would not intervene, whatever way Japan might choose to settle her disputes.[2]

Saigō saw little chance of a confederated government at that time but mentioned no other solution. In contrast Iyo-no-kami, a few days earlier, had said that he, Chōshū, and Satsuma were in agreement that Japan should become a confederated empire with the Mikado for its head. He admitted having read the translation of Satow's articles on British policy. And Satow confirmed his personal belief that this was the only solution for Japan's dilemma.[3]

Satow also learned before leaving Hyogo that the Shogun planned to invite the foreign representatives to Osaka when he would receive a letter from the French Emperor—an effort, it was said, to counteract Satow's proposal in *English Policy*, for

[1] Satow MSS. *Diary*, i, opp. p. 23, 8 Jan. 1867, written before Keiki was made Shogun; *Diplomat*, pp. 176, 178–9.
[2] F.O. 46/78, Satow's *Memorandum*, 17 Jan. 1867, re. conversation with Saigō at Hyogo, 11 Jan. 1867.
[3] Satow MSS. *Diary*, i, opp. p. 23, 8 Jan. 1867; *Diplomat*, p. 179.

a coalition of the leading clans, and to enhance the Shogun's prestige. Saigō requested that Sir Harry send for him and his colleague, Komatsu Tatewaki, at that time in fulfilment of Parkes's promise to see Shimazu and other daimyo when in Osaka.[1]

Before the Shogun's conference could be convened, however, the death of Emperor Kōmei on 3 February 1867 made way for a successor who was destined to lead the modernization of Japan. This was Kōmei's fifteen-year-old son, Mutsushito, who already gave promise of some liberality towards foreigners, having ventured to be vaccinated the previous year.[2] The traditional ceremonies connected with his accession, delayed until April the visit of the foreign envoys to Osaka.

Ostensibly Keiki had invited the Western representatives to his headquarters to present their credentials and to discuss important affairs. It was clear to Parkes and his colleagues, however, that such an audience would bolster the prestige of the Shogunate. They therefore refused to accept the invitation until assured by Keiki that Hyogo would be opened under all circumstances and that their audience should conform as far as possible to the precedents of European courts. Keiki not only agreed, saying his object was to promote the fulfilment of the treaties of which the opening of Hyogo was a part, but promised to overcome the Mikado's opposition to it, and to notify all daimyo publicly that they were free to trade there.

In the meantime Parkes dispatched Algernon Mitford and Ernest Satow by ship to Hyogo to inspect the arrangements for the reception of the foreign representatives and to gather more political information. Again Parkes ordered them to stress Britain's neutrality in Japan's internal conflict when talking with either party.[3] In Hyogo Mitford and Satow found the merchants anticipating a peaceful opening of the port and an increase of prosperity.[4] In Osaka, a city of 370,000 people, the government officials received the young emissaries with unprecedented courtesy and deference of manner, although the

---

[1] Satow, *Diplomat*, pp. 181, 184. F.O. 46/78, Satow's *Memorandum*, 17 Jan. 1867, encl. in Parkes's No. 8 of 1867. Ishii, *Meiji Ishin no Kokusaiteki Kankyō*, p. 463.

[2] F.O. 46/78, Parkes to Stanley, No. 25, Yedo, 14 Feb. 1867.

[3] Ibid., No. 1, Yedo, 16 Jan. 1867; No. 27, Yedo, 14 Feb. 1867.

[4] F.O. 46/78, Mitford to Parkes, *Argus* off Hyogo, 10 Feb. 1867, encl. in Parkes's No. 29, 28 Feb. 1867.

Governor of Osaka gave them little information.¹ Representatives of both the Shogun and the opposition daimyo visited them. They experienced some difficulty with Shibata Gōchū over the use of European court forms in arranging for the visit of the foreign representatives but began a lasting friendship with the Shogun's most loyal supporters, the Aizu *han*, whose anti-foreign sentiments were giving place to an interest in sending young men to Yokohama to study English and English commerce.²

Satsuma's representative, Komatsu Tatewaki, was more eager to talk with the Englishmen than were any members of the *Bakufu*. In well-guarded interviews he undertook, in company with Yoshii Kōsuke, another Satsuma officer, to undermine British support for the Shogunate. He not only disparaged Keiki's motives for inviting the foreign representatives to Osaka but cast doubt upon the opening of Hyogo and Osaka. Such an extension of foreign trade, he said, would counter the repressive policy of the *Bakufu* with respect to the Mikado and his Court by bringing them into contact with foreign ideas. Even then, he lamented that the potentially able young Emperor was denied all useful knowledge, including association with the liberal *kuge* who would like to see Hyogo opened up and who in many cases had been imprisoned.³

Komatsu went on to say that the principal daimyo regarded with 'distrust and jealousy' the schemes which aimed to increase the power of the Shogun. They would like to see 'the constitution of Japan restored to a single and intelligible monarchy'. Their dislike of the Shogun's government was neither 'revolutionary' nor 'captious'. The *Bakufu* had used its power badly, proving itself 'equally traitorous to Japan and to foreigners'.⁴ For example, the Convention of 1866 had not yet been published to the nation. And according to Satow, he stated that 'the object of Satsuma and other daimyo was not to overturn or destroy the *Bakufu* but only to prevent it from abusing its

¹ Ibid., Mitford to Parkes, Yedo, 26 Feb. 1867, encl. 2 in Parkes's No. 29 of 28 Feb. 1867. Satow, *Diplomat*, p. 187.

² Ibid., pp. 190–1; MSS. *Diary*, ii. 10–11, 17 Feb. 1867. F.O. 46/78, Mitford to Parkes, Yedo, 26 Feb. 1867, encl. 2 in Parkes's No. 29 of 28 Feb. 1867.

³ Ibid. Satow, MSS. *Diary*, ii. 9, 16 Feb. 1867; *Diplomat*, p. 189.

⁴ F.O. 46/78, Mitford to Parkes, Yedo, 26 Feb. 1867, encl. 2 in Parkes's No. 29 of 28 Feb. 1867.

power, that he hoped to see the Mikado restored to the ancient honour of his line because that would be a real benefit to the country'.[1]

At the end of this interview Komatsu raised a question which both Satow and Mitford recorded later in their memoirs.[2] In his original report to Parkes, Mitford wrote that Komatsu said:

> There is a question which I wish to put to you. When the Ministers come to Osaka my Prince, the Princes of Tosa, Echizen, Uwajima, and other powerful Daimios will be at Kioto. Now should your Minister say to himself that it is customary for Treaties to be made between Sovereigns only, and propose to make one with the Mikado, the Daimios will lend him all their support, and this will be the death blow to the assumed Sovereign power of the Tycoon. What do you say to that?

Mitford replied:

> This is not a matter which we four sitting over the fire can settle. Great Britain does not interfere in the internal feuds and factions of foreign nations. We wish to see Japan prosperous both for her own sake and for ours, but any thing that the Daimios wish to be done for their Country must be done by themselves.

> We do not want you to fight for us [said Komatsu], all we want is to raise the dignity of the Mikado, and thereby that of the nation. Let Sir Harry Parkes only say that he wishes to make a treaty with the Mikado and the Daimios to a man will carry it out.

Mitford repeated that the British never took part in the civil struggles of foreign countries; the daimyo must not look to Britain 'to help them in their intrigues'.[3]

It thus becomes evident that Satow's proposals had taken root among the opposition daimyo. Satsuma was testing out Britain's official support for the proposals and found it lacking. Satsuma was also aiming to confuse the British by denying the daimyo plan to overthrow the *Bakufu*. At the luncheon after the interview Inoue Bunda appeared in disguise to give Mitford an invitation from his daimyo for Parkes to visit Chōshū—a clear indication of the continuing secret co-operation between Satsuma and Chōshū.[4]

---

[1] Satow, MSS. *Diary*, ii. 9–10, 16 Feb. 1867.

[2] Ibid. *Diplomat*, p. 190, which follows closely his *Diary* of 16 Feb. 1867. Redesdale, op. cit. i. 388.

[3] F.O. 46/78, Mitford to Parkes, Yedo, 26 Feb. 1867, encl. 2 in Parkes's No. 29 of 28 Feb. 1867.

[4] Ibid. Satow, *Diplomat*, p. 190.

Sir Harry was not tempted to encourage Satsuma's proposal for a British treaty with the Mikado. He insisted that there was no question of the validity of the treaties as made with the Shogun and ratified by the Mikado and that no new constitutional law which the daimyo might seek to establish could invalidate these earlier obligations. Concurrently he was advising the Shogun's ministers that the recognition of the rights of all classes was necessary to the permanence of their power, that it was natural for the daimyo to want a voice in the affairs of the country, and that the treaties provided for their free participation in foreign trade. Parkes apparently believed at this time that the Shogun could conciliate the opposition daimyo by extending to them a place in the government and a share in foreign trade. Parkes restated his determination to remain neutral in Japan's internal struggle and rejoiced in Mitford's opportunity at Osaka to attest this by exchanging civilities with the *karō* of the Prince of Aizu, known for illiberality towards foreigners. He wrote to the Foreign Office that any changes in the Japanese government, such as the resumption of greater power by the Mikado, or the imposition of constitutional checks by a national council on the then almost absolute power of the Shogun, should emanate from the Japanese themselves and 'not be effected by foreign instrumentality'. He still doubted that the daimyo were prompted by higher motives than individual interest and saw few signs of their willingness to work together for 'intelligible government'.

Mitford's report led him to believe that both the Shogun's government and the opposition daimyo, for different reasons, were sincere in their desire for the visit of the foreign representatives to Osaka; that the people and the facilities of that area gave promise of a more extensive intercourse with a commercial and industrial population than afforded by Yokohama and Nagasaki; and that the proposed ceremonies for the audience would be suitable with a few amendments.[1]

At the same time Admiral King after his visits to the Princes of Chikuzen and Chōshū urged caution in accepting as real the sudden conversion of formerly anti-foreign daimyo to a desire for trade and intercourse with foreigners. Although the Prince

[1] F.O. 46/78, Parkes to Stanley, No. 29, Yedo, 28 Feb. 1867.

and people of Chikuzen (called Skuzen by King) had received King and the officers of the squadron with great kindness and the daimyo had assured King of his desire 'to cultivate the friendship and good will of Foreigners', the Admiral had felt at Mitajiri in Chōshū the lack of 'cordiality and good fellowship', and want of freedom from suspicion which he had enjoyed at Kagoshima, Uwajima, and Fukuoka. King and Parkes held to their belief, however, that the visits of H.M. ships to the ports of friendly daimyo would help to remove the distrust and suspicion felt by many Japanese towards foreigners.[1]

Negotiations at Osaka

The Shogun's audiences with the foreign representatives were scheduled for May. Léon Roches had preceded his colleagues to Osaka in March when in several interviews with Keiki, he arranged for French direction of the arsenal at Yokosuka and for the establishing at Yedo of a French military mission. He had also proposed drastic administrative and financial reforms in the Shogun's government, which included curtailing the powers of the *tozama han*. Upon his return to Yedo he reported favourably on the Shogun's intelligence and friendly manner and his assurance that Hyogo would be opened on time. He tried, unsuccessfully however, to dissuade Parkes on grounds of national disturbances from insisting on the opening of Yedo and Osaka.[2] Thus well informed by his staff as well as by Roches, and impressively accompanied by H.M. squadron, a detachment of fifty men from the British guard, and his mounted escort, Sir Harry arrived at Osaka on 18 April 1867. The Dutch representative went with him. The American and French soon followed.[3]

Parkes took the lead in the negotiations with the Shogun's ministers. Their obviously conciliatory intentions made it possible for the first time to reach agreement quickly. By 25 April Parkes was permitted to issue a public notification to

[1] F.O. 46/79, Parkes to Stanley, No. 34, Yedo, 1 Mar. 1867. Ad. I/6006, King to Adm., 30 Jan. and 1 Mar. 1867.

[2] F.O. 46/79, Parkes to Stanley, Nos. 53, 54, 55, 56, Yedo, 30 Mar. 1867. Beasley, *Documents*, p. 87. Medzini, op. cit., pp. 214–15.

[3] F.O. 46/80, Parkes to Stanley, No. 71, Yedo, 14 Apr. 1867. Ad. I/6006, Keppel (Vice-Adm. Sir Henry Keppel took command of the China Station in Apr. 1867) to Adm., 10 May 1867. Satow, *Diplomat*, p. 197.

British subjects that the two cities and two ports would be opened on 1 January 1868. Arrangements for the selection of foreign sites in these cities, the survey of the anchorages at Osaka and Hyogo, and the creation of a municipality in each place were further agreed upon. Although men from Satsuma, Awa, and Uwajima also came to see the British—a fact recorded by Satow but not by Parkes—Satow thought 'everything seemed to point to the triumph of the Shogun over his opponents'.[1]

Keiki had indeed taken a new line which purported to turn 'the treaties of friendship into a reality'. Before the foreign ministers arrived at Osaka he had already petitioned the Imperial Court to sanction the full observance of the treaties and permit the opening of Hyogo as promised, in consideration of the changed world conditions and for the sake of the national honour and prestige of Japan.[2] In its refusal, at the instigation of Satsuma's emissary, Ōkubo Toshimichi, the Court said that no decision could be taken about Hyogo without the opinion of the great daimyo being expressed in council.[3] Keiki's second appeal to the Court on 26 April met with no greater success and on 3 May the Court prohibited the opening of Hyogo until Imperial orders were issued.[4] Yet on 29 April Keiki had received Parkes in private audience when he promised to adhere strictly to the treaties and expressed his regret at the 'indefensible proceedings' of those parties who put difficulties in the way. He asked Parkes to tell Her Majesty the Queen that he (Keiki) would do all in his power to prevent a repetition of them. He now believed that eight- or nine-tenths of the voices in Japan were in favour of foreign intercourse. He thanked Parkes for the help given to Japanese students recently sent to England and for the naval instructors requested in 1866.[5] He asked advice regarding the class of ships best suited for Japan and admitted the order for an ironclad in France, which the *Rōjū* had denied.[6]

After the Shogun, an excellent horseman, had delighted in seeing the lance and sword drill by Parkes's mounted escort, a

[1] F.O. 46/80, Parkes to Stanley, No. 74, Osaka, 26 Apr. 1867. Satow, *Diplomat*, p. 198.
[2] Ibid. Beasley, *Documents*, pp. 308–10, Shogun Keiki to Imperial Court, 9 Apr. 1867.   [3] Ibid., pp. 307, 310.   [4] Ibid., pp. 310–11.
[5] See pp. 253–6, regarding naval instructors.
[6] F.O. 46/80, Parkes to Stanley, No. 78, Osaka, 4 May 1867.

formal dinner in European style followed. The Japanese Com-missioners for Foreign Affairs and pages of honour waited upon the British and the Shogun presided at the banquet. All were impressed with the 'great natural distinction and kindly courtesy' of the truly aristocratic Tokugawa Keiki. Parkes noted the contrast between his attitude and 'the cold reserve rendering mutual confidence unattainable, shown always by the Gorojiu'. He now believed that Keiki's administration would mark a favourable epoch in the conduct of Japan's internal affairs as well as an improvement in foreign relations. And the Foreign Office in London rejoiced in this prospect.[1]

The Shogun received the foreign diplomats and captains of the foreign squadrons a few days later—a stiff and formal occasion where Parkes's requests for arrangements were care-fully observed. Convinced that the Shogun's position did not warrant the title of sovereign, Parkes used the term *Highness* in his address, with no protest from the Japanese although the other representatives continued to call Keiki 'sovereign'.[2]

The British remained five weeks in Osaka, mingling freely with its friendly people and gathering information about the prospects for trade there and at its seaport, Hyogo, twelve to fourteen miles distant. Satow and Sidney Locock, secretary of the embassy, visited the Guild of the Foreign Goods Merchants and learned of the increasing demand of the Japanese people for foreign articles, of transport arrangements, and of their costs between the open ports and Osaka. They further dis-covered a supply of fair coal available for foreign steamers and tea and silk for their home-bound freight.[3]

The British also learned more about the anti-Togukawa movement. Parkes talked with three agents of Satsuma. Satow held conversations with Date Muneki, who had been summoned to the Council which began to assemble in Kyoto on 15 May.[4] Both sources assured the British that the daimyo would not

[1] F.O. 46/80, Parkes to Stanley, No. 78, Osaka, 4 May, 1867 and F.O. remark at end. Redesdale, op. cit. i. 393–4. The British at this time always used *Gorojiu* instead of *Rōjū* for the Shogun's most senior officials.

[2] F.O. 46/80, Parkes to Stanley, Nos. 79 and 81, Osaka, 6 May 1867. Redesdale, op. cit. i. 395–6. Satow, *Diplomat*, p. 200.

[3] Ibid., p. 202. P.P. H. of C. 1867–8, lxix, 237–50. Locock's *Report on the Ports of Osaka and Hyogo*, Yokohama, 10 June 1867.

[4] F.O. 46/80, *Memorandum* of Parkes's Interview, 13 May 1867; Satow's *Memorandum*, 17 May 1867.

oppose the opening of Hyogo because of anti-foreign prejudice
or to embarrass the Shogun. Date considered the opening of
the cities desirable in that it would enable all Japan to share in
intercourse with the West. He complained that the daimyo had
been kept in wilful ignorance by the Shogun, who had urged
that the ports should not be opened and who must apologize to
both the Mikado and the daimyo for this deception. He said
the main object of the daimyo was to reach an understanding
regarding the relative powers of the Mikado, Shogun, and
daimyo. Their desire was to achieve a voice in affairs and to
have the supremacy of the Mikado acknowledged. They admitted Keiki might have to relinquish some power or appear to
do so. Parkes says that he stressed with both the Shogun's
ministers and the daimyo the importance of peaceful deliberations and the need for unity for the good of the country. He was
delighted to learn again that both sides wished to settle the
matter themselves without foreign counsel.[1]

Satow was in touch with Saigō and knew that the obvious
rapprochement between the British and the Shogun was disturbing
the opposition party. He recognized that the opening of Hyogo
under the same conditions as Yokohama meant the defeat of
the programme of the daimyo and he 'hinted' to Saigō that
'the chance of a revolution was not to be lost'.[2] There is no
evidence, however, that Parkes knew or approved of such a far
from neutral insinuation.

More information came from William G. Aston, a student
interpreter, who reported on conditions in the Straits while
on a trip to Nagasaki abroad H.M.S. *Serpent*. He disproved the
report that Chōshū had been arming the south side of the
Straits and found the batteries on the north side substantially
the same as in December, except for the removal of a few less
useful guns. In all about twenty-five guns were in position.
Chōshū's territorial holdings had not changed and most of the
troops had been withdrawn. The practice of searching junks
passing through the Straits had been generally discontinued.
From Endō Kinsuke, who spoke in Kido Kōin's absence, Aston
learned that Chōshū counted on Satsuma's influencing Kyoto

[1] F.O. 46/80, Satow's *Memorandum*, 17 May 1967; Parkes to Stanley, No. 92,
Yedo, 12 June 1867.
[2] Satow, *Diplomat*, p. 200.

in Chōshū's favour and 'seemed to think that if no settlement of the Chōshū question were now made, Satsuma would give them (Chōshū) active assistance'.[1]

In reporting the accomplishments at Osaka after his return to Yedo, Parkes noted the increase of cordiality of the *Bakufu* officials, owing to orders from Osaka for the removal of restraints formerly imposed on intercourse between native authorities and foreign representatives. Members of the *Rōjū* now visited each of the foreign representatives and congratulated them on the new era in their relations with the Shogun. They asked for Parkes's help in getting more lights to the approaches at Hyogo and the Inland Sea and appointed officers to accompany a British captain for the exploration of the west coast to locate the most eligible port for foreign trade in that area.[2]

Decrees announcing the Court's sanction of the opening of Hyogo and of a lenient policy towards Chōshū simultaneously on 26 June facilitated such co-operation.[3] Furthermore, the Shogun appointed an envoy to reside in London and fulfilled his Osaka promise by announcing on 1 July that the new ports would be opened at the end of six months. The latter was an open reversal of the late Emperor's will, and a set-back for the plans of Satsuma and his followers who even dared protest against the Court's action—having insisted that Chōshū should be pardoned first in order to allay national unrest, but really to enable Chōshū to strengthen the opposition when the ports were opened. For Keiki it proved to be a Pyrrhic victory. It clearly intensified the struggle for power within Japan and strengthened the anti-*Bakufu* movement. Satow noted at the time how ready the armed classes were to use their weapons.[4]

British Observations in the Summer of 1867

While Tosa led a movement for the peaceful restoration of the Mikado's power and Satsuma plotted with Chōshū for the

[1] F.O. 46/80, *Memorandum* of W. G. Aston of cruise on H.M.S. *Serpent*, Nagasaki 3 June 1867, encl. in Parkes No. 101, 1867. The decision for a military coup staged by the two *han* to overthrow the *Bakufu* was not made, however, until 1 July 1867. Craig, op. cit., p. 341.   [2] F.O. 46/80, Parkes to Stanley, Yedo, 12 June 1867.

[3] Beasley, *Documents*, pp. 89–90, and 319 for text of Imperial Court's letter to the *Bakufu*, 26 June 1867.

[4] Ibid., pp. 319–20 for protest of four daimyo. Craig, op. cit., p. 338. F.O. 46/81, Parkes to Stanley, Nos. 115 and 131, Yedo, 27 June and 13 July 1867 and encls., *Memorandum* by Satow and Proclamation for opening of the ports.

military overthrow of the Shogunate, the search for a good
port to be opened on the west coast provided opportunities for
the British to travel in unknown parts of Japan to ascertain the
opinion of more daimyo, and to express the British view on the
internal conflict. Of ten or eleven places inspected by Commander Bullock of H.M.S. *Serpent* and W. G. Aston of the
legation staff, only two, Niigata and Nanao, afforded any
commercial promise.[1] Parkes himself set out in July to inspect
them, accompanied by Satow and Mitford. Niigata, primarily
a trading centre of forty thousand, lacked a good harbour but
had the advantage of extensive communications with the
interior. Its governor welcomed its opening to foreign trade and
proposed possible sites for foreigners. Nanao, in contrast, had an
excellent harbour, most tempting to Sir Harry, but the officers
of its daimyo, the Prince of Kaga, opposed its opening to
foreign trade under the direction of the Shogun. They were
willing to provide facilities for foreign ships but did not
wish *Bakufu* officials in their territory. With this clue to
Kaga's political sentiment, Parkes and his assistants left
for Osaka. While the minister went by sea via Nagasaki,
Satow and Mitford took the overland route through the
territories of Kaga and Echizen to evaluate their commercial
resources.[2]

There is no indication that Parkes or his Japanese-speaking
emissaries, Satow and Mitford, were kept abreast of the rival
schemes which were competing in Kyoto during the summer and
autumn of 1867 for the establishment of a new political order.
Neither were the British trying to influence what was taking
place there. But Parkes and his assistants were untiring in their
efforts to find out the political allegiance of individual daimyo
and clansmen. In discussions with the people of Kaga and
Echizen, Satow and Mitford found that many had read Satow's
articles on British policy but support for his proposals was by
no means general or complete. Contrary to Satow's ideas,
officials of the wealthy, isolated territory of Kaga seemed
basically content with the *status quo*. They did not seek to

[1] F.O. 46/81, Parkes to Stanley, No. 134, Yedo, 22 July 1867. Ad. I/6006,
Keppel to Adm., 16 Aug. 1867 and encl.
[2] F.O. 46/81, Parkes to Stanley, No. 138, Nagasaki, 17 Aug. 1867. Satow,
Diplomat, pp. 232–7; MSS. *Diary*, ii. 50, 9 Aug. 1867. Redesdale, op. cit. ii. 397–8.

overthrow the Shogunate but merely to limit its authority and they favoured the opening of Hyogo and Osaka.[1]

There was no friendliness for the foreigners in Echizen, nor in Ōmi, where *Bakufu* officials refuted Satow's ideas. And before reaching Osaka the young Englishmen narrowly escaped being murdered by a band of Tosa, Satsuma, and Chōshū men, who in spite of the professed pro-British leanings of their daimyo, represented a continuing widespread anti-foreign sentiment within the clans. Additional proof of such feeling awaited them at Osaka where Sir Harry Parkes arrived with word that brawling samurai, suspected of being Tosa men, had murdered two bluejackets of Her Majesty's sloop *Icarus* when they were asleep on the porch of a tea house in the native section of Nagasaki.[2]

Although both Keiki and the ex-daimyo of Tosa, Yamanouchi Toyoshige (Yōdō), promised to seek out the guilty, Parkes and Satow remained for a while in the Osaka area, pushing the apprehension of the criminals and gathering political insight.[3] Through Saigō they learned of a *Bakufu* plan to monopolize all the trade of Hyogo and Osaka by placing it in the hands of a guild of twenty designated Japanese merchants and then granting to France a monopoly of the guild's trade. Parkes's anger at this news and consequent protest to *Rōjū* Itakura Katsukiyo, Iga-no-kami, resulted in the issue of a new proclamation annulling the guild. But Satow and later Gotō Shōjirō of Tosa doubted that it would be carried out, given the diplomatic pressure which produced it.[4]

In another discussion with Saigō concerning French connivance with the *Bakufu* for quelling the opposition daimyo, Satow, apparently without official authorization, offered British assistance to Satsuma and Chōshū in their effort to restore the Imperial power. He proposed it as a possible deterrent to action by Napoleon III, again stating that the British aimed at a

[1] Satow, MSS. *Diary*, ii. 49–50, 54–55, 8 and 9 Aug. 1867; *Diplomat*, pp. 243–4. F.O. 46/81, Mitford's Report, Osaka, 22 Aug. 1867, encl. No. 1 in Parkes No. 147, 26 Aug. 1867.

[2] Satow, *Diplomat*, pp. 245–51. Redesdale, op. cit. ii. 405–7. Ad. I/6006, Keppel to Adm., 18 Aug. 1867.

[3] F.O. 46/81, Parkes to Stanley, Nos. 152 and 154, Yedo, 11 Sept. 1867.

[4] Ibid., No. 156, Yedo, 11 Sept. 1867. Satow, MSS. *Diary*, ii. 66, 25 Aug. 1867; *Diplomat*, pp. 256, 267. Jansen, op. cit., p. 320 mentions the deal with the French in accordance with Saigō's own report but the British sources omit it.

single sovereign for Japan 'with the feudal lords under him so that Japan's national polity would be similar to that of Britain'. But Saigō was equally opposed to both British and French intervention in Japan's affairs. He made it clear to Satow that Japan would make every effort to reform her political structure without foreign assistance.[1]

Although Satsuma men delighted in arousing the British against the French they were not averse to trafficking with the French themselves. They not only exhibited their products as an independent country at the Paris International Exhibition in 1867, but engaged through Count de Montblanc about twenty Frenchmen as naval and military officers and engineers for the service of Satsuma. Some of these had arrived in Nagasaki by October 1867, a fact which made Satow question Satsuma's generally understood partiality for British views on Japan's domestic struggle. Had this engagement of Frenchmen indicated a change of policy? Niiro Nakazo (Gyōbu) assured him that the whole province was loyal to its early decision to adopt English methods, and the Frenchmen would probably have to be sent back.[2]

En route to Tosa Parkes and his party visited Satow's friend, the Prince of Awa, at Tokushima. Being invited to dine with the great daimyo within his castle signified more friendship and 'unrestricted intercourse' than any other daimyo had yet expressed. The Prince was much in favour of opening Hyogo as a way of stimulating industry among the people and had his troops drilled according to the English system. Parkes attributed his good feeling towards the British to 'the favourable impression Satow had gradually created'.[3] This may mean that Parkes now knew about Satow's pamphlet on *English Policy*, but he makes no reference to it.

In Tosa Parkes and Satow talked politics with Gotō Shōjirō, whose intelligence and force of character impressed them both. He expressed interest in the English parliament, constitution,

---

[1] Jansen, op. cit., pp. 320–1. Satow, *Diplomat*, pp. 253–5 gives a slightly different account of this conversation.

[2] F.O. 46/82, Parkes to Stanley, No. 172, Conf'l., Yedo, 1 Oct. 1867. According to Capt. Bullock, H.M.S. *Serpent*, the Frenchmen were paid a year's salary and sent home; 46/83, Parkes to Stanley, No. 221, Conf'l., Yedo, 15 Dec. 1867. Satow, *Diplomat*, pp. 277–8.

[3] F.O. 46/81, Parkes to Stanley, No. 163, Yedo, 15 Sept. 1867. Satow, MSS. *Diary*, ii. 69–72, and opposite p. 31 Aug. and 1 Sept. 1867.

and electoral system, making it evident that he, the influential ex-daimyo Yamanouchi, and Saigō were all considering the British system. After this on 6 September Parkes returned to Yedo.[1]

Satow went on to Nagasaki with orders to follow up the investigations by the *Bakufu* and Tosa in the *Icarus* affair. At Shimonoseki he saw Inoue Bunda, who was completely silent on political developments. The absence of guns and warships, and signs of prosperity gave nothing to indicate that Chōshū was still at war with the *Bakufu*. In Nagasaki Satow dined with Itō Shunsuke (Hirobumi) and Kido Jun'ichirō (Kōin) at Consul Flowers's house. Perhaps in mistrust of Satow and meaning to mislead him, these Chōshū men insisted upon the honesty of their prince in all his doings and again denied he had ever considered the overthrow of the Tokugawa government. Here Satow recognized deliberate deception as the British had long had 'indisputable evidence that the abolition of the Shogunate was the cardinal point in the policy pursued by the western daimios acting in concert'.[2] Niiro Gyōbu of Satsuma also pretended to believe that civil war would not break out. He merely admitted its possibility when at that moment three thousand troops from Kagoshima were on their way to Osaka and thence (under Saigō's command) to Kyoto to be used against the Shogunate.[3] Two days later in conversation with Joseph Heco, Satow learned of a document said to be signed by Satsuma, Tosa, Geishiu,[4] Bizen, and Awa which had been presented to Keiki requiring him to resign his office and allow the government to be reconstituted.[5]

Satow made additional use of his visit at Nagasaki to meet the samurai of various southern clans. He found the Higo leaders professing a great devotion to England and boasting of purchasing British rifles and warships. He returned to Yedo on 12 October accompanied by Endō Kinsuke of Chōshū who had been secretly in England in 1863 and now masqueraded as Satow's pupil, alias Yamamoto Jinsuke. He had some

[1] Satow, *Diplomat*, pp. 267–8, 270.

[2] Ibid., pp. 271–2; MSS. *Diary*, i, 1, Parkes to Satow, 6 Sept. 1867; ii. 79, 12 Sept. 1867. Kido was also known as Katsura Kogorō.

[3] Jansen, op. cit., p. 323.

[4] Geishiu represented Chōshū.

[5] Satow, *Diplomat*, p. 272; MSS. *Diary*, ii. 80, 14 Sept. 1867.

evidence that the suspected Tosa men had not murdered the British seamen, but no clue to other culprits.[1]

Satow's reports and the failure of all parties at this time to round up the murderers of the British sailors made Parkes most uncertain of the Japanese political situation and of what policy he should pursue. Although he had displayed his most arrogant and offensive manners in demanding from the Japanese the discovery and punishment of the criminals, he admitted to London that it was difficult to determine what pressure to impose on 'this quasi Government which will stimulate its energies without impairing its stability or to ascertain how far repeated failures of justice are attributable to supineness and bad faith or to want of power and authority'. As late as 30 October he insisted upon the Shogun's sending a special commission to Nagasaki to remain there until the murderers were located and hoped thereby to strengthen *Bakufu* authority in that area.[2] Obviously he was not contemplating its immediate overthrow.

By this time also the *Bakufu* had met Parkes's wishes liberally in preparing for the coming foreign settlements at Hyogo and Osaka despite disquieting rumours caused by ill-disposed factions.[3] Regulations for foreign residents in Yedo after 1 January 1868 were agreed upon.[4] The ratification of Japan's recent treaties with Belgium, Denmark, and Italy presaged increasing foreign contacts and widening foreign commerce as the time for the opening of the new ports drew near.[5] And the question of a trading centre on the west coast was soon settled by the decision of the powers to accept Niigata, with a supplementary port opposite on the island of Sado.[6]

[1] Idem., *Diplomat*, pp. 272–5, 279–80.

[2] F.O. 46/82, Parkes to Stanley, No. 178, Yedo, 30 Oct. 1867. It was not until the end of 1868 under a new government, however, that the murderers were proved to have been Chikuzen men and reparations which included the sentencing of their daimyo to seclusion and the payment of indemnities to the sailors' families, were made. Dickins, op. cit. ii. 76. Jansen, op. cit., pp. 307–8, F.O. 46/98, Parkes to Stanley, Nos. 297 and 313, Yokohama, 2 and 13 Dec. 1868.

[3] F.O. 46/81, Parkes to Stanley, No. 159, Yedo, 14 Sept. 1867.

[4] F.O. 46/82, Parkes to Stanley, No. 182, Yedo, 30 Oct. 1867.

[5] F.O. 46/81, Parkes to Stanley, No. 153, Yedo, 11 Sept. 1867; 46/82, same to same, Nos. 174 and 175, Yedo, 14 and 15 Oct. 1867.

[6] Ibid., Parkes to F.O., Private, Yedo, 14 Nov. 1867.

The Resignation of Keiki

Parkes had considered doubtful the report circulated in mid-October that the Shogun had abdicated.[1] He apparently overlooked Satow's information about the document asking Keiki to resign. This *Memorial*, the work of moderate reformers led by Tosa men, was presented on 28 October to the *Rōjū* Itakura Katsukiyo and to the Court. Yamanouchi Yōdō had planned it with Gotō Shōjirō and had written introductory and supplementary statements. Gotō, its spokesman, stressed the need for prompt action as war against the Tokugawa was an imminent alternative. The *Memorial* attributed Japan's internal friction and difficulties with foreigners to the dual authority of her administration and asked that the governing powers of the Shogunate be restored to the Emperor and a foundation thus be laid 'on which Japan may take her stand as the equal of all other countries'. Brief suggestions for a new constitution followed. These invested authority to govern the whole country in the Imperial Court and provided for all legislation to originate with a bicameral deliberative council in Kyoto. Here lords and nobles were to compose the upper house; rear vassals and even commoners, the lower. A pro-foreign policy was also advocated.[2]

Emphasis on Japan's need for a basic revision of her government was equally a part of the Imperial decree which had authorized military action against the *Bakufu*, a document instigated by Satsuma and written in early November 1867 by Tamamatsu Misao at the order of Iwakura Tomomi, now a reinstated leader of the anti-Shogun faction at the Imperial Court.[3] The young Emperor may or may not have seen or approved this punitive plan of the Satsuma–Chōshū leaders nor an accompanying decree which at the same time restored the Chōshū daimyo to favour, but a leak to the *Bakufu* of their existence and word to Keiki relayed from Gotō that war was imminent hastened Keiki's answer to Tosa's *Memorial*.[4]

---

[1] F.O. 46/82, Parkes to Stanley, No. 177, Yedo, 15 Oct. 1867.

[2] Jansen, op. cit., pp. 315–17, 325–6. Murdoch, op. cit. iii. 768–9, gives 27 Oct. for date of presentation.

[3] Iwakura Tomomi had been sentenced to five years' confinement because of his activities in 1862 in promoting the marriage of the Emperor's sister with the Shogun, an effort to unite the Court and the *Bakufu*.

[4] Jansen, op. cit., pp. 329–30.

On 8 November 1867 Tokugawa Keiki surrendered his administrative authority to the Imperial Court before an assembly of daimyo and important *han* officials summoned to his Nijō Castle in Kyoto. He took this step, he said, for the sake of national security and internal harmony and in the interest of getting the opinion of the country. All present signed a note-book indicating their approval. On 9 November Keiki's decision was presented to the Court just as the Imperial sanction of war on the *Bakufu* and its supporters, the Aizu and Kuwana *han* reached Satsuma and Chōshū. Thousands of troops were soon *en route* from Kagoshima and Chōshū to Kyoto and vicinity.[1]

The Court accepted Keiki's resignation of administrative power the next day and gave him instructions for the future. He was expected to protect and defend the Empire, to deal with foreign affairs in conference with the daimyo, and to communi-cate with the Court on routine business through the established channels. All major decisions were to be postponed until the conference of daimyo could be held. Aware that he was given responsibility without authority, Keiki resigned his position as Shogun on 19 November. Even this did not satisfy Saigō and his war-thirsty conspirators. The Tokugawa lands, revenues, and private property could still make Keiki dominant in any conference of daimyo. These too must be surrendered, they said, through another Imperial decree.[2]

The first official report of these events reached the British on 14 November. The *Rōjū*, Ogasawara Nagamichi, told Parkes confidentially of changes in Japan's government. Daimyo, he said, would be admitted and consulted on all important ques-tions. The Shogun's right to decision would continue but be subject to confirmation by the Mikado. The details were not worked out. When he knew more about them, he might need information and advice on some points from Parkes. 'The resemblance between Japan and England had suggested the possibility of some of their institutions being assimilated to ours.' Parkes replied he had always advocated this. It would increase both the stability of the government and the prosperity of the country.[3]

---

[1] Ibid., pp. 330–1. Murdoch, op. cit. iii. 769–70.   [2] Ibid., pp. 770–1.
[3] F.O. 46/82, Parkes to Stanley, No. 192, Conf'l., Yedo, 14 Nov. 1867.

Two days later a Commissioner of Foreign Affairs came to Parkes in the dead of night to say that the Shogun had voluntarily restored the supreme direction of affairs to the Mikado. A general council of daimyo would be convened to assist the Mikado and ministers with the Shogun in the leading position to work out details of a new constitution. Keiki believed reforms could thus be effected without conflict. On the eighteenth Ogasawara read to Parkes a review of the Shogunate's relations with foreign powers from the beginning and recounted the opposition of the daimyo to the foreign treaties and thence to the Shogunate. Keiki thought jealousy had motivated the daimyo and that the restoration of the government to the Mikado would help to unite the country. He hoped the treaties would be faithfully carried out and the new ports opened as agreed. The foreign representatives all received copies of the manifesto of the Shogun to the Mikado and of two Imperial decrees: (1) accepting the Shogun's resignation and (2) announcing that in the future all important affairs of state, including foreign relations, would be in the hands of a general council with officers appointed by the Imperial Court to handle at once the ordinary business with the daimyo, while an assembly of daimyo was ordered at Kyoto.[1]

A few days later came reports of troops of the Shogun and forces of the daimyo assembling in Kyoto. Ogasawara made light of this, saying affairs were progressing satisfactorily. The Mikado instructed the Shogun to continue his usual course until a parliament of daimyo could meet. The Tosa *Memorial* with its scheme for constitutional reform and emphasis on good faith towards foreigners was given to Parkes. He thought this to be the first definite statement of the goals of the liberal party and sent it on to London with notes of approval. Both the domestic and foreign position of the ruling group seemed favourable. Parkes applauded the Shogun for seeing the necessity of more comprehensive institutions and his willingness to take a leading share in giving the country a new constitution.[2]

---

[1] F.O. 46/82, Parkes to Stanley, No. 194, Yedo, 27 Nov. 1867. Satow, *Diplomat*, p. 282. W. W. McLaren, *Japanese Government Documents* (Tokyo, 1914), in T.A.S.J. xlii, Pt. I, pp. 1–2, for texts of Shogun's resignations, and Mikado's acceptance. The dates given in McLaren differ from those of Murdoch and Jansen.

[2] F.O. 46/82, Parkes to Stanley, No. 194, Yedo, 27 Nov. 1867.

With great optimism he wrote to Consul Flowers:

I think there is a prospect of the Japanese working out a most important change in their constitution, amounting to an entire revolution in the organization of the State, in a peaceable manner. It will be very creditable to them if they do so. The Tycoon has set an admirable example of a sacrifice of power, and the daimios will have to follow suit. We may in that case hope to see a strong central Government having jurisdiction over the whole of Japan, and which can control the daimios as well as concede them their just rights.[1]

On 28 November he sent a telegram to the Foreign Office summarizing what had occurred.[2] In a letter he asked for a letter of credence to the Mikado, admitting that he had never presented his letter of 28 March 1865 to the Shogun.[3] At the same time he and his colleagues agreed to the *Bakufu* request to defer the opening of Yedo and Niigata until 1 April 1868.[4]

The *Japan Times' Overland Mail* of 28 November reported the resignation of Keiki and the Mikado's instructions to him. The journal took great satisfaction in this event. It had advocated the change for two years and had frequently detailed its advantages. The air was rife with rumours even including the murder of the Shogun. This journal believed that 'the party opposed to the opening of only the Shogun's ports' was supreme in the country but that it was yet to be decided whether 'the old power of the Mikado should be re-established and the treaties with foreigners observed in their true spirit—or whether a futile suicidal effort shall be made to drive us altogether from Japan'.[5]

Parkes soon learned from Ogasawara and the *Bakufu* ministers who returned from Kyoto that the Mikado had directed Keiki to keep his title and handle foreign affairs until the assembly at Kyoto. Two hundred and sixty daimyo had been summoned to meet in January to deliberate on all questions and send their views to the Mikado. Keiki was expected to take part in the council but all decisions appeared to be left to the Mikado. Keiki was determined not to let his personal affairs hinder what

---

[1] Dickins, op. cit. ii. 77–78, Parkes to Flowers, Yedo, 27 Nov. 1867.
[2] F.O. 46/82, Parkes to Stanley, No. 196, Yedo, 28 Nov. 1867.
[3] Ibid., No. 197, Yedo, 28 Nov. 1867.
[4] Ibid., No. 195, Yedo, 28 Nov. 1867. Copy of the official *Notification* was enclosed in Parkes's No. 210 of 1867.
[5] 28 Nov. 1867 issue of this paper at Harvard.

was best for the country. Ogasawara assured Parkes all would
go well. There was no cause for anxiety. 'What we most earnestly desire and pray for', he said, 'is that the Governments of
the Treaty Powers will with their usual friendliness give us
their assistance in our endeavours to unite our nation'.[1]

Men from Tosa and Satsuma also sought to communicate
with the British.[2] Satow's and Mitford's trip to Osaka and
Hyogo to find quarters for the legation and observe final
arrangements for the opening of both cities, gave them further
knowledge of political developments. On 14 December a
Satsuma representative, Yoshii Kōsuke, predicted the approach
of hostilities. The coalition made up of Satsuma, Tosa, Uwajima, Chōshū, and Geishu (Aki) probably supported by Higo
and Arima was determined to gain their points by extreme
measures. Ten thousand *Bakufu* troops at Kyoto were confronting about half that number from Satsuma and Tosa—then
divided between Kyoto and Osaka.[3]

Opinions differed even among the western daimyo in mid-
December regarding the inevitability of war. The plans of
Ōkubo, Saigō, and Iwakura for a military coup remained a
secret from Gotō and others until 27 December. Hence Gotō
could tell Mitford on 15 December that he was not confident
that the necessary changes in the government could be made
without a struggle while Komatsu thought they could. Gotō
cast some suspicion on the 'apparently patriotic and disinterested conduct' of Keiki perhaps in an effort to unite the
wavering elements in Tosa. He continued to argue for a parliament consisting of an upper and lower house to meet the needs
of Japan and leaned towards the English form. From Saigō and
Iwashita Masahiro, another Satsuma samurai, Satow and Mitford learned little except that Satsuma had bought the *Kiang Su*
of the Anglo-Chinese flotilla—obviously a formidable adversary to the Shogun's navy. Discussions of the *Icarus* affair and
penalties for the murder of foreigners made Mitford conclude
that foreigners could 'not be too much upon their guard in the
present state of the country'.

---

[1] F.O. 46/83, Parkes to Stanley, Nos. 205, 213, 218, Yedo, 5, 14, 15 Dec. 1867
and Ogasawara's Report encl. in No. 213 of 14 Dec. 1867.

[2] Satow, *Diplomat*, pp. 283–4.

[3] Ibid., pp. 286–7; MSS. *Diary*, ii. 98, 16 Dec. 1867. F.O. 46/83, Mitford's
Report to Parkes Osaka, 22 Dec. 1867, encl. in Parkes No. 225, 29 Dec. 1867.

Perhaps the most significant facts in Mitford's report were that no date had been fixed for the convocation of daimyo in Kyoto, and that the majority could not be expected in the capital at that time. The confederated daimyo who were already there or shortly expected might therefore resist further delay and act independently, forcing the results of their deliberations upon any princes who might object to their decision. In either case civil war would result.

In conclusion, Mitford assured Parkes:

Mr. Satow and myself in our dealings with the Japanese of both parties, have faithfully obeyed your instructions as to maintaining a strict political neutrality. We have shown no more than the natural interest of spectators in the contest; and I believe that our hearers will have drawn from what we have said but one inference—that England is the very good friend of Japan under whatsoever form of government she may be ruled so long as Treaty Engagements are fulfilled and the rights of foreigners respected.[1]

Itō Shunsuke (Hirobumi) forecast war almost immediately in order to deprive the Shogun of his vast domain. He dared to ask whether Sir Harry's arrival and the opening of Hyogo and Osaka could be postponed as foreign residents would be endangered by the conflict. Without authority, Satow said 'No', and with even less caution continued, that 'as long as the insurgent forces did not attack the residences of foreigners, they might do as they liked with the Tycoon, but if they interfered with us they would have a couple of English regiments and all the foreign men-of-war to fight against as well as the Tokugawa troops'. This was scarcely the statement of a neutral. Itō promised to tell Satow in advance when the time for action became imminent.[2] Obviously by now the British knew what to expect but Parkes's letter to the Foreign Office indicated none of this other than to report the landing of fifteen hundred Chōshū men between Osaka and Kyoto on 23 December and the arrival of the Prince of Chōshū escorted by five or six vessels from Satsuma.[3] Parkes threw his weight against the *Bakufu* as their position weakened, however, by pressing for the round-up of the murderers of the *Icarus* sailors and threatening to send a couple of regiments into Osaka unless

[1] Ibid.   [2] Satow, *Diplomat*, pp. 291–2.
[3] Ibid. p. 292. F.O. 46/83, Parkes to Stanley, No. 225, Osaka, 29 Dec. 1867.

the *Bakufu* removed all its troops from the city because of the danger of their collision with foreigners.[1]

Lord Stanley's Policy

In London, of course, Victoria's government was two months behind in its knowledge of events in Japan. Lord Stanley was holding fast to his policy of neutrality, but having unlimited faith in Parkes, approved what Parkes reported he was doing.[2] There seems to be no evidence that the Foreign Office was told of Satow's encouragement of the anti-*Bakufu* movement, nor of the continuing sales of British guns and ships to Satsuma.[3] Parkes's clear statement of the collective action of the daimyo of Satsuma, Tosa, Echizen, and Uwajima against the efforts of Keiki to resume absolute power and the consequent probability of a prolonged civil conflict, however, led Stanley to weaken his stand.[4] He wrote:

. . . while it is desirable that you should continue to abstain from taking any decided part in the internal affairs of Japan you may without doing so, promote as far as you can any system which, by securing to the Daimios a fair share in the commerce of Japan, will enlist their sympathies in behalf of foreign nations and so promote the development of trade.[5]

The Japanese minister appointed by the *Bakufu* had recently arrived in England. He tried to explain to Stanley the policy of the Shogun to maintain friendly relations with the powers and to fulfil his engagements regarding the opening of the ports, the consequent problems created by the daimyo, the form of government peculiar to Japan, and Japan's claim to the Ryūkyū Islands. He sought the support of foreign representatives in Japan for the Shogun's liberal policy which would be advantageous to both the powers and Japan. He also sought to

[1] Satow, MSS. *Diary*, ii. 104, 30 Dec. 1867. The foreign representatives made similar requests to Satsuma and Chōshū. Satsuma complied but Chōshū troops, unable to enter Kyoto until granted the right by the Court, remained in quarters said to have been assigned by the *Bakufu*. F.O. 46/91, Satow's *Memorandum*, 31 Dec. 1867, encl. in Parkes No. 5, 5 Jan. 1868.

[2] See the entire series F.O. 262, F.O. to Parkes, 1865–7.

[3] J.M. MSS. (Japan Letter Book ii), Shanghai Office to Glover & Co. at Nagasaki, 24 Aug., 10 Sept., 14 and 26 Oct., and 18 Dec. 1867; Shanghai Office to Ryde Holme, 1 Nov. 1867 for contracts.

[4] F.O. 46/82, Parkes to Stanley, No. 166, 1 Oct. 1867.

[5] F.O. 262/124, Stanley to Parkes, No. 179, 28 Nov. 1867.

establish 'Majesty' as the only title acceptable for the Shogun, and considered Britain's effort to alter this mistaken but painful. Stanley replied that the British reciprocated the friendly feelings of the Shogun and understood his difficulties. They would 'give the Tycoon such support as they could properly give to the legitimate authority. But no foreign nation could interfere between daimyo and the Tycoon. Neither would Britain take part in intrigues against the Tycoon'.[1]

Britain's support of the now friendly Shogun had already been demonstrated by her agreement in conjunction with the other powers to postpone the payment of the remaining portion of the Shimonoseki indemnity for two years at the request of the *Bakufu*. The outstanding sum of approximately $1,500,000 was to be repaid with interest by May 1869.[2] Furthermore the Shogun's brother, Prince Mimbutaiko, had been royally entertained in England and shown the naval and military institutions, schools, and colleges in December while the plot to overthrow the *Bakufu* took final form in Japan.[3]

The Opening of Osaka and Hyogo

The political upheaval caused no apparent interruption in the preparations for the opening of Osaka and Hyogo. Trade continued as usual. Reports of the danger in Osaka were proved false.[4] Both cities were in a holiday mood, celebrating in advance the coming of the foreigners with seven days of feasting, merrymaking, and processions. They anticipated a new prosperity.[5] Parkes, however, alarmed by the assembling

---

[1] F.O. 262/124, Stanley to Parkes, No. 184, 14 Dec. 1867.

[2] Ibid., Nos. 141, 156, and 159, 3 Sept. 1867, 10 and 18 Oct. 1867. The Foreign Representatives made no claim for the Indemnity during the political and military disturbances of 1868 and 1869. They agreed to the proposal of the Imperial government to defer all payments and to ask no interest until May 1872 when the Japanese would raise the duty on silk and tea—a date which was extended until 1874. The Japanese paid the last three instalments between Apr. and Aug. 1874 and the foreign powers claimed no interest; 262/162, Clarendon to Parkes, No. 119, 7 Oct. 1869 and encls.; 46/181, Parkes to Derby, No. 152, 18 Aug. 1874; 262/254, Derby to Parkes, No. 150, 21 Dec. 1874.

[3] Windsor MS. (B 24), Stanley to Victoria, 26 Nov. 1867. F.O. 262/124, F.O. to Parkes, No. 189, 26 Dec. 1867 and encl.

[4] Ad. I/6006, Mitford's *Memorandum* Osaka, 7 Dec. 1867, encl. in Keppel to Adm., 19 Dec. 1867.

[5] Redesdale, op. cit. ii. 413–14. F.O. 46/83, Parkes to Stanley, No. 218, Yedo, 15 Dec. 1867.

of armed clansmen in Osaka and Hyogo and the possibility of their unruly behaviour towards foreigners, determined on a show of Western force. He was not convinced that the 'parties coming now into power' would honour the treaties. He knew some daimyo still opposed the extension of foreign intercourse. Were these troops to be used against the Shogun or against foreigners? He and the other foreign representatives therefore requested their respective naval commanders to assemble at Hyogo about mid-December as many ships of war as possible. The British minister was determined that 'all classes in Japan should be satisfied of the ability of Her Majesty's Government to ensure respect for the engagement of the treaties to which this country is pledged'. Admiral Keppel complied. He too, hoped that the assembling of so formidable a force 'would insure respect for our treaty rights, and save the necessity for enforcing the same'.[1] Such was the British faith. Sir Harry arrived with his staff at Osaka on 24 December.[2]

Hyogo and Osaka were opened peaceably to foreign trade on New Year's Day 1868. Twelve British, one French, and six American warships assembled for the event. At Parkes's request all fired a royal salute at noon at Hyogo in honour of the occasion. This was returned by the Japanese men-of-war.[3]

Days filled with rumours of great political changes in Kyoto followed. Keppel wrote that it was difficult to tell which party was responsible for the government of Japan. A rupture between the contenders seemed imminent.[4] Actually the seven-hundred-year-old Shogunate had come to its end.

[1] Ad. R.O. (Japan 49), Keppel to Adm., 4 Dec. 1867 and encl., Parkes to Keppel, Yedo, 22 Nov. 1867.

[2] Satow, *Diplomat*, p. 292.

[3] Ad. I/6052, Keppel to Adm., 6 Jan. 1868. F.O. 46/91, telegram, Parkes to Stanley, No. 4, Osaka, 5 Jan. 1868.

[4] Ad. I/6052, Keppel to Adm., 6 Jan. 1868; Parkes to Keppel, 5 Jan. 1868. F.O. 46/91, Parkes to Stanley, No. 5, 5 Jan. 1868.

IX

BRITISH POLICY DURING THE RESTORATION, CIVIL WAR, AND NORTHERN REBELLION, 1868–1869

The Overthrow of the Shogun

ON 3 January 1868 a coup sanctioned by the Emperor replaced the Tokugawa guards at his palace gates with troops of Tosa, Satsuma, Aki,[1] Echizen, and Owari. A small group of nobles, daimyo, and councillors destined for office in the new government were admitted to an audience with the young Mikado. To them he read his great decree abolishing the Shogunate and restoring supreme power to the Imperial Throne. The offices of the Shogun's intermediaries with the Court were also abolished and a new provisional government was proclaimed. Gotō of Tosa, Saigō and Ōkubo of Satsuma, and Iwakura Tomomi, the most brilliant member of the Court, were entrenched in power.[2] An Imperial edict had pardoned Chōshū's daimyo in November and on 2 January 1868 Court orders permitted his well-trained troops to enter Kyoto.[3] Although Keiki is said to have been told of this plot a few days in advance, he made no effort to stave off the crisis.[4] After a conference with Aizu and other *fudai* daimyo, the ex-Shogun and all his enraged followers retired hurriedly to Osaka on 6 January 1868 without Imperial permission.[5]

Two days later Parkes forced an interview with Keiki in company with Roches, having refused to let the French minister take precedence over him.[6] Keiki said that he resigned his governing powers to facilitate necessary governmental

[1] Hiroshima or Geishū are sometimes used instead of Aki. All were parts of the territory of the daimyo family of Mōri and represented Chōshū in the anti-*Bakufu* policy.　　　　　　　　　　　　　[2] Murdoch, op. cit. iii. 772–3.
[3] Craig, op. cit., pp. 345–6.　　　　　　　[4] Murdoch, op. cit. iii. 772.
[5] Black, op. cit. ii. 111–12. McLaren, op. cit., pp. 3–4 for Keiki's protest and explanation to the Court on 7 Jan. 1868.
[6] Satow, *Diplomat*, p. 301.

reforms by peaceful means. When accepting his resignation, the Mikado had ordered him to resume both civil and military powers until the will of the nation was known. He resented therefore the hasty action of the five clans at Kyoto on 3 January without waiting for the decisions of the already assembling daimyo. He told of the high-handed demand of the five daimyo that he, Keiki, resign his office of Shogun, his rank of *Naidaijin*, and give up two million *koku* of revenue. When he saw these five daimyo had broken faith, he withdrew his troops to Osaka to avoid the use of force near the palace of the Mikado. He was convinced that the Mikado's decree which commanded him to confer with three daimyo in Kyoto on foreign questions of importance was forged. As evidence, he had in writing that the Mikado, when asked the names of the daimyo, replied he did not know. Hence he was not bound to obey the decree. He knew there was dissension among the daimyo. Some who had come to attend the assembly had already gone home. As from the beginning his purpose was to abide by the judgements of the assembly of daimyo. But this assembly 'must be a genuine one and must not consist of Satsuma and a few of his adherents only'. He did not know whether these daimyo would attack him or not. Neither could he say what or where was the government of Japan at that moment. He knew the young Mikado, the undoubted sovereign of Japan, was at the mercy of the Satsuma faction, who might issue decrees in his name, but which did not come from him. He intended to protest to the Mikado that such a government was in fact no government. He did not pledge himself to abide by the answer he would receive.[1]

On 10 January all the foreign representatives assembled for an interview with Keiki at his castle. They declared they would remain neutral in the current dissensions regarding Japan's form of government; they hoped that a stable national government would be formed which would guarantee the fulfilment of Japan's international engagements; and they asked to be officially and promptly informed of the government with which

[1] Gaimushō Chōsakyoku (Foreign Ministry Research Bureau), *Dai Nihon Gaikō Monjo* (Japanese Foreign Office Archives), 73 vols. (Tokyo, 1936–63), (hereafter cited as *D.N.G.M.*), i. 159–65, Doc. 65, Memorandum of Meeting of Parkes and Roches with Keiki, 8 Jan. 1868. F.O. 46/91, Locock's *Memorandum* on same meeting, encl. in Parkes to Stanley, No. 9, Osaka, 10 Jan. 1868.

they must deal in their official capacity.[1] Keiki again explained the terms and motive of his resignation and stressed his continuing responsibility to carry out all the engagements made with foreign powers until Japan's form of government should be settled by the decision of a general council. He asked that the powers not concern themselves with Japan's national affairs nor hinder the course of 'just principles'. He hoped for the continuation of Sir Harry's friendship and expressed appreciation of his help in organizing the Japanese Navy.[2]

At this time Satow and Mitford were again in surreptitious communication with Satsuma and other anti-*Bakufu* leaders on the progress of the revolution. They received the correct texts of the Kyoto decree. They knew that many of the great daimyo opposed the 'violent proceedings' of the Satsuma party and were insisting on the convocation of a general council. It was evident to Satow that the five clans had precipitated the coup in order to have their plans a *fait accompli* when the daimyo assembled. The Tokugawa party was making preparations for war and the five clans were ready to march on Osaka.[3]

Word came to Parkes from a *Bakufu* commissioner of foreign affairs that hostilities had already broken out in Yedo between the *Bakufu* and Satsuma men. The latter were said to have attacked traders, police, and the British legation, hoping to involve the ex-Shogun with foreigners.[4]

A Tosa man discussed with Satow the question of the recognition of the Mikado's government by the foreign ministers. Here again Satow wielded influence. He explained that the initiative in this matter was the responsibility of the new government. They should notify the *Bakufu* that they were informing the foreign ministers of their assumption of the direction of foreign affairs and then invite the latter to Kyoto. This would establish the Mikado's position before the world.[5]

---

[1] *D.N.G.M.* i. 169–75, Doc. 69.

[2] F.O. 46/91, Parkes to Stanley, No. 9, Osaka, 10 Jan. 1868 and encls. Satow, *Diplomat*, pp. 303–4. Ad. I/6052, Keppel to Adm., H.M.S. *Rodney*, Yokohama, 14 Jan. 1868.

[3] Satow, *Diplomat*, pp. 304–6. Redesdale, op. cit. ii. 424.

[4] F.O. 46/91, Parkes to Stanley (probably No. 17), Osaka, 29 Jan. 1868. There is no confirmation that the British legation was attacked.

[5] Satow, *Diplomat*, pp. 307–8.

Keiki's decision to resort to force and his subsequent defeat soon left little doubt about the position of the Kyoto government. Parkes learned of Keiki's purpose through two memoranda which the ex-Shogun wrote to the Mikado, and which the *Rōjū* sent to Parkes. Here Keiki complained that his surrender of power had failed in its purpose in that the council of daimyo had not assembled and that the Mikado was a mere instrument in the hands of one or two ambitious clans. As a result Japan's foreign relations were endangered. He demanded the surrender of Satsuma's retainers, otherwise he would resort to force. The *Bakufu* ministers insisted the contest would be limited to the Shogun's attack on Satsuma. Keiki was not opposing the Mikado but fighting in his name.[1]

The Tokugawa forces left Osaka for Kyoto on 26 January, having posted guards for the protection of foreigners. They far outnumbered those of Satsuma and Chōshū, which made up the majority of the Imperial army. The latter, however, were well trained and equipped with Western weapons. Their orders to block the roads at Fushimi and Toba caused their encounter with Keiki's troops on 27 January. Three days of hard fighting resulted in the routing of the *Bakufu* soldiers, who retreated to Osaka. Here Keiki faced his defeat. He notified the foreign ministers late in the evening of the thirtieth that he could no longer protect them and escaped in disguise the next morning by boat to Yedo. In equal haste the foreign ministers packed their archives and fled by boat to Hyogo to await developments.[2] Parkes telegraphed this news to London before leaving Osaka.[3] At Hyogo the Governor, Shibata Gōchū (Masanaka), asked all the consuls to embark as he could not guarantee their safety. On 3 February he and all other *Bakufu* officials left the port.[4]

Early Negotiations with the Imperial Government: the Bizen Affair

Before the Mikado's government had made official contact with the foreign representatives proof of the anti-foreign sentiment within its own ranks caused great embarrassment.

---

[1] F.O. 46/91, Parkes to Stanley (probably No. 17), Osaka, 29 Jan. 1868 and encls.

[2] Murdoch, op. cit. iii. 778–80. Redesdale, op. cit. ii. 425–7. Satow, *Diplomat*, pp. 310–13.

[3] F.O. 46/91, Parkes to Stanley, No. 18, Osaka, 30 Jan. 1868.

[4] Ibid., No. 20, Hyogo, 12 Feb. 1868. *D.N.G.M.* i. 263–5, Doc. 105.

On 4 February a party of Bizen men *en route* from Hyogo to Osaka fired on a group of foreigners as they passed through the new foreign quarters in Kobe. Exact details of the incident are not clear as Japanese and Western sources differ. Sir Harry Parkes quickly organized a formidable resistance made up of his guard and mounted escort, forty British sailors, eighty marines, and a few American marines from U.S.S. *Oneida* who were later reinforced by more American marines and some French seamen. Parkes himself led his guards against the Bizen samurai, who fled to the hills before anyone was killed on either side. Nevertheless the hostile intent of the Japanese troops was clear. Only their ignorance of the use of their new Western rifles prevented a massacre. The foreign representatives took united action. They issued a protest to the Bizen *Han*, demanding an explanation and threatening, in the absence of full reparation, to take measures involving the whole of Japan. They ordered as a material guarantee the seizure of all Japanese steamers in Hyogo harbour—the actual number varies in different accounts. And they asked their military commanders to assume the protection of the city.[1] On the next day they repeated this demand in notices posted in Hyogo and Kobe, and sent to Osaka and other parts of Japan. At the same time they announced their seizure of the Japanese ships and their assumption of measures of protection but assured the Japanese villagers, townsmen, and unarmed people that these measures would not affect their normal activities.[2]

Although Satow was in communication with his friends in the Imperial party, the foreign representatives received no official word from the Mikado's government until 7 February when Higashikuze Michitomo, a noble restored to court favour after five years of exile, arrived in Hyogo with Iwashita and Terashima of Satsuma, Itō of Chōshū—all foreign affairs officers—and a small retinue bearing an announcement from the Emperor. The meeting of these men with the foreign representatives on 8 February had lasting significance. As Parkes had

---

[1] *Nichi-Ei Gaikō Shi*, i. 105. Oka Yoshitake, *Reimeiki no Meiji Nihon; Nichi-Ei Kōshō Shi no Shikaku ni oite* (The Meiji Era; The Period of Dawn in Japan Viewed from the History of Negotiations with Britain), (Tokyo, 1964), pp. 7–9. F.O. 46/91, Parkes to Stanley, No. 22, Hyogo, 13 Feb. 1868. Black, op. cit. ii. 146–50. Satow, *Diplomat*, pp. 319–20.

[2] *D.N.G.M.* i. 213–16, Doc. 87.

been asked to arrange the meeting, he became the intermediary between the Imperial government and his diplomatic colleagues, much to the annoyance of Roches whose loyalty to Keiki made his position in relation to the new political set-up increasingly embarrassing.[1]

The Mikado's proclamation—long urged by Parkes, Satow, and Mitford, and influenced by a draft written and presented to Satsuma men by Satow and Mitford—now cancelled for ever the Shogun's recently repeated claim to conduct Japan's relations with foreign powers.[2] The Emperor notified the powers briefly that he had accepted the Shogun's return of the governing power in accordance with the Shogun's request. He now held supreme power in the conduct of Japan's internal and external affairs. The title of Emperor must be substituted for that of Tycoon in the treaties already made. New officers were being appointed by him to conduct foreign affairs. He indicated without question that the treaties were binding on his government. The foreign representatives insisted that all conventions and agreements with the Shogun subsequent to the treaties be equally accepted by the Mikado. Higashikuze said this was implied in the announcement and promised a supplementary letter of confirmation.[3]

At this time the Western representatives reported the Bizen attack on the foreign community and presented their demands. They called for a written apology from the Mikado's government combined with the assurance of protection for all foreigners in Japan against similar future aggression, and the execution of the Bizen officer who ordered the attack, in the presence of officers from the legations concerned.[4] Higashikuze acquiesced, promising that the matter would be handled in accordance with the public opinion of the countries concerned. The Imperial government would assume responsibility for future anti-foreign incidents, and Satsuma and Chōshū forces would be ordered to protect Kobe. On these grounds the foreign representatives withdrew their troops and released the Japanese steamers. At the same time they warned of grave

[1] Satow, *Diplomat*, pp. 321, 323. Medzini, op. cit., p. 220.

[2] Satow, *Diplomat*, p. 315.

[3] Ibid., p. 324 for text; MSS. *Diary*, ii. 134, 8 Feb. 1868. F.O. 46/91, Parkes to Stanley, No. 23, 13 Feb. 1868.

[4] *D.N.G.M.* i. 246–50, Doc. 102.

consequences, should the Japanese government not fulfil this pledge.[1]

Concurrently with Higashikuze's announcement to the foreign powers, the Meiji government proclaimed to the Japanese people on 8 February that it would pursue an 'open door' friendly policy towards foreigners instead of hostility and exclusion. It promised to take appropriate steps to rectify the harmful points in the Tokugawa treaties and to conduct its relations with foreign countries in accordance with the law of the universe. It appealed to the nation to unite, to strengthen its military power, and enhance the nation's prestige abroad.[2] In Kobe placards signed by Iwashita, Itō, and Terashima informed the Japanese that the Mikado would uphold the treaties, and demand proper behaviour towards foreigners.[3]

These were appalling and disappointing commands to the general Japanese public who had expected the new government to carry out the isolationist policy and expel the barbarians. Why the Restoration leaders, who so recently expressed anti-foreign sentiments, had changed their minds was not understood.[4] Since the Bizen *Han* had supported the new government, although related to Keiki, and had been firm expulsionists since 1862, the still insecure Meiji leaders had difficulty in deciding to accept the foreign demands and in winning the consent of the Bizen daimyo for the execution of a samurai. Finally on 2 March the government notified the foreign envoys, who in the interim had stubbornly refused to negotiate any other matter, that their demands for the Kobe incident were accepted in full. Parkes's subsequent efforts in conjunction with the Dutch consul to make an appeal to the Emperor for the commutation of the death sentence in the name of the foreign powers were defeated by his other colleagues. That night Taki Zensaburo, accused of giving the order to fire on the foreigners, committed *seppuku*[5] at Hyogo in the presence of Mitford and Satow. The courage and dignity of the condemned man as he obeyed orders impressed the British. When taking leave of his *han* he called upon them not to harbour

[1] F.O. 46/91, Parkes to Stanley, No. 22, Hyogo, 13 Feb. 1868. Oka, *Reimeiki no Meiji Nihon*, p. 10.
[2] Ibid., pp. 5–6.   [3] Satow, *Diplomat*, p. 326. Black, op. cit. ii. 152.
[4] Oka, *Reimeiki no Meiji Nihon*, pp. 5–6.
[5] *Seppuku*, suicide by disembowelment.

resentment against foreigners and showed no fear of his honourable death.[1]

British Neutrality during the Civil War

During the course of settling the Bizen affair the Meiji government's supporters had taken control of Nagasaki without disturbing the business of the port.[2] Provisional customs-house arrangements with Itō, now in charge, were made at Hyogo. Foreign merchants had returned to Osaka.[3] The foreign treaties and all subsequent engagements were ratified in the name of the Mikado.[4] And the Mikado had declared war against the ex-Shogun.[5] Satow advised Godai Tomoatsu, a Satsuma official and an old acquaintance from the Kagoshima engagement, 'to get a letter demanding neutrality on the part of all foreign representatives sent at once' in order to prevent the delivery to the Tokugawa of the ram *Stonewall* from the United States and two ironclads expected from France.[6] In consequence the Mikado promptly requested that all foreign representatives preserve a strict neutrality during the rebellion, his first official admission that the civil contest had begun. Parkes thought all his colleagues wanted an effective neutrality, knowing it would be difficult to protect their nationals at the open ports if they could be entered by belligerent troops transported in foreign vessels.[7] When writing to Keppel of the outbreak of hostilities, he said:

The policy of H.M. Government in regard to this domestic strife is to preserve a strictly neutral position and to demand from any and every party that may be in power at those points at which by Treaty we reside and trade, full respect for all our rights and good usage for the persons and property of H.M. subjects. I have little doubt that this policy of neutrality may be pursued without difficulty as the danger of collision with Foreign Governments by either of the contending parties would tell too greatly in favour of their opponents to be lightly incurred by one or the other.[8]

---

[1] Oka, *Reimeiki no Meiji Nihon*, pp. 10–15. F.O. 46/92, Parkes to Stanley, Nos. 48 and 49 Conf'l., Hyogo, 11 Mar. 1868. Satow, *Diplomat*, pp. 343–6. Redesdale, op. cit. ii. 432.

[2] F.O. 46/91, Parkes to Stanley, No. 30, Hyogo, 15 Feb. 1868.

[3] Ibid., No. 31, same date. [4] Satow, *Diplomat*, p. 331.

[5] F.O. 46/91, telegram, Parkes to Stanley, copy in No. 36, Hyogo, 15 Feb. 1868.

[6] Satow, *Diary*, ii. 139, 13 Feb. 1868.

[7] F.O. 46/91, Parkes to Stanley, No. 29, Hyogo, 15 Feb. 1868.

[8] Ad. R. O. (Japan 49), Parkes to Keppel, Hyogo, 15 Feb. 1868.

Parkes recognized, nevertheless, the probability of danger to British subjects and property during the war from the increased activities of *rōnin* whom neither party could control and whom either party might use for deeds of violence which they themselves would not acknowledge. Hence, he asked Admiral Keppel to maintain in Japan a standard of not less than six or seven effective vessels not including gunboats. Britain, he said, had six points to protect: Osaka, Hyogo, and Nagasaki were already in the control of the Imperial government while Yedo, Yokohama, and Hakodate remained in the hands of the Toku- gawa. It was necessary, he warned, to watch the British mer- cantile marine to prevent breaches of the neutrality which was essential to the safety of the foreign community.[1] Parkes had no illusions about the possible misdemeanours of his own or the Japanese people.

The British minister issued the following notification to all British subjects on 18 February 1868:

OFFICIAL NOTIFICATION

Whereas the Undersigned has been officially informed that hostilities have commenced in this country between His Majesty the Mikado and the Tycoon, and whereas a strict and impartial neutrality should be observed by all British subjects in the contest between the said contending parties, the Undersigned, H.B.M. Envoy Extraordinary and Minister Plenipotentiary in Japan, hereby calls upon all Subjects of Her Majesty to abstain from taking part in any operations of war against either of the contending parties, or in aiding or abetting any person in carrying on war for or against either of the said parties, and to avoid the infringement of any British Law or Statute made and provided for the purpose of maintaining neutrality in foreign or civil contests or of the Law of Nations relating thereto.

The Undersigned hereby publishes for the information of Her Majesty's Subjects the following three sections of the Statute made and passed in the 59th year of the reign of His Majesty King George III, commonly called the Foreign Enlistment Act, and further warns all subjects of Her Majesty that if any one commits any violation or contravention of the Law of Nations relating to Neutral or Belligerent Rights, as for example, by entering into the Military Service of either of the said contending parties in any capacity, or by serving in any capacity on board any ship or vessel

[1] Ibid.

of war, or transport, of or in the service of either of the said contending parties, or by enlisting or engaging in any such service, or by procuring or attempting to procure other persons to do so, or by fitting out, arming or equipping any ship or vessel to be employed as a ship of war or transport by either of the said contending parties; or by carrying officers, soldiers, despatches, arms, military stores, or materials, or any article or articles considered and deemed to be contraband of war, according to the Law or Modern Usage of Nations, for the use or service of either of the said contending parties —then and in all such cases, every British Subject so offending will incur and be liable to the several penalties and penal consequences imposed or denounced by the Statute aforesaid or by the Law of Nations, and may forfeit all claim to Her Majesty's protection and to the rights and privileges of the Treaty concluded between Great Britain and Japan.

Given under my hand at Hiogo this 18th day of Feb. A.D. 1868.

(Sgd) Harry S. Parkes[1]

In support of this policy of non-intervention Admiral Keppel recalled from Yedo Commander Tracy and his assistants, the ex-Shogun's recently appointed British naval instructors.[2] The naval commander was hopeful that the civil war would open a brighter future for Japan. He considered the still existing anti-foreign party weak in comparison with the new rulers who saw in the opening of the country to foreign trade their chief means of supporting their army and navy. He was already convinced that a British naval depot should be established at Yokohama with a force equal at least to half that of the China Station. He proposed arrangements to provision two thousand men, on the ground that such a permanent establishment would be in line with the current activities of British and foreign merchants in Japan who were sinking their capital in expensive buildings and other investments in the belief that the whole country would be opened up to unrestricted commerce as a result of the civil war.[3]

Parkes's notification and Keppel's withdrawal of the naval instructors met with scant approval by the British merchant community at Yokohama who saw in the profession of neutrality 'a distinct though indirect act of hostility against the party

---

[1] *D.N.G.M.* i. 363–79, Doc. 151. Here the full text of the three extracts of the Act of 3 July 1819 called the *Foreign Enlistment Act* is given.

[2] See p. 256.

[3] Ad. I/6052, Keppel to Adm., 24 and 25 Feb. 1868.

of the ex-Shogun and a useful support to the new government recognized at Kobe'. The prohibition of the purchase or charter of foreign ships to transport troops worked hardship on the Tokugawa party but not on the Imperial forces and the refusal of the ironclad *Stonewall* to the former, now announced by the American minister, deliberately crippled the ex-Shogun's naval power in relation to that of his opponents.[1] Sympathy for the Shogun's cause was by no means rare, even among the foreign representatives who remembered Keiki's proven friendship and co-operation during the recent months and had little faith in the daimyo party where anti-foreign outbursts, so long a standard practice, still took place. They wished to see the Mikado use the Shogun as the instrument of his newly acquired power.[2] With the exception of Parkes and the Dutch minister, they all refused to accept the first invitation of the Mikado to an audience in Kyoto, considering it undesirable to increase their relations with the Mikado until the position of the Shogun was known.[3]

Parkes's Faith in the Imperial Government: his Audience with the Mikado

According to the contemporary journalist, John Black, it was Parkes who now gave the new government 'all the moral support in his power', believing that 'with one indisputable ruler exercising the sole authority', with whom foreign sovereigns could be in direct communication, 'the principal obstruction to peaceful intercourse' would be overcome.[4]

The new government had convinced the British of its strength in relation to that of the ex-Shogun. It had fully respected the treaty rights. Good order had prevailed in Nagasaki, Hyogo, and Osaka, which were held by Satsuma and Chōshū.[5] The Mikado's officials had acted promptly after the Bizen outrage.[6] With equal dispatch the demands of M. Léon Roches following

---

[1] *Japan Times' Overland Mail*, 12 Mar. 1868, copy at Widener Library, Harvard.   [2] Black, op. cit. ii. 155.

[3] F.O. 46/92, Parkes to Stanley, No. 62, Conf'l., Osaka, 19 Mar. 1868. Satow, *Diplomat*, pp. 349–50. Oka, *Reimeiki no Meiji Nihon*, pp. 19–20.

[4] Black, op. cit. ii. 156.

[5] Ad. I/6052, Keppel to Adm., H.M.S. *Rodney* at Hong Kong, 25 Feb. and 9 Mar. 1868. Paske-Smith, *Western Barbarians*, pp. 175–81 gives a primary account of the Imperial government's take-over in Nagasaki.

[6] F.O. 46/92, Parkes to Stanley, No. 48, Hyogo, 11 Mar. 1868.

the murder of eleven French seamen by Tosa men on 8 March at Sakai were fulfilled.[1] The British minister considered this proof of the desire of the Mikado's government for friendly relations with foreigners and evidence of its power to control unruly and dangerous armed classes.[2]

Sir Harry, Roches, and the Dutch representative, van Polsbroek, who had remained at Hyogo when their colleagues returned to Yokohama, now accepted a renewed invitation to an audience with the Mikado since the Sakai incident had interrupted the previous arrangements. Parkes regarded this visit as 'the crowning work' of the last three months as it meant the formalizing of relations with the Mikado's government.[3] He knew nothing, of course, of the opposition and fears at the Court which lay behind both invitations and the public announcements that an audience would take place. Concern about attack from anti-foreign elements in Kyoto made many Japanese officials afraid to make preparatory arrangements for hotel accommodation for the three envoys. To prevent violence against the foreigners the government issued two decrees on 19 March which gave the travel schedule of the diplomats and called upon the people to understand the government's purpose and refrain from unlawful acts against foreigners. Shinto priests had instructions on the day of the audience to hold ceremonies on four sides of the palace where they prayed for the prevention of misfortune.[4]

The British were royally received at Kyoto. The leaders of the new government, Sanjō, Iwakura, Itō, Date, and Gotō, as well as several of the princes, professed great friendship for foreigners and expressed their appreciation of England's early recognition of the sovereignty of the Mikado. Iwakura admitted the recent hatred of foreigners by the Mikado and court nobles and their opposition to the pro-foreign policy of the Shogun, which he assured them had now ceased. Even the people in Kyoto appeared friendly towards them.[5] Nevertheless, when on his way to the palace on 23 March accompanied by his

[1] Oka, *Reimeiki no Meiji Nihon*, pp. 23–27.

[2] F.O. 46/92, Parkes to Stanley, Nos. 55 and 61, Hyogo, 11 and 18 Mar. 1868.

[3] Dickins, op. cit. ii. 84–85.

[4] Oka, *Reimeiki no Meiji Nihon*, pp. 16–23, 27–30.

[5] F.O. 46/92, Parkes to Stanley, No. 64, Kyoto, 25 Mar. 1864. Satow, *Diplomat*, pp. 357–8.

mounted escort, sixty British infantry, and a guard of Higo samurai, Parkes and his procession were suddenly attacked by two Japanese swordsmen. Twelve men were wounded. Parkes and Satow both had narrow escapes. Parkes's belt was cut. The nose of Satow's horse was clipped off. Confusion reigned. The Higo guards disappeared into the crowd. Gotō Shōjirō, Satow's Tosa friend and now a member of the Ministry of Foreign Affairs, jumped from his horse and, with Nakai Hiroshi, promptly killed one assailant. Another was bayoneted but before his execution gave evidence that the attack was against all foreigners—he did not know one nationality from the other.[1]

The Mikado's Court was shocked by the news of this assault on its chief foreign advocate. Some of the highest ministers, including Higashikuze, Date, and the Prince of Hizen, came to present their condolences and regrets to Parkes that evening. The next day they brought written apologies and offered very full reparations. These included indemnities to the wounded men and pensions to their families should death result from their injuries. Parkes replied that he left the matter in their hands, as he thought 'a greater outrage had been committed upon the Mikado than upon himself'. To Lady Parkes he wrote, 'Out of this Affair I expect to get a law rendering attacks on foreigners by two-sworded men—hitherto looked upon as heroism—punishable by an infamous death'.[2] He again secured the promise of the Japanese ministers to issue such a decree which should also make public the government's desire for friendly relations with the foreign powers.[3]

Convinced of the government's sincerity and the wisdom of clemency on his part, Parkes consented to an audience with the Mikado on 26 March. The ceremony was brief, conforming closely to that of European courts. Parkes replied to the Emperor's welcome and expression of regret about the occurrence of the twenty-third that the memory of the latter would be effaced by today's 'gracious reception'. He praised His

[1] Dickins, op. cit. ii. 87–95, for Parkes's letter to Lady Parkes, 24 Mar. 1868 and Mitford's account. Parkes's letter to Stanley No. 65, supposed to report the event, has been cut from the F.O. file. Satow, *Diplomat*, pp. 358–60, 363. Oka, *Reimeiki no Meiji Nihon*, pp. 31–32. *Nichi-Ei Gaikō Shi*, i. 106.

[2] Ad. I/6052, Keppel to Adm., 19 Apr. 1868. Dickins, op. cit. ii. 88, 94.

[3] *D.N.G.M.* i. 490–6. Doc. 209. Satow, *Diplomat*, pp. 361–2.

Majesty for 'taking the best measures to place the foreign relations of Japan upon a permanent footing by establishing a strong central government . . . and by adopting the system of international law universally recognized by other states'. Parkes was impressed that this and the audience with the French and Dutch representatives on the twenty-third were the Mikado's first communications with the outside world, the first breakaway from his traditional strict seclusion when he was regarded as a demigod by his people.[1] On the thirty-first Parkes and Satow returned to Yokohama, leaving Mitford in Osaka to keep in communication with the Court and advise the samurai class at Kyoto on the English parliamentary institutions as some, like Gotō, hoped to build Japan's new government on a representative system.[2] Before his departure from Hyogo, Parkes agreed with Roches and van Polsbroek not to press for the opening of Yedo and Niigata to foreign trade under the current disturbed conditions and issued a notification to that effect, a decision most satisfactory to the temporary governor of Yedo.[3]

The Imperial Decree Banning Anti-foreign Violence

In fulfilment of its promise, the government presented to the foreign representatives on 27 March the draft of an Imperial decree to control attacks on foreigners. This proclaimed that the restored monarchical government would honour Japan's foreign treaties in accordance with the rules of international law and ordered the whole nation to act in accordance therewith. It declared that persons guilty of murdering foreigners or committing violence towards them would not only be acting against His Majesty's orders but would jeopardize the national dignity and good faith of Japan with the treaty powers 'with whom His Majesty has declared himself bound by relations of amity'. Such offenders were to be punished in proportion to the gravity of their offence. If samurai, their names should be erased from the roll.[4]

---

[1] F.O. 46/92, Parkes to Stanley, No. 66, Kyoto, 26 Mar. 1868. Satow, *Diplomat*, pp. 362–3.   [2] Ibid., p. 363. *D.N.G.M.* i. 517–20, Doc. 223.

[3] F.O. 46/92, Parkes to Stanley, No. 73, Yokohama, 8 Apr. 1868.

[4] Translation of decree given in Paske-Smith, *Western Barbarians*, pp. 182–3. *D.N.G.M.* i. 506–7, Doc. 216.

Parkes approved this text and asked that British consular officers be informed of the places where the decree would be posted in Hyogo, Osaka, and Nagasaki. Fear of retaliatory action by the anti-foreign elements in Japan, however, led the government to issue a less drastic decree on 30 March. Mitford's opposition to this—although he understood the government's difficulties—led to weeks of negotiations before the Kyoto authorities consented to post the original decree throughout the country. Even then they softened its impact by combining it with a couple of innocuous proclamations.[1]

British Influence at the Surrender of Yedo

Ominous conditions awaited Parkes and Satow upon their return to Yokohama at the end of March. In secret nocturnal meetings in Yedo, Katsu Kaishu,[2] a liberal reformer among Keiki's councillors who had earlier commanded the *Bakufu* navy, brought Satow up to date on recent developments within the Tokugawa party. As early as 4 March Keiki had issued a proclamation to his followers saying he would submit to the orders of the Mikado and forbidding them to oppose the Imperial troops. He had retired to a monastery in Ueno. Aizu and his supporters had returned to their home at Wakamatsu, still determined to resist the approaching troops of the Mikado. Many other daimyo, recently residents of Yedo, had gone back to their territories or given their allegiance to the Mikado in Kyoto. Tokugawa men of lesser rank were doing likewise. The vanguard of the Imperialist troops had already arrived in the neighbourhood of Yedo when the British minister reached the area. The commander-in-chief, Prince Arisugawa himself, was said to be half a day's journey away. The city was in an apprehensive mood not knowing what demands were to be made on Keiki. People were moving their household goods but the stores were still open. On 4 April the forts in the Bay of Yedo

---

[1] *D.N.G.M.* i. 515–17, Doc. 222. Oka, *Reimeiki no Meiji Nihon*, pp. 39–40. Redesdale, op. cit. ii. 464–5.

[2] Katsu Kaishu is known also as Katsu Rintaro, Katsu Awa, and Katsu Yoshikuni or Yasuyoshi. He had advocated the return of the Shogun's political power to the Emperor and the creation of an assembly of daimyo in Kyoto which would debate policy matters under the Emperor, a plan similar to that of Tosa. Sakata Yoshio and John Whitney Hall, 'The Motivation of Political Leadership in the Meiji Restoration', *Journal of Asian Studies*, xvi. (Nov. 1956), 46.

were given over to the Mikado's forces, after the guns bearing on the city were dismounted.[1] An Imperial expedition had been dispatched by sea to take possession of Hakodate expecting to deliver a summons to the Prince of Aizu *en route*.[2] The foreign representatives now accepted the Mikado's government as an established fact.[3]

In Yokohama the appearance of numerous stragglers from the Imperial forces before responsible officials from Kyoto had arrived to take over the government of the town, led the foreign representatives to request their naval commanders to assume temporarily the defence of the city and to ask the Mikado's ministers to provide measures for restoring order and security to the area and regular facilities for communicating with their government.[4] Thereafter no two-sworded man could enter the city without a stamped passport and complete order was secured.

For weeks Katsu Kaishu, with Keiki's permission, had carried on negotiations with the Court's representatives, Ōkubo and Saigō, about the demands to be made on Tokugawa Keiki. Parkes had counselled clemency, arguing that capital punishment of Keiki and his followers would impair the standing of the new government with the powers. His angry refusal to supply Western doctors for a field hospital in the Yokohama area in preparation for the Imperial attack on Yedo Castle led Saigō to call off the siege. The British minister insisted that since the *Bakufu* was known to be willing to surrender unconditionally its castle, estates, and warships to the Imperial army (*kangun*), an attack on its castle would be a serious crime against justice and humanity. It was consequently decided that the Imperial occupation of the ex-Shogun's capital should be undertaken without destruction and jeopardy to the lives of its more than a million inhabitants.[5]

On 26 April the terms of the Mikado's ultimatum were

[1] Satow, *Diplomat*, pp. 364–5. F.O. 46/92, Parkes to Stanley, No. 72, Yokohama, 9 Apr. 1868.

[2] Ibid., No. 68, Yokohama, 9 Apr. 1868.

[3] Ad. I/6052, Keppel to Adm., H.M.S. *Rodney* at Yokohama, 18 Apr. 1868.

[4] F.O. 46/92, Parkes to Stanley, No. 75, Yokohama, 9 Apr. 1868. Ad. I/6052, Keppel to Adm., 9 Apr. 1868. *D.N.G.M.* i. 536–48, Doc. 232. Oka, *Reimeiki no Meiji Nihon*, pp. 44–45.

[5] Osatake Takeki, *Bakumatsu Gaikō Hishi Kō* (Secret Diplomatic History of the End of the *Bakufu*), (Tokyo, 1944), pp. 163–73.

finally presented to Keiki. Parkes's influence for moderation is also evident in these demands. The Emperor required the ex-Shogun to retire to Mito and live there in seclusion. His castle at Yedo was to be evacuated and given to the Owari clan. The resident retainers had to retire outside the walls and remain in seclusion. His assistants in the rebellion were to be punished. All warships and firearms were to be surrendered under the promise that later a suitable proportion would be returned. He was given until 3 May to accept.[1] Urged by Katsu to agree and convinced that he was acting for the good of the country, Keiki surrendered and left Yedo on the third. Daimyo troops then occupied the city. Keiki's followers, however, did not capitulate. Aizu was collecting a great force in his own territory strengthened by other daimyo and malcontents. Enomoto Takeaki, a naval officer of the *Bakufu*, had escaped with eleven ships of the Tokugawa navy and was joined by runaway troops. A trial of strength was inevitable.[2]

Parkes's Presentation of Credentials

Conditions now seemed sufficiently settled for Parkes to present his credentials to the Mikado which had reached him at the end of March. The Imperial authorities for Yokohama, Higashikuze Michitomo and Nabeshima Naohiro, had arrived and taken charge. Imperial government troops now replaced the foreign guards who had recently maintained order.[3] The Mikado was temporarily in Osaka where he had seen the sea, reviewed the Japanese fleet, and observed a foreign warship for the first time. The city, unlike Kyoto, would make possible a display of British naval prowess on the occasion of the presentation ceremony. Parkes wanted to impress on 'the mind of the

[1] Ad. I/6052, Keppel to Adm., 2 May 1868, Encl. 2 gives text of the Mikado's demands translated by Satow. F.O. 46/93, Parkes to Stanley, No. 104, Yokohama, 2 May 1868.

[2] Ibid., Parkes to Hammond, Private, Yokohama, 13 May; Parkes to Stanley, No. 114, 14 May 1868. Sakata and Hall, op. cit., p. 49. These authors believe that the Tokugawa forces had power then to resist and perhaps defeat the Satsuma–Chōshū coalition and that Keiki's peaceful surrender of Yedo was the turning-point in the Restoration.

[3] F.O. 46/93, Parkes to Hammond (Private) and Parkes to Stanley, No. 106, Yokohama, 13 May 1868. Oka, *Reimeiki no Meiji Nihon*, pp. 44–45. The two officials were called *Saibansho Sōtoku* and *Saibansho Fuku-Sōtoku*, literally Director and Deputy Director of the Yokohama Court.

young Mikado who will then be brought for the first time in direct relations with Foreign Sovereigns, a just sense of the rank and dignity of the Queen and also of the power of the nation which is the first to offer to Japan this proof of friendship'. Thus he wrote to Admiral Keppel when asking him to assemble several vessels at Osaka.[1] Meanwhile he had Mitford in Osaka request an audience with the Mikado to deliver his letter of credence, stressing that it was 'a spontaneous proof of good feeling on the part of Her Majesty's Government and the first letter to be addressed by any sovereign to the Mikado'.[2]

The events at Osaka were unique. A salute fired from the fort honoured Parkes when he landed on the eighteenth. High officials welcomed him at a reception. Old acquaintances now in positions of power—Gotō, Date, Sanjō, and Kido—discussed with him the current persecution of Catholic Christians at Nagasaki and the recently renewed edict against Christianity,[3] while preparations for the ceremony were being made. On 22 May Admiral Keppel assembled off Osaka six British men-of-war in company with the French corvette *Dupleix*. The presentation took place at one o'clock at a Buddhist temple,[4] the temporary headquarters of the Mikado. Bodies of Japanese troops preceded and followed the British procession which consisted of Parkes, his staff, Admiral Keppel, the officers commanding Her Majesty's ships, and 160 marines. At the temple, the uncle of the Mikado, Prince Yamashina, and high ranking military and civilian officers received them. As they advanced down the long throne room, the young Emperor arose from his seat on a canopied dais to remain standing during the ceremony. Sir Harry bowed, spoke briefly of Britain's friendship, and handed his credentials to the Mikado. Itō Hirobumi translated his address and the Emperor's response. Sir Harry introduced his staff and Admiral Keppel, who in turn presented his suite. All went smoothly. The British retired backwards out of the presence into the antechamber, bowing as they went.[5]

---

[1] Ad. I/6052, Keppel to Adm., See note p. 232, H.M.S. *Rodney* at Yokohama, 2 May 1868 and encl., Parkes to Keppel, 29 Apr. 1868.

[2] *D.N.G.M.* i. 595–7, Doc. 259.   [3] See pp. 484–5.

[4] This was the Higashi Honganji.

[5] F.O. 46/93, Parkes to Stanley, No. 117, Yokohama, 30 May 1868. Ad. I/6052, Keppel to Adm., Hyogo, 24 May 1868. Satow, *Diplomat*, pp. 369–72.

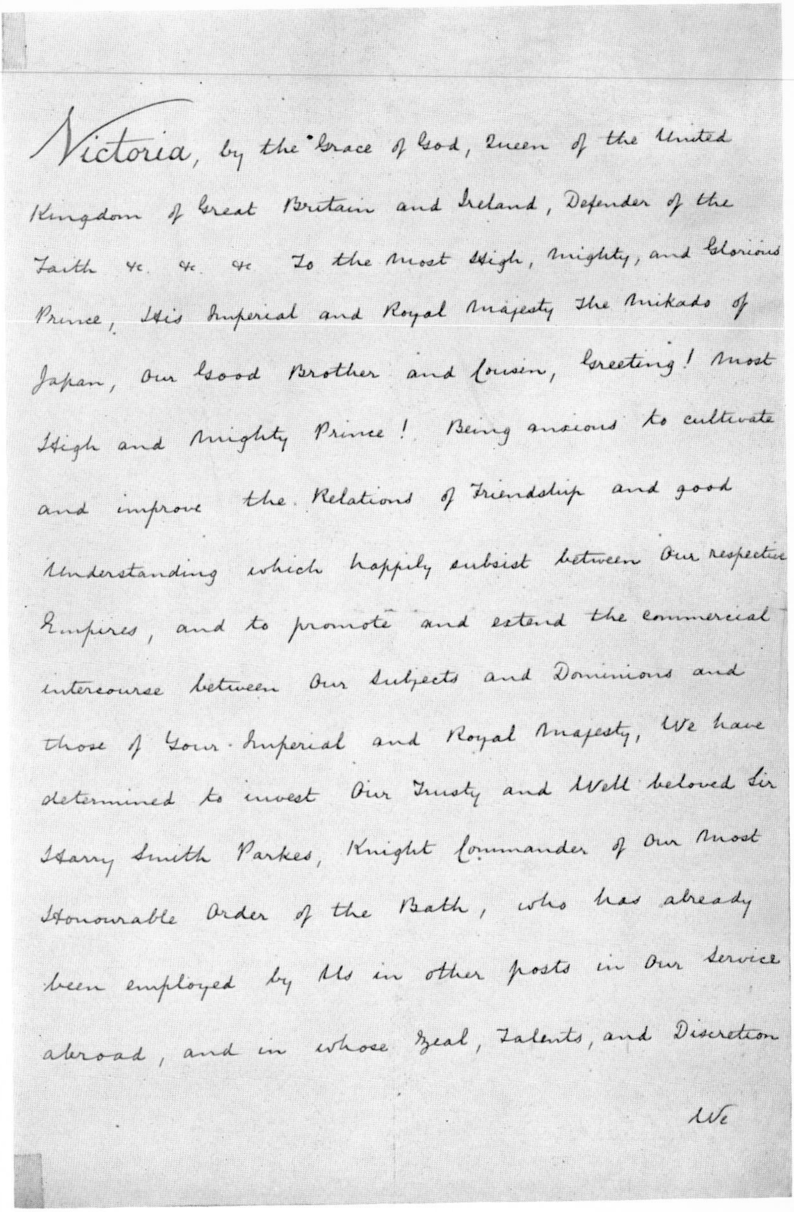

PLATE 4

Victoria, by the Grace of God, Queen of the United Kingdom of Great Britain and Ireland, Defender of the Faith &c. &c. &c. To the Most High, Mighty, and Glorious Prince, His Imperial and Royal Majesty the Mikado of Japan, Our Good Brother and Cousin, Greeting! Most High and Mighty Prince! Being anxious to cultivate and improve the Relations of Friendship and good Understanding which happily subsist between Our respective Empires, and to promote and extend the commercial intercourse between Our Subjects and Dominions and those of Your Imperial and Royal Majesty, We have determined to invest Our Trusty and Well beloved Sir Harry Smith Parkes, Knight Commander of Our Most Honourable Order of the Bath, who has already been employed by Us in other posts in Our Service abroad, and in whose Zeal, Talents, and Discretion

We

Parkes's Letter of Credence to the Mikado

We have the most perfect Confidence, with the Character of Our Envoy Extraordinary and Minister Plenipotentiary to Your Imperial and Royal Majesty, and have directed him to reside in Your Country in that Capacity. — Sir Harry Parkes will have the honour of presenting this Our Royal Letter of Credence to Your Imperial and Royal Majesty, and will in obedience to Our Orders, assure You of Our most sincere Friendship, and of Our ardent wishes for Your long life and continued Happiness. — He is fully informed as to all matters which concern the interests of Our Subjects trading to or residing in the Dominions of Your Imperial and Royal Majesty, and he will use his best efforts to perpetuate that Harmony and friendly intercourse which it is Our earnest desire should ever prevail between the two great Empires. — We accordingly request that Your Imperial and Royal Majesty will receive Our said Envoy Extraordinary and

Minister

Minister Plenipotentiary in a favourable manner, that You
will grant him free access to Your Presence, and that You
will give entire credence to all that he shall have occasion
to represent to You in Our Name. _ And so We recommend
Your Imperial and Royal Majesty to the Protection of
The Almighty. _ Given at Our Court at Osborne, the
Fourth day of February, in the Year of Our Lord One
Thousand Eight Hundred and Sixty Eight, and in the
Thirty First Year of Our Reign.

Your Imperial and Royal Majesty's.

Affectionate Sister and Cousin

Victoria R

Stanley

That evening Date entertained the British in his official residence at a banquet in European style. His hospitality was returned the next day when Admiral Keppel gave a luncheon on board H.M.S. *Rodney* for Prince Yamashina, the *kuge*, and daimyo. When the guests came aboard, all the ships manned yards. At the luncheon toasts proposed by the Mikado's uncle and Keppel were drunk to the Queen and the Mikado. The visitors inspected with interest every part of the *Rodney*. They were fascinated by the ship's band and its noisy music. To their great delight the bandmaster of H.M.S. *Ocean* composed a march and a Japanese national anthem which he dedicated to the Mikado. Their curiosity about the West extended to a request to see a negro and a European cat. At the close of the afternoon they went around H.M.S. *Ocean*, thence returning to the shore under a general salute of nineteen guns, Her Majesty's ships manning the yards.[1] On 25 May the British minister and staff went back to Yokohama. A new order in Anglo-Japanese relations had begun. Parkes became doyen of the foreign representatives with the departure of Léon Roches on 23 June and Maxime Outrey was the new minister of a more cautious French government.[2]

Rebellion in the North

Six months of momentous change in Japan followed. The British and other foreign ministers had little direct influence on these internal developments except that their treaties and their presence demanded constant consideration from the Mikado's young, insecure government. After the capitulation of the Shogun and the Imperial occupation of Yedo, the government struggled against the well-organized and cour- ageous opposition of a confederation of northern daimyo under the leadership of the Aizu *Han*. The rebellion ended in early November with the surrender of Aizu and its stronghold, Wakamatsu Castle, followed by the capitulation of one or two other daimyo.[3]

---

[1] Satow, *Diplomat*, p. 372.

[2] F.O. 46/94, Parkes to Stanley, No. 127, Yokohama, 11 June 1868. Black, op. cit. ii. 230.

[3] F.O. 46/96, Parkes to Stanley, No. 209, Yokohama, 22 Aug. 1868 encloses official documents published in *Kyoto Gazette* covering hostilities of Aizu and followers; 46/98, same to same, Nos. 276, 280, 286, 291, and 292, Yokohama,

Enomoto's capture of Hakodate on 6 December with the Tokugawa steam fleet, 'runaway soldiers' from the defeat at Wakamatsu, and several French officers, was considered a piratical expedition—an independent enterprise unauthorized by the Tokugawa *Han*. These forces took over the government of Hakodate, hoping to establish a Tokugawa colony on the island and act as guardians of 'the northern gate of the Empire'. Their dream was short-lived. The Imperial fleet brought them to complete submission in mid June 1869. Imperial clemency, however, spared the lives of the leaders, who later became officials of the new Japan.[1]

Instructions from Lord Stanley and a new Order-in-Council had insisted upon British neutrality during both the civil war and the northern rebellion in spite of the fact that Queen Victoria's hurried recognition of the Mikado's Government before the outcome of its contest with the *Bakufu* was known had deliberately strengthened the Imperial cause.[2] Shortly before Parkes presented his credentials to the Mikado, a letter from the Foreign Secretary restated Britain's official policy:

> Her Majesty's Government have only one object in Japan—the maintenance of friendly intercourse and trade with the ruling Powers and the people of the country. They have no intention of identifying themselves with any party that may spring up or of aiming at any influence beyond what is required for upholding their Treaty Rights. These rights you will steadily uphold though without enforcing them by any other means than by argument and representation in moderate terms, unless you secure express instructions from me to do so.

Stanley considered the British naval forces in Japanese waters amply sufficient for the personal protection of British subjects and possessions. He wanted no recurrence to the use of force unless as a clearly evident last resort for the protection of life

---

4, 12, 17, and 18 Nov. and No. 300, 2 Dec. 1868 for termination of the civil war. Black, op. cit. ii. 212–24, 237–8, 245.

[1] F.O. 46/97, Parkes to Stanley, No. 260, Yokohama, 15 Oct. 1868; 46/98, same to same, No. 281, Conf'l., Yokohama, 12 Nov. 1868; 46/99, Nos. 320 and 329, Yokohama, 18 and 30 Dec. 1868; 46/109, Parkes to Clarendon, Nos. 103, 118, 123, and 124, Yedo, 11 and 28 May and 7 June 1869; 46/110, same to same, Nos. 135, 139, and 141, Yedo, 25 and 29 June and 12 July 1869. Black, op. cit. ii. 238–9, 259–64.

[2] F.O. 262/141, Stanley to Parkes, No. 30, 18 Feb. 1868, for Stanley's stand on the civil war.

and property, and no grounds for any accusation that England had interfered in Japan's internal affairs or exercised her influence for the benefit of one party rather than another in the state. In the same letter Stanley approved Parkes's conduct at the time of the deposition of the Shogun, apparently oblivious to the encouragement the British had given the Imperial cause.[1] He was now well informed regarding Roches's machinations with the Shogunate and the criticism they had engendered recently in France.[2] He must have known of Roches's reports of British sympathy with the daimyo party but may have concluded that Parkes in the long run had been right.[3]

An Order-in-Council passed at Windsor on 14 May 1868 replaced that of 18 February, issued upon the outbreak of hostilities between the Mikado and the Shogunate. References to the Shogun and the treaty with him were now deliberately omitted. The new Order merely provided that should any British subject during the hostilities carried on between the Mikado and other belligerents, without the licence of Her Majesty, take part in any operation of war in the service of the Mikado, or of other belligerents within the Japanese dominion, or aid and abet any or either of the contending parties by delivering or causing to be delivered to either of them any ship fitted out or armed to be employed in military or naval service against the other, he would be guilty of a misdemeanour and on conviction thereof, be liable, at the discretion of the convicting court, to punishment by imprisonment not exceeding two years with or without hard labour, and with or without a fine not exceeding five thousand dollars or by this fine only.[4] Parkes published the official text in a *Notification* to all British subjects on 13 July 1868.[5]

The foreign representatives had agreed as early as 28 February to make every effort to prevent the delivery to either contending party of warships arriving in Japanese waters which had been purchased from their nationals. Her Majesty's

[1] Ibid., Stanley to Parkes, No. 40, 10 Mar. 1868.
[2] Ibid., Siebold to Hammond, Paris, 28 Jan.; to Lyons, 6 Feb.; to F.O., 11 Feb. 1868, encl. in F.O. to Parkes, 10 and 11 Feb. 1868.
[3] See p. 176. Medzini, op. cit., p. 220.
[4] F.O. 262/141, Stanley to Parkes, No. 61, 26 Apr. 1868. Order-in-Council 14 May 1868 at Court at Windsor, *D.N.G.M.* i. 829–34, Doc. 376.
[5] Ibid., pp. 828–9.

Government held that such interference by British consuls or naval officers was hard to justify in accordance with European rules of international law, but left enforcement action to Parkes's discretion, when acting with the representatives of other powers for the safety of their residents in Japan.[1] The request of the Tokugawa Governor of Kanagawa that foreign consuls prevent men from Satsuma and Chōshū from taking passage in foreign vessels to Kanagawa led Stanley to say it was beyond the power of British authorities in Japan to prevent men of the two clans with no apparent hostile purpose passing from one port to another. British subjects might be warned against transporting these men but could not be punished as other nations did not prohibit the conveyance of passengers on their vessels.[2] Parkes's action on this is not recorded.

The British envoy moved quickly when he learned of the seizure of Hakodate by the exiled Tokugawa followers, who called themselves *kerai*. In reply to their desire to be regarded as belligerents by the foreign powers and knowing that the Imperial government intended to resist their occupation of Yezo, Parkes called a meeting of his diplomatic colleagues. All agreed to protect their resident nationals at Hakodate but not to interfere in the contest. Those without warships refused to give an opinion on the status of the *kerai*. Britain and France agreed to send one warship each to Hakodate but maintained that the *kerai* were not belligerents as far as foreign ships were concerned. They thus denied the exiles the right of capture, search, or blockade but at the same time prohibited British and French ships from carrying to Hakodate troops or munitions of war for either party.[3] Parkes's communications with the exiles whose leaders he trusted gave him confidence that foreigners would be safe at Hakodate.[4] He and Outrey immediately refused the Japanese government's request that their merchant ships stop visiting Hakodate. And the resident British consul, R. Eusden, explained to the *kerai* leaders the requirements of British shipping at that port.[5]

On 9 January 1869 protests from Iwakura regarding the

[1] F.O. 262/141, Stanley to Parkes, No. 72, 19 May 1868.

[2] Ibid., No. 73, 19 May 1868.

[3] F.O. 46/99, Parkes to Stanley, Nos. 316 and 324 Conf'l., Yokohama, 16 and 18 Dec. 1868.   [4] Ibid., No. 320, 18 Dec. 1868.

[5] Ibid., Nos. 331 and 337, 30 and 31 Dec. 1868.

British and French policy of neutrality in the government's contest with the *kerai* led Parkes to explain it was not neutrality since the rights of belligerents were denied—it was merely 'non-interference' in accordance with British and French policy to keep out of the internal affairs of Japan.[1] Arguing that the war was over, Iwakura continued to press for the revocation of the Western neutrality notifications and America's release of the ram *Stonewall* to the Mikado's government. Although the foreign representatives in a joint communiqué conceded the war had ended, they delayed until 9 February to withdraw simultaneously their neutrality policy.[2] At the same time the United States handed over the *Stonewall* to the Imperial authorities, thus providing minor assistance in the Imperial defeat of the *kerai* in June 1869.[3]

The Mikado's Government

During the civil war and northern rebellion the leaders of the Restoration had to establish a new government and give Japan a constitution. Their long-range goals were clear: the supremacy of the Emperor over a stable central government, and the development of military and industrial power sufficient to enable Japan to hold her own in the community of nations. They had little to build on when Keiki surrendered Yedo in May 1868: no funds, the *Bakufu* treasury was bankrupt; no Imperial military power other than the forces of several *han*, each responsible to its local commander; no Imperial administration beyond Kyoto, where the young Emperor of fifteen and his Court had 'prestige without power'; and although many daimyo had united to overthrow the *Bakufu*, they were divided among themselves, jealous and suspicious of each other, and aware of sharp divisions of opinion within their own domains. Moreover these feudal lords presided over independent local administrations, usually managed by their ablest samurai, and were unaccustomed to the interference of any central authority. Only men of great intelligence, vision, courage, and ruthlessness could have brought order, even gradually, out of this chaos. Such were the vigorous young samurai of the south and west with both military and administrative experience, who in many

---

[1] F.O. 46/106, interview between Parkes and Iwakura, 9 Jan. 1869, encl. in Parkes to Stanley, No. 5, Conf'l., Yokohama, 13 Jan. 1869.
[2] Satow, *Diplomat*, pp. 401–8.   [3] F. O. Adams, op. cit. ii. 170, 175–9.

instances had plotted the Restoration—Ōkubo and Saigō of Satsuma, Kido and Itō of Chōshū, Gotō and Itagaki of Tosa, Etō and Ōkuma of Hizen. These men in conjunction with the two court nobles, Sanjō Sanetomi and Iwakura Tomomi, and the former *Bakufu* negotiator, Katsu Kaishu, became the moulders of the new political order during many shifts in their personal positions.

The central government established provisionally in January 1868 changed often during the period here considered and did not reach a permanent form until the Constitution of 1889. In order to emphasize the absence of military control associated with the hated Shogunate, an Imperial prince and court nobles were assigned the highest posts in the three offices of the Mikado's first government. Prince Arisugawa became *Sōsai* (Controller) with Sanjō and Iwakura as his deputies. The *gijō* (senior councillors) who had deliberative and administrative functions, consisted of two Imperial princes, three *kuge*, and representatives of the five daimyo whose troops now guarded the palace gates, Satsuma, Tosa, Hiroshima, Owari, and Fukui. *Kuge* and samurai of lower rank from these five clans, soon joined by Chōshū men, made up the *sanyo* (junior councillors). Thus conflicts among aspiring daimyo were avoided and real power was still exercised by Ōkubo, Kido, Gotō, and other young samurai who served inconspicuously in the Controller's Department. In February eight administrative departments were added. Over them *gijō* presided with *sanyo* as assistants who did the actual work. This necessitated the appointment of many more *sanyo* from other *han* until over a hundred held office. The next month the government summoned representatives from all the *han* to serve as a consultative assembly—an effective device 'for gauging public opinion and rallying support' as well as an effort to provide a basis for reconciliation with the defeated Tokugawa and to win the help of their trained officials for the national administration.[1] The government also established an official news organ, the *Kyoto Gazette*, which published the constitution of February with the names of officials and promised to keep the people informed of government action.[2]

---

[1] Beasley, *History*, p. 101. McLaren, op. cit. Pt. I, 4–6.

[2] Ad. I/6052, encl. No. 1 in China Letter No. 181 of 1868. F.O. 46/93, Parkes to Stanley, No. 80, Yokohama, 18 Apr. 1868 for Satow's translation from the *Gazette*.

On 6 April the young Emperor proclaimed, in what is known as the *Charter Oath*, the working principles and 'anti-feudal aspirations' of his monarchy. This became the first article of the more permanent form of government established by Imperial Proclamation in June 1868, called the *Seitaisho*, and often referred to as 'the first Constitution'. After serious study of Chinese, European, and earlier Japanese systems, it was designed to replace the tentative arrangements of the early months of the new régime. Iwakura Tomomi, Fukuoka Kotei from Tosa, and Kido Kōin of Chōshū were the authors of the text of the oath as well as the constitution. By the oath the Emperor had promised a constitution and laws established for the national weal whereby:

1. Deliberative assemblies shall be widely established and all matters decided by public discussion.
2. All classes, high and low, shall unite in vigorously carrying out the administration of affairs of state.
3. The common people, no less than the civil and military officials, shall each be allowed to pursue his own calling so that there may be no discontent.
4. Evil customs of the past shall be broken off and everything based upon the just laws of Nature.
5. Knowledge shall be sought throughout the world so as to strengthen the foundations of imperial rule.[1]

Following these general principles the constitution in ten more articles provided for the machinery and defined the powers of the government. All powers and authority were vested in a *Dajōkan* (Council of State) where provisions for the separation of powers were soon annulled by an interlocking of both men and functions between the legislative, executive, and judiciary.[2] Seven departments were established to exercise the powers of the *Dajōkan*: a Deliberative Assembly divided into an upper and lower house; an office of the President of the Council; and five departments of state, those of the Shinto

---

[1] *Sources of the Japanese Tradition* compiled by Tsunod aRyusaku, Wm. Theodore de Bary, and Donald Keene (New York, 1958), pp. 643–4. Borton, *Japan's Modern Century*, p. 72. Sansom, *The Western World and Japan*, p. 318, emphasizes the vague character of this Proclamation and the several possible interpretations.

[2] Beasley, *History*, p. 102.

Religion, Finance, War, Foreign Affairs, and Justice, to which an office of Civil Affairs (later called the Home Office) was added in 1869. Other articles sought to establish the supremacy of the Imperial government throughout Japan, delegating certain powers to it and denying other functions to the feudal authorities such as the bestowal of honours, the coinage of money, the employment of foreigners, and the contracting of alliances with each other or foreign states.[1]

The Princes of the Blood and Court and territorial nobility continued to hold the highest office but a reduction in the number of positions at the lower levels drastically cut the representation of the *kuge* and excluded many of the feudatories from the government. Only seven domains now took part through the work of nineteen samurai who exercised real power as advisers on every hand.[2]

Procedures which further strengthened the Imperial authority and concentrated power more openly in the hands of the four western *han* followed the end of the fighting in 1869. Most important was the abolition of feudalism. In March of that year at Kido's instigation, Satsuma, Chōshū, Tosa, and Hizen offered their fiefs to the Emperor, in an effort 'to preserve intact both one central body of government, and one universal authority' and asked that His Majesty issue such decrees as were needed to deal with their lands and their people. The immediate approval of the Court and some compulsion led other daimyo to do likewise. By August 1871 when an Imperial Rescript completely abolished all *han* and converted them into *ken* (prefectures) only seventeen of the 276 domains had not already surrendered their lands to the Mikado's government.[3] Another order compelling all daimyo to move with their families to Yedo (now the capital) soon reduced further the danger of local opposition.[4] Satisfactory financial compensation for the loss of their position kept the daimyo content but the stipends for their dispossessed samurai were too inadequate to insure the general support of the samurai for the new order.[5]

The Deliberative Assembly met for the last time in October

---

[1] McLaren, op. cit., pp. xl, 8–10.
[2] Sansom, *The Western World and Japan*, p. 320. Beasley, *History*, p. 102.
[3] McLaren, op. cit., pp. 29–33. Borton, *Japan's Modern Century*, p. 77.
[4] Sansom, *The Western World and Japan*, p. 326.
[5] Beasley, *History*, p. 109.

1870, and was officially abolished in 1873.[1] In another re-organization of the government in 1871 the *Dajōkan* was divided into three boards. The *Sei-in*, or Central Board, became the executive and policy-making body, wielding most of the power. Its membership sometimes overlapped with the *U-in* or Right Board which was made up of the heads of departments. And the *Sa-in*, or Left Board, became the feeble remnant of the legislative branch promised in the *Charter Oath*. Its powers were strictly advisory and limited to the consideration of 'projects of law proposed by the *Sei-in*'.[2] The open discussion of all mea-sures in widely convoked assemblies had been abandoned. In 1872 a law making possible the conscription of men at twenty and fixing the peace-time force at 36,000 gave the central authority a regular army and brought forward a great military leader, Yamagata Aritomo of Chōshū, who in 1873 became full Minister of War.[3] A new system of taxation in 1873 based on a reassessment of the value of land and payable in money began to provide the Imperial government with a much-needed income.[4] And changes in the names of the orders of nobility and the abolition of the old functional categories—samurai, farmer, artisan, and merchant—led to a growing sense of national unity. *Kuge* and feudal lords were given the same rank and were called *kazoku*. After 1872 the remainder of the people became commoners (*heimin*)—another humiliation for the numerous proud samurai who were also no longer required to wear swords and after March 1876 were forbidden to do so.[5]

The gifted samurai who had led the Restoration, however, rose to open control of the high offices after the abolition of feudalism. Thus in 1871 Ōkubo became Minister of Finance, Soejima Taneomi of Saga, Minister of Foreign Affairs, and Kido, Saigō, Itagaki, and Ōkuma, members of the *Dajōkan*. From the beginning of the Ministry of Industry (Public Works) in 1870 Itō was in virtual control and became minister in 1873 when Ōkubo took over the Home Office and Ōkuma succeeded

---

[1] McLaren, op. cit., p. 21.
[2] Ike Nobutaka, *The Beginnings of Political Democracy in Japan* (Baltimore, 1950), p. 41.
[3] Borton, *Japan's Modern Century*, pp. 84–85. Beasley, *History*, p. 112.
[4] Ibid., pp. 109–10.
[5] Ibid., p. 111. McLaren, op. cit., p. 32. Sansom, *The Western World and Japan*, p. 330. *Japan Weekly Mail*, 8 Apr. 1876.

him as Minister of Finance. The pretence of governing by Court and feudal aristocrats had ceased. Japan was to be ruled by an oligarchy with Sanjō and Iwakura at the top—in general, men of modest origin who would in time create a new peerage.

Such was the government, harassed by advocates of popular rights and modified from time to time, with which Parkes worked until 1883.[1] The long conversations which he, Mitford, and Satow had had with Gotō Shōjirō and others about representative government had borne little fruit. Neither did the Japanese translation in 1868 of Albany de Fonblanque's book *How We Are Governed* (1862) do more than indicate an interest in the English system.[2] The framers of the 1868 Constitution had modelled it upon the pre-feudal constitution of Taihō (A.D. 701–4), a national source which would have political appeal to a still divided Japan.[3] When translating the new text in August, Satow detected traces of American political theories which he attributed to the influence of Ōkuma and Soejima of Hizen who had been pupils of the American missionary, Dr. Guido Verbeck. He predicted many changes ahead.[4]

In consequence of Parkes's advice that export and import duties be levied and wharves for foreign ships established at Osaka, the Meiji government agreed to open Osaka as a port and notified the foreign representatives to this effect in early September 1868.[5]

Yedo became increasingly important as the centre of administration and plans were made for the Mikado's arrival.[6] In September 1868 the Emperor declared the city to be his official residence and changed the name to Tokyo (Eastern Capital) although the city was distressed by the presence of 30,000 Tokugawa men without rice or money who were in constant conflict with the Mikado's officials.[7]

The Mikado was enthroned in Kyoto that October when all

[1] McLaren, op. cit., pp. li–lxx.

[2] Yoshino Sakuzo, Ed., *Meiji Bunka Zenshū* (Collection of Materials Related to Early Meiji Culture), 24 vols. (Tokyo, 1928–55), vii. 27–105. The Japanese title was *Eisei Ikan* (How The British Are Governed).

[3] McLaren, op. cit., p. xxxvii.   [4] Satow, *Diplomat*, pp. 377, 381.

[5] *Nichi-Ei Gaikō Shi*, i. 104.

[6] F.O. 46/96, Parkes to Stanley, Nos. 208 and 231, Yokohama, 22 Aug. and 19 Sept. 1868.

[7] F.O. 46/97, Parkes to Stanley, No. 243, Yokohama, 7 Oct. 1868. Black, op. cit. ii. 224.

foreign consuls were entertained by Japanese authorities at Osaka.[1] Parkes felt optimistic about the future, believing there was reason to hope the Mikado's authority would be established universally. He wrote, 'Of course wars in the council will follow the existing wars in the field but in the end I trust Japan will become a nation, instead of the confederation of petty princes which it has been during the period of our experience'.[2]

On 6 November the foreigners at the open ports all celebrated the Mikado's birthday. At Yokohama Parkes and Sanjō reviewed the British troops—a colourful occasion of self-conscious pomp and ceremony.[3] Japan extended her relations with the West through a treaty with Sweden signed on 11 November. The Mikado entered Yedo on 26 November 1868 escorted by a thousand foot soldiers, mounted officers, and government officials—a procession marked by simplicity and lack of colour which inspired a religious silence among the crowds as the descendant of the Sun Goddess passed in his plain white wood, closed *norimono*, invisible to his reverent subjects.[4]

New Year's Day 1869 witnessed the opening of Yedo and Niigata to trade and foreign residents after a postponement in September because of the continuing civil disturbances. The Court encouraged the growing friendship between the government and the foreign powers by 'inviting' all the representatives of the treaty nations to an audience with the Emperor at his new residence in the ancient palace of the Shogun at Yedo.[5]

At this time Iwakura turned to Parkes for advice on affairs of state. In a confidential interview on 9 January at the Emperor's marine villa he acknowledged the support which England's early recognition had given the Mikado's government and asked Parkes to speak freely on any points in Japan's administration which might be guided by British experience. Parkes wrote Stanley, 'I scarcely think I am going too far in regard to the feeling evinced by the Prime Minister[6] on this

---

[1] F.O. 46/97, Parkes to Stanley, No. 266, Yokohama, 21 Oct. 1868.

[2] F.O. 46/98, Parkes to F.O., Private, Yokohama, 4 Nov. 1868.

[3] Ibid., Parkes to Stanley, No. 289, Yokohama, 17 Nov. 1868. Black, op. cit. ii. 232–4.

[4] F.O. 46/98, Parkes to Stanley, No. 307, Yokohama, 2 Dec. 1868. P.P. H. of C. 1870, lxx. 1–3 for account in the *Japan Times* of 28 Nov. 1868.

[5] F.O. 46/106, Parkes to Stanley, Nos. 3 and 4, Yokohama, 13 Jan. 1869.

[6] Iwakura was really Minister of the 'Right' (*Udaijin*), not 'Prime Minister'.

occasion as more encouraging from its evident reality than any other occurrence that has come to my notice in my communication with this Government'. He believed he had gained the confidence of the Mikado's government and could anticipate greater intimacy and intercourse in the furture.[1]

Others also were encouraged. The contemporary British journalist, John R. Black, marvelled at what the 'new and politically untried men', many converted expulsionists, had already accomplished for the good of the country.[2] And the *North China Herald* concluded its review of Japan in 1868 with this paragraph:

On the whole, though our trade has suffered from the political convulsion which has agitated the Kingdom, we may consider that both our commercial and political relations with Japan have been placed on a more firm and satisfactory basis during the past year; and for this result we are greatly indebted to the ability, fearlessness, and energy displayed by H.B.M. Minister.[3]

The Emperor himself recognized Parkes's assistance to his government. He expressed his appreciation of the British minister's 'advice and counsels' when he received the Duke of Edinburgh in a private interview at Yedo Castle on 4 September 1869. This important occasion climaxed a series of elaborate entertainments arranged in honour of His Royal Highness. Long-established traditions were broken to show the Duke the rarest courtesies. Major daimyo had taken part in the festivities. Even Mito had sent a representative. And now for the first time the Emperor met face to face a prince of European royal blood and had received him on a basis of complete equality.[4]

Parkes viewed these proceedings with fresh optimism. Shortly before the Duke's visit, alarming demonstrations of anti-foreign sentiment, not only by *rōnin* and samurai but among the Mikado's palace guards, had made him question the will and

Thus he ranked third in the *Dajōkan*, the Minister of the 'Left' (*Sadaijin*) and the Prime Minister (*Dajō-daijin*) being his superiors.

[1] F.O. 46/106, Parkes to Stanley, No. 5, Conf'l., Yokohama, 13 Jan. 1869.
[2] Black, op. cit. ii. 226–8.

[3] *North China Herald*, 'Retrospect of Political and Commercial Affairs in China and Japan, 1868,' p. 16.

[4] P.P. H. of C. 1870, lxx. 43–46, Parkes to Clarendon, 30 Sept. 1869 and encl. I. Japanese accuont in *D.N.G.M.* ii. Pt. II, 366–408, Doc. 349.

PLATE 5

A House in the British Settlement in Takanawa, 1868
By Andō Hiroshige

the ability of the Imperial government to control an open
defiance of its proclaimed pro-foreign policy. But in the respect
and tributes paid to the British duke, Parkes found proof of the
new government's determination to accept Western precedents
in the conduct of its foreign relations.[1]

Retrospect

Japan had inaugurated a new order. How much Parkes and
the members of the British legation aided its establishment is
difficult to measure. From Alcock's time onward it had been
clear, in spite of several overtures to the contrary, that the
Japanese wanted to settle their internal conflict without
foreign intervention. And the opposition to the Shogun's dictatorship was sufficiently great to have overthrown the *Bakufu* in
time, regardless of any foreign influence. The introduction of
foreign trade and other stipulations of the foreign treaties
merely hastened the event, giving the opposition daimyo
further cause for grievance against the Tokugawa government
while at the same time embarrassing the Shogunate in its
relations with the Court and weakening it financially through
the exaction of indemnities as penalties for its inability to
protect foreign life and property.

Parkes made great efforts to understand the issues in the
conflict. He knew before the end of 1865, as leading British
merchants had discovered earlier, that the alleged hostility of
the great western daimyo to the foreign treaties and their
declared opposition to the opening of Hyogo and Osaka were
a cover for their attack on the supremacy and trade monopolies of the Shogun. He determined to be neutral in the
obviously approaching civil conflict months before Clarendon's
instructions restating British orders to that effect reached Japan.
At the same time, however, the British Foreign Secretary
commanded Parkes to encourage the daimyo to work with the
Mikado and *Bakufu* to end the exclusive and restrictive system
which might cause civil or foreign war and to exact the observance of the treaties and protection of British subjects from all
parties. Furthermore almost concurrently Clarendon promised
France that Parkes would do nothing 'to encourage the daimios

[1] P.P. H. of C. 1870, lxx. 43, Parkes to Clarendon, 30 Sept. 1869. For anti-
foreign acts and Parkes's protests to the government, see Oka, *Reimeiki no Meiji
Nihon*, pp. 51–85.

to subvert the authority of the Tycoon'.[1] Outwardly Parkes followed these commands to the letter until the resignation of Keiki in November 1867. He secured the right of daimyo to trade at the open ports by the tariff Convention of 1866. He refused to try to open negotiations with the Mikado for a council of daimyo and to come out for a treaty with the Mikado as Satow and Satsuma agents proposed. He did personally visit some of the western daimyo with the Shogun's approval and he encouraged Keiki to make concessions regarding their demand for a share in the government. Consistently he applauded Keiki's abdication and his desire that the government of Japan should be reorganized in line with the wishes of a national assembly of daimyo in which he, Keiki, expected to have a leading part. Parkes was obviously interested in a coalition government under the Mikado, whom he recognized as the undoubted sovereign of Japan, with the Shogun as a principal minister.[2] He believed a strong central government should replace the medieval feudal structure to benefit the development of Japan, as well as Britain's chief concern, the expansion of foreign trade.[3]

The evidence that the British encouraged the daimyo party in the plan to abolish the Shogunate lies in articles in the British press and in the far from neutral statements supporting this aim made and recorded by Satow during his interviews with the Satsuma, Tosa, Uwajima princes and their agents when collecting information for his chief. Whether Parkes acquiesced in this cannot be established from the available documents. Parkes always instructed Satow to maintain that Britain would not interfere in Japan's internal affairs and cared not which party was in power as long as the treaties were carried out. While Satow persistently claimed that he had done so, his own *Diary* and memoirs almost boast of his actions to the contrary.[4] He also not only admitted his growing sympathy for the daimyo party as early as 1864 after the allied attack on Shimonoseki, and stressed the supremacy of the Mikado and the illegitimate pretensions of the Shogun to power, but disparaged any effort to bolster up the Shogunate and advised

[1] See p. 176.
[2] Parkes to Flowers, 14 Oct. 1866, quoted in Dickins, op. cit. ii. 69.
[3] See pp. 210–11.　　　　　　　　　[4] Satow, *Diplomat*, pp. 129, 157, 159.

direct relations with the Mikado and daimyo. Both contemporary and later accounts attribute a wide influence to Satow's articles in the *Japan Times* when translated in pamphlet form, as the accepted statement of British policy, in spite of the fact that Parkes never followed his main recommendation for a treaty with the Mikado and the confederate daimyo. Mitford of the British legation and the respected barrister and one-time proprietor of the *Japan Mail*, F. V. Dickins, who alone had access later to Parkes's private papers, stress Satow's influence on Parkes's policy.[1] It is therefore hard to believe that the British minister did not know what his subordinate was saying and did not secretly support him, although none of the Foreign Office manuscripts gives such evidence.

British sympathy for the daimyo cause, whether official or not, could not have brought about the overthrow of the Shogunate. But from the time of Keiki's abdication, British action deliberately strengthened the nascent Imperial government. Parkes's hurried request for a letter of credence to that government even before he could know what form it would take made Britain the first of the powers to recognize it. His prompt initiation, through Satow, of the allied neutrality policy at the outbreak of civil war, weakened the Tokugawa's defence by denying them the delivery of the ships purchased in the United States and France. His successful efforts in preventing the vindictive Saigō from executing Keiki and destroying Yedo strengthened the new authorities in the eyes of the nation and the world. And by withdrawing the neutrality proclamation and thus releasing the U.S. ram *Stonewall* for the government's use in February 1869, he hastened the defeat of the *kerai*.[2]

Parkes became in his time the foremost foreign adviser and critic of the Mikado's government as it forged a new national life and foreign policy. On some phases of this the British wielded an important influence before Parkes left his post for his assignment in China in 1883. It is with these areas the following chapters are concerned—not with the question of treaty revision or Japan's relations with Korea, which also involved Parkes, but were not settled during his ministry.

[1] Dickins, op. cit. ii. 61. Redesdale, op. cit. i. 377. Shinobu, op. cit. xxvii, 687–9.
[2] Ibid. 875–6.

X

BRITISH INFLUENCE ON THE JAPANESE NAVY

Japanese Navies before the Restoration

JAPAN had made some efforts towards a national navy before she signed the commercial treaties of 1858. Perry's formidable arrival had convinced the *Bakufu* of the urgency of sea defence. A letter from the Dutch government advising the Shogun to build a navy on the European model hastened action.[1] In October 1853 the *Bakufu* repealed the ban of 1638 on the building of large ocean-going vessels and granted to all daimyo permission to build warships. It chose a national flag distinguished by a red ball representing the sun on a white background, began the construction of forts at Shinagawa, and cast a number of large cannon.[2] In May 1854 the *Bakufu* itself built a ship, the *Hōō Maru*, according to an English model at Uraga port.[3] The next year it opened a naval training-school at Nagasaki where Dutch instructors were employed until March 1859 to teach Japanese cadets. Here, too, the *Bakufu* built a dockyard and iron foundry. In the same year, 1855, the Dutch presented Japan with the *Kankō Kan*, a small steam warship of 150 horsepower and six guns which was used later as a training-ship in connexion with a naval training-school, opened in 1857 at Yedo under Japanese graduates of the school at Nagasaki.[4] By 1858 the Japanese government had bought

[1] Yamamoto Gombei, in Ōkuma Shigenobu, Compiler, *Fifty Years of New Japan* (Kaikoku Gojūnen Shi), English version edited by Marcus B. Huish, 2 vols., (London, 1909). i, 223.

[2] Yamaguchi Ken [Shozan Yashi, pseud.], *Kinseishi Ryaku* (Summary History of Modern Times), (Tokyo, 1872), Eng. translation by E. M. Satow, Yokohama, 1873, under title *Kinse Shiriaku* (A History of Japan from the First Visit of Commodore Perry in 1853 to the Capture of Hakodate by the Mikado's Forces in 1869), p. 3.

[3] Katsu Yasuyoshi, Ed. *Kaigun Rekishi* (*History of the Navy*), 9 vols. (25 books) (1899), i. 20. Ueno Kiichiro, *A Hundred Years' History of Ships*, 2 vols. (Tokyo, 1957–8), i. 7.

[4] Yamamoto in Ōkuma, *Fifty Years of New Japan*, i. 223–4. For a more detailed

two warships of 12 guns each from Holland and one of 340 tons from Britain. England had given the Shogun the yacht *Emperor*, later equipped with four guns and finally renamed the *Banryū*. Perhaps six more government-owned warships were built somewhat according to European ideas in native docks at Kagoshima, Yedo, Shimoda, Nagasaki, and at Hakodate before the opening of the ports. The workmanship was faulty and the dates of their construction are not always known.[1]

The *han* were equally active in the building of ships. Satsuma and Mito were the earliest to recognize the need for a navy and to study ship construction from Dutch works. In 1848 the Daimyo of Satsuma ordered the translation of a Dutch book on the steamship. With this as a guide his successor, the great Shimazu Nariakira (1851–8), built three model steamships in 1852.[2] After the repeal of the laws restricting the size of vessels in 1853, he advanced a programme to build fifteen warships including three steamers. The next year the *han* built the first Western-style warship, a ten-gun vessel, the *Shohei Kan*, which Nariakira presented to the Shogun. Nariakira's awareness of the 'geographical similarities' of England and Japan and of England's naval predominance in the West led him to propose not only that the British Navy be considered as a model for Satsuma and thence for Japan but also that the British colonial empire offered valuable lessons in forms of expansion.[3]

Mito started the construction of the Ishikawajima shipyard at Yedo in 1854 where a Western-style ship, a sailing vessel, the *Rising Sun*, was completed in August 1856. Both Satsuma and Mito had no direct foreign technical help, while Saga, the third leader in ship construction, employed some Dutch assistance.[4]

The purchase of ships abroad developed rapidly in the sixties. Both the *Bakufu* and the leading clans hurried to acquire warships and other vessels of their own. The ministers told Alcock

account of Dutch training and influence on the *Bakufu* navy, see John C. Perry, *Great Britain and the Imperial Japanese Navy 1868–1905*, unpublished thesis (Harvard University, 1961), pp. 19–25.

[1] Yamamoto in Ōkuma, *Fifty Years of New Japan*, i. 223–4. Katsu, op. cit. xxiii. 1–3. Ueno, op. cit. i. 7.

[2] Thomas C. Smith, *Political Change and Industrial Development in Japan; Government Enterprise*, 1868–80 (Stanford, 1955), pp. 9–10.

[3] Perry, op. cit., pp. 28–30.   [4] Thomas C. Smith, op. cit., pp. 9–11.

that in so doing they hoped to develop trade with China and other countries. He thought, however, that their awareness of Russian designs on their northern territory caused their hurry to acquire large European warships.[1] By 1863 the government and the *han* together are said to have possessed five men-of-war, all of which belonged to the Shogunate; thirteen screw steamers, six paddle steamers, two barques, two brigs, and two schooners —a total of thirty vessels which had cost them $2,357,800.[2] Most of these ships were built in England or America. Jardine, Matheson and Company handled contracts with Satsuma and the Shogunate for British vessels and guns.[3] Profits were generous; for example, $40,000 on a contract for $183,847 worth of guns.[4] Alcock noted that the Japanese never seemed to get good bargains.[5]

The *Bakufu* distinguished itself in 1866 by building at the Ishikawajima shipyard the first steam warship in Japan, called the *Chiyodagata*, and by making the first regular voyage by steamship between Yedo and Osaka with the *Kishō Maru*, a transport of 517 tons purchased in England.[6] At the time of its collapse the *Bakufu* fleet consisted of eight all Western-built warships; eleven auxiliary ships built in Japan, mostly small barks and schooners; and twenty-three (or twenty-five) foreign-built auxiliary ships, twelve of iron and eleven of wood, ranging from sixty-six to 996 tons. Fifteen of this total had been built in England, twelve in the United States, four in the Netherlands, and one in Prussia.[7]

Next to the *Bakufu*, Satsuma became the largest purchaser of foreign ships. During the last years of the Shogunate, the *han* bought a total of seventeen Western ships. Fifteen were built in England. Thirteen were ironclads. Their horsepower ranged from 45 to 300; their tonnage from 160 to 1,015. All the clans together had bought or built ninety-four ships.[8] These

[1] F.O. 46/12, Alcock to Russell, No. 37, Conf'l., Yedo, 3 Apr. 1861.

[2] Black, op. cit. i. 218–19.

[3] J.M. MSS. (Nagasaki, 1863–4), Glover & Co. to Hong Kong Office, Nagasaki, 13 Mar. and 27 Oct. 1863, 7 Mar. 1864.

[4] Ibid. (Nagasaki, 1866), Glover to (probably) W. Keswick, Nagasaki, 10 Mar. 1866.

[5] F.O. 46/13, Alcock to Russell, Conf'l., Yedo, 25 Aug. 1861.

[6] Ueno, op. cit., pp. 12 and 18. Katsu, op. cit. xxiii. 2. Katsu, however, does not list the *Chiyodagata* as a warship. Ibid., p. 3.

[7] Rear-Adm. Saitō in Alfred Stead, Ed. *Japan by the Japanese* (Tokyo, 1904), pp. 122 ff. Katsu, op. cit. xxiii. 2. The *Stonewall* is excluded here.

[8] Yamaguchi Kazuo, *Bakumatsu Bōeki Shi* (History of Foreign Trade in the

combined with those of the *Bakufu* gave Japan in 1868 a total of 138 ships of which 111 had been imported.

The First British Naval Mission

The training of naval officers was as important to Japan as the acquisition of ships. The *Bakufu* request for British help in this endeavour was preceded by diplomatic embarrassment. Here Her Majesty's Government was in part to blame in that it had made no reply to the Shogun's request of December 1864 for military instructors for Japanese troops.[1] After waiting a year, Shibata Gōchū made application for instruction in all branches of service to France during his mission to Europe in 1865.[2] This was immediately granted. The Japanese then asked Parkes for permission to send twenty young men to study in British military schools instead of having British instructors come to Japan. Parkes was not averse to this proposal. In a private letter to London, reporting the appointment of the French military mission, however, he suggested that should the Japanese government prefer French officers on shore, it might look to England 'for similar assistance afloat'. He was determined to wield equal influence with France in Japan.[3] About a fortnight later the British government consented to Japan's employing British military instructors,[4] much to the embarrassment of the *Rōjū*, who willingly admitted their mistake in applying to France before hearing from Great Britain, but felt unable to break their engagement with France and did not want two systems of military instruction. Parkes then proposed that they ask Britain for naval instructors instead. Further complications arose by the arrival from the United States of Japan's new warship *Fujiyama* where French officers were already employed to drill the crew. Declaring this arrangement temporary, the *Rōjū* sought Parkes's help in persuading these naval officers to leave. Roches co-operated and withdrew

Closing Days of the *Bakufu*), (Tokyo, 1947), pp. 94–96, 108–9. Authorities vary about the number of ships possessed by the clans. Adm. Saitō in Stead, op. cit., p. 122, gives only seventy-two ships for their total fleet of which thirty-nine were ironclad.

[1] See p. 148.   [2] See p. 174.

[3] F.O. 46/58, Parkes to Russell, No. 82, 30 Dec. 1865; Parkes to F.O., Private, same date. Redesdale, op. cit. i. 378–9.

[4] F.O. 46/65, Parkes to Clarendon, No. 5, Yokohama, 17 Jan 1866.

the French officers in May.[1] He even recommended that British naval instructors be invited. He knew full well that Britain would not tolerate France's further domination of both services, especially in the light of the advice and assistance France was giving in the construction of the shipyard at Yokosuka.[2]

On 1 July the *Rōjū* made their official application to Parkes for a naval teaching mission. They said they had learned from the Dutch at Nagasaki something of 'nautical astronomy, surveying, mathematics, practical seamanship and steam', that the French had taught them 'the general routine of the Navy and the practice of great guns', that they had a tolerably correct idea of the naval discipline of the different navies of Europe, but they needed to learn more about the 'methods of naval warfare and the art of manoeuvring ships'. They asked for fourteen men who would include one officer skilled in tactics and experienced in actual warfare, one officer acquainted with naval routine and the general duties of a master, one gunnery officer, one engineer officer, one naval instructor 'skilled in mathematics who could also teach languages', one boatswain, two gunners, three first-class able seamen, and three trumpeters and drummers for making signal calls. Their pay should be settled in England.

Their students were to be selected from those who had studied English, French, or Dutch and who had some acquaintance with naval warfare. The Japanese wished instruction to be given aboard ship where the students would live. A warship, probably the *Kankō Kan*, and one or more ships would be anchored at Yokohama for this purpose. Instruction would be scheduled for certain hours. The instructors were to live on shore.[3]

Her Majesty's Government in London willingly complied with this request.[4] A carefully selected group of men under Commander R. E. Tracey left for Japan in March 1867 on H.M.S. *Rodney* to be at the service of the Japanese government for two years. Their monthly salaries were high for that period:

[1] F.O. 46/69, Parkes to Clarendon, No. 123, Nagasaki, 24 July 1866.

[2] *Yokohama-shi Shi Kō*, ii. 379. See Perry, op. cit., pp. 65–72, for account of French assistance and the duplicity of Roches.

[3] Ad. I/5992, F.O. to Adm., 4 Oct. 1866 and 2 encls., Japanese Ministers to Parkes, 1 July 1866 and *Memorandum on Naval Instruction*, June 1866. Katsu, op. cit. xix. 2–3.

[4] F.O. 262/106, Stanley to Parkes, 23 Oct. 1866. Ad. 13–57, Adm. to F.O., 18 Oct. 1866.

£65 for the Commander, £50 for each of the other three officers, £16 each for one gunner and one boatswain and £8 apiece for the remaining seamen, gunners, and instructors.[1] The Japanese government also agreed to bear the expense of the passage of the men to and from Yedo, their maintenance in Japan, and the equipment for training their navy.[2] While in the service of Japan these men were still under the command of the British Commander-in-chief of the China Station, to whom they were to report quarterly concerning the progress of their work with the Japanese. In the absence of Vice-Admiral Sir Henry Keppel, then in charge of the station, they were to turn to the British minister for advice or assistance. The Admiralty Board ordered Commander Tracey to arrange with the Japanese authorities for the instruction in the various duties they desired for the Japanese officers and men and to observe the course they approved—always remembering to consult 'the peculiar habits and customs of the people' with whom his mission worked in an effort to earn their goodwill and to carry out his duties satisfactorily.[3] The instruments and books which were required for their instruction and for which the British asked reimbursement cost £520 17s. 3d.[4]

Sir Henry Keppel reported that a naval college and accommodations for Commander Tracey and his associates were being constructed in Yedo. He had inspected the site and advised some alterations. His comment on the Japanese Navy was not flattering. The fourteen vessels possessed by the *Bakufu* for war purposes, he said, were in bad order and required experienced officers, especially engineers. The Japanese officials, however, were most anxious to receive instruction.[5]

The training mission arrived in October 1867. Financial

---

[1] Ad. 13–58, Adm. to F.O., 4 Jan. 1867. F.O. 262/123, Stanley to Parkes, No. 8, 10 Jan. 1867.

[2] Ad. I/6006, Keppel to Adm., 20 Dec. 1867. A letter from Stanley, however, states that H.M. Government bore the cost of transporting the instructors to Hong Kong and that they travelled from there to Yedo by a commercial steamer for £85. F.O. 262/124, Stanley to Parkes, No. 185, 14 Dec. 1867.

[3] F.O. 262/124, encl. in Hammond to Parkes, No. 58, 29 Mar. 1867, Instructions Adm. to Tracey, 25 Mar. 1867.

[4] F.O. 262/124, Stanley to Parkes, 9 July 1867.

[5] Ad. I/6006, Keppel to Adm., 13 July 1867. The number of ships of war here varies from Katsu's report. A vessel for 'war purposes' was not always an armed ship.

arrangements were completed with the *Bakufu* before it began work. On 21 November the British instructors met seventy-one Japanese students. A tight schedule from seven o'clock in the morning until ten o'clock at night was enforced six days of the week. Instruction included courses in administration, gunnery, the use of rifles and sabres, navigation, and surveying for both officers and student sailors. Wednesdays were reserved for practice on ship.[1]

The work began well. Admiral Keppel visited the school in December and reported satisfaction with the way Commander Tracey and his assistants had commenced their duties. They had been invited to meet the Shogun at Yedo Castle—a meeting which Katsu himself and high Japanese officers had attended.[2] But their task came to a sudden end.

The abolition of the Shogunate and the Imperial Restoration in January 1868, followed by the outbreak of civil war in which the Western powers proclaimed neutrality, meant that the Shogun's school for naval training under British instructors had to be closed. Sir Harry Parkes ordered Commander Tracey with his officers and men to retire to Yokohama until the re-establishment of peace.[3] The officers of the ex-Shogun continued their pay until Yedo fell to the Imperial forces. By September there was still no prospect of an internal peace when the Mikado's government could use the mission's services. Commander Tracey appealed to Keppel for permission to return to England. Keppel's letter supporting this request reached Parkes simultaneously with a similar proposal from the Japanese ministers. Parkes and Keppel agreed it was unfair to ask the Mikado's government to maintain a mission while all its advantages were withheld. Although the Japanese offered to pay the full salaries of the instructors until they reached home in addition to the costs of their passage, Parkes concluded an arrangement whereby they received only half pay and their travel expenses. The mission embarked for England on 7 October 1868.[4]

---

[1] Katsu, op. cit. xix. 10–12.

[2] Ibid. p. 12. Ad. I/6006, Keppel to Adm., 21 Dec. 1867.

[3] Katsu, op. cit. xix. 16–17. Ad. I/6072, F.O. to Adm., 6 May 1868, encl. Parkes's letter to F.O., 11 Mar. 1868.

[4] Ad. I/6053, Keppel to Adm., 17 Sept. 1868, encl. Higashikuze to Parkes, 11 Sept. 1868. F.O. 46/97, Parkes to Stanley, Nos. 233 and 234, Yokohama, 7 Oct. 1868.

The men schooled so briefly by the Tracey Mission proved the value of their British training in action during Enomoto's final struggle at Hakodate. At that time the Meiji government also recognized the importance of sea power and the inadequacy of what was left of its own and the Tokugawa fleet.[1] A strong navy became the goal of the makers of modern Japan and Britain their chosen teacher.

The Early Meiji Navy

Before the restoration of peace in 1869 Katsu Kaishu, who knew well the limitations of the Tokugawa fleet, drafted a programme for a strong Japanese navy.[2] With great understanding of the historical development of European navies—those of Holland, England, Russia, and France—and an awareness of the increasing war potential of the new ironclad steam battleships, he urged upon Japan a powerful navy as the primary means of establishing her rightful place among the nations of the world. His arguments already indicate an intense nationalism not lacking in imperialist ambitions.

A powerful naval force, he believed, would enable Japan to defend her land against invasion, exile the foreign troops then stationed by England and France on her territory, and keep Russia from the Northern Sea. With sufficient naval power, Katsu predicted Japan would be able to conquer Korea and make it her colony, then occupy west China and thus check Russia's obvious intention—illustrated by her recent conquest of Manchuria and efforts to invade the northern frontiers of Japan, China, and Korea—to create a vast country which would dominate the Asian and European continents. He feared the intention of England and America to propagate Christianity in Japan—a heresy which he said perplexed the Japanese people and which Japan must be powerful enough to prohibit. A strong navy, he argued, was more important than an army for Japan, even as it had been for England, whose prosperity he attributed to her concentration on building a large fleet. He appealed to the Japanese people—a nation, he said, of fifty million with a national income of ninety million *koku*—

---

[1] Joseph H. Longford, 'The Growth of the Japanese Navy', *The Nineteenth Century*, liv (Sept. 1903), pp. 475, 477–81.

[2] For Katsu Kaishu see p. 231.

to use their wealth to build a strong navy and thus to be able to compete with the five big powers, England, France, Russia, Austria, and Prussia.[1]

Katsu's programme required seven years for completion. It provided for sixty ships equipped with steam engines to include three ironclads first class, six ironclads middle class, six ironclads small class, twelve wooden ships middle class, twelve wooden ships small class, eighteen wooden gunboats, and three ironclad transports. It asked for fifty-six sailing vessels for transport to be used for carrying coal and food and to train officers and sailors. The complement of men required was 12,000.[2]

Some ships were to be built in Yokosuka near Yokohama, others to be imported from Western countries. Their cost was to be met through taxation in Japan and by reduction in government expenses. Katsu envisaged naval bases at Yedo and at a good place between Osaka and Kobe.[3]

Katsu proposed the establishing of naval schools where Japanese students should read English books and learn the art of navigation from Englishmen. He did not want the Japanese merely to imitate the English, however, but to adopt their good points and establish a particular Japanese navy. He expected to depend mainly on the English and the Dutch for guidance in setting up the schools, in establishing an examination system, and in making rules for discipline on warships. After taking into consideration both the American and French procedures he recommended adopting the best from all four countries in the establishing of essentially Japanese rules.[4]

Katsu's plan left out little connected with the building of a strong naval force. He discussed hospitals, dockyards, the provision of nourishing food and clothing for the men, classes of officers and sailors, salaries, size of crews, ceremonies, signals, criminal law on board ship, prize, and punishment. He reviewed the changes in Western navies from wooden to ironclad ships

---

[1] Diet Library, Tokyo, MS. (included in the Iwakura Papers), Katsu Kaishu, *Programme for Establishing of a Navy 1868*, Preface, pp. 1–7. Here Katsu is referring to Russia's advances along the north bank of the Amur River since 1854 and her acquisition of the Maritime Province between the Ussuri River and the Pacific by her treaty with China signed at Peking in 1860. Thirty million is a more accurate estimate of the Japanese population at this time. See p. 24.

[2] Katsu, *Programme . . . 1868*, pp. 9–11.   [3] Ibid., p. 12.

[4] Ibid., pp. 22–24ff.

and the percentages of national incomes devoted to naval development in 1867. He showed that if Japan paid 1,100,000 *koku* for her navy, it would be only one-sixth of what England spent and would not be sufficient to repel a Russian invasion. He finally appealed to all Japanese to co-operate in saving money to build the needed naval and military forces.[1]

The new Meiji government accepted much of this programme. Its initial navy was composed of warships handed over by the defeated *Bakufu* and those requisitioned from Satsuma, Chōshū, Saga, and other clans.[2] The *Bakufu* contribution had little value. Five of the fourteen Tokugawa ships seized by the rebels under Enomoto were lost *en route* to Yezo and three were wrecked or burned in the final battle at Hakodate.[3] Others were in poor condition having been worn-out craft sold to the Shogun or daimyo by Western powers.[4] New ships had to be built and a navy department organized.

Mysterious reports of ships being built in British shipyards for the Japanese government soon began to concern the Foreign Office and Admiralty Board in London. J. M. James informed the Lords Commissioners that he had been appointed by the Prince of Higo through Messrs. Glover and Company to take command of an iron-plated corvette being built in Aberdeen for the Japanese.[5] This appears to have been the *Ryūjō*, a three-masted ship-rigged composite corvette, armour belted, of 2,530 tons displacement which mounted ten guns.[6] Built by Messrs. H. Hall and Company of Aberdeen to the order of Glover Brothers of Nagasaki for the Kumamoto *han*, the ship was completed in 1869 and given to the Meiji government in 1870. A second gun vessel, built by the same firm for the

[1] Ibid., pp. 40, 43 ff.   [2] Yamamoto in Ōkuma, *Fifty Years of New Japan*, i. 224.

[3] F.O. 46/97, Parkes to Stanley, No. 244, Yokohama, 7 Oct. 1868; 46/124, Newspaper review of 1869 encl. in Parkes to F.O., No. 15, 1870. Kōshaku Shimazū-ke Henshū Jo (Editorial Office of the House of Prince Shimazu), compiler, *Satsuma Kaigun Shi* (History of Satsuma Navy), 2 vols. (Tokyo, 1929), ii. 263–4. Kaigun Yushūkai (Naval Reserve Officers' Association), compiler, *Kinsei Teikoku Kaigun Shi Yō* (Outline History of the Navy of Modern Japan), (Tokyo, 1938), pp. 544–50.

[4] J.M. MSS. (Nagasaki, 1864), T. Glover to W. Keswick, 5 Oct. 1864. Ad. I/6052, Keppel to Adm., Yokohama, 2 May 1868. Here Keppel says the U.S. ironclad ram *Stonewall*, renamed *Azuma*, represented part payment of a claim made by the *Bakufu* against the U.S. for a number of useless vessels supplied to the Shogun. See p. 239.

[5] Ad. I/6068, James to Adm., 12 Oct. 1868. J. M. James is not mentioned in the *Navy List* for 1868 but Comdr. J. W. James appears on p. 17.

[6] Perry, op. cit., p. 99.

Yamaguchi *han* in 1870, called the *Unyō*, was also presented that year to the new government.[1]

Parkes's inquiries about rumours of other orders for ships built in England for the Japanese government led to less satisfactory replies. Private shipyards were reluctant and not dependable about releasing information to Admiralty officers concerning war vessels for foreign governments. Thus statements that Messrs. Dudgeon's Yard, Millwall on the Thames, had begun the construction of three more gun vessels for the Japanese in September 1868 and completed them in July and August 1869 were not confirmed by any facts concerning by whom the ships were commissioned or where they were in 1870. Their names, *Pepita*, *Conchita*, and *Manuelita*, have no resemblance to those of Japan, and do not appear on the Japanese lists of gunboats built in Britain for Japan in those years.[2]

The shipbuilding companies furthermore were not always certain of the destiny of the ships which Japan ordered. In 1880, for example, Yarrow and Company, Ltd. of Glasgow supplied the hull of a vessel for the Japanese government which was shipped in pieces and re-erected in Japan. But neither the use of this ship—a little craft 100 feet long by 12½ feet beam which cost £1,920—nor its form of propulsion was known to its builders in Britain.[3]

In 1872 separate departments of the Army and the Navy replaced the Department of War which had handled the affairs of both services. Katsu Awa became the naval minister. New regulations for the unification of naval affairs and the construction and purchase of ships followed. The Japanese navy then consisted of seventeen vessels having an aggregate displacement tonnage of approximately 13,812 tons. Except for the two iron-clads, the ram *Azuma*, and the *Ryūjo*, and the wooden gunboat made in England for Saga in 1867, they were small wooden craft, out of date and nearly useless.[4]

---

[1] F.O. 46/133, Adm. to F.O., 18 Feb. 1870 and encl. Adm. Saitō in Stead, op. cit., p. 126.

[2] F.O. 262/184, F.O. to Parkes, 22 Feb. 1870, encl. report on the investigation of the gunboats by Luke, Surveyor for the Admiralty, 15 Feb. 1870. *Kinsei Teikoku Kaigun Shi Yō*, pp. 821–3. Adm. Saitō in Stead, op. cit., p. 126.

[3] Letter from Yarrow and Company, Ltd. to Grace Fox, 6 July 1962.

[4] Yamamoto in Ōkuma, *Fifty Years of New Japan*, i. 225. *Kinsei Teikoku Kaigun Shi Yō*, pp. 544–50.

The construction of two small wooden steamships under French direction at Yokosuka inaugurated in 1872 the Meiji building programme.[1] The Japanese developed rapidly the techniques of shipbuilding and repairs. They laid down the keels of their first real warship, the *Seiki* (897 tons) and of the Imperial yacht *Jingei* (1,450 tons) in 1873 at Yokosuka and launched them respectively in 1875 and 1876.[2] By 1876 little foreign assistance was needed. By 1883 they had built one sloop (720 h.p.), one gunboat (650 h.p.), and two corvettes of 1,267 h.p. each.[3] As early as 1873 an English naval captain considered the facilities for repairing vessels at the Yokosuka dockyard to be as good in a general way as at a dockyard in England.[4] In 1882 there were two docks in use and a third scheduled for completion in 1883. There was a building slip where wooden vessels of 1,000 tons were produced, and a boiler, and machine shop, foundry, and forge made possible the repair of engines of moderate size. The Japanese also began the manufacture of gunpowder and established ordnance works in these early yards.[5]

The new facilities, however, could not supply enough ships to meet Japan's naval needs, which became increasingly apparent as civil strife and growing tensions with China over Formosa and Korea disturbed the country. When the possibility of war heightened in the early autumn of 1874 Japan frantically ordered warships by telegram from the Ahrent and Malcomb companies in England at a cost of about £55,000. The Navy Department also asked the Ahrent Company to purchase 5,000 stand of Henry Martini rifles with bayonets—an order placed with the Braendlin Armoury Company of Birmingham.[6] In

Ogasawara Nagayo, *Life of Admiral Togo*, trans. by Inouye Jukichi and Inouye Tozo (Tokyo, 1934), p. 59. Japanese figures for the tonnage of these ships vary greatly. Why the *Unyō*, the second gunboat built at Aberdeen in 1870, is not included here is not known.

[1] Adm. Saitō in Stead, op. cit., p. 126.

[2] Yamamoto in Ōkuma, *Fifty Years of New Japan*, i. 226. Rear-Adm. Fujii Terugoro, 'Progress of Naval Engineering in Japan', *Transactions of the Institution of Naval Architects*, liii, Pt. II, Table 2, opp. p. 194.

[3] Ibid., Table 2, opp. p. 194.

[4] Ad. I/6262 encl. in Vice-Adm. C. F. A. Shadwell to Adm, 30 July 1873.

[5] F.O. 262/396, Samuel Long's *Report* encl. in F.O. to Parkes, 15 Aug. 1883, p. 6. Yamamoto in Ōkuma, *Fifty Years of New Japan*, i. 226.

[6] L.C. micro. (R 34 F 45181), Taiwan Jimu: Navy, 1874, vol. 4, Na 10644, *Rondon, 9 gatsu 11 nichi zai-Ei Dairi Motono Moritō kōshinsho batsu*. (Excerpt of

September 1875 the Japanese minister in England, Ueno Kagenori (October 1874–November 1879), and the agent of the Japanese government, Edward James Reed, M.P. for Pembroke and a former superintendent of construction for the Admiralty, signed contracts for an ironclad warship with engine at £193,500 and for two steam corvettes, at £240,350. Ueno requested that the first payment of £76,700 be sent by wire through the Oriental Bank within a fortnight.[1] These vessels were completed in February 1878. The twin corvettes *Kongō* and *Hiei* (ironclad wooden ships, 2,535 h.p., 2,248 displacement tons, crew complements 255) were built respectively at Kingston upon Hull and at Pembroke. The *Fusō* ('an armoured iron vessel, 3,650 h.p., 3,717 displacement tons, 295 crew complement') was laid down at Poplar. In accordance with Reed's contract, the officers and crews assigned to bring these ships to Japan were all Englishmen except the nine Japanese naval students who had recently finished their training in England. Among the latter was the future Admiral Tōgō Heihachirō, then a cadet who returned to Yokohama in May 1878 aboard the *Hiei*.[2] Britain's alarm that Japan might have intended to sell those warships to Russia was soon proved groundless.[3] The Minister of Marine approved their performance and had no desire to part with them.[4] Neither Russia nor Japan had thought of such a deal.[5]

At this period Britain was making great efforts to secure detailed information concerning the administration, expenditures, ships in service, complements, and current construction of the navies of the world. The Foreign Office noted that apparently the Japanese Navy was making 'considerable progress' but that their only information was scanty and limited to that obtained from the commander-in-chief of the China Seas.[6]

telegram dispatched by Motono, acting minister of Japan in London, 11 Sept. 1874.) For war scare see pp. 297–307.

[1] Gaimushō (Ministry of Foreign Affairs), MSS., Copies of *Telegrams*, No. 432, 1875, p. 71, Ueno to Terashima, London, 24 Sept. 1875, 6.35 p.m., Nagasaki, 25 Sept. 1875, 10 p.m. For Oriental Bank, see pp. 378 and 383–6.

[2] Ogasawara, op. cit., pp. 59–61.

[3] F.O. 46/229, Parkes to Salisbury, No. 38, Yedo, 15 Apr. 1878.

[4] F.O. 46/230, Parkes to Salisbury, No. 65, Yedo, 1 July 1878.

[5] Baron Rosen, *Forty Years of Diplomacy*, 2 vols. (London, 1922), i. 38.

[6] F.O. 262/318, F.O. Conf'l. Circular No. 40, and *Memorandum* 25 June 1878.

By 1883 Captain Samuel Long, R.N., was able to make a report on *Japanese Ports and Naval and Military Resources*. The detailed facts concerning the navy were taken from an official list compiled on 1 July 1882 which the Japanese Minister of Marine gave to Sir Harry Parkes. Long wrote that Japan had by this time twenty-eight vessels carrying 138 guns, with crews numbering 3,924 officers and men. Nine of these ships had been built in England or Scotland. A tenth, a new unarmoured sloop, the *Tsukushi*, purchased in England in July 1883 by the Japanese government, was then on her way to Japan. Twelve vessels were built in Japanese dockyards, at Yokosuka or Yedo, and six in other foreign ports.[1] This list was probably not complete regarding the ships of British origin. A Japanese authority gives nineteen ships built in Britain, and acquired by the Imperial Navy between 1868 and 1883. Sixteen of these were apparently still in service in 1883. They ranged in size from a very small boat of forty tons to the *Fusō*.[2]

Training the Meiji Navy

In accordance with Katsu's advice the Meiji government turned mainly to England for the training of its naval officers. Two British instructors were employed in January 1870 in the recently established naval training-school, *Kaigun Sōren Sho*,[3] at Yedo. One was Francis Brinkley, a lieutenant in the British Army, as well as a scholar and linguist who taught gunnery, mathematics, and foreign languages. The scarcity and general inaccuracy of his Japanese interpreters led him to hasten to learn to teach in Japanese and to write a text for the study of English.[4] His colleague was a retired officer of the Royal Marine Light Infantry, Lieutenant Albert G. S. Hawes, who was asked to 'organize the system of instruction and discipline to be observed in the Japanese men-of-war'. In doing so, he dared to break with many Japanese traditions. On the only training-ship, the *Ryūjo*, he taught the fundamentals of order, cleanliness, and

[1] F.O. 262/396, Long's *Report* encl. in F.O. to Parkes, 15 Aug. 1883, p. A 2 and Appendix I.
[2] *Kinsei Teikoku Kaigun Shi Yō*, pp. 821–3. There are many differences in the names of ships in the Japanese and English lists.
[3] The *Kaigun Sōren Sho* became the *Kaigun Heigaku Ryō*, the naval preparatory school attached to the Imperial Naval College of 1873. Perry, op. cit., p. 98.
[4] For Brinkley as a journalist, see p. 431.

discipline to *han*-conscious, sword-bearing samurai, at first arrayed in flowing robes. He introduced uniforms and abolished the wearing of swords; he stressed the political danger in the current practice of choosing all the officers and men on any ship from one *han* and gradually introduced men from different *han* into the complements of the various ships; and he sent efficiency ratings of his student officers to the Japanese government. The *Ryūjo* set the standard for other ships to which Hawes's trained officers went as instructors. After two years at the Naval Training School Hawes left to undertake the organization of the Imperial Marine Light Infantry and was recommended for an honorary promotion by his own government.[1]

Hawes's early work laid the foundations of the Imperial Naval College for which the government built spacious quarters in 1872 and sought more naval instructors in England. The Japanese minister in London, Terashima Munenori, asked for ten officers and twenty petty officers who could teach all the varied branches of naval science and seamanship, leaving the selection of the men to the British. Granville, then Foreign Minister, and Parkes supported this request and tried to make service in Japan attractive, suggesting that the men selected be allowed credit for sea time during this work for the Meiji government.[2] Although the Admiralty refused this arrangement largely for financial reasons, it appointed in July 1873 a mission of thirty-three men under the direction of Commander Archibald Lucius Douglas to serve in Japan for three years.[3]

By the contract concluded with Rear-Admiral Kawamura in London in 1872 and signed by Terashima, Commander Douglas was responsible during the three years to the Japanese Minister of Marine. He was not even permitted to inflict punishment on any subordinate or seamen for the violation of regulations or other misconduct without this minister's written consent. All members of the mission were forbidden to engage

---

[1] P.P. H. of C. 1874, lxv. 83–85, R. G. Watson, 'Report on the Present Educational System of Japan', 30 Nov. 1873. Here the author seems to combine Hawes's and Brinkley's work in the Naval Training School and that in the later school for the marines. *Japan Weekly Mail*, 10 June 1876. Perry, op. cit., pp. 98–101. F.O. 46/153, Adams to Granville, No. 74, Yedo, 30 Apr. 1872.

[2] F.O. 46/156, Parkes to Hammond, London, 3 Dec. 1872, encl. draft of agreement prepared by Japanese minister. *Japan Weekly Mail*, 10 June 1876.

[3] Perry, op. cit., p. 105.

in any business beyond their work as instructors or to interfere with business or politics in Japan. Their annual salaries ranged from £960 for Douglas to £108 for the humblest sailor. The Japanese government provided their housing and small sums for 'kit, travelling, and furnishing allowances' but the men were responsible for their food and personal expenses. The Japanese government could break its contract at any time upon payment of the full amount stipulated in the agreement.[1]

The Imperial Naval College opened in the fall of 1873 with a faculty of fifty-one members under Commander Douglas. Although only 31 years old, Douglas was already a commanding figure, strict and quick-tempered, but kind and understanding in his dealing with his subordinates.[2] His British staff consisted of Lieutenant Charles William Jones; Navigating-Lieutenant Charles William Baillie; Chief Engineer Frederick Sutton, two more engineers, two gunners, two boatswains, one carpenter, and twenty-three petty officers and seamen.[3] Most of the remaining faculty were Japanese who had been trained in Holland during the last years of the Shogunate.

The students—at first 129 men—were selected from the graduates of Kaigun Heigaku Ryō, or from graduates of other schools by special permission from the Japanese Navy. They were required to be under seventeen, to read and write Japanese, to read Chinese, and to have studied English and mathematics. They proved to be badly prepared, however, in trigonometry and arithmetic and deficient in English. Their instruction, nevertheless, and even honour awards and certificates were in English. They were taught every branch of seamanship, gunnery, navigation, surveying, and the related branches of mathematics and science. Three years were spent in the college as cadets and one year on a sea-going training ship.[4]

Douglas, like Hawes, put emphasis on training at sea which

---

[1] Sawa, K. and Hifumi, T., *Kaigun Heigaku Ryō* (Institute of Royal Strategy), (Tokyo, 1942), pp. 214–15. Archibald C. Douglas, 'The Genesis of Japan's Navy', The Japan Society, London, *Transactions*, xxxvi. 20–1.

[2] Perry, op. cit., p. 106.

[3] Douglas, op. cit., p. 21. P.P. H. of C. 1874, lxv. 82. Watson, 'Report on the Present Educational System of Japan', 30 Nov. 1873.

[4] Sawa and Hifumi, op. cit., pp. 219–27. *Japan Weekly Mail*, 10 June 1876. Here the full programme of study, food, recreation, etc., is available.

followed that of a British battleship. Several training-ships were fitted out, the *Kenkō* (formerly H.M.S. *Beagle*) for harbour duty, the *Tsukuba* (previously H.M.S. *Malacca*) for ocean cruising, and two others for training seamen. Each year a class of from twenty to forty-five students, having reached the age of eighteen, was sent on a cruise. They made their first ocean voyage —a cruise in the *Tsukuba* to San Francisco in 1875.[1] Apparently these early cadets became promising midshipmen quickly. Vice-Admiral Willes, Commander-in-Chief of Britain's China Station, reported that when drilling, they were 'admirably smart, rapid, and silent', that 'their performance on deck could not have been surpassed on British ships'.[2] Among them in May 1875 was the famous admiral of the future, Itō Sukenori.[3] Gun drill took place within the grounds of the college where two batteries had been fitted up and where guns of the Armstrong pattern similar to those of the British service were used.[4] The cadets were proud to have the British system as their guide and eager to achieve equal standards and world fame for the Japanese Navy.[5]

Branch schools for naval surgeons, paymasters, and engineers under British teachers had been organized during the first three years to augment the work of the College.[6] The Meiji government renewed the contract of the Naval Mission in 1876 with an additional provision that all members would resign in case Japan became involved in war.[7] More British naval officers were appointed as instructors on the training-ship cruising abroad. These included Retired-Commander L. P. Willan, R.N., Lieutenant Thomas H. James, R.N., an engineer, and some warrant and petty officers.[8]

The Japanese, however, intended all foreign instructors to be temporary. They wanted to run their institutions themselves as soon as they understood Western methods. Hence employ-

[1] *Japan Weekly Mail*, 10 June 1876. Douglas, op. cit., p. 27.

[2] Ad. I/6575, Willes to Adm., No. 281, Yokohama, 23 July 1881.

[3] Douglas, op. cit., p. 23.   [4] *Japan Weekly Mail*, 10 June 1876.

[5] For example, see speech of a cadet on the occasion of the Mikado's visit to the College. Quoted Perry, op. cit., p. 110.

[6] Watson, 'Report', p. 83. Douglas, op. cit., p. 27. Perry, op. cit., p. 97. See pp. 464–5, 478.

[7] F.O. 262/284, Derby to Parkes, No. 32, 16 Mar. 1876.

[8] Adm. Saitō in Stead, op. cit., p. 132. F.O. 46/205, Parkes to Derby, No. 63, Yedo, 3 Apr. 1876.

ment in Japan, although often lucrative, offered no professional security for Westerners. Commander Douglas had resigned in July 1875 in the interest of better promotional prospects, but with the satisfaction of knowing that his work had been approved and appreciated by the Emperor as well as by Parkes and the commander-in-chief of the China Station.[1]

On Parkes's recommendation, Commander Charles William Jones succeeded Douglas as director of the Imperial Naval College.[2] Jones died in 1877.[3] Lieutenant Baillie and Mr. Sutton were the chief officers when in April 1879 the Japanese government terminated in advance its contract for the services of the twenty-three remaining members of the British naval mission.[4] Sir Harry Parkes believed that Reed, the contractor for the three British-built warships, had influenced the Japanese authorities to do this. He had offered them men of his own selection and was expected to return to Yedo to reorganize the Japanese Navy and dockyards. At the same time the Japanese minister in London was advised to engage retired British warrant and petty officers to serve under Japanese naval authorities rather than under a senior British officer as the departing mission had done.[5] New arrangements were also made with some members of the original mission.[6] For example, Navigating-Lieutenant Thomas H. James was to remain in Japan and hold his appointment directly under the Japanese government for three more years as instructor on board a training-ship.[7]

In the face of the current local criticism of Japan's termination of her contract, the *Japan Mail* rose to her defence. It stressed Japan's rapidly developed knowledge and intercourse with foreign countries since the need for the mission arose. The editors recognized that Japan had reached the point where she could 'provide for herself through her own representatives, that educational assistance for her own country which formerly she

---

[1] Perry, op. cit., p. 121. For Emperor's address of appreciation to Douglas, see encl. in F.O. 46/193, Parkes to Derby, No. 96, 3 Aug. 1875.

[2] F.O. 46/190, Parkes to Derby, No. 27, Yedo, 8 Feb. 1875; 46/193, Parkes to Derby, No. 96, 3 Aug. 1875.

[3] Black, op. cit. ii. 456.   [4] *Japan Weekly Mail*, 19 Apr. 1879.

[5] F.O. 46/246, Parkes to Salisbury, No. 115, Conf'l., Yedo, 23 May 1879.

[6] F.O. 262/332, Salisbury to Parkes, No. 81, 4 July 1879.

[7] Ibid., encl. in No. 130, Adm. to F.O., 19 Nov. 1879.

sought through the Foreign Ministers resident here'. She did not intend 'to dispense with foreign instruction for her fleet but simply to deal directly with the individuals themselves rather than through the Government to which they belonged'. She had fully expressed her appreciation to England, to Sir Harry Parkes, and to the members of the Mission for the help they had given her.[1] The new policy was a natural step towards the elimination by 1882 of all foreign naval instructors except teachers of foreign languages.[2]

Japanese Cadets on British Training Ships

While the Naval Academy was developing under British teachers in Japan, Japanese cadets were also being trained on board British ships. A review of the six warships in H.M. 'Flying Squadron' at Yokohama in April 1870 so impressed the Meiji government with the British naval organization and tactics[3] that the Department of Military Affairs asked that two Japanese cadets accompany the Squadron to England at Japanese expense to learn about the internal economy of an English man-of-war.[4] Both Parkes and the Squadron's Commander, Rear-Admiral Geoffrey T. P. Hornby, agreed. The British Foreign Office advanced an allowance of from £20 to £25 a month to meet their mess and other expenses during the voyage. Itsuki Ichirō of Tokushima *Han* and Maeda Jūrō-zaemon of Kagoshima were selected to serve respectively aboard the steam frigates H.M.S. *Phoebe* and H.M.S. *Liverpool*.[5] Before their departure the Emperor gave Hornby and his officers a formal audience, then a very rare honour for foreigners.[6]

Itsuki, then over twenty-one, survived the voyage. Maeda committed suicide *en route*. The Admiralty refused Itsuki per-

---

[1] *Japan Weekly Mail*, 19 Apr. 1879.

[2] Yanaga Chitoshi, *Japan Since Perry* (New York, 1949), p. 117. John Perry points out in a letter to the author that Chief Gunner's Mate Hammond was retained to teach gunnery after 1882.

[3] The 'Flying Squadron', then on a voyage around the world, is listed as 'Detached Squadron' in the *Navy List* of 1870.

[4] F.O. 46/125, Parkes to Clarendon, No. 66, Yedo, 21 Apr. 1870.

[5] Ad. Index 18073–52–26, Hornby to Adm., 18 Apr. 1870. F.O. 46/133, Adm. to F.O., 13 June 1870. Sawa Kannojō, *Kaigun Shichijūnen Shidan* (*Seventy-Year History of the Navy*), (Tokyo, 1942), p. 4.

[6] F.O. 46/125, Parkes to Clarendon, No. 67, Yedo, 21 Apr. 1870.

mission to train on board H.M.S. *Britannia*, the training-ship for British cadets, but gave him the opportunity to study mathematics and the theory of navigation at one of the academies in Portsmouth and to visit dockyards and factories. While doing so he was borne on board H.M.S. *Hercules* as supernumerary sub-lieutenant for victuals only.[1] He returned to Japan in 1874 and reached the rank of captain before his death in 1891.[2]

The Meiji authorities asked that more Japanese students be permitted to study on shore or on ships in England. Parkes supported the request since he believed the United States was granting a similar one.[3] In 1871 twelve students were ordered to England. Among them Tōgō Heihachiro, the future naval hero of the Russo-Japanese War, has left records of the experience. The Admiralty Board refused to accept these men at the English Naval College or for service aboard a British battleship because of limited accommodation.[4] Parkes's subsequent recommendation that they be admitted on board a sea-going training-ship probably resulted in Tōgō and others entering the Thames Marine Officers training-ship, *Worcester*, which prepared students for either the Royal Navy or the merchant marine. From this ship they could go to Nelson's ship, the *Victory*, then used for gunnery and rifle practice. Tōgō left the *Worcester* for the new, small sailing ship, *Hampshire*, on which he made a voyage to Australia in 1875 and returned to England via Cape Horn, a voyage of 30,000 miles covered in seven months. After this practical experience in navigation, he was permitted to study mathematics at Cambridge and remained in England until 1878 when he went back to Japan on the new corvette, *Hiei*.[5]

Men of the highest social rank sought the opportunity to train aboard British ships. At his government's request, H.I.H. Arisugawa Takehito was permitted to embark on H.M.S.

---

[1] F.O. 262/185, Adm. to F.O., 29 Nov. 1870.   [2] Sawa, op. cit., p. 4.

[3] F.O. 46/126, Parkes to Princ. Sec. of State for For. Affairs, No. 117, Yokohama, 22 Aug. 1870.

[4] F.O. 262/205, Granville to Parkes, No. 2, 9 Jan. 1871. Ogasawara, op. cit., p. 56. Perry, op. cit., p. 116, says that a greater number went to England and twelve to the U.S. between 1868 and 1883.

[5] F.O. 46/152, Parkes to Granville, London, 22 Feb. 1872. Ogasawara, op. cit., pp. 56–60. Perry, op. cit., p. 102.

Iron Duke, the flagship of the China Station, for naval training. Strict instructions from the Admiralty accompanied his permission. His family rank could not be recognized on board nor official visits permitted in his princely capacity. He was to be subjected to the same discipline and regulations as the other young gentlemen serving on board. He was withdrawn from the *Iron Duke* upon her departure for England in September 1880, owing to irregularities of the Japanese naval authorities, but permitted to complete his studies at Greenwich Naval College.[1]

Surveying Operations

The British and the Japanese co-operated in surveying the coasts and waters of Japan. Even during the rebellion in the north in 1869 the harassed Meiji government offered Commander Edward W. Brooker every facility possible to carry on aboard H.M.S. *Sylvia* his survey of the Kuroshima Straits and the Japanese coast.[2] A year later the Japanese asked Parkes for the services of an English surveyor to assist them aboard a Japanese steamer in making a survey of the Yezo coast. The British realized that such a survey was essential for trips to Sakhalin and that the Admiralty charts of Yezo and the Kurile Islands were inadequate. Both nations were concerned about Russian movements in this area. Parkes wanted the Admiralty to sanction a general survey of the entire Yezo coast for which the Japanese government offered help.[3]

The survey was begun in the spring of 1871 under conditions specified by the Admiralty. On Vice-Admiral Kellett's advice a British ship, H.M.S. *Sylvia*, took the main responsibility. The Japanese agreed to provide a vessel, officered and manned, to accompany her; to store supplies of coal at convenient places, to arrange conveyance and accommodation on shore when needed, and to provide pilots for the coast and protection for detached parties when employed inland. The British officer in

[1] F.O. 46/246, Parkes to Salisbury, No. 133, Yedo, 28 July 1879; 262/332, No. 114, Salisbury to Parkes, 2 Oct. 1879 and encl., Adm. to F.O., 20 Sept. 1879; 46/258, Kennedy to Granville, No. 154, Yedo, 13 Sept. 1880, and No. 194, Yedo, 15 Dec. 1880.

[2] Ad. I/6095, Keppel to Adm., 12 June 1869. F.O. 262/162, F.O. to Parkes, No. 107, 25 Aug. 1869.

[3] F.O. 46/126, Parkes to Clarendon, No. 93, Yedo, 4 July 1870; same to same, No. 95, 11 July 1870. Ad. Index 18073–52–26, Kellett to Adm., 4 July 1870, S. 17. 3.

charge was on no account to allow himself to become involved in any complications which might arise between the Japanese authorities and the subjects of any other foreign power which might be engaged in similar activities along the coasts of Japan.[1] Commander Henry St. John was given command of the survey. The Japanese supplied an efficient ship, the *Keang-su*. Their co-operation and great civility throughout the work made it a successful joint enterprise which was completed in September 1871.[2] Commander St. John reported most favourably on the Japanese officers who worked with him.[3]

Both England and Japan recognized the need for more extensive charts of the Japanese coast. Some parts were as yet entirely unsurveyed. Although in 1872 the Japanese began making independent surveys of their coasts, the British refused to withdraw their surveying ship from Japanese waters until the Japanese could give decided proof of their ability to conduct operations which previously only the maritime nations of Europe and America had undertaken.[4] By 1877 the two governments were exchanging charts of the Japanese coasts and the British Admiralty gave Japan its charts of the Kurile and Ryūkyū Islands, Sakhalin, and Korea.[5] The two nations agreed to a direct exchange of charts between their hydrographic offices in 1879.[6]

Assessments of Japan's Naval Strength

The rapid development of the Japanese fleet and its Western-trained complements attracted the interest of world opinion. Writers on naval affairs began to recognize this Eastern navy as one of the navies of the world and generally regarded the English-built ships, the *Fusō*, *Kongō*, and *Hiei*, as its main strength. Their figures for the numbers of additional armoured and unarmoured vessels, however, differ not only with the

---

[1] F.O. 262/185, Adm. to Kellett, 12 Oct. 1870, encl. in F.O. to Parkes, 18 Oct. 1870; 46/137, Parkes to Granville, No. 14, Yedo, 28 Jan. 1871.

[2] Ad. I/6191, Kellett to Adm., Nos. 90 and 126, 8 Mar. and 15 Apr. 1871. F.O. 46/141, Adams to Granville, No. 67, Yedo, 13 Sept. 1871.

[3] F.O. 46/142, Adams to Granville, No. 97, Yedo, 21 Oct. 1871.

[4] F.O. 262/222, Adm. to F.O., 27 May 1872, encl. in F.O. to Adams, 3 June 1872.

[5] F.O. 46/218, Parkes to Derby, No. 88, Yedo, 18 June 1877; 262/301, Derby to Parkes, No. 72, 16 Oct. 1877.

[6] F.O. 262/332, Salisbury to Parkes, No. 38, 17 Mar. 1879.

Japanese figures but with each other.[1] Obviously the Meiji government was reluctant to reveal either its weakness or its strength.

The British in Japan also held different opinions about the Meiji navy. Lieutenant Thomas James, who served for five years as cadet instructor for the Japanese government under the Admiralty's sanction, considered the condition of the Japanese Navy in 1881 highly unsatisfactory. Although in the beginning it had provided for disestablished samurai, he now thought it primarily an instrument of patronage controlled by the Satsuma *Han*. Discipline was completely lacking. If war were declared at this time, James maintained that Japan could with difficulty obtain efficient complements from among her whole fleet to man the only three effective ships. Even then, the *Fusō*, *Hiei*, and the *Kongō* were not up to standard condition. He considered the remaining ten ships inadequate even for the defence of Yedo harbour. His observation of the behaviour of cadets returning from the annual cruise convinced him that the Japanese had no aptitude for sea life. And he warned the Foreign Office representative in Yedo against the favourable reports regarding the Japanese Navy made by British naval officers visiting Yokohama. The studied efforts of the Japanese to produce a favourable impression of their naval service upon British officers made it impossible for the latter to get at the defects of the service. The British Chargé, Kennedy, accepted James's judgement. It confirmed the current opinion that in the event of complications in the Far East neither the alliance nor hostility of Japan could be an important factor for years to come.[2]

But Vice-Admiral Willes regretted Kennedy's sending of James's report to London. He dissented entirely from its views —those of a man 'in the pay of the Japanese Government'. His own opinion of the Meiji naval force was 'very high'. He was astonished at the advance made by the Japanese Navy since 1861 and regarded the order and discipline of their training-

[1] Leiut. Edward W. Very, U.S.A., *Navies of the World* (New York, 1880), pp. 96–99, 318, 424–5. J. W. King, *The Warships and Navies of the World* (Boston, 1880), pp. 417–24. *Revue Maritime et Coloniale*, lxxviii, July 1883, p. 87.

[2] Ad. R.O. (China Station Records, vol. 76), Kennedy to Willes, Yedo, 21 Sept. 1881, and encl., Kennedy to Granville, No. 110, Conf'l., 20 Sept. 1881.

ship, *Tsukuba*, as worthy of the envy of some European nations.[1] Neither the Foreign Office nor the Admiralty appeared disturbed over either opinion, although both were aware of their difference.[2]

The *Japan Weekly Mail* held that Japan needed a navy sufficient for her defence even though she was in no condition to 'support any large unproductive expenditure'. Its editors produced a detailed plan for the building of an efficient fleet with emphasis on the excellence of British shipwrights and of Armstrong guns.[3] Japan herself, apparently aware of her need for greater naval power as difficulties with China over Korea grew, planned in 1882 to build six large, twelve medium-sized, and twelve small warships, and twelve torpedo boats, less than half of which were completed by 1885.[4]

Great Britain had laid the foundations of this growing fleet. At Japan's request British shipyards had built her best warships and British teachers had trained her officers and seamen. But as in all areas where she sought foreign assistance, Japan had defined the naval programme and kept its direction in her own hands, ready to dispense with such help at will. Although Britain was her model, the navy in the making was to be distinctly Japanese.

[1] Ad. I/6575, Willes to Adm., No. 394, conf'l. 29 Sept. 1881; Willes to Adm., No. 157, 25 Mar. 1882.
[2] F.O. 262/364, F.O. to Kennedy, No. 92, Conf'l., 22 Dec. 1881.
[3] *Japan Weekly Mail*, 11 June 1881.
[4] Yamamoto in Ōkuma, *Fifty Years of New Japan*, i. 226.

XI

BRITAIN AND EARLY MEIJI RELATIONS WITH CHINA

I. THE SINO-JAPANESE TREATY OF 1871

The Negotiations

As early as August 1870 Parkes was informed of Japan's plans for a mission to China.[1] By October the Foreign Minister, Sawa Nobuyoshi, told him about the widening scope of the mission. It would seek acquaintance with general conditions in China, especially a knowledge of her foreign trade and intercourse with foreigners. The mission planned to negotiate at Shanghai about the government of Japanese settlers there and then to go to Peking to attempt to establish a recognized basis for commercial relations between Japan and China which were then being carried on only informally. Parkes applauded Japan's initiative in thus seeking to terminate the system of exclusion observed by both countries for two centuries. He noted that Chinese residents in Japan outnumbered those of any other nation, and that their annual trade then worth eight million dollars would greatly increase if allowed to develop naturally with the establishing of free intercourse between the two countries.[2]

The British heard nothing more about this preliminary effort of Japan to sound out China on the possibility of negotiating a treaty. A Japanese emissary, Yanagihara Sakimitsu, arrived in Tientsin in late September 1870. He found the Chinese ministers receptive to his overtures. They saw clearly that their island neighbour should be granted trading privileges similar to those China had accorded the Western powers. Moreover, as Li Hung-chang, Viceroy of Chihli, pointed out, Japan could perhaps be a source of help to China in resisting the

---

[1] F.O. 46/126, Parkes to Granville, No. 127, Yedo, 29 Aug. 1870.
[2] F.O. 46/127, Parkes to Granville, No. 152, Yedo, 8 Oct. 1870.

West. At least she might be prevented from serving as a base for aggression against China. And it seemed better to deal with Japan independently than to wait until she had the support of foreign powers. The *Tsungli Yamen* (Chinese Foreign Office), therefore, said it would be willing to receive a Japanese negotiator, promising in the interim to study the draft treaty which Yanagihara had submitted. With this understanding, Yanagihara left Tientsin on 12 November.[1]

Seven months later Francis O. Adams, acting in Parkes's absence, reported in the light of a letter from Sir Thomas Francis Wade, the British Minister in Peking, and of a confidential interview with the Japanese Finance Minister, Date Muneki, that the formal mission for China would leave shortly. Its object, according to Wade, was to conclude a commercial treaty and an agreement between China and Japan to act defensively against the foreigners. Date, who was to lead it, expressed more concrete ideas about the hoped-for treaty. He aimed at an agreement similar to those of the West with China except for special extraterritorial provisions which would cover Japanese in China but keep Chinese in Japan under Japanese jurisdiction. His draft differed from that of Yanagihara. He denied any thought of an offensive or defensive alliance against foreigners such as Wade indicated.[2] Three weeks later Adams was officially informed of the mission and the good offices of the British chargé d'affaires and consul in China were requested.[3]

News of the conflicts between the negotiators—Li Hungchang and Date and their assistants—never reached Adams that summer. The Chinese sought to avoid the errors, already too evident, which they had made in their treaties with the West while the Japanese proposed as a model China's treaty with Prussia and a set of commercial regulations assimilating those of China's treaty with the United States. The Chinese were adamant in refusing to include a most-favoured-nation clause, and to open the interior of either country to trade. Being determined to prevent Japan from combining with a third power against China, they insisted upon an arrangement for

---

[1] T. F. Tsiang, 'Sino-Japanese Diplomatic Relations 1870–1894', *Chinese Social and Political Science Review*, xvii. (1933), Anp. 4–6.

[2] Ibid., p. 11. F.O. 46/139, Adams to Granville, No. 17, Conf'l., Yedo, 19 June 1871.   [3] F.O. 46/140, Adams to Granville, No. 27, Yedo, 3 July 1871.

material good offices in case either nation became involved with a third power (Article II of the treaty). Japanese opposition in each case was successfully overcome.[1]

The agreement, known as the Treaty of Tientsin, and its accompanying commercial regulations were signed on 13 September 1871, with the understanding that ratifications would be exchanged within a year. Neither Japan nor China ever published an official translation.[2] In the treaty series put out by the Japanese Foreign Office, two English translations are given, the language of which varies considerably. One is that of the Maritime Customs Office in China, the other by John H. Gubbins, Acting Japanese Secretary of the British legation in Yedo, which was published in the *Japan Weekly Mail*, 16 October 1886.[3]

The Treaty of Tientsin

This was Japan's first attempt to establish treaty relations with an Asiatic country since the seventeenth century. She sought without success an unequal treaty modelled on Western patterns through which she would gain as Europe had done at China's expense. Its terms are important for this study because they indicate how much both nations had learned by 1871 of Western predatory diplomacy and because they became the point of departure for active Sino-Japanese relations in which the British would become involved. The treaty contained eighteen articles.

Article I proclaimed perpetual friendship between the two nations and provided for mutual non-aggression against each other's territories (which the Chinese interpreted to cover Korea).[4] Article II, which so disturbed the British, declared 'now that friendly relations subsist between the two countries this friendship shall without fail, be of an intimate and reciprocal character. Should either State experience at the hands of another country injustice or slighting treatment, on communication being made to the other State the latter shall give assistance or shall use her good offices in mediating between the two countries. Thus friendship should be increased.'[5]

[1] Tsiang, op. cit., pp. 9–11.   [2] Ibid., p. 11.
[3] *Kyū Jōyaku Isan*, i, Pt. 1, 393–409.   [4] Tsiang, op. cit., p. 11.
[5] *Kyū Jōyaku Isan*, i, Pt. 1, 395, Gubbins trans. in *Japan Weekly Mail*.

Japan and China further agreed to refrain from interference in each other's internal administration; to the exchange of ministers plenipotentiary who should reside only at their capitals and travel elsewhere in the interior; to trade only at fixed ports and in accordance with specified regulations; and to reciprocal consular jurisdiction in the open ports. In the absence of a consul the local authorities of the country in question were to exercise control over the subjects of the other, and offences by nationals of either country in the interior of the other were to be handled by the local authorities alone.[1]

Both countries prohibited the wearing of swords by their merchants, the entrance of warships into non-open ports, rivers, lakes, or river ports of the interior, and forbade consuls to engage in trade or to act as consuls for a state not connected with the treaty, a most disturbing practice of Western nations in the East. It was also decreed that flags carried by ships of the two countries should be of fixed design and should a ship of one falsely assume the colours of the other and commit an illegal act, both the ship and the cargo were to be confiscated.[2] The appended trade regulations provided for the opening of eight ports in Japan and fifteen in China.[3]

British Criticism

After weeks in which no report of the treaty had been given to Western representatives, rumours of official disapproval of the action of Date led Adams to question Iwakura. He learned that Date had agreed to an article whereby each country would assist the other 'in cases of insult or aggression offered to them by Foreign Powers' and would act as mediator in such instances —the very thing which Date had denied six months earlier. Adams protested. This was a serious matter. He trusted the Japanese government would not ratify it. Iwakura argued that China had a similar article in her treaty of 1858 with the United States, but assured Adams that Japan had no thought of military co-operation with China. Adams soon proved to Iwakura as well as to Date that the obligations of the two parties in the

[1] Arts. III, IV, VII, VIII, IX.
[2] Arts. XI, XIV, XVI, and XVII.
[3] *Kyū Jōyaku Isan*, i, Pt. 1, 411–13, trans. by John Gubbins, *Japan Weekly Mail*, 27 Nov. 1886.

Sino-American treaty differed regarding assistance and mediation, while in the Sino-Japanese agreement both nations
promised to assist each other or to mediate. If ratified by Japan,
he said, this meant that Japan would have to assist China
should the recent massacre at Tientsin result in war. Iwakura
showed alarm. He pleaded for secrecy about the article and
promised to follow Adams's advice. A second mission to China
was contemplated to point out Japan's objections to the ratification of the treaty.[1]

The first copy of the treaty to be seen by Adams came not
from Iwakura as promised but was brought from China by the
Austro-Hungarian minister.[2] Armed with it, Adams talked with
Prime Minister Sanjō about the article dealing with mutual
assistance. Again in confidence the Prime Minister reported that
the government considered the article ambiguous and never
intended to mean assistance in war. Adams advised deleting
the article. Ambiguity, he said, should be avoided, and if this
clause were ratified as it stood, other powers would regard it
with grave suspicion.[3] The American chargé in Yedo also
urged deletion of the article.[4] In contrast, the Russians regarded
the whole treaty lightly. M. De Stremoukoff considered it an
effort to imitate the European powers and to have been
dictated by feelings of ostentation. He thought it might be a
means of opening fresh ports in China to foreign commerce, for
should Japanese be admitted to Chinese ports, ships of other
treaty powers could not be excluded.[5]

Efforts at Revision

Japan's own dissatisfaction with the treaty extended beyond
Article II. The government opposed the provisions for criminal jurisdiction over Japanese subjects in China, owing to the

---

[1] F.O. 46/143, Adams to Granville, No. 126, Conf'l., Yedo, 7 Dec.; Private
9 Dec.; and Most Conf'l., 16 Dec. 1871. Later Adams pointed out that China had
put before Date a false version of the Sino-American Treaty; 46/151, No. 12,
Conf'l., Yedo, 12 Dec. 1871.   [2] Ibid., No. 6, Yedo, 8 Jan. 1872.

[3] Ibid., No. 12, Conf'l., Yedo, 12 Jan. 1872.

[4] T. F. Tsaing, op. cit., p. 13.

[5] F.O. 262/222, Augustus Loftus to Granville, No. 38, St. Petersburgh, 3 Apr.
1872, encl. in F.O. to Adams, 17 Apr. 1872. Here probably Petr Nikolaevich
Stremoukhov, Director of Asiatic Department of the Russian Ministry of Foreign
Affairs, is meant.

'imperfect state of Chinese criminal law', the absence of a most-favoured-nation clause, and the prohibition of sword-carrying.[1] Yanagihara was sent in May 1872 to negotiate changes but in spite of protracted conversations, accomplished little. Japan had just sent a mission under Iwakura to the United States and Europe, hoping to eliminate the extraterritorial provisions and tariff controls embodied in her treaties with the West. She did not want to incorporate similar limitations in her treaty with China. She argued that since Japan and China could render each other good offices without it, Article II was unnecessary, and she asked that the prohibition of sword-carrying be deleted. China, however, had little sympathy with proposals for change. As Wade pointed out, she had not sought the treaty and would never have dreamed of it without Japan's solicitation. The treaty had been signed. Negotiations were pacific. Nothing had been conceded without an equivalent. China regarded the rejection of conditions to which, after negotiation, she had agreed, as offensive.[2] She refused to omit or alter Article II but declared it did not mean 'material assistance'.[3] She did consent, however, to withdraw the sword-carrying prohibition and promised to accept corresponding changes in the tariff and jurisdictional provisions if Japan succeeded in so revising her treaties with the West. But such revisions were to be made through an exchange of notes after the exchange of ratifications. The two countries agreed to await the return of Iwakura's mission to exchange ratifications.

For other reasons the Japanese government soon decided to hasten this exchange and combine it with the discussion of other matters with China.[4] It dispatched the Foreign Minister, Soejima Taneomi, to Peking in the spring of 1873 to congratulate the Chinese Emperor on his marriage on behalf of the Japanese Emperor, and to exchange ratifications of the treaty of 1871. Soejima gave up the concessions which Li Hung-chang

[1] Ariga Nagao, 'Diplomacy', in Stead, op. cit., pp. 154–5. Tsiang, op. cit., p. 13. *D.N.G.M.* iv. 263–6, Doc. 165.

[2] F.O. 262/224, Wade to Granville, No. 21, Peking, 4 June 1872, encl. in F.O. to Robert Grant Watson (H.M. acting chargé), Yedo, 20 Aug. 1872. Tsiang, op. cit., p. 13.

[3] F.O. 46/155, Watson to Granville, No. 69, Yedo, 4 Aug. 1872. Tsiang, op. cit., p. 13.

[4] F.O. 46/166, Watson to Granville, No. 64, Conf'l., and No. 68, Yedo, 7 and 8 Mar. 1873.

had made to Yanagihara the year before and exchanged ratifications with him on 30 April 1873 in Tientsin.[1] The text of the treaty was exactly that which had been agreed upon in 1871. British and American pressure for the deletion of Article II had failed. In spite of Japanese attempts at revision, the treaty remained unaltered until the Sino-Japanese War of 1894–5.[2]

2. THE JAPANESE EXPEDITION TO FORMOSA, 1874

The Political Setting

No obligation under the Treaty of Tientsin discouraged Japan's long-standing expansionist ambitions which involved inroads on Chinese suzerainty, if not her sovereignty. The nationalist or war party in control of the government after 1871 sought to allay the rising discontent of the samurai class by activities abroad. Their programme involved the annexation of the Ryūkyū and Bonin Islands, punitive expeditions to, if not the conquest of, Korea and Formosa, and an uncompromising attitude towards Russia regarding Japan's territorial rights in Sakhalin.[3]

The expedition to Formosa in 1874 represented a compromise in the programme of the militarists but it gave them their first taste of success. After their Western mission (1871–3) Iwakura, Ōkubo, Kido, and others convinced the Emperor that Japan's resources should be devoted to domestic reconstruction in line with Western institutions, rather than to distant military adventures. His Majesty therefore called off the projected expedition to Korea and ordered negotiation of the difficulties.[4] General Saigō Takamori, Foreign Minister Soejima Taneomi, Etō Shimpei, and two other important members of the Council of State resigned in protest on 25 October 1873.[5] The new council members, again a group of strong men, crushed a

---

[1] Tsiang, op. cit., pp. 14–15. *Kyū Jōyaku Isan*, however, gives 9 Mar. 1873 as the date of exchange of ratifications.

[2] Ariga in Stead, op. cit., p. 155.

[3] Sansom, *The Western World and Japan* p. 332. Japan claimed the portion of Sakhalin south of 50 degrees of latitude. Ariga in Stead, op. cit., pp. 149–51.

[4] Hilary Conroy, op. cit., pp. 42–46.

[5] F.O. 46/168, Parkes to Granville, No. 90, Yedo, 27 Oct. 1873. Idditti Junesay, *The Life of Marquis Shigenobu Ōkuma, a Biographical Study on the Rise of Democratic Japan* (Tokyo, 1956), pp. 155–7. Iwata, op. cit., pp. 163–74.

rebellion in Saga under the leadership of the disgruntled Etō in February 1874 but could not resist the pressure of the militarists for an invasion of Formosa.[1] It would at least give vent to the energies of disturbing elements and remove them from the country for a period. Furthermore, it could be explained as a righteous undertaking in terms of Western precedents. The Japanese militarists even believed that sympathy for the venture could be expected from the West.

As trade increased in the Far Eastern seas many ships had been wrecked on the wild, uncharted eastern and southern coasts of Formosa, and their crews murdered by the head-hunting natives. Although the Peking government professed to administer Formosa as a prefecture of the province of Fukien since the Ch'ing conquest of the island in 1683, it had not incorporated the mountainous eastern and south-western areas into the administrative units of the prefecture. Here the savage aborigines lived by hunting and fishing and preyed upon hapless voyagers with impunity, while thousands of turbulent immigrants from the mainland to the arable areas of the north and west of the island raised rice and sugar for China's coastal provinces.[2] A British report on Formosa in 1869 described the Chinese colonists as only a few degrees less savage than the natives and the Chinese officials as little above 'a state of barbarism themselves'.[3] These mandarins not only did nothing to control or punish the natives for their crimes against castaways but were known to have abetted them. And Peking itself had generally ignored these brutalities, considering the aborigines 'raw' or uncivilized and expecting them in time to seek assimilation in the universal Chinese Empire.[4] There was no Chinese town on the east coast south of Sauo or any evidence of Chinese authority in the area when a Ryūkyūan ship bearing tribute to China was wrecked on the southern coast on 18 December 1871. The savage Botan (Boutan) tribe murdered fifty-four of its crew. Twelve escaped to report the crime to a representative of Ryūkyū in Foochow who in turn sent a report

[1] Ad. I/6300, Shadwell to Adm., 25 Feb. 1874, encl. letters from Parkes. Idditti, op. cit., pp. 162–3. Dickins, op. cit., p. 191.

[2] Kerr, op. cit., p. 357. Sophia Su-fei Yen, *Taiwan in China's Foreign Relations 1836–1874* (Hamden, Connecticut, 1965), pp. 8–9, 16–20.

[3] P.P. H. of C. 1868–9, lxiv (4097–II), 35.

[4] Yen, op. cit., p. 19.

to Shuri, the capital of Ryūkyū.[1] This gave Japan her excuse to invade Formosa.

The relations of the Ryūkyū people to the centralized Meiji government had been a problem since the Daimyo of Satsuma had surrendered his feudal privileges. It will be remembered that the Ryūkyūs had paid tribute to both China and Kagoshima since the seventeenth century and as a feudatory of the Satsuma *Han* had become a channel for a valuable trade. In January 1872 the Yedo authorities dispatched two leading Kagoshima officials to adjust current economic and political issues with the Council of State at Shuri, aiming to transfer the traditional obligations of the Ryūkyūan kingdom from Kagoshima to the Meiji government. Following months of tedious discussions when the Imperial emissaries had advised the Ryūkyūan king 'to pay his respects' to the Mikado and review their mutual problems in Yedo, the report of the murder of the fifty-four Ryūkyūans reached Shuri. Although the Ryūkyūan government agreed to petition Yedo to redress its injuries, the king, wanting to avoid a public demonstration of his subordination to the Japanese Emperor, sent his uncle and leading minister to represent him in the Japanese capital. There on 16 October 1872 his emissaries were presented with an Imperial decree which made their homeland an integral part of the Japanese empire. The Ryūkyū Islands were declared an Imperial *han*, their king a peer of Japan, who should administer the *han*. In November the Meiji government notified foreign powers of Japan's assumption of responsiblity for the kingdom of Ryūkyū and a memorial, issued in Shuri in the king's name in March 1873, after the return of the envoys, acknowledged the new status of the islands.[2]

Concurrent with the incorporation of the Ryūkyūs as an Imperial *han* Japan's naval and military forces demanded the right to punish the Formosan tribes which had murdered the Ryūkyūan castaways in 1871. The threat of their launching an independent expedition without Imperial authority caused the foreign minister, Soejima, who was also aware of Western

[1] Kerr, op. cit., p. 356. Yen, op. cit., p. 157.

[2] Ibid., p. 159. Kerr, op. cit., pp. 360–4. The king abdicated under extreme pressure from Yedo in 1879 when the Ryūkyūs lost all semblance of feudal status and were declared a prefecture of Japan. Ibid., pp. 365–84. Kerr, in contrast to Yen, gives 14 Nov. 1872 as the date of the presentation of the Imperial Decree.

interests in Formosa and of China's claim to the whole island although she controlled only half of it, to restrain these aggressive elements with an attractive promise. He told them that after he had settled some questions (with China) by diplomatic means, 'they would be called upon to occupy aboriginal territory, to colonize it, and to consolidate that area as the southern gate of the Japanese Empire'.[1] Such was his commitment when he was sent to China in 1873 as ambassador plenipotentiary to exchange the ratifications of the Sino-Japanese Treaty of 1871.

British Interests in Formosa

Parkes and his colleagues in Japan and China were interested in every move of the Japanese and Chinese towards or against each other because they wished to maintain peace in the Orient. A conflict between Japan and China at this time would jeopardize Britain's growing trade and restrict her position in each country.

The British also had interests in Formosa. Parkes himself had been there, making a hazardous trip in 1857 into the wild inland country occupied by savages to investigate the situation of three British citizens who had been detained there nine months after the wreck of the H.M.S. *Sarpent*.[2] Townsend Harris had even asserted in 1857 that the British desired to possess Formosa when he was trying to make Japan sign the commercial treaty with the United States.[3]

Although there seems to be no substantial evidence that the British government considered the occupation of the island at this time, it is true that Jardine, Matheson & Company and other British firms were engaged there in trade in the early 1850s and British merchants in China pressed for the opening of Formosan ports in 1857 before the negotiations of the Treaties of Tientsin. In consequence, Taiwan-fu (Taiwan-foo) and Tamsui (Tamsuy) were opened to trade in 1860 according to the Conventions of Peking. Robert Swinhoe, who had explored and reported on the resources of Formosa for Britain in

[1] Yen, op. cit., p. 161.
[2] L.C., LeGendre MSS. (iii. 47-D6), *Memorandum* 11, copy, Parkes to Gideon Nye, Esq. (an American merchant), 22 Aug. 1857.
[3] Beasley, *Documents*, pp. 161–2. Statement made by Harris at his interviews with Hotta Masayoshi, 12 Dec. 1857.

1858, established the first foreign consulate at Taiwan-fu with the rank of vice-consul in July 1861. He and his staff were the only representatives of a treaty power on the island that year. In November Swinhoe moved his office to Tamsui to which Keelung (Kelung) was joined as a dependent port and opened to trade in 1863. The growth of the foreign merchant community at all the open ports necessitated in 1864 the reopening of a British consulate in the south at Takow, the port of entry for Taiwan-fu. And early the next year a vice-consulate was again authorized at Tamsui. Agents of many foreign firms and Christian missionaries took up residence in the western ports. Acrimonious conflicts with the local mandarins became frequent. In 1862 Swinhoe proposed the acquisition of the eastern portion of the island as a penal colony for Great Britain, but received no encouragement from the Foreign Office. Prussia voiced ambitions in 1865 to possess the aboriginal lands and eventually all of Formosa. No efforts to do so followed but Japan became aware of the danger.[1]

The value of the foreign trade of the Formosan ports amounted in 1864 to £705,737. Opium, cotton, and silk manufactures led the imports; rice and sugar the exports. Camphor stood second among the exports of the north.[2] By 1869 both Alcock, then Minister in China, and the Board of the Treasury in London believed that Britain's annual trade with the island, amounting to less than £200,000, did not justify the maintenance of consular establishments. Plans to close them after negotiations with China for ports on the Yangtze River in exchange for those on Taiwan incurred such opposition from the other British diplomatic agents in China and British merchants in Formosa that the Foreign Office reversed its decision to disestablish the consulates in December 1870.[3] In 1873 the exports and imports of Takow-Taiwan-fu reached £602,826, those of Tamsui and Keelung, which were all British, £473,964,

---

[1] Yen, op. cit., pp. 75–77, 91–92, 94–99, 100–6. Great Britain, *Foreign Office List*, 1873, p. 182. James W. Davidson, *Island of Formosa, Past and Present* (London, New York, and Yokohama, 1903), pp. 174–8, 188–201.

[2] P.P. H. of C. 1865, liii. 273–6, 263–4. *Commercial Reports from H.M. Consuls* in Takow and Tamsui including Keelung for 1864 (hereafter cited as Cons. Reports). For Tamsui, imports: £249,677, exports £113,363; for Takow-Taiwan-fu, imports £203,649, exports £139,048.

[3] Yen, op. cit., pp. 114–20.

and were increasing in all ports the next year.[1] Britain commanded the lion's share of the tonnage in both the north and south of the island but was acutely aware of competition from Germany in the seventies.[2]

Soejima's Mission to China: Preparations for the Expedition

Japanese and British sources admit that the mission of Soejima to exchange ratifications of the treaty of 1871 had many motives. The foreign minister intended to press for a personal reception by the Emperor—a break from the traditional kowtow which the Western representatives in Peking were also trying to arrange in the spring of 1873—and he sought to clarify the relations of China to Ryūkyū, Formosa, and Korea.[3] Soejima told Robert Grant Watson that he would obtain satisfaction for the massacre of forty-six [*sic*] shipwrecked Ryūkyūans by the Formosan savages the previous year. If the Chinese government admitted jurisdiction over the aboriginal Formosans, it was to punish the offenders. If not, the Japanese government was determined 'to take necessary measures to obtain satisfaction'.[4] The American Secretary of State was similarly informed of Japan's intentions.[5] Yet in Soejima's letter of credence of 19 December 1872 to the Chinese government, he was empowered only to exchange ratifications of the treaty of 1871 and on behalf of the Emperor of Japan to congratulate the Chinese Emperor upon his recent marriage.[6]

China's appreciation and goodwill resulting from Japan's recent rescue of 232 Chinese coolies from a Peruvian vessel, the *Maria Luz*, engaged in the coolie trade of Macao, made the spring of 1873 a propitious time for the Japanese foreign minister to approach the government in Peking on these

---

[1] At Essex Institute, Salem, Mass., Cons. Report (China, No. 6, 1874) for Takow-Taiwan-fu 1873, p. 105; for Tamsui and Keelung, p. 118. Here the figures differ slightly with those given in P.P. H. of C. lxxvii, 1875, Cons. Reports for 1874 (China No. 5) for Tamsui and Keelung, p. 68; for Takow-Taiwan-fu, Pt. II, p. 100.

[2] P.P. H. of C. 1877, lxxxiv (China, No. 5, 1877), 85, 93, Cons. Reports for 1876.

[3] F.O. 46/166, Watson to Granville, No. 68, Yedo, 8 Mar. 1873. Ariga in Stead, op. cit., pp. 159–61. Tsiang, op. cit., p. 16.

[4] F.O. 46/166, Watson to Granville, No. 64, Conf'l., Yedo, 7 Mar. 1873, Most sources give fifty-four Ryūkyūans.

[5] LeGendre MSS. iii. 47-D6, Appendix 3, F. F. Low to H. Fish, Peking, 13 June 1873.

[6] *D.N.G.M.* vi. 140–1, Doc. 88.

delicate questions.[1] After Soejima had exchanged ratifications with Li-Hung-chang at Tientsin, he and other members of his mission, Lord Yanagihara, and an American adviser, General Charles LeGendre,[2] went to Peking where Soejima presented his credentials to the *Tsungli Yamen* and requested an audience with the Emperor. Delays over the granting of this led Soejima to announce his departure in three days and to take the *Tsungli Yamen* off guard by sending Lord Yanagihara, who was not mentioned in his letter of credence, to raise his territorial questions.[3]

In the meantime, Thomas Wade, now British minister in Peking, when calling on Soejima asked about the policy of the Meiji government towards the Formosan aborigines who had murdered both foreign and Ryūkyūan castaways. The Japanese ambassador declared China had never administered the aboriginal territory and had no right to claim it. Although Soejima said nothing about Japan's policy, Wade should have guessed what to expect.[4]

On 21 June 1873 a brief conversation took place between Yanagihara, with an interpreter, and two or three Chinese ministers. Macao, Ryūkyū, Korea, and Formosa were the chief topics. No written agreement of any kind was reached. The import of what was verbally understood differed drastically for the participants.[5] Both nations claimed suzerainty over the Ryūkyū Islands: Japan, on the strength of Satsuma's overlordship since the early seventeenth century and her recent incorporation of the islands; China, because of her tributary relationship with Ryūkyū since 1372.[6] Yanagihara spoke cautiously, using at first vague terms to indicate Japan's intentions regarding the aborigines of Formosa. He acknowledged that Formosa had been Chinese territory since the Ch'ing dynasty but stated that the Chinese government had never

---

[1] Tsiang, op. cit., p. 16. Ariga in Stead, op. cit., pp. 158–9.

[2] For background and importance of LeGendre, see Appendix III.

[3] Ariga in Stead, op. cit., pp. 160–1. Tsiang, op. cit., pp. 15–17. The audience was finally given in accordance with a preliminary agreement between the *Tsungli Yamen* and the other envoys at Peking, and Soejima was the first to be received because he alone claimed the rank of ambassador.

[4] *D.N.G.M.* vi. 177–8, Doc. 95. Yen, op. cit., p. 185.

[5] Tsiang, op. cit., pp. 16–17. Iwata, op. cit., p. 192.

[6] Kerr, op. cit., pp. 66–70, for China's claim to the Ryūkyūs as a tributary state.

subdued the eastern part of the island nor controlled its aboriginal inhabitants. Because these barbarians attacked and murdered Japanese subjects who were shipwrecked on their shores in the winter of 1871, he said, the Japanese government intended 'to send officers there to call them to account'.[1] Ambassador Soejima wished to warn the Chinese government in advance to prevent endangering friendly relations between the two countries.

The Chinese admitted their local authorities governed only the 'ripe barbarians'; the others, called 'raw aborigines', were still 'beyond the reach' of their government and culture. Hence their government had not chastized them.

Yanagihara further pointed out that these same savages had in the past plundered and murdered other stranded foreign subjects and since the Chinese government had taken no steps against them, they were becoming more atrocious. Japan recognized that this could lead to their subjection as well as the land under China's control by some other country, which would mean the loss of Formosa as Hong Kong and other lands had been lost, and would seriously menace the southern seas of Japan. Hence, Yanagihara said, the Japanese government had decided to dispatch an expedition to govern (*seisuru*) the guilty tribes. Soejima, as foreign minister, had caused the expedition to be postponed, however, until he could inform China of Japan's purpose in Formosa. He wished to assure the Chinese government that when the barbarian lands lying beyond China's jurisdiction were put under Japan's control there would be no interference with China's internal affairs. The Japanese people were so enraged by the crime against the Ryūkyūans that unless their government acted against the savages, the people might take it upon themselves to invade the island and thus disturb the peace between the two countries. Since China's ministers had said that the 'raw aborigines' were beyond the reach of their government, Yanagihara declared Japan would treat them 'as an independent nation'.[2]

It seems incredible that if Yanagihara reported his interview

[1] '. . . tsukai o dashite sono tsumi o towan to su. . .' *D.N.G.M.* vi 178, Doc. 95. Ariga in Stead, op. cit., p. 162, translates this 'expeditionary force'.

[2] *D.N.G.M.* vi. 178 ff., Doc. 95. Japan Gaimushō (Foreign Office), *Nihon Gaikō Nempyō Narabini Shuyō Monjo* (1840–1945) (Chronological Table of Japan's Diplomacy and the Chief Documents), 2 vols. (Tokyo, 1955), i. 72.

correctly, China failed to find in his statements Japan's intention of more than civil action in Formosa.[1] Yet Li Hung-chang
concluded from a Chinese report of this conversation that if, as
stated, the *Tsungli Yamen* had declared that the case of the
Ryūkyūan castaways was no concern of the Japanese government since Ryūkyū was a tributary of China, the matter had
been handled satisfactorily. An appeal for redress could come
from Ryūkyū itself. The Chinese also doubted 'the military
capacity' of the Japanese to deal with the aborigines and dismissed the question.[2]

When Soejima returned triumphantly to Japan, Parkes
thought that Japan would launch a military expedition. He
reported that China had denied the responsibility for the
murder of the Ryūkyūans and he believed the Japanese were
being instigated by Charles LeGendre, who had been with
Soejima in Peking.[3] That LeGendre instigated the expedition
is an exaggeration—Japan's military designs on Formosa were
older than LeGendre's period in the Far East[4]—but LeGendre
had a first-hand knowledge of the island and a point of view
which were valuable to the Japanese war party. He whole-
heartedly encouraged the Formosan operation, perhaps in
retaliation for his disappointment in China.[5]

Before the expedition could be organized, however, resignations in the cabinet in opposition to Iwakura's renunciation
of the Korean military programme brought more cautious
ministers into power. In October 1873 Terashima Munenori
succeeded Soejima at the Foreign Ministry; Ōkuma Shigenobu
became Minister of Finance, Katsu Kaishu, Minister of the
Navy, and Ōkubo Toshimichi took over the Ministry of the
Interior in late November. Unable to resist the pressure of
the restless samurai, these men proceeded secretly with plans for
the Formosan venture, aided by LeGendre who whetted their
ambitions with schemes for the annexation of the whole of
Formosa to be hidden in negotiations with China over the
control of the aboriginal territory, and with visions of Japan as
the great civilizing nation in Asia.[6]

---

[1] Tsiang, op. cit., pp. 28–29. Yen, op. cit., p. 216.
[2] Ibid., pp. 189–90.
[3] F.O. 46/167, Parkes to Granville, No. 62, Conf'l., Hakodate, 18 Aug. 1873.
[4] Iwata, op. cit., pp. 189–90.
[5] Conroy, op. cit., p. 38.   [6] Yen, op. cit., pp. 194–6.

Previous to the cabinet crisis an intelligence mission had been dispatched to the island to collect information. By February 1874 Ōkubo and Ōkuma, aided by advice from both Americans and Japanese, presented to the *Dajōkan* a detailed plan for action preliminary to the military occupation for which the Council voted Y 500,000.[1] The government established a special office called the Bureau of Aboriginal Affairs of Formosa under the direction of Ōkuma Shigenobu and made Nagasaki the base of operations in line with recommendations made by Japan's intelligence mission sent to Formosa in the fall of 1873. It entrusted Yanagihara with the diplomatic negotiations at Peking and appointed Lieutenant-General Saigō Jūdō (Tsugumichi), younger brother of Saigō Takamori, commander of the forces, with General LeGendre as his adviser.[2] Two Imperial decrees of 5 April to Saigō instructed him to 'seek redress for the Ryūkyū people, to use military force if necessary, and to insure safety of Japanese mariners in that area'. But he was 'to confine his military activities to the aboriginal territory; to civilize the tribes after the punitive measures were done; to avoid involving the Chinese or foreigners in Taiwan; to leave negotiations to Yanagihara in Peking; to use LeGendre to smooth out difficulties with the aborigines and foreigners and to economize the costs'.[3]

The expedition consisted of 3,000 troops, 1,000 to be sent ahead with artisans to build encampments, and 2,000 assembled at Nagasaki by 24 April. There were three gun vessels and three troopships, one of which had gone ahead to Amoy. An American vessel, the *New York*, and an English steamer, *Yorkshire*, had been chartered to transport troops. Three hundred women were said to have travelled with the soldiers. In addition to LeGendre, the Japanese appointed other American assistants. Lieutenant-Commander Douglas Cassel, U.S.N., and Lieutenant James R. Wasson, formerly of U.S. Army Engineers, who had been for some time attached to the Yezo Colonization Department, were engaged as staff officers to Saigō. And Edward H. House, a correspondent for the *New York Herald*,

---

[1] Ibid., pp. 197–205.
[2] Idditti, op. cit., p. 164. Ariga in Stead, op. cit., p. 168. Ariga calls Legendre 'Lysander', a name which appears in no other English source. Yen, op. cit., p. 204.
[3] Ibid., p. 205.

became a reporter for the expedition.[1] In its orders for Cassel, the Japanese government directed the expedition to land at Sia-liau (She-liao) and to arrange an encampment for only 3,000 troops, hoping that the inhabitants of the Liang-kiau Valley and the tribes under Tooke-tok (Tauketok) would assist the Japanese. Otherwise, 25,000 troops would be sent.[2]

British Reaction to the Expedition

To Parkes it was obvious the Japanese were aiming at occupation. Although Terashima Munenori did not acknowledge this, he told Parkes of the government's plans to send ships and regular troops to Formosa, justifying the expedition on the ground that the Chinese government had told Soejima the previous year that China had no authority over the Formosan aborigines. The Japanese admitted China had not been asked to concur in the expedition. A minister, they said, was being sent to China to discuss matters, who would arrive in Peking some weeks after Japanese troops had reached Formosa.[3]

Parkes and others foresaw difficulties arising between China and Japan over Japan's high-handed action. Parkes not only telegraphed and wrote confidentially about this expedition to Wade on 4 April but asked the Japanese foreign minister not to employ British ships for carrying troops or military stores in hostile action against Chinese territory before they were cleared. At the same time he telegraphed Vice-Admiral Shadwell at Hong Kong to watch the developments.[4]

With Parkes's information at hand, Wade told the *Tsungli Yamen* of Japan's military undertaking on 18 April, inquiring whether the aboriginal lands in Formosa were Chinese territory and whether Japan had previously asked China's permission for this expedition. China at once claimed jurisdiction over the whole island and complete ignorance of Japan's plans. Wade then tried to thwart Japan's efforts to hire British ships and pilots in Shanghai by ordering British consuls to caution

[1] Edward H. House, *The Japanese Expedition to Formosa* (Tokyo, 1875), pp. 16–17. Conroy, op. cit., p. 55.

[2] LeGendre MSS., Official Letters, 1874–5, iv. 23. For Tooke-tok, see Appendix III, p. 575.

[3] Ad. I/6300, Encl. in Shadwell's No. 114, Parkes to Shadwell, 6 Apr. 1874; Shadwell to Adm., No. 125, 3 May 1874 and encl., Parkes to Shadwell, Conf'l., Yedo, 14 Apr. 1874. F.O. 46/178, Parkes to Granville, No. 61, Yedo, 6 Apr. 1874.

[4] Ibid. Yen. op. cit., p. 212.

British subjects against making such arrangements and to restrain them from service for China against Japan.[1]

Upon hearing of China's claim to sovereign rights over the aborigines, Parkes likewise telegraphed British consuls not to clear British vessels ladened with Japanese troops or munitions to any port in Formosa or China before China had publicly declared her consent to the expedition, and informed the Japanese foreign minister of his instructions. He re-emphasized this several weeks later when he informed the British consul at Nagasaki that British subjects must not participate in the expedition, believing from what the consul had written that it was by no means temporary in character. Eight hundred workmen, it was reported, had been included with the troops. Some men took their families, thinking they were going to settle in the great sugar island of Formosa.[2]

In spite of Parkes's and Wade's efforts to the contrary, the Japanese government succeeded in hiring Captain A. R. Brown, a Scot, the commander of a Japanese lighthouse tender since 1868, to take charge of the shipping of men and supplies to Formosa in 1874. Brown personally commanded the *Takasago Maru* which carried Saigō Jūdō himself and hundreds of Japanese troops to Sia-liau.[3]

Mr. Bingham, the new United States Minister to Japan, however, reversed the position of his predecessor by opposing the employment of United States vessels in this service, removing the *New York* from the expedition, and ordering LeGendre, Cassel, and Wasson to be detained from going to Formosa until the written consent of China to the expedition was secured by the Japanese government.[4] Vice-Admiral Shadwell dispatched the *Hornet* to watch proceedings at the Formosan ports.[5]

---

[1] F.O. 17/673, Wade to Granville, No. 62, Peking, 24 Apr. 1874; Wade to Derby, No. 72, Peking, 30 Apr. 1874.

[2] F.O. 46/179, Parkes to Derby, Nos. 78 and 92, Yedo, 5 and 22 May 1874. *D.N.G.M.* vii, 65–66, Doc. 50.

[3] Rutgers University MSS., Richard Henry Brunton, *Pioneer Engineering in Japan, A Record of Work in Helping to Relay the Foundations of the Japanese Empire (1868–1876)*, condensed and annotated with an introductory chapter and postscript by William Elliott Griffis (cited hereafter as Brunton MS.), xxii. 90. Perry, op. cit., pp. 113–14. Captain Brown served the Japanese government later as Chief Superintendent of the Marine Office and was awarded the Order of the 'Rising Sun' fourth class on 23 April 1881 for his services in the Formosan campaign. *Japan Weekly Mail*, 30 April, 1881.

[4] *D.N.G.M.* vii, 45–46. Doc. 29, F.O. 46/178, Parkes to Derby, No. 71, Yedo, 25 Apr. 1874. [5] Ad. 1/6300, Shadwell to Adm., 16 May 1874.

The British *Japan Herald* saw little likelihood of foreign sympathy for Japan's professed aims—the advance of civilization by punishing savages, protecting navigation, and opening Formosa to trade. Experience had proved, the British paper argued, that the commercial policy of Japan was less liberal than that of China. Since the latter held all ports of Formosa and had admitted foreigners to them all, 'foreign interests would certainly not gain by a change of ownership'.[1] But Wade in Peking is said to have feared the inflation of China's pride should she succeed fully in Formosa and to have determined to prevent it.[2]

Japanese Action in southern Formosa

British and American opposition caused the Japanese to pause.[3] Terashima told Parkes the expedition would be postponed until a Japanese minister could explain to China that Japan had no hostile intentions towards her.[4] Ōkubo rushed orders to Saigō to halt proceedings and await further directions. He himself hurried to Nagasaki to discuss matters with Saigō and Ōkuma. But restraining Japanese soldiers bent on adventure and national glory needed more than civilian orders from Yedo. Saigō dispatched one ship with troops on 27 April. Four more left on 2 May. The American staff officers accompanied them. Ōkubo arrived the next day to face a defiant Saigō.[5] The General refused to give up the expedition. 'If you stop me', he said, 'I will not answer for the conduct of my men; but if you will let me go, I will take the whole responsibility on myself.'[6] He made important concessions, however, in his discussions with the civil authorities. On 4 May he agreed in writing to detach Cassel and Wasson from the expedition, to send LeGendre back to Yedo, and in accordance with the Imperial instructions, to limit the expedition to the punishment of the savage tribes whose land would be held by a small security

---

[1] F.O. 46/178, *Japan Herald*, 11 Apr., encl. in No. 66, Yedo, 14 Apr. 1874. For *Japan Herald*, see pp. 417-21.

[2] Yen, op. cit., p. 215.

[3] Nippon Shiseki Kyōkai (Japan Historical Association), *Ōkuma Shigenobu Kankei Bunsho* (Documents related to Ōkuma Shigenobu), 5 vols. (Tokyo, 1933), ii. 302, letter, Sanjō to Ōkuma, 19 Apr. 1874.

[4] F.O. 46/178, Parkes to Derby, No. 71, Yedo, 25 Apr. 1874.

[5] Conroy, op. cit., p. 55.

[6] Idditti, op. cit., pp. 164-5. Iwata, op. cit., p. 198.

force.[1] Upon his return to Yedo Ōkubo reported that the situation at Nagasaki had been most unfortunate but if it led to serious difficulties with China and embarrassed Japan's relations with other nations, he himself would undertake to negotiate a settlement.[2]

Saigō thus forced the government to support the expedition. On 19 May the *Dajōkan* announced officially its decision to dispatch its troops. At the same time Yanagihara left Japan to negotiate with China in Peking.[3] The Japanese press declared on 22 May that Japan's object was to deal with the outrages of the savage tribes and to take steps to secure the safety of navigation in southern Formosan waters. Another document officially sanctioned for the foreign press maintained that the 'Japanese Government intended no hostility to China but wished China to join her forces with Japan's to give new life and vigour to East Asia to surpass all other countries in the world'. Clearly echoing LeGendre's teachings, Japan declared she wished to punish these savage tribes before some other nation used this as a pretext for subjugating them and occupying their territory.[4]

Japan quickly accomplished her purpose in Formosa. Her achievements can be followed here, however, through the accounts of Japanese sympathizers only.[5] The first troops arrived at Liang-kiau Bay on 6 May. Two days later they pitched their camp at a place near Sia-liau selected by Cassel, Wasson, and Fukushima, the Japanese consul at Amoy. The Chinese residents offered no opposition and the aborigines, excluding the offending Botans and their allies the Kusukuts (or Kousakuts), welcomed the Japanese expedition and gave it guides and enlisted in its service. On 10 May Admiral Akamatsu Noriyoshi arrived with 500 men. He, Cassel, and Wasson interviewed Yee-suk (Isa), the leader of the natives since Tooke-tok's death, who warned them against excursions into the hostile Botan country. Disregarding this advice, some Japanese had skirmishes with the Botans in their territory on 17 and 22 May when sixteen

---

[1] *D.N.G.M.* vii. 61–62, Doc. 46. Conroy, op. cit., pp. 55–56.
[2] *D.N.G.M.* vii. 83–84, Doc. 58.
[3] F.O.46/179, Parkes to Wade, Yedo, 19 May 1874, encl. in Parkes, No. 95, 1874.
[4] Ibid., Parkes to Derby, No. 98, Conf'l., Yedo, 29 May 1874, and encls.
[5] e.g. House, op. cit., and newspaper accounts inspired by LeGendre and United States officers with the expedition.

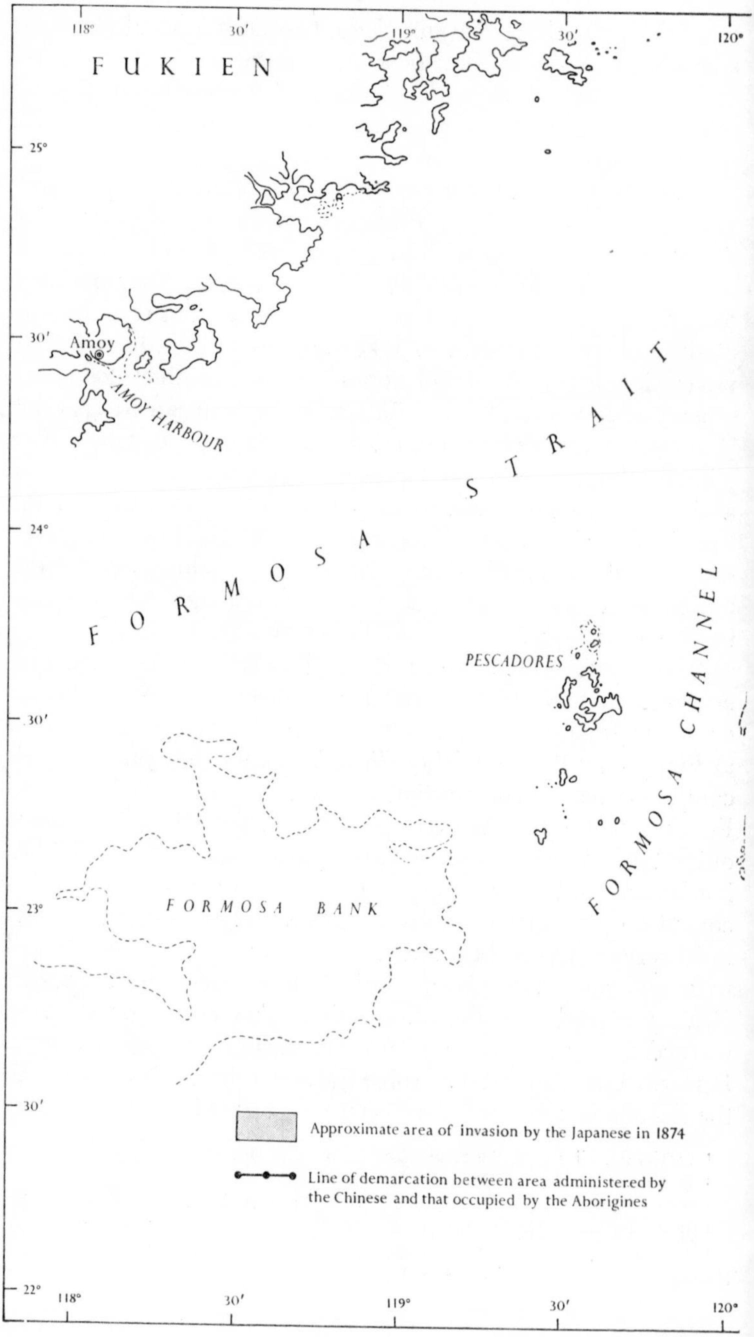

MAP 2 FORMOSA

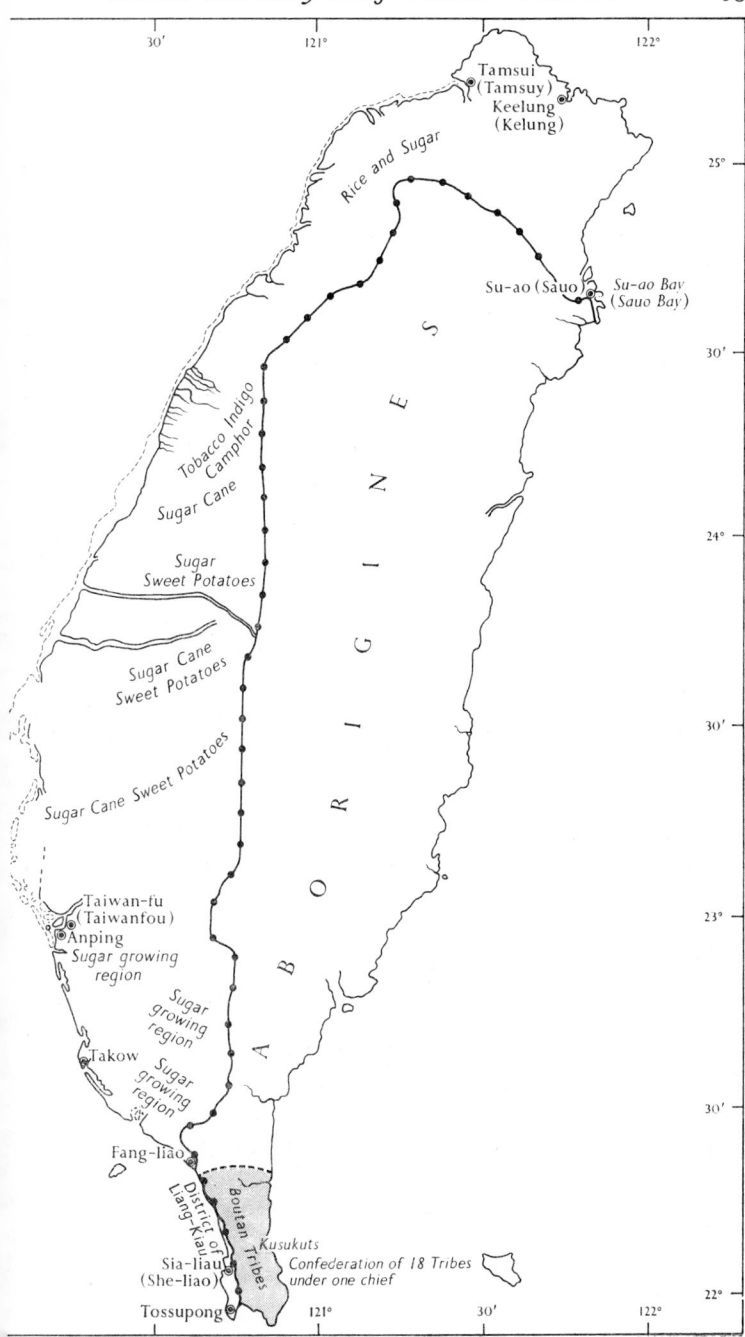

30'   121°   122°

Tamsui
(Tamsuy)
Keelung
(Kelung)

25°

Rice and Sugar

Su-ao (Sauo)   Su-ao Bay
(Sauo Bay)

30'

A B O R I G I N E S

Tobacco Indigo
Camphor

Sugar Cane

24°

Sugar
Sweet Potatoes

Sugar Cane
Sweet Potatoes

30'

Sugar Cane Sweet Potatoes

Taiwan-fu
(Taiwanfou)
Anping
Sugar growing
region

23°

Sugar
growing
region

Takow   Sugar
growing
region

30'

Fang-liao

District of
Liang-Kiau

Boutan Tribes

Kusukuts

Sia-liau
(She-liao)   Confederation of 18 Tribes
under one chief

22°

Tossupong   121°   30'   122°

Source: General Charles W. Le Gendre, 1870

Botans, including the chief, the chief's son, and six Japanese were killed. The Japanese returned to camp bringing twelve heads taken from the killed and wounded.[1]

General Saigō arrived 22 May. On the 25th, Saigō, Cassell, Wasson, House, and others conferred with Yee-suk and four lesser chiefs. They declared their intention to exterminate the Botans and the Kusukuts and demanded the help of Yee-suk and the friendly tribes through the capture and handing over of any of the enemy who should take refuge in their territory. Yee-suk promised to do so but he and his tribesmen objected to the Japanese proposal that they lease at their own price a piece of their tribal lands on the 'east coast' of southern Formosa to provide a safe landing place for foreign ships in stormy weather. The Japanese were free to land in perfect peace anywhere on the south of the island, Yee-suk said.[2]

Saigō's main task now became the destruction of the Botan and Kusukut settlements in the interior country. It was already clear that the numbers of the enemy were not great. Both the extent of the population and the political organization of southern Formosa had been greatly misjudged. At the time of the arrival of the Japanese there were only 2,360 effective men among all the eighteen tribes in the Liang-kiau Valley according to estimates of the 'headmen' of the settlements. The hostile Botans and Kusukuts were the largest single groups, numbering 250 and 190 men respectively.[3] Against them the Japanese could mass 3,500 troops. But to track down these wily savages in their wilderness was hazardous. There were no reliable maps—the most authentic chart being that of LeGendre, compiled in 1870, which did not give precise details of the Botan region. The Japanese had to contend with excessive heat, sodden paths, swollen streams, rocky cliffs, and stunted wilderness as they marched to attack their enemy on the first and second of June, accompanied by the three Americans as observers. *En route* to the Botans' stronghold they came upon the graves of the murdered Ryūkyūans which were explicitly marked. After twenty-four hours in this jungle they reached the

---

[1] House, op. cit., pp. 45–74. The *Tokei Journal*, 20 June 1874, encl. in F.O. 46/180., Parkes's, No. 117, 1874.

[2] The *Tokei Journal*, 20 June 1874. House, op. cit., pp. 75, 97–103.

[3] Ibid., p. 105.

evacuated villages of the Botans and Kusukuts and burned them. A few inhabitants firing from ambush were killed but most had escaped into the mountains. Detachments were left to guard these abandoned places and control the jungle paths. The main body of troops returned to their headquarters at Sia-liao.[1] A telegram from Nagasaki to Yedo on 12 June announced the completion of the subjugation of southern Formosa.[2] Saigō fulfilled his agreement in not going beyond that very small area.

The destruction of the Botans and Kusukuts had brought all the aborigines to a sense of helplessness. They had seen their country overrun which they had thought was impregnable. At a conference with the Japanese on 9 June their chiefs yielded reluctantly to the Japanese request to occupy a piece of land on the eastern shore as a 'temporary' base in the event of continuing tribal hostilities, but refused payment of any kind. Here on 11 June the Japanese established another camp, which was unexpectedly witnessed by an English gunboat. By the end of July all the hostile southern tribes had acknowledged their submission to the Japanese. An outbreak of fever soon decimated the Japanese troops so seriously that reinforcements were required during the long, hot summer. But friendly relations with the natives developed while Saigō and his men awaited the results of the negotiations in Peking.[3]

Parkes lamented the possible effects of the rapid success of this expedition upon Japan's internal politics. If it terminated soon, trouble among the samurai might start again and the government might then decide upon an ill-advised expedition to Korea. A bad harvest could also cause trouble.[4] It was clear that the civilian leaders of the government did not have control over Japanese military commanders in times of crucial decisions, as the departure of the Formosan expedition from Nagasaki had proved.

On 18 June Terashima in an interview with Parkes justified the expedition, admitted the futility of stationing a Japanese garrison on Formosa, and said Japan had no intention of

---

[1] House, op. cit., chs. 20–23. House seems to exaggerate the difficulties of the jungle for the hardened Japanese invaders because of his sympathy for their cause.

[2] The *Tokei Journal*, 20 June 1874.

[3] House, op. cit., pp. 142–4, 149, 151, 215–17.

[4] F.O. 46/180, Parkes to Derby, No. 112, Yedo, 16 June 1874.

taking any land. His country planned to chastise the savages and in talks with China induce her to take measures needed to prevent the repetition of such crimes.[1]

Wade, reviewing the whole episode, made an early and far-reaching judgement. He had decided that 'morally and politically, it was Britain's duty to favour rather the establishment of China's authority over Formosa by negotiation, than the annexation of the island to Japan by force of arms'.[2] He was also convinced that the Japanese on Formosa were determined, with or without the consent of the government in Yedo, to attempt the conquest of Formosa, knowing the unpreparedness of the Chinese, their timidity and abhorrence of action. The Japanese were gaining time by making the right of China to the ground they occupied a matter of discussion. China's position, he said, was full of contradictions. They complained of acts of war but evaded any admission of rupture. Such indecision suited British interests.[3]

China's Response: Negotiations with Japan

China had indeed moved slowly. Although on 8 April Thomas Wade informed the Peking government of Japan's dispatch of ships and men ostensibly against the aborigines in southern Formosa, the *Tsungli Yamen* waited to respond until 11 May when the arrival of a Japanese troopship at Amoy and a letter of 30 April from Li Hung-chang with suggestions for action, had confirmed the news. China's ministers of foreign affairs then wrote Terashima in astonishment. They had understood from Soejima a year earlier that Japan merely planned to send a mission to the Formosan aborigines 'to desire from them the good treatment of her people in future, if they ever go to their territories, and not in any way to wage war upon them'. The Chinese declared that China had jurisdiction over the aboriginal lands and asked if Japan intended a military expedition to Formosa, why had she failed to consult China beforehand?[4]

On 14 May the Emperor issued a decree appointing the director of the Foochow Arsenal and Dockyard, Shen Pao-chen,

[1] *D.N.G.M.* vii. 125–7, Doc. 77.
[2] F.O. 17/674, Wade to Derby, No. 125, Conf'l., Peking, 24 June 1874.
[3] Ibid., No. 139, Peking, no day, 1874.
[4] Yen, op. cit., pp. 212–18. *D.N.G.M.* vii. 72–77, Doc. 55.

Special Imperial Commissioner for Formosan Affairs, with diplomatic and military powers and orders to proceed to Formosa with ships and men. The assignment of P'an Wei, the Provincial Treasurer of Fukien, as Shen's assistant soon followed. But so slow was the communication between the capital and the coast that Shen did not receive word of his own appointment until 31 May.[1] Critical appraisals of China's military resources, proposals to win the moral support of Western powers, and preparations for an eventual military contest with Japan began immediately. Meanwhile Yanagihara undertook diplomatic negotiations with P'an Wei in Shanghai in June and struggled with the ministers of the *Tsungli Yamen* in Peking during August—all without success. Japan and China merely clarified their points of view and demands upon each other through instructions, letters, and interviews.[2]

On 8 July the *Dajōkan* arrived at a not unanimous decision to risk war with China to justify its expedition to Formosa and seek if possible China's recognition of Japan's incorporation of the Ryūkyūs and the opening of Korea. The ministers of the army and the navy were ordered to make a war plan. But the instructions to Yanagihara of 15 July for use in negotiating with the *Tsungli Yamen* made possible an alternative to military action. Convinced by its French legal adviser, Gustave Boissonade, that its expeditionary force to Formosa was legal under existing international law, and strongly influenced by LeGendre, the Japanese government issued the following orders: Yanagihara should explain to China's ministers that (1) the territory then occupied by Japan's punitive expedition was 'truly unclaimed aboriginal territory'; (2) 'the purpose of the Japanese government was to subdue the aborigines, clearly mark the border between the aboriginal territory—which would be renamed Takasago—and Chinese Taiwan and colonize the land for humanitarian reasons'; (3) should the Chinese oppose a divided island, however, 'and propose to receive the aboriginal territory from the Japanese, then an adequate amount of compensation should be demanded'; and (4) 'if the aboriginal territory were to be ceded to China, an agreement should be

---

[1] Yen, op. cit., pp. 218–20.
[2] For details of the negotiations including Saigō's ill-advised efforts to negotiate with P'an Wei at Sia-liau, see ibid., pp. 220–44.

concluded along with the third condition—to guarantee the safety of future navigators'.

Among many accompanying instructions the government pointed out that if China preferred to settle the issue by war, Japan would not hesitate to fight. But negotiations should proceed with dignity to insure a proper future judgement of Japan. And in case the aboriginal territory should be offered to China, nothing below $6,000,000 Mexican should be considered for compensation. While holding the upper hand, Yanagihara should also demand the settlement of the problems over the Ryūkyūs and Korea. LeGendre was to be in Fukien to explain Japan's policy to Chinese officials. The decision for war or peace should be referred to Yedo.[1]

Yanagihara had not yet met the members of the *Tsungli Yamen* in Peking when on 1 August Ōkubo succeeded after great effort and devious strategy in getting himself appointed High Commissioner and Minister Extraordinary and Plenipotentiary to succeed Yanagihara in the conduct of negotiations at Peking. As war became more probable and Japan's military prowess was at best uncertain, Ōkubo wanted personally to resolve the Formosan issue with China, since he had assumed the responsibility for sending Japan's troops to Formosa.[2] His instructions dated 2 August stated that the Imperial orders and basic policies sent to Yanagihara remained essentially unalterable but gave Ōkubo power to use his discretion in carrying them out. Although the chief object of his negotiations was to be the maintenance of peace, he was allowed to decide on war if unavoidable. He was empowered to supervise Japan's civilian and military personnel stationed in China and to make use of and direct the services of LeGendre who had been sent ahead to Fukien.[3] A letter signed by the Emperor on 5 August further enabled Ōkubo to negotiate with the minister of state appointed by the Emperor of China and to conclude and sign a treaty of

[1] Ibid., pp. 231–5. MS. Gaimushō, Tokyo, *Yanagihara Kōshi to Sanshoku Ōfuku Naikan* (Conf'l. correspondence between Yanagihara Sakimitsu, Minister, and the Sanshoku, June–Nov. 1874). Included on L.C. Microfilm of the Japanese Foreign Office Archives, No. M. T. 1–1–2–6. (Hereafter cited as Yanagihara *Correspondence*). Instructions of 15 July 1874 taken to Yanagihara by Tanabe. T. These instructions are condensed in *D.N.G.M.* vii. 155–7, Doc. 95.

[2] Yen, op. cit., pp. 244–6. Iwata, op. cit., pp. 205–8.

[3] *D.N.G.M.* vii. 171–3, Doc. 104.

agreement in the name of the Emperor of Japan.[1] He arrived
in Peking in company with Boissonade, LeGendre, and others,
on 10 September 1874, after Yanagihara's negotiations had
reached a temporary deadlock.[2]

During the preceding months China had consistently claimed
sovereign rights over the aboriginal lands, asserting in consequence that it was her responsibility, not Japan's, to punish
the aborigines for their crimes against the Ryūkyūans, whose
kingdom was China's tributary. She demanded the withdrawal
of Saigō's troops, declaring that Yanagihara had not informed
her in 1873 of Japan's intention to send a punitive military
expedition to the aborigines, and in doing so Japan had violated
the treaty of 1871. Yanagihara refuted this accusation with a
quotation from his conversation with the *Tsungli Yamen* on
21 June 1873 and steadily maintained that the aborigines were
not under the administration or culture of China.[3] By 24 August
he wrote to Prince Kung that further negotiations were useless.
He would insist on Japan's sovereign right 'to punish the
aborigines on the unclaimed land and to assimilate them eventually into Japanese culture'. China, having said she would
undertake to control the savage lands as soon as Japan withdrew
her troops, now declared her determination 'to manage' her
aboriginal domain without Japan's interference.[4] Through the
initiative of China's leading Minister of Foreign Affairs, Wen-
hsiang, however, expressions of mutual willingness to continue
negotiations with the hope of preserving amity had prevented
a rupture when on 10 September Ōkubo arrived. The *Tsungli
Yamen* also had reason to anticipate a solution for the problem,
since Wade had informed it of Japan's intent to negotiate for
the payment of compensation in return for the withdrawal of
her troops—a concession which Li Hung-chang had already
recommended for consideration.[5] But war seemed more probable than peace to the foreign representatives in China and
Japan.

[1] Yanagihara *Correspondence*, Instructions and credentials for Ōkubo, 5 Aug.
1874.
[2] Iwata, op. cit., pp. 210-11.
[3] Yen, op. cit., pp. 220-1, 229, 237-9.
[4] Ibid., pp. 240-2. *D.N.G.M.* vii. 191-3, 195-6, 197-201, Docs. 119, 123, 125,
127, 128.
[5] Ibid., vii. 214, 216-19, Docs. 133, 136, 137. Yen, op. cit., p. 251.

British Concern and Offers of Mediation

Although Parkes had had several interviews with the Japanese ministers, he had secured only contradictory information regarding Japan's intentions. About 18 July Iwakura declared Japan would not withdraw from Formosa even if China requested it.[1] On 27 July Terashima justified the expedition on Japan's original grounds that the land of the aborigines was beyond China's jurisdiction, but conceded Japan would withdraw her troops immediately if a satisfactory agreement could be reached with China.[2]

In August Terashima reported that Yanagihara had instructions to negotiate a settlement on condition that China would take over positions held by the Japanese on Formosa, undertake to keep the savages in order, and admit Japan's right to punish them by the expedition then in Formosa. If China accepted, Japan would retire from Formosa and claim no indemnity.[3] With the dispatch of Ōkubo to Peking, Parkes feared that the conduct of the Sino-Japanese discussions was attended with considerable danger, that the two nations might drift into a conflict which they both professed to wish to avoid.[4] Before leaving Japan Ōkubo implied in a talk with Parkes that the Japanese desired some material consideration for the withdrawal of their troops. Parkes clearly understood the government's problem. Its political opponents considered withdrawal a sign of weakness. They might attack and overthrow the government. War with China could seem a lesser evil, although war would mean increased taxation and probably a revolt of the overburdened agricultural classes. At least the government sought to be ready for it, having bought a large Pacific Mail steamer and two English steamers, and having raised its force to 6000 in Formosa.[5]

At the same time China's military preparations added to the alarm. Merchants in Amoy expected a Japanese invasion and closed their shops in panic.[6] Vice-Admiral Shadwell had written

[1] F.O. 46/180, Parkes to Derby, No. 126, Yedo, 18 July 1874.
[2] *D.N.G.M.* vii. 162–5, Doc. 100.
[3] F.O. 46/181, Parkes to Derby, No. 138, Yedo, 3 Aug. 1874.
[4] Ibid., No. 148, Yedo, 13 Aug. 1874.
[5] F.O. 46/182, Parkes to Derby, No. 167, Yedo, 12 Sept. 1874, encl. conf'l. Memorandum on Formosa, by Vice-Admiral Shadwell of 26 Aug. 1874.
[6] Tsiang, op. cit., pp. 22–23. House, op. cit., p. 176. Ariga in Stead, op. cit., pp. 168–9.

to London saying that Japan showed no signs of leaving Formosa. In fact, she seemed to be establishing a colony there. He thought that China could not submit to such an invasion of her territory and the establishment of foreign jurisdiction against her will. A diplomatic rupture was inevitable. But China would talk first in order to gain time for needed preparations. In the event of war he feared privateering on both sides with little respect for rights of neutrals. He would need reinforcements on the station to protect trade.[1]

Wade, too, was convinced that war was imminent and all foreign interests, both commercial and missionary, would suffer. He proposed arbitration to both the *Tsungli Yamen* and Yanagihara.[2] He suggested that the *Tsungli Yamen* appeal to the foreign powers to neutralize for a given time the coasts and rivers of China. The powers interested in her integrity should be asked to assist her in preserving it until she was able to maintain it herself. But such co-operative assistance from the powers would involve trouble and expense and they could accept no such commitments without the assurance of a *quid pro quo*. He gently suggested they might be invited to establish a protectorate. China's refusal was sharp. Such action on her part would offend her dignity. Wade pressed further for the terms China would offer if Japan were willing to arbitrate. He proposed China's payment of the war costs as a possible concession.[3] On 12 September he wrote to Parkes asking if the Japanese minister should seek his good offices in the Formosan issue, would there be anything advantageous to Britain or foreign interests which he could ask in return. Parkes suggested that the Japanese give foreigners the same rights of travel and trade in the interior of Japan they had in China—a demand which he must have known would have been anathema to Iwakura and others.[4] Thus, China and Japan both had good reasons to suspect foreign interference and at first showed little or no interest in Wade's offer of 'good offices'.

[1] Ad. I/6300, Shadwell to Adm., No. 171, 7 July 1874.
[2] F.O. 17/675, Wade to Derby, Nos. 176 and 178, Peking, 10 and 13 Aug. 1874. *D.N.G.M.* vii. 187–8, Doc. 116.
[3] F.O. 17/676, Wade to Derby, No. 222, 16 Nov. 1874, part of which is given in P.P. H. of C. 1875, lxxxii (C 1164). This letter reviews at length Wade's policy throughout the whole affair.
[4] F.O. 46/182, Parkes to Derby, No. 168, Conf'l., Yedo, 12 Sept. 1874.

British Assistance in the Conclusion of a Treaty

Ōkubo's negotiations with Prince Kung and the ministers of the *Tsungli Yamen* during September made little progress in Peking. He demanded concrete evidence for China's claim to jurisdiction over the land of the aborigines and disproved the information given in reply—both the statement in the *Taiwan Fu-Chih* (Gazetteer of Taiwan-fu) and the collection of local taxes said to be evidence of China's administrative measures in the area. The lack of any effective local administration, many outrages committed on foreigners by the savages, and the statement of the *Tsungli Yamen* to Yanagihara in Peking in 1873—all, he said, indicated the absence of Chinese sovereignty in the territory. China had given no evidence acceptable under international law to prove otherwise. Hence, Japan had not invaded Chinese territory and China's insistence that Japan had violated Article I of the Treaty of 1871 was inadmissible. Wen-hsiang refuted every statement of Ōkubo's, explaining China's system of gradualism in assimilating aboriginal subjects and declaring that the state system of China—older by far than Western international law—'allowed freedom for China to govern aborigines as it saw fit'. Ōkubo continued to express his desire for a peaceful settlement.[1]

War seemed so imminent that Parkes cancelled his plans for a trip and ordered a British warship to remain in Nagasaki. Upon receipt of this information from the British naval commander, Wade questioned Ōkubo about the likelihood of war on 26 September and offered his services in persuading China to settle the dispute if Japan were willing to evacuate her troops under given circumstances. Ōkubo gave him no information and declined his help, still hoping to find a peaceful solution in direct communication with China. Wade pointed out that Britain's more than two hundred commercial firms in China having an annual trade of 'four hundred millions in gold' must be protected in case of hostilities. He would go to Shanghai after ten days to make preparations in consultation with the British admiral.[2] On the 25th Wade had sent the word of

---

[1] *D.N.G.M.* vii. 219–25, 227–36, 241–5, Docs. 139, 142, 143, 146, for negotiations 14–27 Sept. 1874; Doc. 200, Pt. III. 332–4 Ōkubo's report, November 1874. Yen, op. cit., p. 257. For greater details of the negotiations based on wide use of Chinese and Japanese source material, ibid., pp. 252–64.

[2] *D.N.G.M.* vii. 240–1, Doc. 145, Conversation of 26 Sept. 1874. Yen, op. cit., p. 267.

Parkes's concern about war to the *Tsungli Yamen*, which curtly indicated, Wade thought, that the Chinese ministers believed him working in the interests of Japan. And again they refused his offer of mediation. To Prince Kung he urged arbitration, recommending that China induce Japan to withdraw her troops, even if it meant the payment of an indemnity.[1]

Ōkubo threatened to leave Peking on 5 October unless the dispute was settled: the conflict over China's claim to jurisdiction over the aborigines had reached an impasse.[2] On the 9th Yanagihara rejected Wade's suggestion that the dispute be submitted to the adjudication of several neutral nations in accordance with the practice of the West.[3] Wade thought war more likely than peace, but it was still possible that he and his French colleague, M. de Geofroy, might influence China to grant conditions under which Japan could withdraw honourably.[4]

On 10 October Ōkubo repeated forcibly his opinion that since China had not enforced law and order in the aboriginal lands, she had no right to claim them any longer and used the case of the *Rover* as proof of China's unwillingness to take responsibility in that territory. He said China had violated her treaties with foreign nations promising protection of foreigners in that her policy of gradually civilizing aborigines did not provide for such protection. But since Japan did not want to infringe on another nation's territory or station her troops in such a region, and because she sincerely wanted peace, he proposed a 'solution which would be convenient to both parties: China should redefine her boundary line and place the aboriginal territory of Taiwan (Formosa) outside the new demarcation line'. He demanded an answer in five days. Otherwise China's adamant claim of jurisdiction over the aborigines' territory would be considered as China's will to break off friendly relations with Japan.[5] China agreed to co-operate in the interest of mutual friendship and asked for an extension of the deadline on her reply.[6]

---

[1] F.O. 17/676, Wade to Derby, No. 201, Peking, 2 Oct. 1874.
[2] *D.N.G.M.* vii. 252–8, Doc. 152.   [3] Ibid., 258–60, Doc. 153.
[4] F.O. 17/676, Wade to Derby, No. 206, Peking, 16 Oct. 1874.
[5] *D.N.G.M.* vii. 261–4, 332–4, Docs. 155 and 200, Pt. III, Note from Ōkubo to the *Tsungli Yamen*, 10 Oct. 1874 and Ōkubo's Report, Nov. 1874. Yen, op. cit., pp. 269–70. For *Rover* case see Appendix III, p. 575.
[6] *D.N.G.M.* vii. 265–6, 334, Docs. 157 and 200, Pt. III.

It was not surprising that China soon rejected bitterly the revision of her Formosan boundaries and accused Japan of intending to seize the aboriginal lands. But a letter from the Grand Secretary, Wen-hsiang, on the 16th recognized Ōkubo's desire for peace and proposed a meeting to discuss measures which would satisfy both parties.[1] In the meantime Ōkubo talked with Wade and the French minister. He now explained to them the issues in the dispute and gave them copies of his communications with the *Tsungli Yamen*. In answer to their questions about the conditions on which Japan would withdraw her troops, he said Japan wanted no territory but her honour must be vindicated and compensation for her human sacrifices and financial outlay must be given.[2] Several days of negotiations for a compromise began on 18 October. Wen-hsiang presented a plan in answer to Ōkubo's demands. Here China excused Japan on the basis of her ignorance of China's sovereign rights in the aboriginal lands, promised not to hold the case against Japan when the troops were withdrawn, to handle the aborigines thereafter, and 'to pay compensation to those Japanese who had suffered at the hands of the aborigines'. Ōkubo demanded an indemnity of 3,000,000 Mexican dollars. China stated Japan had spent only $500,000 or a little more (the amount of Japan's first appropriation for the expedition), asked that it be called relief money for the families of the murdered Ryūkyūans, and that it be paid after the withdrawal of Japanese troops. She refused Ōkubo's demand for a written guarantee for the payment of the money. On the 23rd Ōkubo declared he would leave Peking. He said, 'Japan has no other way but to proceed with her original plan and annex the territory which she now occupies'.[3]

Here Wade stepped in. When Ōkubo called to say good-bye Wade persuaded him to withdraw the troops, to call the indemnity 'relief money', and even reduce the amount, but Ōkubo insisted upon a written assurance for payment.[4] Wade then hurried to the house of the Grand Secretary and 'urged him

---

[1] Yen, op. cit., p. 274. *D.N.G.M.* vii. 271–5, Docs. 161 and 162.

[2] Ibid., 267–71, Docs. 159 and 160. Tsiang, op. cit., pp. 32–33. For further details, see Yen, op. cit., pp. 271–2.

[3] *D.N.G.M.* vii. 277–98 Docs. 166, 169, 170, 172, and 173, Ōkubo's conversations 18–23 Oct. 1874. Yanagihara *Correspondence*, Yanagihara to *Sanshoku*, Ōkuma, and Terashima, 25 Oct. 1874. Yen, op. cit., 274–8. [4] *D.N.G.M.* vii. 298–9, Doc. 174.

to move Prince Kung to say at once what amount of money China would pay' and 'in what way the payment should be guaranteed'. If all other means failed and Japan's High Commissioner would consent, Wade said that he himself would guarantee the payment promised. Ōkubo did not require the payment to be called an indemnity for war expenses but compensations to the families of the murdered Ryūkyūans as the Chinese had suggested. On 25 October the *Tsungli Yamen* told Wade to offer the Japanese Commissioner 500,000 taels (about 750,000 Mexican dollars)—100,000 for the families of the murdered Ryūkyūans and 400,000 for the 'roads' and buildings which would be left in Formosa. In return for this concession Ōkubo demanded China's recognition of Japan's action as righteous, the obliteration of all evidences concerning the case, and China's payment of the total 500,000 taels to Japan before Japan would agree to withdraw her troops from aboriginal Formosa. Wade induced him to agree to China's payment of half the amount in advance of withdrawal and the remaining sum upon the total withdrawal of Japan's troops. The next day, 26 October, Wade received China's approval of these arrangements and reported it to Ōkubo.[1]

Five more days of negotiation resulted. The problems were (1) to so word the agreement that neither power, Japan or China, appeared dependent on the bidding of the other, (2) to agree upon the dates for the evacuation of Formosa by the Japanese, and the payment of the money by China, (3) to guarantee the performance of these acts. The two nations arrived at a mutual understanding and signed an Agreement, reinforced by a Guarantee, on 31 October 1874. Ōkubo left for Formosa on 1 November.[2] Prince Kung sent a circular dispatch to all the legations enclosing copies of both documents.[3]

In the Agreement of Peking, China accepted Japan's action in Formosa as a humane endeavour to afford 'security to her own

---

[1] *D.N.G.M.* vii. 306–9, Docs. 178 and 179. F.O. 17/676, Wade to Derby, No. 222, Peking, 16 Nov. 1874. Yen, op. cit., pp. 278–80. 'Roads' was a glorified term, as nothing more than footpaths existed. Davidson, op. cit., p. 155.

[2] F.O. 17/676, Wade to Derby, Nos. 208 and 219, Peking, 1 and 16 Nov. 1874. Yanagihara *Correspondence*, Yanagihara to *Sanshoku*, Ōkuma and Terashima, 2 Nov. 1874.

[3] F.O. 46/183, Encl. in Parkes to Derby, No. 202, Yedo, 23 Nov. 1874. P.P. H. of C. 1875, lxxxii (C 1164), 2–3. Ariga in Stead, op. cit., pp. 170–1.

subjects'. She promised to pay a certain amount to compensate the families of the Japanese who were murdered on Formosa and another sum for the 'roads' and buildings erected by the Japanese which she would retain for her own use. And she undertook to control the savage tribes in southern Formosa so as to protect navigation from further atrocities by them along their coasts. Both Japan and China agreed to cancel all their correspondence concerning the question and to drop the discussion for ever. The Guarantee acknowledged Wade as mediator, and stated that China would pay 100,000 taels at once as relief for the families of the murdered Ryūkyūans and 400,000 taels upon the evacuation of the Japanese forces. A definite day was set for the withdrawal and the concurrent payment of the remainder of the indemnity.[1]

British, Japanese, and Chinese Evaluations

The British government approved Wade's action. The Japanese government showed its gratitude publicly.[2] The Mikado received Parkes in private audience when he expressed his appreciation of Wade's good offices and requested him to convey to Mr. Wade 'his thanks for his timely and effective assistance'.[3] Ōkubo himself visited Parkes, requesting him to thank Wade. At this time he admitted to having demanded 3,000,000 dollars from China but since China had agreed to a smaller sum, he was not disturbed since he had secured the safety of future navigation in Formosan waters by agreement and the justification of Japanese proceedings in Formosa.[4] In London the Japanese minister called on Derby to express officially the thanks of his government for the part taken by Mr. Wade in preventing a rupture between China and Japan.[5] China's complete silence is meaningful in contrast to Japan's effusive appreciation. Obviously Japan felt triumphant. Parkes's and Wade's reports to London bear this out.

[1] *Kyū Jōyaku Isan*, i, Pt. 1, 628–32, English translation made at British Legation, Peking.
[2] F.O. 46/183, Parkes to Derby, Nos. 196 and 198, 13 and 16 Nov. 1874. P.P. Yedo, H. of C. 1875, lxxxii (C 1164), 1, Derby to Wade, 19 Nov. 1874. F.O. 262/254, Derby to Parkes, No. 145, 19 Nov. 1874.
[3] P.P. H. of C. 1875, lxxxii (C 1164), 1–2, Parkes to Derby, Yedo, 16 Nov. 1874.
[4] F.O. 46/183, Parkes to Derby, No. 206, Yedo, 30 Nov. 1874. Here Parkes says 3,000,000 taels, which is an obvious error.
[5] P.P. H. of C. 1875, lxxxii (C 1164), 2, Derby to Parkes, 14 Jan. 1874.

The Japanese government promoted three days of festivity in honour of the homecoming of the commissioners from Peking, which included a state reception by the Emperor.[1] In an address to His Majesty, Ōkuma took credit for his country and himself for the success Japan had achieved. Four great ends had been accomplished, he boasted: the wrongs suffered by Japan's shipwrecked subjects were redressed; the position of the Ryūkyūs was clarified and rendered independent of China; the security of world mariners in Formosan waters was ensured; the dignity and influence of Japan were vindicated.[2]

Differences of opinion regarding the success and consequence of the expedition were, however, not lacking in Japan. A group of samurai had addressed the Mikado, declaring Japan's inability to fight a war with China, shortly before a report of the Agreement of Peking reached Japan.[3] The Minister of Marine had opposed the Formosan policy of the government and felt that its success at Peking might make it arrogant and unreasonable. He withdrew from the *Dajōkan*.[4] Kido, a strategic member of the Council, had resigned in April in protest on the grounds that Japan could not afford such a military venture.[5] A clipping from the Japanese press stated that only because of the miserable weakness of China had Japan escaped great danger, and another warned against subsequent rash action in Korea.[6] Such views perhaps led the government to abandon the plan for a triumphant entry of the Formosan expeditionary force into Yedo. Instead, it landed the troops at Nagasaki and returned them to their former stations.[7]

Wade's letters give a picture of the reaction of the Chinese. In a confidential report to Derby on 6 December, more than a month after the signing of the Agreement, he said nothing should yet be published about the Agreement between Japan and China. He suspected that release of the details of the transaction in which he was largely concerned would be distasteful to his colleagues in general and not very acceptable

[1] F.O. 46/183, Parkes to Derby, No. 205, Yedo, 30 Nov. 1874.
[2] F.O. 46/190, Parkes to Derby, No. 31, Yedo, 22 Feb. 1875.
[3] F.O. 46/183, Parkes to Derby, No. 193, Yedo, 9 Nov. 1874.
[4] Ibid., No. 204, Conf'l., Yedo, 30 Nov. 1874 and encl.
[5] Idditti, op. cit., p. 165. Iwata, op. cit., p. 195.
[6] F.O. 46/183, Parkes to Derby, No. 205, Yedo, 30 Nov. 1874.
[7] Ibid., No. 220, Yedo, 21 Dec. 1874.

to the Chinese 'whose tone it appears to me, although they had really the best of the bargain, is the tone of people by no means pleased with the arrangements'.[1]

Chinese appreciation, however, was not entirely lacking. Wade found the Governor and Governor-General at Foochow ready to acknowledge his good offices in June 1875. They chuckled in exultation over the fact that 800 Japanese had left their bones in Formosa, victims of disease and climate during the brief campaign.[2]

Parkes, after a long correspondence with Wade, reflected on the settlement. He said he had not been prepared to find that China when threatened by Japan would feel unable to deal with her and would consent to the payment of a money consideration. He thought Ōkubo had played a bold game with much adroitness but his anxiety to avoid pushing matters to extremes was shown by his readiness to accept a small sum. The Japanese government, he said, would have been ready to agree to no money from China, and China felt humbled by the concession now that the danger was over.[3]

Wade sent further long detailed reports on the proceedings of the whole affair to London. The Secretary of the Foreign Office thought they contained nothing to call to Lord Derby's attention and that it was unnecessary to 'trouble the Queen, Mr. Disraeli or the Cabinet'. Derby noted, 'I have looked into it but see no reason for going through this mass of papers on which no action is to be taken. Thank Mr. Wade. The papers need not go on.'[4] Obviously, the expansionist efforts of the island empire of the Pacific caused little concern in the England of the new imperialist, Benjamin Disraeli. British trade with China and Japan had not been seriously disturbed. That was what counted.

[1] F.O. 17/677, No. 237. On 2 Feb. 1875 he asked to have this letter disregarded, and saw no objection to publishing the whole correspondence, not marked confidential, F.O. 17/697, No. 27.

[2] F.O. 17/699, Wade to Derby, No. 108, Foochow, 10 June 1875.

[3] F.O. 46/190, Parkes to Derby, No. 32, Yedo, 22 Feb. 1875.

[4] F.O. 17/676, F.O. note of 25 Jan. 1875 on Wade's secret and confidential letter to Derby, No. 223, Peking, 27 Nov. 1874.

PART TWO

ECONOMIC AND TECHNOLOGICAL DEVELOPMENTS

MAP 3. JAPAN
Showing areas with which the British were in some way concerned, 1859–83

XII

TRADE AND INDUSTRY

IT was evident from the beginning of the foreign treaties that the economic development of the open ports would differ for geographical as well as political reasons. Hence in this study they shall be considered separately as centres of British trade and activity.

1. YOKOHAMA

Yokohama, a small fishing village of 101 houses at the opening of the port, was destined to become, within ten years, the centre of Japan's foreign commerce.[1] Located eighteen miles from the *Bakufu* capital and within easy reach through Kanagawa of the Tōkaidō, the main artery of interior traffic, in an area directly governed by the Shogunate, it was not only the most central port, but also one most affected by the vagaries of *Bakufu* domestic and foreign policy.

British Firms

Although the foreign consulates remained at Kanagawa for a year or two in stubborn resistance to the arbitrary action of the Shogunate, it has been shown that the merchants chose the deeper harbour and trade facilities which the *Bakufu* had prepared for them at Yokohama. By the early winter of 1860 thirty foreign traders had rented land there and within a few months more than two hundred Japanese had opened shops.[2] The great majority of the foreign merchants were British from the start and throughout the years here considered. A minimum of forty-six British firms were established in Yokohama before the end of the Shogunate.[3] Few of these have survived until today. Fewer still have records of their early history owing to the ravages of fire, earthquakes, and war.

[1] *Yokohama-shi Shi Kō*, vii. 6.
[2] Tanabe Taiichi, op. cit., p. 109. Otsuka, op. cit., p. 24.
[3] *Yokohama-shi Shi Kō*, vii. 49–52, for list. Paske-Smith, *Western Barbarians*, Appendix 13b, p. 362–3 gives fifty-one British firms in Yokohama between 1859–68 but has obvious omissions.

Jardine, Matheson & Company was the leading British firm. William Keswick represented their interest in Yokohama and Kanagawa in the winter of 1859 and soon built House Number One on the Yokohama bund. J. S. Barber joined him that first summer.[1] S. J. Gower succeeded Barber in the spring of 1862, when Keswick probably became a member of the firm in Hong Kong.[2] Three years later C. S. Hope became the Yokohama agent until H. P. Austin took over that office in 1867. These agents rapidly built up a profitable business in imports, exports, shipping, and insurance, although the name of the firm does not appear in the Yokohama section of the Hong Kong *Daily Press* annual, the *Chronicle and Directory*, until 1868, when it is listed as 'merchants' and agents for three insurance companies, the Alliance Fire Insurance Company, the Canton Marine Insurance Company, and the Hong Kong Fire Insurance Company.[3] Dent and Company, Jardine's foremost competitor in the China trade and insurance business, established House Number Three on the Yokohama bund in 1859. They failed in the financial crisis of 1866 and no records are known to exist.[4]

Butterfield and Swire, Ltd., China merchants, then a new firm in the Far East, soon became Jardine's major rival.[5] In

[1] J.M. MSS. (Japan Letter Books). Letters from the Shanghai Office to J. S. Barber at Kanagawa begin as early as 31 Aug. 1859, although Fujimoto, op. cit. i. 327–31 dates his arrival as 1862.

[2] *Jardine, Matheson and Company, afterwards Jardine, Matheson and Company Ltd., an Outline of the History of a China House for a Hundred Years, 1832–1932* (privately printed, 1934), p. 61. But on p. 35 Keswick is said to have been made a partner in 1858–9. Reason for this difference in dates is not clear.

[3] The directories, sometimes called hong lists, were published annually by the British newspapers in the China and Japanese ports. Only a few scattered copies have survived and are a main source, although not always accurate, for lists of foreign residents in China, Japan, and the Philippines, their occupations and addresses. These annuals were commercial in purpose, supplying information on international treaties, trade regulations, complete customs tariffs, postal rates, comparative tables of weights and measures, the calendar, etc. A few of the early issues may be found in the British Museum, among the Jardine, Matheson archives at Cambridge, and in H. S. Williams's private library at Kobe. The 1872 issue by the *Japan Gazette* is in the Business School Library at Harvard and in microfilm in the Library of Congress.

[4] Greenberg, op. cit., pp. 30, 141, 201. G. C. Allen and A. G. Donnithorne, *Western Enterprise in Far Eastern Economic Development* (London, 1954), pp. 35, 120. Paske-Smith, *Western Barbarians*, pp. 266, 362.

[5] As fires in Yokohama and London during World War II destroyed simultaneously the records of Butterfield and Swire's activities in Japan, little of that

PLATE 6

WILLIAM KESWICK

September 1866 John Samuel Swire of John Swire and Sons, Ltd., a Liverpool merchant company with branch offices in New York and Melbourne, established this house in China in partnership with R. S. Butterfield of Butterfield's Woollen and Worsted Mills of Keighley, Yorkshire. It opened for business in Shanghai on 1 January 1867. Four months later Mr. Swire arranged for a branch office in Yokohama where the American firm of Augustine Heard and Company had been serving as agents for John Swire and Sons, Ltd. Here operations began on 1 August 1867 with Richard Norman Newby, a woollen goods man from Yorkshire, as manager. At first the firm was mainly concerned with importing English cotton and woollen piece goods and exporting tea to New York and Melbourne. The partnership with Butterfield lasted only a year. It was formally dissolved by deed dated 1 August 1868 but the dissolution was never gazetted and for reasons unknown Butterfield's name was retained in that of the firm although he received back his initial capital, approximately £15,000.

Several men managed the Yokohama branch in rapid succession during the early years. J. Keith Angus followed Newby in February 1869 and turned the office over to J. H. Scott in July. At the end of that year Angus again took charge until Butterfield and Swire appointed Thomas Merry, a silk man from Reiss & Co., Shanghai, in April 1870. Upon his death in 1872 and that of his successor, J. R. Turner, the same year, W. D. Harrison of the Liverpool office became manager until May 1873 when James Dodds took over the office and remained there until about 1900.

Butterfield and Swire had found new offices with larger

history can be told here. Only one letter book of the firm's London–Japan correspondence has survived, that for Yokohama covering May 1869–Feb. 1870, which consists chiefly of periodic market reports to John Swire & Sons and other British textile exporters. The above account is based on materials most generously given the author by Messrs. John and A. C. Swire and Mr. James H. Scott of John Swire & Sons Ltd., London. They include extracts from the following: James Henry Scott, *A Short Account of the Firm of John Swire & Sons Ltd.* (privately published, London, 1912); Notes by Mr. A. V. T. Dean from the firm's archives; T. J. Lindsay, *A Short History of Taikoo* (privately printed, Hong Kong, 1966); and three pamphlets: *Butterfield and Swire: 1867–1957*, *A Short History* reprinted from *The Blue Funnel Bulletin* of Jan. 1957; *The China Navigation Company 1872–1957*, *A Short History* reprinted from *The Blue Funnel Bulletin* of Jan. 1958; and Lt.-Comdr. B. L. Butcher, R.D., R.N.R. ret'd., *In China Seas, A History of the China Navigation Company* reprinted from *Sea Breezes*, Feb. and Mar. 1964.

godowns necessary in Yokohama in 1869 in spite of the adverse effects of Japan's disturbed political conditions on the import trade. The firm opened branches in the chief China ports in the seventies and eighties and in 1887 set up an office in Kobe for which it leased in perpetuity lot No. 103 from the Japanese government.[1] By that time it had also established firm trading connexions with the leading merchants in the interior of China as well as along the coast.

Although in 1883 the closing of Swire Brothers in New York meant the loss of the New York tea trade, Butterfield and Swire soon found compensation through importing sugar to Japan from the Taikoo Sugar Refinery Company, Ltd., which John Swire and Sons, Ltd. founded in Hong Kong in 1882. The firm acted as agents in Yokohama for the Blue Funnel Line (Ocean Steamship Company founded in 1865–6 by Alfred Holt)[2] and the China Navigation Company which John S. Swire had formed in 1872 with a capital of £360,000. Through these agencies began Butterfield and Swire's interest in shipping which after 1902 became so extensive that they discontinued their trading operations altogether.[3]

A third British pioneer in Japan which, like Jardine, Matheson & Company and Butterfield and Swire, is still of world prominence today was W. R. Adamson and Company, already recognized by Jardine's as a potential rival in the Japan trade in March 1859.[4] They established a house in Yokohama in 1859 or shortly afterwards, although they were still a young concern, having been registered in London and established in China in 1858. They first appear on the shipping list of Yokohama in 1864 as consignees for the British steamer *Elgin*, 396 tons from Shanghai, but are listed only once in the directories of the sixties, that of 1865.[5] In 1867 the name was changed to Adamson, Bell and Company. Under the management of F. D'Ifanger in Yokohama and Kobe in the seventies, the firm became internationally known for its extensive shipping operations. At the same time it imported piece goods from

---

[1] Lease dated 11 July 1887 now in Tokyo office.
[2] Francis E. Hyde with the assistance of J. R. Harris, *Blue Funnel, A History of Alfred Holt and Company of Liverpool from 1865 to 1914* (Liverpool, 1956), pp. 18–19.
[3] Ibid., pp. 33–34.
[4] J.M. MSS. (Shanghai, Private), J. Whittall to J. Jardine, 5 Mar. 1859.
[5] Williams, op. cit., pp. 205–6. Paske-Smith, *Western Barbarians*, p. 346.

PLATE 7

JOHN SAMUEL SWIRE

Manchester and Bradford as well as sugar, metals, and machinery, while exporting tea, silk, and general produce from Japan. Financial difficulties in 1891 resulted in the firm's many interests and connexions being taken over by Dodwell, Carlill and Company, which in 1898 became Dodwell and Company, Ltd., of today.[1]

Aspinall, Cornes and Company, established in Yokohama in 1861, has survived as Cornes and Company until the present. F. Cornes and W. Aspinall amalgamated to form this company but all the early records of their activities have been lost.[2] They were agents in Japan for the Peninsular and Oriental Steam Navigation Company in 1863, and the agents for the Royal Exchange Assurance Corporation (established in 1720) for which they advertised in 1881 that they would accept risks and 'issue policies payable in Europe and America'. For many years they were also Lloyd's agents.[3]

The Peninsular and Oriental Steam Navigation Company, the first British shipping firm to establish a regular line of steamers to Japan, began its operation in the summer of 1859, when their little 'barque-rigged, iron hulled vessel, sail and steam of 80 horsepower' called the *Chusan*, after active service in the East since 1852, was put on the Shanghai–Japan run. Many merchants with their stocks and household goods first reached Yokohama aboard her decks.[4]

Passage rates from Yokohama were:[5]

	Shanghai	Hong Kong	Southampton
First class	$130	$210	$800
Second class	65	100	400

In 1864 Thomas Sutherland (later Sir Thomas Sutherland), a young business genius in the firm's Hong Kong office, organized not only the Hong Kong and Shanghai Banking Corporation, but also established the P. and O. mail line between China and Yokohama with a little 600-ton steamer, the *Corea*.[6]

Other British firms in Yokohama before 1868 which no longer

[1] Edward Warde, Ed., *The House of Dodwell* (London, 1959), pp. 4–5, 95.

[2] Williams, op. cit., p. 205. *Yokohama-shi Ski Kō*, vii. 49.

[3] *Japan Weekly Mail*, 17 Dec. 1881, Author's interview with Mr. H. S. Williams of Kobe.   [4] Williams, op. cit., pp. 210–11.

[5] Paske-Smith, *Western Barbarians*, p. 225.

[6] Allen and Donnithorne, op. cit., p. 107. Boyd Cable, *A Hundred-Year History of the P. and O.* (London, 1937), p. 173.

exist and about which we know still less, are listed as Macpherson and Marshall, 1860, agents for Imperial Fire Insurance Company 1861; Frey and Cooke (later Cameron and Cooke), shipwrights, 1861; William McDonald, broker, 1861; C. H. Richards and Company, 1862; Downie and Company (later Fletcher and Company), 1864; W. A. Baillie, shipchandler; C. Parker, photographer; Bagley and Company; Mrs. Pearson, ladies' tailor; E. C. Kirby and Company; Ross, Barber and Company; and many more.[1]

British Trade under the Shogunate

Advertisements in the English press indicate the many goods and services which the foreigners were bringing to Yokohama during this period. The nationality of these entrepreneurs is so seldom given, however, that usually the British cannot be singled out. The notice of the formation of the partnership of Hansard and Keele, both Britishers, in the auction business on 21 February 1862 and the advertisements of their services indicate what they at least were doing in the port of Yokohama. Here they declare themselves to be:

Auctioneers and General Agents, More particularly for the public Sale of Import Cargoes, Damaged Goods, and of Land interests, Houses, etc.

Main Street, No. LXXVIII

Messrs H. & K. are now prepared to execute commissions in the above business. They have ample storage accommodation for goods intended for sale.

They will also be happy to undertake any business connected with the private sale or leasing of properties.

In the same issues of the *Herald* they listed the following goods for sale which could be seen at their auction rooms:

Champagne, Jacquesson's in pints, Montebello's in pints, Port Wine (Worthington's), John Alberty Cognac, Claret, California White Wine, Old Q Brandy, Old Tom Gin, V. H. Gin, Dr. Mill's Bitters, Ale (Bass Pyramid Trade mark in casks of 4 dozens), Lime Juice, Preserved Potatoes, Pilot Bread, Soap in boxes of 18 lbs., Sperm Candles, Iron Bedsteads, Waterproof Clothing, Saddles and Bridles, etc. etc. etc.[2]

[1] *Yokohama-shi Shi Kō*, vii. 49–52. Paske-Smith, *Western Barbarians*, p. 362–3. *Japan Herald*, 23 Nov. 1861.

[2] *Japan Herald*, 8 and 29 Mar. 1862, copies in L.C.

London firms soon began to advertise their wares directly in the Yokohama press. Thus Frederick Algar, 11 Clement's Lane, Lombard Street, London, 'Colonial, Newspaper and Commission Agent', offered to supply the colonial press with 'Newspapers, Book Type Ink, Presses, Paper, Correspondents' Letters and any European Goods on London Terms'.[1] By 1873 many more such announcements were appearing. Burgoyne, Burbridges and Company, 'Export Druggists' of Coleman Street, London, offered manufactures of every description of chemical, pharmaceutical, photographic, and other preparations, including patent medicines, surgical instruments, etc. They claimed to be conversant with the Japanese market and were prepared to receive commission orders for any articles of British manufacture.[2] Among others were Harrison and Sons, Export and General Stationers of 59 Pall Mall and 1 St. James Street, London; Crosse and Blackwell of Soho Square offering many delicacies from jams and soups in tins to 'fresh salmon, oysters and herrings' with the warning that 'jars and bottles should invariably be destroyed when empty to prevent the fraud of refilling them with native productions'; and D. Nicholson and Company of St. Paul's Church Yard, listing silk, woollen and cotton goods, and everything from musical instruments and carriages to sewing machines to be sent via Suez Canal at cheapest rates.[3] There is thus ample evidence that the thirst of the Westerners in Yokohama could easily be quenched. And the luxuries of the West were equally at hand to satisfy their wants and awaken the Japanese to the alleged benefits of the foreign civilization.

Yokohama rapidly became the centre of the silk trade while tea and cotton were also exported in varying quantities during the last years of the Shogunate. Although only 610 bales of raw Japanese silk are said to have reached London in 1859 which were sold at 16s. 6d. to 27s. per pound, the potentials of Japanese silk were recognized and the trade promoted by Jardine, Matheson and other firms in the first months of the open ports.[4] Nevertheless, Acting Consul Vyse complained in his first six

---

[1] Ibid., 8 Mar. 1862.   [2] *Japan Mail*, 1 Nov. 1873, microfilm in L.C.
[3] *Japan Weekly Mail*, 10 Oct., 26 Dec. 1874.
[4] Paske-Smith, *Western Barbarians*, pp. 215–16. J.M. MSS. (General Series, Shanghai), I. Whittall to W. Keswick, 28 Nov. 1859.

months' report that the price of the raw silk was too high for export: no Japanese merchant was allowed to deliver more than six piculs a day; and contracts entered into by Japanese and British merchants and stamped at the British consulate were often null and void as to the agreed price of the article. But such obstacles did not seriously hamper the British merchants.[1]

As early as November 1859 James Whittall considered Kanagawa-Yokohama to be Japan.[2] By July 1860 he was ordering Keswick to build 'a good substantial house' there because he thought Kanagawa would always afford it.[3] The prospect of large quantities of silk that summer at attractive costs to yield generous profits in London made Jardine's want to secure as much as possible and to advise Keswick 'to act boldly in making advances into the country'. A fatal disease among the silk worms in Europe had increased that market for oriental silk. Whittall sent Keswick $150,000 at one time for investment.[4] Whittall also directed Keswick to go in for insurance and sanctioned as much as $100,000 on any one vessel if a good risk.[5]

At the same time Acting Consul Vyse in his report on trade at Yokohama in 1860 told of problems arising from the lack of a bank in Yokohama. Purchases could be made only against Mexican dollars to be laid down there 'either in specie or saleable imports'. Clean credits on London were unavailable. They had to be negotiated in Shanghai and the dollars sent to Japan which, of course, contributed to higher costs. Some prices, e.g. those for ginseng, tea, and mushrooms, had doubled. Although adversely affected by the rebellion in China and the government's interference in all commercial transactions, trade in 1860 was on the whole encouraging. It was clear the Japanese wanted produce and manufactures superior to their own and could pay remunerative prices for them if the export business flourished. The import trade was still small but would become, Vyse thought, a profitable branch of commerce. Exports were even more promising. Reliable figures for the extent of the foreign trade were not obtainable, but it was clear that the

[1] P.P. H. of C. 1860, lxix (2673), 7–8, Vyse to Alcock, Kanagawa, 15 Feb. 1860.
[2] J.M. MSS. (General Series, Shanghai, 1859), J. Whittall to W. Keswick, 30 Nov. 1859.
[3] Ibid. (Shanghai, Private), J. Whittall to W. Keswick, 13 July 1860.
[4] Ibid., 23, 29 July, 19 Aug. 1860.   [5] Ibid., 16 Sept. 1860.

PLATE 8

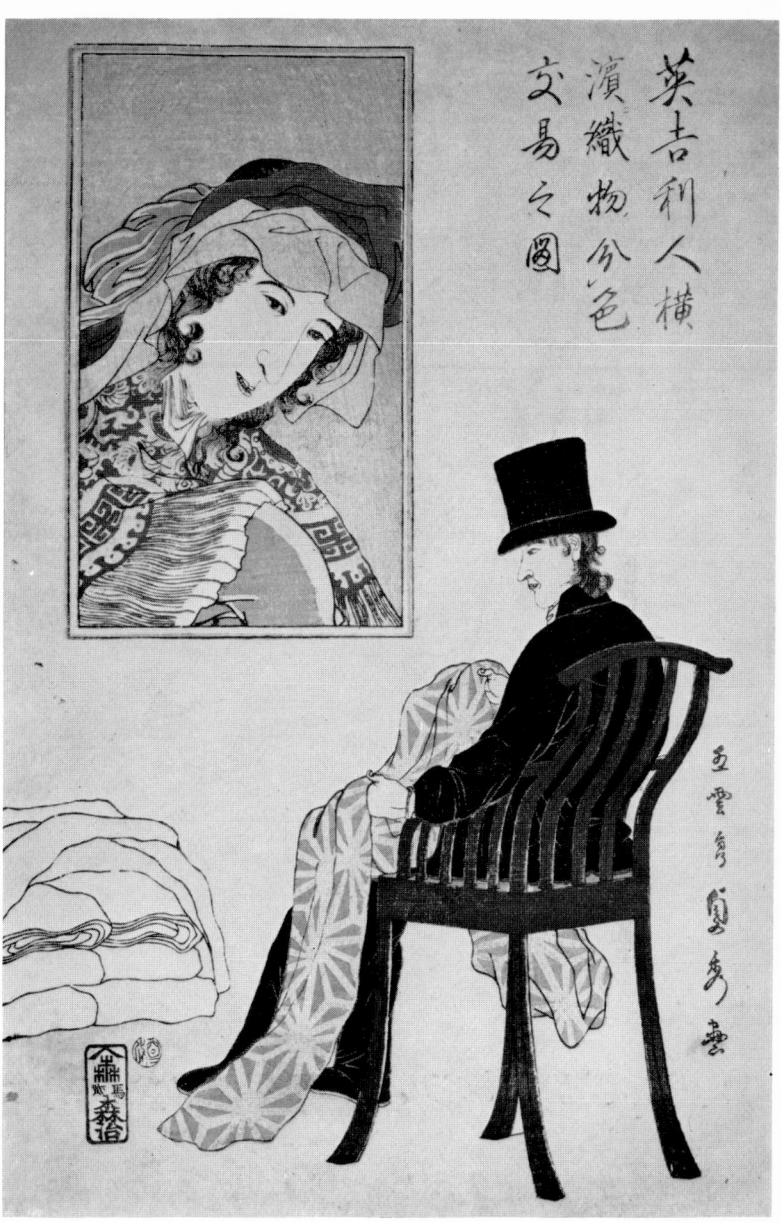

An English Cloth Merchant at Yokohama, 1861
By Utagawa Sadahide

British controlled over half the imports and exports. Japan's direct trade with Great Britain and her colonies had also taken the lead over the direct American trade to San Francisco. The major requirements for the promotion of commerce in Yokohama, Vyse said, were: a bank for European and American credits and a regular mail service between Yokohama and Shanghai via Nagasaki.[1]

Results of the London Protocol in 1862 were evident in the reduction of duties on wines, glass ware, iron, etc., but the promise that the goods of daimyo should come freely to market was not fulfilled. It was evident to the consul and probably to many merchants that the antagonism to foreign countries which the Shogun attributed to the semi-independent daimyo was 'factitious' and 'that foreign trade as between the two parties was a struggle'. At the same time they realized that the controlling influence exercised by the Shogun had its benefits for the foreign traders in preventing their involvement in difficulties arising from the antagonisms among the individual feudal chiefs.[2]

Political alarms and anti-foreign hostilities at Yedo did not seriously repress the growth of trade at Yokohama.[3] Even in 1863 when political disturbances convulsed Japan and foreign trade itself was in dispute, the largest trade yet known was developed at Kanagawa in spite of recurring periods of panic. Jardine's made use of the political tensions to invest heavily. Agents of the daimyo, taking advantage of the pressure Britain was bringing to bear on the *Bakufu* during the summer, brought large stocks for sale 'under arrangements far more liberal than those usually enforced by the Government'—an innovation which the government sought to stop as soon as the pressure was removed. The *Bakufu* then undertook to make the established guilds at Yedo the only channel through which silk could be brought to Yokohama, and to levy increased taxes on this and other valuable staples, and thus restore its authority to do so and retain the principal source of its profits in the foreign trade.

The great increase in exports in 1863 as well as in shipping arose from the demand for cotton as a result of the American

[1] P.P. H. of C. 1862, lviii. 91, 275, 279, and 283-4; 1862, lxiv. 41. Vyse gives reasons for unreliable customs house figures.

[2] P.P. H. of C. 1864, lxi. 160, 158, Cons. Report for Kanagawa, 1863.

[3] J.M. MSS. (Kanagawa, 1861), W. Keswick to Company, 17 Feb. 1861.

Civil War and the blockade of the southern states. Cotton exports increased from 4,616 piculs in 1862 to 46,697 piculs in 1863—a temporary development, of course, but one which the British consul thought proved the aliveness of the Japanese people to the advantages of foreign trade. Steamships were also in increasing demand at Yokohama from both the government and daimyo in 1863.

The increase in the foreign population in 1863 not only by permanent residents but by the presence of the large squadron afloat, manned by 2,000 men, and numerous French and English guards, varying in strength from 300 to 500 men, led to a marked rise in the cost of living, making Yokohama second only to Shanghai in expensiveness among the Eastern ports. Real-estate values rose, house rents doubled, and lots without buildings sold for about $8,000. A memorandum on the ground rentals for 1862 shows that the British were paying $10,255.40 in rentals as against $7,551.99 paid by Americans, Dutch, French, and Prussian nationals altogether. Fortunately the tone and standing of the foreign community had improved as those primarily motivated by an interest in gold and active in the export of cobangs in 1859 and 1860 had left the country.[1]

The year 1864 brought still greater prosperity to Yokohama, in spite of the government's drastic interference with the silk trade and Nagato's closing of the Inland Sea with the consequent destruction of the batteries at Shimonoseki. The bimonthly arrival and departure of P. and O. steamers was welcomed. Exports, imports, and the direct trade with England increased.[2] More foreign residents including ninety British settled in. Raw silk and raw cotton were the chief exports. Satsuma's agents not only tried to buy ships but defied the government's ban on the yarn trade by allowing Japanese and foreign merchants to use Satsuma's vessels with flags bearing Satsuma's crest to break through the *Bakufu* blockade. The severity of the government's control over the export of silkworm

[1] J.M. MSS. (Yokohama, 1863), S. J. Gower to J. Whittall, 7 Feb., 11 Apr., 4 May 1863; W. Keswick to A. Perceval, 3 June 1863; S. J. Gower to W. Keswick, 3 Aug. and 31 Oct. 1863. P.P. H. of C. 1864, lxi. 157–65, Cons. Report for Kanagawa, 1863.

[2] P.P. H. of C. 1865, liii. 303, Cons. Report for Kanagawa 1864. Estimates of imports being $5,443,594 as against $1,595,170 for 1863—exports $8,997,484 in constrast to $5,134,184 in 1863.

eggs was released in consequence of the fatal disease attacking the worms in Europe. A vigorous revival of trade followed the opening of the Inland Sea.[1]

Yokohama grew rapidly. Between 1865 and 1868 its population averaged 20,880 people and 8,580 houses had been built.[2] No reliable figures for the trade of these years were recorded. Those given for 1865 and 1867 were so much below a reasonable estimate of what developed as to be unacceptable, and the records for 1866 of both the customs house and Chamber of Commerce (organized in 1864)[3] were destroyed in the great fire in November which consumed over $2,000,000 worth of property, including Jardine, Matheson's house and godown on lots No. 1, 22, and 23.[4]

The general economic developments at Yokohama during these last three years of the *Bakufu* none the less are clear. Gower had contracted in 1865 for the monopoly of the silk crop of one daimyo for three years for Jardine's and hoped for more business from such sources.[5] Trade in 1866 was generally disturbed by the banking and credit panic in England. The value of the silver *ichibu* fell from 240 to 316 per $100 Mexican and the Yokohama market was glutted with foreign goods purchased at high prices in England. Japan's increasing demand for foreign manufactures combined with a rapid growth of the arms trade led to an excess of imports over exports for the first time in 1867. At least 102,333 stands of arms were imported into Kanagawa that year when respectable English firms began to compete in that lucrative field, although it usurped the place of more legitimate and permanent sources of profit. Large quantities of rice, duty free, from Hong Kong and Saigon had

---

[1] P.P. H. of C. 1865, liii. 286–92, 296, Cons. Report for Kanagawa, 1864. J.M. MSS. (Yokohama, 1864), S. J. Gower to W. Keswick, 15 Mar. and 31 Oct. 1864; (Yokohama, Private), S. J. Gower to A. Perceval, 1 Apr. 1864; S. J. Gower to J. Whittall, 14 Apr., 27 Apr., 9 Aug. 1864; (Japan Letter Book i), Shanghai Office to S. J. Gower, 26 Aug. 1864. Ishii Takashi, 'Saikōku Daimyō to Sakoku Kaikoku' (Western Daimyo and the Closing and Opening of the Country), *Nihon Rekishi* (Japan History), July 1959, p. 3. [2] Koizuka, op. cit. ii. 49.
[3] Paske-Smith, *Western Barbarians*, p. 219. *Japan Times*, 3 Nov. 1865.
[4] P.P. H. of C. 1866, lxxi. 242–50; 1867, lxviii. 252–7; 1867–8, lxix. 304–14, Cons. Reports for Kanagawa, 1865, 1866, and 1867. J.M. MSS. (Yokohama, 1866), C. S. Hope to E. Whittall (brother of James Whittall who apparently took over the Shanghai Office when James Whittall moved to Hong Kong in 1864), 1 Dec. 1866.
[5] Ibid. (Yokohama, 1865), S. J. Gower to E. Whittall, 17 Jan. 1865.

to be imported that year also because of the bad harvest in 1866. In spite of the decline in the shipments of cotton when the American Civil War ended, the direct trade with England continued to grow. Japanese tea, however, proved more suitable for America than Britain, causing the tea trade to develop more slowly than expected.[1]

In 1867 also the government's over-issue of Japanese currency to meet its political exigencies caused silver coin to fall as low as 3·45 *ichibu* to one Mexican dollar, a depreciation of about thirteen per cent. on the comparative bullion value. This was sufficiently cheap to make it profitable to export the silver coins as bullion for recoinage in Hong Kong and Calcutta. 'Considerable quantities' left the country which resulted in exchange keeping at nearly a 'fixity' value. The consul reported further that the Mexican dollar was then the only foreign coin passing current in Yokohama, that it could be called 'the measure of value'. All contracts and payments with foreigners were made in it and Japanese currency as far as foreigners were concerned was simply 'a marketable commodity like anything else, rising and falling with the supply and demand existing among the native trading population'.[2]

Other Business and Community Activities

The British in Yokohama were not always concerned with trade. About 1863 an early English resident, W. A. Curtis, introduced the cultivation of foreign vegetables—lettuce, cabbage, Irish potatoes, carrots, onions, asparagus, tomatoes, radishes, and strawberries—in the rich soil in the hilly district of Yokohama. His success led to Japanese farmers in the Negishi and Isogo districts obtaining seeds and raising these vegetables for foreign customers.[3]

The British were active in community organization and diversions—regattas, a volunteer fire brigade, an elected municipal council, the Bluff Gardens, the building of a hospital, the Yokohama United Club, a Race Club, and amateur theatricals. Cricket matches, paper hunts, and field sports were all a part of the recreation of the young foreign settlement by 1864.[4]

---

[1] Cons. Reports 1865, 1866, and 1867. Thomas C. Smith, *Political Change and Industrial Development in Japan: Government Enterprise, 1868–1880*, p. 24.
[2] P.P. H. of C. 1867–8, lxix. 308, Cons. Report for Kanagawa, 1867.
[3] *Yokohama-shi Shi Kō*, vii. 688.
[4] Paske-Smith, *Western Barbarians*, pp. 268–70.

An Englishman interested Japanese craftsmen in the manufacture of Western furniture which the growing foreign community demanded. Around 1872 there were three or four such furniture makers in Yokohama. Another Englishman, William Copeland, established in 1872 the first Japanese brewery at Amanuma in the hilly district of Yokohama. The success of 'Spring Valley Brewery' led to the building of other breweries, especially the 'Hokkaidō Kaitakushi Bakushu Jōzōsho'. It reduced the import of Western beer and laid the foundation for the Asian beer market. Still other Englishmen are credited with starting a dairy with thirty American cows in Yokohama for foreigners only and with teaching a Japanese the English method of baking bread.[1] The relations between this commercial community and the legation at Yedo—even with the consuls—were, however, not the best. Alcock in desperation over some early predatory practices had called the merchants the 'scum of the earth'—a phrase not easily forgotten. Only members of a legation could visit Yedo until 1868 unless invited by a diplomat.[2] And it is said that the members of the foreign service were denied membership in the Yokohama clubs. Social cleavages were at least mutually sharp.

The Early Meiji Trade

The Restoration brought increased prosperity to the port. In 1868 the arms trade reached great heights. An estimated $757,501 worth of munitions was delivered during the six months ending 31 December 1868. Smuggling accounted for the importation of still greater quantities but when confronted with that fact, the Chamber of Commerce refused to make it their concern.[3] The British also did an extensive business in cloths and woollen manufactures. The currency continued to depreciate—340 *ichibu* to $100 or at a discount of nine per cent. below bullion value. Japan was drained of its coins while silver bars were imported at high prices to replace them.[4] The concurrent

---

[1] *Yokohama-shi Shi Kō*, vii. 655, 665-7, 680-2, Paske-Smith, *Western Barbarians*, p. 358, lists Copeland as an American.

[2] Ibid., p. 267. Williams, op. cit., p. 221.

[3] Cons. Report for Kanagawa, 1868, p. 3. Yokohama Chamber of Commerce, Half Year Report, 31 Dec. 1868; Minutes, 29 June 1868.

[4] Cons. Report for Kanagawa, 1868, pp. 3, 6.

issues of paper money which continued in 1869 produced alarm about the currency. Imports suffered. And the increase in shipping did not indicate a proportionate increase in trade as many ships left in ballast. An improvement in the methods at the Customs House for assessing and collecting duties, however, made the returns more correct.[1]

Native counterfeits of the trade mark of a British firm, Bass and Company, in 1871 led to a national order forbidding such practices and exacting punishments for the guilty. And the founding of the Chamber of Commerce of Japan the same year afforded control over as well as the protection of native merchants.[2] Japan offered to supply models of native carriages, carts, and modes of conveyance as well as specimens of Japanese drinking and smoking implements for the London International Exhibition of 1873.[3]

The British were soon faced with acute competition from French and German manufactures. They also found that it was not necessary to go to Europe for supplies, that China was ready on the least margin of profit to supply Yokohama with any goods. Hong Kong answered the demand for yarn, Shanghai for shirtings. Furthermore the native holders of silk began to consign their product to Europe on their own account rather than accept the lower prices offered by the exporters.[4] By 1879 Britain still dominated the import trade for all open ports, but the United States had the lion's share of the exports owing to her increasing demand for silk and tea. Britain controlled 57 per cent. of the import traffic that year and $58\frac{1}{2}$ per cent. in 1880. But London's early monopoly of the silk trade had ended. France and America now controlled it.[5]

In 1881 all silk transactions suffered from the formation of a new silk guild in Yokohama which tried to centralize the entire silk trade in that port and prohibited all outside sales on

[1] P.P. H. of C. 1870, lxv. 12–13. Cons. Report for Kanagawa, 1869. MSS. Butterfield and Swire (Japan–London Correspondence, 1869), J. Keith Angus to B. and S. at Shanghai, Yokohama, 16 June 1869; same to Messrs. Tabler & Co. at Manchester, Yokohama, 25 June 1869.

[2] F.O. 46/142, Adams to Granville, No. 105, Yedo, 4 Nov. 1871. P.P. H. of C. 1872, lix. 67, Cons. Report for Kanagawa, 1871.

[3] F.O. 46/156, Watson to Granville, No. 144, Yedo, 11 Nov. 1872.

[4] Cons. Report for Kanagawa, 1873, pp. 55–56.

[5] Ibid. 1879, pp. 21, 27; 1880, pp. 32, 40–42; 1883, Pt. II, p. 145.

15 September. British consul Wilkinson told of the opposition of the foreign merchants who boycotted the silk trade through this guild. There were no sales of silk in Yokohama for several months, until the outstanding issues were reconciled with the Japanese merchants. The guild was abolished in November 1881.[1]

A steady decline in Yokohama's import market began in 1881, owing partly to the loss of some direct foreign trade to Hyogo, to fluctuations in the native currency, and to Japan's difficulties in Korea. Exports rose until 1883 when they, too, declined in spite of the increased stability and improved value of the Japanese paper money.[2] By that year Yokohama had an average annual population of 76,135 persons and a foreign community, excluding Chinese, of 1,287 people, 595 of whom were British.[3]

2. NAGASAKI

British Merchants

Paske-Smith's account of the early years of Nagasaki as an open port needs little amplification here.[4] The British led its trade and civic organizations from the start. Representatives of Jardine, Matheson and Company and Dent and Company were two of the first applicants for house room in 1859. By the end of 1861 thirty-seven of the total fifty-seven foreign merchants who rented land in Nagasaki were British. Among them in addition to Jardine's and Dent's were other well-known merchant houses, Alt and Company, Arnold and Company, Glover and Company, Lindsay and Company, Major and Company, and the Peninsular and Oriental Steam Navigation Company.[5] Messrs. Alt and Major served with an American, Franklin Field, on Japan's first municipal council elected in Nagasaki in April 1861. The resident foreign merchants also formed a Chamber of Commerce in June 1861 and appointed Messrs. R. Arnold, T. B. Glover, and W. J. Alt to act as their executive

---

[1] P.P. H. of C. 1882 lxxii. 38–39, Cons. Reports for Kanagawa, 1881. Koizuka, op. cit. ii. 644.

[2] Cons. Report for Kanagawa, 1881, pp. 50, 52; 1882, pp. 1, 4, 10, 11, 17, 22, 23; 1883, Pt. II, pp. 135, 150–1, 155, 157.

[3] Ibid., 1883, Pt. II, p. 158. Koizuka op. cit. ii. 49.

[4] Paske-Smith, *Western Barbarians*, pp. 229–65.

[5] Ibid., pp. 243–4 gives the entire list for 1860–1.

committee. A foreign club, an Episcopal Church, and an overland bi-monthly postal service to Yokohama were established in 1862.[1]

While the foreigners organized a community life their trade prospered. British consuls complained regularly, however, that reliable figures for the extent and value of imports and exports were unobtainable, owing to the mismanagement of the Japanese customs house. The lower duties granted to the Chinese and their unhampered smuggling led their new Western competitors to resort to dishonest practices in self-defence. They undervalued their goods from thirty to fifty per cent. of their actual price and understated their weight and quantity in their customs declarations, taking advantage of the Japanese ignorance of foreign imports. They represented articles legally dutiable at twenty per cent. as being in the five per cent. class, and often smuggled in those of small size. Bribery of the officials was not unwelcome. Goods for household use were allowed to be removed without permit from the ships. And the customs authorities for their returns overvalued the Mexican dollar in taels in relation to the market value of taels. In consideration of all these irregularities, it was estimated that 'at least 50 per cent. could be added to the market valuations to give the approximate return of the commerce'.[2] By studying the books of the Shanghai customs house, however, Consul Morrison was able to state with assurance and pride that the import trade of Nagasaki for the last six months of 1859 was £150,000 and exports upwards of £200,000.[3] In 1863 the consul estimated Nagasaki's imports at £505,971 which included ships bought by Japan and bars of Peking gold imported by the Chinese Guild. Exports were said to reach £347,000.[4] Britain's share in the trade is not given.

Imports comprised sugar, woollens, cotton camlets, drinkables, sapan wood, Chinese medicinal herbs, indigo, and vermilion. Vegetable wax, silk, rape seed, tea, and gall nuts

[1] Paske-Smith, *Western Barbarians*, pp. 203, 261–3.

[2] P.P. H. of C. 1863, lxx. 224–7, Cons. Report for Nagasaki, 1862; 1866, lxxi. 22, Cons. Report for Nagasaki, 1865. Paske-Smith, *Western Barbarians*, p. 204. By 1865 the Japanese were persuaded to appraise the value of goods in *ichibu*.

[3] P.P. H. of C. 1862, lviii, 88–90, Morrison's revised report for Nagasaki for 13 June to 31 Dec. 1859, encl. by Alcock to F.O., Yedo, 26 Apr. 1860.

[4] Paske-Smith, *Western Barbarians*, p. 206.

were exported to England via Shanghai while rice, fish, *bêche-de-mer*, shrimps, isinglass, flour, peas, wax, and seaweed were shipped to Hong Kong. The Japanese government controlled the trade in copper, awabi, and iriko.[1] Four-fifths of Nagasaki's trade came or went through Shanghai. Consul Winchester reported only a small amount of direct trade with Holland and two or three ships a year destined for England. Most British ships went to the neighbouring ports of China and Japan. Freight rates were profitable: from January until April 1862, $6 to $7 per ton (forty cubic feet) for the voyage from Nagasaki to Shanghai and $8 to $10 to Hong Kong. Summer rates were less.[2]

The correspondence of Jardine, Matheson and Company with their agents in Nagasaki reveals the excitements and vicissitudes of British trade, shipping, and financial activities in southern Japan. Although their name, with that of James Keswick as their representative, appears in the list of foreign renters in the port in 1860–1, the name of the firm is not found among the early consignees of ships calling at Nagasaki (June–September 1861), nor does it appear among the British firms listed in the Nagasaki section of the Hong Kong *Chronicle and Directory* from 1865 through 1868.[3] They remained, however, actively concerned with the business of the port after their preview in the early months of 1859. K. R. Mackenzie, also among the first foreign renters, continued to look after their interests until June 1861 when Glover and Company, an equally early renter, became their agent and correspondent. Mackenzie, however, seems to be closely associated with the firm again through Glover by 1867.[4]

Accounts of buying 1,500 piculs of wax at $8.75 per picul, of gold cobangs (*kobans*) at $3.30 to $3.35, which could be sold at from sixteen to twenty per cent. profit, of the successful barter of manufactured goods for produce, of short deliveries in overland orders and uncontrollable pilfering of cargoes between

---

[1] Ibid., pp. 204–5. P.P. H. of C. 1862, lviii. 88–90, revised Cons. Report for Nagasaki, 1859, *Bêche-de-mer*, a sea slug, a Chinese delicacy; iriko, dried small fish used for seasoning in Japan; awabi, abalone, mollusc.

[2] P.P. H. of C. 1863, lxx. 224–5, Cons. Report for Nagasaki, 1862.

[3] Paske-Smith, *Western Barbarians*, pp. 244, 340–1.

[4] Ibid., pp. 243–4. J.M. MSS. (Nagasaki, 1867), K. Mackenzie to J. Whittall, 21 Jan. 1867; (Yokohama, Private), J. Whittall to W. Keswick, 12 Mar. 1870.

shore and ship as well as the advisability of sending produce south as the Shanghai market was over-supplied, fill Mackenzie's letters in 1860. The local coal, especially when mixed with Welsh coal, had already impressed the engineers of men-of-war and private steamers as being well adapted for sea-going steam vessels.[1] In September the business in imports and silk had been so great that the market was nearly bare of both; nearly 3,500 bales of silk had been settled for the previous month. Mackenzie recommended as a good use for dollars the advancing of funds to Russian men-of-war visiting and perhaps wintering at Nagasaki—against bills on Barings under Steiglitz's credit. The profits were attractive. Even a ten per cent. exchange profit had been possible.[2] Jardine's instructed Mackenzie to take a share in such business at 5s. 4d. per dollar, on their account and remained interested in tea, silk, wax, and cuttle fish to the extent of 1,000 piculs or more.[3] The company was obviously cautious. Their interest lay in establishing a sound trade—not speculative adventures.[4]

Glover and Company were the leading British firm in Nagasaki before the Restoration. According to the *Chronicle and Directory* for 1865 they had a staff of sixteen men, being twice as many as that of Alt and Company, the second in size. They were agents for six insurance companies in China, Batavia, and London, including Lloyd's. They had representatives in Yokohama and Shanghai, carried on a banking business of their own, and by 1868 were agents for the Hong Kong and Shanghai Banking and Oriental Bank Corporations.[5]

Thomas B. Glover, the head of the firm, was an entrepreneur at once imaginative, daring, and energetic who early established valuable contacts with the high officers of the daimyo of the south-west and kept informed about Japan's internal politics.[6]

[1] J.M. MSS. (Nagasaki, Private), K. Mackenzie to J. Whittall, 4 Jan. 1860; (Nagasaki, 1860), K. Mackenzie to Hong Kong Office, 15, 16 Jan., 23 Feb. 1860; (Japan Letter Book i), Shanghai Office to K. Mackenzie, 5 Apr., 25 June 1860.

[2] Ibid. (Nagasaki, Private), K. Mackenzie to J. Whittall, 8 Sept. 1860; (Nagasaki, 1860), same to same, 15 Oct. 1860.

[3] Ibid. (Shanghai Private, Draft), J. Whittall to K. Mackenzie, 22 Sept. 1860.

[4] Ibid. (Japan Letter Book i), Shanghai Office to T. Glover, 19 June 1861.

[5] *Daily Press, Chronicle and Directory*, Hong Kong, 1866, 1868, 1869, 1870. Paske-Smith, *Western Barbarians*, p. 220.

[6] Ibid., p. 156, Morrison to Alcock, Nagasaki, 14 Apr. 1863. According to the

PLATE 9

THOMAS B. GLOVER of Glover and Company

The Traffic in Ships

As early as 1861 the Tokugawa government and the Daimyo of Satsuma began buying foreign merchantmen. Other daimyo soon followed. Nagasaki became a centre for such purchases.[1] Glover and Company promoted this lucrative business but from their extant correspondence with Jardine's it is not possible to tell which sales and what profits were credited to Jardine's account. In 1862 the *Bakufu* themselves undertook to explore the potentials of foreign trade at Shanghai and Hong Kong. They bought a British schooner, the *Armistice*, from her 'captain owner', Henry Richardson, and hired him to captain their first overseas commercial adventure in over two centuries.

Nagasaki Prefectual Library, little authoritative material on the life of Thomas Blake Glover is known to exist. No intensive research about him has been done. Documents containing brief biographical sketches of Glover are scattered in private papers in villages, etc., and a few items, including two court documents, are in the Prefectual Library. A pamphlet published by the Tourist Division of the Municipal Government of Nagasaki at the time of the unveiling of a bust of Glover in 1961 gives these facts: Thomas Blake Glover was born in Scotland in 1838. His father was said to be a naval officer with whom he came to Shanghai in 1858 [no officer named Glover appears in the *Navy List* for 1858]. There young Glover became interested in trade and moved to Nagasaki on 19 Sept. 1859. He soon established a merchant firm, T. B. Glover and Company, to import firearms, ships, and machinery in exchange for such exports as marine products, gold, silver, raw silk, and tea. The firm developed into a major concern with as many as twenty leased lots. Glover is credited with all the varied activities discussed in the present work; the promotion of the Meiji Restoration by supplying the pro-Imperial forces with munitions and ships, protecting some of the revolutionary samurai, furthering the Satsuma–Chōshū alliance, and aiding young Japanese students to study abroad. This and his interest in the development of industry through his tea processing plant, the Kosuge dockyard, which the government bought in 1869, the Takashima coal mine, and his negotiation for the Hong Kong mint, all led to the Meiji government's conferring on him in 1908 the Second Order of the Rising Sun. His connexions with the Jardine, Matheson Company are not mentioned in this brief account but he is said to have helped create the firm of Holme, Ringer and Company in 1868, to which he turned over the trading side of his many-sided operations [Williams, op. cit., p. 204, gives 1863 as the date this company was founded]. In his later years he served the Mitsubishi Company in an advisory capacity and moved to Tokyo. He died there on 16 Dec. 1911 and is buried in the International Cemetery at Sakamoto-chō. He married Tsuruko Dankawa of Osaka by whom he had a daughter, Ohana, and a son, Tomisaburo, who became an executive in the Holme, Ringer & Company and the managing director of the Nagasaki Fisheries and Steamship Company. He also carried out his father's plan to make a collection of fish with emphasis on the coastal area of Nagasaki, which is now kept at Nagasaki's Liberal Arts College. Glover's mansion at Nagasaki, the oldest existent Western house in Japan, is now designated as a 'cultural asset'.

[1] P.P. H. of C. 1863, lxx. 225, Cons. Report for Nagasaki, 1862. Paske-Smith, *Western Barbarians*, pp. 222–3.

They renamed this wooden, three-masted ship of 358 tons the *Senzai Maru*, asked British protection for her voyage, and dispatched her from Nagasaki under the Japanese flag with a cargo of coal, seaweed, isinglass, and Japanese wares to an astonished bund at Shanghai.[1] Both daimyo and *Bakufu* bought more ships as the internal political tensions increased. Coal was taken in barter against the steamers. Only during the uncertainties of the weeks preceding the bombardment of Kagoshima did the demand for ships let up.[2] The local people had remained friendly throughout the period of Chōshū's antiforeign activities and gave no indication of carrying out the Mikado's expulsion order.[3] And the smoke had scarcely settled at Kagoshima when Thomas Glover sold to Satsuma the S.S. *Sarah* for $75,000 and was expecting a renewed demand for steamers.[4]

Glover's anticipations were fulfilled. In the following March he reported Satsuma's purchase of S.S. *Scotland* and Dent's steamer *Fuhkien* at $130,000 and $55,000 respectively. The next year Glover became Satsuma's exclusive purchasing agent for steamers and other goods, an arrangement kept secret from the Dutch.[5] Steamers and sailing vessels carrying from two to eight guns accounted in value for more than half of Nagasaki's imports in 1865. Twelve ships were sold for $699,500—small vessels amounting in all to 8,960 registered tonnage. Glover and Company sold five of them.[6] Many other daimyo now bought ships. Hizen, Iyo, Kokura, Higo, Kurume, Kishū, Tosa, Kaga, Ōzu, as well as Satsuma purchased eighteen of the twenty-two ships bought by the Japanese in 1866. Eighteen of this total were

---

[1] Paske-Smith, *Western Barbarians*, pp. 223–3. Nihon Keizaishi Kenkyūjo (Research Institute for Japanese Economic History) (Tokyo), Honjō Eijirō, Ed., *Bakumatsu Ishin* (Bakumatsu and Meiji Restoration Periods), (Tokyo, 1942), ii. 14–15, its Keizai Shiwa Sōsho (A Series of Accounts of Economic History). F.O. 46/23, Neale to Russell, No. 3, Yokohama, 3 June 1862.

[2] J.M. MSS. (Nagasaki, 1863), Glover and Company to J.M., Hong Kong Office, 13 Mar. 1863; J. M. Armstrong to Thomas Hunt and Company, 13 May 1863; Glover and Company to J.M., Shanghai Office, 26 May 1863; W. M. Robinet to Thomas Hunt and Company, 20 Aug. 1863.

[3] Ibid., Glover and Company to J.M., Shanghai Office, 10 July 1863.

[4] Ibid., T. Glover to Hong Kong Office, 27 Oct. 1863.

[5] Ibid. (Nagasaki, 1864), Glover and Company to Hong Kong Office, 7 Mar. 1864; (Nagasaki, 1865), T. Glover to W. Keswick, 2 Sept. 1865.

[6] P.P. H. of C. 1866, lxxi. 22–23, Cons. Report for Nagasaki, 1865.

British.[1] Twenty-one of the total twenty-five ships sold to daimyo were also British vessels in 1867 when in spite of the imminent political revolution, imports and exports of the port nearly doubled those of the previous year. The Japanese paid high prices on long-term credit for these ships, with which they began their own business plying between Nagasaki and the ports of adjacent provinces.[2] Thus Tosa's financial agent at Naga-saki, Iwasaki Yatarō, in association with Gotō Shōjirō, had built up a fleet for his daimyo which included at least six steam-ships. With other vessels it became the nucleus of the Mit-subishi Kisen Kaisha after the Restoration.[3]

The British were also associated with the beginnings of the shipbuilding industry at Nagasaki. J. Mitchell, a British subject, was the first shipwright to begin business in Japan with the construction of a Western rigged schooner at Nagasaki in 1861. Iron works established at Akunoura, Nagasaki, by the Sho-gunate under Dutch tutelage in 1855 combined with a dock built later under two Englishmen, Nicholson and Boyd, were the foundation of the present yard of the Mitsubishi Zōsenjo. The Industrial Department of the Meiji government took over the shipyard in 1871, purchased the patent slip at Kosuge from T. B. Glover for $120,000, and constructed a dock $426\frac{1}{2}$ feet long at Tategami. By 1872 these were called the Nagasaki Works. Here about a dozen small wooden steamships of less than five hundred tons and the wooden steamboat *Kosuge Maru* of 1,500 tons were built before 1887 when after a three-year lease of the yard the Mitsubishi Company obtained its full ownership.[4]

The Arms Trade

Another important factor in the increase of imports in the last year of *Bakufu* rule was the demand for arms and ammuni-tion. The British consul estimated their value at $1,400,505 in

[1] P.P. H. of C. 1867, lxviii. 36, Cons. Report for Nagasaki, 1866.
[2] Ibid., 1867–8, lix. 287, Cons. Report for Nagasaki, 1868.
[3] Paske-Smith, *Western Barbarians*, p. 224.
[4] Ibid., p. 225. *The Mitsubishi Gōshi Kaisha* (The Mitsubishi Company Ltd.), (Tokyo, 1911), pp. 109–11. Matsumura Kanichi, Compiler, *Mitsubishi Jūkōgyō Kabushiki Kaisha Shi* (History of Mitsubishi Heavy Industries), (Tokyo, 1956), p. 731.

1867 in contrast to $304,406 the previous year.[1] Glover and Company had had an early interest in this arms trade, contracting for orders for both the Yedo government and native princes. These orders included a field battery of twelve-pounder guns for a daimyo, two small gunboats to be built in England—buyer not given—price $125,000 each, and money to be paid in thirds in advance; a *Bakufu* contract for $183,847 worth of guns at a profit of $40,000, and 907 packages of guns and ammunitions. Jardine's instructed Glover and Company to hold the last in trust for them and on no account to deliver the guns to the Japanese without payment in full in cash. They were anxious to close the transaction and wanted no delay for a chance improvement in the current rates of exchange.[2]

Banking Services

Jardine's correspondence with Glover also throws light on their involvement in banking services and the treasure trade in Nagasaki. Glover's patron, the Daimyo of Satsuma, was not only the largest purchaser of ships, but by 1865 the leading trader among the daimyo.[3] His knowledge of the benefits of overseas commerce through his political connexions with Ryūkyū and independence of *Bakufu* restrictions on trade made him fearless in expanding Kyūshū trade with the West.[4] His officers and others turned to the British for funds. As early as September 1863 James Whittall gave permission to K. R. Mackenzie to grant the Satsuma officials a loan of 'about $120,000 to $130,000 at one per cent. per month for the purchase of silk and other cargo' which was to be shipped on Satsuma's account through Mackenzie's now independent firm, to Jardine's at Shanghai and disposed of as Edward Whittall, head of that office, thought 'most advisable'. Funds for the loan were to come from money due on the sale of two ships.[5]

---

[1] P.P. H. of C. 1867–8, lix. 288, Cons. Report for Nagasaki, 1867.

[2] J.M. MSS. (Nagasaki, 1865), Glover and Company to Armstrong Company, 28 June and 30 Dec. 1865; (Nagasaki, 1866), T. Glover to W. Keswick (?), 10 Mar. 1866; (Japan Letter Book ii), Shanghai Office to Glover & Company, 24 Aug. 1867.

[3] F.O. 46/58, Satow's Report encl. in Parkes to Russell, No. 80, Yokohama, 29 Dec. 1865.

[4] Robert K. Sakai, 'The Satsuma–Ryūkyū Trade and the Tokugawa Seclusion Policy', *Journal of Asian Studies*, xxiii. (May 1964), 391–403. Ishii, op. cit. in *Nihon Rekishi*, July 1959, p. 3.

[5] J.M. MSS. (Nagasaki, Private), K. Mackenzie to E. Whittall, 23 Sept. 1863.

Glover was willing on his own authority to advance Satsuma's officers $30,000 to purchase silks in the interior. He considered the terms good and thought he had secured the friendship of the daimyo. By encouraging and helping those daimyo both at Nagasaki and Yokohama who now were anxious to take the silk trade out of the hands of (native) brokers and bankers who advanced them money, and put it in the hands of their own officers, he hoped to secure silk for Nagasaki.[1] Later that same year James Whittall arranged for the 'Satsuma people' to have £70,000 or £100,000 for purchases in London provided the articles bought were forwarded through Messrs. Matheson and Company.[2] Glover held to his faith in Satsuma's financial reliability even when Jardine's began to be sceptical, arguing that all the drafts presented by Satsuma's officials in England had been paid on presentation, and reporting they had arranged for a very large loan for their Prince to pay off his debts. Glover even planned to accept an invitation from this daimyo to visit him at Kagoshima and to propose that he obtain a loan on his lands in order to extend his trade and build steamers. When the Satsuma officers returned from England and when more ports were opened, he anticipated large orders from the Kagoshima Daimyo and other princes, as he thought himself 'the only person . . . personally known to the Princes'.[3]

In his efforts to secure the trade of the princes, however, Glover met serious competition from the agent of the Dutch government Trading Society who appeared to have unlimited funds to advance at 'little over home interest' and who charged only five per cent. commission. Glover found it difficult to make sufficiently profitable terms to justify the trouble entailed in getting the business of the daimyo, but his belief in the future of Japan made him pursue it. He told Keswick that commissions of $7\frac{1}{2}$ per cent. were too high and should be lowered to attract a larger trade.[4] He understood Keswick's concern about Satsuma's delay in paying his debt to the Company, but did not want to raise the interest for fear of damaging his relations with this daimyo. He sent Ryūkyū sugar for trial sale in Shanghai to

[1] Ibid. (Nagasaki, 1865), T. Glover to W. Keswick, 25 Aug. 1865.

[2] Ibid., T. Glover to E. Whittall, 3 Nov. 1865.

[3] Ibid. (Nagasaki, 1866), T. Glover to W. Keswick, 1 and 21 Feb. 1866. See pp. 186–8, for Glover's visit.

[4] J.M. MSS. (Nagasaki, 1866), T. Glover to W. Keswick, 10 May and 2 July 1866.

be credited to Satsuma's account. He accepted gold cobangs in part payment from the daimyo, and in November 1867 took a mortgage on the steamer *Kenshin* as security for the $50,000 which the daimyo still owed. But this was not sufficient. In the political uncertainties of the following months, Jardine's asked Glover to obtain repayment or more adequate guarantee.[1] Here the Jardine record ends. Presumably the Meiji government paid this along with the debts of other daimyo.[2] Jardine's connexions with Glover and Company probably drew to a close in 1870 when Whittall had lost confidence in their business policies and directed the liquidation of Glover's debt of about $110,000 to Jardine's during that year.[3]

Industrial Development

British loans brought British machinery to Japan. Satsuma had used his borrowed funds in part to further the development of Western industry in his domain, so imaginatively begun by his great predecessor Shimazu Nariakira. In 1865 he had in operation three furnaces of the reverberatory type and machinery run by water for boring the solid iron gun barrels cast from them. As a consequence an armament industry prospered in Kagoshima in addition to the collection of small workshops established before 1858 called the *shuseikan*, which produced iron tools for carpentering and agriculture, refined sugar, and manufactured leather articles and paper.[4] In conjunction with Glover in 1866, Satsuma constructed a slip dock which the British consul welcomed as a valuable asset to shipping interests.[5] He also established three English sugar factories, employing British engineers on Ōshima in Ryūkyū and Glover expected a fourth steam factory at work there by 1867.[6]

[1] J.M. MSS. (Nagasaki, 1866), T. Glover to W. Keswick, 11 Aug. 1866, T. Glover to J. Whittall, 30 Aug. 1866; (Japan Letter Book ii), Shanghai Office to Glover & Company, 1 Nov. 1867, 28 Feb. 1868.

[2] Horie Yasuzō, *Gaishi Yunyū no Kaiko to Tembō* (Retrospect and Outlook of Foreign Investment), (Tokyo, 1950), pp. 8–9.

[3] J.M. MSS. (Private Letters), J. Whittall to W. Keswick, Yokohama, 22 Jan., 12 Mar. 1870.

[4] Thomas C. Smith, 'Introduction of Western Industry to Japan', *Harvard Journal of Asiatic Studies*, xi. 138–9.

[5] Nagasaki, *Shiyakushō* (Nagasaki Municipal Office), *Nagasaki Sōsho* (a series about Nagasaki), 4 vols. (Nagasaki, 1926), iii. 382. P.P. H. of C. 1867, lxviii. 240, Cons. Report for Nagasaki, 1866.

[6] F.O. 46/67, Parkes to Clarendon, No. 49, Yokohama, 16 Mar. 1866. J.M.

As the founder of Japan's modern textile industry Satsuma has won still greater fame. Probably in 1866—authorities differ about the exact year—he bought a spinning and weaving factory consisting of 3,640 spindles and 100 looms from Pratt Company of Manchester and had it installed in Kagoshima by seven English technicians. One of them, Edward Z. Holme, supervised the operation and taught the native employees. His contract illustrates the caution of the Satsuma officials. They agreed to pay him an annual salary of eight thousand Mexican dollars in four instalments beginning 1 January 1866, to provide reasonable shelter, and to make him responsible for his furniture and food. The contract expired November 1867 but could be renewed annually at the request of both parties. The mill was in good working order by 1868. It employed more than two hundred Japanese workmen whom Holme found so apt that they learned to work the looms in five or six months without European aid, and their daily production amounted to nearly four hundred pounds of yarn.[1]

Through Glover and Company the British also had a close relationship with the Saga clan where the Daimyo, Nabeshima Kansō (1814–71), had taken an early interest in Western industrialization and the importation of Western knowledge, particularly in connexion with his responsibility for the defence of Nagasaki. As coal became a profitable export for use by foreign ships and capital funds were needed, the Saga authorities turned to Glover and Company for financial help and technical and commercial guidance, to organize a joint undertaking to exploit the Takashima coal mine on Takashima Island about ten miles off Nagasaki harbour, which belonged to one of the retainers of the Nabeshima family. A contract negotiated by Joseph Heco[2] was signed 6 May 1868 by Thomas Glover and

MSS. (Nagasaki, 1866), T. Glover to W. Keswick, 2 July 1866. Paske-Smith, *Western Barbarians*, p. 224.

[1] Tsuchiya Takao, *Ishin Keizai Shi* (Economic History of the Restoration), (Tokyo, 1942), pp. 182–3; *Hōken Shakai Hōkai Katei no Kenkyū* (A Study of the Disintegration of Feudal Society), (Tokyo, 1927), p. 512. Thomas E. Smith, op. cit., in *Harvard Journal of Asiatic Studies*, xi. 150. Paske-Smith, *Western Barbarians*, p. 217. Cons. Report for Nagasaki, 1868, p. 35.

[2] Joseph Heco (Hamada Hikozo, 1837–97), the Japanese who in 1850 was rescued from shipwreck by an American ship and became an American citizen while in the United States until 1859. He then returned to Japan to become an interpreter in the American consulate and was useful in diplomatic and consular

the Saga authorities. The British agreed to provide the necessary capital, half of which was to be 'a first charge against the profits which were thereafter to be shared equally'. In June they hired an English civil engineer, Mr. Morris, who was joined later by two working miners from England. For the first time in Japan, modern mining machinery was introduced—steam driven winches for raising coal from the 150-foot pits, a steam pump for draining purposes, safety lamps, a ventilating system, and a small railway to haul the coal from the pit mouth to the pier. A Saga clansman managed the production and Glover and Company handled the marketing under the watchful eye of Joseph Heco.[1]

The British engineer, Henry Brunton, visited the mine in December 1868. He found three hundred men raising daily about two hundred tons of good bituminous coal which sold at $4.50 a ton, while coal imported from England cost $7.50 a ton. He thought this was the only instance where Japan permitted a European to mine this mineral in Japan. Parkes's efforts to persuade Terashima Munenori, a member of the foreign ministry, to allow its mineral resources to be used had brought only the rebuff that Japan's minerals must remain unexploited until the Japanese themselves could work them.[2] By December 1869 the mine had produced a total of 46,454·96 tons of bituminous coal, said to be superior to Welsh coal for fuelling ships. In January 1870 James Whittall of Jardine's, after a visit to the mine with Glover, reported a yield of only ninety tons a day, but the expectation of five hundred tons daily when two newly arrived practical engineers got into operation.[3] By October 1871 the cumulative yield reached 422,640·83 tons.

Glover and Company continued their connexion with the

business. He soon resigned to enter business in Yokohama and edit a newspaper, *Kaigai Shimbun* 1864–6. He went to Nagasaki, had contacts with Kido and Itō, and took part in international negotiations, not only for the Takashima mine operation but for the transfer of the U.S. ship *Stonewall* and the Hong Kong mint to Meiji ownership. Later he entered the Ministry of Finance and compiled the regulations for the National Bank under Shibusawa.

[1] Etō Kōji, 'Takashima Tankō ni Okeru Nichi-Ei Kyōdō Kigyō (Japanese-British Joint Enterprise at the Takashima Coal Mine) in *Bakumatsu Keisai Shi Kenkyū* (Study in Bakumatsu Economic History), ed. by Nihon Keizaishi Kenkyūjo (Institute for Research in Japanese Economic History), Tokyo, 1935, pp. 27–28, 43–47. Thomas C. Smith, op. cit., in *Harvard Journal of Asiatic Studies*, xi. 151.

[2] Brunton MS. Sec. i. 64.

[3] J.M. MSS. (Private, Yokohama), J. Whittall to W. Keswick, 22 Jan. 1870.

mine until 1873 and then received $400,000 for their interest when the Meiji government bought it and managed it for ten months. Gotō Shōjirō purchased it as a private venture in 1874 and in April 1881 it was transferred to Iwasaki Yatarō.[1]

The Treasure Trade

Glover's ambition and energy were exceeded only by his optimism in the treasure trade. In 1864 he believed he had 'all but arranged' to take the long-standing monopoly of the government's gold trade out of the hands of the Chinese Guild. He had sold one hundred gold bars at $220 a bar as an experiment and had received an order for a monthly supply of one thousand bars. He asked Jardine's to send him one lot of one thousand pieces to be packed and marked as Mexican dollars in order to avoid discovery by American competitors. At the same time he asked whether Keswick would consider an advance of $200,000 to the *Bakufu* on government security, thinking it a profitable investment and a possible means of securing the contract for supplying all the gold to the Japanese government.[2] But the *Bakufu* was cautious. After comparing musters of gold offered by Jardine's with that of the Chinese it accused the former of being nine per cent. alloy and asked that the price be reduced accordingly. Glover, however, believed that Jardine's gold was very little inferior to that imported by the Chinese and blamed the Chinese for obstructing foreign interference with their long-held monopoly. He remained sure of selling the sample order.[3] In 1865 he was blocking American efforts to gain a *Bakufu* annual contract for two thousand bars of silver to be delivered in lots of five hundred pieces and preferably paid for in copper, silk, and tea. Concurrently he was asking Keswick to supply him with silver required to be 990 thousandths fine at a slight reduction in the price, hoping to win the order for Jardine's.[4]

---

[1] Etō Koji, op. cit., p. 50. Stanleigh H. Jones, Jr., 'Early Industrialization in Japan: The Example of the Saga-Han', *Columbia University East Asian Institute Studies*, No. 6 (New York, 1959), pp. 16–19.

[2] J.M. MSS. (Nagasaki, 1864), T. Glover to W. Keswick, 5 Oct. 1864.

[3] Ibid., T. Glover to K. Keswick, 25 Nov.; T. Glover to E. Whittall, 2 Dec. 1864 and 5 Jan. 1865.

[4] Ibid. (Nagasaki, 1865), T. Glover to W. Keswick, 24 Aug. 1865. Jardine's answer is unknown.

The decline in the import trade in 1865 in Nagasaki led Jardine's Shanghai office to send Glover $100,000 Mexican to be entirely invested in *ichibu* and shipped to their agent, C. S. Hope, in Yokohama.[1] The payment of the Shimonoseki indemnity soon attracted the alert Glover as an opportunity to bring copper into the market legitimately. The *Bakufu* was paying the three million dollars in copper cash which it deposited in two of the Yokohama banks for sale on its account and had the amount realized placed in the indemnity account. Glover at once made arrangements to buy supplies of copper from this source.[2] But in the extant letters of 1866 and 1867, Glover fails to note at this time the rapid increase of imports and British shipping resulting from the growing demand for munitions, rice, sugar, and cotton and leading to a great excess of imports over exports. To balance this trade, *ichibu* were remitted to Yokohama and large quantitites of *nishu* (half *ichibu* gold pieces) and *nibu* were sent to China. From $700,000 to $800,000 worth of these old gold pieces were bought up at ninety-eight per cent. over their issued value and readily sold in Shanghai and Hong Kong at a profit.[3] It is hard to believe that Jardine's and Glover had no part in this.

Trade Developments, 1869–1883

While the cotton mill and the Takeshima mine prospered and the population of the port was estimated at eighty thousand, Nagasaki trade responded adversely to the unsettled conditions following the Restoration, the opening of Osaka and Hyogo, the fluctuations in the native currency, and the decline in the demand for arms in 1869. The trade became more sound in character the next year. The opening of the Suez Canal led to a line of steamers, other than mail steamers, leaving China for England regularly by that route, carrying merchandise at moderate freight rates and bringing back manufactures from England to Shanghai for Nagasaki. Steamers came into demand again. Daimyo bought five British vessels in 1870. Coal became

[1] J.M. MSS. (Japan Letter Book i), Shanghai Office to Glover and Company, 11 July 1865.

[2] Ibid. (Nagasaki, 1866), T. Glover to W. Keswick, 10 Feb. 1866.

[3] P.P. H. of C. 1867, lxviii. 240; 1867–8, lxix. 290, Cons. Reports for Nagasaki, 1866 and 1867. In the former 'nishu' is spelt 'nushus'.

the principal export of Nagasaki. The Takeshima mine nearly doubled its production in 1873 over 1872, but the British consul lamented that so many other mines in the vicinity were undeveloped. The Formosan Expedition in 1874 brought a new temporary demand for munitions. Competition between the Mitsubishi and Pacific Mail Lines to keep freights low for the major part of the year enabled buyers to seek larger markets where selection was better, and bring goods to Nagasaki at nominal cost, thus cutting the import trade.[1] In 1875 the British consul saw no hope for the improvement of the port's trade until roads and other communication with the interior were improved. The increase in the Mitsubishi mail steamers plying between Shanghai and the Japanese ports, however, was impressive. Ninety-one of them, representing a tonnage of 127,023, had entered Nagasaki that year. A second private mine, the Hashima, worked by foreign machinery, was opened in 1876 and the Meiji government hired Mr. Potter, an English mining engineer, to improve the system in the Muke mine, already worked for two hundred years. Excessive taxes without compensations in public improvements interfered with commerce in the late seventies and the depreciation of Japanese currency caused a further decline in imports. But more British ships—a total of 216—with greater aggregate tonnage entered Nagasaki in 1880 than at any time since the opening of the port, owing to its becoming a port of call for several British steamship lines, the Pacific and Oriental Steam Navigation Company, the 'Ocean Steam Navigation Company', and the Glen Line. Native shipping was also on the increase. Eight hundred and twenty-two Japanese vessels with a total tonnage of 280,751 came into the port in 1880 in contrast to 656 ships of 296,736 [*sic*] tons the previous year. The dry dock opened in 1879 was used by fifteen ships. By 1883 Nagasaki stood third among the open ports in Japan with regard to trade, but led them all in the number and tonnage of ships, being the main source of the coal supply for the east of Asia. 310,038 tons valued at $1,115,090 had been sold that year despite the

---

[1] In Oct. 1870 Iwasaki Yatarō, founder of the Mitsubishi Corporation, had opened a marine transport service at Osaka called *Tsukumo Shōkai*, which was the beginning of the Mitsubishi shipping business. Matsumura Kanichi, op. cit., p. 731.

general depression which caused both exports and imports to decline. In spite of Japanese efforts to prevent it, British, Russian, and German ships were seeking business at unopened ports, Kuchinotsu and Karatsu, while the nascent trade with Korea since the treaty of 1876 had been suddenly checked.[1]

3. HAKODATE

Hazards to Foreign Trade, 1859–1883

The picturesque fishing village of Hakodate attracted few foreign merchants. But Alcock's predictions about its potentials for commerce proved true.[2] There were no trade returns from the port in 1859. Five Russian warships, two American merchantmen, one American whaler, and five British merchantmen entered the port between Hodgson's arrival in October and the end of December. Four of the latter had left with fair cargoes.[3] Jardine's *Troas* had found little to buy since Lindsay and Company's agent had bought up all the seaweed. Keswick therefore recommended that a representative be on the spot to purchase *bêche-de-mer*, seaweed, and peas, expected in quantities next year, and prevent Lindsay's agent from having the market to himself.[4] The Japanese merchants were pleased with big profits but disturbed by the use of foreign currency and were deciding their own exchange rates.[5]

Hodgson reported constant interference with trade at the customs house until December 1859, but amicable relations with the Japanese people.[6] The consul's unruly temper and habitual drunkenness, however, soon brought complaints about him from the Japanese governor (*bugyō*) as well as from the foreign

[1] Cons. Reports for Nagasaki, 1868–83. F.O. 46/124, Parkes to Clarendon, Yokohama, 12 Feb. 1870 and encls. 1 and 2. 'The Ocean Steam Navigation Company' is probably an error and the Ocean Steamship Company founded by Alfred Holt in China 1865–6 is meant. The figures for the tonnage of 1879 and 1880 also seem to have been reversed. See Cons. Report for Nagasaki, 1880, p. 60.　　　　　　　　　　　　　　　　　　　　　　　　[2] See p. 67.

[3] P.P. H. of C. 1860, lxix (2673), 7, Hodgson to Alcock, Hakodate, 31 Dec. 1859.

[4] J.M. MSS. (Kanagawa, 1859), W. Keswick to J. Whittall, 21 Nov. 1859.

[5] *B.G.K.M.* xxix. 27–28, Doc. 15, Hakodate *Bugyō* to *Rōjū*, 21 Nov. 1859 and xxxi. 151, Doc. 50, Communication, Dec. 1859.

[6] Ibid. xxx. 11–13, Doc. 113, Alcock to Japanese Commissioner of Foreign Affairs, Yedo, 19 Dec. 1859. P.P. H. of C. 1860, lxix. (2673), 7, Hodgson to Alcock, Hakodate, 31 Dec. 1859.

community which led to his recall in the early autumn of 1860. His redeeming act seems to have been the collection of the plants of Hakodate area which he sent to Kew Gardens in London.[1]

How much Hakodate trade developed in 1860 is not known. Hodgson reported the sale of 100,000 *ichibu* worth of exports which realized 300,000 *ichibu*, a rate of profit considered too great to last but proof of the existence of sufficient Japanese produce to encourage a profitable trade. At the same time Stevenson, Willie and Company, merchants, were asking for British textiles, canvas, and window glass.[2] The next British consul, James J. Enslie, lamented a decrease in Hakodate's trade in 1861 in comparison with that of the previous year. Only seventeen merchantmen had been in port. He attributed this to the scarcity of some articles, e.g. iriko and awabi, restricted by government monopoly, and the overstocking of the China market with others, such as lumber. The great demand for oak, elm, and pine in 1860 to build houses for the refugees in Shanghai, had ceased, and the price of wood fell with consequent losses to both Dent and Company and Lindsay and Company. Salt fish and fish oil, always important exports, varied in quantity according to the weather. Peas and potatoes in too great supply caused further losses, when exported to China, but a kind of brandy distilled from potatoes was in great demand in Hakodate among the Russian and merchant seamen. The vast mineral resources of the island, sulphur, coal, and lead, were undeveloped, or in the case of lead, ineffectively mined.

European imports consisting mainly of chintz, camlets, vermilion, and medicine were seriously restricted by the government's exaction of an extra duty of twenty per cent. from Japanese merchants before they were permitted to sell them to their own people. High prices resulted, but foreign money was plentiful owing to the excess of exports. Government monopolities of Yezo produce and secret speculations caused articles to disappear with consequent losses to merchants.[3] Thus silk

[1] Hakodate Municipal Library, *Japanese-Anglo Relations Centering on Hakodate*, narrated on the occasion when the crest of the former British Consulate was presented to Hakodate City, 30 Aug. 1940 (Hakodate, 1940), pp. 5–6.

[2] F.O. 46/8, Alcock to Russell, No. 46, Yedo, 29 July 1860, encl. letter from merchants to Hodgson, 11 July 1860.

[3] P.P, H, of C. 1862, lix. 109–11, Cons. Report for Hakodate, 1861.

and copper had vanished from the market by the close of 1862 owing to lack of confidence in the Europeans whose firms were now required to make advances in money to get these products. All kinds of people had flocked to Hakodate—now the capital of Yezo—enticed by public works still uncompleted by the government. Hatred and rudeness to foreigners were general for which the crude and arbitrary behaviour of the foreigners themselves was much to blame.[1]

Only seven foreign merchants, however, had settled in Hakodate by 1865.[2] Business did not pay. The dangerous winds and currents of the Tsugaru Straits kept both foreign ships and Japanese junks from this port. Its beautiful harbour had not been surveyed. Buoys and a lighthouse did not exist. No demand for imports developed. The main export market—that to China and southern Japan—often responded adversely to the current political disturbances. And articles in demand for direct European trade, fish oil, tobacco, copper, skins, were usually in short supply. The *Bakufu* officials continued to interfere with the Japanese merchants by heavy fines and duties and tried to prevent intercourse between foreigners and nearby daimyo who indicated an interest in trade. Foreign merchants also suffered from the unfavourable exchange rate for dollars and felt aggrieved by the exchange benefits of the consulates.[3] Smuggling on a large scale developed in consequence of the government's interference and accounted for a great part of Hakodate's trade. Consul Vyse reported instances of customs house officers visiting foreigners at night in order to sell copper, in defiance of the prohibition. The absence of an interpreter who could speak or write English or Dutch in 1865 added to the inconvenience of the traders. Yet the British consul was convinced that Hakodate would increase rapidly in trade and population and perhaps become the most important port in Japan for the trade of China if the government's obstructions were removed.[4]

Jardine's records of their dealings with Hakodate during these

[1] P.P. H. of C. 1862, lix. 112; 1863, lxx. 204–5, Cons. Reports for Hakodate, 1861 and 1862.

[2] *Daily Press, Chronicle and Directory*, Hong Kong, 1865.

[3] P.P. H. of C. 1864, lxi. 139–56, Cons. Report for Hakodate, 1863, encl. letters from local merchants.

[4] P.P. H. of C. 1866, lxxi. 7, Cons. Report for Hakodate, 1865.

early years are too scarce to permit a reliable account of their activities. Along with Lindsay and Company and Dent and Company, they experimented with the export of lumber, seaweed, deer skins, deer horns, fish oil, rape seed oil, etc., and imported coal with limited success.[1] They were never mentioned among the merchants resident in Hakodate in the yearly issues of the Hong Kong *Chronicle and Directory* from 1864 to 1868.[2] There seems no evidence that the company kept a resident agent in the port as Keswick had advised. C. S. Hope, their Yokohama agent, reporting from Hakodate in October 1864, doubted that it would 'become a port of importance'.[3]

In 1866 the government's monopoly of iriko and awabi ceased. Their export more than doubled and a lucrative business direct with China seemed imminent. No banks had yet been established. Trade continued to be principally transacted through Shanghai, Nagasaki, and Yokohama, which supplied Hakodate with treasure to balance its exports. Encouragement regarding the development of Hokkaido's mineral resources came with the *bugyō*'s application to Yedo for authority to work the Iwanai coal mine under foreign superintendence.[4] An Englishman, Erasmus Gower, was appointed to this task, which was delayed by the developments of civil war in 1868.[5]

As the Tokagawa Shogunate came to its end the contemporary guide to the open ports of China and Japan gave a grim picture of life and trade in this remote city. 'The only things generally considered worth buying', it said, 'are the celebrated Hakodate "whatnots", square or triangular in shape, and consisting of a series of small tables graduated in size from two feet to eight or ten inches square. They are lacquered and gilt, and are useful for displaying the numberless small curiosities which visitors are apt to buy in Japanese towns and the price asked—some 26 to 38 boos—is not exorbitant.' It maintained that more

---

[1] J.M. MSS. (Hakodate, Private), Fred. Wilkie to Thomas Hunt & Company at Shanghai, 26 July 1863; (Hakodate, 1864), John H. Duns to J. M. & Company, 26 Nov. 1864. Duns represented Lindsay & Company according to the *Directory* of 1865. [2] These issues are in the J.M. archives.

[3] J.M. MSS. (Hakodate, 1864), C. S. Hope to W. Keswick, 5 Oct. 1864.

[4] P.P. H. of C. 1867, lxviii, 219–23, Cons. Report for Hakodate, 1866.

[5] Cons. Report for Hakodate, 1868, pp. 40–42. F.O. 46/81, Parkes to Stanley No. 151, Yedo, 11 Sept. 1867, encl. Mitford's report on mines.

extended communication would be needed before Hakodate could take prominent place among the treaty ports of Japan.[1]

The period of the Restoration and civil war brought more ships and greater tonnage to Hakodate than at any time during the twenty-five years here considered. Jardine's records report that copper was freely sold there in 1868, that there was a considerable demand for arms, and as the war moved to the north a growing market for blankets and camlets.[2] Although the number of vessels entering the port did not necessarily mean an increase in trade, as many only stayed a few hours on their way to the western coast with arms and munitions, nevertheless it seems clear that Hakodate's trade as well as shipping and tonnage reached their peak in 1869, more than doubling that of the previous year. The Tokugawa squadron brought in silk and copper for export. Silkworm eggs came from Niigata. And most important for the future, a native carrying-trade developed whereby Japanese merchants chartered foreign ships to go up and down the coast. Twenty-eight British ships entered the port on Japanese charters including government charters. Seventy-one merchant ships came in under the British flag as against fifty-nine of all other Western nations and bore nearly half the entire tonnage. Steamers made up forty-two of the total merchant carriers. A new order in the nature of shipping was beginning. Along with it came the Meiji government's first effort to colonize Yezo. And the British men-of-war stationed at Hakodate from December 1868 left in October 1869.[3]

The trade boom was short lived for the British and other foreigners. Both exports and imports decreased alarmingly in 1870 and until 1883 never approached the level of 1869. The regular service of the United States Pacific Mail steamers with their greater tonnage capacity led to the reduction of British ships and tonnage, and Japanese trading companies

[1] N. B. Dennys, et al., *The Treaty Ports of China and Japan* (London, 1867), pp. 614–15, 617.

[2] J.M. MSS. (Hakodate, 1868), Howell and Company to Shanghai Office, 19 Aug. 1868.

[3] P.P. H. of C. 1870, lxv. 71–73, 81. Cons. Report for Hakodate, 1869. Although no trade figures at this time are completely reliable, they indicate the information available to the consul. For 1869 foreign imports are said to have amounted to $789,926.52, and exports $990,711.54. There are no figures for British trade alone. Ibid., pp. 77–79.

using their own ships had a similar result. Both exports and imports fluctuated from year to year giving little hope for a steadily rewarding trade. When the Pacific Mail steamers stopped running northward in 1875 Britain regained the lion's share of Hakodate's foreign shipping and tonnage but that was now largely restricted to the transport of produce to Chinese ports.[1] By 1880 the Mitsubishi Company steamers had dominated the coastal and local carrying-trade, which a year later showed an aggregate of 598 vessels entering and clearing the port with a total of 283,166 tons exclusive of over one hundred Japanese sailing vessels ranging from eighty to one hundred tons. Direct trade with Britain and Europe scarcely existed.[2] British exports from Hakodate vastly exceeded her imports as the import trade was controlled by Japanese merchants who preferred to purchase goods for home consumption in Yokohama and import them in native vessels at high freights rather than contract with foreigners for supplies in Hakodate. In 1883 the British consul saw no possible hope for any improvement in the foreign import trade of the port and reported the foreign export trade decreasing and unremunerative. For the latter, he held the Japanese custom of sending goods to Yokohama where they claimed to receive higher prices for produce destined for China and elsewhere, partially responsible in addition to world conditions.[3]

Obviously it was not the British nor any foreign influence which caused the growth of Hakodate. The Meiji government promoted colonization zealously in Yezo; establishing schools— 146 by 1882 in Hakodate district—; building roads, hospitals, and prisons, and a railway to connect Otarunai with Sapporo and the coal mines of Poronai. Japanese companies provided the coastal shipping and mail services—the latter under Mitsubishi running weekly in 1883 between Yokohama, Kobe, Oginohama,[4] and Hakodate. They also built up a significant native

---

[1] Cons. Reports Hakodate for 1870-9. The Pacific Mail Steamship Company of New York founded in 1867 a regular service between San Francisco, Yokohama, and Hong Kong. Their impressively large steamers carrying passengers, mail, and freight, offered severe competition to British and other lines. Black, op. cit. ii. 46-48. MSS. Butterfield and Swire (London/Japan Correspondence), J. H. Scott to John Swire & Sons, Yokohama, 30 Dec. 1869.

[2] Cons. Report for Hakodate, 1880, pp. 5-6; 1881, pp. 6-7.

[3] Cons. Report for Hakodate, 1883, pp. 119-20.

[4] Otarunai is a port north of Hakodate, Oginohama, a port on the Bay of Sendai.

export-import trade, said to total $15,087,178 in 1882 in con-trast to $515,504, the figure given for the entire foreign trade of the port in that year. By 1882 the fishing village of 1859 had become a community of 26,908 residents within a district of 119,778 people which attracted a floating population of 12,672 non-registered residents.[1]

British Activities in Hakodate

During these years the European and American community had never reached a total of fifty. Here the British always constituted the most numerous nationality and a few of them made a lasting impact on the area. The most versatile and colourful personality was Thomas Wright Blakiston (1832–91) of Lymington, Hampshire, who came to Hakodate in 1861 to stay until 1884. He had been an artillery captain, serving in the Crimean and Anglo-China wars. He was also a zoologist and former explorer of the Canadian Rockies and the Upper Yangtze River, when he entered into trade, lumbering, and shipping in Hakodate. He established Blakiston, Marr and Company to trade with Russia and China, manufacture ice, and process timber for market.[2] In 1864 he imported a steam sawmill and European engineers to erect it. In announcing their arrival to the superintendent of customs at Hakodate he invited the government to place its mechanics on the plant to learn steam machinery under these engineers and encouraged the officials and Japanese people to visit and 'inspect his mill'.[3] In 1871 he had negotiated a contract with the Meiji govern-ment for a sawmill and steam engine for the government of Hokkaido and was arranging for its delivery.[4] Contemporary advertisements indicate that his firm was dealing in paint, selling and renting real estate, and offering for sale the salvage from ships wrecked off the coast.[5] His activities also included the inspection of the stores, ordnance, and material of the ill-fated H.M.S. *Rattler* which sank off the Hokkaido coast

[1] Cons. Report for Hakodate, 1879, pp. 5–6; 1882, pp. 1, 4, 6, 7; 1883, Pt. II, pp. 121, 124–7.
[2] Dai Jinmei Jiten (Biographical Dictionary), 10 vols. (Tokyo, 1954), viii. 689.
[3] Hakodate Municipal Library, Blakiston, Marr MSS., Blakiston to Sup., 21 May 1864.
[4] Ibid., B.M. Co. to Chief Officer, Foreign Dept., 6 Oct. 1871.
[5] *Hakodate Shimbun*, 27 Feb., 7 June, 24 Aug. 1878.

north of Sapporo;[1] the making of plans for the harbours of Hokkaido; the founding of a regular shipping service between Hakodate and Aomori; and planning a water system for Hakodate.[2]

Blakiston came into conflict in 1875 with the local commissioner of colonization over his firm's issue of coupons (*shōken*), a kind of private paper currency in the form of ten sen, twenty sen, and one yen notes, promising to pay the bearer Japanese money on demand, which it expected to use in connexion with a project to establish a commercial route connecting Hakodate, Yokohama, and Shanghai. Such *shōken* had been issued by foreign trading companies before as well as by local daimyo. Since the banking regulations of 1872, however, prohibited this action by the clans the commissioner considered it applicable to Blakiston, Marr and Company and prohibited the use of their *shōken*. After widespread discussion and the foreign ministry's denial of the commissioner's right on such grounds to suspend such foreign *shōken*, Parkes and the foreign minister agreed that this practice should be stopped. Parkes ordered Eusden to prohibit the use of Blakiston, Marr's coupons and a regulation of the finance ministry of 14 March 1876 suspended the circulation of this foreign commercial paper money.[3]

Blakiston's most lasting influence on Hokkaido bore no relation to his business interests, which eventually suffered seriously from his inability to collect the generous loans he had made to Japanese civilians, and thus caused him to leave Japan.[4] Blakiston, the scientist, after observing the animal life of northern Japan, proved that the Straits of Tsugaru were the demarcation line between the animals of northern and middle Asia. His friend John Milne, the British seismologist, who often visited him in Hokkaido, named the boundary the 'Blakiston Line'—facts about which appear in Blakiston's article ' Zoological Indication of Connection of Japan with the Continent.'[5]

[1] Blakiston, Marr MSS., Blakiston Report, 25 Oct. 1869.
[2] Okada Kenzō, *Hakodate Hyakuchin to Hakodate* (One Hundred Facts and Historical Events of Hakodate), (Hakodate, 1956), pp. 84, 116.
[3] Okada, K., op. cit., p. 84. Hokkaidō, *Hokkaidō Shi* (History of Hokkaido), 7 vols. (Tokyo, 1937), i. 131; iii. 531. *Japan Weekly Mail*, 14 Aug. 1875, p. 690. For *sen* notes see p. 404.   [4] Okada, K., op. cit., p. 116.
[5] Denkichi Koga, *Hokkaidō Kyōdoshi Kenkyū* (A study of the Local History of Hokkaido), (Sapporo, 1932), pp. 294–5. *T.A.S.J.*, xi, Pt. I for Blakiston's article. For John Milne, p. 468.

Blakiston made a collection of 1,314 birds of Japan, which is now in Hokkaido University. He sent other specimens to England, France, and America, and in co-operation with H. Pryor he published a catalogue of the birds of Japan.[1] In 1873 he escaped from a sinking ship, the P.M.S.S. *Ariel* wrecked on a reef off Toyoma Point on Japan's east coast, and made his way overland through unexplored country to Aomori to get a steamer to Hakodate, a distance of about 350 English miles. He recorded carefully the nature, resources, and inhabitants of this then unknown area and recommended the opening of a port on the Bay of Sendai.[2] He interested the Japanese in meteorological observations and led to the establishing of Japan's first meteorological station at the home of his friend Fukushi Unokichi. And he inaugurated the annual sailboat race in Hakodate harbour for the purpose of developing sailing techniques.[3] Memories of Blakiston's services linger on and many local ceremonies have been held in his honour.[4]

Other Englishmen also made an impression on the port. Alexander P. Porter, a former sea captain, arrived from Shanghai in 1859 to be the manager for Dent and Company. When Alfred Howell succeeded him sometime before 1865, he went into trade with China for himself and remained in the city for thirty years, making many friends among the Japanese people. The colonization commissioner appointed him chief of Hakodate port in charge of foreign ships and Chinese people in 1871 at 2,400 *ryō* a year. He measured the depth of Hakodate harbour and constructed buoys to aid the anchoring of ships. The port regulations which he established aroused objections from the foreigners, however, and his position was abolished the next year. In the *Gazette Hong List* for 1872 and the *Japan Directory* of 1879 he is registered as 'Commission Merchant, General Agent, and Marine Surveyor'. He also ran an agency for an English marine insurance company which he transferred to the Mitsubishi-sha in 1882. His efforts to colonize seed oysters in Hakodate waters and to establish outdoor feeding for pheasants in Tsugaru failed. He accumulated many debts which were

---

[1] *Japanese-Anglo Relations Centering on Hakodate*, p. 6.
[2] *T.A.S.J.* ii. 198–222, 'A Journey in North-East Japan'.
[3] Denkichi, op. cit., pp. 295–6.   [4] Okada, K., op. cit., p. 84.

cleared by two devoted English and Japanese friends before he left Hakodate for Yokohama where he died.[1]

After Dent's failure, Alfred Howell established Howell and Company, which appears to have been Jardine's agent in 1869 and which is listed in 1872 and 1879 as an insurance company with three members.[2]

A fourth important British figure in Hakodate was J. H. Thompson, who founded the Thompson shipyard in 1865 in Toyokawa-chō. He built Western-style ships, schooners, and boats. In partnership with another Englishman, George Bewick, he formed a company which was listed as 'ship builders, naval contractors, butchers and ships compradors'. Selling foodstuffs to foreign ships proved so profitable that the construction of ships declined and after Thompson's death in 1888 the shipyard was closed down.[3]

At least one other Englishman should be mentioned as an influential member of the little foreign community of the north. He was John Batchelor, an Episcopal missionary (C.M.S.) to the Ainu people who also worked among the Japanese in Hakodate. His name appears in the Hakodate Directory of 1879 but he may have begun his study of the indigenous Ainu earlier. He published an *Ainu–English, Japanese Dictionary* which included a grammar of the Ainu language, several works on the Ainu life and lore, and an Ainu translation of the Gospel of St. Matthew.[4]

British consuls came and went frequently in the sixties. Some, like Hodgson and Vyse, had to be replaced—the former for drunkenness and ill temper, the latter because of his connexion with the desecration of Ainu graves in areas beyond the foreign concession, and the sending of the bones to his brother in England, much to the dismay of the British government and to

[1] *Japanese-Anglo Relations Centering on Hakodate*, pp. 6–7. Okada, op. cit., p. 127.

[2] J.M. MSS. (Letter Book ii), Shanghai Office to Messrs. Howell and Co., 22 Jan. 1869. *Japan Gazette Hong List and Directory. Japan Directory*, 1879 in Hakodate Library.

[3] Ibid., and *Anglo-Japanese Relations Centering on Hakodate*, p. 7. Okada, K., op. cit., p. 128.

[4] John Batchelor, *An Ainu–English, Japanese Dictionary and Grammar* (Tokyo, 1889 and 1905); *The Ainu and their Folklore* (London, 1901); *Chikoro Utarapa ne Yesu Kiristo Ashiri Ekambakte, a Matteu Orowa no Asange Pirika* (translation from the Ainu unobtainable), (Tokyo, 1889), and articles in *T.A.S.J.* x, xvi, xxiv, and the *Church Missionary Intelligencer*, ix. 445.

the horror of the families of the interred. Vyse was asked to resign from the consular service, the bones and skulls were returned to the governor of Hakodate, and one thousand silver *ichibu* were paid to the aggrieved Ainu relatives.[1]

Richard Eusden, who arrived in Hakodate in July 1867 as acting consul, was the outstanding British official there during our period. He had held this post in Hakodate during a few months in 1861. Before and after this he served in the legation in Yedo as Japanese secretary and interpreter, and in other capacities. He became consul at Hakodate on 1 January 1868 and acted as German, French, and Austrian consul as well. He and his wife took a lively interest in the growing city, making many friends among the Japanese people. His small stature led to an affectionate nickname, 'mame consul' (baby consul). Mrs. Eusden encouraged and supervised the construction of the first public garden in Hakodate and taught Western methods of laundry in the schools. She and the consul played prominent parts in welcoming the Emperor to Hakodate in 1876. Their departure in 1880 was generally regretted.[2] Their successor, John Quin, left no personal record.

4. HYOGO AND OSAKA

The Early Trade

Although civil war overshadowed the opening of Hyogo and Osaka British merchants hastened to test the anticipated opportunities of these interdependent cities and famed centres of native trade. In a report of June 1867 Sidney Locock, Secretary of the British Legation, had already described not only the industries, great resources, and desire for foreign articles in the area but some of the difficulties foreign trade would encounter. Osaka, a city of 373,514 inhabitants dominated by money-lenders and wholesale and retail merchants, was located three miles from the mouth of a river so shallow that foreign vessels could not ascend it. Ships of all sizes, however, could find shelter and excellent anchorage in the bays of

---

[1] *Hokkaidō Shi*, ii. 793. F.O. 46/65, Parkes to Clarendon, No. 15, 31 Jan. 1866 and F.O. 46/88 is entirely devoted to this discreditable incident, 1866–7. Dickins, op. cit. ii. 68–69.

[2] Great Britain, *Foreign Office List*, 1883, p. 92. *Anglo-Japanese Relations Centering on Hakodate*, pp. 5–6.

Hyogo and Kobe twelve or fourteen miles to the west. The Japanese had selected Kobe (about twenty miles overland from Osaka) for the foreign settlement. It was a wise choice because of an extensive basin with docking facilities well adapted for landing goods. The two cities were thus essential to each other and the difficulties of transport between them—usually via cargo boats loaded from seagoing vessels off the Osaka bar— were to be shared by native and foreign merchants alike.[1]

The *Regulations for Trade* appended to the Treaty of Yedo were enforced in Hyogo when it opened on 1 January 1868. Since Osaka was opened only to foreign trade and not as a port, no foreign vessel could anchor there. Until arrangements could be made for a customs house all foreigners wishing to import goods into the city had to enter them at the customs house at Hyogo according to the *Regulations of Trade* and pay duty there unless paid on the same at another open Japanese port. Likewise all exports by foreigners had to be cleared and the duty paid at Hyogo before being shipped on any foreign vessel.[2] Francis C. Myburg became the first British consul for the consular district of Hyogo and Osaka with residence at Hyogo.[3] The vice-consul, John F. Lowder, lived at Osaka, which was opened as a port to the shipping of foreign powers on 1 September 1868.[4]

The first British merchant said to have begun business in the Kobe–Osaka area was a man named House who arrived in Osaka in December 1867 and tried to sell weapons to the representatives of the feudatories. He went to Kobe as soon as it was opened to import Western textiles and miscellaneous goods.[5] Messrs. Glover and Company were also among the earliest arrivals. In answer to their letter of 10 February 1868 optimistically reporting the prospects for trade and unrealistically anticipating 'Peace for some time to come', the Shanghai office of Jardine, Matheson and Company asked for full details

---

[1] P.P. H. of C. 1867–8, lxix. 237–50.

[2] *Regulations for Trade and Residence of Foreigners at Osaki, 1 Jan. 1868*. Text in *Japan Gazette Hong List and Directory*, 1872.

[3] Parkes's *Notification*, Osaka, 1 Jan. 1868. Myburg died three weeks later.

[4] Ibid., Yokohama, 30 July 1868.

[5] Murata Seiji, *Kōbe Kaikō 30-nen Shi* (Thirty Years after the Opening of Kobe Port), 2 vols. (Kobe, 1898), i. 297. The romanization of his name may not be correct.

regarding the political situation as well as arrangements for the sale and price of land. The firm said 'we have every intention of purchasing a good site if procurable on reasonable terms'.[1] Although the area was disturbed by the Bizen affair a government notification assuring the natives of safety and protection and inviting them to trade with friendly feelings towards foreigners led to 'considerable quantities of tea, copper, and silk being offered and every evidence of a smart trade springing up'. This continued until the murder of the French seamen at Sakai on 8 March. All chance for trade except in arms and munitions of war of every description was then upset. The probable author of this report was again Glover, who went on to say that copper was no longer a government monopoly but could be sold by anyone at the market rate. As Japan had masses of it, quantities would find their way to Shanghai and Hong Kong. He predicted that 'silk, tea, copper, perhaps vegetable wax, and tobacco' would form the staple exports for Europe, and copper, isinglass, seaweed, *béche-de-mer*, and *paon-yu* for China. It was not yet settled whether the export of copper cash would be allowed.[2]

By May Glover was admitting that all branches of trade were neglected owing to the temporary residence of the Mikado with many daimyo in Osaka, rumour of more fighting, and 'the extremely dear price and scarcity of money'.[3] He was sure, however, that Osaka was the place 'where an immensely large trade' would be done because it was the residence of 'all the monied merchants of Japan whose trade is to advance the daimyo money on the produce of their countries'. He thought the portion of produce sent to Yokohama would now be disposed of in Osaka and advised Jardine, Matheson against 'building to any extent in Yokohama'. Glover and Company already had 'establishments' in both Osaka and Hyogo and recommended that Keswick send Jardine's own man to Osaka at the commencement of the silk season to conduct their purchases and 'secure an influence'.[4]

[1] J.M. MSS. (Letter Book ii), Shanghai Office to Glover and Co., 21 Feb. 1868.

[2] Ibid. (Hyogo, 1868), to Shanghai Office, 21 Mar. 1868. The end of this letter is missing so there is no signature. *Paon-yu*, literally, 'peacock jade', is a pseudo-emerald.

[3] Ibid. (Osaka, 1868), Glover and Co. to Shanghai Office, 10 May 1868.

[4] Ibid., T. Glover to W. Keswick, 11 May 1868.

Since the opening of the cities foreign merchants had been living in temples or had leased at very high rents Japanese houses or godowns, sake breweries, or warehouses connected with them, as no preparation had been made for their residence in either city.[1] During the summer gold and arms in great quantities were shipped from Shanghai to Glover and Company at Hyogo while they and others waited for a chance to build more permanent quarters.[2] By September the land designated for the foreign settlement at Kobe had been raised above sea level, drained, and made ready for the erection of buildings. Lots were first sold at auction on 10 September at the customs house. The lowest selling price of lots on the bund was 8 *ichibu* per *tsubo*. Aspinall and Cornes, agents for the North Fire and Life Insurance Company and the Pacific and Oriental Steam Navigation Company, bought lot No. 1. Glover and Company bought No. 11 at 13 *ichibu* per *tsubo* as well as No. 84 on wide Kyōmachi for which they paid 32¼ *ichibu* per *tsubo*, the highest of all prices. E. H. Hunter, another English firm, bought No. 29 in the same area at 8¼ *ichibu* per *tsubo*. Two more sales of lots followed, on 1 June 1869 and 16 May 1870. Lots were first sold in the Osaka settlement on 15 September 1868. Prices were higher than at Kobe because foreigners thought Osaka would be the greater centre of trade.[3]

As the civil war ended with the surrender of the Aizu clan in November the prospects for foreign trade increased. During the summer T. B. Glover had negotiated successfully for the Meiji government's purchase of the Hong Kong mint and its installation in Osaka.[4] New demands for gold and silver followed. At an interview with the Japanese officials in charge of purchasing metals for the coining of Japanese money, Glover was asked to import 600 *piculs* of San Francisco silver and 5,000 bars of Peking gold a month to meet the current consumption and was promised it would be purchased at once.[5] Although he advised against such a large transaction at the start he was soon convinced of a continuing and profitable demand for

---

[1] *Japan Chronicle, Jubilee Number, 1868–1918*, pp. 10–11.

[2] J.M. MSS. (Japan Letter Book ii), Shanghai Office to Glover and Co., 24 June and 31 Aug. 1868.

[3] *Japan Chronicle, Jubilee Number, 1868–1918*, p. 16. *Tsubo* = about 36 square feet.

[4] See p. 402.

[5] J.M. MSS. (Osaka, 1868), T. Glover to H. B. Johnson in Shanghai, 3 Dec. 1868.

gold. Besides the needs of the mint he was offered outside contracts for one or two hundred bars of gold at $240.00 to $245.00.[1]
He calculated the profits from gold and silver for the mint at
from four to six per cent. a month and urged Keswick to put
through the contract before the banks could 'step in and spoil
our rates'.[2] Thus the treasure trade became a major item in the
commerce of Hyogo-Osaka from their first year as open ports.

In spite of the political disturbances, poor communication
between the cities, and the depreciated state of the currency,
combined with the marked indifference of the wealthy native
merchants to contacts with foreign traders, the amount of
foreign trade carried on in 1868 was not discouraging. Several
compilations of figures exist. None are completely accurate, and
none distinguish British trade from that of other countries.
The customs house statistics, considered an underestimate
because of laxity in the enforcement of customs dues, give
$449,388 as the value of the exports and $687,752 for imports.
Figures produced by the foreign merchants and compiled by
the *Hyogo News* state that the direct foreign trade amounted to
$388,096 in exports and $822,404 in imports. In addition
there was still larger trade with the open ports of Japan.[3]

1869–1875

The development of the two cities during the next fifteen
years was vastly different. Those who believed that Osaka would
become the great foreign commercial centre were doomed to
disappointment. The conveyance between Hyogo–Kobe and
Osaka remained unsatisfactory and in 1869 the scheme for
improving Osaka harbour was abandoned. The British consul
recognized that Hyogo would become the shipping centre but
thought Osaka would remain the market. The anchorage at
Hyogo had already been improved and the foreign settlement
at Kobe had prospects of becoming one of the best in the East.
Few ships bound directly for Europe or America came to these
ports as yet but a startling increase in the coastal shipping
already proved that Hyogo and Osaka were important markets

---

[1] J.M. MSS. (Osaka, 1868), T. Glover to H. B. Johnson in Shanghai, 16 Dec.
1868.

[2] Ibid., T. Glover to W. Keswick, 17 Dec. 1868.

[3] Cons. Report for Hyogo-Osaka, 1868, pp. 23–25. *Japan Chronicle, Jubilee
Number, 1868–1918*, p. 33.

for the disposal of imports originally sent to Yokohama and other places. The general shipping of Hyogo in its second year, 1869, exceeded that of Yokohama in her tenth year. There was also in 1869 an improvement in the import of staples such as cotton, woollen manufactures, and sugar and it seemed clear that tea would become the main export of the port. The continuing depreciation of Japanese currency and fluctuations in exchange, however, led merchants to dubious banking speculations and checked normal commercial transactions.[1] In February Jardine's had written Glover that they considered the mint authorities 'already liable to make good the loss on their depreciated issues affair, each succeeding issue appearing to contain a greater percentage of alloy than the one preceding. The last receipts from Hyogo will not realize more than taels 20 per 100 in this market.'[2]

Although all trade figures remained inadequate and unreliable it is clear that both imports and exports increased with a prevailing unfavourable balance for Japan. Direct trade with England grew. More than one and a third million dollars in gold and silver were imported in 1870 which aroused hope for the issue of good gold and silver money. Foreigners were optimistic about the prospects of the port. Hyogo proper and Kobe were now united by a line of Japanese houses on the main road. All remaining lots in the foreign settlement were disposed of at the third land sale. The area was drained, paved, and lighted. The British owned nearly half of it. Branches of two British banks, the Hong Kong and Shanghai and Oriental Bank Corporations, were established. Natives moved rapidly into the settlement, the population increasing from approximately 1,000 in 1868 to 40,000 in 1873.[3] Industries sprang up in Osaka—two steam rice mills, a powder mill, and copper smelting works.[4]

The great success of the mint and new currency policies inspired confidence. The *kinsatsu* (gold notes) issued in 1868 circulated at par in 1873. The old gold and silver coins were no longer in use; neither were the new gold and silver yen

---

[1] P.P. H. of C. 1870, lvx. 23–27, Cons. Report for Hyogo and Osaka, 1869.

[2] J.M. MSS. (Japan Letter Book ii), Shanghai Office to Glover and Company at Hyogo, 19 Feb. 1869.

[3] P.P. H. of C. 1871, lxvii. 25–31, 45, Cons Report for Hyogo and Osaka, 1870. *Japan Chronicle, Jubilee Number*, pp. 34, 36 f.

[4] P.P. H. of C. 1871, lxvii. 31–32, Cons. Report for Hyogo and Osaka, 1870.

generally in circulation among the Japanese people. Paper money, the *kinsatsu* and *yensatsu* (yen notes), were the circulating medium. To them were added notes of ten, five, and one yen, issued by the Mitsui bank which on presentation at the office were payable in gold yen. The Hong Kong and Shanghai Bank also aided local trade with the issue of $100, $50, $10, and $5 (Mexican) notes payable to the bearer. Kobe and Osaka were at last connected by railway. Four British marine insurance companies and nine fire insurance companies competed in Hyogo with eighteen of the former and seven of the latter established by other Westerners or Chinese. The total trade of Hyogo in foreign vessels exclusive of treasure was estimated in 1873 at £1,773,664, that of Osaka £273,226. Of this Britain's share at Hyogo amounted to £583,403, at Osaka £70,998. Native-owned steamers with foreign captains and engineers already provided regular communication between Osaka, Hyogo, Yokohama, and Yedo as well as some ports on the Inland Sea and were gradually monopolizing the coasting trade.[1]

The failure of the Ono Bank and other large Japanese firms in Osaka had a depressing effect on business in 1874. Even so, both imports and exports increased at Hyogo. And there was a vast export of treasure.[2] The number of foreign ships entering the ports, however, declined. The Pacific Mail Steamship Co. supplied a large proportion of the tonnage, although its monopoly of the important local traffic between Hyogo, Yokohama, and Shanghai since 1868 was now challenged by two Japanese lines. Among British firms, the Hyogo Gas Company had completed its plant and under contract with the Municipal Council was satisfactorily lighting the public lamps; the Japan Papermaking Company, with its head office in London, had erected large works to convert rags and other material into pulp for the use of paper-makers in Europe and America; and E. C. Kirby of Yokohama, having established the Kobe Iron Works and a shipyard at Ono in 1873, was promoting industry and

---

[1] Cons. Report for Hyogo and Osaka, 1873, pp. 15, 16, 20, 25–27.

[2] Cons. Report for Hyogo and Osaka, 1874, pp. 68–69, 71. Total imports at Hyogo in 1874 were estimated at $5,288,868; exports at $4,396,360; but treasure to the extent of $3,983,627 was exported as against $1,618,272 imported.

training Japanese in all branches of engine-making and ship-building. The many and varied industries of Osaka were apparently directed and owned by Japanese.[1]

The Decline of Osaka

From 1875 onwards, for perhaps twenty-five years, the foreign trade of Osaka remained insignificant. Its railway connexion with Hyogo and its still unimproved harbour led to the centralization of foreign trade at Hyogo. Almost its entire foreign community moved to the more prosperous port. The few remaining British residents were generally employed at the railway works near Kyoto, at the mint, and in the colleges.[2] Not a single British firm was left in Osaka in 1876, and no foreign vessel called at the city. Native trade and industry prospered. Almost daily Japanese steamers laden with Japanese goods or foreign merchandise from Yokohama entered or cleared from or to the Inland Sea. Although this native trade in foreign products increased the foreign merchants showed little interest in it, since the imports were chiefly sugar, drugs, and other Eastern produce and the exports mostly for the Chinese market.

By 1882 the Osaka trade was almost entirely in the hands of Chinese and the foreign settlement, Kawaguchi, had become the headquarters of Christian missionary organizations. The major British contribution to the city's economic life was the Osaka Iron Works founded by E. H. Hunter, which built and repaired ships. The works covered six acres of land and included a dry dock which was capable of docking vessels 220 feet long and drawing nine feet of water. Here thirteen sailing vessels were built in 1882 and two wooden steamers in 1883, one of 500 tons and one of 210 tons, for Inland Sea traffic. Two steamers of 400 tons and 650 tons respectively and a foreign barque were also docked and repaired.[3]

Growth of Hyogo-Kobe, 1875–1883

Although Hyogo felt the adverse effects of the depression of 1875 and the Japanese currency fluctuations in 1880 and

[1] Cons. Report for Hyogo and Osaka 1874, pp. 50, 57, 59, 63–65.
[2] P.P. H. of C. 1876, lxxvi. 25–26, Cons. Report for Osaka, 1875.
[3] Cons. Reports for Osaka, 1876, 1878, 1879, 1880, 1881, 1882, and 1883. *Japan Chronicle, Jubilee Number, 1868–1918*, pp. 33 and 35.

1881, its foreign trade grew almost steadily, rising from Y 1,113,740 in 1868 to Y 12,961,842 in 1883. In 1876 the P. and O. steamers first called regularly at Kobe on the trip between Hong Kong and Yokohama. The foundations of the great shipping and shipbuilding centre of the future were already laid by 1883 when Japan's exports again exceeded her imports and the value of her money was being stabilized.[1] Exports rose and fell according to the foreign need for rice and the American demand for tea. Fans made in Osaka became an important item for export. The British found they could not compete with France and Germany in the manufacture of *mousselines-de-laine* which in 1875 comprised one-fifth of the total imports. That same year the Pacific Mail Company sold the steamers it had been running since 1868 between Shanghai and Yokohama to the Mitsubishi Steam Navigation Company. The vessels continued the same trade under the Japanese flag but ceased to be registered in the foreign shipping of the port. By 1881, a year of great hardship for importers, the Hyogo trade was conducted almost entirely in steamers bound via the Suez for London and New York. The sailing vessels which touched there were American carriers of kerosene. The shipbuilding industry prospered. In 1882 Messrs. Kirby and Company of the Ono Iron Works constructed the first iron vessels in Japan and the Government Works at Kobe built three steamers of an aggregate tonnage of 650 tons. At the death of the English proprietor in December 1882 the Ono Iron Works became the property of the Naval Department of the Japanese government which carried on its work with most of the same personnel.[2]

During the sixteen years since Hyogo had opened, the amount of shipping entering the port had varied in accordance with the political and financial conditions in Japan. As the period here considered came to a close the British were still the dominant Western nation at the port. Their sailing ships had given place to steamers coming via the Suez Canal, and most of these went to and from England or the British colonies, stopping at intermediate Japanese ports, principally with general cargoes. The British and Americans had yielded much

---

[1] *Japan Chronicle, Jubilee Number, 1868–1918*, pp. 36–36a, estimates of value of Kobe trade 1868–83 from Japanese Customs Reports.
[2] Cons. Reports for Hyogo, 1875, 1878, 1879, 1880, 1881, 1882, and 1883.

of the coastal shipping to Japanese companies. In 1883 fifty-two of the 124 British vessels which entered Hyogo were steamers of the P. and O. Steam Navigation Company, with an aggregate burden of 75,810 tons; fifty-seven, totalling 74,625 tons, were steamers of other lines; and fifteen, of 8,863 tons, were sailing ships. Competing with them and using the facilities of the port were 462 Japanese steamers and six sailing vessels representing a total of 379,342 tons in addition to fifty-three ships from other Western nations with a total of 48,415 tons. Japan's future as a maritime nation was already assured and Britain had pointed the way.[1]

5. NIIGATA

British interest in Niigata was seriously restricted by the city's limited facilities for foreign trade. No group of avid merchants hastened to the opening of its port on 1 January 1869, a year later than designated by the London Protocol because of the civil war. James Troup was appointed to the British consular office as acting consul from 5 August 1869 to 26 September 1871.[2] His report for the port in 1869 was discouraging. No ship had come direct from any foreign country. The only trade had been with other open Japanese treaty ports. Only seventeen foreigners, exclusive of Chinese, had taken up residence. There were none from Britain. The returns from the customs house were as usual unreliable, but figures furnished by the foreign merchants and native junk managers were approximately correct. About sixty per cent. of the goods brought by British and non-Japanese ships had been sold. Cotton and woollen manufactures and cotton yarn held the most important place. Imported manufactures to the value of $788,000 had been brought overland. Total foreign imports were estimated at over $1,300,000. Rice was the main export in British and other non-Japanese ships. The circulation of spurious coins, made by Aizu, Sendai, and other northern daimyo during the civil war, caused difficulty and confusion. Paper money was the ordinary medium of exchange. Prices were cheaper than in any other port.[3]

[1] Cons. Report for Hyogo, 1883, pp. 101-2, 113.
[2] Great Britain, *Foreign Office List*, 1883, p. 194.
[3] P.P. H. of C. 1870, lxv. 82–87, Cons. Report for Niigata, 1869.

The development of Niigata was obviously dependent on the creation of a harbour. Its river did not admit European ships owing to a dangerous bar at its entrance and 'the open unprotected condition of the Niigata roadstead'. The idea that the good harbour at Sado Island nearby would meet the needs of Niigata shipping was soon disproved. The island was small, thinly populated, and had no attractions as a place of business, no produce of any kind, and no trade suited to foreign tastes. Insurance companies vetoed Niigata with premium rates in many cases higher than England, and refused insurance on goods sent to and from Sado. By 1871 Consul Enslie wrote that the efforts of some influential firms to give Niigata a chance because of its nearness to districts rich in copper, lead, gold, silver, petroleum, gas, rock salt, and rice, had stopped. Only one firm, a German house, was left. Trade and shipping were gradually decreasing and would probably stop in a few years. Although the total produce of the seven provinces, of which Niigata was the natural centre, approached £4,500,000, the problem of transport had to be solved before foreign trade could be enlarged. To send the two staple articles, copper and rice, overland to Yokohama would raise the price of rice 200 per cent. and copper $16\frac{1}{2}$ per cent.[1]

John Gubbins inspected the mines in Sado, then flooded with water. Five or six years were needed to bring the mines into working order. An Englishman, Mr. J. Scott, was in charge of the machinery for crushing the quartz and new smelting works then approaching completion.

Three years later, up to the spring of 1874, there were only five foreign residents in Niigata, two Germans, one Dutchman, one Frenchman, and Mr. Moss, an Englishman who taught in the local school. Niigata, however, was growing and prospering. Japanese were moving in from other towns. An energetic Japanese governor had laid out new streets, provided them with lamps, and repaired the canals. A prison, a hospital, and a school were erected. Japanese junks carried on the trade in native goods and produce. The trade in foreign goods depended on road communication with Yedo. Probably to facilitate this and communication in general the Mikami route was being

---

[1] P.P. H. of C. 1872, lix. 76–84, 90, Cons. Report for Niigata, 1871.

repaired. Although 'trade in foreign goods and foreign manufactures in foreign bottoms' were not extensive, the British
consul believed that Niigata would some day 'take rank with
the principal towns of Japan'.[1]

By 1876 no direct foreign trade had yet developed at this
western port; the small coast trade for a year or two carried on
in foreign ships had entirely ceased. The same trade in Japanese
steamers was small and out of proportion to the number of
ships engaged in it. A choice between admitting that Niigata
was unsuitable for foreign trade or finding means to make it a
practical port for foreign vessels seemed necessary. The smallness
of the existing foreign interests hardly justified the expense of
keeping up the machinery of an open port. Imports in Japanese
steamers and sailing vessels of foreign build amounted to
$94,090, exports to $58,850. Niigata had not fulfilled the
purpose for which it was opened.[2]

In 1877 only three foreign ships, two British and one Danish,
came into Niigata, with a total burden of 859 tons. There were
six British members in the foreign community of fifteen people.[3]
Vice-Consul Troup was transferred to Nagasaki as consul and
if the *Foreign Office List* is correct no resident consul was appointed
to take his place.[4] Up until 1879 the commercial reports on
the port were signed by men holding positions elsewhere
who made brief visits to Niigata to check on its development.
Thereafter no annual reports on the city for the remainder of the
period here discussed have been found in English or American
libraries.

In 1878 the Japanese finance minister assured Parkes that
the proposed work for clearing the bar of the river would
commence the next spring. A good harbour could then be
expected and foreign and native trade would develop. It was
now recognized that from the end of March until mid-October
vessels could load and unload at Niigata without difficulty.
The foreign import trade was still slight and strictly confined to
reimports from other open ports. There was a fairly extensive
business in foreign-made articles carried on by Japanese

[1] Cons. Report for Niigata, 1874, pp. 3–6.
[2] P.P. H. of C. 1877, lxxxiv. 64, 73–76, Cons. Report for Niigata, 1876.
[3] Ibid., 1878, lxxv. 78–80, Cons. Report for Niigata, 1877.
[4] Great Britain, *Foreign Office List*, 1880, p. 195.

merchants in the city and the surrounding districts. And the transport of merchandise overland by pack horses from Yokohama could be arranged at nominal rates. Exports in 1878 soared in value to $524,167 because of large shipments of rice to Hong Kong, the China ports, Manila, and Yokohama. The difference in prices of rice in Niigata and outside places made possible a reasonable margin for profit. Sixteen foreign ships, including nine British—total tonnage 13,846—had entered and cleared. Seventeen Mitsubishi steamers and sailing vessels with an aggregate tonnage of 17,880 tons had called, usually on their way from Yokohama via Hakodate. Shippers and merchants, however, could not consider this increase in trade in relation to 1877 indicative of steady future development. The movements of the steamers were too uncertain; freight rates were too high; and the port manager was too inefficient to make trade in these bottoms as remunerative as it should be.[1]

The only currency used in the entire *ken* was paper money (yen). This, according to W. A. Woolley, who visited Niigata briefly as Acting Vice-Consul in 1879, was a major cause of the collapse of the foreign import business the next year. Unaccustomed to the low value of paper money ruling in the other open ports in 1879, the native merchants refused to pay sufficiently high prices to enable the foreign importer, who usually paid for his goods in dollars, to realize a profit. Only one British steamer arrived during the season and few purchasers were found for its limited cargo valued at Y 9,170. The ship cleared for Manila carrying rice worth Y 47,302—the main export in a foreign vessel that season. In contrast the Mitsubishi steamers brought in foreign and domestic products valued at $674,085 and exported $672,880 worth of rice and small quantities of other native produce. This meant a total increase of exports and imports over 1878 of nearly a million dollars. But it was all in the hands of the Japanese and was likely to remain there until the new harbour and breakwater were built and foreigners could bring in their goods more cheaply and obtain desirable return freights.[2]

---

[1] P.P. H. of C. 1878–9, lxxii. 66–72, Cons. Report for Niigata, 1878.

[2] P.P. H. of C. 1880, lxxv. 1–8, Cons. Report for Niigata, 1879; 1886 lxvi. 1–2, Report of J. S. Quin for Niigata and Sado, 1879–June 1884 shows no direct foreign trade at Niigata after 1879.

6. JAPAN'S FOREIGN TRADE 1859–1883

In spite of the inaccuracies of the statistics for Japan's foreign trade in the late *Bakufu* and early Meiji periods, admitted by the British consuls in their contemporary reports and evident today in the differences in the figures compiled by both Japanese and British authorities,[1] the figures show trends generally agreed upon and have historical value as the basis on which business risks and economic policy were undertaken. It is clear that from 1859 until 1866 Japan's exports exceeded her imports and both rose steadily—the former from $1,200,000 in 1859 to $16,054,000 in 1866, the latter from $750,000 to $12,510,000.[2] Britain had the lion's share in this trade although, separate figures for her exports and imports at each treaty port for this period are not often known. Ishii Takashi has estimated that for the three years 1863–5 she controlled respectively 79, 94, and 88 per cent. of the total exports and 73, 83, and 81 per cent. of the total imports of Japan.[3] The consuls and merchants found much satisfaction in these developments, the former writing optimistic reports home, the latter in many cases laying the foundations of great fortunes. Even in England where the Japan trade during the Shogunate never amounted to even one per cent. of Britain's total imports or exports, both the government and the merchants considered Japan an important commercial frontier to be expanded and defended within the terms of the Treaty of Yedo.[4] Japanese cotton filled a great need in 1863 and 1864 when the American Civil War cut off the American supply of cotton. Japanese raw silk and silkworm eggs saved the silk industry in Europe when a widespread disease nearly destroyed silk culture in France and Italy. And both the *Bakufu* and the daimyo proved profitable customers for British ships, arms, and ammunition as the civil conflict in Japan became inevitable.

The situation changed rapidly in 1867 when Japan's balance of payments became unfavourable. With the exception of 1868

[1] Compare the figures of Horie Yasuzō in *Nihon Shihonshugi no Seiritsu* (The Formation of Japanese Capitalism), (Osaka, 1939), pp. 108, 194, cited in T. C. Smith, *Political Change and Industrial Development in Japan: Government Enterprise, 1868–1880*, p. 24, with Borton, *Japan's Modern Century*, p. 57.

[2] Figures from Borton, *Japan's Modern Century*, p. 57.

[3] Ishii Takashi, *Bakumatsu Bōeki Shi no Kenkyū* (Study of History of Trade in the Late *Bakufu* Period), (Tokyo, 1944), p. 80.   [4] For figures see Table I, p. 368.

and 1876, her imports exceeded her exports until 1880 by an annual average of Y 5,746,000.[1] Cotton and woollen manufactures, arms, munitions, sugar, and sometimes rice were then her chief imports. Silk, silkworm eggs, tea, and vegetable wax led her exports. According to British records her total foreign trade, excluding the treasure which annually left the country, grew from $28,076,062 in 1867 to $64,041,872 in 1880.[1] In 1881 when Japan's exports nearly equalled her imports—Y 30,219,000 as against Y 30,797,000—Parkes sent Granville summaries of Japan's foreign trade for the past fifteen years with his explanation of the causes of what he called its 'stationary condition'.[2]

The British minister took a dreary view of these figures. 'The commercial capacity of the country depends of course upon its productive power', he said, 'and that measured by its foreign exports falls below the expectations that have naturally been formed of a country so favourably situated as Japan. Taking the value of the foreign exports at $30,000,000, the production of the country over and above its own wants averages about 86 cents, or say 3*s*. 6*d*. per head of the population of 35,000,000. This denotes a low state of national enterprise, and no great material advancement may be looked for so long as three great obstacles to improvement exist.

'These are the absence of capital'—the employment of foreign capital was forbidden by law; 'the excessive dearness of transport in the interior'—the cost of sending a ton of goods 50 miles into the interior on the backs of men or pack horses equalled that of sending it from Japan to Europe; 'and the great fluctuations in the depreciated paper which forms the currency of the land'. The last, Parkes continued, 'occasion fluctuations of corresponding violence in the price of all commodities and of the necessaries of life, they render all business transaction hazardous and uncertain, they effectually impede the prosecution of all industries which require time for development, and they cause honest but laborious trade to be forsaken for the attractions of gambling on the currency exchanges'.

---

[1] T. C. Smith, *Political Change and Industrial Development in Japan*, pp. 24–25. These figures differ from those of Sir Harry Parkes which show a favourable balance of trade also for 1871 when according to a synopsis of the consular reports for that year Japan's imports totalled $17,745,605 and her exports $19,184,805. P.P. H. of C. 1882, lxxii. 96, *General Report of the Foreign Trade of Japan*, 1881.

[2] See Table II, p. 369.

As to transport, Parkes pointed out that given Japan's extensive coastline which 'leaves no part of the country distant more than 100 miles from the sea, the carrying needs of the country might be met to a great extent by marine transport. But native shipping, being limited in amount, and mainly confined to two privileged Companies, is also abnormally costly, and the service of cheap foreign tonnage is forbidden to the people.' The latter are therefore unable to convey heavy produce to the treaty ports, where it would be readily bought by foreigners if obtainable at remunerative rates. Parkes also recognized that in her lighter commodities, tea and silk, which formed the bulk of her exports, Japan was competing with India and China and was handicapped by restraints which prevented the Japanese producers from dealing directly with the foreigners at the treaty ports while the latter could neither deal with the former in the producing districts nor visit them for commercial purposes.

'While this state of things continues', Parkes wrote, 'and the Japanese retain their present economical opinions, which deprive trade of the freedom that is essential to its vitality and run it into the narrow groove of monopolists and guilds, the commerce of the country must be expected to remain in a comparatively stationary condition.' Since it was obvious that Japan could not buy more than she could pay for, that her power to purchase had to be measured by her power to export, Parkes asked that British exporters perceive that their shipments for some time past had been in excess of demand, and that Japan could consume only a limited amount of foreign imports, even when supplied at prices which left no profit to the exporter.[1]

Matsukata's policy of retrenchment soon followed Parkes's advice for importers. In 1882 and 1883 Japan exported more than she imported. And an improvement in the preparation of the returns of the customs house made it possible for the first time to learn with approximate correctness in 1883 the share of each treaty power in the Japan trade. The value of Japan's imports was Y 27,974,000, that of her exports Y 35,694,000 in 1883, the year Sir Harry Parkes left Japan. Great Britain at that time controlled 45·56 per cent. of the former and 13·53 per

[1] P.P. H. of C. 1882, lxxii. 88-89.

cent of the latter.¹ Cotton and woollen manufactures, metals,
kerosene, and sugar were now the chief imports. Raw silk, tea,
coal, dried fish, and rice dominated the exports. Here the
American demand for tea and of France for silk caused
Britain to take third place in Japan's export trade.² And in
relation to Britain's total foreign trade the trade with Japan
still had only fractional importance.³

TABLE I

*Great Britain: Imports from and Exports to all Countries
and Japan, 1859–1883*

(In thousands of £)

	British imports from All countries	Japan	Per cent. from Japan	British exports to All countries	Japan	Per cent. to Japan
1859	139,708	97	0·07	106,042	3	0·002
1860	167,571	168	0·10	117,988	(a)	
1861	164,809	539	0·32	114,493	44	0·04
1862	160,434	592	0·36	120,744	(a)	
1863	164,235	1,284	0·78	141,932	126	0·09
1864	181,208	1,424	0·78	156,908	667	0·42
1865	198,231	615	0·31	167,285	1,654	0·98
1866	223,085	274	0·12	181,738	1,560	0·85
1867	214,449	318	0·14	172,440	1,694	0·98
1868	227,700	181	0·08	174,061	1,219	0·70
1869	225,044	167	0·07	185,123	1,592	0·86
1870	238,425	96	0·04	188,689	1,777	0·94
1871	238,071	109	0·04	228,013	1,746	0·76
1872	275,321	184	0·06	248,980	2,147	0·86
1873	290,277	561	0·19	239,857	1,884	0·78
1874	287,920	573	0·19	219,740	1,364	0·62
1875	289,516	378	0·13	204,957	2,594	1·26
1876	290,822	657	0·22	186,627	2,191	1·17
1877	304,866	734	0·24	176,594	2,460	1·39
1878	290,835	629	0·21	173,491	2,906	1·67
1879	284,049	451	0·15	182,274	2,998	1·64
1880	318,711	532	0·16	204,887	3,813	1·86
1881	305,483	676	0·22	210,402	3,152	1·49
1882	313,589	721	0·22	214,323	2,408	1·12
1883	328,210	663	0·20	215,036	2,601	1·21

(a) Less than £260.

SOURCE: Great Britain, Board of Trade *Statistical Abstract for the United Kingdom*,
17th number, 1854–1869 (London, 1870), pp. 22–31, and 31st number, 1869–83
(London, 1884), pp. 36–37.

¹ See Table II, p. 369. For Matsukata, see p. 410.
² P.P. H. of C. 1884–85, lxxxi. 178–90, *Summary of the Foreign Trade of Japan,
1883*.   ³ See Table I.

TABLE II

Japan: Imports from and Exports to all Countries and Great Britain, 1873–1883

(In thousands of Yen)

	Japanese imports from		*Per cent. from* Gr. Brit.	*Japanese exports to*		*Per cent. to* Gr. Brit.
	All countries	*Gr. Brit.*		*All countries*	*Gr. Brit.*	
1873	27,617	11,907	43·11	21,142	5,169	24·44
1874	22,925	10,520	45·88	18,780	3,233	17·21
1875	29,332	14,655	49·96	17,968	2,478	13·79
1876	23,478	11,089	47·23	27,225	7,017	25·77
1877	27,063	15,658	57·85	22,976	6,298	27·41
1878	32,564	19,227	59·04	25,525	3,857	15·11
1879	32,508	16,841	51·80	27,389	4,054	14·80
1880	36,176	19,574	54·10	27,418	2,545	9·28
1881	30,797	16,365	53·13	30,219	3,514	11·62
1882	29,168	13,956	47·84	37,236	4,982	13·37
1883	27,974	12,745	45·56	35,694	4,832	13·53

SOURCE: Japan Bureau of Customs, *Returns of Foreign Trade of Japan for the Eighteen Years from 1868–1885 Inclusive* (Tokyo, 1885), pp. 261–2. In 1881 these figures were first accepted by the British Board of Trade and published in the *Statistical Abstract for the Principal and other Foreign Countries in each year from 1874–1883*, 12th number (London, 1886), p. 149. Before 1881 the British *Statistical Abstract* cited gives no figures for Japan's foreign trade. And British figures in the Consular Reports, e.g. those for 1867–81 on p. 96 in the Cons. Report for 1881 (Japan No. 1 (1882), Pt. II), differ from those of the Japanese for some of the years perhaps because of varying exchange rates when converting dollars into yen.

XIII

THE ENGINEERING PROJECTS OF
RICHARD HENRY BRUNTON

Lighthouses

THE need for Western engineers was inevitable in Japan's efforts to make her ports and coasts safe for the navigation of Western ships in fulfilment of her promise in the Convention of 1866. British and French naval authorities recommended the sites most in need of lights and the apparatus required. Parkes sent these suggestions to the *Rōjū* on 17 November 1866, urging the promotion of the work. Eleven lights were soon agreed upon, three of which were commissioned in France and completed by the engineer in charge of the Yokosuka arsenal. The *Bakufu* asked Her Majesty's Government to provide estimates for the cost of eight lighthouses and assured it of payment. The matter was referred to the Board of Trade, which hesitated to order apparatus before Japan had organized a lighthouse service and trained some keepers. Arrangements were also delayed by having to get the consent of the daimyo in whose territories some lights were to be erected as well as their agreement to share in the costs.[1] After consultation with Trinity House[2] the Board of Trade commissioned Messrs. D. and T. Stevenson (M.M.Inst.C.E.), the engineers to the Commissioners of Northern Lights, on 6 November 1867 to select the personnel to design and construct the lighthouses and introduce the lighthouse service into Japan. The Board of Trade was to manage and supervise the arrangements while Messrs. Stevenson had charge of the construction of the lights.[3] Meanwhile Parkes had ordered in August 1867 the apparatus for five more lights which the Japanese government authorized

---

[1] F.O. 46/72, Parkes to Stanley, No. 213, Yedo, 30 Dec. 1866. F.O. 262/123, Stanley to Parkes, 4 May 1867. Black, op. cit. ii. 276.

[2] The department in London in charge of pilots, lighthouses, and buoys.

[3] Richard Henry Brunton, 'The Japan Lights', *Minutes of Proceedings of the Institution of Civil Engineers* (hereafter cited as *Japan Lights*), Session 1876-7, Pt. I (London, 1877), p. 2. Brunton gives six lights ordered while Parkes gave eight.

for lighting the Inland Sea and the approaches to Kobe and Osaka.¹ The Shogunate had already forwarded to the Board an instalment of £10,729 3s. 4d. on the cost of the lighthouses for Yedo Bay with the promise of a similar sum in three months, when the government of Japan passed into the hands of the young Emperor Meiji.²

In spite of the civil war the new régime continued the light-house programme with Parkes as intermediary with the Board of Trade. On 24 February 1868 Richard Henry Brunton, a twenty-seven-year-old civil engineer who had been educated in the private schools of Scotland and had had ten years' experience in railway and building services in Great Britain, was appointed chief engineer. He had a five-year contract to work under the orders and instructions of the Minister or Vice-Minister of Public Works of the Japanese government at $450 a month. A rider to this agreement signed in Edinburgh on 25 May 1868 gave Brunton complete authority in his department in carrying out the orders of the Ministry of Public Works, promised to raise his salary to $600 on 1 September 1870, required two years' notice on the part of the government or Brunton before breaking the contract, and made provisions regarding dismissal, illness, holidays, and travel expenses for himself and his family.³

The young engineer arrived at Yokohama on 8 August 1868 with two assistants, Blundell and Mcbean and the equipment for the lighthouses. Although the Meiji government gave a reception in their honour upon their arrival, Parkes was the only medium of communication between them and the Japanese authorities for many months. He conducted all financial operations and threw his great energy into inaugurating the work without delay. He requisitioned H.M.S. *Manila* to assist the Japanese government in an inspection of the sites on which it was agreed the lighthouses should be built.

¹ Brunton MS., p. 2; *Japan Lights*, p. 3.
² F.O. 46/82, Parkes to Stanley, No. 180, Yedo, 30 Oct. 1867; 262/141, Stanley to Parkes, No. 3, 6 Jan. 1868. Brunton MS., p. 2.
³ Waseda University, Tokyo, Ōkuma Kinen Shakai Kagaku Kenkyūjō (Ōkuma Memorial Institute of Social Sciences), *Ōkuma Shigenobu Monjo* (Papers of Ōkuma Shigenobu), (hereafter cited as Okuma MSS.), C 144 and C 145. Brunton requested the raise with greater security and more benefits in 1870. Note by Griffis on Brunton MS., p. 5.

The lighthouse headquarters, consisting of dwellings, offices, stores, and workshops, were located at Yokohama. Because of the inexperience of the Japanese in carrying out large building operations, it was decided to obtain representative masons, plumbers, machinists, and several light keepers from England.[1] By November Brunton was requesting three more engineers and one workman. The lack of skilled hands was retarding his programme.[2] But progress could be noted by the beginning of 1869—the erection of the light at Kannonzaki half-way up the Bay to Yokohama, the temporary light on the tip of Awa at Nojimagasaki, the first point sighted by ships approaching Yokohama; the purchase of a small British ship *Sunrise* to act as a lightship at the entrance to Yokohama harbour as well as to give lighthouse service; and the beginning of construction with the help of British arkwrights on a lightship which was launched on 24 June 1869 for use at Hakodate.[3] Buoys were placed at Yokohama and Shimonoseki in 1869 and applications for three lighthouses and more lighthouse apparatus were sent to the Board of Trade.[4] By 1870 the Japanese were requesting lighthouse apparatus for Hyogo, Osaka, and the entrance east and west to the Inland Sea, apparently repeating the Shogun's authorization of 1867, which Brunton ordered from Messrs. Stevenson and Company.[5]

Procurement of such apparatus through the British government stopped in 1871. The Japanese wished to deal directly with the contractor.[6] The Japanese also wished to dispense with the English and European lighthouse keepers who had been essential in the beginning until the Japanese learned the work and the importance of a strict routine in the maintenance of the lights. With the reorganization of the Lighthouse Depart-

[1] Ad. I/6094, Keppel to Adm., 12 Jan. 1869. Brunton MS., pp. 5, 6–7. F.O. 46/96, Parkes to Stanley, No. 211, Yokohama, 22 Aug. 1868.

[2] F.O. 46/98, Parkes to Stanley, No. 287, Yokohama, 17 Nov. 1868.

[3] Borton, *Japan's Modern Century*, p. 75. Brunton MS., Sec. xxv. 104.

[4] F.O. 46/111, Parkes to Clarendon, No. 183, Yedo (?), 30 Sept. 1869. Board of Trade, H.4941 contains the correspondence for 1869 on the manning and equipping of these stations.

[5] F.O. 46/124, Parkes to Clarendon, No. 41, Yedo, 12 Mar. 1870. The rapid development of the programme is fully recorded in F.O. 1870, 46/125; 1871, 46/137, 139, and 146; and 1872, 46/151, Adams to Granville, No. 10, Yedo, 10 Jan. 1872, encl. list and report by Brunton.

[6] F.O. 46/141, Adams to Granville, No. 68, Yedo, 13 Sept. 1871; 262/205, F.O. to Adams, No. 46, 29 Nov. 1871.

ment and a newly appointed Japanese official in charge in 1871, Brunton agreed to having two Europeans at the head of only the most important stations since the Japanese wanted their people to learn to hold the second place wherever possible.[1] Altogether forty-seven foreigners—engineers, supervisors, metal workers, instructors, and lighthouse keepers, and teachers were employed by the Meiji government in the first years of the lighthouse project.[2] Statistics for 1873 show that thirty-one lighthouses, two lightships, five buoys, three beacons, and two steam tenders were already in operation. The programme continued to grow with Brunton as superintendent until 1876 when thirty-six lighthouses, two lightships, thirteen buoys, and three beacons had been established and the coast of Japan was comparably as safe as any in Europe.[3]

Brunton's assistant, another Englishman, succeeded him in 1876 in conformity with the advice of the Board of Trade, that the lighthouses should continue for a year or two under experienced foreign supervision until strict discipline could be developed among the native keepers.[4] But Japanese engineers trained abroad or in the new College of Engineering at Tokyo soon replaced all the foreigners in the lighthouse service.[5]

During the course of the lighthouse construction Brunton's difficulties had been great. Not the least was the manifestation of anti-foreign sentiment at many levels in spite of the Meiji government's instructions to local authorites to provide every assistance to the lighthouse project. Thus an 'ignorant, bumptious' functionary appointed to accompany the inspection of lighthouse sites in 1868–9 'bought one vessel and chartered

[1] F.O. 46/140, Parkes to Granville, No. 47, Yedo, 21 Aug. 1871.

[2] Borton, *Japan's Modern Century*, p. 76. Brunton, *Japan Lights*, p. 19 gives only twenty-nine Europeans as the number who helped him during the first eight years. *Meiji Bunka Zenshū*, xvi. 355–7, lists for 1872 the names, length of appointments, and salaries of the foreigners employed in the Lighthouse Department of the Ministry of Engineering from 1868 onwards. Thirty-three out of forty-five were said to be British.

[3] W. E. Griffis, *The Mikado's Empire* (New York 1887, p. 620. Brunton, *Japan Lights*, pp. 22, 24; MS., Sec. xxxiv. 152 gives larger figures which included apparatus on hand to be established.

[4] F.O. 46/191, Parkes to Derby, No. 39, Conf'l., Yedo, 8 Mar. 1875; 262/269, Derby to Parkes, No. 57, 1 June 1875 and encl. from Board of Trade; 46/207, Parkes to Derby, No. 120, Yedo, 18 July 1876.

[5] For description of Engineering College 1873–7 see *Japan Weekly Mail*, 9, 16 Feb. 1878. For inauguration of Imperial College of Engineering see F.O. 46/230, Parkes to Salisbury, Yedo, No. 79, 13 Aug. 1878.

another in order to avoid travelling on a British ship' and did nothing to help the construction of lighthouses.[1] The increase of anti-foreign feeling resulting from the failure of the Iwakura mission of 1871 led even the government's lighthouse functionary to assume a haughty, autocratic attitude, forcing Brunton to struggle against indignities and making Europeans 'mere drudges without authority'.[2] Some of the anti-foreign actions caused Parkes to fear for the safety of foreign shipping.[3] There were many changes in the Japanese officials appointed over the lighthouse office—actually fifteen during Brunton's eight-year period. Some gave instructions without reference to Brunton's schemes which openly clashed.[4] And the cost of the lighthouse construction was kept secret—a covering for the widespread corruption in the use of public money which was not considered discreditable.[5]

The two British engineers who accompanied Brunton to Japan in 1868 resigned at the end of 1869, finding that their salaries of $150 a month were equal to about one-third of their value in England, owing to the very high cost of European food and clothing. Although their salaries were immediately doubled, the inconveniences experienced as engineers in Japan were great enough to prevent them from remaining as Brunton's assistants.[6] In explanation, Brunton wrote to Parkes:

A man arriving in a country like this has many causes for discontent. The nature of his duties disappoint him. He is required, owing to his being the only engineer, to do trifling pieces of work which perhaps years before had been given over to his juniors in the office. On account of the want of many skilled foremen, he is often required personally to supervise work and to explain the minutest details to men unwilling to execute them and to whom the work they are engaged is perfectly new and uninteresting. He has to deal with people tantalizingly slow and lazy and who are wonderfully retentive of their own system of working which it is needless to say is subversive of all the principles of mechanics, and he has his patience severely tried in his dealings with them. Every stone, piece of wood, nail or other small article has to be got by the engineer

---

[1] Brunton MS., p. 55.   [2] Ibid., Sec. xxix. 121 ff.
[3] Ibid., pp. 146–7.   [4] Ibid., p. 94.
[5] Ibid., Sec. xxi. 87–88. Although Brunton gives a total cost of $2,242,800 up until end of 1875 (*Japan Lights*, p. 25), in his manuscript (Sec. xxxiv. 152) he says no accurate figures were known.
[6] F.O. 46/124, Parkes to Clarendon, No. 34, Yokohama, 25 Feb. 1870.

and accounted for by him entailing a considerable amount of trouble. His duties lead him to remote corners of the country for many weeks at a time where he is surrounded by none but natives and is supplied with provisions by the steamer on her monthly visits.

The difference between this and making plans for some large construction in England, putting it into the hands of a trustworthy contractor, and being there and then relieved of all trouble in regard to it can be easily conceived. His advance in position disappoints him. A man does not leave all the ties of home without hope that he is very considerably bettering himself.

If $300 per month be his salary he looks upon it as an equivalent for £800 a year or thereby. But every skilled artizan gets $150 per month here and engineers on steamboats get $200 per month and found in food, bank clerks also getting from 200 to 500 dollars per month. All European articles of food and clothing are three times the price they are at home and of course amusement is out of the question. Therefore a man who exchanges say, £300 a year at home for £800 a year here with the prospect of bettering himself is greviously disappointed. These things should be explained directly to anyone coming here and he should not be allowed to come out in ignorance of them.[1]

Telegraphs

Brunton did more than build lighthouses in Japan. Within a year of his arrival he was asked to construct the first telegraph lines in the Far East—a twenty-two-mile connexion between Yokohama and Yedo, soon followed by another between Osaka and Kyoto, together amounting to 100 miles of wire. The Meiji government instructed him to order the necessary material and appliances from England and to employ an expert who could do the work and teach the Japanese to run the system. The material arrived in September 1869. G. M. Gilbert superintended the building of the lines and initiated Japanese operators in the use of the dial and key. Messages were sent in English and Japanese, the latter requiring forty-two characters. Both the Swiss and Austrian governments had been involved with the Shogunate in a concession for the erection of telegraphs throughout the country which Parkes forestalled after the Restoration. Brunton and his staff, however, used the apparatus and large quantity of wire supplied by Austria to erect a telegraph between

[1] Ibid., encl. Brunton to Parkes, Yokohama, 21 Nov. 1869.

the Imperial Palace and various government offices in Yedo.[1]
And as early as 1871 he was recommending machinery to
connect the police stations in Yedo by telegraph.[2]

Such innovations were not made without opposition. Many
Japanese foretold failure. The popular mind associated the
project with necromancy and Christian propagandism. Sabo-
tage was to be expected. 'Two sworded roughs' hacked at some
posts in the beginning and ignorant people often broke down
the line so that guarding it was difficult. By spring 1870, however, the single wire was hardly adequate to handle the demand
for transmitting Japanese messages between Yedo and Yokohama.[3] A year later the Japanese foreign minister was negotiating for a line between Yedo and Nagasaki which when
completed in 1872 made possible telegraphic communication
with London through the Great Northern Telegraph. Hyogo
and Osaka were then connected with Yedo and a line to
Hakodate was established in 1874.[4] In 1883 195 telegraph offices
had been opened, 2056 *ri* of lines were in operation, and
2,678,860 messages were transmitted.[5]

Other Projects

At the request of the authorities Brunton also designed a
system for drainage and road-making in Yokohama which was
carried out in 1870 to the great benefit of the community. But
his schemes for supplying pure water to the city, for lighting
the settlements at night, and for providing concrete jetty
accommodation were rejected by the Japanese.[6] He made many
important surveys but those of the harbours of Osaka and
Niigata resulted in proposals for improvements which were too
costly for the Japanese. His map of Japan compiled from
Japanese data in 1876, showing towns, villages, rivers, moun-

[1] Brunton MS., Sec. ii. 7–9.

[2] Ōkuma MSS., C147, Brunton to Ōkuma, 21 Jan. 1871.

[3] P.P. H. of C. 1870, lxx. 95, Parkes to Clarendon, Yedo, 21 Apr. 1870. Henry
Dyer, *Dai Nippon, The Britain of the East* (London, 1904), p. 145.

[4] The Great Northern Telegraph Company was a Danish concern. It connected
the European network with Nagasaki as its end station. F.O. 46/139, Parkes to
Granville, No. 67, Yokohama, 22 May 1871. Cons. Report for Hyogo and Osaka
1873, p. 26; 1874, p. 61.

[5] Dyer, op. cit., p. 147. A *ri* is 3·927 kilometres.

[6] Black, op. cit. ii. 277–8. F.O. 46/142, Adams to Granville, No. 94, Yedo,
21 Oct. 1871; 46/52, same to same, no. 32, Yedo, 5 Feb. 1872. Brunton MS.,
Secs. i, iii, iv, v.

PLATE 10

Asakusa Temple and Telegraph Office, 1874
By Okada Kuniteru

tains, roads, etc., at a scale of twenty miles to an inch, with the Japanese names romanized, was considered the standard work of its kind.[1] In all Brunton claimed to have erected over forty important public buildings. During their construction he had become so impressed with the aptitude, intelligence, and efficiency of Japanese carpenters that he had been able to dispense with European assistance altogether and later recommended Japanese carpenters for work in England.[2]

His ingenuity and energy were dauntless. When the first illuminating apparatus for the lighthouses was lost in a wreck off Formosa in 1869 and Parkes insisted upon going ahead with the project without awaiting replacements from England, Brunton directed Japanese coppersmiths to make kerosene-burning lamps according to his design, to be erected as temporary lights on the more important headlands.[3] And with only Japanese mechanics whom he taught to cut iron plates, make holes for rivets, and to fit and rivet together the whole girders, he built the first iron bridge without mishap in Japan.[4]

Black believes 'fickleness hidden under the mask of economy' led the Japanese to notify Brunton in March 1875 that his services would not be required at the end of another year. Nevertheless his work was appreciated. Itō Hirobumi made this clear. The Mikado gave him an audience, followed by a banquet at the palace, when he was presented with a cheque for £500 in gratitude for his work.[5]

[1] Brunton MS., Sec. ix. 39.
[2] Letter from Brunton 5 Jan. 1875 in *Japan Weekly Mail* of 2 Mar. 1878, p. 193.
[3] Brunton MS., Sec. xxiv. 102.
[4] Ibid., Sec. v. 17–19. Borton, *Japan's Modern Century*, pp. 75–76.
[5] Brunton MS., Sec. xxvi. 108–10, 150–1. Black, op. cit. ii. 277.

XIV

BRITISH BANKS, LOANS, AND BANKERS

The British Banks

BRITISH banks did not follow immediately the establishing of branches of the great merchant firms in the Japanese treaty ports. The leading British houses, Jardine, Matheson and Company and Dent and Company, carried on their financial operations through Shanghai and Hong Kong and profiting by the Tokugawa's overvaluation of silver in terms of gold had little need of banking facilities in the years immediately following July 1859. Towards the end of 1860 the Chartered Bank of India, Australia and China, established by Royal Charter in 1853 and operating in Shanghai by August 1858, had sent its Shanghai manager to Nagasaki to report on the prospects for setting up an agency in Japan. He advised against it on the grounds that conditions were not yet ripe for such an enterprise.[1] Rival British banks in India and China soon took the risk. In 1863, encouraged by the growth of the Japan trade, the Chartered Mercantile Bank of India, London, and China opened a branch in Yokohama under the management of Robert Brett. The next year the Central Bank of Western India followed suit with Charles Rickerby in charge of its Yokohama office. Branches of the Commercial Bank Corporation of India and the East with Charles S. Lynill as agent and the Oriental Bank Corporation, managed by J. G. Rickard, were founded in 1865.[2] Messrs. Marshall and Macpherson, British merchants

---

[1] Information from MS. by J. Leighton-Boyce formerly of the Chartered Bank in London. Compton Mackenzie, *Realms of Silver* (London, 1954), pp. 20–22, 94–95.

[2] Hong Kong, *Daily Press, Chronicle and Directory 1865* (hereafter cited as the *Directory*), Paske-Smith, *Western Barbarians*, p. 220. *Yokohama-shi Shi Kō*, vii. 54. Here the date of the Commercial Bank is given as 1863 and the Oriental as 1868. Both seem inaccurate. John Morrison succeeded Charles Rickerby as agent of the Central Bank of Western India in 1865 according to the *Directory* of 1866. Mr. Leighton-Boyce also mentions the Hindustan among the first banks in Yokohama but it does not appear in the Directories.

in Yokohama since 1860, had represented the Hong Kong and Shanghai Banking Corporation there until 7 June 1867, when it set up a branch under John Grigor. By that time the financial crisis of 1866 had caused all except the Oriental and Mercantile banks to close their doors.[1]

The officers of the Chartered Bank of India, Australia, and China looked over the situation in Japan again in 1866 but hesitated to open an office in Yokohama not only because of Japan's obvious political uncertainties but because the bulk of the available exchange business had been secured by the Oriental and Mercantile banks and prospects of profits were limited. Until 1880 Japan appeared little more than 'a potential field for securing sterling bills'. By then, however, competition from other banks had declined. The Mercantile Bank had withdrawn from Yokohama in 1879 and the Oriental, suffering from bad debts and poor management, was no longer an obstacle. Although the Hong Kong and Shanghai Bank now had control of the most lucrative business, the Chartered Bank decided to send T. H. White, head of its Hankow Branch, to open an office in Yokohama in September 1880. Up until the end of the period here considered, its success was limited, owing to the supremacy of the Hong Kong and Shanghai Bank. Ten years later, however, the position of the Chartered Bank was assured in the rapidly expanding economic position of Japan.[2]

No British or other banks are listed in the Directories for Nagasaki or Hakodate before the Restoration. Glover and Company carried on banking operations during the early years at Nagasaki. Mr. J. R. Jones of the Hong Kong and Shanghai Bank believes, however, that this bank opened a branch in Nagasaki in 1865. In 1868, 1869, and 1870 Glover and Company are listed as its agents as well as those for the Oriental Bank.[3]

Although Western business developed in Kobe and Osaka, no British bank established a branch in either city until more than

---

[1] Leighton-Boyce MS. Advertisement *Japan Times*, 30 Nov. 1867. The *Directory*, 1868. In 1867 the Comptoir d'Escompte de Paris, also having been represented previously by a mercantile agent, opened a branch in Yokohama. Hereafter the Hong Kong and Shanghai Banking Corporation will be cited as the Hong Kong and Shanghai Bank.   [2] Leighton-Boyce MS.

[3] Paske-Smith, *Western Barbarians*, p. 220. *Directory*, 1865, 1866, 1868, 1869, 1870. Letter from Mr. Jones to the author.

two years after it was opened to the West. Agencies represented both the Hong Kong and Shanghai and Oriental Banks, Messrs. Adrian and Company acting for the former. On 7 May 1870 the Hong Kong and Shanghai Bank opened an office in Kobe with Mr. Henry Smith in charge. Business grew slowly, however, and by 1878 there were only two Europeans on this bank's staff, its agent and a cashier. A Kobe branch of the Oriental Bank Corporation was established on 1 September 1870 under the direction of Mr. D. A. J. Crombie, but by 1878 it likewise had only two Europeans on its staff. Messrs. Browne and Company represented the Chartered Bank of India, Australia, and China in Kobe for many years before it established its branch there in 1895.[1]

Few records of the early operations of these British banks are to be found in England or Japan. The Oriental and the Mercantile Banks in the sixties and early seventies were the most important. Both helped to finance the development of Japan's foreign trade and the dealers from whom the European and American merchants obtained their supplies.[2] Their main business consisted of buying and selling of bills on England, Shanghai, and Hong Kong. The condition of the silk trade determined largely the volume of their transactions. Before the establishment of the Yokohama Specie Bank in 1880 these British banks also conducted, in conjunction with the foreign merchants, most of the foreign exchange operations of Japan. Since the official rate of exchange fixed for the *ichibu* was thought to be unfavourable they kept their accounts in Mexican dollars until 1871. They loaned money on the security of Japanese silver, charging from six to ten per cent. interest per annum.[3]

Although British authorities have said that the branches of the foreign banks of issue established in Japan did not issue notes.[4] there is strong evidence that they did so primarily for

[1] *Japan Chronicle, Jubilee Number, 1868–1918*, p. 34. Mackenzie, op. cit., pp. 217–18. Mr. Jones gives 1869 as the date when the Hong Kong and Shanghai Bank opened its branch in Kobe.

[2] George C. Allen, *A Short Economic History of Modern Japan 1867–1937*, (New York, 1963), p. 35.

[3] Allen and Donnithorne, op. cit., pp. 215–16. Mackenzie, op. cit., p. 97. The date 1871 may be too early as it was not until 1873 that the Oriental Bank announced its willingness to keep current accounts and receive fixed deposits in gold and silver yen. L.C. Micro., *Japan Mail*, 24 Dec. 1873.

[4] Allen and Donnithorne, op. cit., p. 215.

the convenience of their foreign customers—but the Japanese, having confidence in the Western banking facilities, made use of them. As early as 1873 the British Consul in Hyogo, Abel Gower, reported that local trade was much indebted to the Hong Kong and Shanghai Bank for its issue of 100, 50, 10, and 5 Mexican dollar notes payable to the bearer. He said they had put an end to the needless loss of time and labour entailed by the inspection of Mexican dollars and had diminished the influence of the Chinese shroffs.[1]

A series of decrees in 1876 indicates the government's effort to prevent the use of these foreign bank notes although they contained no such specific prohibition. On 8 April 1876 the *Ōkurashō* (Finance Ministry) issued a decree, ordered by the *Dajōkan* at the suggestion of Ōkuma and the First National Bank (*Daiichi Ginkō*), which declared that notes issued by the foreign banks in Japan had been used as money in the treaty ports. Since these banks were not under Japanese government control, it was difficult to know either the extent of the capital of the foreign banks or the amount of their notes. Should such banks fail, the people holding their notes would lose their money. To prevent such loss, the decree declared that the specie of the treaty powers and the national bank *Yōginken* (silver notes) issued by the Japanese government were to be used for trade at the treaty ports, Yedo and Osaka.[2] On 24 April the *Ōkurashō* issued the same decree for the whole country. On 4 May the Governor of Kanagawa district published a proclamation for that area in line with the *Ōkurashō* decree of 24 April. This was reissued on 23 July because the people were still using the foreign notes.[3] The British press found the alleged lack of Japanese knowledge about the foreign banks absurd since these banks published the amount of their capital in the newspapers.[4]

Three of the four foreign banks—the Oriental was the exception—retaliated by announcing in the *Japan Herald* of 26 July

[1] Cons. Report for Hyogo and Osaka for 1873, p. 26.
[2] Okada Shumpei, *Meiji Zenki no Seika Seisaku* (Currency Policies in Early Meiji Period), (Toyko, 1958), 39–40, 43–45. Meiji Zaisei Shi Hensankai (Association for editing financial history during the Meiji period), *Meiji Zaisei Shi* (The Financial History of the Meiji Period), 15 vols. (Tokyo, 1904–6), xii. 402–6. *Yōginken* had been issued in 1870 and 1872 in Yokohama for foreign trade purposes but were never issued in Kobe or elsewhere. Okada Shumpei, *Bakumatsu-Ishin no Kahei Seisaku*, p. 87.   [3] *Meiji Zaisei Shi*, xii. 404–5.
[4] *Japan Weekly Mail*, 10 June 1876. *Japan Herald*, 26 July 1876. For example of

that they would not accept from their customers Japanese bank notes after 1 August.[1] Soon afterward a Meiji government official, Tokunō, required the Kanagawa and Hyogo governors and Mitsuigumi (the forerunner of the Mitsui Bank) to investigate the results of the decree in their areas. It had no influence in Kobe because *yōginken* were used there very little if at all. In Yokohama *yōginken* were used much more because of the investigation but, even there, its success was decidely limited.[2]

Advertisements of the Hong Kong and Shanghai Bank in 1874, early 1875, and again from 1878 until 1881 in the *Japan Weekly Mail* indicate the Bank's resources, interest rates, and discount policies. On 1 May 1874 this corporation had a paid-up capital of $5,000,000 and a reserve fund of $1,000,000. It had branches and agencies in Hong Kong where its chief manager, James Greig, resided, and in Shanghai, Yokohama, Bombay, Calcutta, Foochow, Hankow, Hyogo, Amoy, and Saigon. In Yokohama interest of two per cent. per year was allowed on the daily balance of current deposit accounts, while on fixed deposits the rate for three months was three per cent. per annum, for six months, four per cent., and for twelve months, five per cent. The local manager, Herbert Cope, announced that credits would be granted 'on approved securities and every description of Banking and Exchange Business transacted'. Drafts would 'be granted on London and the chief commercial places in Europe, India, Australia, America, China and Japan'.[3] During January 1875 the reserve fund was reduced to $775,000 and W. H. Harris became the manager of the Yokohama branch.[4] By 13 April 1878 the acting manager, A. M. Townsend, announced new branches of the Bank in London, San Francisco, Manila, and Singapore and a rise in the interest rate to four per cent. on fixed deposits for three months.[5] As from 15 June 1880 the manager, John Walter, advertised that this rate was again only three per cent., that a branch had opened

early statements of the paid-up capital and reserve fund of the Hong Kong and Shanghai Bank, see *Japan Weekly Mail*, 23 May 1874, 9 Jan. 1875, 20 Mar. 1875.

[1] *Meiji Zaisei Shi*, xii. 408–9.

[2] Ibid., pp. 411–13.

[3] *Japan Weekly Mail*, 9 May 1874, and remaining issues in 1874.

[4] Ibid., 9 Jan. and 20 Mar. 1875.

[5] Ibid., 17 Aug. 1878, and weekly thereafter until 19 June 1880.

in New York, and that the Bank would issue 'circular notes' for the use of travellers in addition to its other services. Its reserve fund was now $1,500,000.[1] By 25 August this fund was said to be $1,600,000;[2] on 26 February 1881 it was reported as $1,800,000.[3] In that year also, its fixed and current deposits totalled £32,932,000 in contrast to those of its rivals; the Oriental's being £8,768,000 and the Chartered Bank's £4,022,000.[4]

A little of the history of the Oriental Bank Corporation may also be noted. More than any other bank its name appears in the diplomatic correspondence and in the economic histories of this period, but none of its own archives are known to have survived. Chartered in London in 1851 it became the predominant bank in the East during the years immediately following the financial crisis of 1866.[5] Its business in Yokohama flourished. Its London paper was preferred by remitters. Alone among the exchange banks its shares consistently stood above par. Its operations expanded rapidly through branches in Australia, New Zealand, South Africa, and Mauritius and by 1874 to Port Elizabeth.[6]

The balance sheet for the year 1875 indicated a paid-up capital of £1,500,000 and a reserve surplus fund of £450,000. Its net profit was £174,069 after defraying current expenses and providing for all bad and doubtful debts. It paid dividends of six per cent. for the half year ending 30 June 1875, and of five per cent. for that ending 31 December. The decrease in profits in 1875 was attributed to the steady decline in Eastern

---

[1] Ibid., 26 June 1880, and weekly until 21 Aug. 1880.

[2] Ibid., 28 Aug. 1880, and weekly until 24 Dec. 1880.

[3] Ibid., 26 Feb. 1881, and weekly until 24 Dec. 1881. There were no advertisements of the bank during 1882 and early 1883.

[4] J. W. Maclellan, *Banking in India and China*, p. 734, photostat record secured by Mr. John Keswick from the Hong Kong and Shanghai Bank.

[5] The fall in the price of cotton in Liverpool in May 1866 led to the failure of many Eastern banks within a few days.

[6] Leighton-Boyce MS. A. S. J. Baster, *The Imperial Banks* (London, 1929), pp. 104–6, 258; *The International Banks* (London, 1935,) pp. 161, 163–4. *The Banking Almanac, Directory, Year Book and Diary* for 1862 (hereinafter cited as *The Banking Almanac* for 1862), ed. by D. M. Evans (London, 1862), p. 161, gives South Sea House, Threadneedle St., E.C., as the Bank's headquarters and lists branches in Auckland, Bombay, Calcutta, Colombo, Galle, Hong Kong, Kandy, Madras, Mauritius, Melbourne, Shanghai, Singapore, Sydney, and Wellington. Its London bankers were the Bank of England and Union Bank of London. By 1884 it had branches also in Cape Town, Durban, Port Elizabeth, Hyogo, and Yokohama.

exchanges, as well as 'to the provision which had to be made for the fall in the value of Indian Government Rupee paper', and to the generally depressed state of commercial and monetary affairs during the year.[1] The dividend was again only five per cent. in June 1876—a falling-off said to result from exceptional circumstances such as fluctuations in the Indian, Hong Kong, and Shanghai exchanges and the failure of the sugar crop in Mauritius—not from any falling off in the usual branches of business.[2] By 1878 a marked decline was evident. Its South African business had proved unprofitable and was transferred to the newly formed Bank of Africa, Ltd. Through the progressive devaluation of silver in the last quarter of the nineteenth century, the forced revaluation of its funds in the East, the absorbing of bad and doubtful debts, and unsuccessful adventures in the floating of Chilean loans, the once great bank lost half a million pounds. Its credit was already damaged when it had to meet the continued depreciation of silver, which cost it another £800,000 in the early eighties. And enormous losses were incurred from unproductive property and securities acquired through default on loans and advances, as well as from the unwise investments in sugar in Mauritius and coffee in Ceylon. It was forced to suspend payments in 1884, causing serious difficulty to many depositors. And although soon reconstructed as the New Oriental Bank Corporation, it survived only until 1893.[3]

In its hey-day the Oriental Bank had rendered important services to Japan and the foreign communities. Until instructions were received from the governments of the recipient powers, the Oriental and Mercantile Banks were each entrusted with a deposit of $250,000 which together constituted the *Bakufu* payment of the first instalment of the Shimonoseki indemnity.[4] When dollar certificates became necessary to satisfy the need of Yokohama traders who, unaccustomed to the use of bills issued by foreign banks, were victims of forged bills and who found the carrying of actual dollars in their

---

[1] *Japan Weekly Mail*, 10 and 17 June 1876, pp. 526, 550. In 1862 its dividend had been ten per cent. with a bonus of seven per cent. *The Banking Almanac* for 1862, p. 160.　　　　　　　　　　　　　　[2] *The Times*, London, 20 Oct. 1876.

[3] Leighton-Boyce MS. Baster, *Imperial Banks*, pp. 258–9. *Japan Chronicle, Jubilee Number, 1868–1918*, p. 34. Maclellan, op. cit., pp. 734, 738–9.

[4] P.P. H. of C. 1866, lxxvi. 55, 56, 58.

pockets burdensome, the Board of Trade (Tsūshōshi) originally produced certificates of poor design and material, for issue by the Yokohama Kawase Kwaisha (Exchange House) in accordance with a government order of 1870. Here the Oriental Bank stepped in, ordering from Perkin and Bacons of London the manufacture of 5, 10, 20, 50, 100, 500, and 1,000 Mexican dollar certificates to the amount of $1,500,000. These were then issued by the Yokohama Kawase Kwaisha (which became in 1872 the Second National Bank) to the full amount for dollars received from foreign banks in payment of bills presented to them by exporters. The government's careful supervision of these transactions and insistence upon the declared reserve of dollars being maintained meant that few of the certificates were presented for conversion. They served the Yokohama traders so well that their circulation persisted until 1890 in spite of the Convertible Bank Note Act of May 1884 which had prohibited their issue after 1 May 1885.[1]

Of more importance were the connexions of the Oriental Bank with the first foreign loans made to the new Meiji government. When the *Bakufu* fell in 1868 its debt to the French Société Géneralé for a loan of half a million Mexican dollars contracted in 1865 for the construction of the Yokosuka Iron Works and Shipyards remained unpaid. The effort of the French government to embarrass the Meiji authorities by insisting that the Société Géneralé press for its money, made it necessary for the new government to arrange for payment at any cost to avoid foreign encroachment on its control of Yedo and the loss of the entire property. When Mitsui and other companies refused them the necessary funds Ōkuma, Komatsu, and Terashima turned to Sir Harry Parkes for help. Through his introduction to the manager of the Oriental Bank they arranged for a loan of 500,000 Mexican dollars at fifteen per cent. interest for three years. This in turn was paid back by 1870 by funds made available by W. J. Alt, an English merchant in Yokohama who loaned the government $400,000, and a Dutch company which supplied $100,000.[2] The Oriental Bank

[1] Soyeda Juichi, 'A History of Banking in Japan', in *A History of Banking in All Leading Nations*, ed. by the *Journal of Commerce and Commercial Bulletin*, 4 vols. (New York, 1896), iv. 436–7.

[2] Hori, *Gaishi Yunyū no Kaiko to Tembō*, pp. 10–11. Tsuchiya Takao, 'Bakumatsu Dōranki no Keizaiteki Bunseki' (Economic Analyses of the Restless Period of

also handled the two foreign loans made to the Meiji government in its early years.[1]

The Railway Loan and Railway Construction

Foreign pressures for building railways in Japan began during the last days of the *Bakufu*. French and American schemes for their construction fell through with the end of the Shogunate.[2] Parkes and the British engineer, Henry Brunton, thereafter stressed the need for railways and improved communications in conversations with the young Meiji ministers. The rate of travel then averaged only twenty miles a day and the difficulties in transporting rice often resulted in distress in one province while another suffered for an outlet for its produce. But the progressive members of the government, Iwakura, Itō, Ōkubo, and Matsukata, had to overcome strenuous opposition, factional and otherwise, including that of Saigō Takamori, before they could secure a majority of opinion in favour of immediate railway construction, which they recognized as a political, economic, and military necessity.[3] This was achieved in November 1869 when the *Dajōkan*, following Parkes's advice, decided that the government itself should build and manage the railways and envisage the construction of an extensive system eventually connecting Yedo with Osaka and with northern and western Japan. Brunton, the British engineer, recommended that a beginning be made with the building of a pilot railroad between Yedo and Yokohama, which he estimated would cost $950,000 and yield a net annual return of at least ten per cent. His advice was accepted. As the needed funds were lacking, Date, Minister of Finance, Ōkuma, Vice-Minister, and Itō, Assistant Vice-Minister, were appointed to negotiate for a loan from England and to take charge of the railway work.[4]

the End of Tokugawa), *Chūō Kōron*, xi, Oct. 1932, 91. *Nichi-Ei Gaikō Shi*, i. 133–4.   [1] See pp. 390–4.
    [2] Ōshima Fujitarō, *Kokutetsu* (The National Railways), (Tokyo, 1956), pp. 21–22. Asahi Shimbun Sha (Ashi Newspaper Co.), ed., *Meiji-Taishō Shi* (Meiji-Taisho History), 6 vols. (Tokyo, 1930), iii. 196–7. Makino Terutomo compiled this volume.
    [3] *Yokohama-shi Shi Kō* vii. 398–404. F.O. 46/114, Parkes to Clarendon, No. 228, Yedo, 4 Dec. 1869. P.P. H. of C. 1870, lxx. 95–99, Parkes to Clarendon, Yedo, 21 Apr. 1870. T. C. Smith, *Political Change and Industrial Development in Japan: 1868–1880*, pp. 42–43.
    [4] Tetsudō Shō (Ministry of Railways), *Nihon Tetsudō Shi* (History of Japanese

During the previous summer Horatio Nelson Lay, C.B., a former British government employee in China who had rendered distinguished service under Lord Elgin and Sir Frederick Bruce and had been commissioner of the Chinese Imperial Maritime Customs, arrived in Japan. His avowed purpose was to offer the Japanese government £3,000,000, which he claimed large English capitalists wished him to lend to either the Chinese or Japanese government. He had failed to do so in China and now turned to Japan, preferring to keep secret the names of his financial backers. Parkes introduced him to the Japanese ministers.[1] By December Lay had made arrangements with the Meiji government to finance the building of Japan's first railway. In an agreement of 14 December 1869 he contracted to provide the Japanese government by 31 July 1870 with a loan of £1,000,000 as part of the expenses of constructing the line from Yedo to Hyogo with a connecting branch to Yokohama and a line between the Biwa Lake and the Port of Tsuruga. The principal and interest at twelve per cent. were to be secured on the Japanese customs and net receipts of the railway. Repayment was promised in twelve annual instalments beginning 27 July 1873. Elaborate provisions made possible the payment of interest and instalments of principal in copper, lead, or other produce to be shipped and sold in China or in bank bills on London at the will of the Japanese government.[2] With no reference to this agreement, an Imperial Decree of the same date appointed Lay commissioner for the Japanese government to raise and negotiate a loan of £1,000,000 on any terms and from any persons he 'shall think fit'.[3] Both documents were signed by Date, Ōkuma, and Itō. A third agreement of 22 December referred to the above documents as if they were one act and authorized Lay to retain £300,000 out of the million for the purchase of the railway plant, and to appoint engineers for construction, etc. A further agreement of 28 December confirmed these three documents and added a war clause which had been omitted from the first. These documents were written in English. Lay himself drafted them. He was

Railways), 3 vols. (Tokyo, 1921), i. 15–16. Ōshima, op. cit., p. 22. Inouye Masaru in Ōkuma, *Fifty Years of New Japan*, i. 430. *Meiji-Taishō Shi*, iii. 196–7.

[1] F.O. 46/126, Parkes to Clarendon, No. 104, Conf'l., Yedo, 31 July 1870. Inouye Masaru in Ōkuma, *Fifty Years of New Japan*, i. 430.

[2] *D.N.G.M.* ii, Pt. 3, 323–37, Doc. 589.   [3] Ibid., pp. 316–23, Doc. 588.

apparently unperturbed by the double position in which he had placed himself, or he deliberately misled the Japanese. He thus became both the contractor for the loan for his financial constituents in London and the commissioner for the Japanese government to raise the loan. The Japanese later said that they did not understand the precise meaning of the Decree of 14 December but that Lay had explained it was 'a necessary adjunct' to the first agreement of that date and 'was required that he might prove to his friends that he had received full power from the Japanese Government to borrow and receive money'.[1] Owing to his knowledge of Chinese, Lay boasted he was able to get to the high officials and to keep his movements shrouded in secrecy. A Bill in Chancery later filed against Lay and two of his partners by two other partners indicates the extent of the profits which Lay hoped to make from this dual role.[2] The Japanese, equally desirous of secrecy, and believing they were securing a private loan, had no idea that this second document of 14 December could empower Lay to go on the money market and publicly pledge their customs and railway when opposition to the building of railroads and all innovation was still rampant in the country.[3]

Upon his return to London to secure the funds and engage the engineers, Lay chose to raise the money on the stock exchange under contract number two (the Imperial Decree of 14 December) rather than collect the funds from friends in accordance with agreement number one. He published in London on 23 April 1870 a prospectus of the loan giving decree number two as his authority and announcing a loan of £1,000,000 to be raised on interest of nine per cent. and at a discount of two per cent.[4]

On 25 April 1870 *The Times* carried the following announcement:

The London Stock Exchange, as centre of the financial negotiations of the world, is about to open a new connection. A loan of

[1] F.O. 46/126, Parkes to Clarendon, No. 97, Conf'l., Yokohama, 21 July 1870; Parkes to Hammond, Private, Yedo, 25 July 1870.
[2] Ibid., Parkes to Clarendon, No. 104, Conf'l., Yedo, 31 July 1870 and encl. showing agreement with Japanese government as Lay's partners understood it and three per cent. profits expected. *The Times*, London, 26 Feb. 1873.
[3] F.O. 46/126, Parkes to Clarendon, No. 97, Conf'l., Yokohama, 21 July 1870. *Meiji-Taishō Shi*, iii. 196–7. *Nichi-Ei Gaikō Shi*, i. 131.
[4] F.O. 46/126, Parkes to Clarendon, No. 97, Conf'l., Yokohama, 21 July 1870.

1,000,000£ for the Imperial Government of Japan, contracted under the authority of Mr. Lay, as special commissioner is introduced by Messrs. J. Henry Schröder and Company. The price is to be 98, the rate of interest 9% per annum: the principal redeemable at par within 13 years by annual drawings. The object is to connect by railway Yedo, the captial of the Empire, with Yokohama, Osaka, and the port of Tsuruga—points which comprise several million inhabitants and the most active trading communities of the country. As a special security the entire Customs Duties of the Empire, said to amount to 600,000£ or 700,000£ per annum, are to be assigned, together with the proceeds of the intended lines, which are to be completed within 3 or 5 years: and the Oriental Banking Corporation who have had long experience of pecuniary intercourse with the Japanese government and people, are to be the agents for the receipt and transmission of these funds.

Although to external nations Japan is as yet a comparatively strange country, its capacities have been illustrated by the enormous development of its trade both with England and the United States during the past few years and the conclusions of the various merchants engaged in this new and attractive branch of commerce seem favourable alike to commercial sagacity and good faith of the Government and people.

Thus far Lay had acted as the Meiji government's commissioner but at the same time he tried to retain his position as contractor, and in delivering the money thus raised to the Japanese government, wished to charge them with interest at twelve per cent. in terms of agreement one. Parkes, when at possession of the documents, immediately questioned the ethics of such proceedings. He asked for instructions. 'Was Lay as commissioner for the Japanese government not bound to do his best for them and deliver to them the money on the same terms he received it having acted in their name and on their faith and credit?' But in meeting Ōkuma's protests, Parkes refused to give an opinion until officially required to do so.

Parkes had confidence in Lay's honesty about the funds at his disposal but did not examine carefully his arrangements with the Japanese, and never 'endorsed' them as Lay asserted in the Bill filed in Chancery. In fact Parkes made it clear to Lay that he did not approve of Lay's clause in the agreement of 14 December providing for the payment of interest on the loan in metals or any other produce instead of allowing it to enter the general market, and he resented Lay's misrepresenting to him the money at his disposal. At the same time he appeared sceptical of Japan's professed misunderstanding of the meaning of the Imperial Decree and indifferent to Lay's proceedings at the beginning in 1869.[1] Obviously he did not want to take a definite position on the issue without instructions from Clarendon. He wrote: 'I feel that it would be convenient that I should be instructed by your Lordship whether his (Lay's) position as a contractor in regard to this loan is compatible with that of a commissioner of the Japanese Government and whether when serving in the capacity of the latter he is entitled to the profits of the former.'[2]

The Japanese authorities were greatly disturbed by Lay's action in England, especially the publicity given to the security pledged for the loan, believing that the loan was to be raised quietly among Lay's friends. They fully recognized that they had been deceived by Lay's explanation of their Decree of 14 December. Public protests against the loan were so violent that Itō and others feared physical danger.[3]

Lay's appointees, Edmund Morell, chief engineer, and others engaged in England arrived in April. Work on the eighteen miles between Yedo and Yokohama had already begun and the railroad bonds were being sold in London when the Meiji government issued on 29 June 1870 a public proclamation cancelling Lay's commission and withdrawing 'all powers given to him' to raise or negotiate money on their behalf or in their name to enter into and execute any deeds, contracts, bonds, or mortgages, etc. on the ground that Lay had made use of the powers improperly obtained from them and had in their name and on their behalf 'solicited subscription to a Loan of one million Pounds sterling from the general public in London whereby he has vitiated and rendered void and of no legal effect whatever his aforesaid agreement with our Government'.

In the same edict, the Japanese government appointed the Oriental Bank Corporation in London to be its agents and attorneys to settle with Lay and his associates, to manage the said loan, to pay the interest and instalments thereon when due, to take charge of the securities pledged for the same in the

[1] F.O. 46/126, Parkes to Clarendon, No. 97, Conf'l., Yokohama, 21 July 1870.
[2] Ibid., and No. 104, Conf'l., Yedo, 31 July 1870.
[3] *Meiji-Taishō Shi*, iii. 196–7.

interests of the several bondholders as well as to further the construction of the railways, and for that purpose, appointing, or removing, and paying the required personnel.[1]

To the Oriental Bank, the Japanese government gave further instructions and delegated power. The ministers said they were determined 'to consider and maintain in every way the rights and interests of the holders of the Bonds' of their Sterling Loan and 'strictly to carry out the arrangements legally entered into with them' on the Japanese government's behalf by Mr. Lay. They preferred, however, to cancel the whole arrangement and return the money to the bondholders, or if that were impossible, to have the Oriental Bank buy up all the bonds on the best terms it could secure. Could either be done, they would then need to offer the public a new loan or series of loans on proper securities for an amount sufficient to complete the estimated cost of the railways—say not more than £3,000,000 sterling. They preferred to have the money raised in instalments of £500,000 so as to meet the current outlay as the work progressed. They planned to apply to railway construction such money as they could spare from other resources and wished to borrow only what was absolutely necessary. The Bank was to exercise its discretion in their best interest.

In fact the Bank was asked to decide whether buying up the bonds or returning the money would be expedient. If not it was requested to arrange with the holders of bonds issued in terms of Lay's prospectus, 'as to taking charge of the lien on the customs and railway receipts on their behalf'. Further the Bank was asked to appoint and deal with an eminent consulting engineer and all other engineers and personnel for the maintenance and proper working of the railways for the duration of the loan, as at that time it was doing for the mint.[2] Thus a great British bank played a major part in the construction of Japan's first railroad. The Bank appointed C. F. J. Stuart chief manager of its London headquarters, John Robertson manager of the Yokohama branch, and W. W. Cargill travelling supervisor, to take charge as their representatives and commissioners.[3]

[1] *D.N.G.M.* iii. 495–500, Doc. 278.
[2] Ibid., pp. 500–2, second document in 278. For mint see pp. 402–6.
[3] Inouye Masaru in Ōkuma, *Fifty Years of New Japan*, i. 432. *The Banking Almanac* for 1862, p. 202. *Japan Gazette Hong List*, 1872, pp. 10, 16.

In London the bonds issued on 25 April were at first eagerly subscribed, selling at 1¼ to 1¾ pm.[1] The price went as low as four per cent. discount as the time approached for an instalment of fifteen per cent. to become due.[2] This was met with entire promptitude on 5 May. The largest number of investors were believed to be men with some knowledge of Japan through trading and other connexions who considered nine per cent. interest a fair cover for risk and not likely to be swayed by market fluctuations.[3] By 3 June the bonds were selling at from one per cent. discount to par and a considerable amount of the loan had been paid up by the parties to whom it was allotted.[4] *The Times* did not note the dismissal of Lay nor the subsequent commissioning of the Oriental Bank by the Meiji government. By 22 August the Japanese railway bonds introduced by Messrs. Schröder and Company were selling at par although all other foreign securities were still much below the prices current when the Japanese loan was brought out. The recovery of these bonds from their discount price was attributed to the steadily encouraging reports from Japan which indicated that while Europe was convulsed by war, Japan was 'emerging from centuries of fanaticism to take a prominent place among commercial nations', a statement which *The Times* reinforced by a detailed review of Japan's progress since the Restoration.[5] A total of £930,000 was turned over to the Japanese government after £29,750 for the costs of floating the loan and £20,250 for cancelling Lay's contract had been paid.[6]

While public confidence in Japanese credit was being built up in Britain the construction of the railway began. The section between Yedo and Yokohama was started at both ends at once. A 3 ft. 6 in. gauge was decided upon according to the advice of British engineers. The land for the Yedo station was being cleared and all possible facilities were afforded Mr. Morell.[7] In July 1870 work began on the twenty miles between Osaka and

---

[1] *The Times*, 26 Apr. 1870.　　　　　　　[2] Ibid., 4 May 1870.
[3] Ibid., 6 May 1870.　　　[4] Ibid., 3 June 1870.　　　[5] Ibid., 22 Aug. 1870.
[6] *Nihon Tetsudō Shi*, i. 26. A different set of figures for the payment to L,ay, etc. is given in Ōkurashō (Finance Ministry), Ouchi Hyoe and Tsuchiya Takao Editors, *Meiji Zenki Zaisei Keizai Shiryō Shusei* (Collection of Historical Documents of Finance and Economics of the Early Meiji Period) (hereafter cited as Ōkurashō, *Documents*), 20 vols. (Tokyo, 1934), x. 190. But *Nichi-Ei Gaikō Shi*, i. 132. agrees with the above.
[7] *Japan Mail*, 21 May 1870, reprinted in *The Times*, 6 July 1870.

PLATE 11

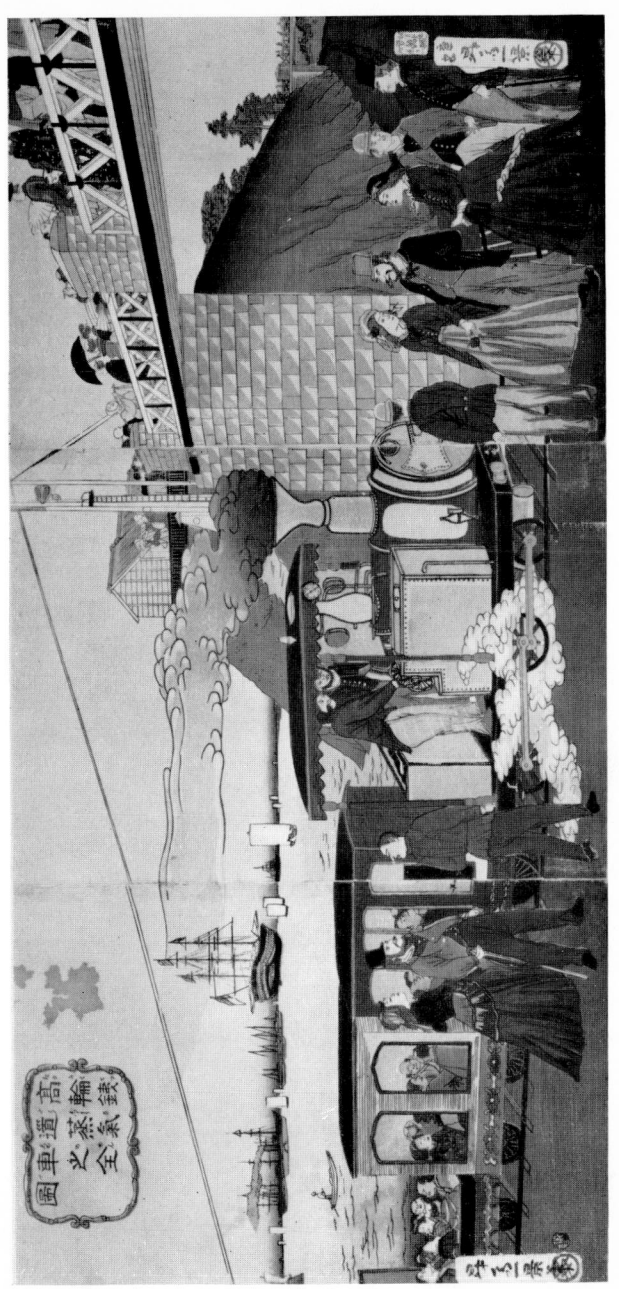

The First Railway Train at Takanawa, 1872. By Shōsai Ikkei

Kobe and finished in November 1873. The section between Yedo and Yokohama, completed in September 1872, was officially opened by the Emperor, who generously recognized the work of Ōkuma and Itō and rewarded officials concerned with the construction.[1] During the previous two years at least fifty-one Englishmen had been employed in this initial railway project, now under the direction of Inouye Masaru, who since August 1871 had been superintendent of the Railway Bureau in the new Department of Public Works.[2] Morell had gained the confidence of the Japanese and was teaching them how to run their railway.[3] By 1877 the contracts with the office of the Oriental Bank had expired although the number of foreign employees had reached its maximum at 120. Strenuous efforts to reduce their cost by training more Japanese to take over their work made it possible for Japanese to replace successfully the English engineers in 1882.[4] Meanwhile the Kyoto–Osaka line had been completed and was officially opened by the Emperor in February 1877 in a great ceremony attended by the foreign diplomatic corps who found the Kyoto crowds friendly and orderly—a vast contrast to their behaviour in 1868.[5] The total mileage of eastern and western lines was now seventy-one. The Kyoto–Ōtsu section was ready for use in July 1881 and that to Tsuruga in 1884—altogether twenty-seven more miles—a great achievment in the face of financial stress and public opposition.[6]

The Second British Loan

In the early Meiji years both the government and the public wanted to avoid borrowing abroad out of fear of political encroachments arising from Japan's well-known financial instability. Such general opposition did not, however, prevent the Japanese government from again turning to England for a public loan in 1873. Here its purpose was to raise £2,400,000

[1] Inouye Masaru in Ōkuma, *Fifty Years of New Japan* i. 433.

[2] Ibid. Oyatoi Gaikōkujin Ichiran (Foreigners Employed by Meiji Government), pamphlet of 1872 reproduced in *Meiji Bunka Zenshū*, xvi. 347–64.

[3] F.O. 46/124, Adams to Granville, No. 88, Yedo, 3 Oct. 1871.

[4] *Japan Weekly Mail*, 6 May 1882.

[5] F.O. 46/216, Parkes to Derby, No. 23, Yedo, 12 Feb. 1877. Dickins, op. cit., ii. 246–7. Inouye Masaru in Ōkuma, *Fifty Years of New Japan*, i. 434, gives the date of this ceremony as Feb. 1878, an obvious typographical error.

[6] Inouye Masaru in Ōkuma, *Fifty Years of New Japan*, i. 436–9.

for adjusting the pensions of daimyo and retainers by establishing an employment fund for all who had renounced their feudal privileges and had surrendered their lands and the 'registers' of their people to the government.[1]

An Imperial Order designated the Oriental Bank Corporation as agent. The loan was floated in London, the books being opened on 13 January and closed on 18 January 1873. Seven per cent. bonds of £100 denomination were offered at an issue price of £92/10 to be redeemed in twenty-four years. The enormous sum of £9,664,900 is said to have been subscribed. Proceeds turned over to the Japanese government amounted to £2,220,000. The first interest was paid on 1 July 1873 and thereafter every six months on the first of the month.[2]

Parkes's Proposal for a Third British Loan

To meet Japan's growing financial difficulties arising in part from the over-issue of inconvertible paper currency, Sir Harry Parkes in 1879 suggested to Ōkuma, then Minister of Finance, that Japan not only establish a central bank with capital subscribed by both Japanese and foreigners but also contract for a new loan of fifty million yen in England. He recommended John Robertson, the manager of the Yokohama branch of the Oriental Bank Corporation, as the man best qualified to negotiate the loan and help solve Japan's problems. After serious consideration in Ōkuma's government of 1880 Parkes's proposal for this third British loan as a means to the resumption of specie payments was rejected by the new government of 1881. It was generally agreed that another foreign loan under the existing deterioration in the Japanese currency would be a further burden on the national economy. Matsukata Masayoshi, now Finance Minister, declared that asking the help of foreigners to solve a domestic problem would be prejudicial to the reputation and honour of Japan. The dangers involved would far outweigh any short-term benefits—a judgement concurred in by the *Japan Weekly Mail*.[3]

[1] Matsukata Masayoshi in Ōkuma, *Fifty Years of New Japan*, i. 375. *Meiji-Taishō Shi*, iii. 439.

[2] *The Times*, 11 and 16 Jan. 1873. *Meiji Zaisei Shi*, viii. 619–24. Borton, *Japan's Modern Century*, p. 84.

[3] Horie Yasuzō, *Gaishi Yunyū no Kaiko to Tembō*, pp. 31–32. *Japan Weekly Mail*, 17 Sept. 1881.

Allan Shand and the Daiichi Ginkō

While British banks were controlling the foreign exchange and discount business in the open Japanese ports, at least one British banker was exercising an important influence on Japan's newly established national bank system, recommended by Itō Hirobumi upon his return from America and Europe at the end of 1870. The Meiji government decided to adopt the American system in December 1871 and appointed two of the great merchant houses, Mitsuigumi and Onogumi, in August 1872 to establish the First National Bank (*Daiichi Kokuritsu Ginkō* or *Daiichi Ginkō*). Regulations to govern the bank were drafted by Shibusawa Eiichi (later Viscount), the chief tax official in the Ministry of Finance, on the model of the American national bank laws, and were proclaimed as law on 15 November 1872. The first shareholders' meeting took place in June 1873. The initial capital was Y 2,440,800. Mitsuigumi and Onogumi controlled the shares and the directorate. Shibusawa was General Superintendent with power to supervise the activities of all the officers of the bank, who were made up of two presidents two vice-presidents, two managing directors, etc., to represent equally the Mitsui and Ono companies. The bank opened on 20 July 1873.[1]

Shibusawa knew well the importance of establishing efficient methods of book-keeping and accounting in the new bank and the general lack of such knowledge among its founders and officers. He therefore turned to an Englishman, Allan Shand, a former employee of the Chartered Mercantile Bank of Yokohama, who in 1872 was appointed to a minor position in the bank-note department of the Meiji Ministry of Finance. Here he established a school of banking administration (*Ginkō-gaku Kyoku*) where he trained employees of the ministry and of the *Daiichi Kokuritsu Ginkō* from its start in Western methods of book-keeping and prepared many of Japan's important bankers for their future work: for example, Sasaki Yūnosuke, the second president of the *Daiichi Ginkō*. Shand's Manual, *Ginkō Boki Seihō* (Detailed Bank Book-keeping Manual) published by the

---

[1] Daiichi Ginkō Hachijūnenshi Hensanshitsu (Committee for Compilation of Eighty Year History of the First National Bank), *Daiichi Ginkō Shi* (History of the First National Bank), 2 vols. (Tokyo, 1957–8), i. 129–31. Obata Kyugoro, *An Interpretation of the Life of Viscount Shibusawa* (Tokyo, 1939), pp. 90–93.

Ministry of Finance in August 1873, led the newly opened *Daiichi Kokuritsu Ginkō* to adopt the Western methods of book-keeping and to abolish all the former money orders, discount procedures, the preparation of financial reports, etc. Shand's caution and conservatism, called by the Japanese his 'steady first' policy, was typical of that of the contemporary British commercial banks. And although the Japanese National Bank Act was modelled on the American system the actual banking operations were developed in the English manner.[1]

In November 1874 the bankruptcy of Onogumi, one of the two main shareholders of the Bank, shook the foundations of the young institution and led to a drastic reform of its policies. Shand was appointed by the banking department of the Ministry of Finance in March 1875 to investigate the books of the Bank and its branches, in accordance with Article 17 of the National Bank Act. This, the first governmental inspection of a bank in Japan, revealed complete lack of uniformity and confusion in the book-keeping practices of the first years of the national banks. Violations of the Bank Law had occurred, such as: the granting of large loans (Y 1,300,000) to Onogumi and lesser amounts to some individuals without security. The currency reserve was not sufficient to meet a sudden demand by depositors for their money. The influence of Onogumi was too great, the evaluation of the Bank's buildings and lands was too high, and the main building itself was not suitable for Western banking procedures.

As a result of Shand's findings and a memorandum from the banking department of the Finance Ministry the stockholders of *Daiichi Ginkō* at an extraordinary meeting in August voted for a series of reforms. These included the reduction of the Bank's capital from Y 2·5 million to Y 1·5 million, the uniform handling of loans and abolition of special favours to individuals; thorough investigation before granting loans; the selection of directors because of ability, not for special connexions; the expansion of the money-order business, etc. New directors in accordance with new rules were elected at this time and Shibusawa became president.[2]

---

[1] *Daiichi Ginkō Shi*, i. Preface, by Sakai Kyōnosuke and pp. 4, 177–82, 204, 720–2.   [2] Ibid., pp. 203–4.

Shand also proposed a wider distribution of shareholders and an expansion of business, both to include merchants, in an effort to further the Bank's acquaintance with trade and commerce. Here President Shibusawa showed great reluctance, maintaining that no merchants understood banking. He even hesitated to open checking accounts with them. He did, however, consent to Shand's idea of holding periodic meetings with merchants at the Bank to discuss the business of the Bank and commerce, a first step, Shand thought, in the right direction.[1]

When in 1874 the bank petitioned the ministries of finance and foreign affairs for permission to handle the foreign exchange needs of Japanese legations and consulates overseas, it was denied because of Shand's opposition, based on the still shaky foundation of the Bank. Likewise in March 1875, Shand's disapproval persuaded the finance ministers to refuse the Bank's application to open a foreign exchange office in Shanghai, which had been urged by the Japanese consul there as a step towards making Japanese money the chief currency in use in the Far Eastern coastal trade. Shibusawa was for ever grateful to Allan Shand for his sound opposition in this instance.[2]

Shand continued to be a close friend and consultant to Shibusawa during the latter's presidency of the *Daiichi Ginkō* and to make a major contribution to the development of the banking system of modern Japan, which in 1882 included the establishment of a central bank, the Bank of Japan.[3]

[1] Ibid., pp. 187–94, 203–4, 214–35.

[2] Ibid. 185–6, 721. Obata, op. cit., p. 97. Okada Shumpei, *Meiji Zenki no Seika Seisaku*, pp. 185–6.

[3] Obata, op. cit., p. 97. Soyeda in *History of Banking*, op. cit. iv. 462–4.

XV

CURRENCY POLICIES AND THE MEIJI MINT

Currency Problems

To gain both domestic and foreign confidence the young Meiji government recognized the immediate need to reform the debased, counterfeit, and widely varied currency which it had inherited from the *Bakufu* administration. The time had also come, according to the Tariff Convention of 1866, for the alteration in the exchange rate of $100 to 311 silver *ichibu*, used since 1860 in payment of import duties. A Government Proclamation on 13 March 1868 declared the circulation of the Mexican dollar lawful and fixed the exchange rate at one dollar to three *ichibu*. A second order on 4 August 1868 made the rate $100 to 293 *ichibu*.[1] The reform of the native currency was much more difficult. Many kinds of gold, silver, iron, and copper coins and nearly 1,700 types of gold, silver, and rice certificates of an approximate value of Y 146,790,000 were in circulation. Favourable exchange rates between gold and silver even at the Restoration made it possible for foreign merchants to exchange foreign silver for Japanese gold at a profit of 100 per cent. Quantities of gold were leaving the country; for example, a half-million gold pieces (*ryō*) were exported in January 1869.[2]

In the early months of 1868 the government had sponsored an official investigation of the currency with a new mintage in

---

[1] Shinjo, op. cit., p. 15. *Nichi-Ei Gaikō Shi*, i. 112–13, for description of debased and counterfeit currencies. English text of Proclamation in *Japan Gazette Hong List*, 1872, p. 45. Matsui Kiyoshi, *Kindai Nihon Bōeki Shi* (History of Modern Japanese Trade), (Kyoto, 1959), pp. 300–1. Ōkurashō, *Documents*, xiv. 39.

[2] Borton, *Japan's Modern Century*, pp. 73–74. Here yen, although not coined until 1870, probably means the same as Mexican dollars, since when coined it had exactly the value of a Mexican dollar, 416 grains 9/10 fine silver, and an exchange rate of one dollar for one yen was established 22 Nov. 1870. Matsui, op. cit., p. 301. One *ryō* = one koban. A *ryō* was originally a unit of weight in China and represented the weight in gold of the Japan koban first struck in 1601. Shinjo, op. cit., p. 16.

mind. Since the quality and weight of the Japanese coins were proved inferior to those of the West and would jeopardize the development of foreign trade, the Meiji authorities decided in April or May 1868 to arrange for the issue of a new coinage.[1]

Before this could be done, however, the government had to meet the deficits arising from the excess of its expenditures over its revenues and supply capital for the development of industry in accordance with an Imperial Ordinance of 9 June 1868. To do so it resorted to the issue of millions of paper notes called '*kinsatsu*' (gold notes) to be redeemed in thirteen years. They rapidly depreciated, reflecting lack of faith in the new administration and opposition from the nobility and the samurai. The new notes were exchanged for the debased coins at a heavy discount—as great as fifty-five per cent. in 1868. Notes amounting to 48,000,000 *ryō* were in circulation by the end of 1869. Over-issue of notes within the clans for their local use, small denomination civic department notes, authorized by Imperial Ordinance in October 1869, and many counterfeits also flooded the country. Internal and external trade suffered.[2]

The British minister entered a protest as foreign commerce was further threatened by reports that new coins issued in Osaka by the harassed government in the winter of 1869 were deliberately debased below the standard agreed upon in 1866. Parkes inquired about the truth of such assertions and urged measures to check the excessive fluctuation in the market rates of native coin.[3] On 3 April the Italian, French, and German ministers made second protests against the new coinage.[4] Date and Higashikuze could onlyh edge in their reply. Their expression of regret that the recent gold and silver coins (*nibukin* and *ichibugin*) had troubled foreign commerce accompanied a promise to report in full on the situation when Ōkuma, who had been sent to Osaka to investigate the facts, returned. Should debasement of the currency be proved, the authorities

---

[1] Honjō Eijirō, *Meiji Ishin Keizai Shi Kenkyū* (Study of Economic History of the Meiji Restoration), (Tokyo, 1930), pp. 504–5. Count Matsukata Masayoshi, *Report on the Adoption of the Gold Standard* (Tokyo, 1899), pp. 1–2.

[2] Matsukata, op. cit., pp. 17–22. George C. Allen, *A Short Economic History of Modern Japan*, p. 39. Takaki Masayoshi, *A History of Japanese Paper Currency* (Baltimore, 1903), pp. 9–34.

[3] *D.N.G.M.* ii. Pt. 1, 26–29 and 336–8, Docs. 13 and 91, Parkes to Higashikuze, Yokohama, 19 Feb., and Parkes to Date, Yokohama, 2 Apr. 1869.

[4] Ibid., p. 348, Doc. 95.

said the guilty persons would be punished. In view of the current circumstances, however, the government would discontinue the minting of *nibukin* (2 gold bu) and *ichibugin* (silver *ichibu*). It planned to strike a new coinage and would appreciate the considered suggestions of the foreign representatives.[1] On 8 July 1869 the Foreign Ministry announced to all the consulates that the production of paper money had stopped. The government had ordered the destruction of the machines which made it. A new coinage would be minted into which the paper currency then in circulation would be convertible. Paper money could be used for taxes. And anyone who set up rates for the exchange of this paper currency for gold or who hindered its circulation would be punished.[2]

An Imperial Ordinance of 7 July and a letter from Date to Parkes confirmed the government's decision to do away with the evils of fiat currency. The ministers intended to redeem the 32,500,000 *ryō* in paper money already issued during the next three years or pay interest at six per cent. on what remained unredeemed after 1872.[3] Parkes made no objection to this policy. He pointed out, however, that although the Japanese authorities had a right to issue paper money and make it legal tender, they exceeded their right when they attempted 'to prevent paper money finding its own level', and when they sought 'to force it upon their subjects and indirectly upon the foreign merchants, on the same terms as coin'. He declared: 'It is neither by Decrees nor by other compulsory measures that paper money can be made to circulate at a par value, but only by means of public confidence in the Government by which it is issued.' The government's action in opposition to this rule was 'seriously interfering with that liberty of commerce and intercourse between foreigners and Japanese' which the treaties were established 'to foster and protect'. The fact that the Japanese authorities were initiating such measures with full awareness that they would be prejudicial to foreign trade until

---

[1] *D.N.G.M.* ii, Pt. 1, 409–10, Doc. 107, Date and Higashikuze to the Foreign Representatives, 11 Apr. 1869.

[2] Ibid., p. 938–40, Doc. 255, Date, then Foreign Minister, to the Foreign Representatives.

[3] For text of Ordinance, Matsukata, op. cit., pp. 23–24. No copy of Date's letter to Parkes has been found but Parkes's reply makes clear its contents. Figures differ for the amount of paper money already issued.

they should be 'accepted with entire confidence by the people' made Parkes ask how long must foreign merchants wait for such a result. He said there was no confidence on the part of the people at that time or 'why should so many of them have suddenly discontinued their business and thus nearly occasioned a stoppage of foreign trade?'

The British minister advised that 'in dealing with financial difficulties' a government can expect to gain the confidence of its own people and of the subjects of foreign powers, 'not by coercive measures' but 'by furnishing them with a full and fair explanation of the state of the country, its income and expenses, and the financial resources and plans of the Government'. He recommended to the Japanese authorities the adoption of this course. He asked again for a prompt satisfactory answer to his several letters and those of his colleagues, requesting an explanation of the continuing circulation of large quantities of debased coin issued by the government as well as by some of the daimyo which, he said, were as detrimental to commerce as an over-issue of inconvertible paper money.[1] This letter brought results slowly.

On 14 August 1869 Ōkuma Shigenobu, then Assistant Finance Minister, notified all the diplomatic missions that to eliminate the debased currency and assist foreign trade a new mint would be established and a new currency produced by December. With this he forwarded samples of the form, size, and weight of the coins being considered.[2] On 26 August Sanjō Sanetomi, now Minister of the Right, met with the foreign representatives to arrange for an examination of all *nibu* then held by foreigners. Parkes in consequence issued notifications and instructions regarding these decisions to all British consuls in Japan. He announced that the Japanese government would determine and certify the quality of all *nibu* then owned by foreigners. Those equal to the government standard (established by treaty in 1866) would circulate freely in the future, while those of inferior quality would be gradually exchanged by the government for *nibu* of government standard. Until so exchanged, the inferior coins would be accepted in payment of duties. British subjects were ordered to furnish their resident consul

---

[1] *D.N.G.M.* ii, Pt. 2, 75–83, Doc. 273, Parkes to Date, Yedo, 19 July 1869.
[2] Ibid., pp. 291–6, Doc. 330.

with a statement of the number of *nibu* in their possession the day following the receipt of the notification. Their statements were to be sent that same day to the local *saibansho* (court). On the following day, Sundays excepted, the owner of the *nibu* was to be told at the *saibansho* when to present his *nibu* for examination. The two qualities were to be distinguished by different seals or stamps and returned to their owner. The government engaged to redeem the inferior *nibu* as rapidly as possible. After the date of this notice the government would refuse to receive *nibu* that had not been examined and certified. All *nibu* accepted by British subjects thereafter must also be examined at the *saibansho* and, if found equal to the government standard, certified. How fully this was carried out is not clear. The coins circulated until 1874.[1]

British Influence on the Meiji Mint

A new national coinage soon followed. Early in 1868 the Meiji government had purchased through Thomas B. Glover of Nagasaki the British mint in Hong Kong, then valued at $60,000. This machinery arrived and was established in Osaka in November 1868. An Englishman, Thomas Waters, was appointed that autumn to supervise the construction of the mint and the preliminary work began.[2] In March 1869 the government established a Mint Department to be responsible for the control of all matters relating to the currency as well as the production of coins, under the jurisdiction of the *Dajōkan*. At the same time the *kinza* and *ginza* where currency had been minted since the beginning of the Tokugawa Shogunate on a half-governmental, half-private contractual basis, were abolished, and the government assumed full responsibility for the coinage.[3]

The government's decision to adopt Western methods of minting and to hire British technicians led to tentative agree-

---

[1] *D.N.G.M.* ii, Pt. 2, 356–64, Doc. 347. There were two kinds of *nibu* (2 bu coins) in circulation. *Nibugin* (silver) 1854–74. *Nibukin* (gold) 1867–74. *Nihonshi Jiten* (Dictionary of Japanese History), (Tokyo, 1960).

[2] Ōkurashō, *Documents*, xiii. 53. J.M. MSS. (Hyogo, 1868), Glover and Co. to J.M. Co., 14 Feb. 1868; (Osaka, 1868), T. B. Glover to W. Keswick, 28 May 1868; (Hyogo, 1868), Glover and Co. per K. R. Mackenzie to J.M. & Co., Hong Kong, 31 Oct. 1868. Here Mackenzie says the mint machinery will be 'landed from the ship in a day or two'. Jardine, Matheson received a commission of five per cent. on the $60,000.   [3] Honjō, *Meiji Ishin Keizai Shi Kenkyū*, p. 505 ff.

ments on 4 November 1869 between members of the foreign and finance ministries, Parkes, and John Robertson, manager of the Oriental Bank in Yokohama, regarding the employment of those men. At the same time, the samples proposed for the new currency were adopted.[1] The Foreign Ministry announced its plans for a new currency to all diplomatic missions on 11 December 1869.[2] All progress was much delayed, however, because in early December 1869 a fire destroyed the mint machinery which had been imported from Hong Kong.

Undaunted, the Meiji authorities decided to build another mint at Osaka, importing the necessary equipment from England through the Oriental Bank Corporation, the total cost of machinery and construction eventually amounting to 955,200 *ryō*. The new mint was completed in the late autumn of 1870. Upon the recommendation of the Oriental Bank the government had appointed the former master of the Hong Kong mint, Major William Kinder, to be director of the Japanese mint, and concluded a contract with him on 3 March 1870 to expire in February 1875. By this Kinder was made responsible for the supervision of all departments within the mint, the establishing of principles and regulations for running the mint, and measures to prevent losses by the Japanese government as well as the Oriental Bank. He was charged with the supervision of Japanese as well as European employees and the approval of all public notices before issuance. It was the Oriental Bank, however, which was to act as the agent of the Japanese government in the employment of ten Europeans, including Kinder, as mint engineers.[3]

Upon the advice of Robertson and Kinder the government decided that the currency should be based on silver. Silver was plentiful in the East while gold was scarce. Ōkuma, who had drawn up the new monetary plans, hoped that since silver was a means of international settlement, Japan's new currency would thus gain international acceptance.[4] In December 1870 the government announced that a one yen silver coin weighing

---

[1] *D.N.G.M.* ii, Pt. 3, 18–19, Doc. 507. Here the terms of employment in full may be found.   [2] Ibid., p. 298, Doc. 581.

[3] Ōkurashō, *Documents*, xiii. 53–56. According to *Daiichi Ginkō Shi*, i. 48–49, the European engineers were all British.

[4] Thomas F. M. Adams in collaboration with Iwao Hoshii, *A Financial History of Modern Japan* (Tokyo, 1964), pp. 5–6.

416 grains equal to that of the Mexican silver dollar would be the base of the new currency. Ten auxiliary coins were agreed upon—four of silver, three of gold, and three of copper. The coins were to be round, not oblong as formerly, and a decimal system was adopted.[1] The new mint opened in March 1871 amid an elaborate ceremony which Parkes and all the foreign representatives attended. The British minister and others expected it to bring about a much-needed reform in the currency.[2] Confusion, however, rather than effective reform followed.

The gold standard was being considered in Europe and the United States. Germany adopted it in 1871. These facts and a bill introduced and debated but not passed by the House of Representatives in the United States which recommended an international system of coinage based on gold led Itō to persuade the Meiji government to adopt a gold standard based on the metric system for Japan a few weeks after the opening of the mint.[3] The concerted opposition of the foreign representatives to this change had no influence.[4] Gold coins valued at two, five, ten, and twenty yen, all legal tender to any amount, of which one yen should be the standard unit of value, were ordered into circulation, causing new dies to be struck and increasing the burdens on Kinder and his inadequate staff and machinery. The recent silver yen coin remained in use for payment of import-export duties and other taxes at the treaty ports but was not available for internal taxes. Its relative legal value to the gold yen at the treaty ports was 100 silver yen to 101 gold yen.[5]

Mexican dollars continued to be current everywhere so that foreign merchants saw no advantage in applying to the mint for silver yen where they were charged two per cent. for coinage.

[1] Honjō, *Meiji Ishin Keizai Shi Kenkyū*, pp. 506–9. Okada Shumpei, *Meiji Zenki no Seika Seisaku*, p. 55. 1 yen = 10 sen; 1 sen = 10 rin; 1 rin = 10 mō; 1 mō = 10 shi.　[2] F.O. 46/138, Parkes to Granville, No. 54, Yedo, 21 Apr. 1871.

[3] Matsukata, op. cit., pp. 2–5, for text of Itō's recommendation; pp. 6–10, text of Imperial Ordinance. T. F. M. Adams, op. cit., pp. 5–6.

[4] F.O. 46/140, F. O. Adams (now chargé during Parkes's home leave) to Granville, No. 36, Yedo, 18 July 1871. This protest by the British chargé and other foreign representatives was opposed by the Lords of the Treasury in London who thought the gold standard in the East most desirable and that the example set by Japan, if persisted in, might prove most beneficial. 262/222, Encl. in No. 19, William Laird to F.O., 30 Nov. 1871.

[5] Matsukata, op. cit., p. 9. F.O. 46/142, Adams to Granville, No. 114, Yedo, 18 Nov. 1871, and Kinder's *First Quarterly Report on Japanese Mint*.

The foreign ministers considered the abandonment of the silver standard as planned in 1870 a serious mistake, and warned the Meiji authorities that they would insist upon the strict observation of the treaty stipulations.[1] Sudden changes in regulations regarding currencies in which customs dues should be paid angered the foreign merchants and goods piled up on wharves at Yokohama until a new agreement was reached between the Japanese foreign minister and the foreign representatives allowing time to adjust to the new but justified requirements.[2]

Kinder's report for the year ending 31 July 1872 stated that the coinage of gold had far exceeded the expected demand and new machinery was required, 2,100,256 pieces having been struck with a value of Y 14,488,981. One yen silver pieces were made until April 1872 when Kinder was instructed to limit until further orders the coining of silver entirely to subsidiary coins, five, ten, twenty, and fifty sen pieces. Both the gold coins and silver yen had been assayed and found to be within the prescribed limits. The lack of skilled workmen in some operations had been a severe handicap but since from the beginning of the mint the object had been to instruct and advance Japanese in the work of coinage, Kinder had with great reluctance not recommended the appointment of additional foreign officers. By 1872 he had only twelve in his department. He was glad to note improvement in Japanese engravers and workmen and looked forward to the coinage equalling that of the United States within a short time.

Kinder told of the Emperor's visit to the mint for three days in July 1872 during his first tour of the principal seaports of his south-western domains. His Majesty had inspected the various departments showing special interest in the details of coinage. He had admitted Kinder to a special audience when he expressed his appreciation for all Kinder had accomplished.[3] Many thousands of people followed the Emperor in showing

[1] F.O. 46/140, Adams to Granville, No. 36, and No. 37, Conf'l., Yedo, 18 July 1871.
[2] F.O. 46/142, Adams to Granville, No. 91, Yedo, 6 Oct. 1871; 46/143, Parkes to Hammond, Winchfield, 5 Dec. 1871.
[3] Kinder's Report of 28 Aug. 1872 and appendixes, in *Japan Weekly Mail*, 1 Feb. 1873, pp. 71–72, 74, 76, encl. in F.O. 46/165, Watson to Granville, No. 31, Yedo, 10 Feb. 1873. Samuel Mossman, *New Japan, The Land of the Rising Sun* (London, 1873), pp. 455–6.

interest in the mint. Kinder reported 19,500 Japanese and 224 foreign visitors during the first six months of 1874.[1]

Although Kinder's achievement at the mint and the responsibility assumed by the Oriental Bank had gained respect for the Japanese coinage at home, the Japanese wished to run their mint themselves and do away with all foreign direction as soon as possible. Hence, much against Parkes's and other British judgement, their contracts with Kinder and the Oriental Bank were not renewed when they expired in February 1875.[2] Six Westerners remained for a while as advisers but only two, and they were British, were employed by the mint in 1880, among a native staff of 605 officers and men.[3]

Parkes lost interest in the mint when the government 'gave up the plan of coining dollars (silver yen) for the East and went in for a gold standard and a gold coinage which nobody cared for out of Japan'. He wrote: 'Now it does not matter a bit to foreigners who works the mint nor how it is managed. Its coinage can only be used for internal purposes, and will probably be nearly confined to copper.'[4]

The British exercised no apparent influence on the subsequent financial policies of the authorities in Tokyo. When in 1873 the government found it could not fulfil its promise of July 1869 to redeem its paper currency (*kinsatsu*), it decided to issue government bonds called *Kinsatsu* Exchange Bonds, bearing interest at six per cent. and payable in gold, in exchange for the paper money. These bonds in turn promoted the establishment of national banks which issued convertible notes on the security of these *Kinsatsu* Exchange Bonds and specie equal to four-tenths of their capital—a plan which failed to withdraw from circulation the inconvertible paper, as intended.[5] More experiments followed: the recoinage of the silver yen of 416 grains in 1874;[6] the issue of the silver trade dollar of 420 grains in 1875 in the vain hope of driving out and replacing the

[1] Ōkurashō (Finance Ministry) *Kōkoku Zōheiryō Shuchō Daisanshūnen Hōkokushō* (Reports for Second to Fourth Years of Imperial Mint), (Tokyo, 1874), p. 34.
[2] Ōkurashō, *Documents*, xiii. 56. *Japan Weekly Mail*, 8 Aug. and 17 Oct. 1874.
[3] F.O. 46/256, Kennedy to Salisbury (Foreign Minister since 2 Apr. 1878), Yedo, 9 Feb. 1880. *Japan Weekly Mail*, 17 Jan. 1880.
[4] Dickins, op. cit., ii. 195, Parkes to Sir Brooke Robertson, 14 Dec. 1874.
[5] Matsukata, op. cit., pp. 24–25. Takaki, op. cit., pp. 47–48.
[6] Naikaku Kampō Kyoku (Government Gazette Bureau of the Cabinet),

Mexican dollar;[1] and the national bank regulations of 1876 which made possible the founding of many more national banks with power to issue notes secured only by government bonds and inconvertible government paper money. These bank-notes thus became just 'another kind of inconvertible paper money'. Many new national banks and their extensive issues of paper notes further complicated the government's financial problems.[2] To meet the costs of the Satsuma rebellion in 1877, the government issued Y 27,000,000 in inconvertible paper currency out of the reserve kept for exchanging 'worn-out paper notes'.[3] The next year Ōkuma made the silver yen and trade dollar legal tender throughout the country. Before 1878 ended the coinage of the trade dollar was suspended and the mintage of the silver yen of 1874 resumed.[4] Public confidence and trade suffered from all these changes, although a British report on the finances of Japan, January 1873–30 June 1877, sought to show that in the light of her progress already made, Japan's financial position did not appear 'unsatisfactory'.[5]

By the end of 1878 a total of Y 165,697,598 in government paper and bank-notes were in circulation against a specie reserve of Y 17,837,729.[6] Although for a few years after 1872 the paper notes had circulated at par with specie within Japan, their inconvertible character and the over-issue in 1877 led to their rapid depreciation. A serious inflation followed throughout 1880. Gold and silver left the country. The excess of imports was alarming. Prices rose, that of rice in 1881 being more than double what it was in 1877. And private gambling on currency values, much deplored by the responsible British press, flourished. Average interest rates soared from 10·03 per cent. in December 1876 to 14·10 per cent. in December 1881 when the highest rate was eighteen per cent. In April 1881, one silver yen commanded an average one yen, seventy-nine sen, five rin in paper currency.[7]

Hōrei Zensho, M. 7 (Collection of Laws and Regulations, 1874), (Tokyo, 1887), pp. 28–29, Imperial Ordinance No. XXXIV, 20 Mar. 1874.

[1] Imperial Ordinance No. XXXV, 28 Feb. 1875. T. F. M. Adams, op. cit., p. 6.

[2] Matsukata, op. cit., pp. 25–26. Soyeda in *History of Banking*, iv. 426.

[3] Takaki, op. cit., p. 44. Imperial Ordinance No. LXXXVII, 27 Dec. 1877. Matsukata, op. cit., p. 26.

[4] Imperial Ordinances No. XII, May 1878, and XXXV, 26 Nov. 1878. For all these ordinances see Matsukata, op. cit., pp. 9–12.

[5] P.P. H. of C. 1877, lxxxi. 211, Report by Augustus H. Mounsey, encl. in Parkes to Derby, Yedo, 5 Mar. 1877.   [6] Table VIII. Matsukata, op. cit., p. 29.

[7] Ibid., p. 40 and pp. 13–16, 34 for Tables II, III, IV, IV, X. Takaki, op. cit.,

British Opposition to the Yen as Legal Tender in Hong Kong

It was during this hazardous period that the Japanese government sought on 18 February 1878 to establish the silver yen as legal tender in Hong Kong, perhaps to compensate for its financial concerns at home. Ando Tarō, the Japanese consul in Hong Kong, who was pressing the issue upon the British authorities in the colony, wrote optimistically to his government in the winter of 1878 that he already had the support of the governor of the colony and the approval of the Hong Kong and Shanghai and Oriental Banks.[1] He knew the decision rested in London, however. And the bankers were awaiting the decision of the British government regarding the coinage of British dollars for trade in the Orient, and the legalization of the American trade dollar as recommended by the Hong Kong Chamber of Commerce. Although they admitted the possible value of the yen as an adjunct to the currency of the colony, they were not yet ready to accept it.[2] Parkes doubted the ability of the Japanese government to supply a coin of fixed weight, purity, and denomination in sufficient quantity to meet the needs of the Eastern trade and questioned whether public confidence in the maintenance of the standard of Japan's coin could be increased since native officers managed the mint.[3] Again, while in London on home leave, he discouraged such recognition of the yen as premature in view of the uncertainty of Japan's supply of silver and the depreciation of paper currency, until greater reliance could be placed on the measures of the Japanese government regarding currency and finance.[4] Concern for the position of the Mexican dollar may have influenced Parkes's thinking, as the British consuls in Yokohama and Hyogo reported that since 19 September 1879 the foreign banks had accepted the silver yen on a par with the Mexican dollar and it had virtually expelled the latter from circulation in Japan.[5]

p. 51. *Japan Weekly Mail*, 27 Sept. 1879 and 10 Apr. 1880. Soyeda in *History of Banking*, iv. 521.

[1] *N.G.M.* xi. 315–16, 320–1, Docs. 151 and 154. With vol. x of the *D.N.G.M.* series, which covers the documents of 1877, the title of the series is changed to *Nihon Gaikō Monjo (N.G.M.)*

[2] F.O. 46/229, Parkes to Derby, No. 18, Yedo, 4 Mar. 1878.

[3] F.O. 46/231, Parkes to Salisbury, No. 101, Yedo, 11 Oct. 1878.

[4] F.O. 46/256, Parkes to Salisbury, London, 12 Jan. 1880.

[5] P.P. H. of C. 1880, lxxv. 8, 31, Cons. Reports for Hyogo and Kanagawa, 1879.

On 9 February 1880 the British government refused Japan's proposal to make the yen legal tender, without giving its reason.[1] Parkes's advice probably led to this decision. At the time, however, it was attributed to the uninformed opinion of Sir Charles Fremantle, the Master of the London Mint, who opposed the measure principally on the ground 'that there was no trade of any consequence between Japan and Hong Kong'. The appeals of the Governor of Hong Kong, Sir John Pope Hennessy, to Fremantle to change his view and to the British government had no effect although his wish to make the Japanese silver yen legal tender in Hong Kong now had the firm support of Thomas Jackson, the Chief Manager of the Hong Kong and Shanghai Bank, the Hong Kong Chamber of Commerce, and the Chinese bankers.[2]

The matter was still under discussion two years later. Although Ōkuma Shigenobu, Minister of Finance 1873–80, in his detailed reports on Japan's expenditures and revenues had explained and tried to justify his country's currency measures in the midst of great difficulties,[3] although the estimates of revenues and expenditures for Japan's annual budget were now made public,[4] and although the Director of the Osaka Mint, Mr. Ishimaru, showed in his annual report a marked increase in Japan's imports of silver in 1881 over 1880, and reported the consensus of the national mints in London and Philadelphia that the standard of weight and fineness of all Japanese coins had been satisfactorily maintained, the British government, even under the Liberal Gladstone, did not reverse its judgement. 'Want of confidence in the permanence of both the quality and the supply of silver yen' was still thought to influence the policy of the English authorities.[5]

[1] *N.G.M.* xiii. 535–7, Docs. 223 and 224, Pancefote to Mori (Japanese Minister in London), F.O. 9 Feb. 1880; Kennedy to Inoue Kaoru, Yedo, 18 Mar. 1881.

[2] Ibid., pp. 537–43, Doc. 225, encls. in Andō (Japanese Consul in Hong Kong) to Inoue, 10 May 1880. Okada Shumpei, *Meiji Zenki no Seika Seisaku*, pp. 225–34.

[3] Count Ōkuma Shigenobu, 'Revenues and Expenditures' Report for Eight Fiscal Years 1868–June 1875, *Japan Weekly Mail*, 14, 21 Feb., and Editorial Comment upon the report, 5 June 1880.

[4] For examples see F.O. 46/247, Parkes to Salisbury, No. 102, Yedo, 12 Sept. 1879 and encls. *Japan Weekly Mail*, 13, 20, 27 Aug. 1881.

[5] Digest of Ishimaru's Report, *Japan Weekly Mail*, 22 Apr. 1882, pp. 479–80. *Report of the Commissioner of the Imperial Mint for the Year Ending 30 June 1881* (Hyogo, 1882), pp. 4, 31–32.

Francis Brinkley, the conscientious, able editor of the *Japan Mail* papers, both upheld the quality of the yen at this time and saw clearly the advantages of its being legal tender in Hong Kong. He knew that Japan's lack of silver mines should have little bearing on the question because of her proximity to the inexhaustible supplies in America and China, but he had this to say to the Japanese about the British action:

To conduct large coining operations with thoroughly reliable accuracy and regularity, demands a degree of scientific and practical attainments for which sober-minded persons cannot yet persuade themselves to give the Japanese credit. If the English Government could have been sure that Japan would be content to leave the management of their mint in the hands of efficient foreigners until no shadow of doubt remained as to native competency, there would probably have been less hesitation about declaring the silver yen a legal tender in Hong Kong. But unfortunately rumour refused to sanction any such assurances. It was no secret that in the matter of the mint at any rate the late Minister of Finance [Ōkuma] sacrificed expedience to sentiment, and set greater store by the name of independence than by the ability to be independent.

Brinkley advised the Japanese authorities to regard the English decision as final and to make the increased popularity of the silver yen a paramount object.[1] To do this he proposed specific methods in addition to his earlier recommendations for the resumption of specie payment.[2]

Reform in this direction had already begun with the appointment of Count Matsukata Masayoshi as finance minister in October 1881. His aims to contract the currency, to build up a growing specie reserve, and ultimately to make the irredeemable paper notes convertible led to the government's decision to establish on 10 October 1882 the Central Bank of Japan in accordance with Matsukata's *Memorandum* of March 1882. New taxes were levied to increase revenues. A surplus thus acquired was used half and half to redeem inconvertible paper money and to add to the reserve fund to secure specie from abroad. A drastic fall in prices and general disturbance to all business resulted, causing widespread distress and depression. But by 1885 the government had reduced its paper currency to approxi-

[1] *Japan Weekly Mail*, 10 June 1882.
[2] Ibid., 27 May 1882.

mately Y 88,345,096 and could maintain about Y 42,260,000 of specie in reserve. By 1886 specie and paper were at par.[1] This spectacular recovery and Japan's assurance that the Imperial Mint would gladly coin yen in any amount at a charge of one per cent. had no effect on London's opposition to making the yen legal tender in Hong Kong. Another attempt in Hong Kong and Singapore to do so in both colonies met a summary refusal from the British Foreign Office in November 1887, based on the opposition of the Colonial Office authorities[2]— this in spite of the fact that the silver yen had been in use as legal tender in Singapore since 17 January 1874.[3]

[1] Matsukata, op. cit., p. 70; for text of *Memorandum* on his policy see ibid., pp. 43–67. Takaki, op. cit., p. 58. *Japan Weekly Mail*, 31 Mar. 1883, pp. 201–3.

[2] *N.G.M.* xiii. 548, 549, 552–3, Doc. 225.

[3] Okada Shumpei, *Meiji Zenki no Seika Seisaku*, p. 235.

PART THREE

BRITISH INFLUENCE ON
JAPANESE CULTURE

XVI

THE BRITISH PRESS IN JAPAN
1861–1883

'In its endeavours to lead and educate the people in politics, in commercial development, in national expansion, the Japanese press has invariably pointed to Great Britain as a model and example. . . . It is English journalism and its unique traditions that the best section of the Japanese press constantly keeps in mind in its humble efforts to be a worthy factor in the elevation of its beloved countrymen.'[1]

English Newspapers

THE beginnings of English newspapers in the newly opened Japanese cities were necessarily modest. Prompt reporting of world events was impossible in the Far East in the eighteen sixties, the nearest telegraph being at Colombo. Papers from India and England were the main sources for foreign news. But such news was old when it arrived in Japan. Typical of the period is the announcement in the *Japan Commercial News* of 9 March 1864 reporting that the London mail of 5 January would be due in Hong Kong on 11 March, in Shanghai on 18 March, and in Yokohama on the 25th. Postal rates were high. Letters from Nagasaki to England via Suez cost twenty-four cents per half-ounce, newspapers eight cents. So precious was news that anyone receiving a budget of papers sent them to the early editors for the interest of the entire community.[2] Furthermore the number of English readers in any Japanese port was small and mails between the ports were infrequent. Although a twice-monthly overland postal service between Nagasaki and Yokohama was begun in March 1862, by which newspapers could be carried for half an *ichibu* per ounce, the number of potential English readers in the whole of Japan would have discouraged most editors.[3] Four

---

[1] Zumoto Motosada, founder of the *Japan Times*, 1897, in Alfred Stead, op. cit., p. 557. [2] Paske-Smith, *Western Barbarians*, pp. 260, 263.
  [3] *Japan Herald*, 8 Mar. 1862, in the Library of Congress. Half an *ichibu* equalled about 16½ cents.

hundred and fifty copies of a leading paper in Yokohama was the maximum number printed daily in 1870. Actually financial difficulties caused the failure of a number of the early papers.[1]

Albert W. Hansard, the pioneer in English journalism in Japan, made his newspapers an adjunct to other business. On his way east from England he had had some newspaper experience in New Zealand where he had published the *Southern Cross* and had acquired the printing machinery which he brought to Japan in 1861. According to contemporary advertisements he set up in Nagasaki a general printing establishment to supply circulars, cards, receipt and order forms. He also became a public auctioneer of 'Property of every description' and provided for the storage and display of goods offered for auction or private sale. And he was the Nagasaki agent for the *London and China Telegraph*.[2] He launched the *Nagasaki Shipping List and Advertiser* on 22 June 1861. This two- to four-page paper, measuring about eighteen by twenty-eight inches, came out on Wednesdays and Saturdays. Subscription was twenty dollars a year.

Hansard aimed to meet the need for commercial information in several communities as well as to satisfy an increasingly world-wide desire for knowledge about Japan. In his opening editorial he promised intelligence 'not only about our trade and commerce and social progress' but also 'about original and interesting particulars of the beautiful country in which we are living—and its interesting people'.[3] His motto was 'Onward, press onward'. He devoted the first six and a half columns of the issue of 10 July 1861 to advertisements of firms, articles for sale, hotels and rooming-houses in Nagasaki, Deshima, and Shanghai. An announcement of divine service every Sunday at the British Consulate follows and is succeeded by a brief section on correspondence, the dates of shipping from London to

[1] Ebihara Hachirō, *Nippon Ōji Shimbun-Zasshi Shi* (The History of European-language Newspapers and Magazines in Japan), (Tokyo, 1934), pp. 73–78.

[2] Ono Hideo, 'Waga Kuni Shoki no Gaiji Shimbun' (Early Period of Foreign Newspapers in Japan) which is the introduction to *Bakumatsu Meiji Shimbun Zenshū* (Collection of Late *Bakufu* and Meiji Newspapers) [5 vols. (Tokyo, 1934), i. 1–2], ed. by Osatake Takashi, Meiji Bunka Kenkyū Kai (Institute for Studying Meiji Culture). *Nagasaki Shipping List and Advertiser*, 10 July 1861, p. 1, given in Paske-Smith, *Western Barbarians*, Supplement II.

[3] Ibid. Supplement I. *Japan Herald*, 23 Nov. 1861, pp. 2–3.

Shanghai, the weekly calendar and weather report, and a note to subscribers. There is an editorial on the Kanagawa trade returns for the half-year 1861 which had been published as a supplement to the *North China Herald* of 8 June 1861, a long account of the first meeting of the Municipal Council in Nagasaki, a detailed report of the local market, and two columns of foreign news dealing with England, and the civil war in America. The fourth page covered shipping intelligence—arrivals, departures, and the shipping in Nagasaki harbour.[1]

Hansard had the full support of the British Consul, George Morrison, for this venture. In a letter to the Governor of Nagasaki, Morrison wrote that the forthcoming paper would be the medium for public notifications from the British legation and British consulates in Japan. He also told the Governor that Hansard would be glad 'to instruct two or three respectable young gentlemen' on the Governor's recommendation 'in all that relates to the art of printing'.[2]

The life of this Nagasaki paper was brief—twenty-eight issues only. Although the support of subscribers in Nagasaki and China had brought Hansard financial success, his ambition to produce a 'journal for Japan' could not be achieved in Nagasaki. Yokohama had already surpassed Nagasaki as a commercial centre and was much nearer Yedo, the seat of official information. Hansard therefore transferred his enterprise to Yokohama. There on Saturday, 23 November 1861, he inaugurated a weekly newspaper, the *Japan Herald*, 'under the same Proprietorship, Editorial and General Management and with the same staff and material' as its Nagasaki predecessor. Subscriptions were seventy-five cents per copy or $25·00 per year payable in advance.[3]

Hansard made his principles clear in the opening editorial. He intended to be thoroughly independent. No pressure could be devised which would make his paper a vehicle of personal abuse or 'the organ of a party to the unfair exclusion of the

---

[1] *Nagasaki Shipping List and Advertiser*, 10 July 1861. This photostat copy in Supplement II of Paske-Smith, *Western Barbarians*, is the only copy of the paper known to exist.

[2] Ebihara, op. cit., pp. 15–16. Paske-Smith, *Western Barbarians*, pp. 258–9.

[3] Ibid., Supplement I. *Japan Herald*, 23 Nov. 1861, p. 2. A second photostat of this issue is attached to the 5 Mar. 1864 number of the *Daily Japan Herald* in the Meiji Shimbun Zasshi Bunko at Tokyo University.

views of others'. The *Japan Herald* would 'aim at becoming the medium for conveying at the earliest possible moment, such information as we may be able to obtain on all matters of public importance, and of their fair and open discussion in a temperate and consistent tone.' He requested all the legations and the community to assist in making the paper a 'public medium of intelligence' which would be an important addition to the Eastern Press—'with an influence for much good and of great interest' not only in Japan—'but *at home*, in China, India, and in all parts of the world'. His new paper followed closely the format and the distribution of news items adopted by the *Nagasaki Shipping News and Advertiser.*

The surviving copies of the *Japan Herald* fail to list the editorial staff. John Reddie Black, a Scot, and former naval officer and merchant, is known to have been one of the first editors-in-chief whose editorials gave the paper prestige over its forthcoming competitors. He was assisted by I. Y. Pin and J. H. Brooke, an Australian and 'the first trained journalist to make Japan his field'.[1] In his book, *Young Japan*, Black tells nothing of his part in the publication of the *Herald*.[2] Japanese writers, however, consider his contributions to this and later journals of prime importance to contemporary developments in Japan. His frank, kindly criticism of the Japanese government became a recognized benefit to the *Bakufu* and early Meiji officials.[3] It is not clear whether Black was responsible for the support which the *Herald* gave the Shogunate against the rising Imperial cause in 1865 although he was thought to be sympathetic to the Tokugawa government.[4]

Hansard announced in February 1862 that O. R. Keele, his partner in the auction and commission business, would henceforth 'share jointly in the interest, management, and responsibility' of the *Japan Herald*.[5] Five years later in 1867 Hansard returned to England where he died. A. T. Watkins followed him as the publisher of the *Herald* but was soon succeeded by J. H.

[1] Ebihara, op. cit., pp. 19, 24–26, 67–68. Ono, op. cit., in *Bakumatsu Meiji Shimbun Zenshū*, i. 6–7. *Kobe Chronicle*, 23 Mar. 1941.

[2] Black, op. cit. i. 70–71.

[3] Ebihara, op. cit., pp. 51–52. *Kokumin Hyakka Daijiten* (National Encyclopedia), 12 vols. (Tokyo, 1936), xi. 462.

[4] Ono, op. cit., in *Bakumatsu Meiji Shimbun Zenshū*, i. 2–3.

[5] *Japan Herald*, 21 Feb. and 8 Mar. 1862. Copies in Library of Congress.

Brooke who bought the paper in 1867. Black left the journal in the same year to establish a newspaper office of his own.[1]

The publication of competitive newspapers caused several changes in the *Herald*'s policies. The *Japan Express*, a paper financed and published by Americans, challenged its position without success in 1862.[2] Its monopoly, however, was menaced in July 1863 when another English weekly appeared. This was the *Japan Commercial News*, edited and published in Yokohama by a Portuguese, F. da Roza. Although the editorials of this newcomer were considered inferior to those of the *Herald*, its articles on Japan were selected for translation for the *Bakufu* and attracted many readers.[3] Hansard therefore sought fresh limelight. On the morning of 6 December 1863 he came out with the *Daily Japan Herald*, a four-page sheet similar in size and format to the weekly but devoted primarily to the advertisements of Western firms and announcements of interest to them.[4]

It is clear from these advertisements that life was not necessarily dull in the early days of Yokohama. A wide range of goods and services was available to the Western community. The Yokohama Hotel announced its opening to the public on or before 1 February 1864 'with entirely new fittings' which would include 'two splendid bowling alleys and five of Phelan's best slate bed Billiard Tables'.[5] The Restaurant Aux Trois Frères Provencaux promised 'that orders for dinners and pastry for town' would be executed with greatest care.[6] Items listed for sale included: 'Photographic supplies and pictures; marine insurance by Aspinall, Cornes & Co. on First Class vessels to the United Kingdom or to various ports of China'; 1,500 volumes of new and popular standard books from the 'eminent publishing

[1] Ono, 'Waga Kuni Shoki no Gaiji Shimbun', p. 6. Ebihara, op. cit., pp. 68–70.
[2] Ono, 'Waga Kuni Shoki no Gaiji Shimbun', p. 4. One copy has been found in the French Foreign Office Archives.
[3] Ebihara, op. cit., pp. 20–24, 27–29. Copies of the *Japan Commercial News* are unknown except for clippings or extracts enclosed by British Foreign Office officials or naval officers in their reports home, e.g., extracts for 26 Aug. 1863 and 9 Mar. 1864.
[4] Ebihara, op. cit., p. 29; 20 Oct. 1863, however, is the date given for the first issue of the *Daily Japan Herald* in *A Short History of the Japan Times* (In commemoration of the 15,000th Issue of the Daily and Revision of Its Title), (Tokyo, 25 Mar. 1941), p. 65. A file of the *Daily Japan Herald*, 8 Jan. 1864, No. 61 to 24 June 1864, No. 202, is at Tokyo University. Some time between 20 Oct. and 6 Dec. 1863 is therefore probably correct for the first number of the paper.
[5] Ibid., 15 Jan. 1864.   [6] Ibid., 21, 29 Jan., 5, 10 Feb. 1864.

house of Routledge, Warne and Routledge', and luxuries such as morocco travelling bags, Albert Gold Guards, gold scarf and finger rings, watches, shirt studs, riding, racing, and fencing equipment as well as ladies' white satin and kid boots and shoes, black lace flouncing, wreaths, flowers, and opera cloaks.[1]

Crafts and business advertised in the *Daily Japan Herald*. One man sought work as 'ship builder, carpenter, and blacksmith', others as civil and mechanical engineers, silk inspectors, and pharmacists.[2] The daily columns included brief notices of local fires, murders, attacks on foreigners, and the collection of garbage.[3] Shippers were continuously warned to weigh silk carefully before shipping by P. and O. steamers because of frequent 'discrepancies between the weight of bales as ascertained on board steamers and that in the bills of lading'.[4] Enthusiastic comments supported the performance of an equestrian troop from Shanghai on 28 March 1864. The show lacked 'vulgarity, claptrap, and improprieties'. Dress seats were $3.00, those in the second circle $2.00.[5]

Editorials occasionally crept in with the advertisements. Thus the reduction of duties was discussed and a re-evaluation of Colonel Neale's policy regarding Satsuma.[6] The paper sought to correct for China and the home market the 'sensation vending' of its rival the *Commercial News* such as the statement that 'the Mikado having abdicated, was about to come to Yedo with his friend, the Tycoon, to aid him in his government'. 'Nonsense', laughed the *Herald*; this shows 'utter ignorance of the Government of Japan'.[7] In another issue the editors expressed great sympathy for an unoffending Japanese fisherman who was assaulted and injured by a drunken private in Britain's 20th Regiment and suggested that the men of the Regiment reimburse the fisherman's family for loss of their usual support. 'A trifle would serve the purpose', they thought, and 'be highly useful, perhaps, in respect to the position of esteem in which we all desire to be held amongst the industrious and kindhearted villagers whom we frequently encounter in our rambles in the

---

[1] *Daily Japan Herald*, 8, 21, 23, 27, 29 Jan., 3, 17 Feb. 1864.
[2] Ibid., 18, 19 Feb., 2 Mar. 1864.
[3] Ibid., 11 Jan., 23 Feb., 23, 24 Mar. 1864.
[4] Ibid., 11, 27 Jan., 4, 5, 25 Feb. 1864.   [5] Ibid., 30 Mar. 1864.
[6] Ibid., 30 Jan., 7 Mar. 1864.
[7] Ibid., 14 Apr. 1864.

neighbourhood.'[1] The price of all this daily information and opinion was $2.00 a month. And the paper prospered until another competitor caused another change in its form.

This was the *Japan Gazette*, a daily evening paper which appeared in Yokohama on 12 October 1867. Herein John R. Black and B. N. Heght undertook to publish current local news in addition to the periodic news from abroad. Their immediate success led the owners of the *Herald* papers to abolish both their weekly edition and their daily advertising sheet in favour of a competing evening daily, called the *Japan Daily Herald*.[2] The date of the first issue is unknown.[3] In its new form the *Herald* held to its critical attitude towards the Japanese government. Thus it opposed Japan's invasion of Formosa in 1874 and expressed contempt for General Charles LeGendre and the 'American mercenaries' who were lending aid in embroiling China and Japan with whom their country was at peace. It declared: 'Japan should not be encouraged to make war upon false pretences in order that she may filch territory from her Chinese neighbour.'[4] The paper was distinguished for its reprints of articles on Japan which were appearing in leading English journals, such as 'The Romance of the Japanese Revolution' in *Blackwood's Magazine* and for its criticism of Fred Marshall's article in the *Fortnightly Review* which had attacked British policies in Japan.[5] The *Herald* followed the current practice of all English papers of the time in publishing a summary, probably fortnightly, for overseas consumption[6] and it continued to put out annually a *Hong List and Directory* which its founder had begun in 1862.[7] By 1879 this contained lists of the diplomatic and consular establishments, foreign firms and residents throughout Japan, the proposed arrivals

---

[1] Ibid., 24 June 1864.

[2] Black, op. cit. ii. 87–88. Ebihara, op. cit., p. 68. Nihon Shimbun Kyōkai (Japan Newspaper Association), *Chihōbetsu Nihon Shimbun Shi* (*History of Local Japanese Newspapers*), (Tokyo, 1956), pp. 116, 159, 161.

[3] Copies of the *Japan Daily Herald* for 4 Apr. 1874 (No. 3201) to 31 Oct. 1874 (No. 3380) and Mar. 1877 (No. 4089) to June 1881 (No. 5412) are in Meiji Shimbun Zasshi Bunko. Broken files for 1874, 1875, and 1881 are in the Ueno National Library.   [4] *Japan Daily Herald*, 14, 15, 27 Aug. 1874.

[5] Ibid., 16, 17, 18, 19 Aug., 5 Sept. 1874. *Blackwood's Magazine*, June 1874, pp. 696–712. *Fortnightly Review*, July 1874, pp. 133–45.

[6] This was called the *Japan Herald Mail Summary*. Broken files May 1874 to Nov. 1877 are in the British Museum. I have not seen them.

[7] *Japan Herald*, 8 Mar. 1862. In Library of Congress.

and departures of the Mitsubishi Mail Steamship Co.'s ships running between Yokohama and Shanghai, a chart of the settlement of Yokohama, the Bluff, and native town, and an almanac for the year—a volume which a contemporary journal considered the best work of its kind yet published in Yokohama.[1]

Before discussing the nature of the *Japan Gazette*, a still earlier and briefer competitor of the *Herald*, the first *Japan Times*, deserves consideration. It was the successor of the *Herald*'s rival, the *Japan Commercial News*, which had suspended publication in the late spring of 1865. At that time Charles Rickerby, an English resident of Yokohama since 1862 and the local manager of the Central Bank of Western India, gave up his financial post and jointly with J. R. Anglin, C. L. Westwood, and B. Seare, purchased the printing-plant and goodwill of da Roza's paper. They published the first issue of the *Japan Times* on 8 September 1865 at Yokohama.[2] It consisted of four pages about the size of the first *Herald* and claimed to be 'A Commercial, Political and General Weekly Newspaper'. Charles Rickerby, the real editor and proprietor, expressed his determination to be independent and to seek the truth regardless of personal hazards. He assured his mercantile readers, however, that their interests would be his first consideration. He would spare no effort or expense 'to render the *Japan Times* a useful guide and reliable reference on all matters connected with the trade of the country'. His sources of information, both native and foreign, were to be authentic. He intended to secure correspondents in London, Paris, and China 'whose original letters would doubtless be more interesting than the stale reproduction of news and opinions of journals which all receive for themselves and which is all that has hitherto been attempted in Japan'. He was fully conscious of his duty as the servant of the 'one great protector of liberty—THE PRESS— knowing that the consciousness of acting up to the motto: "*fais ce que dois, advienne que pourra*" is the best consolation in adversity as it is the sweetest morsel of success'.[3]

---

[1] *Japan Weekly Mail*, 18 Jan. 1879.

[2] Ebihara, op. cit., p. 63. Ono, 'Waga Kuni Shoki no Gaiji Shimbun', p. 6. Paske-Smith, *Western Barbarians*, pp. 271, 357. *Chihōbetsu Nihon Shimbun Shi*, p. 161. Only a broken file of the *Japan Times*, 8 Sept. 1865 to June 1866 in the Ueno National Library, and a few isolated copies in the British Foreign Office Archives have been found.   [3] *Japan Times*, vol. i, No. 1, 8 Sept. 1865. Black, op. cit. i. 377–8.

The *Times* staff also put out a daily sheet called the *Japan Times Daily Advertiser* which first appeared on 13 September 1865.[1] Although it lived up to its name as a commercial medium it carried official notifications[2] and important news items such as the opening of the telegraph between St. Petersburg and Peking,[3] and the Mikado's formal sanction of the treaties of 1858.[4] An equally important enterprise of the same editors was the *Japan Times' Overland Mail* which they published approximately every two weeks for dispatch by each Pacific Mail Steamer to Europe.[5] This was a small paper, averaging about twelve pages, thirteen by eight and a half inches in size. It devoted a third of its space to advertisements, market reports, and shipping news. The remainder included a review of the previous fortnight, the topics of the day, sprightly editorials on burning issues, some correspondence and news from Nagasaki.[6]

The *Times* papers quickly revealed their political colours. In this they were aided by Ernest Satow, the young interpreter in the British legation. At Rickerby's request he wrote for the weekly, cloaking his identity in the customary anonymity of the writers of that day. A long editorial of 1 December 1865, attributed to Satow, dealt with the importance of the Convention of Osaka showing that 'Japan is now for the first time, really and legitimately open to foreign trade' since the Mikado has sanctioned the treaties with the West. It stresses the fact that the 'sovereignty of the Tycoon was a shadow and his title a mockery'. Numerous weaknesses of the Shogun's pretensions to sovereign power in Japan since 1859 are cited. And the Mikado's sanction of his treaties is interpreted to mean that the Tycoon is 'relegated to his proper position as a subordinate though important official in the government of Japan'. The last half of the discourse is given to the probable consequences of the opening of Osaka to trade in 1868, to warning young and sanguine merchants, and to scorching criticism of the exaction of the indemnity for the Shimonoseki affair.

[1] A broken file is included with the *Japan Times* in the Ueno National Library.
[2] *Japan Times Daily Advertiser*, 10 Jan. 1866.   [3] Ibid., 4 Jan. 1866.
[4] Ibid., 14 Feb. 1866. It will be remembered that the Mikado's consent to the treaties was given on 22 Nov. 1865.
[5] A nearly complete file of volume v, No. 56, 4 Jan. 1868 to volume vii, No. 108, 30 Dec. 1869, is in the Meiji Shimbun Zasshi Bunko.
[6] *Japan Times' Overland Mail*, 4 Jan. 1868.

This article, considered by Japanese sources to have first expressed the *Times*'s support of the Imperial cause and to have represented the official British point of view,[1] is far less specific than the three articles which Rickerby's paper published between 16 March and 19 May 1866. Probably it was not included in the now famous pamphlet, *Eikoku Sakuron* (British Policy).[2] Satow may not have written it, although it foreshadows his later more constructive programme. Nevertheless, this editorial in conjunction with Satow's subsequent writings firmly established the allegiance of the *Times* on the side of the Restoration. Keiki's resignation in November 1867 was interpreted as the beginning of the political reforms the editors had advocated for two years.[3] In consequence the *Times* had become not only the rival but the political opponent of the *Herald*, the supporter, if not the subsidized spokesman, of the *Bakufu*.[4]

Rickerby became known for the 'scoops' in his articles on the Tokugawa régime. His papers even decried Britain's policy of neutrality during the civil war of 1868. In this the *Japan Times' Overland Mail* made no secret of its commercial motives. It wrote:

If it is right to pay custom duties at Kobe and Nagasaki to a Mikado in his minority and at Yokohama to an ex-shogun, defeated, dismissed and disgraced, why should not duties be paid at Hakodate to any northern chief who is strong enough to take possession . . . . We have honestly advocated the abrogation of the Treaties of 1858 with the Shogun because we have believed them to have been made under false impressions and because we have judged them to be restrictive of trade and incentive to civil war. And we have honestly advocated the conclusion of fresh treaties with the Mikado and the confederated *Daimios*, Southern and Northern together, because we saw in such a settlement, extension of trade, development of the resources of the country and peace for the people. But double coexistent treaties we cannot approve . . . . we hold that our primary object in invading India, China, and Japan is our own benefit, the extension of trade, the opening of fresh markets for our teeming

[1] Osatake Takashi, *Bakumatsu Gaikō Monogatari* (Tales of Late *Bakufu* Diplomacy), (Tokyo, 1926), pp. 34–35. *Bakumatsu Meiji Shimbun Zenshū*, i. 367. Yamamoto Fumio, *Nihon Shimbun Hattatsu Shi* (*History of the Development of the Press in Japan*), (Tokyo, 1944), p. 28. These Japanese translations of the article are so condensed that they give inaccurate impressions of its content.
[2] See pp. 179–82.
[3] *Japan Times' Overland Mail*, 28 Nov. 1867. Copy at Harvard University.
[4] Ebihara, op. cit., pp. 72, 76.

looms. Holding such views, it is necessarily immaterial to us whether Shogun or Mikado is to be upheld. But it is clear, one should be, both cannot be—and as clear that until we decide which power to recognize as the supreme, we should satisfy neither and that our trade cannot flourish. Our neutrality is a standing invitation to their hostility.[1]

The editors of the *Times*, however, could change their minds. By 12 March 1868 they were willing to admit that the *Notification* requiring strict neutrality of all foreigners resident in Japan and suspending the article in the treaties of 1858 whereby only the Shogun's government could purchase munitions, had virtually ended the war. At the same time they upbraided the foreign representatives for the treacherous way they had thus treated their first ally, the Shogun. He should have been told that the treaties of 1858, made in error, were no longer binding. Fresh treaties with the Mikado should have been announced and the Shogun's opposition challenged.

The *Times*'s criticism of the foreign ministers as a group was mild in comparison with its denunciation of the British minister, Sir Harry Parkes. His visit to the Shogun in 1867 and his arrangements for the opening of Osaka and Hyogo without prior consultation with the merchants came in for bitter reproach as detrimental to trade.[2] No effort to understand the reasons for Parkes's policy was apparent. The editorials of the *Japan Times' Overland Mail* obviously intensified the cleavage between British officials and the commercial community. Knowing that their words would reach London, the editors declared: 'It is a great misfortune for English merchants and indeed for commercial men generally, that England is not represented in Japan by an abler man at this critical time. Sir Harry's rashness and vacillation together have made shipwreck of whatever reputation he had. He has shown himself to be no diplomat at all.'[3] The hostility of Yokohama's newly founded Chamber of Commerce towards the ministers and especially towards Parkes was emphasized. They were all accused of not only neglecting to show the Japanese nobles in what esteem merchants were held in Europe, and thus by the force of example, leading them to a proper appreciation of their own commercial group,

---

[1] *Japan Times' Overland Mail*, 27 Feb. 1868.
[2] Ibid., 28 Nov. 1867, 18, 29 Jan. 1868.   [3] Ibid., 18 Jan. 1868.

but they had lost no opportunity . . . . to debase the foreign merchants in Japanese eyes. The journal asserted that 'men sent by foreign governments to Japan to protect and advance foreign mercantile interests should recognize the fact that they are the servants of the merchant class and not its masters'.[1]

The consular courts received similar condemnation. A trivial case, *Regina* versus *Short*, precipitated an open appeal to the home government. Here the consul, after repeated warnings, had fined Short $5.00 for infringing municipal regulations by allowing filthy material to run from his compound to the street. This judgement was upheld by Chief Judge Edmund Hornby, in the Court of Shanghai. The *Japan Times' Overland Mail* took the occasion to 'expose the imbecility of the Consular Courts' —to seek a serious inquiry and in time the consequent abolition of a 'corrupt and utterly inefficient system of administration of the laws'—in which the protection of liberty and property lie 'at the mere discretion of judges without knowledge of law, without respect for forms, with no apparent guide for their conduct of cases brought before them than their own temper, observation and caprice'. In taking this stand the Yokohama paper followed four London journals (the *Morning Post*, the *Examiner*, the *Pall Mall Gazette*, and the *All Year Round*) which were at that time exposing corruption in the Foreign Office and its consular appointments.[2]

Corruption in the Japanese customs came under equal fire. The *Japan Times' Overland Mail* stated that not more than one-fifth of the proceeds reached the treasury. No one would pay duty on goods who could avoid doing so. The whole theory of free trade opposed the principle behind such payments. Native officials with all opportunities for the examination of goods passed goods at the valuation given by the merchant and allowed one description of merchandise to be palmed off upon them as well as another. Underpaid native officials were subject to bribery and paid themselves from the revenue they were expected to collect. Squeezes were multitudinous. The editors doubted 'whether profits derived by the native government from foreign trade have done more than pay for the indemnities we have exacted from it and the necessary expenses of preparing land for our residence while for all other inconvenience and

[1] *Japan Times' Overland Mail*, 9 Apr. 1868.   [2] Ibid., 2 May 1868.

damages consequent on our irruption here, no compensation whatever remains'. But dues on foreign trade were important as a means of raising revenue. Reform in collection was obviously essential. The prime need of the Mikado's new government was revenue. A foreign inspectorate of customs, the editors suggested, would remedy the evils of the current system and provide the government with a new power for borrowing money. They urged the ministers of the treaty powers to support this solution and recommend it to the Mikado.[1]

The *Times* papers made historically valuable contributions in their summaries of the major events of each year published in January of the succeeding year.[2] Evaluations of men and events crept in. By 1869 Parkes had won the approbation of the editors by his prompt recognition and moral support of the Mikado's government and for his rise to the position of the Emperor's most trusted foreign counsellor.[3]

According to Black, Rickerby's papers might have been a power in the land, had his lack of tact not overshadowed his talents.[4] As it was, his subscribers were always few even though his well-written opinions commanded attention in wide circles.[5] Financial pressures were therefore the probable reason for suspension of publication of the *Times* trio during the autumn of 1870.[6] About seven years later, 5 January 1878, Rickerby inaugurated a *Japan Times, New Series* which lasted until July of the same year.[7] Here again he espoused the principles of its predecessor, declaring it his right and duty to continue criticizing the government in a friendly manner, and hoping that his 'advice would not be thought intrusive'.[8] In both his first and second series, he published important studies in serial form. Thus Ernest Satow's *Diary of a Member of the Japanese Embassy to Europe, 1862–3* came out in the *Japan Times* of 1865[9] and Captain Frank Brinkley's *Times of Taiko* appeared in weekly instalments in 1878.

[1] Ibid., 30 May 1868.
[2] e.g. ibid., 4 Jan. 1868, 13, 27 Jan. 1869. *Japan Times*, 5 Jan. 1866.
[3] *Japan Times' Overland Mail*, 22 Aug. 1868, 27 Jan. 1869.
[4] Black, op. cit. i. 377–8.
[5] Ono, 'Waga Kuni Shoki no Gaiji Shimbun', p. 6.
[6] *A Short History of The Japan Times*, p. 66.
[7] A file of the Jan. to June 1878 issues is in the Sophia University Library.
[8] *Japan Times, New Series*, 5 Jan. 1878.
[9] *Japan Times*, 1865, Nos. 6, 7, 8, 11, and 14.

While the *Times* papers rose and fell the *Japan Gazette* was becoming an established institution. Several business men supported Black in starting this evening daily.[1] Here, as when editor of the *Herald*, he often criticized the Japanese government but in a way which was usually regarded as helpful.[2] He joined forces with the *Herald* in opposing treaty revision.[3] The earliest surviving copy of the *Gazette* seems to be that of 1 June 1868.[4] By this time the paper contained eight pages, approximately seventeen by twenty-four inches. Foreign and domestic news covered less than two of these. Information brought by the London mail of 10 April was summarized. More recent items came from India, Australia, and Hong Kong. The peace of Europe was thought to rest upon Napoleon III's solution of the domestic disturbances of France. Local items told of the opening of the Yokohama General and a smallpox hospital with first-class beds at $4.00 a day. The *Gazette* condemned the brutality of masters to servants and reported a great fire in Hakodate and a decision in the British Consular Court. The rest of the paper was devoted to advertisements.

The *Gazette*'s type outshone that of the *Herald* as a medium for advertising. By the summer of 1869 many public notices make clear the rising standards of life among the Western community in Yokohama. In addition to the varied and extensive quantities of alcoholic beverages for sale in that city, California fruits, Bombay onions, and caviar from China were offered to tempt exiled palates. An hotel had been opened for foreigners at Yedo which provided not only 'magnificent' accommodation for its patrons but bonded warehouses for the storage of large quantities of silk, tea, or silkworm eggs. Four hotels in Yokohama featured billiard saloons or bowling alleys. Board and a single room at the Phoenix were $8.00 a week, a furnished room $10.00 a month. The proprietors here *sold* 'Good Spring Mattresses'. A two-horse coach left Yokohama for Yedo daily at nine in the morning and returned in the afternoon. The fare was $2.00 each way. 'Concertinas, accordians, flutinas, harmoniums, organs, pianofortes, musical boxes

---

[1] Ono, 'Waga Kuni Shoki no Gaiji Shimbun', p. 6.

[2] Ebihara, op. cit., p. 52.   [3] Ibid., p. 103.

[4] This is in the Library of the Pennsylvania Historical Society in Philadelphia. Scattered copies for 1872–6 are said to be at Yale. Broken files for 1877, 1879, 1880, and 1881 are at Meiji Shimbun Zasshi Bunko and at the Ueno National Library.

and all kinds of Musical Instruments' could be tuned and repaired. And the gardener of the late Tycoon presented for sale a fine collection of his master's 'Plants in rare Porcelaine Pots, such as have never been offered to the Yokohama public before'.[1]

The *Gazette* staff also published a morning sheet and a fortnightly summary as well as a *Hong List and Directory*. The fortnightly edition claimed to be a summary of the 'Political, Commercial, Literary and Social Events of Japan'. It contained from twenty to thirty-four pages. Among the items included were: a brief summary of the events of the past fortnight, several leading articles, reviews of recent issues such as Imperial Government Notifications and the spirit of the Japanese press, 'Occasional Notes', correspondence, reports of cases tried in consular courts, reports from foreign cities—e.g. Wenchow and Vladivostok—shipping, market, and financial intelligence, and a very small amount of advertising.[2]

The fourth important British newspaper in Yokohama, the *Japan Mail*, appeared in daily, weekly, and bi-monthly editions in January 1870.[3] None of the early issues has been found. W. G. Howell, the owner and editor, was considered by some 'the most accomplished journalist ever known in the Far East'.[4] The Meiji government sought his support, in an effort to get accurate reports of conditions in Japan circulated in the West. It instructed Ōkuma Shigenobu, then a member of the *Dajōkan*, to sign an agreement with Howell on 13 October 1873, wherein the government was to purchase 500 copies of every issue of the *Japan Mail* (the fortnightly edition) for distribution to Western countries at a cost of ¥ 5,000 plus ¥ 428 for postage for one year beginning 1 September 1873. Howell was to be responsible

---

[1] Section of *Japan Gazette* for July 1869 in MSS. Clarendon (Foreign Office 23B), at the Bodleian Library in Oxford.

[2] *Japan Gazette Fortnightly*, 19 Jan. and 13 Apr. 1880. Vols. 23, 25, 26, 28, and 29, covering, although with gaps, the period from Jan. 1879 to June 1882 are in the Baker Library at Harvard.

[3] *Japan Weekly Mail*, 20 Jan. 1877, p. 53. Ebihara, op. cit., p. 81. Ono, 'Waga Kuni Shoki no Gaiji Shimbun', p. 6. *Chihōbetsu Nihon Shimbun Shi*, p. 162. Files of the *Daily Mail* for 1874, 1877, 1878, 1879, 1880, 1881, and 1882 are at the Sophia University Library; for 1874–82 at Tōyō Bunko. Files of *Japan Weekly Mail*, 9 May 1874 to 19 May 1883 in Library of Congress; for 6 Jan. 1872 to Oct. 1917 at the Stamford University Library; some for 1879 in Meiji Shimbun Zasshi Bunko; for 6 Jan. 1877 to 21 Dec. 1912, although with gaps, at the Sophia University Library.

[4] Dickins, op. cit. ii. 170.

for the distribution and for informing the government every month regarding the destination and number of copies sent. He also promised to report accurately the facts which the Japanese government wished the world to know about its national administration, economic development, manners and customs of the Japanese people, and relations with foreign countries. He retained the right, however, in accordance with English practice, to express his own opinions impartially on the material given him by the Japanese government, as if he had no connexion with the state. The agreement could be cancelled by the government on three months' notice. This the government eventually did in March 1875 by *Notification Thirty-five*, in spite of the fact that Howell had apparently been just and objective in his handling of Japanese news.[1]

Howell retired from the *Mail* in January 1877. His valedictories stressed his sincere efforts for seven years to make 'his journal the organ of his own mind, fortified, instructed and corrected by the best advice and opinion at his command'. His predominant motive had been his desire for the welfare of the British Empire and the foreign communities in Japan; 'for the promotion of just, generous and sympathetic feelings towards the Japanese; and of good will from them towards ourselves'. A dinner of sixty-four representatives of the Diplomatic Corps, the Bench, the Bar, the Armed Forces, the Press, and all classes of the community testified to his success. Even the editor of the *Herald*, J. H. Brooke, in spite of his disapproval of the politics of the *Mail*, praised its tone and character and its literary and musical criticism.[2] Satow wrote that Howell's departure would be 'a great loss to Yokohama, socially, musically and literarily'.[3]

George Cullen Pearson, a highly regarded member of the English community, bought the *Japan Mail* at a reported price of £3,500 and inaugurated a *New Series* on 27 January 1877.[4] He wished to maintain the tone and reputation of the paper but sought to make it the reflector of many minds and not the spokesman of his alone. He came out in his introductory editorial against the abolition of extraterritoriality and attacked

[1] Ebihara, op. cit., pp. 81–86.

[2] *Japan Weekly Mail*, 20 Jan. 1877, p. 53, and (New Series), 27 Jan. 1877, pp. 11–13.

[3] Satow, MSS. 15/5 *Diary*, Yokohama, 8 Mar. 1877.

[4] Ibid. *Tokio Times*, 13 Jan. 1877.

the Meiji government's policies towards the dispossessed samurai.[1] This brought him at once into disfavour with the American founder of the newly established *Tokio Times*, Edward Howard House.[2] Pearson treated the Satsuma Rebellion, however, with detachment, viewing it in its historical setting.[3] He left the *Mail* in May 1878 having attained popularity among his staff and in the community.[4]

Pearson was succeeded by the prominent barrister, F. V. Dickins, who negotiated with Rickerby a merger of the *Mail* and *Times* publications about six months after Rickerby had begun his *New Series* of the *Times*.[5]

On 29 June 1878 Rickerby reviewed the accomplishments of his first volume and proudly presented his readers with the first index. On 20 July 1878 the merger had been accomplished as the title of the weekly paper of that date, '*The Japan Weekly Mail* incorporated with *The Japan Times*', first indicates. In the same number Dickins announced his retirement as proprietor of the *Daily Mail* and its subordinate issues, stating that Rickerby would henceforth conduct the journals.

Under Rickerby the *Japan Mail* became the open opponent of the *Herald* and the *Gazette*. The name of the *Times* was dropped from the title in July 1879, but advertisements of the *Mail* papers in 1880 stated that they were founded in 1865, the date that Rickerby began the *Times*. Hence the role of the *Times* was not ignored. When Francis Brinkley became editor-in-chief in 1881 the *Mail* papers continued to give a thoughtful allegiance to the Japanese government in contrast to the blatant criticism of their rivals.[6] A German in Japan in 1882 asserted that the *Mail* was the only foreign newspaper which sought to interpret the Japanese position fairly. It seems to have been alone in supporting the government's terms for treaty revision.[7]

The *Japan Weekly Mail* was a journal of distinction, not only because of its literary merits but especially because of the breadth of its interests. At first it claimed to be 'A Political,

---

[1] *Japan Weekly Mail*, 27 Jan. 1877, p. 5.
[2] *Tokio Times*, 3 Feb. 1877. Files for 1877 and latter part of 1879 are in Meiji Shimbun Zasshi Bunko. An almost complete series for 1877–80 is in the Library of Congress.   [3] *Japan Weekly Mail*, 1877.
[4] Ibid., 11 May 1878.   [5] Ebihara, op. cit., pp. 92–93.
[6] Ibid., p. 93. *Kobe Chronicle*, 23 Mar. 1941.
[7] Ebihara, op. cit., pp. 94–103.

Commercial, and Literary Journal', but from July 1879 it termed itself 'A Weekly Review of Japanese Commerce, Politics, Literature and Art'. Its thirty or more folio pages of fine print gave a perceptive picture of life in Japan through both Western and Japanese eyes. The contents included news of Japan and the West, Reuter's latest telegrams, thoughtful editorials on major current issues, accounts of the meetings of Chambers of Commerce and the Asiatic Societies, financial, shipping, and commercial intelligence, and a moderate number of advertisements, as well as poetry, book reviews, double acrostics, and chess problems. This journal sought to interpret Japanese opinion on many questions through translations of generous excerpts from the native press and of official Meiji *Notifications*. The editors reported with fair detachment the Japanese expedition to Formosa in 1874, and printed the official correspondence regarding the settlement of the struggle.[1] They published long studies such as *The History of Japan* by F. O. Adams as well as a work on the relations between England and Japan 1600–1851.[2] They reprinted important articles from English journals such as Macaulay's essay on *Johnson* and 'The Later Blunders of Napoleon III' from the *Pall Mall Gazette*.[3] They included verbatim the proceedings of trials in the British consular courts. They dealt objectively with religious matters— especially the work of Christian missions in Japan and the Japanese response to Christianity.[4] They featured the work of Sir Charles Lyle with an outstanding eulogy at the time of his death.[5] In sharp contrast these journalists were concerned with the sale and prices of Japanese porcelain in London, the statistics of government budgets and railways in Japan, and the intricacies of Japanese currency.[6] They also dealt fearlessly with demands for treaty revision, the press laws, and Japan's policy towards Korea. Published every Saturday evening, the price for a year's subscription to the *Weekly Mail* was $24.00.

The fortnightly, called the *Japan Mail*, was a summary of the weekly editions, intended for transmission to Europe and the

[1] *Japan Weekly Mail*, 9 May, 4, 11, 18, 25 July, 1, 8, 22 Aug., 5, 19, 26 Sept., 10, 17 Oct., 14, 28 Nov., 5, 12 Dec. 1874, 1 May 1875.
[2] Ibid., 11 July, 8, 13 Aug. 1874.   [3] Ibid., 17 Apr. 1875.
[4] Ibid., 15, 29 May, 5, 19 June, 21 Aug. 1875.
[5] Ibid., 24 Apr., 1 May 1875.
[6] Ibid., 12 Feb. 1876, 2 July, 27 Aug. 1881, 10 June 1882.

United States via Suez and San Francisco. The use of the American mail steamers to San Francisco was stressed in the advertisement of 1874. The thirty-one folio pages of the issue of 9 April 1875 included leading articles, reports from the consular courts, notes of the week with comments, and other information which had appeared in the *Japan Weekly Mail* of 27 March and 3 April. News a little more recent, such as the meeting of the Regatta Club of 8 April, and much larger sections on shipping and commercial intelligence, were followed by advertisements of Yokohama firms which would be likely to interest Western readers at home.[1]

The *Mail* had agents in London, New York, San Francisco, Hong Kong, Shanghai, Hyogo, Osaka, and Nagasaki who made it known to a wide public. For many years it was said to be 'the best known paper in Japan'. Though the offices were destroyed by fire on 18 September 1882, and a new plant had to be imported from England, the *Mail* survived with the omission of only one weekly issue. The editor took pride in the fact that his was the only morning daily in English published in Yokohama and delivered at places of business during office hours on the day of publication.[2]

English newspapers were not confined to the major port of Yokohama. Other open cities had their own. The life of many journals in this period was short; and little is known about them since most of the files are missing. The *Nagasaki Express*, established by F. da Braga and an American, Frank Walsh, in 1870, was taken over by C. A. Norman in 1873. He later renamed it the *Rising Sun and Express* and, as editor-in-chief, made it one of the influential papers of the period. It was published every Saturday, each subscription costing $1.00 a month. In line with its contemporaries, most of the space was devoted to advertisements. One or two columns were given to editorial comments on current issues and about a page and a half to news items, correspondence, market and shipping reports. Its expressed aim was to 'excel as a local journal, to furnish the public a trustworthy account of local occurrences, obtained from native

---

[1] *Japan Mail*, fortnightly edition, 8 Dec. 1873, 26 Mar. 1874, 9 Apr. 1875. These three issues in the Library of Congress are all I have found, except the micro-filmed copy mentioned on p. 319.

[2] *Japan Weekly Mail*, 18 Sept. 1882, 5 May 1883.

sources'. It was renamed the *Kyūshū Times* on 5 January 1878.[1]

Another paper called the *Nagasaki Gazette* is mentioned in the *Express* of 9 June 1872 and by a contemporary Japanese newspaper, the *Shimbun Zasshi*, in November 1873. The printing office and the name of the proprietor, A. Louriciro, are listed in the *Japan Gazette*'s *Hong List* for 1872, but no other information has come to light about it.[2]

Three days after the opening of the port of Kobe, 4 January 1868, A. T. Watkins, a former publisher of the *Japan Herald*, brought out the first number of the weekly *Hyogo and Osaka Herald*, which consisted of four small pages and cost two dollars a month. Several other editors succeeded him before Frederick M. Cruchley, a solicitor who practised in the consular courts, became editor and proprietor in April 1869.[3] F. da Braga offered the *Herald* keen competition by publishing twice a week, beginning on 15 May 1868, the *Hyogo News*, which later under the direction of Frank Walsh caused the *Herald* to fail. The victorious *News* became a daily paper in June 1877 and remained supreme in Kobe until about 1890.[4] The office of the *Hyogo News* and its complete files were destroyed by fire in 1889.[5]

Yedo was rather late in possessing an English newspaper of its own. Since foreign residents in the capital city were not numerous, the Yokohama journals had to suffice until some three years after the Restoration. Here again John R. Black was the pioneer journalist. Early in the summer of 1871 he issued from the main office of his Japanese newspaper a weekly known as the *Tokei Journal* which lasted about four years.[6] Its successor,

[1] Ebihara, op. cit., pp. 104–8. *Nagasaki Express*, 30 May 1874. The first five volumes—1870 to 30 May 1874—are in the Ueno Collection at Kyoto University. Files for 1872 are at Meiji Shimbun Zasshi Bunko and at Tōyō Bunko. The *Rising Sun and Nagasaki Express*, 1876–8 and 1881–97 are in the Nagasaki Municipal Library. These last I have not seen.

[2] *Japan Gazette Hong List and Directory* (Yokohama, Jan. 1872), p. 58.

[3] *Japan Chronicle, Jubilee Number, 1868–1918*, p. 15.

[4] Ebihara, op. cit., pp. 70–71. *Chihōbetsu Nihon Shimbun Shi*, p. 311. According to the *Gazette Hong List* of 1872, the *Hyogo and Osaka Herald* was still in existence under F. M. Cruchley and A. H. Blackwell in 1872.

[5] Williams, op. cit., p. 238. Two copies of *Hyogo and Osaka Herald*, 9 Jan. 1869 and 26 Mar. 1870, were in possession of the Editors of the *Japan Chronicle, Jubilee Number, 1868–1918*, p. 15.

[6] Ebihara, op. cit., pp. 52, 114–16. *Chihōbetsu Nihon Shimbun Shi*, p. 126. Copies of the *Tokei Journal* may be found occasionally among the British Foreign Office papers.

the *Tokio Times*, was conducted by an American, Edward H. House, between January 1877 and June 1880. House aimed 'to advance an honourable effort toward progress in Japan, appreciation of Japanese culture and harmony between true interests of foreigners and Japanese alike'. He attacked British economic policy, criticized Parkes bitterly, and argued violently for the abolition of extraterritoriality. He attempted to explain Japanese drama, history, customs, and morals with no great success, and estranged readers owing to his extreme criticism of the West.[1]

Magazines and Cartoons

Although European magazines—among them the *Illustrated London News*—were exported to Japan by the Dutch before the opening of the treaty ports, the British were the first to publish magazines in that country.[2] As early as 1861 Charles Wirgman, an English painter and retired army captain, joined Alcock in Japan as correspondent for the *Illustrated London News*. He exercised his artistic gifts further by publishing the *Japan Punch*, beginning in July 1862. In the first issue he declared that he wished to bring comfort to the foreign residents whose lives were dull. Punning on the name of the Japanese coin of the period, he declared that his magazine would be an official organ, reporting by the order of 'Itziboo-no-kami', amusing episodes that took place at customs houses and boat houses. His discerning epigrammatic observations made him popular. He carried a sketchbook as he moved about, depicting street scenes, local customs, people, and furniture as he observed them. These pen sketches, or brush drawings, were carved in wood and printed on thick double octavo paper. Ten sheets were usually bound together into a modest pamphlet.[3]

The *Japan Punch* was a monthly magazine published irregularly until the spring of 1887 with Wirgman always at the helm.[4] No number or date is given on the early issues. In the

---

[1] Ebihara, op. cit., pp. 117–20. *Tokio Times*, 6 Jan. 1877, 19, 26 July 1879.

[2] C. R. Boxer, 'Sakoku, or the Closed Century', *History Today*, 1957, p. 82.

[3] Ebihara, op. cit., pp. 33–37. *Chihōbetsu Nihon Shimbun Shi*, p. 162. Satow, *Diplomat*, p. 212. *Yokohama-shi Shi Kō*, vi. 784.

[4] The Library of Congress has issues from June 1881 to Dec. 1885. Other segments, some earlier ones, are at the Ueno National Library and at the Yokohama Municipal Library.

first Meiji years, only the year of publication is recorded, but during the eighties both the month and the year are printed on each number.[1] Wirgman's wit and brilliant mind produced independent cartoons which dealt with the Restoration and the middle Meiji era. He concerned himself not only with Japanese customs and politics, but in a very detached manner with the behaviour of Western officials, the rivalries and tactics of local English newspapers, the press laws, and current incidents which have little meaning today.[2] His cartoons brought on Japanese imitators such as Nozaki Bunzo in the pictorial newspaper *Nippon Shi* and in the *Maru Maru Shimbun*. Artists flocked to his studio to learn Western techniques. The works of many early Meiji painters show his influence although few of his own paintings survive. But memories of his humour endure. 'A fellow of infinite jest' is his epitaph in Yokohama's foreign cemetery.[3]

Wirgman is reported to have begun another magazine, called *The Far East*, in 1867 but about this little is known. It may have existed for two years.[4] The same title was chosen by John R. Black for a fortnightly which he began as editor and publisher on 31 May 1870. This was characterized by literary distinction and by the delightful, actual photographs of the Far East which were pasted into it. On 1 July 1873 it became a monthly and continued as such until 1875. There were gaps in regular delivery between July 1875 and June 1876. A new series was begun in 1876. Black published it simultaneously in Yokohama, Shanghai, and Hong Kong. Subscription was $13.00 a year.[5]

A new English monthly 'for Japan and the Far East' called *The Chrysanthemum* appeared in Yokohama in January 1881.[6]

[1] *Yokohama-shi Shi Kō*, vi. 784–9.

[2] *Japan Punch*, June 1881 to Dec. 1883. Paul C. Blum, *Yokohama in 1872, A Rambling Account of the Community in which the Asiatic Society of Japan was Founded* (Tokyo, 1963), p. 39. Many of Wirgman's cartoons and caricatures are reproduced in this work.

[3] *Yokohama-shi Shi Kō*, vi. 795–6.

[4] Ebihara, op. cit., p. 37.

[5] *The Far East*, 'Introduction', i, New Series, July 1876. Issues of *The Far East* for 1 July, 1 Aug., 1 Oct. 1873, 1 May 1875, and New Series vols. i–v are in Tōyō Bunko. Vol. ii, 1 June 1871 to 16 May 1872, and the Reprinted Edition of vols. i–vii by Yushodo (Tokyo, 1966), are in the Library of Congress.

[6] Vols. i–iii are in Tōyō Bunko. Vols. i–ii, 1881–2, and Supplement i, 1882, are in the Library of Congress.

The editors are unknown. Kelly and Co. of Yokohama was the publishing house although it was printed at the firm's Yedo office. This octavo-size magazine was renamed *The Chrysanthemum and the Phoenix* beginning with the first issue of volume III in 1883 and the size altered to double-duodecimo. By this time it had offices in Shanghai, Hong Kong, and London. The anonymous editors aimed high. They wished 'to aid in bringing, so to speak, the poles of Eastern and Western thought into such contact as may result in the diffusion of a genial warmth and light around us'.[1] Missionaries and scholars of both East and West supported the undertaking. Thus the Reverend H. Waddell contributed an article 'On the rendering into Japanese of some Theological and Psychological Terms'. The Reverend W. Imbrie translated the *Kōeki Mondō*,[2] J. W. Gordon, M.D., discussed the legend of Amida Buddha. Tsuda S. described 'the Japanese Audiphone or Otacoustic Fan'. Ernest Satow contributed a translation of 'A Sanskrit Manuscript'.[3] Captain Brinkley wrote 'The House of Kuroda' and 'A History of Japanese Ceramics' (Chapter I) as well as other articles. The Reverend John T. Gulick produced a paper on 'Darwin's Theory of Evolution applied to Sandwich Island Mollusks'.[4] At first the magazine featured reviews of serious books, a section called 'Notes and Queries', short translations from English works (e.g. one from *Aesop's Fables* entitled *Roba to Chin no Hanashi*), a section named 'Voices from the West', and another 'Science, Art, and Literature'.[5] By volume III it was limited solely to scholarly articles. Fascinating as this journal was in its day, and even now, it survived through only six volumes.

[1] *The Chrysanthemum*, No. 1, Jan. 1881.
[2] Ibid.   [3] Ibid., Jan. 1882.   [4] Ibid., Jan. 1883.
[5] Ibid., Jan. 1881.

XVII

BRITISH RELATIONS WITH THE JAPANESE PRESS

Japanese Translations from the British Press

THE *Bakufu* realized early that what foreign newspapers reported about Japan had importance for it. In December 1860 it established a translation unit called the *Kaiyakusha* in its Institute for the Study of Foreign Books (*Bansho Torishirabe-dokoro*) where news from foreign papers was translated, struck off from wood blocks, and sold.[1] Sixteen young Japanese students of Western learning under Yanagawa Shunzō summarized in Japanese articles relating to Japan which had appeared in the local English journals. They chose what should be translated and put it into publications called *Honyaku Hissa Shimbun*. At first these articles were distributed only among high officials and important personnel of the *Bakufu*, but later were rented under specific conditions to certain applicants.[2]

Each of the 'Shimbun' adhered to one, or at most two, of the English journals. Thus the *Yokohama Shimbun* was a translation of the *Japan Commercial News*. It continued under numerous aliases from the spring of 1863 to the summer of 1865.[3] Its successor, the *Nihon Shimbun Gaihen*, published translations from the weekly *Herald*, beginning 30 September 1865 and continuing until early in the winter of 1867. Another Japanese newspaper, said to be a rendering from the *Japan Herald* and called the *Chūgai Shimbun*, appeared from the *Kaiyakusha* for a brief period early in the autumn of 1867. In its Japanese edition the *Japan Times* was known as *Nihon Shimbun* or *Nihon Betsudan Shimbun*. The translations began with the very first number of the *Times*, that of 8 September 1865, and continued for fifty-one

[1] Hanazono Kanesada, *The Development of Japanese Journalism* (Tokyo, 1924), p. 4.
[2] Ebihara, op. cit., pp. 38–41. Yamamoto, op. cit., pp. 28–29.
[3] e.g. *Nihon Bōeki Shimbun, Nihon Kōeki Shimbun, Nihon Bōeki Betsudan Shimbun,* and *Yokohama Bōeki Hyōban.*

consecutive issues until 8 September 1866. Sometimes the *Kaiyakusha* placed in the *Nihon Shimbun Gaihen* translations combined from the *Herald* and the *Times*. For example the fifth issue of 9 November 1865 was based on the *Times* of 4 November 1865 and on the *Herald* No. 193. Items selected for translation in that issue dealt with the movement of foreign warships (there were nine in Osaka), and with Parkes's trip to Hyogo with the ministers from France, Holland, and the United States. The mission of Parkes and the other ministers was to request the Mikado to ratify the foreign treaties. All advertisements were omitted. The various translators all signed their work.[1] Some of their summaries were so brief or inaccurate as to be almost unrecognizable when compared with the original articles.[2]

For a short interval in 1862 the *Bansho Torishirabe-dokoro* published for distribution by a Japanese book seller in Yedo translations of Dutch and Chinese newspapers of 1860 in a sheet called the *Batavia Shimbun*.[3] This sheet competes with the *Kaigai Shimbun* for the honour of being the first Japanese language newspaper. The latter was the publication of Joseph Heco.[4] It consisted of translations of overseas newspapers, being printed from wood blocks on several sheets of heavy paper. Heco started it in the summer of 1865 as a bi-monthly, but because of the anti-foreign agitation of that period, it attracted few subscribers and was discontinued after twenty-four issues.[5]

Others followed Heco's lead in publishing independently Japanese translations of the foreign press. An Englishman named Scott, working in Yokohama, edited a sheet called the *London Shimbunshi* based on translations of London papers before the Franco-Prussian War, possibly in 1867. But little is known of him or his work.[6] Still another effort apart from the

---

[1] *Bakumatsu Meiji Shimbun Zenshū*, i. 348, 373–80. Ebihara, op. cit., pp. 41–44.

[2] e.g. the translation of Satow's article in the *Japan Times* of 1 Dec. 1865 given in *Bakumatsu Meiji Shimbun Zenshū*, i. 367.

[3] Ebihara, op. cit., p. 15. *Yokohama-shi Shi Kō*, vi. 723–4. Nos. 1–23 are in the Ueno Collection, Kyoto University. *Meiji Bunka Zenshū*, xvii. 4.

[4] See p. 337, n. 2.

[5] Ebihara, op. cit., pp. 46–47. F. M. Jones, 'Foreign Influence on the Early Press of Japan', The Japan Society, London, *Transactions*, xxxii. 48. Kimura Ki, op. cit., in *Contemporary Japan*, xxii. 638. Nos. 1–17 of *Kaigai Shimbun* are in the Ueno Collection, Kyoto University.

[6] Ebihara, op. cit., p. 47. Ono Hideo, *Nihon Shimbun Hattatsu Shi* (History of the Development of Japanese Newspapers), (Tokyo, 1922), p. 23. Yamamoto, op. cit., p. 30.

Kaiyakusha was the *Nainai Shimbun*, a translation of Wirgman's *Japan Punch* renderings which began in September 1868 and continued for at least twenty numbers. Even the original cartoons were skilfully copied. But the name of the translator and the members of his staff are yet to be discovered.[1]

British Editors of Japanese Newspapers

Through these varied efforts at translating from the English press the Japanese made clear that they were concerned about local and world opinion. Vernacular newspapers were the next step. Here again British journalists took the initiative. The Reverend M. Buckworth Bailey, a Cambridge graduate and the chaplain attached to the British consulate at Yokohama, edited the *Bankoku Shimbunshi* (All Countries Newspaper) in Yokohama in the winter of 1867.[2] This paper contained about twenty pages, approximately six by nine inches, through which it aimed to bring both foreign and local news to the Japanese people, to correct false information, and to further understanding of the West. Readers were requested to send current strange stories to the editor for verification. In the second issue five pages were devoted to news from England, France, Prussia, Russia, Holland, Belgium, Austria, Italy, Rome, the United States, Mexico, Algeria, and China. Accounts of the arrivals of ships and people in Yokohama, the prices of Japanese commodities in foreign countries, two stories from *Aesop's Fables* with one illustration, the announcement of a telegraph line from Yokohama to Yedo, and a series of advertisements, all by Westerners, of Western goods and services, completed the paper.[3] This was the general format, although the order of the main sections varied from time to time, as the *Bankoku Shimbunshi* progressed irregularly through eighteen issues into the spring of 1869. In it Bailey published serially 'A History of Great Britain from 55 B.C.'[4] He often singled out achievements of Great Britain which Japan might profitably follow: an extensive newspaper press,[5] emphasis on education, good public morals, public health, and trade and industry, rather than on

[1] Ebihara, op. cit., p. 44.   [2] Ibid., p. 47.
[3] *Bankoku Shimbunshi*, 2nd Issue 1867. Broken file in *Meiji Shimbun Zasshi Bunko*. No telegraph line was built before 1869, however. See pp. 375–6.
[4] *Bankoku Shimbunshi*, 6th, 7th, and 8th Issues 1867, 11th Issue 1868.
[5] Ibid., 5th Issue 1867.

military and naval strength in times of peace.[1] He commended the skilful work of an English surgeon who became head of the Government Hospital in Yedo.[2] He did not hesitate to attack the *Japan Times* for its attitude towards the Shogunate.[3] At the same time he thought the civil war following the Restoration would lay the foundation of a New Japan destined for a great future. He urged the Kyoto government to act according to accepted law and not for selfish advantage[4]—an opinion which he himself signed.

Why and when the *Bankoku Shimbunshi* ceased publication are still matters of opinion. Ishii Kendo asserts in the *Bakumatsu Meiji Shimbun Zenshū* that it went through eighteen issues into the spring of 1869 and of these he located seventeen. Several papers using the same title but forging Bailey's name as editor were published for brief periods in the early seventies.[5]

A second British effort to establish a newspaper in the vernacular was made by John Hartley in Osaka in May 1868. This again was a small pamphlet-type paper, printed from wood blocks and called *Kakkoku Shimbun* (All Countries News). An Englishman, Mark Voysey, signs himself as editor, although Hanazono Kanesada declares that Hartley was the editor, and was assisted by a Japanese samurai of the Chōshū *Han*. The first issue, May 1868, contained eighteen pages of foreign news arranged according to the country of origin. Two appendixes followed. Voysey devoted the first to a history of the steamship in England, thus anticipating that Japan would need many such ships. The second described the Western watch. And Hartley's single advertisement of Western books on astronomy, geography, physics, navigation, mining, and steam engines, as well as all kinds of medicines supplied by his shop, ended the number. Though considered to have been superior to Bailey's, this paper was also short-lived. It is conjectured that Hartley was too occupied with his mercantile business to devote sufficient time to it.[6]

[1] Ibid., 4th Issue 1867 given in *Bakumatsu Meiji Shimbun Zenshū*, ii. 318.
[2] Ibid., 16th Issue 1869 given in *Bakumatsu Meiji Shimbun Zenshū*, ii. 443–4.
[3] *Bankoku Shimbunshi*, 8th Issue 1867.   [4] Ibid., 11th Issue 1868.
[5] *Bakumatsu Meiji Shimbun Zenshū*, article by Ishii Kendō, ii. 13–23. Ebihara, op. cit., pp. 48–49.
[6] Hanazono, op. cit., p. 7. Two copies of this issue of the *Kakkoku Shimbun* are in *Meiji Shimbun Zasshi Bunko*.

The Japanese themselves were now energetically publishing many newspapers of their own, having realized their political value during the Restoration. At least sixteen, including the important *Chūgai Shimbun*, edited by Yanagawa Shunzō, appeared during 1868. By 1869 the new Meiji government was issuing regulations requiring government permission for the publication of any newspaper; regulating the contents, forbidding 'Indiscreet comments on Administration and military affairs', and prohibiting libels and religious propaganda.[1] A small weekly, the *Shimbun Zasshi* (The Budget of News), believed to be under the patronage of Kido Jun'ichirō (Kōin), many other weeklies and two dailies, the *Nichi Nichi Shimbun* in Yedo and the *Mainichi Shimbun* in Yokohama (both mean Daily News) did indeed demonstrate Japan's desire for a national press, but the editors did not yet dare to write leading articles or comment seriously on the occurrences of the day.[2]

At least this was the case in 1872 when John R. Black edited and published the most important of the foreign owned vernacular papers, the *Nisshin Shinjishi*. Black had long before wanted to satisfy the earnest desire of the samurai for information and instruction 'about the outside world'. His own abortive effort to do this in 1869–70 and the rapid growth of other Japanese journals in no way discouraged him. He found the columns of the latter 'always defaced with such filthy paragraphs as to render them worse than contemptible to foreigners'. It was his view that the Japanese of that day had for the most part 'no conception of what a newspaper was, nor what were its uses'. Black himself undertook to teach them! His experience throws light on the workings of the government as well as the press in the early Meiji period.

With the enthusiastic assistance of the Portuguese, F. da Roza, Black overcame the difficulties which stood in the way of founding a vernacular paper. Having first secured the necessary licence through proper introduction to the Secretary of State for Education, he built up a staff of highly intelligent samurai—more than sixty of them—under a Japanese editor of social and official distinction. This editor was a former

[1] Hanazono, op. cit., pp. 10, 18.

[2] Black, op. cit. ii. 309–10, 364. Toyabe Sentarō in Ōkuma, *Fifty Years of New Japan*, ii. 396. Zumoto, 'The Press', in Stead, op. cit., p. 552.

vice-governor of Hakodate and a scholar whose refined, if not always intelligible, literary style gave the *Nisshin Shinjishi* prestige among the elite of Japan. All the subordinates were men of equally good family, even the office messenger being a samurai. Only the machine and press-men, and their staffs, were of lower rank.[1]

Obtaining the necessary Chinese characters in the form of movable wood type took much ingenuity. The first 1,200 made had rapidly to be increased to 12,000. Hence several skilled carvers were constantly employed in the office to cut the characters required for incoming articles. Uncut blanks of the proper size were kept in quantities for this purpose. Some months after the first issue of the *Nisshin Shinjishi* a founder who could cast the type in metal was discovered to replace the rough wood blocks at one cent apiece.[2] Black's promise, in his second number, to import from England a printing machine using movable type, was achieved by the issue of 5 February 1874.[3]

The *Nisshin Shinjishi* first appeared in Yedo on 23 April 1872.[4] Black aimed to put before the Japanese people all information useful to their nation—information pertaining to Japan as well as to foreign countries. He acknowledged the support of the Japanese government at the start, and publicly expressed his appreciation.[5] In his editorials, however, he exercised the same critical spirit towards the Meiji government which had characterized his earlier writings for the *Herald* and the *Gazette*. For example, he attacked the arbitrary judgements of Japanese judges, the acceptance of bribes by Japanese officials, and the lack of accepted written law. He urged the government to work on this problem as earnestly as possible. Westerners, he said, would willingly obey Japanese law, if it were settled and the judges were honest. From the start his paper had an obvious influence on Japanese opinion. His criticism of obscene entertainments in Yedo led to closing the shows. His commendation

---

[1] Black, op. cit. ii. 364–7, 448–9.

[2] Ibid., pp. 367–8. The need for this enormous number of separate characters is questionable even though Black himself gives it as fact.

[3] A broken file of the *Nisshin Shinjishi* from the second issue in Apr. 1872 to that of 4 May 1874 is in *Meiji Shimbun Zasshi Bunko*.

[4] Ebihara, op. cit., p. 57.

[5] *Nisshin Shinjishi*, 2nd Issue, 26 Apr. 1872.

of the work of the police brought him personal appreciation. The Japanese even sought his support to achieve local reforms.[1]

The young Meiji government, however, was not unmindful of the growing power of the *Nisshin Shinjishi*. It prohibited Black from publishing any news about the Saga rebellion in Kyūshū in the winter of 1874. Black's acquiescence was followed by an editorial on the inherent dangers both to the Japanese and to foreigners in the suppression of genuine news. He appealed to those authorities who knew the customs of the West to withdraw the order.[2] Within a fortnight the government complied, for which Black was openly grateful.[3] A few weeks later, however, Black criticized Japan's proposed invasion of Formosa, pointing out that it would create discord between China and Japan and would mean a vain destruction of life.[4]

Such criticism seemed legitimate to Black since in late 1872 the Sa-in had made the *Nisshin Shinjishi* its 'official organ' with permission to criticize the government.[5] But Black's increasing influence upon the native press so alarmed the Meiji authorities by 1874 that they determined to silence him. Unable to restrain an Englishman by Japanese law because of extra-territorial jurisdiction, the Sa-in insnared him in a contract. This document found among old *Dajōkan* papers under the heading 'Written Contracts relating to Foreign Employees' establishes these facts. The Sa-in employed Black on 1 January 1875 for two years to investigate various problems. In Article V of the contract Black was prohibited from revealing to either Japanese or foreigners any activities, small or great, within the *Sa-in*, as well as any of the problems he was hired to investigate. If secrets should leak out through him, he would be called to account. By Article VI he was not to be connected with any business whatsoever. Even his newspaper was to be transferred to others.[6] Why the discerning and British-bred Black signed such a contract and thus gave up his paper is a mystery. His own silence on the matter in his memoirs appears ominous. But Black's *Nisshin Shinjishi* had already wielded an irrepressible influence on the native press.

[1] *Nisshin Shinjishi*, 263rd Issue, 19 Mar. 1874, p. 2.
[2] Ibid., 234th Issue, 23 Feb. 1874, p. 3.
[3] Ibid., 241st Issue, 4 Mar. 1874, p. 2.
[4] Ibid., 278th Issue, 20 Apr. 1874, p. 3.
[5] Black, op. cit. ii. 372.　　　　　　[6] Ebihara, op. cit., pp. 59–61.

Japanese journalists were following Black's leads in outspoken criticism of government policy. Simultaneously the rapid growth of native newspapers made them a formidable power throughout the country.[1] The Post Office records for 1874 show that 2,564,229 papers from 34 publishing houses passed through the mails that year. Since some journals published every other day were delivered to the door at as low a rate as 11 cents a month, these figures probably indicate a minor part of the circulation among a population of more than 33 million. As yet no effective censorship inhibited the pens of zealous editors. The Press Laws of 1869, although made more severe in 1873, were not enforced. Unbridled comments on any issue before the public became the order of the day. Newly fledged writers pleaded for representative institutions and religious liberty for the inexperienced Japanese electorate. They spared neither the private lives nor the public acts of their officials and their attacks on them were often shortsighted and irresponsible.[2] Rumours of more stringent regulations to come made even the native press admit the rashness of some editors, because it recognized the overwhelming benefits of freedom of the press on the English pattern.[3] The publication of a petition to the government demanding the disgrace and decapitation of the prime minister, however, forced the government to act.[4]

On the ground that newspaper reporters were liable to err, members of the Japanese press were excluded from the meetings of the Assembly of Local Authorities which convened for the first time in Yedo about mid-June 1875. Storms of protest in both the native and foreign papers were followed by eulogies on the accomplishments of an unfettered press in Japan. The *Nichi Nichi Shimbun* thundered that government suppression of the native press would drive its writers into the welcoming columns of the *Herald*, the *Mail*, the *Gazette*, and the *Echo* where they would join forces with Western journalists in the free

[1] Hanazono, op. cit., p. 23.
[2] Harvard University, Houghton Library, MSS. American Board of Commissioners for Foreign Missions (hereafter cited as A.B.C.) (16–4–1), Annual Report of Japan Mission for 1874, May 1875, p. 18. Uyehara Shigaru, *The Industry and Trade of Japan* (London, 1936), p. 33, gives the population of Japan in 1873 as 33,000,000. For Press Laws of 1873, see the *Japan Mail*, 24 Dec. 1873, pp. 811–12.
[3] Translations from the Japanese press in *Japan Weekly Mail*, 19 June 1875, pp. 530–1.
[4] Black, op. cit. ii. 447–8.

expression of opinion.[1] The government countered with the recasting of the Press Laws on 28 June 1875.

Stringent regulations now prohibited Japanese from making any criticism of the government on pain of from one to more than three years' imprisonment. All articles dealing with 'foreign or domestic politics, finance, the feelings of the nation, the aspect of the times, learning or religion, or matters affecting the rights of officials and people' had to be signed. The use of a 'feigned' name meant imprisonment for thirty days and a fine of ten yen. The penalty was more than doubled if the name of another person had been used. Any newspaper or magazine inciting to the commission of crime was to be considered equally guilty with the person who committed it. Translators of articles from the foreign press were required to give their names, and were punishable according to the laws against slander or incitement to crime if their articles offended in these respects. Memorials and petitions could not be published without the sanction of four government agencies representing central and local authorities.[2] Foreigners were prohibited from owning or editing a Japanese newspaper. Anonymity of editors, proprietors, and printers was forbidden.

The response of individuals and groups to this legislation makes clear the position attained by the native press after Black launched the *Nisshin Shinjishi*. On 19 July 1875 Black was discharged from his government post with three months' salary on the pretext that there was no work for him to do. The new laws forbade him, as a foreigner, to return to his *Nisshin Shinjishi* which had declined during his absence and was discontinued by the end of 1875. But the great editor was not to be defeated. Relying on his extraterritorial rights he challenged the Japanese law in January 1876 by publishing without government permission another vernacular newspaper, the *Bankoku Shimbun* (Universal News) in which he signed his name as editor-in-chief and publisher.[3] This caused an international incident.

---

[1] *Japan Weekly Mail*, 26 June 1875. *L'Echo du Japon* was one of the two leading French newspapers in Yokohama.

[2] *Japan Weekly Mail*, 3 July 1875. Kōsaka Masaaki and David Abosch, Eds. *Japanese Thought in the Meiji Era* (Centenary Culture Series ix), (Tokyo, 1958), pp. 127–8. *Hōrei Zensho* M. 8 (Collections of Laws and Orders, 1875), (*Article 16*, p. 154. [3] Ebihara, op. cit., pp. 61–62. *Japan Weekly Mail*, 22 Jan. 1876, pp. 74–76.

Seven days later the Meiji authorities stopped the publication of Black's newspaper[1] and fined Black in accordance with Article I of the Press Law. Although there is no evidence that Black had any subversive intent, the government held that vernacular newspapers, published by persons not subject to Japan's press laws, might be subversive to internal order and cause grave injury to the public interests. The government appealed to the British minister, Sir Harry Parkes, to prohibit the publication of Japanese language newspapers by British subjects—a reasonable request in view of the recent excesses of the native press. Faith in the basic justice of the British government's response was apparent. Sir Harry saw the absurdity of so interpreting the extraterritorial privilege as to enable the native press to evade the laws of the land by the simple expedient of placing itself under the protection of a foreign power. He used the powers granted him by the Order-in-Council for China and Japan of 1865 (Sec. 85, 86, and 90) to promulgate a regulation in emergency which should be in effect in Japan until disapproved by Her Majesty's Government in London. This *Regulation* made any British subject within the dominions of the Mikado who should publish or print a newspaper in the Japanese language, guilty of an offence punishable by imprisonment up to three months or a fine not exceeding $500.00 or both.[2]

Praise, condemnation, and questions concerning the constitutionality of Sir Harry's act naturally followed both in Japan and in London. The *Herald* attacked the *Regulation* in principle, and condemned Parkes. The *Mail* held that 'the Japanese, and they alone, should be the judges of what should or should not be published in Japan'. 'The liberty of the press', it contended, 'is peculiarly local in its nature. No one can claim that if an Englishman or an American goes to France or Germany, he carries that liberty with him.' The *Pall Mall Gazette* in London agreed with the *Mail* 'that it is neither conformable to reason or justice that foreigners residing in this country [Japan] should have power to override laws deemed necessary to the regulation

---

[1] *Japan Weekly Mail*, 15 Apr. 1876. *Ōkubo Toshimichi Monjo* (Papers of Ōkubo Toshimichi), 10 vols. (Tokyo, 1927–9), vii. 41–42, Ōkubo to Terashima, 22 Feb. 1876.

[2] *Japan Weekly Mail*, 12 Feb. 1876. F.O. 46/203, Parkes to Derby, No. 24, 7 Feb. 1876. Dickins, op. cit. ii. 244.

of the relations between the Japanese government and its own subjects'. The *Nichi Nichi Shimbun* rejoiced in the *Regulation* as a successful step of the Japanese government towards 'bringing foreigners within the pale of Japanese law'—an opinion firmly refuted by the *Mail* on the ground that it was merely a 'concession to reason and justice on a point touching . . . the sovereign rights' of Japan 'as an independent nation'.[1]

Black, in his letter to the Consul, Martin Dohmen, claimed his rights as an Englishman 'to publish anything I like in any language I please; always, of course, subject to the laws of my country, which are ample to pursue me, if I write or publish sedition or libel'.[2] Sir Charles W. Dilke raised the question of government approval of Parkes's *Regulation* in the House of Commons on 23 March and on 10 April 1876, asking whether British ministers in China and Japan were not prohibited under the Order-in-Council of 1865 'from creating offences in China and Japan which are not offences in England or violations of British treaties in those countries'. The British government evaded the issue on the ground that it was awaiting a report from the Law Offices on the information it had received from Japan —a report which was not mentioned again in Parliament during the remaining seven years of Parkes's service in Japan.[3] The government in London, however, approved Parke's *Regulation* on 24 May 1876.[4] This ended English efforts to publish Japanese language periodicals.

The British Press and the Japanese Press Laws

The Japanese press controls occupied the attention of British journalists for many years. Having firmly implanted the concept of a free press in Japan, British writers were torn between a blind loyalty to their own system and a modification of it to meet the realities of current politics in Japan. A complete file of the *Japan Weekly Mail* from 9 May 1874 to 19 May 1883, makes it possible to follow its policies and to glimpse, not without its bias, those of its opponents, the *Herald* and the

[1] *Japan Weekly Mail*, 22 Jan., pp. 75–77, 12 Feb., pp. 141, 144–5, 148–9, 26 Feb., pp. 184–5, 11 Mar., pp. 238–9, 20 May 1876, p. 441.

[2] Ibid., 15 Apr. 1876, p. 328.

[3] *Hansard's Parliamentary Debates*, 3rd Series, ccxxviii, cols. 478 and 1413. H. of C. 23 Mar. and 10 Apr. 1876.

[4] F.O. 262/284, Derby to Parkes, No. 60, 24 May 1876.

Gazette. Howell's paper accepted as a stern necessity the Press Laws of 1875 in view of the irresponsible, incendiary writing of the Japanese press which was using its early liberties to incite the people to rebel against the government. Certainly the new laws were an improvement on the code of 1873 which had enabled transgressors to plead all kinds of excuses for evasion. The *Mail* believed that they still provided ample scope for all purposes of 'practical discussion' and hoped they would be leniently interpreted and administered. Revenge would be inevitable, Howell asserted, if the government made an enemy of the press, for 'the press is in some sense the public voice, and this no government can safely disregard'. He cautioned that Japan under an absolute government should not be compared with contemporary England where law and liberty had been correlated after a struggle of almost two hundred years. A free press is one of the latest fruits of an orderly growth of freedom, and in times like these the Japanese government had to consider not what was good for England but what was good for Japan.[1]

The editors of the native papers appeared to think the laws fairly liberal and looked for moderation in their enforcement. This was not to be. Almost at once editors were fined and imprisoned even for the publication of letters criticizing the Press Laws. The *Mail* held that in all instances the editors should first have been warned.[2] As the number of victims increased, it appealed to the native press 'to obey and conform', to improve the quality of its work, to make an effort 'to train the people with the rudiments of political knowledge and thus, eventually, fit them to take a larger part in the management of national affairs'. It had no sympathy with those whose licence gave the government a warning of the 'mischief which would be done were the Press liberated from all control'.[3] The *Mail* sought, however, a modification of Article XIV which was then being interpreted by judicial authorities 'to forbid all criticism upon laws now existing, or hereafter passed'. 'This', said Howell, 'is utterly unreasonable—destructive of real and proper respect for law, benumbing to the sense of the people as political entities, tyrannical, and most unwise.' A good press 'with which

---

[1] *Japan Weekly Mail*, 3, 10, 31 July 1875, pp. 568–70, 590–2, 649.
[2] Ibid., 14 Aug. 1875, pp. 689, 690–1.
[3] Ibid., 21 Aug. 1875, p. 713, 5 Feb., pp. 123–4, 2 Apr. 1876, p. 351.

honourable men may be honourably associated' could never be attained under such conditions.[1]

But neither punishment nor advice silenced Japanese editors. The *Hōchi Shimbun* wrote: 'Now that the Government has prohibited people from discussing laws which have been once enacted and the acts of the Administration, the people appear all the more bent on discussing both.'[2] By 22 April 1876 thirty public writers were reported in prison of whom a very few were subject to serious punishment. Moderate opinion among Westerners both in Japan and in Europe was repelled by the government's severity. Descriptions of the plight of editors in prison further alienated public sympathy. Such use and abuse of law, the *Mail* pointed out to the Meiji authorities, would destroy any immediate hope of the abolition of extraterritoriality—one of Japan's most cherished goals.[3] Heedless of this warning, however, the government announced in *Notification* No. 98 of 6 July 1876 that 'should any duly registered newspaper' or magazine, publish any matter which may be deemed to interfere with or have a tendency to destroy the peace of the nation, the further publication of such newspaper, or magazine, will be suspended at the discretion of the Naimushō'.[4] The *Mail* concluded this 'got rid of the scandal of imprisonment but left the government with the power of depriving any man of his means of livelihood without any judgement being pronounced against him in a court of law'.[5] Three newspapers were suppressed within a week.[6] Others followed; yet the circulation of newspapers in 1876 increased rapidly—forty-eight per cent. over 1875 and 264 per cent over 1874[7].

The muzzling of the press was but one of the people's grievances against the government. Discontent was widespread: an uprising at Kumamoto in 1876 and the far more serious Satsuma Rebellion in 1877.[8] Throughout this period government censorship tightened over the native press. Reports and

---

[1] *Japan Weekly Mail*, 8 Jan. 1876, p. 25.   [2] Ibid., 11 Dec. 1875, p. 1099.

[3] Ibid., 6 May, 3 June 1876, pp. 393–4, 493.

[4] 'Naimushō' was the Ministry of Home Affairs under the reorganized Meiji government.   [5] *Japan Weekly Mail*, 8 July 1876, pp. 601, 605–7.

[6] Ibid., 15 July 1876, p. 633.

[7] Report of Japanese Post-Master General for year 1 July 1875 to 30 June 1876, given in *Japan Weekly Mail*, 6 Jan. 1877, p. 4.

[8] Ibid., 19 Aug., 4 Nov. 1876, pp. 758, 1009–11.

telegrams covering news of the war were deleted. Japanese editors retaliated by issuing blank columns indicating the amount of news cut out by the authorities. The *Mail* discussed the possible dangers arising from public speculation and the drawing of ill-founded conclusions.[1] British journalists also had difficulties. For their efforts to determine what was happening they were accused of being anti-governmental in their sympathies. Howell's weekly, now under Pearson's editorship, forcibly denied the charge. It had no wish to discredit the government in the eyes of foreigners nor to indicate sympathy with the rebellion. Although it believed that the arbitrary policy of the government towards the samurai had caused the struggle in Kyūshū, it maintained that rebellion was not the way to achieve reform. And though it had paid tribute to Saigō in his eventual defeat—a great man who had made a great mistake—the *Mail* certainly did not condone his action.[2]

With the end of the rebellion the native press resumed its fight for freedom, hoping to aid in reconstruction and social reforms.[3] In June 1878 the government allowed a draft of a revision in the Press Laws to leak out in the semi-official organ, *Akebono Shimbun*. The *Mail* rejoiced in this effort to seek the opinions of the press upon the measure before its final promulgation but showed no enthusiasm for its provisions. Political criticism was still branded as a crime. The editors believed by this time that 'if a good law of libel were established, the press of Japan might be left entirely free'.[4] House, of the *Tokio Times*, on the other hand, upheld the proposed laws as a necessity.[5] Five years passed, however, before there were any legislative changes.

Persecution and injustice actually strengthened the growth and importance of the Japanese press. Nothing could check the type of independent criticism which John Black's *Nisshin Shinji-shi* had inspired. Journalism opened up a new field of work for the thousands of dislocated samurai who brought to it the same boldness in criticizing their government that they had had as two-sworded men. Black found that whenever one editor or writer was imprisoned, there was always a man of ability ready

[1] Ibid., 24 Feb., 7 Apr. 1877, pp. 102–3, 253.
[2] Ibid., 11, 25 Aug. 1877, pp. 685–6, 733–4.
[3] Ibid., 3 Nov. 1877, pp. 982–3.
[4] Ibid., 8 June 1878, pp. 539–40, 542–3.
[5] Ibid., 29 June 1878, pp. 612–13. *Tokio Times*, 8, 22 June 1878.

to take his place immediately and to assume the same risks. Fully conscious of public support, editors founded new papers and brazenly continued their attacks on the government.[1] They even hired 'dummy editors . . . who paid the fine and served the jail sentence for the paper while it continued to appear'.[2] By April 1879 the *Mail* reported that there were more daily newspapers in Yedo than in London. During 1879–80 there were 80 vernacular journals of all types printed in Tokyo, and 112 in the provinces.[3]

The mania for these newspapers was alarming, all the more so since their quality was much in need of improvement. Their information was often inaccurate; they were still filled with 'frivolous or obscene' matter, and they continued to indulge freely in personalities which hindered them from attaining the respected position of the British Fourth Estate. The *Mail* attributed their popularity and success to their 'having drawn upon themselves the attention and, in some respects, the opposition of the Japanese authorities.[4] The *Nichi Nichi Shimbun* condemned its contemporaries for seeking pecuniary benefits while disregarding honest efforts to express the public opinion of their communities.[5] The *Japan Times* pointed to the daily increase in influence of the native papers and lamented that 'its conductors hardly appreciate the enormous and growing weight of responsibility which is accumulating on their shoulders'.[6]

The vernacular papers naturally protested against the fact that laws which denied them freedom exercised no control over the country's foreign press. Thus when the *Mainichi Shimbun* translated from the *Gazette* a criticism of government policy based on incorrect information, the Japanese editor was summoned before the Yokohama *Saiban-sho* (Court of Justice) and sentenced to a year's imprisonment whereas the British editor escaped all censorship. The *Nichi Nichi Shimbun* pointed out that the two editors were guilty of the same offence and advised action against the editor of the *Gazette* in a British court. Since many Japanese subjects read English papers, it main-

[1] Black, op. cit. ii. 449–50.   [2] Borton, *Japan's Modern Century*, p. 186.
[3] *Japan Weekly Mail*, 5 Apr. 1879, 25 Sept. 1880, pp. 418–19, 1254. Other figures are given, 4 Mar. 1882, p. 255.
[4] Ibid., 19 Apr. 1879, pp. 474–5, 8 May, 20 June 1880, pp. 585, 813–14.
[5] Ibid., 26 July 1879, p. 974.   [6] *Japan Times*, 9 Mar. 1878.

tained that seditious material published in them was equally
disturbing to the peace of the country.[1] The *Weekly Mail* under
Brinkley showed sympathy for this point of view; it deplored
the irresponsible and incendiary writing of the foreign journals,
their scurrilous accounts of personalities, and their ignorance
when discussing Japanese affairs.[2] Brinkley courageously
attacked the motives of sections of the Yokohama foreign press
in its crusade against the Japanese government's policy for the
development of a coastwise carrying trade.[3] He proved that the
Gazette had been guilty of plagiarism and that other English
journals had criminally abused their freedom.[4] He asserted that
the bad taste and ill-judged criticism of the Japanese nation in
which these papers indulged had concealed from the Japanese
government and people the advantages of a free press. He
never advocated that the Japanese Press Laws should be
applied to foreign journals, but he did believe the Japanese
government 'ought to be competent to check, within its own
territories, displays of foreign journalism which are calculated
to excite sedition among the people'.[5]

These conflicting opinions divided the British press against
itself, making its rivalries and antagonisms the butt of many
cartoons in the *Japan Punch*.[6] Brinkley, a former naval officer,
was caricatured as a 'Japanese Flunky' wearing an English
uniform and carrying a pen as a walking stick.[7] Even the
Hyogo News clearly intimated that the *Mail* was subsidized by
the Japanese government. Brinkley replied: 'This paper is not
an official organ in any sense of the word. It receives no subsidy
whatsoever from the Government of Japan, and the opinions
expressed in its columns are entirely the outcome of independent
conviction.'[8]

There was no marked improvement in the behaviour or the
conditions of the Japanese press before Sir Harry Parkes's
service in Japan came to an end in September 1883. Following

---

[1] *Japan Weekly Mail*, 2 Nov. 1878, pp. 1172–3.
[2] Ibid., 6, 13 Aug. 1881, pp. 897, 926–7, 932–3, 15 Apr., 29 Oct. 1882, pp. 439,
1126–7.   [3] Ibid., 10 Dec. 1882, pp. 1250–1.
[4] Ibid., 27 Jan., 9 Feb. 1883, pp. 57, 71.
[5] Ibid., 24 Feb., 19 May 1883, pp. 121–3, 61.
[6] *Japan Punch*, Sept. and Dec. 1881, Aug. 1883.
[7] Ibid., Sept. and Oct. 1882.
[8] *Japan Weekly Mail*, 29 Jan. 1881, p. 90.

the Mikado's promise of a National Assembly in 1890, the aims of the nebulous political parties were clarified. Three major organizations emerged for a brief period: the Liberals, the Constitutional Reformers or Progressives, and the Constitutional Monarchists. To one or the other of these every newspaper in the country gave its allegiance.[1] Fukuzawa Yūkichi made clear his faith in newspapers as channels of reform by inserting articles in the reputable papers in favour of the national Diet. He even started a paper of his own, the *Jiji Shimpō*, in which he encouraged his reporters to 'write bravely and freely—but to limit their statements to what they would be willing to say to the victim face to face'.[2] But the long-heralded revision of the Press Laws which came out on 16 April 1883 (*Imperial Notification* No. 12) did nothing to encourage even this kind of criticism.[3]

These regulations, nevertheless, made for greater justice in the exercise of governmental control of the press. Henceforth not only the editor, but the proprietor, director, foreman, or translator on the staff of any journal found guilty of publishing items contravening the *Regulations* were held responsible—a stipulation which put an end to the use of dummy editors whose function had been 'confined to going to prison when necessary'. The Home Minister retained the power to suspend or to stop permanently any journal containing items 'calculated to disturb the public peace or demoralize the people'. In grave cases he could order the confiscation of the plant and the machinery. The *Mail* still held that Press Laws were a necessary evil in Japan at that time, but thought that the Minister's power should have been limited to suspension of the journal, pending judicial investigation and sentence. It applauded the *Regulations* for limiting sentences of imprisonment with hard labour to only a few cases, and for providing that the names of authors should be furnished when required. The provision that sentences pronounced against journals should be printed in full in the succeeding issue, and the stipulation that failure to rectify errors committed against a person at the request of individuals would entail severe punishment, likewise won favourable

[1] *Japan Weekly Mail*, 27 Jan. 1883, Supplement, p. 1.
[2] *Fukuzawa*, op. cit., pp. 343, 345–6.
[3] Text given in *Japan Weekly Mail*, 21 Apr. 1883, pp. 255–6.

comment. This last might prevent 'hypocritical plaints about newspapers suspended for unknown crimes' and 'respectable persons from having their names associated with tidbits of immoral gossip'. Though the *Regulation* prohibiting publication of the proceedings of departments, boards, city and provincial assemblies, and criminal courts was regrettable, it was perhaps meant to correct the gross carelessness and inaccuracy which so frequently characterized the reports of the vernacular press of the time. Looking at the *Regulations* as a whole, the *Weekly Mail* awaited with utmost impatience the day when it would be possible to sweep away half their provisions. It believed that 'Japan can never call herself a thoroughly civilized country until she is in a position to substitute the wholesome restraint of public opinion for the demoralizing coercion of penal statutes'.[1]

British editors dominated the English press in Japan from 1861 until 1883. Through their newspapers and magazines they introduced to the Japanese people the ideals, the skills, the values, and the abuses which two hundred years of experience with a press had taught them at home. Men like Hansard, Black, Rickerby, and Howell stood for independent judgements, honest exchange of opinion, and careful reporting in their columns. They sought to create better understanding between East and West through the free circulation of valid information concerning both civilizations. With the exception of Howell, all were primarily interested in the growth of English commerce and the welfare of the merchant class. This made them fearless critics of their own officials and brutal in attacking leading personalities. Their anonymous editorials and correspondence often made possible the expression of irresponsible and uninformed opinions. A desire to prevent the abolition of extraterritoriality led their journals, during the latter part of the period, to indulge in unwarranted criticism of the Japanese people and government with a view to proving them incapable of assuming the responsibilities which such a revision of the treaties would entail. Such criticism would not have been tolerated by their own government in London, and was clearly an abuse of the 'freedom of the press' which they unjustly claimed as part of their extraterritorial privilege.

[1] Ibid., pp. 248–50.

No Western institution appealed more quickly or more generally to the awakening Japanese nation than the popular press. Within less than fifteen years after the publication of the *Nagasaki Shipping List and Advertiser*, the Japanese people had a powerful, widespread press of their own. Young Japanese journalists seized upon all the traditional British freedoms as goals for Japan, and courageously attacked the new Meiji government in their efforts to attain them. They did not develop simultaneously, however, a sense of reponsibility commensurate with their growing power, for again and again they disturbed the peace of the nation. The clamour of the *Herald* and the *Gazette* urged them on. The Meiji government's attempt to control them by a series of *Press Regulations* was inevitable in view of the existing political instability. But the punishments they meted out had little effect on the growth of newspapers, nor did those punishments blur the aims of the journalists for the free institutions which their contacts with the West egendered.

XVIII

BRITISH INFLUENCE ON JAPANESE SCIENCE AND MEDICINE

Introduction

A STRONOMY, mathematics, and medicine were the principal sciences with which the Japanese had been concerned before the opening of the ports. Their proficiency was greatest in astronomy where no superstitions impeded their progress. In the decades before the arrival of Perry Japanese astronomers were familiar with the most profound European treatises translated into Dutch and had learned the use of many European instruments and even how to make them.[1] To this knowledge English scholars appear to have added nothing of importance in the following half-century. But British scientists in the fields of mathematics, medicine, chemistry, physics, seismology, and engineering, both at their own universities and in the academic and governmental institutions of Japan, did much to train the Japanese in these disciplines of the West.

Few records remain of the personal experiences of these British scientists with their Japanese students. Although many were Fellows of the Royal Society and made recognized contributions to the advancement of scientific knowledge, we are forced to learn of their work in Japan through obituaries and scientific journals rather than from their own correspondence or from accounts by their associates. A review of the positions occupied by British scholars and the men they taught in the years here considered will indicate at least the extent of their opportunities for influencing eager, inquiring minds of awakening Japan. Any account of the work of British scientists alone,

[1] *Manners and Customs of the Japanese*, edited by Mrs. W. Busk (London, 1841), pp. 307–9. National Research Council of Japan, *Scientific Japan, Past and Present* (Tokyo, 1926), essay by Mikami Yoshio, p. 185. Saigusa Hiroto, 'Japanese Astronomy in the Tokugawa Era', *Japan Quarterly*, v. 332–8. David Eugene Smith and Mikami Yoshio. *A History of Japanese Mathematics* (Chicago, 1914). Fujikawa Y., *Japanese Medicine*, trans. from the German by John Ruhrah (New York, 1934), chs. I–VIII.

however, would give a false impression unless it is understood that scholars from the United States, France, Holland, and Germany were currently teaching Japanese students at home and abroad in the same or different fields in an effort to satisfy Japan's thirst for the technical knowledge then possessed by the West.[1]

Japanese Students in England

The first Japanese students to go to England, Itō Hirobumi, Inoue Kaoru and Inouye Masaru (Katsu), Endō Kinsuke, and Yamao Yōzō became distinguished national leaders. Disregarding the rigid law against foreign travel, the Shogunate secretly ordered Itō Hirobumi and Inoue Kaoru to England for study in May 1863.[2] At the same time an equally secret order from the Daimyo of Chōshū and Suwō, their feudal lord, supported them in their desire to see the West. William Keswick of Jardine, Matheson and Company in Yokohama facilitated their departure on a company ship bound for Shanghai.[3] Arrangements by the manager of the firm in Shanghai led to Itō and Inoue Kaoru being assigned to the schooner *Pegasus* as apprenticed seamen and the other three to the schooner *White Adder*. The horrors of his 130 days with Inoue aboard the *Pegasus* have been described by Prince Itō. Unable to explain their interest in navigation rather than seamanship because of language difficulties, the two Japanese gentlemen had to work day and night spreading and lowering sails, washing decks, working pumps, and doing other menial tasks with nothing better than dry bread, salt beef, and coarse tea sweetened with red sugar for food, and with no bedding or lavatory to provide other comforts. Their little schooner of three hundred tons braved the strong winds and high seas off the African coast with the likelihood of capsizing at any moment. A deep and lasting friendship was formed between these two men as they faced together numerous chances of death and unbearable loneliness. Since the *Pegasus* always anchored off shore at the ports of call, in order to escape pay-

[1] Yuasa Mitsutōmo, *Kagakushi* (History of Science), (Tokyo, 1961), p. 104. Erwin Baelz, *Awakening Japan, The Diary of a German Doctor*, ed. by his son, Toku Baelz (New York, 1932), pp. 14, 39. E. S. Morse, *Japan Day by Day 1877, 1878–9, 1882–3*, 2 vols. (Boston, 1917), i. 281.   [2] Yanaga, op. cit., p. 34.

[3] Jardine, Matheson & Co. (Japan) Ltd., *Jardine's Centenary in Japan 1859–1959* (privately printed, Tokyo, 1959), pp. 17–18.

ment of harbour dues, they could never leave the ship.[1] That they had any interest left in Western ways of life when they reached London, exhausted and emaciated, in mid-autumn 1863, is proof of their stamina, both moral and intellectual.

Fortunately a good life in England awaited them under the supervision of Matheson and Company. The head of the firm, Hugh Matheson, met them. Alexander William Williamson, Professor of Chemistry at University College, London, an ardent scientist and magnetic teacher, became their guardian and friend.[2] Itō Hirobumi, Inoue Kaoru, and Yamao Yōzō lived at Williamson's home and owed much of their early training to him. All five students found interest in many phases of English life and learned wherever they went. They visited museums and galleries; they looked at factories and dockyards; and they became friends with English undergraduates.

The return of Itō and Inoue Kaoru to Japan after a year has been noted.[3] Their three colleagues remained in England until 1868 studying industrial techniques which they wanted to introduce in Japan. As a result of their work in engineering, Inoue Masaru laid the foundation of the Japanese railway system, Yamao developed methods of mining engineering, and Endō brought into Japan the European system of minting.[4]

European training became a goal for young men of promise when in 1866 the Shogunate issued a proclamation permitting Japanese of all ranks to visit foreign countries provided they secured passports from their own daimyo or from the government.[5] Even before this T. B. Glover, Jardine, Matheson's agent in Nagasaki, had connived with the Daimyo of Satsuma as well as Chōshū in getting students to Europe. He continued

---

[1] Ibid., pp. 26–28, *A Memoir of the late Baron Itō, formerly Principal Private Secretary to Prince Itō.*

[2] Alexander William Williamson, 1824–1904, was born in London, studied chemistry in Germany, physics and mathematics in Paris, and became professor of chemistry, University College, at twenty-six. He was renowned for his 'classical investigation of the formation of ethers and his remarkably keen insight into the atomic constitution of matter' (Baron Sakurai at University College Fellows' Dinner, 30 Apr. 1937). Williamson was made Foreign Secretary of the Royal Society in Mar. 1873. (MS. Royal Society, A 524). Williamson's scientific papers are also among the manuscripts at the Royal Society (AP 37. 29) but nothing about his work with Japanese students survives. H. E. Roscoe, *Life and Experiences* (London, 1906), p. 36. [3] See pp. 132–5.

[4] *Jardine's Centenary in Japan*, p. 19.

[5] Black, op. cit. ii. 33. See p. 184.

to do so, even to the extent of helping them violate the passport regulation after 1866.[1] Between 1865 and 1870 twenty or more names of Japanese students appear on the calendars which at this time listed all the students in attendance at University College, London.[2] In November 1866 the Shogunate itself sent fourteen students to England from the *Kaiseijo* (the *Bakufu* school for teaching Western languages) in charge of a Mr. Lloyd, the chaplain and naval instructor of H.M.S. *Scylla*.[3] The Shogun's agreement with Lloyd that the students should stay five years came to a sudden end with the Restoration of the Mikado. The Foreign Office advanced funds for their return home for which and for the losses on Lloyd's contract the Japanese government made compensation.[4]

Among these students were the great mathematician of the future, Kikuchi Dairoku, then a prodigy only 12 years old, and his elder brother Mitsukuri Keigo.[5] Satsuma men also sought study in Europe immediately after their humiliating experience with the British fleet at Kagoshima. Among them many became great in the service of their country—for example, Terashima Munenori, Mori Arinori, and Yoshida Kiyonari[6]—and Nagasawa Kanaye, sent to Scotland by the Daimyo of Satsuma under the auspices of T. B. Glover, was the first Japanese to take 'honours' in a British university. This he did at Aberdeen according to a report in the *Aberdeen Herald* of 26 June 1866.[7]

With the open encouragement of study abroad during the early years of Meiji many more men profited by the training of British universities. Even His Imperial Highness Prince Higashi-Fushimi, who had received the Duke of Edinburgh in Japan in 1869, planned a private visit for study.[8] Eighty-seven students had arrived by March 1872 and 150 by August. They were in

---

[1] Paske-Smith, *Western Barbarians*, pp. 264–5.

[2] These calendars are among the fragments of the records of University College in the mid-nineteenth century left after the destruction of World War II.

[3] F.O. 46/72, Parkes to Stanley, Nos. 194 and 196, Yedo, 17 and 30 Nov. 1866. Ad. 13/58, Adm. to F.O., 17 Jan. 1867.

[4] F.O. 262/141, Stanley to Parkes, No. 95, 19 June 1868; 46/97, Parkes to Stanley, No. 259, Yokohama, 15 Oct. 1868.

[5] Baron Kikuchi's *Diary* was destroyed during World War II. This and my later information concerning him, I have received indirectly from his descendants through the help of Prof. and Mrs. Higasi Keniti of Hokkaido University.

[6] Yanaga, op. cit., p. 34.   [7] Black, op. cit. ii. 33.

[8] F.O. 46/127, Parkes to Granville, No. 164, Yedo, 3 Dec. 1870; 262/205, Granville to Parkes, No. 9, 9 Feb. 1871.

general without guidance and of some concern to the British Foreign Office, which wished the Japanese government to make an independent arrangement for their supervision.[1] Some were assisted by advances from Matheson and Company.[2]

Among all these students in England none became more distinguished scholars than Kikuchi Dairoku (1855–1917) and Sakurai Jōji (1858–1939). Kikuchi having returned to Japan in 1868 came back to England to study at Cambridge in 1874, where he graduated with high honours in 1877. He went home to become the first professor of mathematics in the Faculty of Science at the newly established Tokyo Imperial University where he lectured on pure and applied mathematics. He rose to be Dean of that Faculty by 1881, Dean of the College of Science which opened in 1886, President of Tokyo Imperial University in 1898, and Minister of Education in the Katsura Cabinet in 1901. He was created Baron the next year and became a Privy Councillor in 1911. As professor of mathematics Kikuchi did much to advance its study in Japan. In 1877 he was the founder of the Tokyo Mathematical Society which under his direction became the Physico-Mathematical Society in 1884. He was the author of textbooks on geometry and a series of papers on the mathematics of Tokugawa Japan (Wasan) and articles on 'Enri' (measurement of the arc.)[3]

More personal records of the great Japanese chemist, Baron Sakurai Jōji, have been preserved.[4] He was one of ten promising students selected by the Ministry of Education in 1876 from Tokyo *Kaisei Gakkō* (Daigaku Nanko), the forerunner of Tokyo Imperial University, to study abroad for five years. Eight of these ten, including Sakurai, went to England in contrast to the eleven of the previous year who were ordered to the United States, France, and Germany.[5] Sakurai attributed his success

---

[1] F.O. 46/152, Parkes to Hammond, London (?), 26 Mar. 1872; 46/155, unsigned, 24 Aug. 1872. Probably Parkes to Hammond, London, as Parkes was on home leave. [2] F.O. 262/184, F.O. to Parkes, No. 70, 1 July 1870.

[3] Sakurai Jōji 'Mathematical-Physical Science in Japan' in Ōkuma, *Fifty Years of New Japan*, ii. 248–9. Material from the Kikuchi family. Oya Shin-ichi, 'A Short Note on the History of Japanese Mathematics', *Japanese Studies in the History of Science*, i. 1962.

[4] *Omoide no Kazu Kazu, Danshaku Sakurai Jōji Ikō* (Manuscripts left by Baron Sakurai Jōji ed. by his son, Takeo (Tokyo, 1940) (Hibaihin)).

[5] Ibid., 'Eikoku Ryūgaku' (My Study in England), pp. 10 ff., trans. by Higasi Yoshie. The other Japanese students who went to England at this time were:

as a scientist 'first and most of all to the scientific training' he received in University College, London, from 1876 to 1881. Throughout the five years he, too, was a student and devoted admirer of Professor Alexander Williamson. And he sat under Professor Carey Foster and Dr. Oliver Lodge for physics. His record was outstanding from the beginning. At the end of his first year he passed highest in the examinations and won a gold medal in chemistry. The next year he was the prize-winner in a competitive examination for students in chemistry and physics, with the award of a scholarship of £50 for each of the two following years—a great boon to the limited budget granted by his government. He presented a paper at the Chemical Society, London, and another at the annual meeting of the British Society for the Progress of Science in 1879 when he was elected to membership in the Chemical Society. He could not take a degree from the University, however, because he had not matriculated. Degrees came later—a Doctor of Science from Tokyo in 1888 and a Doctor of Laws from Glasgow in 1901.[1]

Sakurai enjoyed the intellectual and social life in England at this period and seized every opportunity to understand the culture which surrounded him. He studied English history, literature, art, and drama, in addition to his courses in science. He listened to Gladstone and Disraeli in Parliament. He read the works of Spencer, Tennyson, Dickens, and George Eliot. He found pleasure in the paintings of Turner and Millais at the Royal Academy, and he sat among the crowds at the Lyceum enchanted by Henry Irving and Ellen Terry. He made enduring friendships among the English people, whose homes he often visited and where he was known to dance all night.[2]

Sakurai returned to Japan in 1881 to become a lecturer in chemistry at Tokyo University. He was promoted to a full professorship the next year which he held until 1919 and where he raised the teaching of chemistry to the European level. He was the founder of scientific chemistry in Japan,

Irie (Hozumi) Nobushige, Sakisaka ——, Okumura Teruhiko (law); Sugiura Jūko (chemistry), Sekiya Kiyokage, Matsuda Reisaku and Taniguchi Naosada (engineering).

[1] London, Extract from University College Committee Minutes, Tuesday, 2 Feb. 1937.

[2] 'Eikoku Ryūgaku' in Sakurai, *Omoide no Kazu Kazu*, pp. 10 ff. Information from Prof. Higasi Keniti, given him in an interview with Baron Sakurai's son.

working at first in organic chemistry, although his 'natural bent of mind was in the direction of theoretical and physical chemistry'. He was an equally gifted administrator, serving as a University Councillor, Dean of the Faculty of Science, and Acting President of the University during the course of his thirty-eight years at Tokyo. Recognition and honours were great. They included the presidency of the National Research Council of Japan, the presidency of the Imperial Academy of Tokyo—a position analogous to that of President of the Royal Society—and the presidency of the Third Pan-Pacific Science Congress in 1926. He became a Privy Councillor and in 1937 he was made an Honorary Fellow of University College, London, being the first foreigner to receive this distinction.[1]

Sakurai's numerous addresses before scientific groups, and all types of schools, colleges, and learned societies make clear the warmth and magnetism of his personality, the breadth of his interest in education at all levels, and his great faith in international intellectual co-operation. Through him thousands of his own people felt the impact of English thought. Sakurai was generous in his appreciation of the teaching of British scientists who were invited to Japan in the early years of Meiji. From them and those from America, he thought, the Japanese had learned to study science for its own sake and that this accounted for the 'rapid and healthy development' of science in Japan.[2]

British Scientists in Japan

To secure these competent teachers the Meiji government appealed to members of the Jardine, Matheson firm in Japan. Although Parkes supported Winchester's recommendations that British instructors be sent to Japan to balance the influence of those from other countries and he and the Foreign Office encouraged the *Bakufu* request for British instructors to staff a college for the study of English, history, literature, mathematics, natural philosophy, astronomy, engineering, and chemistry, the Shogunate fell before the college was established.

[1] London University College Records, *Report of the Proceedings of the Fellows Committee* at their meeting on 17 Nov. 1936, included in the *Minutes* of the University College Committee, 2 Feb. 1937. 'Obituary Note' from Proceedings, Imperial Academy, Tokyo, vol. xv.

[2] Sakurai, 'Mathematical-Physical Science in Japan' in Ōkuma, *Fifty Years of New Japan*, ii. 244; *Omoide no Kazu Kazu*, pp. 296–8.

And the efforts of the British Foreign Office to employ professors for Japan failed owing to the demand for competent scholars in England and India.[1] Through the help of Jardine's correspondents in London, however, young English scientists recommended by Dr. Alexander Williamson, and other scholars were sent to Japan before the organization of Tokyo University.[2]

Among them Henry Dyer (C.E., M.A., D.Sc., 1848–1918), a distinguished graduate of the University of Glasgow, was one of the most influential in the industrial development of Japan. During Iwakura's Embassy in England at the end of 1872, Dyer, at the age of twenty-four, was offered the position of Principal of the Engineering College which the Japanese government wanted to found in Yedo. Itō Hirobumi, then Vice-Minister of Public Works and a member of the Embassy, envisioned a College, called at first *Kōgakkō*, which would train Japanese to design and superintend the works which Japan required as she adopted the industrial methods of the West. Dyer, accompanied by Hayashi Tadasu, Itō's private secretary, arrived in Japan in the late spring of 1873, equipped with a calendar for the new college which the Japanese government accepted without change. Hayashi, representing the Department of Public Works, managed the finances and administration of the College as Chief Commissioner while Dyer was responsible for the educational policy.[3] In this Dyer combined the best in the British and continental systems for training engineers. He introduced highly theoretical scientific courses along with practical experience in workshops. The course lasted six years. A general and scientific programme for two years preceded the theoretical and practical work. It included English language and composition, geography, elementary mathematics, elementary mechanics, elementary physics, chemistry, and mechanical drawing. Instruction was partly professorial, partly tutorial.

By 1877 the government had completed impressive quarters for this college—a main building containing the large examination hall, library, drawing-offices, lecture halls, and class-

---

[1] F.O. 46/81, Parkes to Stanley, No. 112, Yedo, 27 June 1867; 262/141, Stanley to Parkes, No. 14, 25 Jan. 1868.

[2] MS. University College, Sakurai's speech at University College Fellows' Dinner, 30 Apr. 1937.   [3] Dyer, op. cit., pp. 1–3.

rooms, which was surrounded by separate buildings used as dormitories, professors' houses, a museum, and four laboratories devoted to chemistry, physics, metallurgy, and engineering.[1]

Dyer not only organized the curriculum and planned the buildings for the engineering college, called by 1877 *Kōbu Daigakkō* (Imperial College of Engineering), but was professor of engineering himself until his return to Glasgow in 1882. During this time he introduced the telephone to Japan when he installed instruments ordered from London in 1877 to connect his office at the College with the Public Works Department, but telephones were not established for general use until after the period here considered.[2]

Men destined for distinction were members of Dyer's faculty from the start. When Robert Grant Watson, Secretary of the British legation, visited *Kōgakkō* in August 1873 he reported that the professors for the general and scientific course were all British. W. E. Ayrton, University College, London, taught natural philosophy (physics); David H. Marshall, M.A. University of Edinburgh, mathematics; Edward Divers, M.D., D.Sc., F.R.S. Queen's University, Belfast, chemistry; Edmund F. Mondy, A.R.S.M. Royal School of Mines, London, drawing; William Craigie, M.A. University of Aberdeen, English language and literature.[3]

Two of these, Ayrton and Divers, deserve special notice. William Edward Ayrton (1847–1908) taught physics and telegraphy 1873–8. He is said to have introduced electric light into Japan when he equipped the Central Telegraph office with lights during its inaugural ceremony in 1878, although the lighting of an electric arc lamp had been first publicly demonstrated at the graduation ceremony of Tokyo University, 19 December 1877, by Yamakawa Kenjirō, then an assistant professor of experimental physics. With John Perry (1850–1920, M.E. Queen's University, Belfast, D.Sc., LL.D., F.R.S.), who

[1] 'Engineering Education in Japan', *Nature*, 17 May 1877, pp. 45–46. Dyer, op. cit., pp. 89–90. *Kōbu Daigakkō* was merged with Tokyo Imperial University in 1886. For detailed description of the courses, entrance examinations, etc., of the Engineering College, see P.P. H. of C. 1874, lxv, 53–81, R. G. Watson, 'Report on the Present Educational System in Japan', 30 Nov. 1873.

[2] Obituary of Dyer, *Nature*, 10 Oct. 1918, p. 109. Dyer, op. cit., pp. 147–8.

[3] P.P. H. of C. 1874, lxv. 53, R. G. Watson, 'Report on Present Educational System of Japan'.

joined the faculty as assistant professor of civil engineering 1875–82, Ayrton promoted the study of physics not as a special course but to qualify engineers for their profession.[1] They published papers jointly in the *Transactions* of the Asiatic Society and in the *Philosophical Magazine* of London, but not without some contemporary criticism.[2] Ayrton's earliest and ablest pupil was Shida Rinzaburo (1855–92) who recognized the importance of basic science for the progress of industry and made contributions to electrical engineering.[3]

Two Englishmen, Edward Divers (1837–1912), and R. W. Atkinson, were not only the pioneer teachers of Western chemistry in Japan but English works were basic sources of Japan's earliest book on chemistry. The Japanese author Udagawa Yoan, a physician and student of the Dutch language, introduced chemistry to his country in 1837 with the publication of his *Seimi Kaisō*. He grounded this book on the Dutch translation by Adolphus Ypey of *Chemie fur Dilettanten* (Amsterdam, 1803). This in turn was the German translation by Johann Bartholoma Trommsdorf (Erfurt, 1803), of *An Epitome of Chemistry*, the work of an English scholar, William Henry, first published in London in 1801. Although there were many revised and enlarged editions of Henry's book Udagawa followed most closely this first edition and added to it detailed notes from other Dutch sources. Udagawa also described at length Sir Humphry Davy's isolation of sodium and potassium metals of 1807 and his famous study on chlorine (1810). He fully appreciated Davy's work but does not mention Davy's great contemporary, John Dalton, although there is some indication in *Seimi Kaisō*, xvi, ch. 272, that he knew about Dalton's atomic theory (1808–10) from later accounts of it.[4]

[1] Sakurai in Ōkuma, *Fifty Years of New Japan*, ii. 255. Iwanami, *Seiyō Jinmei Jiten* (Dictionary of Foreign Names), (Tokyo, 1956), pp. 239, 1324. Nakamura Seiji, *Tanakadate Aikitsu Sensei* (My Teacher, Tanakadate Aikitsu, (Tokyo, 1943) p. 35.

[2] *T.A.S.J.* iv, Pt. I, pp. 116 ff., 'Specific Inductive Capacity of Gases'; p. 131, 'Importance of a General System of Simultaneous Observations of Atmosphere Electricity'; p. 181, 'On a Neglected Principle that may be Employed in Earthquake Measurements'. Other scientific papers of John Perry may be found among the MSS. of the Royal Society—e.g. AP 66. 29. *Philosophical Magazine*, ix. Fifth Series (Jan.–June) 1889, 292–301, 446–8.

[3] Sakurai in Ōkuma, *Fifty Years of New Japan*, ii. 255. Information from Prof. Higasi Keniti.

[4] Higasi Keniti, *Dipole, Molecule, and Chemistry* (Sapporo, Japan, 1965), pp. 51–53, Sakaguchi Masao, 'Seimi Kaisō no Kenkyū' (Studies on Seimi Kaisō), *Kagakushi*

In his preface to the first edition of *Seimi Kaisō* another Japanese physician and Dutch scholar, Totsuka Seikai, stressed the importance of chemistry as fundamental to the study of medicine and other sciences.[1] A few Japanese soon began work in chemistry but little was accomplished before the Restoration.

Japan's new Code of Education introducing Western sciences systematically into the curriculum in 1872 and the opening of a well-equipped laboratory in 1874 at the *Kaiseijo* brought progress. That same year R. W. Atkinson, the prize student of Professor Williamson of University College, London, was invited to become professor of chemistry at the *Kaiseijo*. There and later at Tokyo Imperial University until 1881 he inaugurated a more advanced study of chemistry as a special branch of science. He taught analytical chemistry, organic chemistry, theoretical and technological, as well as metallurgy, and conducted original research with his students, among whom were the distinguished Sakurai Jōji and Takamine Jōkichi.[2] A number of his papers may be read today in the *Transactions* of the Asiatic Society.[3] He was awarded the Order of the Rising Sun, fourth class, when he left Japan.[4]

Currently with Atkinson, Edward Divers was lecturing on chemistry at *Kōgakkō*. He was transferred to *Rika Daigaku* (College of Science) with professorial rank in 1886 when the Engineering College was merged with Tokyo Imperial University. He worked with Sakurai until 1899, doing important research with his students in inorganic chemistry, particularly on inorganic compounds containing nitrogen and sulphur.[5] Among those he trained were Takamine Jōkichi, Nakamura

Kenkyū (Journal of the History of Science), 1964, lxxii. 145, 151–2, 155–6; 1965, lxxiii. 29; 1966, lxxx. 171. Letters from Prof. Higasi to the author, 15 Jan., 3, 5, 8, and 18 Feb. 1966, and 20 Jan. 1967. The later editions of William Henry's book were entitled *Elements of Experimental Chemistry*, e.g., the seventh edition (London, 1815) now in the Library of Congress.

[1] Photostat of Preface by Totsuka Seikai to 1837 edition of *Seimi Kaisō*, secured by Prof. Higasi.

[2] Sakurai in Ōkuma, op. cit. ii. 257–8. Yuasa, op. cit., pp. 107–8.

[3] e.g. 'Analysis of Surface of Waters in Tokyo', *T.A.S.J.* vii, Pt. IV; 'Notes on the Manufacture of O Shiroi', vi. Pt. II; 'Porcelain Industry in Japan', viii, Pt. II.

[4] Fuzambo's *Kokushi Jiten* (Dictionary of Japanese History), 4 vols. (Tokyo, 1940), i. 159.

[5] e.g. *T.A.S.J.* vi, Pt. II, 'Notes on the amount of Sulphuretted Hydrogen in the Hot Springs of Kusatsu'.

Sadakichi, and Kawakita Nōtatsu. His work was recognized in England when he was made a Fellow of the Royal Society and in Japan when he received the Order of the Sacred Treasure, second class, and the Order of the Rising Sun, third class.[1]

Three British scholars introduced the science of seismology to the Japanese during the latter part of the 1870s. John Milne 1850–1913, F.R.S., Hon. D.Sc. Oxford, F.G.S. a mining engineer, taught geology and mining at *Kōbu Daigakkō* (Imperial College of Engineering) and later at Tokyo Imperial University for nearly twenty years, 1876–94. He carried on important research in seismology, invented a seismograph, established a seismic survey of Japan which embraced 968 stations for observation, and founded in 1880 the Seismological Society of Japan. He applied for a grant for instruments and money from the Royal Society to further his researches in Tokyo but there is no evidence that he received it. The Japanese Diet awarded him a small pension upon his retirement from his university work.[2]

James Alfred Ewing (1855–1935, K.C.B., M.A. Edinburgh, Hon. D.Sc. Oxford, Hon. Sc.D. Cambridge), was professor of mechanical engineering and physics at Tokyo Imperial University 1878–83. With the assistance of T. Lomar Gray, who taught telegraphy at *Kōbu Daigakkō* 1879–81, he investigated the phenomena of earthquakes, and devised and improved instruments for recording and measuring their intensity.[3] Ewing and his students at Tokyo carried on experiments on magnetic induction, reporting their findings on the hysteresis of magnetism in the *Philosophical Transactions* of the Royal Society, London, 1885.[4] Ewing also established an observatory in the lowest part of the Vale of Gedo. His observations there appeared

[1] Yuasa, op. cit., pp. 105–8. *Sekai Dai Hyakka Jiten* (World Encyclopedia), xviii. 113. *Medical Directory* (London, 1874) p. 1036. MSS. Royal Society Nos. 76 and 77, letters of Edward Divers to Prof. G. G. Stokes, 6 and 7 Aug. 1885.

[2] Yuasa, op. cit., p. 195. Iwanami, op. cit., p. 1498. *Who Was Who 1897–1915* (London, 1935), p. 494. F.O. 46/458, *Memorandum* by John Longford, 28 Feb. 1895. MSS. Royal Society No. 176, Sekiya to J. A. Ewing, Kobe, 16 Nov. 1890; Mc 16. 1, application for grant, 4 Jan. 1893. For an example of his publications, see *T.A.S.J.* vii, Pt. I, 'Journey Across Europe and Asia'.

[3] Sakurai in Ōkuma, *Fifty Years of New Japan*, ii. 262. Iwanami, op. cit., p. 1567. Yuasa, op. cit., pp. 195–6.

[4] From comment by Prof. Higasi Keniti, Nov. 1961. Some of his papers, e.g. *The Effects of Stress on the Thermoelectric Quality of Metals*, are at the Royal Society (A.P. 61–63).

in 1883 in the *Memories* of the Science Department of Tokyo University.[1] His statement on a contemporary technological development seems to indicate he was a man of caution. In a lecture on the phonograph which he preceded by lllustrations of telephonic transmission of sound, a local newspaper reports that he took great pains to show that 'no desirable results of a practical nature had yet proceeded from Edison's contrivance'.[2]

One of Ewing's earliest students, Tanakadate Aikitsu, who graduated from Tokyo University in 1882, was sent to Glasgow to study under Ewing's former teacher, Sir William Thomson. He made important contributions to seismology, especially those relating to earth magnetism.[3] Years later at the time of Ewing's death the Japanese paid warm tribute to all he had done in his five years in their country. His picture was hung with that of James Watt in the dining-hall of the Eiraku Club, Tokyo, at the thirty-second celebration of James Watt's birthday in Japan. Tanakadate Aikitsu recounted his teaching of the theory and practice of steam engines and praised the spirit of scientific engineering which he had engendered among his students.[4]

British Medical Leaders, Dr. William Willis and Dr. Joseph Bower Siddall

English medical works concerning surgery, internal medicine, and obstetrics reached Japan in the early 60s through translations into Chinese by an English physician, Benjamin Hobson.[5] Soon both English and American medical practice gained popularity over the Dutch works which had been Japan's source for the study of Western medicine since 1771. Two British physicians attached to the British legation, William Willis and Joseph Bower Siddall, did much to increase Japanese confidence in British medical knowledge.[6]

Dr. Willis (1837–94), of Fermanagh County, Ireland, had a

[1] *Dictionary of National Biography (D.N.B.)* 1931–40, (London, 1949), p. 264.

[2] *Tokio Times*, 30 Nov. 1878.

[3] Sakurai in Ōkuma, *Fifty Years of New Japan*, ii. 255.

[4] Tanakadate Aikitsu, *Kuzu no Ne* (Selected Essays, Speeches, and other Works), (Tokyo, 1938), pp. 221–5. The Japanese students of physics, mathematics, and astronomy had held annual festivals in honour of Newton since 1880 and in honour of Watt since 1900. Ibid., pp. 130–1.

[5] Yanaga, op. cit., p. 81. Aoyama Tanemichi and Fujikawa Ukabu 'The Development of Medicine in Japan', in Ōkuma, *Fifty Years of New Japan*, ii. 294.

[6] Satow, *Diplomat*, p. 31. List of Japanese books on medicine, translated from Dutch works before 1858, published by Suhavaya, Tokyo. (No date.)

medical degree from Edinburgh and was a member of the Royal College of Surgeons when in 1861 he was appointed to the British legation in Yedo to serve as surgeon and assistant interpreter. He was a lifelong friend of Ernest Satow who said of him: 'Perhaps no other man ever exhibited in a greater measure the quality which we are wont to call conscientiousness, whether in his private relations or in the discharge of his duties.' Willis—6 ft. 4 in. tall and heavily built—was absolutely fearless whenever his medical services were needed. Thus in 1862 he was probably the first to rush to the aid of Richardson 'passing for a mile along the ranks of the men whose swords were reeking with the blood of Englishmen' only to find the mutilated corpse of the Shanghai merchant at Namamugi.[1] He managed successfully the smallpox hospital in Yokohama which was established on the bluff in 1864 to check the spread of the disease, and contributed largely to the control of a nascent epidemic.[2]

Willis was made vice-consul at Yedo and Kanagawa on 1 January 1868. He was present at the attack on Sir Harry Parkes on his way to an audience with the Mikado on 23 March 1868 when his skilful surgery was a stroke of good fortune for the wounded men.[3] His medical and surgical knowledge so impressed the Japanese that both parties in the civil war of 1868 sought his services. He attended the Satsuma and Chōshū men in Kyoto after the fighting at Toba-Fushimi and helped the Shogun's wounded troops on their retreat to Osaka.[4] The Meiji authorities asked his help in the case of the illness of Yamanouchi Yōdō in Kyoto, a service which Sir Harry Parkes also readily granted and which benefited the ex-daimyo.[5] He was then asked to be the surgeon at the temporary hospital established in Yokohama in April 1868 for wounded soldiers, the first surgical hospital in Japan. Soon afterwards the Imperial government chose him to accompany its troops during the operations in the north after the surrender of Yedo.[6]

Parkes wrote of Willis to Hammond: 'It is very satisfactory,

---

[1] Satow, *Diplomat*, pp. 31–32. Great Britain, *Foreign Office List*, 1883, p. 204. Oka, *Reimeiki no Meiji Nihon*, p. 172. Brunton MS., pp. 74–75.
[2] P.P. H. of C. 1865, liii, 292, Cons. Report for Yokohama 1864.
[3] Dickins, op. cit., ii. 90, 95. Satow, *Diplomat*, pp. 359–60. See pp. 228–9.
[4] F.O. 46/91, Parkes to Stanley, No. 41, Hyogo, 25 Feb. 1868.
[5] Satow, MSS. 15/2, *Diary*, 13 Feb. 1868; *Diplomat*, p. 349.
[6] *Yokohama-shi Shi Kō*, iii. 594. Oka, *Reimeiki no Meiji Nihon*, pp. 179–97.

though it scarcely forms a subject for surprise when it is known how good a man he is, to see how entirely he earns the confidence of the Japanese wherever he goes and how they beg him to proceed from point to point to the farthest place of interest, Wakamatsu, the capital of Aizu. I entirely approve of his having proceeded there in order that he may give effect to those lessons of humanity towards the wounded prisoners which he has so sedulously inculcated. His journey will be the most interesting travel yet performed by any foreigner in Japan.'[1]

Willis's own account of his service deserves quotation:

I attended personally to the requirements of 600 men and gave directions regarding the treatment of about 1000 others. Of these numbers 900 were of the Mikado's army and 700 of the Aizu Clan. I performed thirty-eight amputations, varying in magnitude from removal of a finger to amputation of thigh at the hip joint. Of those operated upon, about one-half recovered. I extracted twenty-three bullets, and removed dead bone from upwards of 200 patients. The wounds were almost exclusively gun shot injuries. I saw a few instances of spear wounds and sword cuts, but no instance of a bayonet wound. As far as time, and other circumstances would permit, I instructed the native doctors in the treatment of the wounded.

Willis was shocked at the 'deplorable state of filth and wretchedness' in which he found the Aizu men and at the general practice of killing wounded prisoners. As often as possible he pointed out 'the inhumanity of a wanton sacrifice of human life' and stressed the consideration given to wounded opponents in the West. He found armour 300 years old in the Aizu town of Wakamatsu which convinced him there had been no decline in the physique of the soldier class in Japan during three centuries.[2]

In July 1868 the military hospital was transferred from Yokohama to Yedo. A few months later the *Bakufu* Institute of Western Medicine (1861) was reopened and incorporated with the hospital to form what later became the School of Medicine of Tokyo Imperial University. When Willis returned from the north in December the Meiji government asked him to reorganize this hospital as a general hospital and to be the professor of surgery for one year. The British Foreign Office

---

[1] F.O. 46/98 Parkes to Hammond, Private, Yokohama, 2 Dec. 1868.
[2] P.P, H. of C, 1868–9, lxiv, pp. 34–35, *Memorandum* by Dr. Willis, 23 Jan. 1869.

co-operated by granting him a leave of absence, agreeing with Parkes that the post offered him a wide opportunity to influence native opinion in favour of Englishmen and foreigners generally.[1]

Although the Japanese respected Willis's surgical knowledge —he was the first to teach septic surgery in Japan—the young officials, Iwasa Jun and Sagasa Tomoyasu, appointed to advance medical service in Japan, were influenced by Guido Verbeck, an American missionary and scholar, to choose the German school of medicine as the new model for their country. This called for the retirement of Willis, whose work had been much appreciated by the Meiji government and who felt entitled to an assured position. Saigō Takamori eased the task of requesting his resignation by making possible an invitation to Satsuma. Here Willis was asked to help establish and preside over a medical school and hospital at Kagoshima. He resigned his post as vice-consul in December 1869 and made a great success of his work in Satsuma. Among his distinguished pupils were Ikeda Kensai, Sasaki Tōyō, Takagi Kanehiro, Mitamura Hajima, and Kagami Mitsukata. Henry Brunton, the British engineer, reported in 1870 that Willis was much respected by foreigners and Japanese alike but that as a solitary Englishman in Kagoshima he was having to assuage loneliness by reading the *Encyclopedia Britannica* and studying Japanese. He married a daughter of a former vassal of the daimyo by whom he had a son.[2]

It was at Willis's house that Saigō met with Satow in February 1877 and told of the strength of his forces rising in rebellion.[3] Soon after this Willis reluctantly returned to Yedo at the command of the Japanese Foreign Office which could not protect foreigners in Kyūshū during the rebellion. So great was Willis's known friendship with Saigō that it was proposed by Kambara Seiji of Nambu that Willis go to Kyūshū in the service of the Japanese Society for the Wounded and see Saigō at the same time, in an effort to persuade him to capitulate— a plan which Satow discouraged for diplomatic reasons and

[1] Oka, *Reimeiki no Meiji Nihon*, pp. 197–8. F.O. 46/107, Parkes to Stanley, No. 37, Yokohama, 9 Feb. 1869. Fujikawa, op. cit., pp. 63–64.

[2] Oka, *Reimeiki no Meiji Nihon*, pp. 198, 201–3. Brunton MS., pp. 74–75. For Verbeck see p. 503.

[3] Satow, MSS. 15/5, *Diary*, pp. 60–61, 11 Feb. 1877.

because he knew that Willis would not advise his friend to surrender.[1]

Willis went back to England later in 1877 after receiving many honours in Japan. He had been the first European and the first commoner to whom the Mikado presented Imperial brocades and the first foreigner to be admitted within the sacred precincts of Kyoto.[2] A memorial was dedicated to Dr. Willis in 1893 at Kagoshima University Hospital. Here great tribute is paid to him as a major contributor to the progress in medical science in Japan, which was one of the significant fruits of the introduction of Western learning. His care of the wounded in the war for the Restoration is noted and his teaching in the medical school at Kagoshima is said to have laid the foundation for the rapid development of medicine in the prefecture.[3]

Dr. Willis was assisted by Dr. Joseph B. Siddall in his work with the wounded and in establishing the great hospital, Dai Biyōin, in Yedo. A graduate of the University of Aberdeen with highest honours and a former house surgeon of St. Thomas's Hospital, London, Siddall had been appointed surgeon to the British legation in 1868.[4] With Willis he attended the wounded men of the Mikado's army who had been brought to Yokohama in June 1868 for the special attention of Willis. In November, at the request of the Japanese government and with Parkes's sanction, he took charge of the temporary hospital for the relief of the wounded at Yedo. His experiences there reflect the transition going on in medical care.

Goten palace, a large *yashiki* (palace) of a daimyo, had been converted into this hospital. The big central rooms seemed to provide excellent wards, but the Japanese preferred separate rooms though small. It was difficult to keep them in wards as the native surgeons had little concept of the strict order and regularity required in an English hospital. Many of the bedsteads were iron with hair mattresses and sheets and blankets were of first-rate quality. The problem was to get the attendants to keep the beds clean. Nurses averaged one to each patient. Severe cases had two and sometimes three nurses in attendance.

[1] Ibid., pp. 89–90, 13 July 1877.
[2] Obituaries, *British Medical Journal*, 24 Feb. 1894, p. 441. *Lancet*, 1894, i. 507–8.
[3] Oka, *Reimeiki no Meiji Nihon*, p. 171.
[4] *Medical Directory* (London, 1869, 1870, 1871).

They were usually married women who did their work well but were deficient in discipline, feeling obliged to obey their patients who being men were considered superior beings. Their patients were sometimes unexpectedly difficult. They even threatened to decapitate the Japanese chief of the hospital for 'swelling about instead of attending to his duties'. Satow thought Siddall had his hands full.

A dispensary was established on European as distinct from Chinese principles. At first, the drugs came from Holland, later supplies were bought from English chemists at Yokohama. Native surgeons handled the dispensing according to simple prescriptions. There were occasional mistakes, of course, arising from ignorance of different names and of the physical properties of drugs compounded of the same base. Siddall struggled with the problems of drainage and disposal of waste since the attendants insisted upon burying bandages and poultices. He finally refused to see more patients until the filth was removed. Hygienic methods were thus introduced into the Japanese military service.

Siddall found that his Japanese assistants learned quickly the use of splints and to bandage in a manner creditable to a London hospital. He also taught them some surgery, holding a class after amputations at a thigh and making them perform amputations on the foot and leg. Previous to Willis's trip to the north in October 1868, Willis performed all operations and in addition to his consular duties came to the hospital every third and fourth day to explain cases needing an interpreter and to visit his patients.[1]

Vaccination

Although vaccination had been introduced in the Hakodate region by Nakagawa Gorosi upon his return from captivity in Russia about 1812, its efficacy had been proved by the Dutch physician Monike at Nagasaki in 1848 or 1849, and Japanese doctors had founded a vaccination institute in Yedo in 1858 its practice had spread very slowly and against much opposition, in spite of further efforts by several Western doctors.[2]

[1] J. B. Siddall, *St. Thomas's Hospital Reports*, New Series (London, 1874), v. 84–112. Satow, MSS. 15/3 *Diary*, pp. 6, 11–13, 24 Nov., 4–9 Dec. 1868.

[2] George Alexander Lensen, *Report from Hokkaidō* (Hakodate, 1954), p. 26. Black, op. cit. ii. 339. W. N. Whitney, 'Notes on the History of Medical Progress in

Siddall and another English physician, Dr. George Newton, R.N., at the time of the severe smallpox epidemic in the winter of 1870–1, however, were able to convince the Meiji government that compulsory vaccination was the only way to control the disease. Newton offered his services to the Japanese authorities on 2 January 1871, with the intention of establishing free vaccinating stations where all natives should be vaccinated, and supervising smallpox hospitals. Sir Harry Parkes called a meeting of all the English and American medical men, civil, military, and naval, to discuss these proposals with one of the Japanese governors of Kanagawa, which resulted in general support for Dr. Newton's suggestions and the promised co-operation of the Japanese government. On 15 March the Japanese authorities introduced by public notices a system for vaccination which was well received among the people. New stations were opened in Yokohama and nine neighbouring towns where careful medical officers vaccinated children. The Japanese government, however, did not establish smallpox hospitals.[1]

Each doctor and Parkes himself are given exclusive credit for this work which resulted in the Mikado's order in 1874 to vaccinate the entire population and the consequent disappearance of smallpox virtually within fifteen years. The two physicians probably deserve equal recognition. But it was to Siddall that the Mikado awarded the Order of the Rising Sun—an honour then given to a foreigner for the first time.[2]

Lock Hospitals

Dr. Newton was more widely recognized for his organization of lock hospitals in Japanese ports between 1867 and his death in 1871. Concern in London about the prevalence of venereal disease among British troops and sailors in Japan led to instructions for military and naval officers stationed there to confer together on the best means of checking the evil.[3] As a result

---

Japan,' *T.S.A.J.* xii, Pt. IV, 339–44. The vaccination institute became in 1861 the Institute of Western Medicine under the control of the Shogunate.

[1] Ad. I/6150, Kellett to Adm., 25 Jan. 1871. Ad. I/6191, Newton to Vice-Adm. Kellett (now Commander-in-Chief of the China Station), 2 Apr. 1871. Black, op. cit. ii. 339–42.

[2] Obituary of J. B. Siddall, *Lancet*, 18 July 1925, p. 155.

[3] F.O. 262/123, Stanley to Parkes. No. 19, 26 Jan. 1867.

Admiral Keppel offered the Shogun's government the gratuitous services of the naval surgeon, Dr. Newton, if it would build a hospital and make obligatory the periodic examination of all public women. Although the *Bakufu* made a grant towards the building, political troubles delayed work on the hospital. It was finally erected by the Meiji authorities and opened in the autumn of 1868. In the meantime Dr. Newton had conducted a temporary clinic for venereal diseases in Yokohama and had begun the examination of licensed prostitutes—the first time in Japan.[1]

The difficulties in the way of such reforms were many as Dr. Willis and Parkes pointed out. There was a great shortage of competent medical men to carry on regular inspection and the training of native practitioners for daily duties under occasional supervision required a long time. Furthermore the police were not only notoriously corrupt and the authorities apparently indifferent to the ravages of disease from which their people had widely suffered but the keepers of numerous houses of entertainment opposed such government interference with their interests.[2]

Dr. Newton gradually overcame the resistance of the brothel-keepers and found the Japanese authorities so co-operative that they consulted him about introducing his system in other Japanese ports.[3] By May 1871 a lock hospital had been established at Nagasaki where more than fifty-six per cent. of the women examined had contagious venereal diseases.[4] The government promised similar hospitals at Hyogo and Yedo as soon as possible. Newton's report on Yokohama for the first quarter of 1871 proved the value of his early work. Every prostitute in 102 brothels had been examined once a week making a total of 14,450 examinations, and only two per cent. were diseased and detained in the hospital. The Lock Hospital Report for the same period showed that 269 out of 411 men had been cured during the quarter.[5] By 1875 Dr. Hill, Newton's successor, reported the successful operation of lock hospitals

---

[1] Ad. I/6052, Keppel to Adm., Yokohama, 1 June 1868. *Yokohama-shi Shi Kō,* iii. 609–10. F.O. 46/97, Parkes to Stanley, No. 249, Yokohama, 13 Oct. 1868.

[2] Ibid. and encl., Willis's report on prostitution in Japan.

[3] F.O. 46/108, Parkes to Clarendon, No. 78, ? Yokohama, 24 Mar. 1869.

[4] F.O. 46/139, Parkes to Granville, No. 60, Yedo, 1 May 1871.

[5] Ad. I/6191, Newton to Kellet, 2 Apr. 1871.

in Nagasaki, Hyogo, and Osaka, the latter being run entirely by Japanese.[1]

As the British had benefited greatly from these institutions in Japan the British government continued to pay for the services rendered by the British doctor who supervised the system. It was clear to Parkes and the naval commander, Vice-Admiral Ryder, that the cost of maintaining the British medical inspector was more than offset by the benefits accrued to British sailors. Before the introduction of examinations and seclusion of diseased women at Kobe, twelve seamen from H.M.S. *Sylvia* were invalided with their constitutions injured by syphilis in one year. The unannounced visits of the British naval inspector to brothels were thought necessary to check laxity, corruption, and incompetence on the part of the native doctors.[2] Nevertheless, the Japanese foreign minister wanted to dispense with this British doctor even though his service was free. Reports from Parkes were needed in 1879 to win his acceptance of Dr. Lawrenson, as successor to Dr. Hill, on agreement that he would be the last British inspector.[3]

The persistence of unlicensed prostitution in all the treaty ports, however, seriously handicapped the full enforcement of the system.[4] Nevertheless in 1881 the Japanese authorities refused to accept Dr. Fisher as a successor to Lawrenson and insisted upon taking entire control of the lock hospitals. The British chargé d'affaires agreed that British inspectors were no longer needed, the two British physicians returned to England, and Inoue Kaoru, Minister of Home Affairs, promised diligent supervision of the Imperial medical officers at the lock hospitals.[5]

---

[1] F.O. 46/190, Parkes to Derby, No. 16, Yedo, 25 Jan. 1875; 46/191, Parkes to Derby, No. 44, Yedo, 22 Mar. 1875.

[2] F.O. 262/301, Ryder to Adm., Nagasaki, 12 Nov. 1876, encl. in F.O. to Parkes, No. 12, 12 Feb. 1877; 46/217, Parkes to Derby, No. 57, Yedo, 12 Apr. 1877.

[3] F.O. 46/245, Parkes to Salisbury, No. 88, Yedo, 25 Apr. 1879; 46/271, Kennedy to Granville, No. 33, Yedo, 1 Apr. 1881.

[4] F.O. 46/194, Parkes to Derby, No. 144, Yedo, 18 Oct. 1875; 46/221, Parkes to Derby, No. 161, Yedo, 24 Dec. 1877; 46/299, Parkes to Granville, No. 73, Yedo 11 May 1883; 46/193, Capt. St. John to Adm. Ryder, Nagasaki, 11 Aug. 1875, encl. 2 in Parkes No. 115, Yedo, 30 Aug. 1875.

[5] F.O. 46/271, Parkes's *Memorandum*, London, 20 May 1881. Kennedy to Granville, Nos. 50 and 79. Yedo, 21 May and 23 July 1881; 46/273, same to same, No. 137, Yedo, 19 Nov. 1881.

The Naval Medical College

Meanwhile the Meiji government had founded in 1873 a Naval Medical College in Yedo under the direction of an English surgeon, Dr. William Anderson, who was selected for this post by the surgeons of London upon the request of the Japanese. A recent distinguished graduate of St. Thomas's Hospital and an inspiring teacher, Anderson lectured on anatomy, physiology, and surgery for seven years while serving as medical officer in the British legation. He was probably responsible for the rapid development of the medical officers who in 1881 were considered able to run the lock hospitals without British inspection. His recommendation in 1876 for a special establishment to train a body of Japanese surgeons to treat venereal disease who should be ready in three years to meet the need throughout the country, was sent to the Japanese foreign minister and apparently carried out.[1] Anderson learned Japanese and became well acquainted with Japanese life. His interest in the native arts resulted in his collection of Japanese paintings and engravings of historic importance which is now in the British Museum.[2] He wrote authoritative books on Japanese pictorial arts as well as important articles on *kakke*, a disease common in Japan and associated with over-crowding, bad drainage, and bad ventilation.[3] The Meiji government awarded him the honour 'Commander of the Order of the Rising Sun'.

Japanese trained in medicine in England rose to important positions in medical circles at home. Takagi (Takaki) Kanehiro, later Baron Takagi (1848–1920), and his two sons, all went to St. Thomas's Hospital in London, possibly as a result of having met Dr. William Anderson in Japan. They in turn sent other Japanese to that hospital. Takagi himself won honours at St. Thomas's, became a Fellow of the Royal College of Surgeons in 1880, and upon returning to Japan was

---

[1] F.O. 46/207, Parkes to Derby, No. 121, Yedo, 18 July 1876. J. F. Payne, obituary of William Anderson 1842–1900, *St. Thomas's Hospital Reports*, xxx, 330–1, 333. *Medical Directory* (London, 1874), p. 1025.

[2] Brit. Mus. R.AC. 4644/28.

[3] *St. Thomas's Hospital Reports*, vii. 5–30; viii, 247–50. *Japan Weekly Mail*, 19 Jan. 1878. *T.A.S.J.* vii. 155 ff. *Kakke* is a Japanese name for Beriberi, a disease causing dropsy and numbness of the legs common in Yedo and Kyoto during the period here considered.

made Director-General of Medical Services in the Japanese navy.[1]

Other British Doctors

A number of British doctors employed at first as surgeons for the Peninsular and Oriental Steam Navigation Company or in private practice took positions in government or private Japanese agencies during the early years of Meiji. Thomas Charles Thornecraft, Arthur Hanley Clay, and William Turberville Buckle, all surgeons of the P. and O. service, are listed in Japan in 1873. Thornecraft and Clay were partners in private practice in Hyogo-Kobe. Thornecraft became in 1877 surgeon for the Imperial Government Railway at Kobe.[2] Dr. William Renwick (L.M. Edinburgh, 1870) was practising in Yokohama in 1874 and 1875. Between 1876 and 1883 he was surgeon to the Imperial Mint at Osaka, to the Imperial Government Railways, and to the Takashima coal-mine in Nagasaki. Others were sought as teachers in addition to medical practice. Dr. C. James Manning (M.R.C.S. University College, 1874), was surgeon at the Government Civil Hospital, 1877–9, surgeon and lecturer on surgery at the Government General Hospital, Tokyo, 1880, and medical adviser to the British legation as well as to the Japanese Railway and Public Works Department in 1881.[3]

British doctors who were missionaries also made important contributions to the development of medicine in Japan. Most outstanding was Dr. Henry Faulds of the United Presbyterian Mission of Scotland who in 1874 introduced at the mission hospital at Tsukiji in Tokyo Lister's antiseptic system and the treatment of fevers by an exclusive milk diet. While working with patients in this hospital Faulds and his medical students studied their finger-prints and those of other people. As a result Faulds advanced the theory in a letter to *Nature* in 1880 that finger-prints were sufficiently personal and changeless in pattern to identify any offender who left his finger-marks behind him and to disprove the suspected identity of an innocent person.

[1] Victor Gustave, Plarr's *Lives of the Fellows of the Royal College of Surgeons of England*, 2 vols. (London, 1930), ii. 380. *Medical Directory* (London, 1881), p. 1250. Whitney, op. cit. in *T.A.S.J.* xii, Pt. IV, 374.

[2] *Medical Directory* (London, 1873), pp. 1024–57; (1883), p. 1215.

[3] Ibid. (1874), p. 1060; (1876), p. 1130; (1883), p. 1260. For Manning (1877), p. 1155; (1880), p. 1207; (1881), p. 1231.

The originality of this was challenged unsuccessfully for many years.[1]

English influence was further exerted through the continued use of English medical works after German professors ran the medical school. Gray's *Anatomy*, Flint's and Dalton's *Physiology*, Lindells's, Gross's, and Sane's *Surgery*, among other books in English, were read.[2] The adoption of Western medical practice, however, came very slowly throughout the country. In 1882 there were supposed to be 65,000 doctors in Japan among whom only eight hundred were thought to 'have ventured to sacrifice the classical Chinese laws in favour of that which they designated as the Western system'.[3]

Medical Journals

As early as 1874 a Japanese medical journal, *Kinse I Setsu* (Modern Medical News), a bi-monthly under the auspices of Kaitakushō (Office of Colonization) at Yedo had been published to benefit the scattered native practitioners who had some knowledge of Western medical science. Contributions in French, German, and English were solicited for translation into Japanese. Sales increased from 500 to 1,000 copies by the second issue, a clear indication of the pioneer's zest for learning.[4] In 1877 the first medical weekly, the *Tokyo Medical Weekly*, appeared.[5]

The *Lancet*, a leading English medical journal, welcomed the appearance of another Japanese weekly periodical, *I-je-Shimbun* (Medical News), edited by Mizumoto of Tokyo in 1881. The issue of 5 April 1882 was a compromise between native and European styles. Several items gave evidence of Japanese progress in the Western system: a statistical report on the inmates of a lunatic asylum in Kyoto, a novel institution for Japan; a notification of official permission given to a provincial medical college to give European medical qualifications

[1] Whitney, op. cit. in *T.A.S.J.* xii, Pt. IV, 381–2. Sir Sidney Smith, 'Finger Print Pioneer', *The Scotsman*, 21 Mar. 1961. Although Faulds presented his system to Scotland Yard, it was rejected until 1901. George Wilton Wilton, *Fingerprints: History, Law and Romance* (London, 1938), pp. 29–31, 97–121. For the other work of Faulds and other missionaries see pp. 524–6.

[2] Aoyama and Fujikawa in Ōkuma, *Fifty Years of New Japan*, ii. 296.

[3] 'Medicine in Japan', *Lancet*, 14 Oct. 1882, pp. 640–1.

[4] Letter from Stuart Eldridge, M.D., Hakodate, 19 July 1874, in *Japan Weekly Mail*, 1 Aug. 1874.

[5] Fujikawa, op. cit., p. 86.

to its students, and the dispatch of a Japanese surgeon, Mr. Maede, to the Naval Medical School in Korea to initiate the study of Western medicine.[1]

Learned Societies

From 1876 to 1879 the number of foreign teachers of science excluding medicine and engineering had reached its peak in Japan with about twenty-eight men. Eighteen of the total of eighty-six between 1868 and 1889 were British.[2] In 1877 the Japanese established Tokyo Imperial University with two of its four faculties devoted to natural science and medical science. Other new institutions, the Naval Hydrographic Bureau 1871, the Tokyo and Osaka Hygienic Laboratory 1874, the Central Meteorological Observatory 1875, and the College of Engineering, were also training Japanese to dispense with Western instructors. Learned societies had begun with the founding of the Zoological Society and the Society for Mathematics in 1877, to be followed by sixteen more within a decade. The establishing of the Tokyo Academy (Tokyo Gakushikaiin) in 1879, which became in 1906 the Imperial Academy of Japan, further illustrated Japan's adoption of the Western system for the training, association, and recognition of scholars.[3] To its development a few British scientists and their Japanese students had made a major contribution.

[1] *Lancet*, 14 Oct. 1882, pp. 640–1.   [2] Yuasa, op. cit., pp. 104–5.
[3] *Scientific Japan, Past and Present*, pp. 311–59. Sakurai, *Omoide no Kazu Kazu*, 'Fifty Years of History of the Imperial Academy of Japan'. Hashimoto U., 'An Historical Synopsis of Education and Science in Japan from the Meiji Restoration to the Present Day', *Impact of Science on Society*, xiii (1963), 9–14.

XIX

BRITISH INFLUENCE ON RELIGIOUS TOLERANCE

Bakufu Policy

To the advisers of the Shogunate, the probable reintro-
duction of Christianity seemed a major political hazard
accompanying the reopening of Japan to Western trade.
Memories of the seventeenth-century Christian disloyalty and
sectarian strife persisted. The Western faith was suspected,
feared, hated. Although the *Bakufu* failed in its efforts to prohibit the practice of Christianity in Japan through the commercial treaties of 1858, it did not grant general religious
tolerance.[1] The treaties merely permitted Westerners at the
treaty ports to exercise their faith freely and to build churches
for worship within the prescribed territorial limits. And they
prohibited them as well as the Japanese from exciting religious
animosity.[2] Japan's long-standing law forbidding Japanese
acceptance of Christianity held. Government edicts against the
'evil sect' which promised rewards to informers on converts
remained widely posted throughout the country.

This was not an atmosphere to encourage the arrival of
missionaries along with the traders. But the zeal of the long-
established Catholic Orders of France and the rapidly growing
Protestant missionary societies of America was not to be
daunted. For the Catholics Japan was a field to be recovered;
for the Protestants a land to conquer. In 1859 missionaries from
both faiths reached Nagasaki, and Ivan Makhov of the Russian
Orthodox Church arrived in Hakodate as chaplain to the
Russian consulate. His successor, the monk Nikolai, a scholar,
educator, and later evangelist, had nearly ten thousand converts
by 1884.[3]

[1] Beasley, *Documents*, pp. 104, 119, 137, 147, 170–1.

[2] Ibid., p. 187, Art. VIII of U.S. treaty applied to all the treaty powers according to most-favoured-nation arrangements.

[3] Lensen, op. cit., pp. 89–101. Nikolai's full name was Ioann Dmitrievich
Kasatkin.

Here we are mainly concerned with the results of the activities of the French Roman Catholic priests. Prudence Séraphin Barthélemy Girard of the *Société des Missions Étrangères* of Paris entered Yedo in September 1859 as interpreter to the French consul-general. In Yokohama Girard erected a chapel and in Yedo he opened a school. Japanese who visited the church, however, were arrested. The French also built a church in Nagasaki which had been the stronghold of Christianity in the sixteenth and seventeenth centuries. Shortly after the dedication of this building in March 1865, communities of Japanese Christians were discovered in the vicinity and later in other places. They were descendants of the early converts, who were secretly persisting in some traditional forms of Catholic worship. Probably ten thousand gladly submitted to the incoming French priests. Many more, perhaps ten times as many, while adhering to some Christian practices would not accept the ministrations of the representatives of Rome. The secret existence of all, however, had been discovered. Persecution was the inevitable consequence of such defiance of the Japanese law. It began in 1867.[1]

The arrival of about fifteen French priests during that year had greatly increased the Catholic missionary activities in and around Nagasaki. Natives long worshipping in secret were now making open professions of their Christian faith in the village of Urakami four miles from Nagasaki, although ten years previously some members of this community were executed as heretics. On 14 July 1867 more than seventy were arrested and others insisted upon the same punishment. By midsummer at least eighty were in a new prison constructed for them. Officials and Buddhist priests tried in vain to make them recant.[2] Although accounts varied regarding the severity of their treatment, this persecution of religious faith led the French minister, M. Léon Roches, and the foreign consuls at Nagasaki to protest to the Japanese government that this policy would injure its reputation abroad. Roches secured a promise of the prisoners' release from the Shogun on condition that the converts remain

[1] Kenneth Scott Latourette, *A History of the Expansion of Christianity*, 7 vols. (New York, 1937–45), vi. 374–6. Paske-Smith, *Western Barbarians*, pp. 286–7.

[2] Matsuzaki Minoru, Ed., 'Yaso Ketsumatsuki' (Report on the Christians), in *Meiji Bunka Zenshū*, xxii. 3–4, 9–10. The numbers of Christians differ in different accounts.

under police surveillance and that the Catholic missionaries be prohibited from communicating with them.[1] It is also said that Roches had promised that the Catholic missionary activities would cease and advised the French priests to conform to the laws of Japan.[2] As a result the prisoners were set free without abjuring their faith, although they may have pretended to do so.[3] Satow believed the Shogun favoured this action knowing that the Christians were too numerous to be punished. But the dissident daimyo protested against the violation of the laws of Japan in another effort to embarrass the Shogun in his relations with the West.[4]

Parkes at this time took no stand. The Foreign Office in London, however, felt that advice to the *Bakufu* authorities was called for even though the Christians appeared to have deliberately provoked their punishment. Lord Stanley instructed Parkes:

> You may point out in a friendly way that religious zeal is more likely to be inflamed than subdued by persecution and that although it may not suit the Japanese system openly to recognize the profession of Christianity by the natives it would be better to tolerate the exercise of their religion within certain limits rather than acquire throughout Europe and America the reputation of persecuting the faith accepted in those continents and so incur the ill will of all civilized nations to whose feelings religious persecution is now abhorrent.[5]

About the same time a letter from the Shogun to Napoleon III asking that the propaganda of the Roman Catholic priests be stopped led the British and French governments to consider the need for moderation in the efforts of their missionaries to convert the Japanese.[6] But no effective action resulted.

Early Meiji Persecutions

The new Meiji government published afresh the prohibition against Christianity as the 'heretical' or 'evil' sect. Parkes's vehement protests to Prince Iwajima and higher officials were

---

[1] F.O. 46/81, Parkes to Stanley, No. 140, Yedo, 18 Aug. 1867; 46/82, same to same, No. 170, Conf'l., Yedo, 1 Oct. 1867.

[2] Medzini, op. cit., in Harvard University, *Papers on Japan*, ii. 218.

[3] *Meiji Bunka Zenshū*, xxii. 9.

[4] F.O. 46/82, Parkes to Stanley, Nos. 183, 191, Yokohama, 30 Oct., 14 Nov. 1867.   [5] F.O. 262/124, Stanley to Parkes, No. 167, 23 Oct. 1867.

[6] F.O. 46/82, encl. in No. 170, 1 Oct. 1867; 262/124, Lyons (British Ambassador to France) to Stanley, Paris, 8 Nov. 1867.

followed by those of the other foreign representatives. In consequence the Japanese admitted their error in so stigmatizing the faith of the West. They agreed to alter the wording but not to the repeal of the edict. Events in the Nagasaki area were proving that toleration or the open profession of Christianity was still to be feared.[1]

The recently released Christians had used their freedom to carry on an active propagation of their beliefs. Citizens of Nagasaki told of the open profession of the Catholic religion by native converts, of riotous agitation among villagers by fanatical leaders, and of forced conversions by Catholic missionaries. The weak Meiji government feared the spread of the movement to the other treaty ports.[2]

The hostility of the native priesthood, local feuds, and the deep-seated national prejudice against Christianity all united against the over-zealous Japanese followers of Rome. An insurrection in Nagasaki led to the renewal of persecution.[3] The circulation of a libellous pamphlet directed equally against Protestants and Catholics increased popular excitement.[4] People were told that faith in Christ was incompatible with loyalty to the state.[5] The arrival of a French bishop with the new French minister, M. D'Outrey, appeared to the Japanese that the French government had ignored the late Shogun's appeal to check the proselytizing of its missionaries.

An Imperial decree on 15 May 1868 ordered 4,100 native Christians to be distributed for hard labour for three years among thirty-four *han*. The daimyo were to be paid for their maintenance and permitted to employ them in the mines, agriculture, and any other work, while treating them kindly and trying to convert them. If at the end of this period gentle persuasion had not led the Christians to recant, further refusal to do so would condemn them to capital punishment.[6]

[1] F.O. 46/93, Parkes to Stanley, No. 113, Yokohama, 14 May 1868.
[2] Matsuzaki, op. cit., in *Meiji Bunka Zenshū*, xxii. 9. Tokyo, Diet Lib. MSS. *Iwakura-Kō Denki Shiryō* (Materials for Biography of Prince Iwakura), No. 211, Petition from Citizens of Nagasaki, April–May 1868. (Hereafter cited as Iwakura MSS. No. 211.)
[3] F.O. 46/94, Parkes to Stanley, Nos. 130, 132, Conf'l., Yokohama 11 June 1868.
[4] F.O. 46/93, Parkes to Stanley, No. 118, Yokohama, 30 May 1868.
[5] M. Paske-Smith, *Japanese Traditions of Christianity* (London, no date), pp. 103–12.
[6] Paske-Smith, *Japanese Traditions of Christianity*, pp. 123–5. Matsuzaki, op. cit., in *Meiji Bunka Zenshū*, xxii. 5–6. The numbers differ in the two sources.

The foreign consuls at Nagasaki were first to befriend the Christians. They appealed to their ministers in Yedo to complain to the central authorities. In a letter to the Governor of Kyūshū they remonstrated against the rumoured persecutions, asking the Japanese government in a friendly spirit and 'in the name of humanity', not to take such a step. The authorities were adamant. Perverse-minded Japanese who in the face of an old, established Japanese law had become members of the prohibited religion would have to be punished according to the Japanese law if repeated official remonstrances did not cause them to repent and retract their errors.[1]

A representative of the Mikado, Kido Kōin, who was sent to Nagasaki to inquire into the question, made clear the government's point of view. It feared that the great animosity existing between the Christian population and the Japanese of the lower classes would lead to disturbances and civil strife. To preserve order in the country, the progress of Christianity had to be stopped. The authorities hoped severe measures would not be needed. At first they intended to exile among several daimyo only 150 of the confirmed Christians of Urakami. Should such measures be unsuccessful they would resort to more severe punishment. Kido condemned the continuing activities of the Roman Catholic priests but did not see how Japan could get rid of them. A missionary he defined as 'a man who is sent to Japan to teach the Japanese to break the laws of their country'.[2]

Parkes's Personal Influence

The exile of the Christians began in July 1868 when 120 were put on board a Japanese steamer and sent to Chōshū, Fukuyama, or Shinano. All the consuls at Nagasaki remonstrated again to the local authorities.[3] In the meantime Parkes had informed London. He pointed out that the anti-foreign party in Yedo proposed to make Christian proselytism a cause for increasing hostility to foreigners.[4] He thought the concern expressed by the Western representatives had already mitigated the severities since only 120 Christians had been exiled to date.

[1] Paske-Smith, *Japanese Traditions of Christianity*, pp. 113–16 gives texts of letters.
[2] Ibid., pp. 117–19. F. O. Adams, op. cit. ii. 146.
[3] Paske-Smith, *Japanese Traditions of Christianity*, p. 121.
[4] F.O. 46/94, Parkes to Stanley, No. 150, Yokohama, 27 June 1868.

He counselled that Western remonstrances should continue to be urged with 'consideration and discretion'. He understood the Japanese government's position. Roman Catholic proselytism at Urakami had assailed its dignity and authority. It was compelled to act if only to satisfy popular opinion which seemed to be vehemently directed against native converts.[1]

Parkes believed that the French proposal for strong collective protests by the foreign ministers might enlist public opinion against rather than for the Christians. The Mikado had not answered the one formal remonstrance which they had sent. Parkes realized that more protests could imply the protection by the foreign powers of one section of the native population against its own government. He preferred to use his influence on important members of the Mikado's advisers by urging them in friendly conversation to realize that amicable relations with foreign governments were not compatible with the persecution of their religion—a policy immediately approved by the Foreign Office.[2]

Events in time confirmed Parkes's faith in his personal influence with important Japanese ministers. Not only was the wording of the edict against Christianity modified as promised so as to distinguish between Christianity and the 'heretical' sect but the government gave a voluntary pledge in early 1869 to stop the enforcement of severe penalties against native Christians.[3] The foreign representatives applauded the Meiji authorities for the 'humane motives' which prompted this course. They assumed openly that in consequence the Japanese government would suppress the fresh persecution recently reported in the Island of Gotō near Nagasaki.[4] Political expediency, however, took precedence over good intentions.

On the Islands of Gotō more civil disturbances occurred. The French bishop, Petitjean, admitted that old Christian families publicly acknowledged their acceptance of the Christian faith and refused spiritual obedience to the native priests.

---

[1] F.O. 46/95, Parkes to Stanley, No. 183, Yokohama 25 July 1868.

[2] Ibid., No. 202, Conf'l., Yokohama, 21 Aug. 1868; 262/142, Stanley to Parkes, 21 Oct. 1868. Medzini, op. cit., in Harvard University, *Papers on Japan*, ii. 218.

[3] F.O. 46/106, Parkes to Stanley, No. 20, Yokohama, 26 Jan. 1869. *Nichi-Ei Gaikō Shi*, i. 110–11.

[4] *D.N.G.M.* i, Pt. 2, 802–5, Doc. 754. F.O. 46/107, Parkes to Stanley, No. 38, Yokohama, 10 Feb. 1869.

Accounts of brutal persecution in Gotō, although denied by Japanese authorities, disturbed the foreign representatives.[1] Investigation led to more conflicting reports from Western and Japanese officials.[2] Parkes's informant maintained that 400 Christians, men, women, and children, had been arrested on the Gotō Islands. Some were tortured. Seventeen died from hunger and cold. Parkes and all the foreign representatives requested an independent investigation by the central government.[3]

An inquiry resulted which confirmed the use of torture to force confessions in a few cases of suspected persons and the imprisonment of many Christians in large private houses—in one instance seventy-three people including children to a house. Men and women were separated. Some died of illness but none died of cold, an impossibility in Gotō in the spring. The investigator believed that deserters from Gotō had exaggerated the nature of the persecution but admitted that the anti-Christian policy had been stricter in Gotō than in Urakami. Pending instruction from Yedo, this official gave orders to stop severe tortures, adhere to leniency, increase prison houses to avoid congestion, and to provide prompt medical care for the sick, in addition to other reforms.[4]

The Japanese extremists remained adamant in spite of Western criticism. A private member of the new advisory assembly (called parliament by the British) introduced a motion to suppress Christianity by the relentless use of capital punishment. In the discussion which followed the defeat of this motion by 189 to 22 votes there was evidence of growing tolerance which Parkes had already noted in his talks with key authorities.[5]

Although the assembly at the same time passed a motion against Christianity and approved generally of its suppression, the members were concerned about the means to be used. Many speakers recommended education rather than persecution.

[1] F.O. 46/107, Parkes to Stanley, No. 38, Yokohama, 10 Feb. 1869 and encl.

[2] F.O. 46/108, Parkes to Clarendon, No. 60, Yokohama, 9 Mar. 1869.

[3] *D.N.G.M.* ii, Pt. 1, pp. 652–66, Doc. 170. Iwakura MSS. No. 211, Parkes to Date, Higashikuze, and Ōkuma, 18 May 1869.

[4] Ibid., Instructions from Gaimushō (Foreign Office), 6 June 1869; letter from Nagasaki authorities to Gaimushō, 23 July 1869.

[5] F.O. 46/109, No. 121, Yedo, 28 May 1869. Here Parkes notes that the Meiji government had granted a piece of ground at Ōsaka for a Roman Catholic Church and had employed an American Protestant missionary in its service.

Some attributed the growth of foreign religions, both Buddhism and Christianity, to the indifference of the nation—especially the higher classes—to the religion of the state. Others, echoing foreign remonstrances, considered the persecution of the faith of foreigners inconsistent with the maintenance of friendly relations with the foreign powers and likely to offend them. This group recommended the opening of negotiations with the treaty powers 'for the purpose of engaging the latter to refrain from active interference on the ground that religious divisions were injurious to the stability of empire'.[1] Parkes believed that such division of opinion meant that the question would not be left in the hands of the fanatical party but would 'be considered with more intelligence and forbearance than might have been expected from a people and a class who have hitherto been nurtured in one idea on the subject, that of uncompromising hostility'.[2] The hot-headed Parkes thus interpreted with understanding and tolerance an issue which he knew could inflame the British public.

In spite of many confused native reports the British consul in Nagasaki wrote that as a result of the protests of the foreign ministers in May, the plight of the native Christians in the Gotō Islands had been remedied to a large extent. Only eighteen or nineteen of the leaders remained in prison and their conditions had improved.[3] This, however, did not augur general clemency towards the growing numbers of Japanese Roman Catholics. Without discussing the plan with the foreign representatives for fear of opposition, the government in Yedo decided about mid-November 1869 to exile the Christians of the Urakami village of Hizen among various clans and ordered nineteen clans to send their ships to Nagasaki to carry them away.[4] Much to the embarrassment of Protestant missionaries who witnessed their deportation, American and European ships assisted in this enterprise.[5] English reports and later Japanese sources estimate that as a result of this order between three and four thousand men, women, and children were exiled

[1] F.O. 46/111, Parkes to Clarendon, No. 156, Yokohama, 9 Aug. 1869.

[2] Ibid. and encl. translation by Aston.

[3] F.O. 46/113, Parkes to Clarendon, No. 202, Yedo, 22 Oct. 1869.

[4] *Nichi-Ei Gaikō Shi*, i. 112. Iwakura MSS. No. 211, Sawa's *Memorandum* at government meeting, 18 Jan. 1870.

[5] Evarts B. Greene, *A New Englander in Japan* (Boston, 1927), p. 108.

from the villages of the Urakami Valley and Mogi near Naga-saki. The exact destination of the exiles was difficult for the British to discover.[1]

Parkes happened to be in Nagasaki in early January 1870, when the order for the deportation of the Christians arrived from Yedo. In addition to immediate protests to local authori-ties from all the foreign consuls on the spot, Parkes tried to persuade the responsible Japanese officials to delay the proceed-ings until he could communicate with Yedo. Such treatment of the Christian population, he maintained, was inconsistent with the government's promise of leniency towards them.[2] Similar protests by the other foreign representatives resulted in several conferences with the Japanese ministers in Yedo when they agreed to suspend further deportations if the foreign envoys could prevent the Roman priests from visiting the Urakami people. But the foreign effort came too late. Zealous local officials had already distributed 2,810 persons of both sexes among nineteen clans in less than three weeks.[3]

Japan's Official Defence

In these conferences and in private talks with Parkes, the Meiji authorities defended their policy forcibly. Sawa and Terashima, ministers for foreign affairs, sent a memorandum to the foreign representatives which maintained that the behaviour of the Urakami people not as Christians, but as disloyal Japanese subjects, had necessitated their exile. Instigated by the French priests, these people had openly defied the local authorities, insulted the traditional religion and desecrated the shrine to the Imperial ancestor. Being taught to rely on foreign protec-tion, it was supposed that in case of war these converts would side with the foreign invaders. The Mikado's new government had to consider the pressures of a strong anti-Christian party in Japan which was also anti-foreign. To resist this powerful group and openly favour Christianity would, they believed, mean the destruction of the government. The Urakami Chris-tians, 'all people of a low class whose minds are easily worked upon', would 'be quiet when once removed from the influence

[1] F.O. 46/124, Annesley to Parkes, Nagasaki, 15 Jan. 1870, encl. 14 in Parkes to F.O., No. 6, 22 Jan. 1870.
[2] *D.N.G.M.* ii, Pt. 3, 423–4, Doc. 619 F. O. Adams, op. cit. ii. 208–10.
[3] F.O. 46/124, Parkes to Clarendon, No. 6, Yedo, 22 Jan. 1870.

of the priests'. So long as people conducted themselves with outward decorum, the Japanese government would not trouble themselves with their religious convictions.[1]

This *Memorandum* confirmed in different words what Parkes had learned in confidence from a Japanese minister who also pointed out:

Although the Mikado's Government must not lay itself open to the charge of being faithless to its political trust, we are far from treating Christianity in a persecuting spirit. We are well aware that Bibles and prayer books are being extensively circulated: that these books are read by many of our own officers, and I believe it is possible to purchase them in book shops. No attempt has been made to check the circulation of these scriptures and we have employed several missionaries as teachers of languages and we are well aware that they teach other things besides philology but we do not undertake to be keepers of men's consciences. . . . I may even tell you that I have studied the tenets of Christianity and approve them. They appear to me to be superior to those of Shintoism, Buddhism or Confucianism, but at the same time the high aims of Christianity may be perverted, and as taught by the Roman Catholic priests we think it is open to grave objections. England thought the same at one time and found it necessary to interdict the Romish faith. We can hardly be blamed for doing the same for reasons which are not dissimilar to those which then actuated England. On the contrary, we consider we have reason to complain of the French Minister or the French Government for not repressing the mistaken zeal of these priests, and thus exposing us to danger.[2]

Further in the *Memorandum* the government insisted that the removal of the Christians from Urakami was not at variance with its promise to the foreign representatives of leniency towards them, in that they were adequately cared for during travel and provided with sufficient housing and farm lands at their destination. They were allowed to live with their families and no work heavier than that of other people was imposed upon them. The authorities would permit the foreign representatives to ascertain the truth of this. Furthermore, the government

[1] Iwakura MSS. No. 211, *Memorandum* enclosed in letter from Sawa and Terashima to British, French, American, and German ministers, 28 Jan. 1870. Translation of memo. enclosed in F.O. 46/124, Parkes to Clarendon, No. 12, 29 Jan. 1870.

[2] F.O. 46–124, encl. in No. 7, Conf'l., 22 Jan. 1870. Minutes of confidential interview between Parkes and unnamed principal Japanese minister, 20 Jan. 1870.

stated that if the missionaries would observe the treaty stipulations and devote themselves to preaching among their own
countrymen and not disregard the state of affairs in Japan
it would not be necessary to remove many villagers to other
regions to be alienated from their missionaries. It might even
be feasible to return them to their homes. The ministers
earnestly desired that amicable relations with all foreign
countries be promoted more and more without being hindered
by questionable actions, which disturb friendly intercourse.[1]

Parkes considered the explanation reasonable. He knew the
charges against the Roman Catholics were not groundless. The
opposition of the 'highly sensitive' Japanese nation to the
political character of the Catholic teachings which deliberately
withdrew the converts from allegiance to their own government
was understandable. Under the circumstances he thought
'active propagandism' was 'scarcely less to be deprecated than
persecution'. He saw prophetically that with Japan's continuing adoption of Western ideas and with circumspection on
the part of foreign missionaries religious toleration would be
adopted.[2]

Iwakura soon assured Parkes that the removal of the
Christians from Urakami was essentially a domestic question.
No hostility to the foreign powers was intended. Japan wanted
to consider the wishes of the powers, but if pressure were
imposed upon the Meiji government, it must fall before the
pressure or before its own reactionary party. He asked for time
to curb the latter and that foreign powers should not coerce
his government on domestic issues. He promised it would be
faithful to its treaty obligations.[3]

More facts concerning the behaviour of the French missionaries were brought out in another meeting of the foreign
representatives with the Japanese authorities. The priests had
insisted on visiting the native Christians chiefly at night disguised as Japanese. Under their direction five places of worship
had been erected at Urakami. As a result of their teaching their
converts had refused to observe the required state and religious

---

[1] Iwakura MSS. No. 211, *Memorandum* enclosed in letter from Sawa and Terashima to British, French, American, and German ministers, 28 Jan. 1870.
[2] F.O. 46/124, Parkes to Clarendon, No. 7, Conf'l., Yedo 22 Jan. 1870.
[3] Ibid., Private. Yokohama. 23 Feb. 1870. F. O. Adams, op. cit. ii. 213–14.

ceremonies and had destroyed a temple, its altar offerings, and the images of the orthodox faith. The consequent bad feeling which arose among the people of the area caused them to quarrel and fight the converts.

The foreign representatives regretted that the Japanese had not reported their grievances against the missionaries before they had sent whole communities into exile. The French minister, M. D'Outrey, proposed that if the Japanese government would restore these exiles to their homes he would take steps to prevent the Roman Catholic priests from preaching or holding religious services outside the foreign settlements of Nagasaki. The return of the exiles, he said, would recover for Japan favourable opinion in Europe and America and bring justice to a large number of sufferers. But the Japanese officials again pointed out that to bring back the exiles would appear to the entire nation that their government was acting under foreign dictation. National opposition to this might disturb foreign relations and foreign trade.[1] On 23 March they informed the foreign representatives that they could not return the Christians to their homes at that time. It could only be done gradually if the converts abstained from outward observances of their faith.[2]

British Reactions

Parkes continued to view the Japanese explanations tolerantly. He understood their intense national pride, their well-founded fear of Catholic proselytism, and the precarious position of the Emperor's Government. He knew its ministers understood the remonstrances of the West. They now had to decide whether to defer to foreign influence or whether to give greater consideration to strong public pressure at home. He wished to avoid further discussion and more definite British action until he had instructions from London.[3]

H.M. Government presented the facts and Parkes's interpretation of the Japanese action when the question was raised in Parliament on 18 March 1870. An aroused public here learned that the policy of the Meiji government towards the Roman Catholic converts of Urakami, although regrettable, could be justified for valid political reasons. The remonstrances

---

[1] F.O. 46/124, Parkes to Clarendon, No. 35, Yokohama, 26 Feb. 1870.
[2] Ibid., No. 50, Yokohama, 26 Mar. 1870.
[3] Ibid., No. 35, Yokohama, 26 Feb. 1870.

by British officials in Japan had not been too feeble, but had brought promises of leniency towards the exiles.[1]

At the Foreign Office Lord Clarendon approved Parkes's course and interpretation of Japan's action. He asked that Parkes hold the government to its promise to protect the dispersed Christians in their new communities, against persecution because of their religion, that the foreign representatives accept without appearing offensive the Japanese offer of free access to the localities wherein the Christians were distributed, and impress upon the local daimyo their responsibility to treat the Christians well and to protect them from persecution. He further urged that the foreign representatives, and the French minister in particular, should try to convince the Christian converts that loyalty to the state was not incompatible with Christianity.[2]

Months later Parkes told Iwakura that although Her Majesty's Government regretted the deportation of the Urakami Christians, it recognized the unavoidable circumstances which caused Japan's action. It hoped that severe treatment of the exiles would not continue and asked that Parkes be permitted to visit some areas where the converts were detained.[3]

Both Britain and the United States opposed the view of the French M. D'Outrey that 'a strong and united demonstration of force by European powers would be the only effectual mode of preventing the recurrence of such acts and checking the intolerance of the Japanese government'. As no Western Christians had been molested, Parkes maintained that the powers had no right within their treaties to a recourse to force. He believed the situation would improve.[4] He also recognized some truth in the remark of a Japanese minister that the distribution of the converts in nineteen different localities was 'more calculated to facilitate the propagation of Christianity through Japan than their unmolested residence in the locality in which they have hitherto been permitted to reside'.[5]

[1] F.O. 46/133, copy of H.M. Government's reply in the H. of C. to question by James White of 16 Mar. 1870.

[2] F.O. 262/184, Clarendon to Parkes, 20 Apr. 1870.

[3] Iwakura MSS. No. 211, Iwakura's interview with Parkes, 10 Oct. 1870.

[4] F.O. 262/184, Clarendon to Lyons, Nos. 231, 232, London, 28 Mar. 1870; Thornton to Clarendon, Washington, D.C., Apr. 1870 and 20 June 1870 and encl. in F.O. to Parkes, Nos. 32 and 71, 4 May and 4 July 1870.

[5] F.O. 262/184, F.O. to Parkes, No. 42, 22 Apr. 1870 and encl., Clarendon to Lyons, 20 Apr. 1870.

Investigations

True and false reports about harsh treatment and further deportations of the Christians continued to circulate.[1] Parkes himself questioned the Daimyo of Kyūshū about those in his care. The prince regretted having responsibility for these people, gave them so much liberty that some escaped, and wished they would be returned to Nagasaki.[2]

Accounts of cruelty in the Kaga *Han* led Parkes to arrange with the Meiji authorities to send James Troup, Her Majesty's acting consul at Niigata, in company with a Japanese official, Mizuno, to observe and report on the conditions of the exiles in that area.[3] They inspected the accommodation, food allotments, general treatment of the Catholic converts in April 1871 without local interference. They talked privately with the exiles—all in an effort to ascertain how far the government's promises of lenient treatment had been observed. At Kanazawa the provisions for the Christians were adequate but they were unable to find employment. Those who recanted had better food and more freedom of movement until in the twelfth month all were forced to sign a declaration of recantation. In Daishōgi only one old woman had rejected the rewards of recanting, bits of paper money, more food, and freedom to go in and out of assigned quarters. No lands were allotted before recantation in accordance with the local interpretation of the government's instructions. In Toyama the exiles had suffered great deprivation and torture because of their refusal to recant.[4]

Mizuno's report agreed with Troup's. He was shocked at the difference between the local treatment of the Christians and the instructions from Yedo. As a result the government issued a reprimand in the *Government Gazette* of 25 June 1871 for cruel treatment of the 'adherents of the foreign sect' and prohibited its recurrence. Strict orders were sent to the three places in Kaga to obey the government's instructions.[5]

[1] Iwakura MSS. No. 211, Parkes's interviews with Sanjō and Iwakura 8 Jan. and with Sanjō, Sawa, Soejima, and Terashima 10 Jan. 1871. *Japan Weekly Mail*, 28 Jan. 1871.
[2] F.O. 46/127, Parkes to Granville, No. 163, Yedo, 2 Dec. 1870.
[3] *D.N.G.M.* iv. 747–51, Doc. 454.
[4] Ibid., pp. 789–95, Doc. 480, *Memorandum* on Troup's Report.
[5] Iwakura MSS. No. 211, interview between Foreign Minister Sawa and British chargé, 19 Aug. 1871. F.O. 46/141, Adams to Granville, No. 65, Yedo, 9 Sept. 1871.

Western Pressure on the Iwakura Mission

Before Iwakura left on his mission to the West to exchange views on the revision of the treaties of 1858, the British chargé warned him of the probable demand of the foreign powers for the toleration of the Christian religion throughout Japan. The Ambassador Plenipotentiary still maintained that to yield this would be fatal to his embassy and the Japanese government. He said it was absolutely necessary that the Japanese people believe in the divine origin of the Mikado. To this the Christian faith was directly opposed. And many malcontents would seize a move for its toleration as an excuse to overthrow the government. How could he explain this to the treaty powers? Adams recognized the difficulty. He admitted it was not yet safe for the government to permit the free exercise of the Christian faith. He thought the time would come when progress would be more rapid than if forced now.[1]

Reports of the arrest and exile of sixty or seventy heads of Christian families from Shimabara near Nagasaki in December 1871 coincided with the arrival of Iwakura's distinguished embassy—Ōkubo, Itō, Kido, and a large retinue—in America.[2] Protestant missionaries in Japan had already urged upon their home churches the need for pressing the question of religious tolerance upon the Japanese envoys.[3] Officials as well as the general public in America immediately showed great concern about Japan's treatment of her native Christians. Before Iwakura's mission reached England in August 1872 its members recognized that a more liberal religious policy in Japan was needed to increase their chances among the treaty powers for support of their proposals for treaty revision.[4]

The embassy found the British well informed about the recent exile of the Christians.[5] Protestant missionaries in Japan, weary of the ineffective remonstrances of the foreign representatives to stop these persecutions, had signed a memorial urging that all foreign governments demand the repeal of the

[1] F.O. 46/143, Adams to Granville, No. 127, Conf'l., Yedo, 12 Dec. 1871.

[2] *D.N.G.M.* iv. 836–7, Doc. 498. F.O. 46/151, Adams to Granville, No. 16, Yedo, 15 Jan. 1872; 46/152, same to same, No. 50, 4 Mar. 1872. F. O. Adams, op. cit. ii. 307.   [3] Greene, op. cit., pp. 109–10.

[4] Marlene June Mayo, 'The Iwakura Mission to the United States and Europe, 1871–1873', in *Columbia University East Asian Institute Studies* (New York, 1959), No. 6, pp. 33, 39, 40.

[5] *The Times*, 22 Mar. 1870 and 6, 16 Mar. 1872.

anti-Christian law, and indicate 'a fixed determination behind it'. They appointed a representative to bring the issue before the Western governments.[1] A delegation from the Council of the Evangelical Alliance and British Missionary Societies in London waited upon Earl Granville, then Foreign Minister, with this memorial asking for action on behalf of the persecuted Christians.[2]

Fortunately, Parkes was in England on home leave. As a representative of Granville he gave these petitioners a fair interpretation of Japan's position, and gave them a copy of the *Memorandum* of the Meiji government explaining its action. He opposed their desire for coercion. To meet Japanese intolerance with foreign intolerance seemed to him a questionable principle which was likely to revive Japan's traditional animosity towards foreigners. His confidence in the effectiveness of friendly remonstrances still held. Any change in the religious feeling of Japan had to come as a result of a change in the convictions of the people as well as the government of Japan. Parkes believed this would happen if not impeded by ill-considered acts offensive to the existing national faith and feeling.[3] So convincing was his argument that the Church Missionary Society—then represented by the only British missionaries in Japan—concluded that force should not be used against Japan even if 'the cause of Christ should for a season be hindered and delayed'.[4]

At Iwakura's first meeting with Granville at the Foreign Office on 22 November to learn the views of the British government on the revision of the treaties, the British Foreign Secretary at once stressed the importance of religious freedom in England and America and its growing acceptance in Europe. Nothing, he said, would create a more favourable feeling towards Japan among Englishmen than a more liberal religious policy by the Meiji government.[5] Five days later at a longer

[1] MSS., A.B.C. (16–4–1), i, No. 4, letter of ten missionaries to the Revd. David Thompson, 22 May 1871. F.O. 262/222, Parkes's *Memorandum*, 8 Feb. 1872, encl. in F.O. to Adams, No. 15, 14 Feb. 1872.

[2] The Evangelical Alliance was an interdenominational international association of Protestants formed in London in 1846 to promote scriptural Christianity and to combat religious indifference.

[3] F.O. 262/222, Parkes's *Memorandum*, 8 Feb. 1872, encl. in F.O. to Adams, No. 15, 14 Feb. 1872.

[4] *Church Missionary Intelligencer*, Mar. 1872, pp. 74–79.

[5] F.O. 262/224, *Memorandum* of Interview between Granville and Iwakura, 22 Nov. 1872, encl. in F.O. to Watson, No. 59, 28 Nov. 1872. *D.N.G.M.* v. 227–9, Doc. 94.

interview when Parkes was present, Iwakura told Granville of Japan's difficulties in establishing religious freedom because of the disastrous early history of Christians in Japan. He said serious disturbances would result if the ban on Christianity were lifted immediately. The government had abolished the trampling on religious emblems and even the death sentence on Christians since the opening of foreign commerce. Christians were not persecuted now if they were not harmful to the public peace. His government hoped that freedom of religion could eventually be achieved.[1]

Although letters in *The Times* sought to explain the difficult position of the Japanese government and to stress the importance of restraint and consideration in missionary activities,[2] Iwakura's mission was everywhere confronted with embarrassing questions from an aroused and informed people. The revision of the tariff and the abolition of extraterritoriality became obviously impossible as long as Japan persecuted Christians.[3] Finally from Brussels after an anti-Japanese demonstration by Belgian Catholics Itō Hirobumi sent a telegram to his government requesting the release of exiled Christians and the withdrawal of the edict against Christianity.[4]

The Withdrawal of the Anti-Christian Edicts

Meanwhile native support for the tolerance of Christianity had been growing. A leading conservative reformer, Nakamura Masanao (Keiu), published in the *Shimbun Zasshi* (News Magazine) a memorial to the Emperor called *Memorial on the Imitation of the West*. He paid full tribute to the reforms already adopted from the West but regretted that Christianity, the true source of the Western strength and wealth, was not

---

[1] F.O. 262/224, *Memorandum* of Iwakura's interview, 27 Nov. 1872, encl. in F.O. to Watson, No. 67, 13 Dec. 1872. *D.N.G.M.* v. 229–34, Doc. 95.

[2] *The Times*, 15, 16, 28, 29, 30 Jan. 1873.

[3] Kishimoto Hideo and John F. Howes, *Japanese Religion in the Meiji Era* (Centenary Culture Council Series, ii, (Tokyo, 1956), pp. 193–4. Griffis, *The Mikado's Empire*, p. 572.

[4] *D.N.G.M.* vi. 96–97. Doc. 64. The telegram is not included in these documents. Two Japanese historians, however, give it as a fact without the date. See Urakawa Wazaburo, *Urakami Kirishitan Shi* (History of Christians in Urakami), (Osaka, 1943), p. 353. Nezu Masashi, 'Meiji Shonen no Kirishitan Tsuihō to Teimei Kakkoku no Taido' (Exile of Christians in the early Meiji period and the Attitudes of the Treaty Powers), *Shigaku Zasshi* (Journal of Historical Science), June 1935, xlvi. 786–7.

among them. He fearlessly proclaimed that Japan would never make any real advance until she accepted Christianity. He advised the Mikado to be baptized, to become head of the Church and leader of his people professing the Western religion. He believed the sovereigns of the Western countries would then love and respect His Majesty, their people would bless him, and Japan would become the Europe of the East.[1] There was no effort to suppress this memorial, which soon appeared in pamphlet form. Copies had been given to Satow by Kido and Itō who both stated privately that anti-Christian prohibition must be lifted soon.[2]

In February 1872 Inoue, the Vice-Minister of Finance, recommended and petitioned that some three thousand Christians from the Nagasaki area who had been in custody of different prefectures, be released with special consideration. He said they should be allowed to establish homes in the prefecture where they were detained and orders given to the local authorities to afford them a means of livelihood, or they should be permitted to migrate wherever they wished.[3] By April 1872 some of the exiles—probably only those who had recanted—were allowed to return home.[4]

In June the Yedo government issued new instructions to the Development Agencies in all prefectures, stating that Christian believers had been under clemency since the Meiji Restoration. The government's main purpose in reallocating them was to make them recant. Appropriate measures should be adopted to bring this about.[5] At the same time the Vice-Minister of Foreign Affairs maintained that open religious tolerance was still impossible even though it might lighten the work of Iwakura's embassy in England. He admitted that the Japanese government was anxious at a later date to assume jurisdiction over all foreigners which of course would imply full religious toleration.[6] In Hakodate, however, there appeared to be a *de facto*

[1] F.O. 46/143, Adams to Granville, No. 138, Yedo, 29 Dec. 1871. Kishimoto and Howes, op. cit., pp. 190–2. Kōsaka and Abosch, op. cit., pp. 113–17. F. O. Adams, op. cit. ii. 301–3.

[2] F.O. 46/143, Adams to Granville, No. 139, Conf'l., Yedo, 29 Dec. 1871.

[3] Iwakura MSS. No. 211, Recommendations of Inoue, 22 Feb. 1872.

[4] F.O. 46/153, Adams to Granville, No. 77, Yedo, 30 Apr. 1872.

[5] Iwakura MSS. No. 211, Government Instructions, 8 June 1872.

[6] F.O. 46/154, Watson to Granville, No. 26, Yedo, 6 June 1872.

tolerance as the native converts of the Russian Orthodox Church increased and attended services without interference by Japanese authorities.[1]

Early in January 1873 the Meiji government adopted the Gregorian Calendar and attempted to make Sunday a day of rest for officials.[2] In February the new Foreign Minister, Soejima Taneomi, promised the foreign representatives that the edicts against Christianity would be withdrawn and all exiled Christians would be returned home within a month.[3] Ōkuma Shigenobu, a councillor of state, and Soejima explained that because of the deep-seated anti-Christian prejudice still to be overcome, the government had to proceed with great caution. Hence they approached the toleration of Christianity in the negative manner by withdrawing the proclamations against it rather than by issuing a new edict declaring a policy of tolerance.[4]

The *Instruction* of 24 February 1873 merely said: 'The hitherto posted notification shall be removed as it is well known to the general public.'[5] A month later the publicly posted edicts forbidding the profession of Christianity were removed in most areas.[6] The liberation of Christian converts soon followed, with orders for 1,938 people from specified places to be returned to their homes.[7]

Parkes and Downing Street rejoiced. The chief obstacle to Japan's cordial relations with Christian nations had thus been removed by 'moral' means within a few years.[8] Japan's explanation of her recent action, however, soon limited their pleasure.

[1] F.O. 46/155, Watson to Granville, No. 74, Yedo, 9 Aug. 1872. Lensen, op. cit., p. 101.

[2] F.O. 46/165, Watson to Granville, No. 4, Yedo, 10 Jan. 1873; 46/166, same to same, No. 82, Yedo, 24 Mar. 1873. H. Ritter, *History of Protestant Missions in Japan*, English translation by G. E. Albrecht and D. C. Greene (Tokyo, 1898), pp. 46–47.

[3] F.O. 46/165, Watson to Granville, No. 47, Yedo, 22 Feb. 1873. *Japan Gazette*, 20 Feb. 1873. *Japan Mail*, 24 Feb. 1873.

[4] F.O. 46/165, Watson to Granville, Nos. 53 and 54, Yedo, 24 Feb. 1873.

[5] Iwakura MSS. No. 211, Government Instruction to all Prefectures, 24 Feb. 1873. Translation by Aoki Arata formerly member of Japanese foreign service.

[6] F.O. 46/166, Watson to Granville, No. 80, Yedo, 24 Mar. 1873.

[7] Iwakura MSS. No. 211, Government Instruction to all Prefectures, 14 Mar. 1873, and General Directive to Nagasaki Prefecture, 14 Mar. 1873. *The Times*, 19 May 1873.

[8] F.O. 46/166, Parkes to Granville, No. 2, Yedo, 7 Apr. 1873; 262/240, Granville W ats n, No. 33, 18 Apr. 1873.

Soejima explained to Parkes that it would be erroneous for foreign governments to believe that the Japanese government openly tolerated Christianity as a result of the withdrawal of the anti-Christian edict. Japanese might still be punished for professing the faith of the West, if in so doing their behaviour was obnoxious and troublesome. The Japanese government needed to be free to respond to native opinion and could not afford to be charged with openly favouring Christianity.

Although the eventual aim of the Meiji authorities was complete toleration there were contradictions in its current policy. Foreign teachers—in general, missionaries—were asked to teach in government schools on Sundays and to observe only Japanese holidays: a policy intended to remove them from government employ. At the same time Japanese were permitted to attend Christian services in Yedo and the open ports. The Primer for primary schools which featured the anti-Christian edict was recalled and new editions published without it. The Urakami exiles who survived were all repatriated by 22 July 1873. According to English figures the mortality had been seventeen per cent.[1]

Lord Granville met these contradictions with understanding. He instructed Parkes to express the regret of Her Majesty's Government that Japan's tolerance of Christianity was less complete than had been expected. The discrepancy between what Japan had announced in February and what she had actually done was the cause of great disappointment in England.[2]

From 1867 to 1873 Parkes, Clarendon, and Granville had shown wisdom and patience in guiding the Japanese towards a policy of religious tolerance. They had no ulterior motives. Although their success was limited they had retained the goodwill of the Japanese government as they brought its leaders to a realization that their desired equality with the West was dependent upon an established freedom for the Christian faith.

[1] F.O. 46/167, Parkes to Granville, Nos. 37, 41, and 47, Yedo, 7, 8, and 22 July 1873. Iwakura MSS. No. 211, *Directives of the Supreme Council* concerning the removal of the Prohibition Posters and the return of the exiles. No date. A Roman Catholic authority states that of the 6,000 to 8,000 Japanese Christians who were torn from their homes between 1868 and 1873 nearly 2,000 died in prison. Ritter, op. cit., p. 437.

[2] F.O. 262/240, Granville to Parkes, No. 34, 30 Aug. 1873. Iwakura MSS. No. 211, Parkes's letter to Sanjō, 4 Nov. 1873. *D.N.G.M.* vi. 599–600, 256.

XX

BRITISH PROTESTANT MISSIONS

The Pioneers

GEORGE SMITH, Anglican Bishop of Victoria, Hong Kong, kept his eyes open for missionary prospects. On 23 May 1853 he wrote to the Archbishop of Canterbury giving news of Perry's visit to Japan. He himself went to Japan early in 1860 and reported his impressions at length to the Secretary of the Society for the Propagation of the Gospel in Foreign Parts (S.P.G.). He considered the Japanese 'a frank, manly and energetic race, as compared with the generality of Oriental Nations'. Although he recognized 'a deep seated *religious senti-ment* among the Japanese of the middle and lower classes' and found living conditions for missionaries good, he thought it 'unwise, to encourage either in the missionaries themselves or in the Committees of our Church Societies, any sanguine expectations of an immediate enlargement of *direct* Missionary labour'. He had brought with him a large supply of the Gospel of St. Luke, translated in parallel clauses, into Japanese and Chinese but had 'only deemed it expedient as yet to dispose of one copy'.[1] The Bishop's caution was apparently so effective that althouth the S.P.G. had appropriated £1,000 for missions to Japan in 1859, it sent out no missionaries before the removal of the anti-Christian edicts in 1873[2]. And the Church Missionary Society (C.M.S.) had assigned only two men to Japan a few years earlier.

In Protestant missionary activities therefore, as well as gun-boat diplomacy, the British let the United States take the lead in Japan. Even before the ports were opened a few American missionaries stationed in China had made brief visits to Naga-saki and Kanagawa when they were able to teach elementary English to a small number of eager Japanese students. By the end of 1859 six men and their families representing the Epis-

[1] London, S.P.G. Archives, MSS. (*Original Letters Received*, xxiii), George Smith, Bishop of Victoria, to Revd. Ernest Hawkins, Nagasaki, 19 Apr. 1860.
[2] C. F. Pascoe, *Two Hundred Years of the S.P.G.*, 2 vols. (London, 1901), ii. 717.

copal, Presbyterian, and Dutch Reformed Churches in America
had arrived in Japan. Unwelcome newcomers they all were.
Hatred of foreigners was general and as representatives of the
Christian faith missionaries were regarded with extreme suspicion and closely watched. Evangelistic work was impossible
in any direct way. Their first tasks were to learn the language
and to gain the confidence of the Japanese people.[1]

Two outstanding men, Dr. James Curtis Hepburn of the
American Presbyterian Mission at Yokohama and Guido F.
Verbeck of the Dutch Reformed Mission at Nagasaki, established the patterns for Protestant activities in preparing for the
time when Christianity would be tolerated and permission for
its propagation be granted by the Japanese Government.
Hepburn compiled and published by 1867 an English–Japanese
lexicon of 40,000 words. He worked on Japanese translations
of the Bible and in 1862 he set up a dispensary and clinic in
Yokohama which lasted sixteen years. He and his wife held
classes in their own home which grew into two schools, one for
boys, and by 1867 one for girls. He conducted religious services
for the non-Anglican community and served as a go-between
for the missionary and mercantile communities.[2]

Guido Verbeck won the confidence of Japanese authorities
early. He established a school of foreign languages and science
in Nagasaki at the request of the Shogun. In his own home he
taught English through the text of the Bible while becoming a
distinguished speaker of Japanese. He baptized his first converts
and administered communion to them there in May 1866. They
were Murata, Wakasa-no-Kami, his brother, Ayabe, officials
of the Daimyo of Hizen, and Motono, their messenger who,
with Yano Riu, baptised in Yokohama in 1864, constituted the
first Japanese to accept Protestant Christianity.[3]

The united appeal for prayer sent out in 1866 by the American
evangelists resulted in the arrival of the first English missionary

[1] G. F. Verbeck, 'History of Protestant Missions in Japan', pp. 3, 8–9, included in
*Proceedings of the General Conference of the Protestant Missionaries of Japan Held at Osaka,
Japan, April 1883* (Yokohama, 1883).

[2] Ritter, op. cit., p. 22. C. W. Inglehart, *A Century of Christianity in Japan* (Tokyo,
1959), pp. 34–36, 41. Greene, op. cit., pp. 94–97.

[3] Inglehart, op. cit., p. 40. Greene, op. cit., pp. 97–98. W. E. Griffis, *Verbeck of
Japan* (New York, 1900), pp. 102–3, 123–7. Rev. J. H. Ballagh of the American
Dutch Reformed Church baptized Yano Riu, his Japanese teacher in 1864.
Ritter, op. cit., pp. 9–10,

to Japan. He was George Ensor, a graduate of Queens' College, Cambridge, and a priest in the bishopric of London, who reached Nagasaki in January 1869. He represented the C.M.S. of the 'Low Church' party of the Anglican communion. He was joined in 1871 by Henderson Burnside, a recent graduate of the Church Missionary College at Islington. Ensor's reception indicates that many changes had occurred in Japanese attitudes towards missionaries during the preceding decade. Three Japanese whom he had met in London greeted him respectively with two ducks and a friendly note in English, a basket of oranges, and a cake. He also found that the intense passion of the Japanese people for learning English and science gave him access to them. He could and did preach the Gospel in private and urged the Christian life silently by example. He observed that Bibles in Chinese supplied by British and American Bible Societies were freely sold among the educated. He was invited into Japanese homes and had soon arranged with a native to exchange English lessons for Japanese during which he hoped 'to unfold the truth to him'.[1] Within a few months he was visited by men of many classes, physicians, samurai, priests, etc., from many places in Japan. He could speak with them in safety and by May he had sold one thousand Bibles and tracts in Chinese. Some form of religious tolerance appeared to be under official consideration with the support of considerable influence. Buddhism, he believed, was nowhere in the Imperial favour. Shintoism, the religion authorized by the new government, was the ground where the battle would be fought.[2] A C.M.S. missionary, the Revd. W. A. Russell, who visited Nagasaki in May 1869, was amazed at the numbers of Japanese who called on Ensor and took the initiative in introducing the subject of Christianity after having purchased Christian literature from him. He believed that were religious toleration granted that so eager were the Japanese to be Europeanized, that they would readily adopt at least the outward forms of the Christian religion as they had already adopted the European costume.[3]

[1] London, C.M.S. Archives, MSS. (C.T. 10, 6–12), Ensor to C.M.S., Nagasaki, 4 Feb. 1869. British and Foreign Bible Society (B.F.B.S.) 58th *Report*, 1862, pp. 121–2; 64th *Report*, 1868, pp. 200–2.

[2] MSS. C.M.S. (C.T. 10, 6–12), Ensor to C.M.S., Nagasaki, 12 May 1869.

[3] *The Church Missionary Intelligencer*, Nov. 1869, 349–50.

Ensor baptized his first Japanese convert in early April 1869. By September three government officials who had never before seen a missionary asked him for baptism. Two 'grim samurai' wearing long swords also appeared at his home, demonstrating a knowledge of half the Bible, and promised to come again.[1] Such incidents meant progress to the evangelist in spite of the government's resumption of the persecution of the native Catholic Christians in the Nagasaki area and the circulation of a tract attacking the Christian faith and defending Buddhism. Here the few Protestant missionaries were denounced as more injurious than the Roman Catholics not only in doctrine but because they led astray talented young Japanese by spreading Christian doctrines abroad while pretending to teach astronomy, geography, medicine, etc.[2]

Ensor witnessed the deportation of the Urakami Catholics. Although he feared the widespread proselytizing of the relatively numerous Roman priests, he urged that England had a moral responsibility to help the suffering Japanese Catholics and to insist upon religious liberty.[3] He watched with dismay the government's determined efforts to re-establish and regiment the Japanese people into Shintoism.[4] Before his return home because of illness in 1873 he and Henderson Burnside recognized a growing tolerance of Christian missionary activities and experienced a new personal security themselves. Bible classes of twenty-five to thirty natives were being held openly on Sunday afternoons in Yedo with no opposition from the authorities. Even the Emperor had accepted a Bible and acknowledged it with an autographed letter.[5] Burnside could now hold public services at his home which were attended by 'the few Christians, inquirers, and their friends'.[6]

Protestant missionaries in general were finding some rewards for their efforts. In 1872 there were ten baptized Japanese Protestants divided between Nagasaki and Yokohama, all of

[1] MSS. C.M.S. (C.T. 10, 6–12), Ensor to C.M.S., 20 Sept. 1869.

[2] Oxford, Bodleian Library, Clarendon MSS. (F.O. Box 14, in Misc.), encl. in Parkes to Clarendon, 26 June 1869. Also in Satow MSS. 1/4. The tract first appeared in 1867, and was republished in Osaka in spring 1868 when Satow translated it.

[3] MSS. C.M.S. (C.T. 10, 6–12), Ensor to Venn, Nagasaki, 14, 16 Jan., 5 Apr. 1870.   [4] Ibid., Ensor to Committee, Nagasaki, 13 Sept. 1870.

[5] Ibid., Burnside to C.M.S., Nagasaki, 2 Dec. 1872.

[6] Verbeck, op. cit., p. 64.

whom had been tolerated by the authorities. On 10 March of that year a Japanese Protestant Church was organized in Yokohama. Nine very recent converts and two older Christians made up the congregation which called itself 'The Church of Christ of Japan' (Kirisuto Kokwai).[1] The American missionaries anticipated thousands of converts as soon as the government withdrew its opposition. They asked for more evangelists to put into Osaka and southern Japan.[2]

At the Convention of the Protestant Missionaries held in Yokohama in September 1872 important decisions were made. Perhaps the most significant was the appointment of an inter-denominational committee to make an improved translation of the Scriptures into Japanese. Medical service was endorsed as an important way of conducting missionary work and considered in some fields an indispensable pioneer. The early education of a native ministry was further agreed upon.[3] The Convention commended the name and policy of the first Japanese Church, decried denominationalism and pledged its members (who were all Americans) to work for 'identity of name and organization in all future church developments'.[4]

Growth of British Missions, 1873–1883

Into this ecumenical setting British missionaries from six different Protestant societies began to come after the removal of the anti-Christian edicts. British official documents seldom mention their work and the Japanese have written little about them. They were always second in numbers and activities to those of the American societies. But they were not idle as their own archives amply indicate.

An anonymous grant of £2,000 to the C.M.S. in 1872 was

[1] MSS. A.B.C. (Jap. Mission. Supplementary Docs. 1869–1929), 01, 154. Verbeck, op. cit., pp. 52–53.
[2] MSS. A.B.C. (16–4–1), Davis, Greene, Berry, and Gulick to Clark, 30 July 1872. Here the membership in the first Japanese church is given as 17.
[3] MSS. A.B.C. (16–4–1), Japan Mission i, No. 165–6. The British and Foreign Bible Society had not been satisfied with the character of the first Japanese translations of the Bible by B. J. Bettelheim and looked to the missionaries for an amended version. B.F.B.S. 56th *Report*, 1860, p. 132. The S.P.G. found the Bettelheim translations useless and believed even English Bibles would be more useful in Japan. MSS. S.P.G. (Letters, Victoria, 1868–74), Wright to Bullock, 24 Sept. 1874.
[4] Inglehart, op. cit., p. 44.

designated for the enlargement of the Japan Mission.[1] Sir Harry
Parkes himself joined Bishop Russell in stressing the urgent
need for missionaries in Japan, especially at the recently opened
ports of Osaka and Kobe.[2] Between 1873 and 1875 the C.M.S.
sent out six missionaries to the rapidly changing Meiji empire.
The experience of Ensor and Burnside had proved to the Board
in London that men of education and intelligence chosen from
British universities must be sent to Japan—men who could
master the difficult language and interest the inquiring minds
of the Japanese.[3]

Charles Frederick Warren and John Piper, both graduates of
the Church Missionary College at Islington, had had missionary
experience in Hong Kong before being assigned in 1873 to
Osaka and Yedo, respectively.[4] Herbert Maundrell and Walter
Dening, also graduates of Islington and former missionaries
in Madagascar, went to Nagasaki and Hakodate. Henry
Evington, B.A., of Pembroke College, Oxford, joined Warren
in Osaka in 1874 and twenty years later became one of the two
bishops for Japan. Philip Kimball Fyson, a scholar of Christ's
College, Cambridge, with double first-class honours, arrived in
Yedo in 1874, worked in Niigata from 1875 to 1882 when the
mission was given up, returned to Yedo and later (1889)
became principal of the Divinity College at Osaka. Five more
men from the C.M.S. were stationed in Japan between 1875
and 1883.[5]

Piper was appointed Secretary of the Society in Japan with
discretionary power to erect houses for the missionaries not to
exceed £600 to £700 each.[6] He was able to combine these
responsibilities with those of a chaplaincy at Yokohama.[7]
A Mrs. Goodall whose 'Christian character and devotedness'

[1] Eugene Stock, *The History of the Church Missionary Society*, 4 vols. (London,
1899), ii. 604. C.M.S., *Index*, 1872-5, xli. 18.

[2] MSS. C.M.S. (C.J.) *China and Japan Mission Minutes* (hereinafter cited as
C.M.S. *Minutes*), xl. 73. 1 Apr. 1873,

[3] 'Japan as a Mission Field', *Church Missionary Intelligencer*, Jan. 1873, p. 17.

[4] Ibid,, Sept. 1873, 268-9 for 'Valedictory Dismissal' of Warren and Piper.

[5] MSS. C.M.S. *Book of Missionaries*. Stock, op. cit. iii. 236-7. Maundrell replaced Burnside at Nagasaki in 1875. The five additional men were James Williams,
John Batchelor, and Walter Andrews at Hakodate; C. H. Pole at Osaka and Niigata
and later at Hakodate; A. B. Hutchinson at Nagasaki. Walter Dening left the
Society in 1882 because of his unacceptable views on immortality.

[6] MSS. C.M.S. (C.J.) *Minutes*, xl. 73, 3 June 1873; xli. 115, 17 Feb. 1874.

[7] Ibid. xlii. 152, 13 Sept. 1875.

had been established accompanied Maundrell to assist him in Nagasaki. The Society voted £120 for her passage and outfit.[1] Two other women, Miss M. J. Oxlad of the British Society for the Promotion of Female Education, and Mrs. Jane Caspare, a former C.M.S. missionary, assisted the work while acting as governesses in missionary families.[2] Outstations established by the Nagasaki Mission began to prosper in Kagoshima, Saga, and Kumamoto, and several were opened in conjunction with Dening's station at Hakodate.[3] By 1876 the need for preaching-chapels in Hakodate and Osaka was met by grants from the Society ranging from £200 for Hakodate to $500 for Osaka.[4] More than a year later the corner stone of Dening's church was laid at Hakodate. During erection of the building Dening preached near by to about two hundred people on three evenings a week.[5]

The Society for the Propagation of the Gospel decided in June 1872 to participate in 'importing the Gospel to China and Japan'. For this purpose a committee was appointed to raise £5,000 in five years and two anonymous donors made possible the prompt opening of the station.[6] The mission had to begin with unmarried clergymen in accordance with 'the usual practice in missions to the Heathen'. But it was to be established on such footing that the 'addition of a lady possessing qualities essential to the wife of a missionary would increase the efficiency of the mission'.[7] The two bachelors selected were the Revd. A. C. Shaw, M.A., of Trinity College, Toronto, and the Revd. W. B. Wright, M.A., of Trinity College, Dublin. Each agreed to go to Japan at a salary of £250 a year to be raised to £300 if after two years they could speak Japanese fluently. The Society also provided their passage money and outfits.[8] They established the mission's first station in September 1873 at Yedo, in a Japanese house in Mita Machi some distance from the foreign

[1] MSS C.M.S. (C.J.) *Minutes*, xli. 638, 27 Apr. 1875.

[2] Ibid. xliii. 645, 23 Oct. 1877, Stock, op. cit. iii. 216.

[3] Verbeck, op. cit., pp. 109–10.

[4] MSS. C.M.S. (C.J.) *Minutes*, xliii. 190 and 225, 5 and 19 Dec. 1876. Here '$500' may be a mistake for £500 since the Hakodate figures were given in pounds.

[5] MSS. C.M.S. (C.T. 10, 6–12), Dening to C.M.S., Hakodate, 10 Dec. 1878.

[6] MSS. S.P.G. *Minutes*, Standing Com., No. 35, p. 155, 20 June 1872. *Mission Field*, Dec. 1872, p. 380. Pascoe, op. cit. ii. 717.

[7] MSS. S.P.G. *Minutes*, Standing Com., No. 85, p. 277, 30 Jan. 1873.

[8] MSS. S.P.G. *Book of Missionaries*, 1869–87, pp. 52–53.

PLATE 12

S.P.G. Missionaries, 1881

| W. B. WRIGHT | E. C. HOPPER | A. C. SHAW |
| W. F. GARRATT | H. J. FOSS | |

concession.[1] Here in a disused temple they held services for British residents while learning Japanese. Miss Alice Hoar was sent by the Ladies Association in 1875 to Yedo where she began a girls' school and trained women as evangelists.[2] A station was established in Kobe when in 1876 the S.P.G. sent two priests, Hugh James Foss and Francis B. Plummer, who conducted Episcopal services for the Western community every Sunday evening and on alternate Sunday mornings, in addition to their missionary activities. Henry Hughes succeeded Plummer in 1878 and Edmund Charles Hopper joined Foss in 1880 but soon took charge of the Yedo station during the furloughs of Wright and Shaw.[3] Another woman, Miss Shaw, joined the Tokyo Mission in 1878 to teach at the girls' school. Foss worked with Japanese helpers at Kobe, ministering to the English community, teaching the Japanese for whom he built St. Michael's Church in 1881, and founding an outstation on the Island of Awaji.[4] Later he became Bishop of the Osaka jurisdiction.[5]

The year 1873 also marked the beginning of the Japan Mission of the Methodist Church of Canada when the Revd. George Cochran and family and the Revd. D. Macdonald, M.D., and wife were sent to Yokohama. Within the following year Macdonald accepted an invitation to teach, preach, and practise medicine at Shizuoka in Suruga ken while Cochran began to teach in Nakamura's Academy in Yedo and to hold religious services in his own home. Three others joined this mission in 1876 to teach at the academy at Numazu in Suruga ken and to work in Yedo. Miss M. Cartmell was sent by the Ladies Society to the Yedo station in 1882 to develop the school department and to be an evangelist among the women of Yedo.[6]

Two Scottish missionary societies began work in Japan in

[1] Verbeck, op. cit., p. 66. Hineya Yasusada, *Nihon Kinsei Kirisutokyō Jimbutsu Shi* (History of Christian Figures in Modern Japan), (Tokyo, 1935), p. 169.

[2] Verbeck, op. cit., p. 76. H. P. Thompson, *Into All Lands, The History of the Society for the Propagation of the Gospel in Foreign Parts* (London, 1951), pp. 450–1.

[3] MSS. S.P.G. *Book of Missionaries*, 1869–87, pp. 91, 92, 116, 145. Thompson, op. cit., p. 451. *Japan Chronicle, Jubilee Number, 1868–1918*, p. 18.

[4] Verbeck, op. cit., p. 103. Thompson, op. cit., p. 451.

[5] Stock, op. cit. iii. 234.

[6] Verbeck, op. cit., pp. 66, 71, 83, 161. The archives of this mission have not been examined here.

1874, the United Presbyterian Church of Scotland (U.P.S.) and the Edinburgh Medical Mission. As few of their Japan records have survived we know little about the actual experiences of their men in the field. So great was the concern about Japan in Scotland, however, that seventy-two subscribers gave £8,949 for the founding of the mission of the United Presbyterian Church, a record for the initiation of any fund of the Church.[1] The U.P.S. sent out the Revd. Robert Davidson, Dr. Henry Faulds, M.D., and wife, the Revd. Hugh Waddell and wife, and Dr. Williamson, 'associate and adviser', to settle in Yedo in March and June 1874. Dr. Faulds opened a medical dispensary in Tsukiji where a few medical students also congregated.[2] Missionary salaries amounted to £300 for unmarried and £350 for married men.[3] The Revd. S. G. McLaren and wife and Miss A. M. Gamble joined the mission the next year. In 1877 this Presbyterian mission united with the missions of the Presbyterian Church of the U.S. and the Reformed Church in America to form the United Church of Christ in Japan (Nippon Kirisuto Itchi Kyōkai). Eight native churches with a membership of 623 were combined in this union which was a natural development of the interdenominational spirit of the conference of 1872.[4] From thence the work of the Scottish mission was so closely allied with the other missions in this union and with the Japanese churches that except for the special medical work of Dr. Faulds it is difficult to distinguish its individual activities.[5]

The Edinburgh Medical Missionary Society, founded in 1841 as a result of Dr. Peter Parker's reports on Asia's medical needs trained students for medical missionary work and gradually sent them into the field.[6] Theobald A. Palm, M.A.. M.B., with his wife first represented the Society in Japan. They arrived in Yedo in May 1874 studied Japanese diligently, and moved to

---

[1] Elizabeth G. K. Hewat, *Vision and Achievement* (Edinburgh, 1960), p. 294.

[2] National Library of Scotland, Edinburgh, MSS. U.P. (Letter Book 17), H. M. MacGill to Faulds, Davidson, Williamson, Waddell, Edinburgh, 22 Jan. 1874. Verbeck, op. cit., p. 71.

[3] MSS. U.P. S. (Letter Book 18 [Foreign]), extract from *Minutes* of Committee on Foreign Missions, 30 Mar. 1875.

[4] Verbeck, op. cit., pp. 77, 85–89.

[5] Hewat, op. cit., p. 294. For Faulds's work, see pp. 479–80, 524–5.

[6] John Lowe, *Primer of Medical Missions* (no date or place of publication), pp. 9–10, 54.

Niigata in 1875. Palm initiated Protestant missionary work in that port where he soon proved the value of a medical mission as an auxiliary to evangelistic work. He was assisted by Mr. Amenomori, a former pupil of an American missionary, and by Mr. Oshikawa Masayoshi, an elder in the native church in Yokohama. In 1880 Oshikawa moved to Sendai to begin evangelistic work in that area. In spite of the indifference to Christianity presented by Niigata, a city of 46,000, notorious among the Japanese for its immorality, Palm won the confidence and gratitude of the people and the friendship of native physicians who asked for his instruction and assistance. His medical services prospered. A dispensary was opened in the centre of the city and a house was built for the reception of in-patients. Palm also made monthly visits to the country to treat patients in co-operation with native doctors. This medical service not only supported itself but helped to carry a considerable part of the evangelistic expenses. The number of converted Christians, however, was small in relation to the patients. Palm returned to England in 1883 and the mission was taken over by the American Board of Missions in 1885.[1]

A sixth British missionary society, the Baptist Society for Propagating the Gospel among the Heathen, began work in Yedo in February 1879 with one evangelist, W. J. White, a former secular teacher in Japan. By August he had formed a church of five members. He remained the only worker for this society in Japan in 1883.[2]

Figures differ for the total number of Protestant missionaries in Japan at the end of 1882 because of the different months in which the figures were assembled for each mission. A recent counting gives 226 including wives.[3] Of these slightly more than one-fourth were in English, Scottish, and Canadian stations. The great majority here were Anglicans whose work in conjunction with that of the American Episcopal Church and a few Japanese converts had by 1883 led to the establishing of a native Episcopal Church of 761 members occupying thirty-eight

[1] Verbeck, op. cit., pp. 71, 77, 83, 104, 124, 164–5. John Lowe, *Medical Missions, Their Place and Power* (New York, 1886), pp. 136–7. Ritter, op. cit., p. 83. W. T. Thomas, *Protestant Beginnings in Japan 1859–1889* (Tokyo, 1959), p. 131.

[2] Verbeck, op. cit., p. 112. No archives of this mission have been examined here.

[3] Thomas, op. cit., pp. 78–79.

stations—a minor part of the 6,598 said to approximate the total number of Japanese Protestants at that time.[1] These figures should be viewed in relation to those of the Catholic Churches. By July 1883 the Greek Orthodox Christians numbered 8,863 with 148 organized churches, while the Roman Catholics as early as 1881 had 25,633 followers, eighty churches or chapels, and seventy-four schools and orphanages in Japan.[2]

British, Scottish, and American Bible and religious tract societies contributed to the success of the Protestant missions. Before 1876 the Bible societies had been helping with the cost of the Japanese translation of the Bible and sending English and Chinese scriptures to Japanese translators.[3] As early as 1872 the National Bible Society of Scotland (N.B.S.S.) proposed to memorialize Earl Granville 'to secure in the revision of the Treaty with Japan, the repeal of the edicts against Christianity or freedom for religious work'.[4] After a report on conditions in Japan requested from Mr. R. Lilley who was in China, the N.B.S.S. transferred him to Japan, as their first agent there in the spring of 1876. He created the functionary Bible colporteur —a native to distribute or peddle Bibles through the country, called 'Seisho o uri aruku Hito' (Seisho hanbainin).[5] He was joined in 1879 by J. A. Thomson who succeeded him in 1883. Thomson upon arrival began selling scriptures and opening new agencies in the interior. In 1882 the N.B.S.S. sold 5,151 New Testaments and 28,171 parts of the same.[6]

The rival of these Scotsmen, the British and Foreign Bible Society, (B.F.B.S.) worked in Japan through a committee of missionaries from 1876 until March 1881 when the Revd. I. S. Taylor became the Society's first agent. During 1882 this Society sold 1,140 New Testaments, 7,257 parts of the same, and fifty-nine Bibles—a small part of the total—16,578 New Testa-

---

[1] *Proceedings of the General Conference of Protestant Missionaries in Japan*, held in Tokyo, 24–31 Oct. 1900 (Tokyo, 1901), pp. 882–3.

[2] Verbeck, op. cit., p. 185.

[3] *Report*, Japan Bible Society (Nihon Kwai Kyo Kai), Aug. 1961.

[4] Edinburgh, MSS., N.B.S.C., *Minutes*, iv. 281, 1 May 1872.

[5] Ibid., 25 Jan. 1875, v. 228; 6 and 16 Dec. 1875, v. 278, 285. *United Presbyterian Missionary Record*, Edinburgh, 1 July 1884, p. 209.

[6] Verbeck, op. cit., p. 175, MSS. N.B.S.S., *Minutes*, Western Com., vi. 199, 310, 7 Jan., 19 Dec., 1878; vii. 90, 124, 3 May, 5 July, 1880; viii, 71, 11 Nov. 1882.

ments and Bibles sold by all three National Societies in 1882.[1]

The London Religious Tract Society worked under the direction of Lilley of the N.B.S.S. and contributed to his salary and expenses. It reported in 1882 a total circulation of 48,690 volumes of Christian literature of which 34,773 were sold and 13,917 given away.[3] All societies increased their circulation of Christian literature in 1883 and anticipated a growing need for Bible work since many schools were already in missionary hands and a new Japanese law made school attendance for children compulsory.[2]

Obstacles to the Spread of Christianity

Protestant missionaries had similar aims and problems. The instructions issued by the C.M.S. to its missions in June 1868 indicate in general the goals of all British missionaries in Japan. They were:

1. Study the national character of the people among whom you labour, and show the utmost respect for national peculiarities.
2. Keep in mind that race distinctions will probably rise in intensity with the progress of the Mission.
3. As soon as converts can be gathered into a Christian congregation let a native church be organized as a national institution.
4. As the native church assumes a national character, it will ultimately supersede the denominational distinctions which are now introduced by foreign Missionary Societies.
5. The proper position of a missionary is one external to the native church, and his most important duty towards that church is the education and training of native pastors and evangelists, especially in the knowledge and use of the Bible.[4]

Japan presented unusual obstacles to the creation of such a

[1] Verbeck, op. cit., p. 175. Ritter, op. cit., p. 84. B.F.B.S. 78th *Report*, 1882, pp. 248–53, gives 7,909 copies of the Bible whole or in part, mostly in Japanese, sold in 1882, of which 5,524 by colporteurs. Ritter's figures for the total may be very conservative.

[2] MSS. N.B.S.S., *Minutes*, Western Com., vi. 388, 7 July 1879, Verbeck, op. cit., p. 176.

[3] B.F.B.S. 79th *Report*, pp. 201–3. Verbeck, op. cit., p. 175. U.P.S. *Missionary Record*, 1 July 1884, p. 209.

[4] *The Church Missionary Intelligencer*, Apr. 1869, p. 104.

native Christian church. Progress was very slow even during the decade following the removal of the anti-Christian edicts from the public notice-boards. The missionaries who arrived in 1873 and 1874 soon discovered that there was no general tolerance of Christianity. Although the central government was consciously lax in enforcing its laws against native believers, local officials were often strict in their adherence to the earlier practice.[1] As one Japanese judge maintained when he fined native Christians for attempting to discard Buddhist rites at the burial of a fellow convert, Japanese were at liberty to study but not embrace the Western faith.[2]

Although they could hold public services in all the foreign concessions where Japanese attended without molestation, the missionaries found difficulties in reaching the Japanese who lived beyond these areas and the ten *ri* limit surrounding the treaty ports. Should they venture outside these boundaries they would be summoned before their consul and fined for infringing treaty regulations. Renting houses from Japanese for preaching services or Bible classes in the native town or country near Nagasaki, Yedo, Osaka, and Niigata proved almost an impossibility.[3] Hakodate was the great exception. There Dening could live in the native settlement and conduct missionary activities freely in the vicinity. In other ports the difficulty was met by friendly Japanese who opened their homes from time to time for Christian meetings.[4] All the evangelists naturally urged upon their home governments their need for access to the interior of Japan.[5]

Passports granted by the Meiji government in 1874 allowed foreigners to travel beyond the treaty limits for health, scientific observations, and pleasure. These enabled missionaries to visit many parts of Japan but they could not preach the Gospel openly as they passed from town to town nor could they remain long

---

[1] Warren in *Church Missionary Intelligencer*, May 1874, p. 139. MSS. C.M.S. (C.T. 10, 6–12), Burnside to C.M.S., Nagasaki, 31 July 1873; Dening to Wright, Hakodate, 7 Dec. 1874.

[2] MSS. S.P.G. (D. 41, Asia, 1875), Wright to Bullock, Yedo, Holy Week 1875.

[3] Burnside in *Church Missionary Intelligencer*, May 1874, pp. 133, 136, 220–1. Verbeck, op. cit., pp. 137, 164. MSS. S.P.G. (D. 47, Asia, 1878), Wright to Bullock, Yedo, 25 June 1878.

[4] Warren, 'The Present Position of Christianity in Japan', *Church Missionary Intelligencer*, Feb. 1875, p. 43.

[5] MSS. N.B.S.S., *Minutes*, Western Com., viii. 26, 5 June 1882, is one example.

outside the concessions even when Japanese had purchased houses for them.[1] Warren wrote: 'Of course it is quite possible to speak a few words by the way, to answer questions in such a manner as to make statements of Christian truth, and by consistent Christian conduct—which alas! the natives too seldom see in those who profess and call themselves Christians—to exert an influence which under some circumstances cannot but be felt.'[2] Wright found conditions more liberal in 1881 when he preached openly to groups of from forty to sixty Japanese during a month's travel in Shimōsa Province.[3]

The Japanese people themselves confronted Christian missionaries, even those accustomed to Asian and African cultures, with unique problems. Members of the literate middle and upper classes, seeking knowledge of every aspect of Western civilization, were their first potential Christian converts. In contrast to the lower classes, these Japanese were accustomed to freedom of belief in the realm of their native religions and to holding unchallenged convictions. Although Buddhism and the Meiji requirements of the Shinto cult had accustomed them to practices similar to many in Christianity, for example, burial and other rituals, listening to public preaching, and the acceptance of many sects within one faith, the Japanese were in general indifferent to religious matters.[4] Many came to the Protestant missionaries, to their Bible classes and schools, feigning an interest in Christianity in order to learn English. Their logical, sceptical minds made the acceptance of Christian dogmas difficult. Social and family opposition made young believers reluctant to commit themselves. Conversions to the Western faith came slowly, sometimes only two or three annually at a single mission. Instances of converts who repented of their baptism and returned to their old life also caused the missionaries to be extremely careful in ascertaining that their converts had both sincere conviction and adequate knowledge before they baptized or confirmed them.[5] Six years after the removal

---

[1] MSS. S.P.G. (D. 47, Asia, 1878), Shaw to Bullock, Yedo, 20 Mar. 1878. *Church Missionary Intelligencer*, Dec. 1874, pp. 364–73; *Church Missionary Intelligencer and Record*, May 1876, pp. 272–81.

[2] Ibid., p. 273.

[3] *Mission Field*, May 1881, p. 205, Wright's letter of 1 Jan. 1881.

[4] 'Japan as a Mission Field', *Church Missionary Intelligencer*, Jan. 1873, pp. 16–17.

[5] *Mission Field*, May 1880, p. 156, Wright's report at end of 1879.

of the anti-Christian edicts the C.M.S. could report only 128 Japanese Christians divided among its missions at Nagasaki, Osaka, Yedo, Niigata, and Hakodate.[1]

Several forces were at work which explain further these facts. The defensive writings of Confucian scholars as well as the secular philosophies of the West were competing with the teachings of the Protestant missionaries for the minds of the Japanese people. Works of Darwin, Huxley, Spencer, Buckle, Tom Paine, Ingersol, Draper, and others appealed greatly to Japanese students at home and abroad. They were being taught by American and British scholars in the Imperial University and other government schools. On Sundays in public halls lectures attacking both Christianity and theism were well attended.[2] Although Dr. Henry Faulds of the Scottish Presbyterian Medical Mission at Tsukiji made an eloquent defence of the theory of evolution as compatible with the Christian faith and gave other lectures on scientific subjects bearing on religion, most missionaries felt thwarted by the growing popularity of Western materialism, scepticism, and humanistic thought.[3]

Japanese hatred and fear of Christianity on political grounds also continued through 1883 to plague the missionaries. Although Shaw of the S.P.G. believed in 1875 that the Japanese were too well informed to be persuaded ever again that political motives had anything to do with the propagation of Christianity, there is much evidence to the contrary.[4] Buddhist priests alarmed at the foreign religion raised a cry that for the sake of Japan and her laws it must be stopped.[5] Prospective missionaries were warned in 1881 to expect this type of opposition.[6] The Japanese themselves voiced it in print.[7] Among them the most influential

[1] *Church Missionary Intelligencer*, May 1874, pp. 134–5. For annual statistics of C.M.S. see ibid., Dec. 1876, p. 754; May 1878, p. 320; May 1879, p. 310.

[2] D. C. Greene in *Proceedings*, Osaka Conference, 1883, pp. 118–29. Kōsaka and Abosch, op. cit., pp. 180–1. Honda Yōichi and Yamaji Yakichi, 'Japanese Religious Beliefs: Christianity' in Ōkuma, *Fifty Years of New Japan*, ii. 81, 85–87. MSS. S.P.G. (D.47, Asia, 1878), H. J. Foss to Bullock, Kobe, 4 June 1878.

[3] *Mission Field*, May 1879, p. 217, Wright's report, Yedo, 31 Dec. 1878; Nov. 1879, p. 509, Wright's report, Yedo, 30 June 1879. Verbeck, op. cit., p. 124. Wilton, op. cit., p. 27.

[4] MSS. S.P.G. (D. 41, Asia, 1875), Shaw to Bullock, Yedo, 25 Jan. 1875.

[5] *Mission Field*, Mar. 1882, p. 74, Wright's report, Yedo, 30 Sept. 1881. S.P.G. *Missionary Reports*, Mar. 1882, Hopper, Kobe, 30 Sept. 1882.

[6] *Mission Field*, Mar. 1881, pp. 130–2.

[7] *Church Missionary Intelligencer*, Jan. 1882, pp. 47–48 for an address by a Japanese.

was the great educator Fukuzawa Yūkichi. His works *Bummei Ron* (Treatise on Civilization), *Jiji Shogen* (A Word for the Times), and *Yaso Kyō Koku Gai* (Christianity an Injury to the Country), were listed as expressions of the political grounds for Japanese opposition to Christianity.[1]

Japanese and missionaries alike realized that the most exasperating obstacle to Japan's acceptance of Christianity was the bad example set by nominal Christians at the treaty ports. Their arrogant, predatory behaviour and dishonesty in business, their drunken brawls and profanity, and their brutality to natives showed a wide divergence between the profession and practice of the Christian faith.[2] If they represented Christian ethics, the teachings of Confucius, Buddha, and those of the Imperial Ancestors appeared to the Japanese far superior. To prove otherwise, a scattering of missionaries in the great cities of Japan had a lonely and an often unrewarding struggle. The merchant community held them in contempt and delighted in gossip over usually unfounded scandals about them. 'Men of business and leisure', dedicated to diametrically opposite goals, were 'utterly unable to understand a missionary's life, work or purpose.'[3]

Even British official interest in missionary successes was casual. Satow expressed surprise that Maundrell expected commendation for his conversion of twenty-one Japanese, chiefly samurai, during his eighteen months' residence in Nagasaki.[4] And Sir Harry and Lady Parkes, although respected by the missionaries, were not considered 'church people'.[5]

Reasons for Encouragement

In spite of such obstacles and the destruction of their newly built churches by fire—both accidental and incendiary—the missionaries maintained a striking optimism regarding the progress of their work.[6] This was not unfounded. They saw in

[1] Greene in *Proceedings*, Osaka Conference, 1883, p. 121, Honda and Yamaji in Ōkuma, *Fifty Years of New Japan*, ii, 84–85.
[2] *Proceedings*, Osaka Conference, 1883, p. 163. *Church Missionary Intelligencer*, Jan. 1873, p. 15. for quotation from an essay by a young Japanese. *Japan Weekly Mail*, 24 Dec. 1881. *Mission Field*, Sept. 1877, p. 421, Plummer's report, Kobe, 1 May 1877.   [3] Griffis, *The Mikado's Empire*, 344–5.
[4] Satow MSS. 15/6, *Diary*, 24 Feb. 1877.
[5] MSS. S.P.G. (India and Far East, 1877), Wright to Bullock, Tokyo, 9 Apr. 1877.
[6] Verbeck, op. cit., pp. 103 and 131 for burning of Canadian Methodist Church

the greater freedom which they and native Christians had enjoyed since 1873 the opportunity to reach more and more people. They had complete liberty to teach and preach in the foreign settlements. Natives could and did come to them at any time without molestation to learn about Christianity.[1] The fortitude with which some converts held to their faith in spite of family and social ostracism gave the evangelists inspiration.[2] The many types of Japanese who attended Christian services seemed evidence of at least a widespread interest in learning about the faith. Dening wrote of Buddhist and Shinto priests as well as 'merchants, government officers and school masters who have hitherto been too prejudiced to attend' being seen at his services 'again and again attentively listening to long sermons'.[3]

The overall picture was promising. Little scattered congregations were mounting up. The American missionary Dr. Otis Cary pointed out in May 1875: 'There are at this time not less than ten places in Yokohama, twenty-five in Tokyo, ten in Kobe–Osaka district, and five in other places, making fifty in all where regular Christian services are held as often as once a week, with audiences varying from twenty to two hundred in number.'[4]

New legislation was destroying some of the obstacles to the missionaries' work. A law passed on 13 March 1876 made Sunday the national day of rest and Saturday a half-holiday beginning on 1 April 1876. Some government departments had kept Sunday since 1873 but making it a general holiday throughout the land seemed evidence of 'the silent influence of the Christian nations over the minds of the Japanese people.' The evangelists rejoiced that it would give many natives a regular

at Yedo in 1878 and the C.M.S. Church at Niigata, 1880. MSS. C.M.S. (C.J.), *Minutes*, xlv. 572, 27 Jan. 1880 for destruction by fire of C.M.S. house and church at Hakodate, a $9,000 loss.

[1] *Church Missionary Intelligencer*, Oct. 1875, p. 310. *Mission Field*, Mar. 1877, p. 72, Wright to S.P.G., Yedo, 25 Sept. 1876.

[2] *Church Missionary Intelligencer*, May 1874, p. 135; July 1879, p. 437. Verbeck, op. cit., p. 151. Honda and Yamaji in Ōkuma, *Fifty Years of New Japan*, ii. 81. *Mission Field*, Mar. 1877, pp. 71–74, Wright to S.P.G., Yedo, 25 Sept. 1876.

[3] MSS. C.M.S. (C.T. 10, 6–12), Dening to Wright, Hakodate, 15 May 1876; Dening to C.M.S., Hakodate, 24 Dec. 1879.

[4] Quoted by Henry St. George Tucker, *The History of the Episcopal Church in Japan* (New York, 1938), p. 99.

opportunity to hear the Gospel.[1] The difficulties experienced over Christian burial services for Japanese also diminished when in 1876 the government issued new forms of death certificates requiring only the signatures of a doctor and a civil officer and omitting that of a non-Christian priest.[2]

A concern about Christianity also appeared in the rapidly expanding native press. Writers expressed both friendly and hostile attitudes towards the Western faith and boldly advocated liberty of conscience in matters of religion. Mori Arinori, an early minister to the United States, entered into the argument maintaining that 'men should be left free to believe what they like, provided their belief entails no injury upon others'.[3] The sympathy for Christianity which Mori and other leading political figures such as Katsu, statesman and minister of the Navy, Sugi Kōji, pioneer statistician and member of the Home Office, and Ōkubo Ichiō, member of the Ministry of Education, expressed directly or indirectly was obviously another source of encouragement.[4] And the leadership assumed by outstanding Japanese Christians, Niijima Jō, Kozaki Hiromichi, Uemura Masahisa, and Uchimura Kanzō, all converts of American missionaries, pointed to the possibilities of greater success.[5]

A vast popular interest in Christianity suddenly became evident at mass meetings where missionaries lectured on Christian thought. Thousands attended an open assembly in the garden of a restaurant near Ueno Park on 13 October 1880.[6] The C.M.S. and the American Board hired a theatre in Kyoto where they advertised 'a great meeting for Christian preaching'. Ten thousand came.[7] Similar gatherings were held in Osaka and Yedo. The government itself provided a large hall in the capital to attract educated Japanese to lectures on evidences of Christianity. Though many of the audience were

[1] *Church Missionary Intelligencer and Record*, July 1876, p. 440. *Mission Field*, July 1876, p. 176.
[2] Ibid., Oct. 1876, p. 308. S.P.G. *Missionary Reports*, 1877, Wright's report, Yedo, 25 Dec. 1876.
[3] *Japan Weekly Mail*, 22 May 1875, pp. 441–3.
[4] Kōsaka and Abosch, op. cit., pp. 160–6. Otis Cary, *Japan and its Regeneration* (New York, 1899), pp. 91–92.
[5] Kōsaka and Abosch, op cit., pp. 166–78. [6] Ritter, op. cit., p. 93.
[7] MSS. S.P.G. (D. 56, Asia 11, 1881), Foss to Tucker, Kobe, 30 June 1881. *Mission Field*, Nov. 1881, p. 396.

atheists, the building was crowded.[1] The number of converts began to multiply rapidly, rising from 4,367 in 1882 to 11,000 by 1885.[2]

Problems of church administration were at the same time being solved for the British Episcopal missions. From their beginning they had been under the jurisdiction of the Bishop of Victoria (Hong Kong) but a resident American, Bishop Williams of Yedo, had fulfilled his functions in Japan during his long absences in China.[3] Bishop Burdon, the British incumbent, after visiting Japan in 1876 and 1878 recommended to the C.M.S. and S.P.G. the appointment of a resident English missionary bishop for Japan. After some denominational differences, the Archbishop of Canterbury proposed the consecration in England of a bishop to represent the entire Church of England in Japan. His position was to be independent, each society contributing half of his stipend. To this the C.M.S. agreed, limiting its concurrence to the bishop's first tenure of office.[4] A member of the Society so approved the plan that he offered £500 a year for five years to cover its quota.[5] The appointment in 1882 of the Revd. Arthur W. Poole (who graduated from Oxford in 1873, and was a former C.M.S. missionary in India) as the first missionary bishop for Japan, met with great approval.[6] He reached Japan in December 1883 and set out to co-operate with the American Episcopal Church, hoping to achieve as much unity of action as the Presbyterian bodies already possessed in Japan.[7]

Schools, Hospitals, and Publications

Schools, hospitals, and scholarly works rewarded generously the missionaries' efforts. Through these the evangelists exerted a far-reaching influence on both Christian and non-Christian

---

[1] MSS. S.P.G. (D. 64, Asia 11, 1883), Hopper to Tucker, Yedo 11 Jan. 1883.

[2] Kishimoto and Howes, op. cit., p. 237.

[3] MSS. S.P.G. (India and Far East, 1877), Report from Yedo, 27 Sept. 1875.

[4] MSS. S.P.G. (D. 47, Asia, 1878), Burdon to Wright, Hong Kong, Aug. 1878; (India and Far East, 1879), Bishop of Ohio to Archbishop of Canterbury, Cleveland, 26 Apr. 1879; Wright to Tucker, 12 Aug. 1879; (D. 56, Asia 11, 1881), Shaw to Tucker, Yedo, 5 July 1881. *Church Missionary Intelligencer and Record*, Apr. 1882, pp. 223–8, Cantuar to C.M.S., 23 Dec. 1881.

[5] Ibid., May 1882, p. 299.

[6] Ibid., July 1883, p. 441. *Mission Field*, Oct. 1883, p. 351.

[7] MSS. S.P.G. (D. 64, Asia 11, 1883), Poole to Tucker, Yedo, 23 Dec. 1883.

Japanese. Here the British record deserves recognition although it is considerably less than that of the American societies.

Boarding and Day Schools. In 1882 the C.M.S. reported in Nagasaki and its outstations Kagoshima and Kumamoto, a small girls' boarding-school with six pupils and eight day schools, the regular attendance at which approximated thirty-five boys and twenty-five girls; at Osaka a girls' school; at Yedo a school for boys and girls of the poorest class was attended by twenty-five boys and twenty girls. A similar school in Niigata was discontinued in 1883.[1]

Funds were granted for a school at Hakodate which was opened in November 1878. Here 'the women of the mission'— Mrs. Dening, Mrs. Williams, and C. Callas—taught English and sewing for three hours every afternoon. Within two weeks, said Dening, they had nearly twenty students, men and women, who otherwise might never have had contact with a missionary or native converts.[2] Dening also took part in the intellectual life of Hakodate through membership in a literary society. Although the topics for discussion were required to be 'literary' the missionary expected to gain influence gradually over them.[3]

The work of the S.P.G. in Yedo and Kobe was largely evangelistic. The Society reported one church school, three primary schools, and a flourishing boys' and girls' school in Shiba (Yedo) under the charge of Miss Hoar. At Kobe there was a prosperous boys' school where Eurasians, from seven years of age, were admitted, with H. Hughes as headmaster. The attendance at these schools totalled two hundred.[4] When missionaries were absent on furlough, however, the schools were suspended—the case in Shiba in 1883.

Shaw himself protested against the general practice through which missionaries set up schools in their homes where students came nominally to read the Bible but really to learn English. He found such early teaching a hindrance to his own study of

[1] Verbeck, op. cit., p. 152.
[2] MSS. C.M.S. (C.J. 61, 1874–87), pp. 32–34, C.M.S. to Piper, 25 Nov. 1875. *Church Missionary Intelligencer and Record*, July 1879, p. 436, for Dening's report of 10 Dec. 1878. *Hakodate Shimbun*, 22 Nov. 1878. This school is not mentioned in Verbeck's account of the C.M.S. for 1882 probably because Dening and the C.M.S. had severed relations owing to his eschatological ideas.
[3] MSS. C.M.S. (C.T. 10, 6–12), Dening to C.M.S., Hakodate, 24 Dec. 1879.
[4] Verbeck, op. cit., p. 163. These figures are obviously later than those given by the chart opposite p. 184.

the Japanese language and dangerous for the Japanese who might be subjected to grave theological errors because of the missionaries' ignorance of their language.[1] He chose instead to accept the offer of Fukuzawa Yūkichi to live in his house and teach his three children English although he knew it meant 'an entirely solitary life'. The government consented to this on condition that Shaw signed the regular agreement between Japanese and foreigners. Since this did not mention the Christian religion, Shaw's conscience was not disturbed. He refused any salary but required Fukuzawa either to subscribe a sum of money to charity or else take three children of poor parents to be educated in his school, a gesture to offset the general impression that all foreigners in Japan were a money-loving lot. He also taught moral science in Fukuzawa's school, *Keiō Gijuku*.[2] Shaw thus gained admission to a nationally famous school of three hundred boys from good families. To him the teaching of moral science meant 'Christian Science'. He met fourteen boys twice weekly, nine of whom wished for fuller instruction two evenings a week. At the same time he gave weekly public lectures on Christianity in a small rented room on a main street at which the attendance varied. He also attempted to answer the numerous attacks on Christianity in native papers by writing apologies for his faith for publication in the same journals.[3] He soon concluded that the evangelization of Japan could be achieved only through trained native ministers. The multitudes would listen to them, but not to foreigners.[4]

Wright also gave lectures on Christianity in another large public school in Yedo.[5] At the same time a little school in his own home grew rapidly. Within a year it had forty scholars of whom fifteen were boarders. At least two native Christian teachers were on the staff who were asked to 'consider it a blessed privilege to teach and preach the Gospel free of charge'. Secular

---

[1] *Mission Field*, June 1874, pp. 186–7, Shaw's 'Quarterly Report', Yedo, 21 Feb. 1874.

[2] Ibid., Sept. 1874, pp. 260–3, 'Quarterly Report', Yedo, 14 May 1874. Hineya, op. cit., p. 169.

[3] MSS. S.P.G. (D. 41, Asia, 1875), Shaw to S.P.G., Yedo, 17 May and 30 Aug. 1875. *Mission Field*, Dec. 1875, p. 357.

[4] Wright held the same opinion. *Mission Field*, June 1877, 422.

[5] Ibid., Mar. 1875, pp. 71–76, Wright to S.P.G., Yedo, 24 Sept. 1874.

school work, however, was paid for.[1] The school continued to grow. The Bible was taught every morning in Japanese. Scholars even brought their parents to the daily services. The standing committee in London appropriated funds for the benefit of the school.[2]

An S.P.G. school was founded at Kobe in June 1878 to teach boys English and Christian English literature, in opposition to the government high schools where the works of the free thinkers were generally used. Within a year the master, Mr. Hughes, had forty-one boarders and thirty day scholars.[3]

A Christian school founded by a native convert was in operation in 1882 near the Nakatsu mission. Here the parents of fifty scholars offered to build the school and Wright appealed to the S.P.G. for funds to build a chapel with it.[4]

Theological Schools. The need for native ministers had always been apparent. In 1877 the three missions co-operating in the United Church of Christ in Japan founded a Union Theological School in Yedo. Here twenty-five students came from the schools of the co-operating missions. By the end of 1882 the United Church had twenty-five churches with eighteen native pastors and 1,643 adult members.[5]

At Nagasaki in 1877 Maundrell of the C.M.S. started a theological school for special preparation for those who wished to become school masters, catechists, or ordained ministers. Only three students at first undertook to subscribe to the binding conditions of admittance. All had small means of their own so that the Society contributed only five dollars a month per person towards their expenses. Vice-Admiral A. P. Ryder, Commander-in-Chief of the British China Station, visited the school at its completion. His enthusiasm for the place and his conviction that each student should have a room to himself led him and his officers to contribute $100 towards a new wing

[1] Ibid., Dec. 1874, p. 363; Aug. 1875, pp. 353–8, Wright to S.P.G., Yedo, 4 Aug. and 27 Sept. 1875.

[2] S.P.G. *Missionary Reports*, 1876, Wright's report of 25 Dec. 1875; *Minutes* Standing Committee, No. 37, 1875–7, p. 151, 3 Jan. 1876.

[3] MSS. S.P.G. (D. 47, Asia, 1878), Foss to Bullock, Kobe, 4 June 1878; *Missionary Reports*, 1879, Foss, Kobe, 31 Mar. 1879.

[4] MSS. S.P.G. (D. 60, Asia 11, 1882), Wright, on home leave, to Tucker, 8 May 1882.

[5] Ritter, op. cit., p. 77. MSS. C.M.S. (C.J. 10–17), Piper to Wright, Yedo, 3 Jan. 1878.

when it should be needed.[1] Vice-Admiral Robert Coote was equally impressed with the little college when he visited Nagasaki in May 1880. He sent Maundrell $500 with the suggestion that the C.M.S. see the necessity of sending at an early date 'a thoroughly efficient helper in the educational department'.[2]

The C.M.S. also organized a theological school in 1882 for its own students in Osaka which kept them from co-operating in a joint Episcopal Divinity School which the American bishop, Williams, opened in his own home in Yedo after the Missionary Conference of 1878. Here Shaw and Wright of the S.P.G. were among the teachers and the English and American Missions worked together in training native catechists and priests.[3]

A fifth theological school was conducted by the Evangelical Alliance jointly with the Methodist Church of Canada which provided a four-year course of study. Its students also undertook evangelistic work.[4]

Hospitals. Between 1874 and 1883 the hospitals established by the United Presbyterian Church of Scotland (U.P.S.) at Tsukiji in Yedo and by the Edinburgh Medical mission at Niigata rendered a great service. Dr. Henry Faulds's hospital and dispensary at Tsukiji which the U.P.S. had bought for £600 in 1875, had from the start attracted numbers of in- and out-patients and medical students.[5] Faulds was asked by the Japanese government to become the physician of a Japanese prince at a salary of £1,000 a year besides a house built according to his own English design, on condition that he give up his mission work. He resisted such temptation and turned to establishing a medical school in connexion with the mission. But at the time of the cholera epidemic he was invested with official authority in his hospital. He organized a weekly course of lectures in which he himself dealt with physiology. His popular lectures on Darwinism were so successful as to require one of the largest theatres in Yedo. The Meiji government

[1] *Church Missionary Intelligencer and Record*, May 1878, pp. 320–2.
[2] Ibid., Oct. 1880, p. 646.
[3] MSS. S.P.G. (India and the Far East, 1879), Wright to Tucker, Yedo, 20 May 1879. *Mission Field*, Oct. 1883, 'Notes of the Month'. Verbeck, op. cit., pp. 152, 163. Tucker, op. cit., p. 97.   [4] Verbeck, op. cit., p. 168.
[5] MSS. U.P.S. (Letter Book 18), Extract from *Minutes* of Foreign Board Com. Meeting, 10 May 1875. Verbeck, op. cit., pp. 77, 111.

appointed him honorary Surgeon-Superintendent of its hospital in Yedo from March 1874 until he left Japan finally in 1885, a post he held in addition to his work as a medical missionary.

Faulds and his students carried on important medical research and introduced new treatments in his hospital. He performed many eye operations, devised a system of raised characters for the Japanese blind and aided, a group of native philanthropists in founding an asylum for the blind. Fees from his Japanese patients he gave to the mission. Faulds came into conflict with his Mission's Home Board over his determination to edit a journal concerned with medical science 'to aid the intercourse of Christian foreigners with educated Japanese'. His directors considered this incompatible with missionary work. Hence his resignation became inevitable. In accepting it, however, the Foreign Mission Committee of the U.P.S. recorded their appreciation of his 'excellent service'.[1]

In 1882 the annual attendance of 14,000 out-patients at Tsukiji had noticeably decreased owing to the opening of a number of free dispensaries in other parts of Yedo and to the introduction of rather high fees in the hospital itself.[2] The Japan Conference of the U.P.S., therefore, agreed to abandon it. Soon afterwards in 1883 the Board in Edinburgh decided to discontinue the medical department of its mission as of no further use.[3]

This decision was undoubtedly influenced by the speech of Dr. Theobald Palm, head of the Edinburgh Medical Mission at Niigata, when at the Osaka Conference in April 1883 he discussed the results of the widespread acceptance of Western medical practice in Japan. Government medical schools and hospitals employing foreign teachers, he said, had trained a disproportionately large number of medical students. Missionaries were no longer useful as medical instructors. Every village or hamlet had its doctor with some knowledge of Western medicine—sometimes to a surprising degree. Missionary

[1] Wilton, op. cit., pp. 27–28. Ritter, op. cit., pp. 78–79. MSS. U.P.S. (Letter Book 20, Foreign), Buchanan to Faulds, 29 Jan. 1881; Williamson to Faulds 7 Apr. 1881. For Faulds's research, etc., see p. 479–80.

[2] Verbeck, op. cit., p. 165. *Proceedings*, Osaka Conference, 1883, pp. 320–3.

[3] MSS. U.P.S. (Foreign Mission Letter Book 2), Extract from *Minutes* of Japan Local Conf. 21 Dec. 1882; Extract from *Minutes* of Foreign Mission Board Meeting, 31 July 1883.

co-operation with these native or government practitioners had proved impractical except through occasional travel in the country. Although in 1882 he had registered 2,950 patients in his dispensary and 151 in-patients in his hospital, and had seen 162 in consultation on visits to the country, and although several persons had come into the church through the hospital, he believed that the great need for medical missionaries in Japan had passed. They found themselves in competition with government hospitals, often directed by European doctors, or if not, staffed by well-trained Japanese physicians. They had arraigned against them Japanese national pride and anti-Christian prejudice which made Japanese patients 'prefer the paid services of one of their countrymen to putting themselves under obligations to one who is a foreigner and a Christian Missionary'. Palm maintained that in comparison with China, India, or African nations Japan had attained acceptable medical service.[1] Adverse opinion was not lacking at the conference and it seems probable that Palm's opinion was based on local experience.[2] Nevertheless he left Japan in 1884 never to return. His mission was taken over by the American Board of Foreign Missions the following year. Thus the two British Medical missions in Japan came to an end.

Although nothing was done at this time about the training of women nurses, the urgent need for a school to do this was recognized. The accepted practice of using untrained men in serious cases had proved utterly untrustworthy. Shaw pleaded for the appropriation of funds by the S.P.G. for this purpose with the support and promises of assistance by Sir Harry and Lady Parkes, as well as by the principal doctors, and chief surgeon, Dr. Manning, of Yedo.[3] All without success, as the Standing Committee of the S.P.G. in London believed the use of its funds for this purpose would be illegitimate.[4]

Publications. British missionaries participated in the trans-

---

[1] *Proceedings*, Osaka Conference, 1883, pp. 317–21. Verbeck, op. cit., p. 165.

[2] *Proceedings*, Osaka Conference, 1883, p. 324. The fact that 25,000 patients were treated in five mission hospitals and eight dispensaries indicated the Japanese continued to need their service.

[3] MSS. S.P.G. (D. 47, Asia, 1878), Shaw to Bullock, Yedo, 26 Oct. 1878. *Mission Field*, May 1879, pp. 17–18.

[4] MSS. S.P.G. (Japanese Letters Sent—I, 1874–1908), Bullock to Wright, 30 Apr. 1879.

lations of the Scriptures into Japanese and contributed to other scholarly publications which were basic to the teaching of Christianity. Although many were members of the Yokohama and Yedo committees set up in 1872 and 1876 to translate the New Testament, the work itself was done by Americans, mainly by J. C. Hepburn with revisions by D. C. Greene and S. R. Browne. The American Bible Society subsidized its translation and publication. Its completion was celebrated in Yedo on 19 April 1880. The British, however, contributed to the translation of the Old Testament at the request of the Permanent Committee which succeeded the Yokohama and Yedo committees in 1878.[1] P. K. Fyson of the C.M.S. was transferred to Yokohama to work on the translation of the Old Testament. He prepared the translation of Joshua and the Ten Commandments with notes. Piper (C.M.S.) translated the books of Jonah, Haggai, and Malachi, and wrote a *Japanese Reference New Testament*, an independent assignment for the N.B.S.S.[2] Two Japanese members of C.M.S. did the work on Numbers and Jeremiah. Piper and Warren assisted in the translation of the Book of Common Prayer as members of a joint committee of English and American Episcopalians. Piper, Warren, Maundrell, and Dening prepared other Christian works, e.g. *Scripture Catechism* (Warren), *Life of Christ* (Piper), and *Hymn Book* of ninety hymns (Dening).[3] Wright of the S.P.G. prepared in part a first translation of Isaiah and with Shaw brought out two or three Church and other catechisms.[4] McLaren of the U.P.C. not only taught Sacred History and Biblical Literature at the Union Theological School from its opening in 1877 but had ready for publication in 1882 an *Old Testament History* and was at work on a volume of critical introductions to the books of the Bible. Davidson prepared a translation of 2 Kings.[5] The translation of the entire Bible was published in February 1888; the B.F.B.S. and the N.B.S.S. having provided subsidies for the publication of the Old Testament.[6]

The secular writings of the British missionaries also deserve attention. Their letters, reports, and articles written for their boards in London or Edinburgh were often published in the

---

[1] Verbeck, op. cit., pp. 43, 94–98. Thomas, op. cit., pp. 118–19.
[2] Verbeck, op. cit., p. 123.   [3] Ibid., pp. 151–3.
[4] Ibid., p. 164.   [5] Ibid., p. 166.   [6] Thomas, op. cit., p. 119.

journals of the societies. Although the number of subscribers to
these papers for this period is unknown, many people throughout the English-speaking world must have gained their first
knowledge of Japan, its charm and its problems, through these
publications, given the then widespread interest in missions
and the general coverage of missionary activities by the journals.
For example: Warren's detailed descriptions of Osaka and
Kyoto explained the new Western economic and social influences as well as traditional Japanese life and religion in the
two cities.[1] His two articles on *A Pedestrian Tour of Japan* in 1876
gave accounts of Japanese villages, the growth of elementary
schools in rural areas, the hospitality of the country people, the
town and castle at Hikone on Lake Biwa, of Buddhist and
Shinto temples, and of pilgrims on their way to the shrines of
Tenshō Kōdaijin at Ise.[2] Dening's visit to the Ainu tribes in
the interior of Hokkaido brought an awareness of their existence
to many. And his *Journal* covering a later visit to these aborigines
as well as to Sapporo made observations about little-known
northern Japan.[3]

Political developments such as the Satsuma Rebellion and
economic facts such as the Japanese census were also reported
to the English people in a missionary journal.[4] And book
reviews included such works as Sir E. J. Reed's *Japan—its
History, Traditions and Religions*, Miss Isabella Bird's *Unbeaten
Tracks in Japan*, and Sir Rutherford Alcock's *Old and New
Japan*.[5] People interested in missions had access in this way to
the best current information about Japan, information seldom
given as thoroughly in *The Times* or the quarterly reviews.[6]

Some British missionaries also published articles in the
Transactions of the Asiatic Society of Japan proving their
scholarship. Thus Dening wrote on 'Modern Translation into
Sinico-Japanese' and his assistant, John Batchelor, 'Notes on
the Ainu' and 'An Ainu Vocabulary', while Dr. Henry Faulds,

---

[1] *Church Missionary Intelligencer*, Oct. and Dec. 1874, pp. 303–7, 364–73.
[2] *Church Missionary Intelligencer and Record*, May and June 1876, pp. 272–81,
348–52.
[3] Ibid., Jan. 1877, p. 55; May and June 1879, pp. 271–9, 351–5.
[4] Ibid., July 1879, pp. 385–92, Feb. 1879, p. 121.
[5] Ibid., Feb. 1881, pp. 72–87.
[6] Index, *The Times*, 1873–83, indicates a very limited and superficial interest in
Japan.

in addition to his interest in medicine, raised characters for the blind, and finger-prints, found time for 'Remarks on the Dojo' and 'Biological Notes',[1] as well as for a book *Nine Years in Nipon: Sketches of Japanese Life and Manners* (London, 1885) which was highly praised by journals in London.[2] Here again the work of the missionaries reached critical Western readers with fresh facts about Japan.

The Osaka Conference—Retrospect and Prospect

When in April 1883 representatives of the Protestant missions and Bible Societies in Japan assembled in Osaka for a general conference, Christianity appeared on the eve of a national conquest. The delegates viewed the achievements since 1873 with pride and the future with enthusiasm. Christianity had taken root in urban areas as part of the Westernization of Japan. Religious tolerance was increasing and would be complete when extraterritoriality was abolished—a political bargain early predicted by the evangelists.[3] A fine interdenominational spirit existed among the firmly entrenched denominational organizations and jurisdictions.[4] Many missions had co-operated in the translation of the Bible. The two Anglican Societies and the American Episcopalians had agreed upon the Japanese text of the Book of Common Prayer. The former had approved the appointment and joint support of a British missionary bishop. And the Scottish Presbyterians had formed a United Church with the American Presbyterian and Dutch Reformed Churches. But Warren of the C.M.S. pleaded at the Conference for still more concerted effort, more unity of action, a need which both missionaries and native clergy alike seriously confirmed.[5]

To the Protestant missionary achievements of the preceding decade, the founding of native churches, schools, and hospitals, the initiation of education for Japanese girls, and the translation of the Old Testament and other religious works, the British minority had made a proportional contribution. Some had

---

[1] *T.A.S.J.* vi. 183, 205; x. 206, 220; xii. 104.
[2] Wilton, op. cit., p. 28.
[3] MSS. C.M.S. (C.J. 10, 17), Piper to Wright, 9 July 1875.
[4] Inglehart, op. cit., pp. 57, 71. Thomas, op. cit., p. 139.
[5] Warren's speech at Conference, *Church Missionary Intelligencer and Record,* Nov. 1883, p. 671. Ritter, op. cit., p. 103–5.

also served as chaplains to the Western communities and through literary channels had helped to make Japan a reality for the people in England. Unlike the Americans they had had no part, however, in prison reform nor in the founding of the early Japanese Christian newspapers.[1]

From 1875 onwards men like Charles Warren had asked for more missionaries to meet the challenge of Japan.[2] The scarcity of British missionaries was considered shameful in contrast to the preponderance of British merchants and other business men in the Japanese cities. In 1883 Japan appeared unique among non-Christian nations in its need for more evangelists, not because it had fewer than other countries in Asia in relation to its population—it actually had more[3]—but because of the recent progress and still malleable state of the Japanese nation, there existed the possibility of making Protestant Christianity the national faith. G. H. Pole (C.M.S.) wrote from Osaka:

Tis incontrovertible

1. that this country is ripe for the Gospel in a sense that no other country in the world is at this moment

2. that it is manageable in size—its insulated position and its comparatively small population (as compared for instance with China) render its evangelization possible within reasonable limits

3. that the Japanese (and especially the Christian Japanese) are an active and energetic race, who are eminently qualified for missionary work in the neighbouring lands

4. that the speedy winning of this land for Christ would have an electric shock-like effect upon both Christendom and heathendom and would give an incalculable impulse to missionary effort throughout the world.[4]

At the Conference Warren asked for a united appeal to the churches then represented in Japan for specialists to do this work:

educationalists for the schoolroom, theological professors for the college, zealous evangelists for the open field, men of ripe Christian

---

[1] For American work in Japanese prisons see MSS. A.B.C. (16–4–1, vol. 2, *Japan Mission*, No. 121), Otis Cary's report on *Prison Reform*.

[2] *Church Missionary Intelligencer*, Feb. 1875, p. 45.

[3] In Japan one male missionary to every 400,000 people, in China one to every million. *Church Missionary Intelligencer and Record*, Nov. 1883, p. 671.

[4] Ibid., p. 678.

experience and thoroughly acquainted with the native character to guide and help the native churches to the higher Christian life.[1]

The period of preparation was over. Conditions for accelerated work were ripe. Fields for endeavour were defined. British missionaries looked ahead with expectations never yet to be fulfilled.

[1] *Proceedings*, Osaka Conference, 1883, p. 431.

XXI

CONCLUSION

BRITAIN and Japan, 1883. Twenty-five years had passed since fear of British might had forced Japan to open a few ports to Western trade. An influx of men, ideas, and commodities had fired Japanese ambition to lay the foundations of a modern state. The long-standing differences between the two island empires had lessened considerably. With Britain at the height of the world's financial and maritime power and Japan at one of the low points in her political and economic history, their confrontation could easily have ended as conqueror and conquered, had not each government determined to keep it otherwise. Sobered by her mistakes in China, Great Britain aimed to avoid their repetition in Japan while enforcing her unwelcome treaty to its limits and extending her commercial frontier as far as possible within them. Japan on the other hand was equally intent upon maintaining her independence at all hazards while mastering the techniques and political skills of the West. She aimed to meet its encroachments with its own weapons. Thus in the midst of Britain's profit-making and Japan's struggles for political and economic rebirth, the relation between the two nations became essentially that of instructor and instructed for the benefit of both. Even before the treaties and during their early years Japanese officials and scholars had chosen Britain as their nation's model. Recognizing the similarity of Japan's geographical relation to Asia to that of Britain's to Europe, and wishing to emulate British achievements, they set about making Japan the Britain of the East.

By the summer of 1883 the first stage in Japan's realization of that goal was coming to an end. In the past quarter of a century Japan had performed a near-miracle. She had replaced her military dictatorship with an oligarchy of samurai bureaucrats, theoretically subordinated to the will of her hereditary Emperor whom she had restored to supremacy and enshrouded in divinity. She had awakened to the benefits of foreign trade, abolished her ancient feudal order, and created a unified revenue system, a national currency, a conscript army, and the beginnings of an ironclad steam navy. She had opened mines, built factories, railways, telegraphs, lighthouses, a merchant marine, and shipyards, all at first on a small scale but with the vision of a greater future. While her government had financed these undertakings in the beginning it was now turning them over to private native capital but still prohibiting foreign investment. In the cultural sphere Japan was also promoting change. She had adopted the Western calendar, founded a vociferous press, promulgated a new penal code and law of criminal procedure,[1] established schools[2] and universities, studied Western science and medicine, and declared the toleration of Christianity, with little evidence, however, of any general acceptance of the Christian faith. Her population had grown from an estimated 30,000,000 to about 38,000,000.[3]

Encouraged by success and filled with self-confidence Japan was well on her way to greatness and recognition in the family of nations. She now felt ready to dispense with most of her Western instructors. She had hired them at great expense, defined their duties, but had made them responsible to her own officials, and for several years had been gradually terminating their contracts. In a burst of anti-foreign feeling and need for governmental economy she had determined to fill their positions with her own people, often against the judgement of her British advisers. Thus by 1883 most of the work begun by British officers, engineers, and doctors in naval training, lighthouses, the mint, the railways, hospitals and clinics was in the hands of Japanese.

By this time also the death of many of the leaders of Japan's first efforts at modernization—Yamanouchi Yōdō, Etō Shimpei, Saigō Takamori, Kido Kōin, Ōkubo Toshimichi, Date Muneki, and Iwakura Tomomi—had already made places for new men. And in late August 1883 Sir Harry Parkes, Japan's most severe but probably her most influential teacher of the ways of the West, was leaving to become Her Majesty's ambassador

---

[1] Here France was her chief adviser.
[2] In education the Americans wielded the major influence.
[3] Taeuber, op. cit., pp. 23, 27, 41. Japan took no census from 1852 until 1872 when she began the registers of her household population.

in China. As his successor was not expected to arrive in Yedo until late next year, a former secretary of the legation, P. H. le Peur Trench became chargé d'affaires. British influence and popularity had seriously declined, a fact recognized by the *Japan Weekly Mail* and attributed to Britain's obdurate opposition to Japan's desire to abolish extraterritoriality and to raise the tariff, and to the persistence of 'cold disdain' and 'unsympathetic imperiousness' in the attitudes of British diplomats and merchants towards the Japanese. In the light of Japan's achievements since 1858 the *Mail* argued, with reason, that these early treaty arrangements and British manners had outlived their fitness.[1]

There is no gauge by which to measure Britain's influence on this formative period of modern Japan. Relative to that of the other treaty powers it was dominant in economic matters from the opening of the ports, since British residents and British firms outnumbered those of any other Western nation. With the largest naval and military forces available the British chastised Satsuma and took the lead in bringing Chōshū to terms and won respect in both *han* for Western prowess. Politically Britain rivalled and opposed the influence of France during the last years of the *Bakufu* but in 1868 with Sir Harry Parkes as doyen of the diplomatic corps she was unquestionably the leading foreign adviser of the young Meiji government. In journalism, engineering, banking procedures, naval development, railway building, and the early adoption of Western medicine and other sciences the British led the way and supplied the greatest number of foreign employees of the Japanese Imperial government.

That this was true after the United States had taken the major risk in the opening of the Japanese ports and was likely to gain the most from them because of her push towards the Pacific, may be explained by the demands of the war between the States and its aftermath on American resources and initiative and by the proximity of Britain's already established position in China and India.

The breadth and depth of British influence, however, can certainly not be attributed to any great interest in Japan among British political leaders or within the British public at this

[1] *Japan Weekly Mail*, 13 Jan. 1880, p. 4; 30 July 1881, pp. 874–5; 20 Jan. 1883, pp. 38–39.

period. The addition of a few islands to an already extensive commercial frontier without undue cost and elaborate administrative machinery was of minor importance to the government in London. Contrary to Japanese fears and suspicions, that Britain aimed at their annexation before 1868 and afterwards that Britain would invade her territory as a countermove to any aggression upon it by Russia, H.M. Government desired no territory and wished to avoid embroilment in Japan's domestic affairs as well as conflicts with its rival powers in the East. So long as Japan's trade brought profits to even a few British subjects and expensive warfare was avoided, what happened in the little island empire north of the Shanghai emporium, which was to become the most powerful nation of the Eastern Pacific, mattered little to the great empire of the West.

After the arrival of Parkes as British plenipotentiary with increased powers to make policy on the spot, what Britain did was largely determined by the minister and his staff at Yedo and sanctioned in London. There is little or no evidence that the leading British statesmen of the period, Palmerston, Disraeli, and Gladstone, took much interest in Japan. Lord John Russell, when Foreign Secretary, showed some personal concern about British policy there during Alcock's difficulties but Sir Edmund Hammond, the Permanent Under-Secretary of Foreign Affairs, was probably the chief author of British policy in Japan until his retirement in 1873. At least in times of decision, Alcock, Winchester, and Parkes wrote directly and sometimes confidentially to him.

Neither did Parliament nor Britain's powerful daily press[1] concern themselves seriously with Japan except when the Treaty of Yedo was signed and when the British armed forces were involved in 1863 and 1864. The vast accounts of local developments and the problems of British representatives in the treaty ports which were printed in the Sessional Papers of Parliament up until 1870 and in the regular consular reports after 1865, were not easily accessible and aroused little public attention or parliamentary discussion. Through the great monthly and quarterly journals, however, British readers could gain some major information about Japan. These

[1] According to the index of *The Times* covering 1858–83 items on Japan were very rare—months, even years passing without any reference to the country.

periodicals reviewed in detail the occasional books written by British subjects or other Westerners who worked or travelled in the Japanese empire, adding their comments on British policy with suggestions for the future.[1] In general they viewed the Japanese people sympathetically, admitting the wrongs done to them by the treaty powers and marvelling at their progress after 1868 towards modernization but not without an awareness of the continuing corruption among Japanese officials and the dangers of over-hasty change in the country.[2] Such articles, nevertheless, in addition to a few papers on Japanese history, scenery, or artifacts in the same magazines and some news items and delightful pictures in the *Illustrated London News*,[3] formed a very small part of the current literature of the day and indicated only a minor public interest.

Furthermore, most British subjects had never seen a Japanese. Only a very limited number had personal contacts of any significance with the Japanese who came to England as members of diplomatic or trade missions or as students. These visitors were officially entertained and either publicly applauded for their courtesy and charm or regarded as curiosities. But opportunities for friendship and mutual understanding such as Professor Williamson gave to Baron Sakurai and other students were exceedingly rare.

Examples of Japanese art and art industry were brought before the British and European public at international exhibitions, first in 1862 when Alcock introduced his personally selected collection to the London exhibition and later, under Japanese government sponsorship, at Paris in 1867[4] and at

[1] e.g. Lawrence Oliphant, *Narrative of the Earl of Elgin's Mission to China and Japan*, 2 vols. (London, 1859) was reviewed in *Blackwood's Magazine*, Mar. 1860, pp. 255–77 and in the *Edinburgh Review*, Jan. 1860, pp. 96–118; Sir Rutherford Alcock, *The Capital of the Tycoon*, 2 vols. (London, 1863) in *Blackwood's Magazine*, Apr. 1863, pp. 397–413 and the *Edinburgh Review*, Apr. 1863, pp. 517–40; A. B. F. Mitford, *Tales of Old Japan*, in *Blackwood's Magazine*, Apr. 1871, pp. 460–2; Sir E. J. Reed, M.P., *Japan: Its History, Traditions, and Religions, with a Narrative of a Visit to Japan in 1879*, 2 vols. (London, 1880); Isabella Bird, *Unbeaten Tracks in Japan: An Account of Travels on Horseback, chiefly in the Northern District of Japan, including Visits to the Aborigines of Yezo and the Shrines of Nikko and Ise* (London, 1880); and Augustus H. Mounsey, *The Satsuma Rebellion, An Episode of Modern Japanese History* (London, 1879), in the *Quarterly Review*, Oct. 1880, pp. 305–36.

[2] *Edinburgh Review*, July 1872, pp. 259–69.

[3] e.g. *Illustrated London News*, 29 Oct. 1864 and 11 Jan. 1868.

[4] Sir Rutherford Alcock, *Art and Art Industries in Japan* (London, 1878), pp. 1–4.

London and Vienna in 1873.[1] A growing appreciation of Japanese silks, embroideries, lacquer, china, faience, bronzes, and enamels resulted, as well as a modest demand for them in the shops, museums, and private art collections. But as the previous tables have shown, Britain's imports from Japan to the end of 1883 never amounted to even one per cent. of her total import trade and at that time were on the decline, as were her almost equally negligible exports to the Meiji Empire. Japan was merely a distant outpost on the Far Eastern frontier of Great Britain's commercial empire, of minor interest to the British nation, offering no attractions as an additional colony to the Colonial Office, and no more than supplies and repairs to Britain's expanding steam fleet. It is therefore to the influence of a few individuals that the credit belongs for the British contributions to the early development of modern Japan.

Men of varied types and motives represented Britain to the Japanese people: diplomats and admirals of the fleet, merchants and journalists, engineers, doctors, scientists and evangelists, smugglers, debauched seamen, and unscrupulous adventurers. They were a cross section of their own island empire exhibiting both the virtues and vices of their national character in the certainty of their national strength. All were handicapped at first by gross ignorance of Japan and its culture in addition to their preconceptions of how to deal with orientals. Confined to the limited boundaries of the treaty ports and subject only to the jurisdiction of the consular courts, with few or no opportunities to meet or associate with the Japanese *élite*, they worked for their own ends: treaty enforcement, protection of British nationals, honest and dishonest profits,[2] the spread of Western learning and the Christian faith. They often operated at cross-purposes and were mutually hostile. To the Japanese the lives of many were strangely inconsistent with the faith they professed, but they all taught by example the varied ways of the West.

Although British subjects formed the largest part of the Western communities in the open ports their number was always

---

[1] F.O. 46/156, Watson to Granville, No. 174 and No. 176, Conf'l., Yedo, 23 and 24 Dec. 1872.

[2] For a contemporary recognition of dishonest profits see *Blackwood's Magazine*, Sept. 1872, pp. 385–6.

small, ranging from 18 in a total of 35 in Yokohama in 1859[1] to 1,094 in a total of 2,382 in all Japan in 1883.[2] That a few men in these little communities could direct and influence such basic change in the economy and institutional structure of a nation of over 30,000,000 in twenty-five years was only possible because the Japanese themselves wanted to observe and learn and adopt what the West knew for their own national purposes and had the leadership and capacity to do so.

Any appraisal of British policy and influence in Japan during this brief segment of history must rest on the contributions of these men in positions of authority in the local fields of British activity. Contemporary accounts of those troublesome British subjects who in their desire for gain or reckless adventure, exploited and deceived the Japanese and held in contempt a civilization not their own, seldom deal with specific individuals. And the culprits themselves naturally chose anonymity. But their callous, lawless behaviour frequently represented Britain or the West to the Japanese people and caused difficulties for those concerned with a just interpretation of the treaties and the development of Japanese friendship. It was always a factor in Anglo-Japanese relations at the treaty ports and must not be forgotten when the constructive work of the responsible men is here reviewed.

The representatives of the British government who had the responsibility for on-the-spot policy in Japan were, with few exceptions, men of integrity and intelligence, loyal servants of the Crown who sought to adhere closely to their instructions from London and worked hard at their posts. The two ministers, Rutherford Alcock and Harry S. Parkes, were unfortunately influenced by their previous experiences in China. Both believed in the necessity of the presence, threat, or use of force to secure the rights granted by the treaties which Japan had yielded in fear of Western power. Both, with some reason, had

---

[1] *Yokohama-shi Shi Kō*, vii. 8. Accounts of the number of British subjects in Nagasaki in 1859 vary from twenty-five to thirty. Paske-Smith, *Western Barbarians*, p. 256, and I have found no figures for the total Western community in the city for that year. Hodgson, his family, and one merchant were probably the only British residents in Hakodate in 1859.

[2] P.P. H. of C. 1884–5, lxxxi, 189, Cons. Report, *Summary of Foreign Trade of Japan for the Year, 1883*. The British controlled 98 of the 208 Western firms in the treaty ports.

little faith in the honesty or reliability of oriental officials. Both taught the Japanese that treaties once signed must be fulfilled and that military might is the most essential arm of a world power. And Parkes's ' "bullying" or at least haughty self-assertion' was said to have led the Japanese to conclude that 'the adoption of an arrogant attitude on their own part towards all European nations would be prudent and successful'.[1]

Alcock had the most hazardous task, being the first minister to try to enforce Britain's treaty with the Shogun whose limits of authority in Japan neither Alcock nor his superiors in London understood. He was subjected to the calculated duplicity of the *Bakufu* and the assaults of the anti-foreign or anti-*Bakufu* terrorists, denied contacts with the *élite* classes, and was often thwarted in his efforts at justice, by the defiant behaviour of British subjects. Yet by 1863 his analysis of the situation and recommendations for ending Japan's obstructions and opposition to the foreign treaties set the goals for British policy until after the Restoration. The latter included the repeal of the Tokugawa law justifying the murder of foreigners, the Mikado's public sanction of the treaties, the abolition of the Shogun's monopoly of foreign trade and provisions for the opposition daimyo to share in it.

As a result of Japan's increasing anti-foreign activities and expulsion policies following British efforts at the conciliation of the *Bakufu* through the London Protocol, Alcock led his government to approve a restricted use of force to punish the guilty daimyo whose actions the *Bakufu* obviously could not control, while supporting the Shogun as the sole treaty-making power from which Britain could exact the enforcement of her treaty rights. The success of British arms at Kagoshima and of the allied treaty powers against Chōshū seemed to justify Alcock's policy. It convinced the Japanese of the futility of challenging British power and won a rapport with the leading *tozama* daimyo, without disturbing Britain's tenuous relation with the Shogunate. Alcock thus cleared the way for the achievements of his successor, having also devised the Shimonoseki indemnity as a basis for bargaining with the *Bakufu* and having recommended that the new minister be given increased powers

[1] F.O. 262/254, Lytton (British Ambassador to France) to Derby, Paris, 27 Oct. 1874, encl. in F.O. to Parkes, No. 143, 10 Nov. 1874.

to act as local developments required without reference to London.

Before Sir Harry Parkes could reach Japan, Charles Winchester, the British chargé d'affaires, initiated two policies to which the incoming minister gave further support. He reinforced the efforts of the *Bakufu* to stop British merchants from supplying arms to private buyers and trading at unauthorized ports in defiance of the treaty. And he recommended that Britain send competent instructors in the arts of peace and war to help the Japanese in their desire for Western knowledge and to overcome their suspicions of British expectation of a military conflict.

Parkes came to his new post fortified with authority to act as Japanese conditions seemed to require and backed by the presence of British marines, infantry, and a portion of the fleet. He had already won the confidence of the British merchant communities in the Far East and he had the assistance of brilliant young men, especially Ernest Satow and Algernon Mitford, who were students of the Japanese language and culture. As interpreters and observers on many missions for their chief they established contacts with the agents of daimyo or the daimyo themselves and kept him informed of rumoured political developments and the daimyo point of view.

Between his arrival in Japan in June 1865 and the signing of the Tariff Convention just a year later Parkes had secured most of Alcock's objectives: the Mikado's public sanction of the foreign treaties, the Shogun's agreement to abandon his monopoly of foreign trade and to permit without restriction the trade of daimyo agents at the open ports. In addition the *Bakufu* chose to pay the Shimonoseki indemnity instead of opening Hyogo and Osaka immediately as Parkes had proposed, and promised to revise the tariff on a five per cent. basis, to revoke the exclusion policy so that Japanese could travel abroad for trade or study, to introduce numerous facilities and reforms for the benefit of foreign trade and shipping, and to establish a free mint. The free development of foreign trade now seemed assured. But the safety of foreigners was yet to be attained.

Meanwhile Parkes had recognized many factors in the current political unrest: the unquestioned sovereignty of the secluded Emperor over all Japan, the desire of the south-western daimyo for a share in the government, their opposition to the opening of Hyogo and Osaka as a means of attacking the Shogunate, their greed for economic and political power, and the divisions among them. He was equally aware of the weakness of the Shogun in his relations with the Court at Kyoto and the daimyo, his financial embarrassment, and his inability to protect foreigners. Parkes determined to remain neutral in the approaching contest for power and to urge a policy of accommodation on both the daimyo and the *Rōjū*, a policy endorsed by Lord Clarendon, then Foreign Secretary. Downing Street went further, however, in demanding the strict observance of the treaties and the protection of British subjects by the dominant party in every quarter. Parkes held to this neutral position in all his official correspondence and his instructions to his staff who dealt with both parties, in spite of the admitted sympathy of members of the legation for the daimyo party and the restoration of Imperial power.

The British Minister had no illusions about the unreliability of both parties in their relations with foreigners but he respected their general determination to settle their domestic problems without foreign intervention or assistance. He became convinced, however, of Japan's need for a strong central government in which the Mikado, the Shogun, and the daimyo would all have appropriate power, never hesitating to urge this on the *Bakufu* as the solution for its difficulties. He, therefore, rejoiced in the Shogun's return of administrative power to the Emperor and in the plan for a council of daimyo to work out with the Mikado, his ministers, and the Shogun the details of a new constitution. They were statesmanlike steps towards a peaceful realization of the strong central government he had long advocated. Parkes's hurried request to London on 28 November 1867 for a letter of credence to the Mikado merely indicated his support for these developments, not for the military coup to overthrow the Shogun, then planned by the Satsuma-Chōshū coalition in co-operation with the Court noble, Iwakura Tomomi, of which Parkes then knew nothing.

Although by late December the British were told of the intention of the daimyo party to seize power by force, Parkes and his staff were in no way involved in the actual overthrow of the Shogunate on 3 January 1868, nor were they kept informed about the early stages of the Mikado's new government. The

Shogun made his position clear, however. He told the foreign representatives of the treachery he had endured in his sincere effort to bring about a more representative government under the Mikado; he implied his willingness to fight the daimyo who had usurped power, and he asked the foreign representatives not to interfere in the settlement of Japan's governmental questions. Although Parkes and his diplomatic colleagues promised to be neutral, Satow and Mitford kept in secret communication with the men in power at the Mikado's Court, offering them valuable advice on ways of gaining international recognition for the Mikado's government and in proclaiming its support of the foreign treaties and amity towards foreigners.

The British legation was far from neutral in the confused weeks which followed Keiki's defeat by the Satsuma-Chōshū forces and the Mikado's declaration of war on the ex-Shogun. The new government's courageous fulfilment of all the foreign demands consequent upon Bizen's attack on foreigners in Kobe, and the Mikado's national proclamation, promising to uphold the foreign treaties and maintain friendship with foreigners in the face of strong anti-foreign factions throughout the country, led Parkes to give it his open support even before its conflict with the Tokugawa forces was decided. The British knew it was a government forced upon the people by a few militant *han* and that it faced the opposition of many daimyo but believed that, with the supremacy of the Mikado restored, it gave promise of becoming the strong central authority with which the foreign powers could work.

Parkes therefore aided the Meiji authorities in many ways, showing understanding of their difficulties and needs but never ceasing to impress upon them the military strength of Great Britain. He instigated indirectly the treaty powers' proclamation of neutrality during the civil war which handicapped the Tokugawa by preventing the delivery of its three previously ordered foreign-built warships. He was magnanimous when attacked by anti-foreign fanatics on his way to his first audience with the Mikado and secured as a result the Imperial annulment of the ancient law encouraging the killing of foreigners. His early presentation of his credentials to the Meiji Emperor strengthened the position of the Kyoto government in the eyes of the world. His intercession for clemency to the ex-Shogun saved the Imperialists from a dishonourable act and left Yedo uninjured to become the Mikado's future capital. Finally Parkes's consent to the withdrawal of the allied neutrality proclamation in February 1869 hastened the government's defeat of the rebels in the north that June.

With peace established Parkes turned to gaining the confidence of the Meiji ministers and to helping them build a modernized state, while never flagging in his zeal to enforce to the limit British treaty rights. As in the latter days of the *Bakufu* he was sympathetic and co-operative in bringing British instructors of high calibre to train Japanese naval officers. He encouraged the founding of the Imperial Naval College to establish British standards for officers, doctors, and engineers and supported the Meiji government in its request for training its cadets on British ships at sea and in English harbours.

Evidences of Sir Harry's initiative and help in Japan's construction of lighthouses, telegraphs, and railways are even more numerous. He was the liaison with the Board of Trade for the development of the lighthouse programme which brought to Japan the outstanding services of Richard Henry Brunton as chief engineer. And it was through Parkes that Brunton and his assistants communicated with the Meiji authorities and were enabled to progress with the construction of lighthouses during the civil war and northern rebellion. Between 1868 and 1876 Japan became indebted to Brunton and his British workmen not only for her early lighthouses but also for her first telegraphs, a system for drainage and road-making in Yokohama, the scheme for her pilot railway between Yedo and Yokohama, a standard map of Japan, and many public buildings.

Parkes was equally sympathetic to the Meiji government's financial plight. He was instrumental in securing its loan from the Oriental Bank which paid off its debt to the Société Générale promptly, thus preventing the loss of its valuable ironworks and shipyard at Yokosuka. True he introduced Horatio Nelson Lay to the Japanese ministers to help them get the much-needed railway loan. But when Lay tried to play a double role, acting as contractor for the loan for his constituents in London, while at the same time serving as commissioner for the Japanese government to raise the loan, and deceived the Japanese about floating the loan in London, Parkes never hesitated to lay these facts before his Foreign Secretary and to ask for advice in handling the matter. There seems to be no evidence that Parkes or Her Majesty's Government tried to defend Lay when the Japanese government cancelled his commission but the over-generous compensation granted Lay at the time is hard to explain. Fortunately the British Oriental Bank handled a loan satisfactorily in London for the building of Japan's first railway.

The British minister had been concerned with the instability of the Japanese currency since the Tariff Convention of 1866. He took a strong stand against the government's further debasement of the coinage and efforts to make its vast issues of paper money circulate on the same terms as coin in 1869, emphasizing the consequent destruction of confidence in the government and adverse effects on foreign trade. Some reforms followed. The mint promised in 1866 was established under the direction of a British army major. And in 1871 the government issued a new currency based on silver. But when the Japanese suddenly changed to a gold standard within a year against the opposition of Parkes and his foreign colleagues, Parkes lost interest and confidence in the mint and Japan's currency policies and hence opposed the Japanese yen as legal tender in Hong Kong.

Japan's early ventures in international commercial and expansionist policies in imitation of the West met different reactions from the British. Parkes encouraged her initiative in negotiating a commercial treaty with China in 1871 but later British efforts to alter its terms failed utterly. The British minister then took a strong stand against Japan's secret plans to invade aboriginal Formosa which was generally considered Chinese territory. He suspected her intentions and tried to forestall her expedition until she had informed China. In line with Thomas F. Wade, the British minister in Peking, Parkes foresaw the interruptions to British trade which would result from a Sino-Japanese war caused by Japan's aggression in 1874. He and Wade, therefore, prohibited British subjects and British ships from assisting either China or Japan. But neither the Japanese government nor Parkes could restrain their own nationals: the rampant Japanese troops sailed from Nagasaki in defiance of Yedo's orders; a British captain piloted the

Japanese Commander and his forces to Formosa and was later decorated for his services by the Mikado's Government.[1]

Parkes understood the inability of the Meiji authorities to control the discontented, militant samurai, their financial impotence to conduct a war, and their need to save face with their own people by some material compensation, once the expedition to Formosa had taken place. From Britain's point of view, however, Formosa under China's lax authority offered advantages to British trade which its acquisition by Japan might eliminate. On the other hand, a marked victory by China would make her more insufferable towards the West. The need for British arbitration seemed imperative. But neither China nor Japan trusted Wade's offers of 'good offices'. The Chinese ministers already knew of the exorbitant extension of British power in China which Wade had in mind as remuneration. And although Ōkubo probably knew nothing of Parkes's proposals for increased British privileges in the interior of Japan, he, in keeping with general Japanese policy, rejected foreign interference of any kind. It was not until war seemed imminent and neither party wanted it, nor was prepared, that Wade was able to effect a compromise. Japan felt triumphant; China reconciled. The British gained no material rewards but British trade could proceed as usual.

Parkes's sense of fair play and ability to resist the pressures of his own countrymen came to the fore when he prohibited the publication of Japanese newspapers by British subjects. He perceived the gross injustice of permitting Japanese journalists to criticize and undermine their own government through a foreign-controlled journal when prohibited from doing so in their own press.

He was equally objective—even sympathetic—in his handling of the problems of the Japanese authorities when confronted with their persecution and exile of native Roman Catholics near Nagasaki between 1867 and 1873. With great understanding of the support which the spread of Christian proselytism gave to the anti-foreign forces in Japan, the threat it posed to the Yedo government, and the dangers of the foreign powers siding with a section of the Japanese people against their government, Parkes rejected any demonstration against Japan's

[1] *Japan Weekly Mail*, 30 Apr. 1881.

N n

religious intolerance by the forces of the treaty powers in Japan and won among the protesting religious groups in England some understanding of Japan's difficulties arising from illicit proselytism. With Clarendon's approval he sought to deal personally with the Japanese ministers, thus securing some mitigation of the conditions to which the fanatical converts were subjected in their exile. He achieved an honest and co-operative relationship with the Meiji authorities and avoided in his interpretation of Japan's problems a hostile outburst in England against the Meiji government. With Japan's continuing interest in the adoption of Western standards he believed religious tolerance would develop if the illicit practices of foreign missionaries could be controlled. His faith was soon justified. As a result of public pressure on the Iwakura Mission, the Japanese statesmen realized that their desire for the abolition of extraterritoriality and increase of the Japanese tariff would never be possible as long as Japan denied her own subjects religious freedom. In consequence the anti-Christian edicts were quietly withdrawn and the exiled Christians returned to their homes. The British minister was at his best in his handling of this issue which was so highly charged with emotion in both the East and the West.

Sir Harry Parkes was an outstanding figure in the British diplomatic service in the Far East in the nineteenth century. Although he represented the traditional manner of all European governments in dealing with orientals under the early commercial treaties, he was sincerely interested in the development of Japan so long as Britain's treaties and agreements were not jeopardized. Granted that his outbursts of temper and arrogance often offended the sensitive, increasingly self-confident Japanese, the Meiji ministers sought and respected his advice from the beginning of their government. With the Emperor himself they never ceased to recognize and express publicly their appreciation of Parkes's support and help during the difficult early days of the Restoration.[1]

Parkes was penetrating in his judgements of men and political situations. An indefatigable worker himself and of his staff he was always determined to know the facts. Hence the reports written at his request by Satow, Mitford, Aston and others on

[1] F.O. 46/142, encl. in Parkes to Granville, London, 5 Oct. 1871. Dickins, op. cit. ii. 342–3.

the current economic, political, and social conditions in Japan, and their articles on Japanese culture and history in the *Transactions* of the Royal Asiatic Society of Japan are of inestimable value to any understanding of the Japan of his day.

In spite of occasional criticism in the English and Japanese press, and the open enmity of Edward H. House, the editor of the *Tokio Times*,[1] to Britain's free-trade policy and to Parkes himself, the British minister had the confidence and affection of the foreign community for the eighteen years he served in Japan. The leading citizens took pleasure from time to time in expressing their gratitude for his handling of their problems and his protection of their interests.[2] His home government recognized his worth when Queen Victoria invested him with the riband, badge, and star of a Knight Grand Cross of the Order of St. Michael and St. George.[3]

The desires of even a small number of British merchants for more markets and raw materials gave Britain the reason for her interest in Japan. In the light of Alcock's two volumes on the *Capital of the Tycoon*, however, the *Edinburgh Review* concluded in 1863 that the profits of a few British merchants in the Japanese ports brought no benefits to the British people as a whole and were not worth the cost and danger of Britain's involvement in Japan's domestic conflict. The editors recommended Britain's withdrawal.[4] But Her Majesty's Government would never consider such a step. How much the great merchant and shipping houses in Great Britain with branches in China and Japan influenced this decision and subsequent policy in Japan cannot be determined here. Letters from merchants or groups of merchants to British officials in England or Japan are seldom found in the diplomatic correspondence and the Parliamentary Papers of the period; none have been located in the great archives of Jardine, Matheson & Company; and the extant records of the Board of Trade and questionnaires to local chambers of commerce in Britain have yielded nothing. The consular reports and the fortnightly editions of the English newspapers in Japan with their market, shipping, and financial

---

[1] Ibid., pp. 302–4. *Tokio Times*, 6 Jan. 1877, 19 and 26 July 1879; 16 Aug. 1879, excerpt from *Osaka Nippo*.

[2] Dickins, op. cit. ii. 297–9, address of Foreign Community, Feb. 1882; pp. 344–6 farewell address 27 Aug. 1883.

[3] Ibid., p. 296.   [4] *Edinburgh Review*, Apr. 1863, 539.

intelligence for overseas consumption obviously convinced the government early that the growing trade with Japan was an increment to British commerce worthy of its protection and the attendant expense.

At least two British merchants, however, and probably many more who are nameless, exercised an important influence on British policy. Having established early contacts with the representatives of Satsuma and other *tozamo* daimyo, Thomas B. Glover and S. J. Gower, both agents of the Jardine, Matheson firm, learned of the desire of these *han* for a share in the foreign trade of Japan, their resentment of the Shogun's monopolies and restrictions, and the false statements of the *Bakufu* regarding the nature of the opposition to the foreign treaties. Glover became an unofficial liaison between the daimyo and the British officials. Thus consideration of the daimyo point of view was introduced into the making of British policy in London as well as in Japan. The Shogun's permission for the daimyo to trade at the treaty ports followed and British interest in their having a share in a central government under the Mikado resulted.

British merchants taught the Japanese both the honourable and dishonourable commercial practices of the West while supplying them with the machinery, ships, cotton and woollen yarn, and textiles needed to lay the foundation of their new economic order. They hastened the development of the profit motive and the rise of successful business men to social prominence in a society where formerly merchants were considered fourth-class citizens. They introduced new industries, new games, new foods and drinks, and created wants for luxuries of the West which greatly changed the frugal, simple, and artistic lives of many Japanese within access of the treaty ports. They assisted Japanese students in their desire for Western learning. Jardine's, for example, secretly helped them to get to England, provided them with hospitality there, and aided the Japanese government in selecting scientists to teach in Japan. Within the compass of British official policy and sometimes in defiance of it, it was the British merchants in conjunction with their Western competitors who introduced or abetted the most numerous changes in Japanese life and thought in this period.

The influence of British journalists on the modernizing of Japan was particularly obvious. They found Japan without a press and very limited channels for the circulation of news and opinion. In less than a decade after the publication in 1861 of the first English newspaper in Japan, men like Albert W. Hansard of the *Japan Herald*, John R. Black, and Charles Rickerby of the *Japan Gazette* and the *Japan Times* had taught the Japanese the importance of the press in making and leading public opinion. Japanese translations from these English newspapers and Japanese-language journals under Japanese or Western editors soon developed. Both the virtues and the vices of the traditional British press were eagerly adopted. In the name of freedom, responsible and irresponsible, incendiary criticism of the still insecure Meiji government made repressive press laws necessary and led to Parkes's prohibition of the publication of Japanese-language newspapers by British subjects. But nothing could restrain the rapid growth of a powerful Japanese press modelled on Britain's own Fourth Estate.

Equally important, if less spectacular, were the contributions of a few British teachers and doctors in both England and Japan to the study of science, the practice of medicine, and the administration of hospitals in Japan. Kikuchi Dairoku and Sakurai Jōji, two of Japan's greatest scientists, were among the distinguished Japanese students who were trained in English universities; a British scholar, Henry Dyer, became the first principal of the Meiji government's Engineering College and assembled a distinguished faculty which included the physicist William E. Ayrton and the chemist Edward Divers; a very early English text on chemistry served as the basis of Japan's first book on chemistry; and two British seismologists, John Milne and James Ewing, introduced the scientific study of earthquakes in Japan and invented instruments for recording and measuring their intensity.

Outstanding among British doctors was William Willis, the first surgeon on the British legation staff. His help in controlling the smallpox epidemic in Yokohama in 1864, his treatment of the wounded on both sides during the civil war, his introduction of humane consideration for wounded prisoners whom the Japanese had usually killed, and his leadership in reorganizing the military hospital at Yedo where he also introduced the teaching of septic surgery, won for him such respect that when the Japanese government chose the German school of medicine as its national model, Willis was invited to help establish and preside over the medical school and hospital at Kagoshima where his work is still recognized as a major contribution to the development of medical progress in Japan.

To Dr. Willis's assistant in the military hospital at Yedo, Dr. Joseph B. Siddall, the Japanese owed not only the introduction of hygienic methods in medical service but the establishing of a compulsory national vaccination system which he, in co-operation with Dr. George Newton, proposed to the Meiji government during the smallpox epidemic of 1870–1. In addition Dr. Newton, a naval surgeon, paid by the British, set up lock hospitals in the treaty ports for the control of venereal disease with the full approval of the Japanese authorities. Another distinguished British doctor, William Anderson, was chosen by the Japanese to direct their new Naval Medical College in 1873 where he trained Japanese to treat venereal disease and run the lock hospitals. Finally, but by no means of less significance, there was the work of two medical missionaries: Dr. Henry Faulds at the hospital of the United Presbyterian Church of Scotland at Tsukiji in Yedo and Dr. Theodore Palm, the head of the Edinburgh Medical Mission at Niigata. Faulds's innovations were numerous: operations on the eye, Lister's antiseptic system in surgery, the milk treatment for fevers, and the study of finger-prints which led him to conclude that they are sufficiently individual and changeless to be used to identify people. He founded a medical school in connexion with the mission hospital which attracted many students. The Meiji government sought his services, investing him with official authority in his hospital at the time of the cholera epidemic and appointing him honorary Surgeon-Superintendent of its hospital in Yedo from 1874 until his departure from Japan in 1885.

Other British missionaries and members of Bible Societies added to Japan's understanding of the West after 1869. To their schools for boys and girls and Bible classes, often held in their own homes, Japanese came to learn English while feigning an interest in Christianity. Here the evangelists exerted a permanent influence on the education of women in Japan and on the thought of many non-Christian natives while converting a few of them to their faith. British scholars assisted in the translation of the Bible into Japanese and their colporteurs helped in its distribution and that of other Christian literature to the Japanese people. Public lectures by British missionary scholars on Christian thought aroused in the early 1880s a wide interest and resulted in a rapidly rising number of converts. Through their own denominational theological schools or in those under the direction of several Protestant missions, the British missionaries contributed to the training of Japanese clergy and catechists who became leaders in a growing native Christian church.

Britain's policy in Japan was always ambivalent. She professed a desire for friendship with Japan when forcing her commercial treaties upon her but it was friendship on British terms. And even those terms were often violated by British subjects by practices inimical to Japan's welfare. Too frequently they claimed that what was good for Britain was good for Japan. Even so Japan chose Britain as her model in her endeavour to become a respected world power. In this effort she had the generous assistance and co-operation of British diplomats, leading merchants, carefully selected teachers, and scholars. Through observation, imitation, and intensive study her leaders and her people learned for better or worse the ways of the West and adopted them for their own national purposes. By 1880 the *Quarterly Review* could credit her with the 'glory' of 'having first among Asiatic States shown herself capable of marching in the forefront of civilization, almost abreast with the most advanced nations of the vaunted West'.[1]

That a small British community could exercise such far-reaching influence on Japan in such a short period was possible primarily because conditions in Japan were ripe for change and a group of able young Japanese leaders sought British guidance. But with Japan on the periphery of Britain's vast commercial empire and of relatively minor interest to the British government in relation to its world-wide responsibilities, Britain's extensive contributions to the development of modern Japan may well be considered unique in the history of international relations.

[1] *Quarterly Review*, Oct. 1880, p. 336.

APPENDIXES

APPENDIX I

THE TREATY OF YEDO[1]

TREATY of Peace, Friendship, and Commerce between Great Britain and Japan. Signed, in English, Japanese, and Dutch, at Yedo, August 26, 1858.

HER Majesty the Queen of the United Kingdom of Great Britain and Ireland, and His Majesty the Tycoon of Japan, being desirous to place the relations between the two countries on a permanent and friendly footing, and to facilitate commercial intercourse between their respective subjects, and having for that purpose resolved to enter into a Treaty of Peace, Amity, and Commerce, have named as their Plenipotentiaries, that is to say:

Her Majesty the Queen of Great Britain and Ireland, the Right Honourable the Earl of Elgin and Kincardine, a Peer of the United Kingdom, and Knight of the Most Ancient and Most Noble Order of the Thistle;

And His Majesty the Tycoon of Japan, Midzuo Tsikfogono Kami; Nagai Gembano Kami; Inouwye Sinano no Kami; Hori Oribeno Kami; Iwase Higono Kami; and Isuda Hauzabro;

Who, after having communicated to each other their respective full powers, and found them to be in good and due form, have agreed upon and concluded the following Articles:

Art. I. There shall be perpetual peace and friendship between Her Majesty the Queen of the United Kingdom of Great Britain and Ireland, Her heirs and successors, and His Majesty the Tycoon of Japan, and between their respective dominions and subjects.

II. Her Majesty the Queen of Great Britain and Ireland may appoint a Diplomatic Agent to reside at the city of Yedo, and Consuls or Consular Agents to reside at any or all the ports of Japan, which are opened for British commerce by this Treaty;

The Diplomatic Agent and Consul-General of Great Britain shall have the right to travel freely to any part of the Empire of Japan;

His Majesty the Tycoon of Japan may appoint a Diplomatic

---

[1] Lewis Hertslet, compiler, *Complete Collection of the Treaties and Conventions and Reciprocal Regulations at Present Subsisting between Great Britain & Foreign Powers*, 24 vols. (London, 1864), xi. 396–405.

Agent to reside in London, and Consuls, or Consular Agents, at any or all the ports of Great Britain;

The Diplomatic Agent and Consul-General of Japan shall have the right to travel freely to any part of Great Britain.

III. The ports and towns of Hakodadi, Kanagawa, and Nagasaki, shall be opened to British subjects on the 1st of July, 1859. In addition to which, the following ports and towns shall be opened to them at the dates hereinafter specified:

Nee-e-gata, or, if Nee-e-gata be found to be unsuitable as a harbour, another convenient port on the west coast of Nipon, on the 1st day of January, 1860;

Hiogo, on the 1st day of January, 1863.

In all the foregoing ports and towns British subjects may permanently reside. They shall have the right to lease ground, and purchase the buildings thereon, and may erect dwelling and warehouses; but no fortification, or place of military strength, shall be erected under pretence of building dwelling or warehouses; and to see that this article is observed, the Japanese authorities shall have the right to inspect, from time to time, any buildings which are being erected, altered, or repaired.

The place which British subjects shall occupy for their buildings, and the harbour regulations, shall be arranged by the British Consul and the Japanese authorities of each place, and, if they cannot agree, the matter shall be referred to and settled by the British Diplomatic Agent and the Japanese Government. No wall, fence, or gate shall be erected by the Japanese around the place where British subjects reside, or anything done which may prevent a free egress or ingress to the same.

British subjects shall be free to go where they please, within the following limits, at the opened ports of Japan:

At Kanagawa to the River Logo (which empties into the Bay of Yedo, between Kawasaki and Sinagowa), and 10 *ri* in any other direction.

At Hakodadi 10 *ri* in any direction.

At Hiogo 10 *ri* in any direction, that of Kioto excepted, which city shall not be approached nearer than 10 *ri*. The crews of vessels resorting to Hiogo shall not cross the River Enagawa, which empties into the bay between Hiogo and Osaca.

The distance shall be measured by land from the goyoso, or town hall, of each of the foregoing ports, the *ri* being equal to 4,275 yards English measure.

At Nagasaki, British subjects may go into any part of the Imperial domain in its vicinity.

The boundaries of Nee-e-gata, or the place that may be substituted for it, shall be settled by the British Diplomatic Agent and the Government of Japan.

From the 1st day of January, 1862, British subjects shall be allowed to reside in the city of Yedo, and from the 1st day of January, 1863, in the city of Osaca, for the purposes of trade only. In each of these 2 cities a suitable place, within which they may hire houses, and the distance they may go, shall be arranged by the British Diplomatic Agent and the Government of Japan.

IV. All questions in regard to rights, whether of property or person, arising between British subjects in the dominions of His Majesty the Tycoon of Japan, shall be subject to the jurisdiction of the British authorities.

V. Japanese subjects, who may be guilty of any criminal act towards British subjects, shall be arrested and punished by the Japanese authorities according to the laws of Japan.

British subjects who may commit any crime against Japanese subjects, or the subjects or citizens of any other country, shall be tried and punished by the Consul, or other public functionary authorized thereto, according to the laws of Great Britain.

Justice shall be equitably and impartially administered on both sides.

VI. A British subject having reason to complain of a Japanese must proceed to the Consulate and state his grievance.

The Consul will inquire into the merits of the case, and do his utmost to arrange it amicably. In like manner, if a Japanese have reason to complain of a British subject, the Consul shall no less listen to his complaint, and endeavour to settle it in a friendly manner. If disputes take place of such a nature that the Consul cannot arrange them amicably, then he shall request the assistance of the Japanese authorities, that they may together examine into the merits of the case, and decide it equitably.

VII. Should any Japanese subject fail to discharge debts incurred to a British subject, or should he fraudulently abscond, the Japanese authorities will do their utmost to bring him to justice, and to enforce recovery of the debts; and should any British subject fraudulently abscond or fail to discharge debts incurred by him to a Japanese subject, the British authorities will, in like manner, do their utmost to bring him to justice, and to enforce recovery of the debts.

Neither the British nor Japanese Governments are to be held responsible for the payment of any debts contracted by British or Japanese subjects.

VIII. The Japanese Government will place no restriction whatever upon the employment, by British subjects, of Japanese in any lawful capacity.

IX. British subjects in Japan shall be allowed the free exercise of their religion, and for this purpose shall have the right to erect suitable places of worship.

X. All foreign coin shall be current in Japan, and shall pass for its corresponding weight in Japanese coin of the same description.

British and Japanese subjects may freely use foreign or Japanese coin, in making payments to each other.

As some time will elapse before the Japanese will become acquainted with the value of foreign coins, the Japanese Government will, for the period of 1 year after the opening of each port, furnish British subjects with Japanese coin in exchange for theirs, equal weight being given, and no discount taken for re-coinage.

Coins of all description (with the exception of Japanese copper coin), as well as gold and silver uncoined, may be exported from Japan.

XI. Supplies for the use of the British navy may be landed at Kanagawa, Hakodadi, and Nagasaki, and stored in warehouses, in the custody of an officer of the British Government, without the payment of any duty; but if any such supplies are sold in Japan, the purchaser shall pay the proper duty to the Japanese authorities.

XII. If any British vessel be at any time wrecked or stranded on the coasts of Japan, or be compelled to take refuge in any port within the dominions of the Tycoon of Japan, the Japanese authorities, on being apprised of the fact, shall immediately render all the assistance in their power; the persons on board shall receive friendly treatment, and be furnished, if necessary, with the means of conveyance to the nearest Consular station.

XIII. Any British merchant vessel arriving off one of the open ports of Japan, shall be at liberty to hire a pilot to take her into port. In like manner, after she has discharged all legal dues and duties, and is ready to take her departure, she shall be allowed to hire a pilot to conduct her out of port.

XIV. At each of the ports open to trade, British subjects shall be at full liberty to import from their own or any other ports, and sell there, and purchase therein, and export to their own or any other ports, all manner of merchandize, not contraband, paying the duties thereon, as laid down in the tariff annexed to the present Treaty, and no other charges whatsoever. [See Regulations, Page 564.]

With the exception of munitions of war, which shall only be sold to the Japanese Government and foreigners, they may freely buy from Japanese, and sell to them, any articles that either may have for sale, without the intervention of any Japanese officers in such purchase or sale, or in making or receiving payment for the same; and all classes of Japanese may purchase, sell, keep, or use any articles sold to them by British subjects.

XV. If the Japanese Custom-house officers are dissatisfied with the value placed on any goods by the owner, they may place a value thereon, and offer to take the goods at that valuation. If the owner refuses to accept the offer he shall pay duty on such valuation. If the offer be accepted by the owner, the purchase-money shall be paid to him without delay, and without any abatement or discount.

XVI. All goods imported into Japan by British subjects, and which have paid the duty fixed by this Treaty, may be transported by the Japanese into any part of the Empire without the payment of any tax, excise, or transit duty whatever.

XVII. British merchants who may have imported merchandize into any open port in Japan, and paid duty thereon, shall be entitled, on obtaining from the Japanese Custom-house authorities a certificate stating that such payments has been made, to re-export the same, and land it in any other of the open ports without the payment of any additional duty whatever.

XVIII. The Japanese authorities at each port will adopt the means that they may judge most proper for the prevention of fraud or smuggling.

XIX. All penalties enforced, or confiscations made under this Treaty, shall belong to, and be appropriated by, the Government of His Majesty the Tycoon of Japan.

XX. The Articles for the regulation of trade which are appended to this Treaty, shall be considered as forming a part of the same, and shall be equally binding on both the Contracting Parties to this Treaty, and on their subjects.

The Diplomatic Agent of Great Britain in Japan, in conjunction with such person or persons as may be appointed for that purpose by the Japanese Government, shall have power to make such rules as may be required to carry into full and complete effect the provisions of this Treaty, and the provisions of the Articles regulating trade appended thereto.

XXI. This Treaty being written in the English, Japanese, and Dutch languages, and all the versions having the same meaning and intention, the Dutch version shall be considered the original; but it is understood that all official communications addressed by the Diplomatic and Consular Agents of Her Majesty the Queen of Great Britain to the Japanese authorities, shall henceforward be written in English. In order, however, to facilitate the transaction of business, they will, for a period of 5 years from the signature of this Treaty, be accompanied by a Dutch or Japanese version.

XXII. It is agreed that either of the High Contracting Parties to this Treaty, on giving 1 year's previous notice to the other, may demand a revision thereof, on or after the 1st of July, 1872, with a view to the insertion therein of such amendments as experience shall prove to be desirable.

XXIII. It is hereby expressly stipulated that the British Government and its subjects will be allowed free and equal participation in all privileges, immunities, and advantages, that may have been, or may be hereafter, granted by His Majesty the Tycoon of Japan to the Government or subjects of any other nation.

XXIV. The ratification of this Treaty, under the hand of Her Majesty the Queen of Great Britain and Ireland, and under the name and seal of His Majesty the Tycoon of Japan, respectively, shall be exchanged at Yedo, within a year from this day of signature.

In token whereof, the respective Plenipotentiaries have signed and sealed this Treaty.

Done at Yedo, this 26th day of August, 1858, corresponding to the Japanese date the 18th day of the 7th month of the 5th year of Ansei Tsut sinonye mma.

(L.S.) ELGIN and KINCARDINE.

(L.S.)

MIDZUO TSIKFOGONO KAMI.
NAGAI GEMBANO KAMI.
INOUWYE SINANO NO KAMI.
HORI ORIBENO KAMI.
IWASE HIGONO KAMI.
ISUDA HAUZABRO.[1]

(ANNEX.) *Regulations under which British Trade is to be conducted in Japan*

REGULATION I. Within 48 hours (Sundays excepted) after the arrival of a British ship in a Japanese port, the captain or commander shall exhibit to the Japanese Custom-house authorities the receipt of the British Consul, showing that he has deposited all the ship's papers, the ship's bills of lading, &c., at the British Consulate, and he shall then make an entry of his ship, by giving a written paper, stating the name of the ship, and the name of the port from which she comes, her tonnage, the name of her captain or commander, the names of her passengers (if any), and the number of her crew, which paper shall be certified by the captain or commander to be a true

---

[1] The correct Romanization of these Japanese signatures is:
Mizuno Chikugo no Kami
Nagai Gemba no Kami
Inoue Shinano no Kami
Hori Oribe no Kami
Iwase Higo no Kami
Tsuda Hanzaburō.

statement, and shall be signed by him; he shall, at the same time, deposit a written manifest of his cargo, setting forth the marks and numbers of the packages and their contents, as they are described in his bills of lading, with the names of the person or persons to whom they are consigned. A list of the stores of the ship shall be added to the manifest. The captain or commander shall certify the manifest to be a true account of all the cargo and stores on board the ship, and shall sign his name to the same.

If any error is discovered in the manifest, it may be corrected within 24 hours (Sundays excepted) without the payment of any fee, but for any alteration or post entry to the manifest made after that time, a fee of 15 dollars shall be paid.

All goods not entered on the manifest shall pay double duties on being landed.

Any captain or commander that shall neglect to enter his vessel at the Japanese Custom-house within the time prescribed by this regulation, shall pay a penalty of 60 dollars for each day that he shall so neglect to enter his ship.

II. The Japanese Government shall have the right to place Custom-house officers on board of any ship in their ports (men-of-war excepted). All Custom-house officers shall be treated with civility, and such reasonable accommodation shall be allotted to them as the ship affords.

No goods shall be unladen from any ship between the hours of sunset and sunrise, except by special permission of the Custom-house authorities; and the hatches, and all other places of entrance into that part of the ship where the cargo is stowed, may be secured by Japanese officers between the hours of sunset and sunrise, by fixing seals, locks, or other fastenings; and if any person shall, without due permission, open any entrance that has been so secured, or shall break or remove any seal, lock, or other fastening that has been affixed by the Japanese Custom-house officers, every person so offending shall pay a fine of 60 dollars for each offence.

Any goods that shall be discharged, or attempted to be discharged, from any ship, without having been duly entered at the Japanese Custom-house as hereinafter provided, shall be liable to seizure and confiscation.

Packages of goods made up with an intent to defraud the revenue of Japan, by concealing therein articles of value which are not set forth in the invoice, shall be forfeited.

If any British ship shall smuggle, or attempt to smuggle, goods in any of the non-opened harbours of Japan, all such goods shall be forfeited to the Japanese Government, and the ship shall pay a fine of 1,000 dollars for each offence.

Vessels needing repairs may land their cargo, for that purpose, without the payment of duty. All goods so landed shall remain in charge of the Japanese authorities, and all just charges for storage, labour, and supervision, shall be paid thereon. But if any portion of such cargo be sold, the regular duties shall be paid on the portion so disposed of.

Cargo may be transshipped to another vessel in the same harbour without payment of duty, but all transshipments shall be made under the supervision of Japanese officers, and after satisfactory proof has been given to the Custom-house authorities of the *bonâ fide* nature of the transaction, and also under a permit to be granted for that purpose by such authorities. The importation of opium being prohibited, any British vessel coming to Japan for the purposes of trade, and having more than 3 catties weight of opium on board, the surplus quantity may be seized and destroyed by the Japanese authorities; and any person or persons smuggling, or attempting to smuggle opium, shall be liable to pay a fine of 15 dollars for each catty of opium so smuggled or attempted to be smuggled.

III. The owner, or consignee of any goods who desires to land them, shall make an entry of the same at the Japanese Custom-house. The entry shall be in writing, and shall set forth the name of the person making the entry, and the name of the ship in which the goods were imported, and the marks, numbers, packages, and the contents thereof, with the value of each package extended separately in one amount, and at the bottom of the entry shall be placed the aggregate value of all the goods contained in the entry. On each entry, the owner or consignee shall certify in writing that the entry then presented exhibits the actual cost of the goods, and that nothing has been concealed whereby the Customs of Japan would be defrauded, and the owner or consignee shall sign his name to such certificate.

The original invoice or invoices of the goods so entered shall be presented to the Custom-house authorities, and shall remain in their possession until they have examined the goods contained in the entry.

The Japanese officers may examine any or all the packages so entered, and for this purpose may take them to the Custom-house; but such examination shall be without expense to the importer or injury to the goods; and, after examination, the Japanese shall restore the goods to their original condition in the packages (so far as may be practicable), and such examination shall be made without any unreasonable delay.

If any owner or importer discovers that his goods have been damaged on the voyage of importation before such goods have been delivered to him, he may notify the Custom-house authorities of such damage, and he may have the damaged goods appraised by two or more competent and disinterested persons, who, after due examination, shall make a certificate, setting forth the amount per cent. of damage on each separate package, describing it by its mark and number, which certificate shall be signed by the appraisers, in presence of the Custom-house authorities, and the importer may attach the certificate to his entry, and make a corresponding deduction from it. But this shall not prevent the Custom-house authorities from appraising the goods in the manner provided in Article XV of the Treaty to which these Regulations are appended.

After the duties have been paid, the owner shall receive a permit, authorizing the delivery to him of the goods, whether the same are at the Custom-house or on shipboard.

All goods intended to be exported shall be entered at the Japanese Custom-house before they are placed on shipboard. The entry shall be in writing, and shall state the name of the ship by which the goods are to be exported, with the marks and numbers of the packages, and the quantity, description, and value of their contents. The exporter shall certify, in writing, that the entry is a true account of all the goods contained therein, and shall sign his name thereto.

Any goods that are put on board of a ship for exportation before they have been entered at the Custom-house, and all packages which contain prohibited articles, shall be forfeited to the Japanese Government.

No entry at the Custom-house shall be required for supplies for the use of ships, their crews and passengers, nor for the clothing, &c., of passengers.

IV. Ships wishing to clear shall give 24 hours' notice at the Custom-house, and at the end of that time they shall be entitled to their clearance, but if it be refused, the Custom-house authorities shall immediately inform the captain or consignee of the ship of the reason why the clearance is refused; and they shall also give the same notice to the British Consul.

British ships of war shall not be required to enter or clear at the Custom-house, nor shall they be visited by Japanese Custom-house or police officers.

Steamers conveying the mails of Great Britain may enter and clear on the same day, and they shall not be required to make a manifest, except for such passengers and goods as are to be landed in Japan. But such steamers shall, in all cases, enter and clear at the Custom-house.

Whale-ships touching for supplies, or ships in distress, shall not be required to make a manifest of their cargo; but if they subsequently wish to trade, they shall then deposit a manifest, as required in Regulation I.

The word 'ship', wherever it occurs in these Regulations, or in the Treaty to which they are attached, is to be held as meaning ship, barque, brig, schooner, sloop, or steamer.

V. Any person signing a false declaration or certificate, with the intent to defraud the revenue of Japan, shall pay a fine of 125 dollars for each offence.

VI. No tonnage duties shall be levied on British ships in the ports of Japan, but the following fees shall be paid to the Japanese Custom-house authorities:

For the entry of a ship, 15 dollars; for the clearance of a ship, 7 dollars; for each permit, $1\frac{1}{2}$ dollar; for each bill of health, $1\frac{1}{2}$ dollar; for any other document, $1\frac{1}{2}$ dollar.

VII. Duties shall be paid to the Japanese Government, on all goods landed in the country, according to the following Tariff.

CLASS 1.—All articles in this class shall be free of duty:—viz.: Gold and silver, coined or uncoined; wearing apparel, in actual use; household furniture and printed books, not intended for sale, but the property of persons who come to reside in Japan.

2. A duty of 5 per cent. shall be paid on the following articles:— All articles used for the purpose of building, rigging, repairing, or fitting out of ships; whaling gear of all kinds; salted provisions of all kinds; bread and bread stuffs; living animals of all kinds; coals; timber for building houses; rice; paddy; steam machinery; zinc; lead; tin; raw silk; cotton and woollen manufactured goods.

3. A duty of 35 per cent. shall be paid on all intoxicating liquors, whether prepared by distillation, fermentation, or in any other manner.

4. All goods not included in any of the preceding classes shall pay a duty of 20 per cent.

All articles of Japanese production, which are exported as cargo, shall pay a duty of 5 per cent., with the exception of gold and silver coin, and copper in bars.

Rice and wheat, the produce of Japan, shall not be exported from Japan as cargo, but all British subjects resident in Japan, and British ships for their crews and passengers, shall be furnished with sufficient supplies of the same.

Foreign grain, brought into any open port of Japan in a British ship, if no part thereof has been landed, may be re-exported without hindrance.

The Japanese Government will sell, from time to time, at public auction, any surplus quantity of copper that may be produced.

Five years after the opening of Kanagawa, the import and export duties shall be subject to revision, if either the British or Japanese Government desires it.

(L.S.) ELGIN and KINCARDINE.

(L.S.)

MIDZUO TSIKFOGONO KAMI.
NAGAI GEMBANO KAMI.
INOUWYE SINANO NO KAMI.
HORI ORIBENO KAMI.
IWASE HIGONO KAMI.
ISUDA HAUZABRO.[1]

---

[1] See p. 560.

APPENDIX II

Two of the Three Articles by Ernest Satow on English Policy 1866

JAPAN TIMES

A Commercial, Political and General Weekly Newspaper

Vol. 1—No. 28 YOKOHAMA, Friday March 16th, 1866

YOKOHAMA, 16th March, 1866.

ACCUSTOMED as are the foreign merchants of Yokohama to see in their port vessels of war flying the flag of the 'morning sun'—the arrival of a merchant steamer, with the private ensign of an independent Daimio at the main, still cannot occur at present without causing some slight degree of excitement. Such an occurrence has taken place within the last few days. A vessel, belonging to the Prince of Satsuma, which left Hakodate some months since on a surveying expedition to the islands of Sodo and Oki on the north-west coast of Japan, dropped her anchor in this harbour last week and the Captain, in accordance with Art. XIV of our Treaty, proposed to sell European merchants, certain Japanese produce which he had on board.

The native authorities refused to allow the officers and crew to land, and as a necessary consequence the trade intended to be done was likewise prohibited. Here is certainly a case in which the Chamber of Commerce might with good reason lay a charge against the Japanese Government of hindering our commercial intercourse with the agents of a Daimio, appeal to the Article in the Treaty to which we have referred, and call on the Foreign Representatives for their interference. For reasons which we will proceed to state, it is unlikely, however, that such remonstrance would have any effect.

The fact is, as may be learned from blue-books, that in previous years the Japanese Government have been requested to take some measure against the entrance of Daimios' retainers into this settlement, because, in consequence of the unfortunate occurrence during our early intercourse with the country in which the two-sworded class played so large a part, they were generally supposed to entertain hostility and dangerous designs against foreigners. The native authorities, having thus been requested in general terms to take precautions have adopted measures which seem to them sufficient, and cannot be reasonably called upon now to abrogate their own regulations hurriedly and to suit a particular case, and we cannot but acknowledge that, if our intercourse with Daimios' trading agents is circumscribed and subject to espionage, we have ourselves to thank for it in the main.

Far from wishing, however, to accuse the Foreign Representatives of having neglected the interests of their countrymen, we maintain, that in view of our peculiar relations with this country, no other course was open to them. It must be borne in mind that the Tycoon, though claiming to conduct the Government of Japan, is in reality, or was at the time when the first Treaties were made, only the head of a Confederation of Princes, and to arrogate to himself the title of ruler in a country, of which only about half was subject to his jurisdiction, was a piece of extraordinary presumption on his part. It cannot, justly, be matter of wonder that the independent Daimios, already possessing many grounds for dissatisfaction with the Tycoon, should refuse their approval to measures in which they were never even consulted. The natural consequence was a strongly manifested hostility on their part, which gave rise to apprehensions in the mind of the Tycoon's Ministers, as well as of the Foreign Representatives, of indefinable dangers. The entrance of Daimios' retainers into the open ports was therefore strictly prohibited.

As time wore on, the Daimios became alive to the advantages of Foreign trade, and by pressure on the Tycoon, obtained the great concession of a privilege to purchase arms, subject always to the supervision of Yedo officials. This supervision, stigmatized rather unfairly as espionage, was necessary to secure to the Tycoon the acknowledgement of the right which he possessed, according to Treaty, of being sole purchaser of munitions of war (Art. XIV.) and, as it was foreigners who, in the first place desired the total exclusion of Daimios' retainers, they cannot fairly grumble at the present partial restriction of free intercourse with the class whom they had themselves [*sic*] should be entirely excluded from the open ports.

But from being purchasers of arms only, the Daimios have gradually come to be desirous of selling the produce collected in their provinces, doubtless in order to pay for their previous investments and their position in relation to foreign merchants is entirely changed. It is not intended to discuss the policy of erecting these princes into gigantic monopolists, to the exclusion of legitimate traders, from amongst their own subjects; but, if it be considered a desirable thing to let them bring goods to market, let us endeavour to arrange the matter to the satisfaction of all parties concerned.

It is a well ascertained fact that the so-called hostile Daimios are now alive to the advantages of foreign commerce and intercourse with Europeans and it is even alleged that some of them wish to open ports in their own territories. By all means let it be done, so far as is convenient. But consideration will show that it would be impossible, and useless if possible, to have a port in the territory of every independent Daimio, for their number amounts to nearly twenty, far beyond the number of ports required for the development of trade: one or two would perhaps suffice, and it is allowed that the opening of these would be a very useful measure.

So long, however, as we continue to have a treaty with the Tycoon only, and not with Japan, this will never take place. At present the Daimios are not bound by the Treaty, and have no interest in it whatever; they are only called on to acknowledge the existence of treaties with the Tycoon, and to abstain from obstructing their execution.

We gravely and seriously advocate a radical change. What we want is not a Treaty with a single potentate, but one binding on and advantageous to every one in the country. We must give up the worn-out pretence of acknowledging the Tycoon to be sole ruler of Japan, and take into consideration the existence of other coordinate powers. In other words we must supplement or replace our present treaties, by treaties with the CONFEDERATE DAIMIOS of Japan.

There is every reason to believe that a proposal to discuss the matter on such a basis would not only prove acceptable to the princes, but also to the harassed and perplexed Cabinet of the Tycoon, which would be relieved from many of its present embarrassments by the participation of the Daimios in the advantages of trade. It would not be a political revolution, deposing the Tycoon from the position which he arrogated as head of the Government, for that has taken place already. It would be merely recognizing the actual state of affairs.

That the treaties at present in force are not destined to be permanent every one is by this time convinced. We have lately seen the Tycoon acknowledge by his actions that without the sanction of the Mikado they would never be carried out or be recognized by the Daimios, and from this men have naturally and reasonably concluded the Mikado to be the superior. A notion however, has arisen out of this that a Treaty with the Mikado would be a good thing. No doubt to a treaty made with the Daimios, the sanction of the titular Emperor would be necessary, or at least desirable, but he could not enter into a treaty himself, for he would be unable to enforce its observance.

Between the present time and Jan. 1st, 1868, on which date Hiogo is to be opened, there is ample time for negotiations with the Daimios, for discussing every point hitherto in dispute, for settling what new ports shall be opened and in which Daimios' territories, and for establishing our relations generally on a secure and permanent footing. Unless some arrangement is come to before that date, we fear that we shall not enter on residence at the port without resort to coercion and bloodshed. If we would avert such misfortunes, we must treat with the Daimios, for they are responsible rulers of the country equally with the Tycoon.

The Gods themselves cannot fight against the Inevitable and, though somewhat reluctantly, we have no doubt that the Tycoon's cabinet will yield, with very slight pressure, to the conviction that Art. XIV. of the Treaty with their master cannot longer be treated as a dead letter. That Article affirms that:—

'At each of the ports open to trade, British subjects shall be at full liberty to import from their own or other ports, and sell there and purchase therein and export to their own or any other ports, all manner of merchandize, not contraband, paying the duties thereon as laid down in the Tariff annexed to the present Treaty and no other charges whatsoever.'

'With the exception of munitions of war, which shall only be sold to the Japanese Government (i.e. what was then supposed to be Japanese Government:—the Government of the Tycoon) and foreigners, they may freely buy from Japanese and sell to them, any articles that either may have for sale, without intervention of any Japanese officers in such purchase or sale, or in making or receiving payment for the same; and all classes of Japanese may purchase, sell, keep or use any articles sold to them by British subjects.'

Not only has the observation of this article been always consistently refused by the Tycoon's Government, which is natural enough, but we ourselves have been,—ever since the panics in 1862–3, when we requested the Yedo authorities to exclude from the foreign settlement of Yokohama the whole class of Daimios' retainers—thereby very foolishly playing into the hands of the Ministers of the one powerful prince with whom we had made a treaty as titular sovereign of Japan. Recent events have proved that we were in error in assigning to this great Daimio such a position of sovereignty and, as we are certain that the measure of reform we advocate, though a sweeping one, will have the great and unusual advantage of being received with favour by all parties interested— by the Tycoon and his cabinet, as relieving them from domestic trouble and jealousies, by the Daimios as opening to them new springs of wealth, by the people of the country and by foreign traders for the same reason—therefore we earnestly commend the matter to the 'best consideration,' of the Representatives of the Treaty powers, convinced that, not only will the measure be of immense benefit to the country, but that a great stimulus will be also given to our own rising trade with Japan.

THE

JAPAN TIMES

A Commercial, Political and General Weekly Newspaper

Vol. 1—No. 36   YOKOHAMA, Saturday, May 19th, 1866

YOKOHAMA, 19th May, 1866.

WHILE advocating, lately, the abrogation of the existing Treaty with the TYCOON and the substitution of a more equitable and comprehensive convention with the MIKADO and the Confederated Daimios of Japan, we have hitherto contented ourselves with stating the broader arguments in favour of the measure. The idea is a bold and a startling one and it was necessary that the minds of those whose interest in the matter we wished to arouse, should be gradually accustomed to it. The arguments we have to bring forward against the existing state of things are, besides, so numerous that it was impossible to adduce them all within the limited space of one or two articles. Our intention at present, is to go more into particulars than heretofore, and, taking the provisions of the existing Treaty in detail—to strengthen the position we have thought it right to take up, in opposition to the continuance of the present arrangements, by showing how completely wrong was the TYCOON in taking the first step of signing in a character which did not belong to him—how utterly incapable he has since proved himself to be of carrying out his own engagements—and finally, how generally insufficient are the Treaty and Trade Regulations for commercial as well as international purposes.

On the first two points we have already dilated to some extent, though we have still something to [sic] say with regard to them—but it is more particularly to the consideration of the subject from the third point of view that we wish to direct our readers attention to-day.

Students of Japanese politics and literature may, perhaps, accuse us of pedantry in remarking now, that the title of 'TYCOON' is one to which the MIKADO alone has right. But there are many circumstances which prevent the bulk of our readers from the study of these subjects and it is for the many that we write, not for the few. The SHOGOON, or SJOGOON, or SIEGOON, as his name is indifferently spelt, has signed a treaty with the representatives of foreign powers under another and more dignified appellation, to which he has no right. In fact, were there no more cogent reasons to absolve the Western Powers from the observance of the existing Treaty—the fatal technical flaw undoubtedly exists that the Yedo potentate has signed a contract to which the letter of the word makes him no party. We cannot fairly blame the representatives of foreign powers for accepting him as a 'high contracting party' to the Treaty they were anxious to make with this country. Nor can we say with justice that they were deceived by his assumption of a dignity which did not belong to him. It was a matter of total indifference to them (as may be proved by reference to Lord ELGIN's dispatches on the subject) by what title he chose to be called, so long as he really was, as he pretended to be, and as they believed him to be, the real and *bonâ fide* Sovereign of the country. We should be the last to urge upon our diplomatists the occupation of such ground for a revision of the existing Treaty, had we no better stand point—but as we have missed the splendid opportunity afforded us by the proved treachery of the SHOGOON in the affair of Shimonoseki, we need a combination of small *locûs standi* to give our Representatives secure foothold, and we cannot afford to throw away a single *point d'appui*.

We may reasonably object, with justice, to this individual Daimio arrogating to himself the designation of Majesty (*vide* Lord Elgin's dispatches *passim*) which belongs only to sovereigns. If TOKUGAWA is Majesty—what is the MIKADO? the MIKADO, who is always spoken of as the supreme dignitary of the Empire, and the extortion of whose real or pretended sanction to the Treaty made with the SHOGOON is held to be the great diplomatic success of the past year. The SHOGOON, in fact, is always styled 'Highness' by the Japanese themselves and 'Highness' he is—and no more.

Let us note here the effect of this error of designation. The preamble of the Treaty runs thus:—

'Her Majesty the Queen of the United Kingdom of Great Britain and Ireland and his Majesty the Tycoon of Japan, being desirous to place the relations between the two countries on a permanent and friendly footing, &c., &c.'

Here is evidenced the assumption of sovereign power over the whole of Japan, a mistake carefully avoided afterwards, because,— though the TYCOON of Japan is spoken of throughout the whole treaty—reference to the country is always made by the expression 'his territories' or 'his dominions'—phrases which, to the Japanese had a meaning widely different to that assigned to them by our diplomatists. This preamble really should run thus;—

'Her Majesty the Queen of the United Kingdom of Great Britain and Ireland and his *Highness the* SHOGOON being desirous of placing the relations between their *respective dominions and territories* on a friendly footing &c.'

Thus the words of the Treaty would have corresponded to what is actually the fact:—that we have a treaty with the master of Yedo and the eight provinces round it and with a few outlying spots scattered through the islands of DAI NIPPON—but with SENDAI, CHIOSIU, SATSUMA and the other great Daimios, we can claim no more than what they may choose to consider the general duties of man to man may require.

This is absolutely our position at present—one of great difficulty and from which we see no means of extrication but that which we suggest,—the additional complication of the question when OSAKA is opened and we find ourselves in the immediate neighbourhood of the MIKADO and several powerful chiefs, all busily intriguing against the Yedo usurper—we leave our readers to imagine.

Let us now pass the Treaty, such as it is, in review. The first article of any importance is Art. III, providing for the opening of certain ports and towns and we need not again tell the oft-told tale of its persistent and vexatious violation.

'ART. IV.—All questions in regard to rights, whether of property or person, arising between British subjects in the dominions of His Majesty the Tycoon of Japan, shall be subject to the jurisdiction of the British authorities.'

This is very good as far as the 'dominions' of his 'Majesty' the SHOGOON are concerned, but it does not preclude nor would it in the least degree prevent the Prince of OWARRI from decapitating any British subject who ventured to land in his 'dominions' nor him of HIZEN from putting to death with agonizing torture any unfortunates shipwrecked on his coasts, whose skulls he might wish to place in his museum of European curiosities.

'ART. V.—Japanese subjects, who may be guilty of any criminal act towards British subjects, shall be arrested and punished by the Japanese authorities according to the laws of Japan.'

'Justice shall be equitably and impartially administered on both sides.'

The first clause of this has been occasionally put in force, when the offender has happened to live under the jurisdiction of the Yedo officials, but it is a dead letter as regards the retainers of other Daimios—as has been proved in the cases of SATSUMA and CHIOSIU.

We need not weary our readers with again drawing the obvious inference: Art. VI. is a good and necessary one, to wit:—

'ART. VI.—A British subject having reason to complain of a Japanese, must proceed to the Consulate and state his grievance.'

'The Consul will inquire into the merits of the case, and do his utmost to arrange it amicably. In like manner, if a Japanese have reason to complain of a British subject, the Consul shall no less listen to his complaint, and endeavour to settle it in a friendly manner. If disputes take place of such a nature that the Consul cannot arrange them amicably, then he shall request the assistance of the Japanese authorities, that they may together examine into the merits of the case, and decide it equitably.'

The mixed Court, suggested in the latter part of this Article would, if established on a proper basis and guided in its procedure by well-considered rules, be of infinite service. The subject is too large to treat here. At present, experience shows us that this most important part of it has been too frequently overlooked and our Consuls, instead of arranging amicably disputes between foreigners and Japanese, or calling in the native authorities to aid them in deciding cases too difficult to manage alone, have too often relegated the disputants to the Custom-house altogether, a place where justice to the foreigner is utterly unknown.

Art. VII. provides for the recovery of debts and punishment of fraudulent debtors. The subject is too painful to foreign creditors to allow of our dwelling on it.

The celebated Art. VIII—that:—

'The Japanese Government will place no restrictions whatever upon the employment, by British subjects, of Japanese in any lawful capacity' has been and is persistently and continually violated daily and hourly, by the officials of the SHOGOON. The article is noticeable as containing the assumption that the officials at Yedo are the 'Japanese government.'

Articles IX. and X. providing for the free exercise of religion and the currency regulations, we need not here discuss—while to the provisions of Art. XI. we profess utter indifference.

Art. XII. providing for the good treatment of shipwrecked mariners, applies only to the dominions of the SHOGOON and will not protect any castaways on the coasts of other potentates. The Yedo authorities appear to have been conscious of this when they officially requested the foreign Ministers to issue notifications to the effect 'that shipwrecks should only be allowed at the open ports, except in cases of urgent necessity.'

Art. XIII., regulating pilotage, refers only to the open ports. We now come to Art. XIV., engaging that at these open ports,

British subjects may freely import and export goods and trade freely with 'all classes of Japanese,' and without the 'intervention of any Japanese authorities in such purchase or sale, or in making or receiving payment for the same.' This is the most important commercial article in the Treaty. From the opening of the ports it has been consistently violated. Scores of well-authenticated cases can be quoted of its infraction; our trade with Japan is crippled by its being a dead letter, our social intercourse with the people checked, and all advance towards amity rendered impossible. The non-observance of this article is one of the strongest points the Ministers have for demanding a new Treaty, and until reform in this particular is obtained, neither our own trade, nor the resources of this empire can ever be developed.

Art. XV. provides that the Shogoon's Custom-house officials, if disatisfied [sic] with the valuation placed by a merchant on goods passing through their hands—shall value them for themselves and either receive duty on such valuation or take over the merchandize. The patient and defrauded British merchant can best tell his Representatives how this article has been observed.

The same remarks made on Art. XIV. apply with equal force to Art. XVI., providing for the free and untrammelled transit through the country, of goods that have once paid the import duties at the open ports. In addition, we have only to note the magnificent audacity of a chief whose authority extends over only 8 provinces of the empire, engaging that none of his peers shall levy custom dues at their own frontiers! The remaining articles of the Treaty are almost all either insignificant or of no importance to the present discussion. We note the famous Art. XXIII. the 'favoured nation' clause—latest invention of diplomacy, whereby the negotiator tries to supply the deficiencies of his memory or of his imagination. It might be pertinently asked whether the privileges and immunities, relaxation of duties, repeated grants of land for the same purpose, large gifts of extra Itchibou exchange, &c., &c allowed to some individuals of the foreign community by the Custom House are to be considered as sanctioned by the Shogoon's Government. In such case, we think we could name some nationalities who have large arrears to receive, to place them on a par with 'more favoured' nations.

But our subject is exhausted. In the series of articles published in these columns on the question, we have—we maintain—fully and conclusively proved that the Shogoon has deceived the representatives of the Western Powers and fraudulently concluded Treaties, many of whose provisions he is unable to carry out—that other clauses, which he can observe if he will, he persistently violates

—that the continuance of the existing arrangements are likely to lead to a political crisis in Japan and the great disturbance of our trade and that this trade can never, under present regulations, acquire the importance and value which is its due. We leave the question now in the hands of those who have the power of bringing it to a solution; in the earnest hope that at no distant date we may see the present Treaty abrogated, in favour of a more comprehensive and satisfactory one—a fair and equitable Convention with the MIKADO and the Confederate Daimios—the real rulers of Japan.

APPENDIX III

CHARLES W. LEGENDRE

CHARLES W. LEGENDRE, a naturalized American of French descent, had been the American consul in Amoy from 1866 until October 1872, after receiving the brevet title of brigadier-general for distinguished service in the American Civil War. He gained an outstanding knowledge of Formosa through many trips to the island during his consulship, when he noted at length its resources and the habits of the aborigines, even winning the trust and friendship of Tooke-tok (Tauketok), the chief of the eighteen wild tribes with whom he made an unauthorized agreement which guaranteed protection for white castaways in the tribal lands 1867–72.[1] His efforts to investigate in co-operation with the Taiwan mandarins the wreck of the American barque *Rover* off southern Formosa in 1867 and to effect the punishment of the savages who had murdered the captain, his wife, and crew, made him acutely aware of the reluctance of the Chinese authorities to take action against the savages and of the absence of any Chinese control in the aboriginal territory.[2] After failing to fulfil orders from Foo-chow to investigate the *Rover* tragedy in conjunction with LeGendre, the mandarins of Formosa declared the aborigines were beyond their jurisdiction and thus their actions were not subject to the provisions for the protection of foreigners in China's treaty with the United States.[3] LeGendre spent much of the next five years trying in vain to induce the Chinese local and prefectual authorities, and at last the *Tsungli Yamen*, through the intercession of the American minister at Peking, to establish military and administrative authority in the aboriginal lands and to make the coasts of the south safe for navigators and a haven for castaways. He maintained that the Formosan tribes were subject to the authority of China although their lands did not come within the limits of the control of the various Chinese magistrates. It was China's responsibility to punish offences there, whether committed by Chinese or natives. Should China not do so, he

[1] LeGendre MSS. in L.C., *Notes on Travel in Formosa*, 4 vols., written in Tokyo, 1874, iii. 242, 249–50, and for the agreement 283–4.
[2] For detailed account of American, British, and Chinese concern with the *Rover* case, see Yen, op. cit., pp. 126–36.
[3] LeGendre MSS., *Notes on Travel*, iii. 359–61.

warned the mandarins in June 1867 and again in 1872 that the 'foreign powers will take the case in hand'.[1] When he was in Formosa in the winter of 1872 reports of the recent murder of the fifty-four Ryūkyūans and China's continued failure to establish permanent garrisons on the south cape[2] led LeGendre to reach an agreement with the Chinese authorities in Taiwan-fu to recommend in a secret memorandum to Peking the building of a lighthouse at Tossupong and the opening of a road from Fang-liao to the southern tip of the island in order to facilitate China's control in the area and expedite the rescue work of Chinese troops to be stationed at Fang-liao.[3] But when no response had come from Peking by October, he left China, his patience exhausted.

LeGendre arrived in Japan on his way to America shortly after Japan's incorporation of the Ryūkyū kingdom. He found the American minister, Charles E. DeLong, apprised of Japan's concern about redress for the murder of its Ryūkyūan subjects by the Formosan aborigines and much interested in LeGendre's own efforts to secure protection for shipwrecked Westerners in Formosa. Knowing that the tribes near Fang-liao gave no quarter to Chinese or people who resembled them, LeGendre suggested that Japan might negotiate for the protection of her own people. DeLong introduced LeGendre to Soejima who was avid for information about Formosa. In consequence of several conferences with the Foreign Minister when LeGendre advised the Japanese government to negotiate directly with Peking in seeking to gain redress from China, LeGendre was appointed adviser to the Japanese Foreign Office on 28 December 1872, at a salary of Y. 1,000 per month.[4] He and DeLong both knew that Japan was then planning to send 'a small force to Taiwan, which without previous notice to the Chinese government would be able to seize the aboriginal territory and would be difficult to dislodge'.[5] LeGendre wrote in his memoirs, 'I was persuaded to remain in the country to give my advice as to the best way of establishing a series of Japanese colonies on the eastern and southern coasts of Formosa, for the protection of castaways and other purposes'. He rejoiced in this opportunity and submitted a programme for action to the *Dajōkan*. Through it, he believed, his 'long cherished hope of seeing the aboriginal coast of the island made safe for castaways' would be realized and 'the foundation of one of the widest

[1] Ibid., p. 363, n., LeGendre's letter to Governor of Formosa 22 June 1867. Yen, op. cit., pp. 131, 145.
[2] LeGendre, MSS., *Notes on Travel*, iii. 339.
[3] Ibid., pp. 371–8. Yen, op. cit., p. 146.
[4] Ibid., p. 170. *D.N.G.M.* v. 299, Doc. 128.
[5] Yen, op. cit., p. 165.

and surest schemes for the advancement of Western civilization, sciences and arts in the East would be laid'.[1]

Americans in the East, including the United States minister, encouraged the Japanese enterprise and congratulated LeGendre on his appointment to high office under the Japanese Government.[2] Parkes, on the other hand, was contemptuous of LeGendre and critical of the Japanese undertaking. He wrote that the Japanese 'have been led away by their own conceit, and by advice which fitted in exactly with that conceit, and which has been chiefly supplied by that man LeGendre . . .'.[3]

[1] LeGendre, MSS., *Notes on Travel,* iii. 383–4. For LeGendre's advice to Soejima, see Yen, op. cit., pp. 175–80.

[2] LeGendre MSS., *Letters,* Lewis Beardsley, Comdr., U.S.N., to LeGendre, Washington, D.C., 27 Jan. 1873. Tyler Dennett, *Americans in Eastern Asia* (New York, 1922), p. 439.

[3] Dickins, op. cit., ii. 190–1.

GLOSSARY[1]

BAKUFU, SHOGUNATE. The term designating the Shogun's officials collectively and signifying the *de facto* central government of Japan under a Shogun.

BANSHO TORISHIRABE-DOKORO (also read as *Bansho Shirabe Jo*). Office for the study of foreign (or Western) writings.

BUGYŌ. Officials of the Shogunate in the middle and upper levels of the administrative hierarchy. Translated 'governors', 'commissioners', even 'ministers' by the British in contemporary documents.

CATTY. In China, 1⅓ lb.

CHOKUSHI. The Emperor's envoy to the Shogun.

CHŌNIN. The merchant or trading class.

DAIICHI GINKŌ. First National Bank.

DAIMYO. Feudal baron.

DAJŌ-DAIJIN. Prime Minister.

DAJŌKAN. Council of State in the early Meiji period.

FUDAI DAIMYO. Those feudal lords who had supported Tokugawa Ieyasu before the battle of Sekigahara in 1600 when he established his supremacy. They alone were eligible for senior offices in the Tokugawa administrative system.

GAIKOKU-BUGYŌ. Officials of the Shogunate, first appointed on 16 August 1858 'to advise the *Bakufu* on foreign affairs and conduct negotiations with foreign diplomats' at home and abroad. Their 'numbers varied from five in 1858 to a maximum of thirteen later'. Contemporary British officials usually referred to them erroneously as 'Ministers' or 'Governors' for Foreign Affairs. See P.P. H. of C. 1860, lxix. 48–51 and 1864, lxvi. (3242) 12–17.

GOYŌ-KIN. Forced loans.

HAN. A feudal clan, all persons subject to the jurisdiction of one daimyo.

ICHIBU. Silver coin (usually referred to as '*bu*'), minted in Japan from 1837 to 1868 and used until the currency reforms of 1874. That on which the 1858 treaties were based consisted of gold 0·21 per cent., silver 98·86 per cent., and copper 0·93 per cent. and was to be exchanged by weight for Western silver coins at a standard rate of 311 to 100 Mexican dollars. A debased coin but of the same weight, the Ansei *ichibu*, minted by the *Bakufu* in 1859 to reduce the drain of precious metals from the country caused by foreign trade led to disputes with the Western powers.

[1] I am indebted to the glossary in Prof. Beasley's *Documents* for the parts in quotation and the source for some adaptations here.

580 *Glossary*

ICHIBUGIN. Silver *ichibu* debased again in 1869.

JISHA-BUGYŌ. *Bakufu* officials at the top of the *bugyō* rank, who had responsibility for the supervision of shrines and temples.

JŌI. 'Expel the barbarian': the slogan of those groups which opposed the treaties with the West in 1854–8 and 'later became associated with the movement to overthrow the Tokugawa'.

KAIKOKU. 'Open the country': the 'slogan of those groups which supported the conclusion of the treaties with the West in 1854–8 and were later associated with the support for the *Bakufu* against its domestic enemies.

KAISEIJO. Name given to *Bakufu* school for teaching foreign languages in 1863. It was the successor to the *Bansho Torishirabe-dokoro* founded in 1856 at Yedo and became part of Tokyo Imperial University in 1877.

KAIYAKUSHA. Translation unit in the Institute for the Study of Foreign Books (*Bansho Torishirabe-dokoro*).

KAKKE. Japanese name for Beri-Beri, a disease causing dropsy and numbness of the legs common in Yedo and Kyoto during the period here considered.

KAN. A battleship.

KANJI. A Chinese ideograph.

KANJŌ-BUGYŌ. '*Bakufu* officials with special responsibility for finance; usually 5 or 6 in number during late Tokugawa period'.

KANJŌ-KATA. Department of the Treasury, established by the Shogunate in the early eighteenth century.

KARŌ. The principal retainer of a daimyo.

KERAI. Literally, a vassal or follower: name taken by the exiled Tokugawa followers who seized Hakodate in December 1868 after the capitulation of the northern daimyo with the hope of establishing a Tokugawa colony on Yezo.

KINSATSU. Gold notes.

KOBAN. A Japanese gold coin equal to a *ryō* or 4 *ichibu*. It was first used as a medium of exchange about 1600. The British called it a 'cobang'.

KŌBU-GATTAI. 'Court-*Bakufu* unity': the slogan of those groups of daimyo and Court nobles who wished to gain a larger share of political authority without actually destroying the *Bakufu*.

KOKU. A measure of capacity, standardized at 4·96 English bushels.

KUGE. Court families or Court nobility.

MACHI-BUGYŌ. *Bakufu* officials who administered the key cities, e.g. Yedo, Kyoto, Osaka, and Nagasaki.

METSUKE. *Bakufu* officials of slightly lower rank than *bugyō*, who supervised the activities of officials and members of the feudal class beneath daimyo status 'with the special duty of detecting maladministration or disaffection'; in British documents often translated as 'spy' or 'censor'.

MIKADO. The Emperor: term normally used by Westerners in the nineteenth century to distinguish the Emperor from the Shogun.

MOMME. 57·9 gr. silver coin or weight in Japan.

NAIDAIJIN. 'Minister of the Centre', one of the highest offices of the Imperial Court, ranking with those of *Sadaijin* and *Udaijin*. It was always held by a Court noble and in addition was bestowed on the Shogun who took rank at Court accordingly.

NAIMUSHŌ. Department of Home Affairs.

NIBUGIN. Silver coin worth two *bu* 1854–74.

NIBUKIN. Gold coin worth two *bu* 1867–74.

NISHU. Half *ichibu* gold pieces.

NISHUGIN. Half *ichibu* silver coins.

NORIMONO. A palanquin.

ŌKURASHŌ. Department of Finance established by the Meiji government.

ŌMETSUKE. Chief censors or inspectors in the Shogun's government, responsible for supervising the activities of feudal lords and officials of daimyo status.

PICUL. 133⅓ pounds, or 10 catties.

RANGAKU. The study of the Dutch language.

RI. 3·927 kilometres.

RŌJŪ. The most senior of *Bakufu* officials in normal times, 'usually 4 or 5 in number and often called members of the Council of State in Yedo'. Only *fudai* daimyo could be appointed and in the late Tokugawa period, only those with fiefs of 50,000 *koku*.

RŌNIN. ' "Wave men": samurai who no longer owed fealty to a lord, either by force of circumstance (e.g. the transfer or disgrace of their lord) or by choice.'

RYŌ. A gold coin equal to the *koban*, established as the unit of gold currency by the early Tokugawa Shoguns. See p. 27, n. 4.

SADAIJIN. 'Minister of the Left', the second most important member of the *Dajōkan* of the early Meiji government, 1871–1885.

SAIBANSHO. A law court.

SANKE. The three senior branch houses of the Tokugawa family whose fiefs were Owari, Kii, and Mito, and who with the addition of the *Sankyō*, 'formed the group from which the Shogun's successor was chosen when the direct line failed'.

SANKIN-KŌTAI. *Bakufu* system requiring each daimyo to spend four or six months every year in Yedo where his family remained as hostages when he was resident in his fief—a means of controlling the great lords.

SANKYŌ. The 'Three Lords': branch houses of the Tokugawa family, those of Tayasu, Hitotsubashi, and Shimizu. They lived in Yedo, had no fiefs, but received an income from the Shogun's estates. With the *Sanke*, 'they formed the group from which the Shogun's successor was chosen when the direct line failed'.

SANSHOKU. Literally, 'the three ranking positions' in the Meiji Council of State, those of prime minister, the minister of the Left and the Minister of the Right.

SEITAISHO. Form of government established by Imperial Proclamation in June 1868.

SEPPUKU. Suicide by disembowelment; harakiri.

SHOGUN. The generally used abbreviation for *Sei-i-tai-shōgun* (barbarian-subduing generalissimo); 'title first used for the commander of the Imperial forces in the campaigns against the Ainu and taken in 1192 by the Minamoto as that under which they became the *de facto* rulers of Japan. It became hereditary and was used thereafter by successive families who ruled Japan, . . . the Tokugawa being the last of these. . . .' The Shogun ruled in the Emperor's name after investiture by him 'but was entirely outside the control of the Imperial Court and worked through his own administrative system'.

SHŌKEN. Here used to mean a private paper currency issued by foreign trading companies before 1876 and local daimyo in the *Bakufu* period.

SONNŌ. ' "Honour the Emperor": slogan of those who in the late Tokugawa period sought in some degree a restoration of Imperial prerogatives and prestige; subsequently developed into a demand for the complete abolition of the Bakufu.'

SONNŌ-JŌI. ' "Honour the Emperor, expel the barbarian"; slogan of the anti-*Bakufu* movement after 1858.'

TAEL. A Chinese ounce weight as well as an amount of money, equal to ten mace or 1½ ounces of silver. The monetary value varied from province to province and from time to time.

TAIRŌ. 'Regent': the highest office in the *Bakufu*. It was filled only in times of crisis when the incumbent took precedence over the *Rōjū* and in effect conducted all important State business. Only *fudai* daimyo with fiefs of a minimum of 100,000 *koku* were eligible.

TOZAMA DAIMYO. Those feudal lords of daimyo status whose ancestors had not submitted to Tokugawa rule until after Ieyasu's victory at Sekigahara in 1600 and who were always regarded by the Tokugawa as potential rivals or rebels.

TŌZENJI. The temple in Yedo which became the first residence of the British legation in 1859.

TSUNGLI YAMEN. Office of Foreign Affairs in the Chinese government after China's involuntary treaties with the West.

TYCOON. '*Taikun*', the title taken by the Shogun in the Tokugawa period when dealing with foreigners, especially Koreans. After 1854 it was used in its Anglicized form 'tycoon' by foreigners to describe the Shogun in their effort to distinguish him from the Emperor at Kyoto.

UDAIGIN. 'Minister of the Right', one of the three highest offices of the Imperial Court before the restoration and afterwards in the early Meiji government, 1871–1885.

YASHIKI. A mansion.

YŌGINKEN. Silver notes.

SELECTED BIBLIOGRAPHY

MANUSCRIPTS

In England and Scotland

At the Royal Archives, Windsor Castle:
Letters and papers pertaining to the Far East 1854–68.

At the Public Record Office, London:

Foreign Office, General Correspondence, *Japan* (F.O. 46), volumes 1–302, covering 'Domestic Various' for 1856, Lord Elgin's Mission in 1858, and the letters and their enclosures from the British Ministers in Japan, Sir Rutherford Alcock and Sir Harry S. Parkes, from 1859 to 1883.

Foreign Office, Embassy and Consular Series, *Japan, Correspondence*, (F.O. 262), volumes 1–396, covering the letters from the Foreign Office to the British ministers in Japan 1859–83.

Foreign Office, General Correspondence, *China* (F.O. 17), volumes 673, 674, 675, 676, 677, 697, and 699, covering letters pertaining to the Japanese invasion of Formosa in 1874.

Admiralty, Secretary's Department, *Indexes and Compilations* Series III (cited here as *Admiralty Index*), 18073–52–26. In these great indexes, digests of letters now missing among the In-Letters of the Admiralty may be found.

Admiralty, Secretary's Department, In-Letters (Ad. 1/), covering the letters from the Commanders-in-Chief of the East Indies and China Station (after 1864 China Station) and some from the Foreign Office and Board of Trade to the Admiralty Board for the years 1854–83.

Admiralty, Secretary's Department, Out-Letters (Ad. 2/ and Ad. 13/), covering the letters and instructions sent from the Military Branch, Civil Department, the Military Branch, Foreign Stations, and the Port and Standing Orders of the Admiralty Board to the Commanders-in-Chief of the China Station and some letters (Ad. 13/57 and 58) from the Admiralty to the Foreign Office, from 1846 to 1883. The numbers of the packets or volumes in which these letters were found are given in the footnotes.

Board of Trade, General Department:

Japan, Erection of Lighthouses, H4941/69.
Japan, Articles for Importation, 32/61.

Documents acquired by Gift, Deposit, or Purchase.

The Papers of Sir Ernest M. Satow (P.R.O. 30/33) for 1861 to 1884.

The Papers of Lord John Russell (P.R.O. 30/22), vols. 24, 26, 49, and 50.

At the Admiralty, Whitehall:

MSS. on the China Station in the Record Office (Ad. R.O.), vols. 26, 31, 42, 49, and 76. Much of the material here duplicates that in the P.R.O.

At the British Museum:

Add. MS. 44096, Gladstone Papers, xi.

At the Royal Society, London:

Letters and papers of British scientists in Japan, MSS. Nos. 76, 77, 176, A524, AP 37. 29, AP 61. 63, AP 66. 29, and MC 16. 1.

At University College, London University:

Calendars of University College 1865–70.

University College Committee, Minutes, 2 Feb. 1937.

Baron Sakurai's Speech at University College Fellows' Dinner, 30 April 1937.

At John Swire and Sons, Ltd., London:

Letter Book, Yokohama, May 1869–Feb. 1870, Japan–London Correspondence.

At the Chartered Bank of India, Australia, and China, London:

MS. on British Banks in Japan by J. Leighton-Boyce.

At the Church Missionary Society, London:

Letters from missionaries in Japan to the C.M.S., Feb. 1869–83 (CT. 10–6–12).

Letters from missionaries to missionaries in Japan (C.J. 10–17).

Letters from C.M.S. to missionaries in Japan (C.J./61, 1874–87).

China and Japan Mission *Minutes*, vols. xl–xlv.

C.M.S. *Index*, 1872–6, xli.

C.M.S. *Book of Missionaries*.

At the Society for the Propagation of the Gospel in Foreign Parts, London:

Letters from missionaries in the Far East (Letters, Victoria, 1868–74), (D. 41, Asia, 1875), (India and the Far East, 1877 and 1879), (D. 47, Asia, 1878), (D. 56, Asia 11, 1881), (D. 60 Asia, 11, 1882), and (D. 64, Asia 11, 1883).

Letters from London Office to missionaries in Japan (Japanese Letters Sent i, 1874–1908).

Book of Missionaries, 1869–87.

Minutes of Standing Committee, Nos. 35 (1872–3), 37 (1875–7), 39 (1879–80) and 40 (1880–2).

At the Bodleian Library, Oxford:

The Clarendon Papers, 1868–70. Those consulted were found in boxes labelled Foreign Office 14, 20, 23B, and 32, and in Miscellaneous 29, 1868–70.

At the University Library, Cambridge:
In the Jardine, Matheson Archive.
Private letters from Shanghai Office to Hong Kong, 1853–9.
J.M. Ledgers, 1858–9, 1859–60.
Japan Letter Books oi and i, which contain copies of letters from the Shanghai Office to Nagasaki, Yokohama, and Kanagawa, 29 Jan. 1859 to 29 June 1867.
Japan Letter Book ii, 1867–9, which also includes letters to Hyogo and Osaka.
Japan Letter Book iii, 18 Mar. 1872–19 Aug. 1879. Mostly illegible. General and private letters from agents of Jardine, Matheson and Company in Nagasaki, Yokohama, Kanagawa, and Hakodate to the Shanghai or Hong Kong Offices, 1859–72 and from Hyogo and Osaka, 1868–70. All cited here as J.M. MSS. There are many gaps in this correspondence.

At the National Library of Scotland, Edinburgh:
United Presbyterian Church of Scotland Missionary Society (U.P.S.). Letter Books Nos. 2, 17, 1874; Nos. 2 and 18 (Foreign), 1875; No. 18 (Foreign), 1876; No. 19 (Foreign), 1877; No. 20 (Foreign), 1878; No. 20 (Foreign), 1879; No. 20 (Foreign), 1880; No. 20 (Foreign), 1881; Nos. 1 and 21 (Foreign), 1882; and Nos. 1 and 2, 1883. These books contain copies of letters from the Secretary of the Foreign Mission Board to missionaries abroad and occasional excerpts from the minutes of the Board's Committee on Foreign Missions. None of the letters from missionaries, nor any minute books, has survived for these years.

At the National Bible Society of Scotland (N.B.S.S.), Edinburgh:
Minutes, Western Committee, vol. iv, 1872–3; vols. v–vii, 1875–82.

At Rockingham Castle, Leicestershire:
The Papers of Admiral Sir Michael Seymour, K.C.B., 1856–9.

In Japan

At Gaimushō, (the Ministry of Foreign Affairs) Tokyo, Archives Division:
Yanagihara Kōshi to Sanshoku Ōfuku Naikan (Confidential Correspondence between Yanagihara Sakimitsu, Minister, and the 'Sanshoku') June–Nov. 1874. This may also be found in the Library of Congress among the microfilms of the archives in the Japanese Ministry of Foreign Affairs, 1868–1945, under No. M.T. 1–1–2–6.
Copies in English of telegrams sent to and received from Japanese representatives abroad, Western officials, &c., 1873–8.

At Kokuritsu Kokkai Toshokan (the National Diet Library), Tokyo:
Iwakura Kō Denki Shiryō (Materials for the Biography of Prince Iwakura).

At Tōkyō Daigaku Shiryō Hensanjo (Historiographical Institute, Tokyo University):
Dai Nippon Ishin Shiryō Kohon (Manuscripts of Historical Data of the Restoration), 3,000 vols. Vol. mlxxvi was used.

At Ōkuma Kinen Shakai Kagaku Kenkyūjo (Okuma Memorial Institute of Social Sciences), Waseda University, Tokyo:
Ōkuma MSS. C144, C145, and C146.

At Municipal Library, Hakodate, Hokkaido:
The Blakiston, Marr Papers (cited here as Blakiston, Marr MSS.)
List of foreign ships entering Hakodate 1860.

In the United States

At the Library of Congress:
Microfilm Reading Room
In *Reproductions of Selected Archives of the Japanese Army, Navy, and other Government Agencies 1868–1945*, T134. (R45 F45181) *Taiwan Jimu*; navy; 1874; *Taiwan Jiken Shūroku*, vol. 4; NA 10644. *Taiwan Affairs: Memoranda Regarding Relations with China and Other Countries on Taiwan Problem; Report on Murder of Ryūkyū Fishermen by Formosans.*
Manuscript Division.
General Charles W. LeGendre Papers: *Notes on Travel in Formosa*, 4 vols., written in Tokyo, 1874, and Official Letters, 1874–5.

At Harvard University in the Houghton Library:
MSS. of the American Board of Commissioners for Foreign Missions: *The Japan Mission 1871–80* (A.B.C. 16–4–1), vols. i–iv and *Japan Mission, Supplementary Documents, 1869–1929*, vol. oi.

At Rutgers University Library, New Brunswick, New Jersey:
Richard Henry Brunton, MS. on *Pioneer Engineering in Japan, A Record of Work in Helping to Relay the Foundations of the Japanese Empire 1868–1876.* Condensed and annotated with an Introductory Chapter and Postscript by William Elliot Griffis. (Here cited as Brunton *MS.*) The pagination and organization of this work is irregular and confusing, as the efforts at editing it were apparently never completed.

COLLECTIONS OF GOVERNMENT DOCUMENTS
AND OTHER PRIMARY SOURCES

British

Great Britain, Board of Trade, *Statistical Abstract for the United Kingdom in Each of the Last Fifteen Years from 1850–1864*, 12th No., London, 1865; *1854–1869*, 17th No., London, 1870; and *1869–1883*, 31st No., London, 1884.

Great Britain, Board of Trade, *Statistical Abstract for the Principal and other Foreign Countries in each year from 1876–1885–6*, 12th and 14th nos., London, 1888.

Great Britain, Foreign Office, *Commercial Reports Received at the Foreign Office from H.M. Consuls* in Japan and Formosa, 1862–83, (here cited as Cons. Reports). Some of these are found in the Libary of Congress as separate pamphlets, some in bound annual volumes, and some in the Sessional Papers of the House of Commons. Others were located at the Board of Trade in London and at the Essex Institute in Salem, Mass.

Great Britain, Foreign Office, Sir Edward Hertslet, Compiler, *British and Foreign State Papers*, xlix, London, 1867.

Great Britain, Foreign Office, *Reports by Her Majesty's Secretaries of Embassy and Legation on the Manufactures, Commerce, &c. of the Countries in which they Reside*, London, Commercial, No. 4, 1877; No. 17, 1878; No. 3, 1879.

Great Britain, *Hansard's Parliamentary Debates*, 1857, 1859, 1864, 1876.

Great Britain, *Navy List*, 1858, 1868, 1870.

Great Britain, Parliament, House of Commons, *Sessional Papers*, (here cited as P.P. H. of C.). These include the correspondence respecting affairs in Japan 1859–83, special reports by British officials on Japan, and some of the periodic commercial reports of H.M. consuls.

HART, COL. H. G., *The New Annual Army List and Militia List* for 1865, London, 1865 (here cited as Hart's *Army List*).

HERTSLET, SIR EDWARD, K.C.B., Compiler, *The Foreign Office List*, forming a complete *Diplomatic and Consular Hand Book*, London, 1873, 1880, 1883, (here cited as *Foreign Office List*).

HERTSLET, GODFREY E. P., *Hertslet's China Treaties*, 2 vols., 3rd. ed., London, 1908.

HERTSLET, LEWIS, Compiler, *Complete Collection of Treaties and Conventions and Reciprocal Regulations at Present Subsisting between Great Britain & Foreign Powers*, 24 vols., London, vol. xi, 1864.

YOUNG, G. M., and HANDCOCK, W. D., Eds., vol. 12, Part I, *English Historical Documents 1833–1874*, New York, 1956, in David C. Douglas, Gen. Ed., *English Historical Documents*, 12 vols., New York, 1953–9.

Yokohama Chamber of Commerce, *Minutes*, 29 June 1869.

—*Half Year Report*, 31 Dec. 1868.

Japanese

BEASLEY, W. G., *Select Documents on Japanese Foreign Policy, 1853–1868*, London, 1955 (here cited as *Documents*).

Gaimushō Chōsakyoku (Foreign Ministry Research Bureau), *Dai Nihon Gaikō Monjo* (Japanese Foreign Office Archives), 73 vols., Tokyo, 1936–63 (here cited as *D.N.G.M.*).

Gaimushō Jōyakukyoku (Foreign Office Treaty Bureau), *Kyū Jōyaku Isan* (Collection of Old Treaties), 3 vols., Tokyo, 1930–6.

Ishin Shiryō Hensan Kakari (Official Compiler of Restoration Materials), Ed., *Ishin Shi* (History of the Restoration), 6 vols., Tokyo, 1939.

Japan Bureau of Customs, *Returns of Foreign Trade of Japan for the Eighteen Years from 1868–1885 Inclusive*, Tokyo, 1885.

The Japanese Foreign Office, *Treaties and Conventions between the Empire of Japan and other Powers, together with Universal Conventions, Regulations, and Communications since March 1854*, Tokyo, 1884.

McLAREN, W. W., *Japanese Government Documents*, Tokyo, 1914, in *T.A.S.J.* xlii.

Naikaku Kampōkyoku (Governmental Gazette Bureau of the Cabinet), Hōrei Zensho M. 8 (Collections of Laws and Orders, 1875), Tokyo, 1889.

Nippon Shiseki Kyōkai (Japan Historical Association), *Ōkuma Shigenobu Kankei Bunsho* (Documents related to Ōkuma Shigenobu), 5 vols., Tokyo, 1933.

Ōkubo Toshimichi Monjo (Papers of Ōkubo Toshimichi), 10 vols., Tokyo, 1927–9.

Ōkurashō (Finance Ministry), *Kōkoku Zōheiryō Shuchō Daisanshūnen Hōkokushō* (Reports for Second to Fourth Years of Imperial Mint), Tokyo, 1874.

Ōkurashō (Finance Ministry), *Nihon Zaisei Keizai Shiryō* (Materials on Japanese Finance and Economy), 11 vols., Tokyo, 1922.

Ōkurashō (Finance Ministry), OUCHI HYŌE and TSUCHIYA TAKAO, Eds., *Meiji Zenki Zaisei Keizai Shiryō Shūsei* (Collection of Historical Documents of Finance and Economics of the Early Meiji Period), 20 vols., Tokyo, 1934 (here cited as Ōkurashō *Documents*).

Omoide no Kazu Kazu, Danshaku Sakurai Jōji Ikō (Manuscripts left by Baron Sakurai Jōji), Tokyo, 1940 (Hibaihin).

Shihōshō (Ministry of Justice), *Tokugawa Kinrei Kō* (Collection of the Tokugawa Prohibitions), First Series, 6 vols., Tokyo, 1895.

Tōkyō Shiryō Hensanjo (Historiographical Institute, Tokyo University), Ed., *Dai Nihon Komonjo, Bakumatsu Gaikoku Kankei Monjo* (Old Japanese Documents, Documents relating to Foreign Affairs in the Last Days of the Shogunate 1853–68), 32 vols., Tokyo, 1911–62 (cited here as *B.G.K.M.*). Series completed to December 1859.

—— *Dai Nippon Shiryō* (Japanese Historical Materials), Part XII, 34 vols., Tokyo, 1925, xxv.

TSUNODA RYŪSAKU, DE BARY, WM., THEODORE and KEENE, DONALD, Compilers, *Sources of Japanese Tradition*, New York, 1958.

YOSHINO SAKUZŌ, Ed., *Meiji Bunka Zenshū* (Collection of Materials related to Early Meiji Culture), 24 vols., Tokyo, 1928–55.

NEWSPAPERS, JOURNALS, AND SERIALS

The dates of the issues consulted and the location of rare copies and broken files will be found in the footnotes.

Western

Blackwood's Magazine.
British and Foreign Bible Society, *Reports*, 1860–83.
The British Medical Journal.
The China Mail.
The Chrysanthemum, 1881–3.
The Church Missionary Intelligencer, New Series, 1869–75.
The Church Missionary Intelligencer and Record, 1876–83.
The Daily Japan Herald.
The Examiner, A Weekly Paper on Politics, Literature, Music and the Fine Arts, London, 1850–2.
The Far East.
The Fortnightly Review.
The Hyogo and Osaka Herald.
The Illustrated London News.
The Japan Bible Society (Nihon Kwai Kyokai), *Report*, August 1961.
The Japan Chronicle, Jubilee Number, 1868–1918.
The Japan Commercial News.

The Japan Gazette.
The Japan Gazette Fortnightly.
The Japan Herald.
The Japan Mail (fortnightly edition).
Japan Punch, June 1881–December 1883.
The Japan Times, 8 Sept. 1865–June 1866.
The Japan Times Daily Advertiser.
The Japan Times, New Series, Jan.–June 1878.
The Japan Times, Overland Mail.
The Japan Weekly Mail, 9 May 1874–19 May 1883.
The Kobe Chronicle.
The Lancet, London.
The London Gazette.
Mission Field; a Monthly Record of the Proceedings of the Society for the Propagation of the Gospel in Foreign Parts, 1872–84.
The Nagasaki Express.
The Nagasaki Shipping List and Advertiser.
Nature.
The North China Herald.
The Philosophical Magazine.
Proceedings, Imperial Academy, Tokyo.
Punch, London, 1850–2.
The Quarterly Review, lxv.
Revue Maritime et Coloniale.
St. Thomas's Hospital Reports.
The Scotsman, 21 Mar. 1961.
Society for the Propagation of the Gospel, *Missionary Reports,* 1876–83.
The Times, 1850–83.
The Tokei Journal.
The Tokio Times, 1877–80.
Transactions of the Asiatic Society of Japan, Tokyo, 1872–3–1964.
United Presbyterian Missionary Record, Edinburgh, 1 July 1884.

Japanese

Bankoku Shimbun Shi.
Batavia Shimbun.
Hakodate Shimbun.
Kaigai Shimbun.
Kakkoku Shimbun.
Nisshin Shinjishi.

BOOKS AND PAMPHLETS

Western

ADAMS, FRANCIS OTTIWELL, *The History of Japan,* 2 vols., London, 1875.
ADAMS, THOMAS F. M., in collaboration with IWAO HOSHII, *A Financial History of Modern Japan,* Tokyo, 1964.
ALCOCK, SIR RUTHERFORD, *The Capital of the Tycoon,* 2 vols., London, 1863.
—— *Art and Art Industry in Japan,* London, 1878.

ALLEN, GEORGE C., *A Short Economic History of Modern Japan, 1867–1937*, New York, 1963.

ALLEN, G. C., and DONNITHORNE, A. G., *Western Enterprise in Far Eastern Economic Development*, London, 1954.

BAELZ, ERWIN, *Awakening Japan, the Diary of a German Doctor*, ed. by his son, Toku Baelz, New York, 1932.

BASTER, A. S. J., *The Imperial Banks*, London, 1929.

—— *The International Banks*, London, 1935.

BATCHELOR, JOHN, *The Ainu and their Folklore*, London, 1901.

—— *An Ainu–English, Japanese Dictionary and Grammar*, Tokyo, 1889, 1905.

BEASLEY, W. G., *Great Britain and the Opening of Japan*, London, 1951.

—— *The Modern History of Japan*, New York, 1963, (here cited as *History*).

BLACK, J. R., *Young Japan, Yokohama and Yedo, A Narrative of the Settlement and the City from the Signing of the Treaties in 1858 to the Close of the Year 1879*, 2 vols., London, New York, and Yokohama, 1880–3.

BLUM, PAUL C., *Yokohama in 1872, A Rambling Account of the Community in which the Asiatic Society of Japan was Founded*, Tokyo, 1963.

BORTON, HUGH, *Japan's Modern Century*, New York, 1955.

—— *Peasant Uprisings in Japan of the Tokugawa Period*, T.A.S.J., 1937.

BUCKLE, GEORGE EARLE, *The Letters of Queen Victoria*, 2nd Series, 2 vols., London, 1926.

BUTCHER, Lt.-Com. B. L., R.D., R.N.R. ret'd, *In China Seas, A History of the China Navigation Company*, reprinted from *Sea Breezes*, Feb. and Mar. 1964.

Butterfield and Swire 1867–1957, A Short History, reprinted from *The Blue Funnel Bulletin* of Jan. 1957.

CABLE, BOYD, *A Hundred Year History of the P. and O.*, London, 1937.

CARY, OTIS, *Japan and its Regeneration*, New York, 1899.

The China Navigation Company 1872–1957, A Short History, reprinted from *The Blue Funnel Bulletin* of Jan. 1958.

CONROY, HILARY, *The Japanese Seizure of Korea: 1868–1910*, Philadelphia, 1960.

COOK, SIR EDWARD, *Delane of The Times*, London, 1916.

COSTIN, W. C., *Great Britain and China, 1833–1860*, Oxford, 1937.

COURT, W. H. B., *A Concise Economic History of Britain*, Cambridge, England, 1954.

CRAIG, ALBERT M., *Chōshū in the Meiji Restoration*, Cambridge, Mass., 1961.

DASENT, ARTHUR IRWIN, *John Thadeus Delane, His Life and Correspondence*, 2 vols., New York, 1908.

DAVIDSON, JAMES W., *The Island of Formosa, Past and Present*, London, 1903.

DAWSON, W. H., *Richard Cobden and Foreign Policy*, London, 1926.

DENNETT, TYLER, *Americans in Eastern Asia*, New York, 1922.

DENNYS, N. B., et al., *The Treaty Ports of China and Japan*, London, 1867.

DYER, HENRY, *Dai Nippon, The Britain of the East*, London, 1904.

FAIRBANK, JOHN K., REISCHAUER, EDWIN O., and CRAIG, ALBERT M., *A History of East Asian Civilization*, 2 vols., Boston, 1960–5.

FOX, GRACE, *British Admirals and Chinese Pirates 1832–1869*, London, 1940.

Fujikawa Y., *Japanese Medicine*, trans. from the German by John Ruhrah, New York, 1934.

Fukuzawa Yūkichi, The Autobiography of, trans. by Kiyooka Eiichi, Tokyo, 1940.

Greenberg, Michael, *British Trade and the Opening of China 1800–1842*, Cambridge, England, 1951.

Greene, E. B., *A New Englander in Japan*, Boston, 1927.

The Greville Memoirs, A Journal of the Reign of Queen Victoria from 1852–1860, 2 vols., London, 1867.

Griffis, W. E., *The Mikado's Empire*, New York 1887.

—— *Townsend Harris*, Boston, 1895.

—— *Verbeck of Japan*, New York, 1900.

Gubbins, J. H., *The Progress of Japan 1853–1871*, Oxford, 1911.

Hakodate Municipal Library, *Japanese-Anglo Relations Centering on Hakodate*, narrated on the occasion when the crest of the former British Consulate was presented to Hakodate City, 30 Aug. 1940, Hakodate, 1940.

Hanazono Kanesada, *The Development of Japanese Journalism*, Tokyo, 1924.

Heco, Joseph, *The Narrative of a Japanese*, 2 vols., Yokohama, 1892.

Hewat, Elizabeth G. K., *Vision and Achievement*, Edinburgh, 1960.

Higasi Keniti, *Dipole, Molecule, and Chemistry*, Sapporo, 1965.

Hodgson, C. P., *A Residence at Nagasaki and Hakodate 1859–60*, London, 1860.

Holmes, Capt. Henry, *My Adventures in Japan*, London, 1859.

Honjō Eijirō, *The Social and Economic History of Japan*, Kyoto, 1935.

House, Edward H., *The Japanese Expedition to Formosa*, Tokyo, 1875.

Hudson, G. F., 'The Far East' in Vol. x of *The New Cambridge Modern History*, 12 vols., Cambridge, England, 1957–60.

Hyde, Francis E. with the assistance of Harris, J. R., *Blue Funnel, A History of Alfred Holt and Company of Liverpool from 1865 to 1914*, Liverpool, 1956.

Iddittie Junesaye, *The Life of Marquis Shigenobu Okuma, A Biographical Study in the Rise of Democratic Japan*, Tokyo, 1956.

Ike Nobutaka, *The Beginnings of Political Democracy in Japan*, Baltimore, 1950.

Inglehart, C. W., *A Century of Christianity in Japan*, Tokyo, 1959.

Iwata Masakazu, *Okubo Toshimichi, the Bismarck of Japan*, Berkeley and Los Angeles, Calif., 1964.

Jansen, Marius B., *Sakamoto Ryōma and the Meiji Restoration*, Princeton, 1961.

Jardine, Matheson and Company, afterwards Jardine, Matheson and Company, Ltd., an Outline of the History of a China House for a Hundred Years, 1832–1932, privately printed, 1934.

Jardine's Centenary in Japan 1859–1959, privately printed, Tokyo, 1959.

Johnson, A. J., *Johnson's New Illustrated Family Atlas*, New York, 1865.

Jones, F. C., *Extraterritoriality in Japan*, New Haven, 1931.

Jones, Stanleigh H., Jr., 'Early Industrialization in Japan: The Example of the Saga-Han', *Columbia University East Asian Institute Studies*, No. 6, New York, 1959.

Kann, Edward, *Currencies of China*, Shanghai, 1926.

Kerr George H., *Okinawa, The History of an Island People*, Tokyo, 1958.

KING, J. W., *The Warships and Navies of the World*, Boston, 1880.
KISHIMOTO HIDEO and HOWES, JOHN F., *Japanese Religion in the Meiji Era*, Tokyo, 1956, Centenary Culture Council Series ii.
KŌSAKA MASAAKI and ABOSCH, DAVID, Eds., *Japanese Thought in the Meiji Era*, Tokyo, 1958, Centenary Culture Council Series ix.
LANE-POOLE, STANLEY, and DICKINS, F. V., *The Life of Sir Harry Parkes*, 2 vols., London, 1891 and 1894.
LATOURETTE, KENNETH SCOTT, *A History of the Expansion of Christianity*, 7 vols., New York, 1937–45.
LENSEN, GEORGE ALEXANDER, *Report form Hokkaido, The Remains of Russian Culture in Northern Japan*, Hakodate, 1954.
LINDSAY, T. J., *A Short History of Taikoo*, privately printed, Hong Kong, 1966.
LOWE, JOHN, *Medical Missions, Their Place and Power*, New York, 1886.
—— *Primer of Medical Missions* (no date or place of publication).
MACKENZIE, COMPTON, *Realms of Silver*, London, 1954.
Manners and Customs of the Japanese, edited by Mrs. W. BUSK, London, 1841.
MATSUKATA MASAYOSHI, *Report on the Adoption of the Gold Standard*, Tokyo, 1899.
MAYO, MARLENE JUNE, 'The Iwakura Mission to the United States and Europe, 1871–1873', in *Columbia University East Asian Institute Studies*, No. 5, New York, 1959.
MEDZINI, MERON, 'Léon Roches in Japan (1864–1868)' in Harvard University, East Asian Research Center, *Papers on Japan*, ii, Cambridge, Mass., 1963.
MICHIE, A., *The Englishman in China*, 2 vols., Edinburgh, 1900.
MORRISON, G. S., *Our Position and Policy in Japan*, Brighton, 24 Nov. 1863.
MORSE, E. S., *Japan Day by Day 1877, 1878–9, 1882–3*, 2 vols., Boston, 1917.
MOSSMAN, SAMUEL, *New Japan: The Land of the Rising Sun*, London, 1873.
MURDOCH, JAMES, in collaboration with YAMAGATA ISOH, *A History of Japan*, 3 vols., London, 1925–6.
National Research Council of Japan, *Scientific Japan, Past and Present*, Tokyo, 1926.
OBATA KYUGORO, *An Interpretation of the Life of Viscount Shibusawa*, Tokyo, 1939.
OGASAWARA NAGANARI, *Life of Admiral Togo*, trans. by Inouye Jukichi and Inouye Tozo, Tokyo, 1934.
ŌKUMA SHIGENOBU, Compiler, *Fifty Years of New Japan* (Kaikoku Gojūnen Shi), 2 vols., English version edited by Marcus B. Huish, London, 1909.
OLIPHANT, LAWRENCE, *Narrative of the Earl of Elgin's Mission to China and Japan*, 2 vols., London, 1859.
PASCOE, C. F., *Two Hundred Years of the S.P.G.*, 2 vols., London, 1901.
PASKE-SMITH, M., *Western Barbarians in Japan and Formosa*, Kobe, 1930 (here cited as *Western Barbarians*).
—— *Japanese Traditions of Christianity*, London, no date.
PERRY, JOHN C., *Great Britain and the Imperial Japanese Navy 1868–1905*, unpublished thesis, Harvard University, 1961.
PHILLIPS, J. S. R., 'The Growth of Journalism', in vol. xiv, *The Cambridge History of English Literature*, 14 vols., Cambridge, 1916.

PRATT, PETER, *History of Japan*, compiled from Records of the East India Company at the instance of the Court of Directors, 1822, ed. by M. Paske-Smith, 2 vols., Kobe, 1931.

Proceedings of the General Conference of Protestant Missionaries in Japan, Held at Osaka, Japan, April 1883, Yokohama, 1883 (here cited as *Proceedings*, Osaka Conference 1883).

Proceedings of the General Conference of Protestant Missionaries in Japan, Held in Tokyo, 24–31 October 1900, Tokyo, 1901.

REDESDALE, BARON, ALGERNON B. F. M., *Memories*, 2 vols., London, 1915.

RICHARD, HENRY, *The Destruction of Kagoshima, Our Intercourse with Japan*, London, 1863.

RITTER, H., *A History of Protestant Missions in Japan*, trans. by G. E. Albrecht and D. C. Greene, Tokyo, 1898.

ROSCOE, H. E., *Life and Experiences*, London, 1906.

ROSEN, BARON, *Forty Years of Diplomacy*, 2 vols., London, 1922.

ROSOVSKY, HENRY, *Capital Formation in Japan, 1868–1940*, New York, 1961.

SALMON, L. M., *The Newspaper and Authority*, New York, 1923.

SANSOM, GEORGE, *A History of Japan*, 3 vols., Stanford, Calif., 1958–63, (here cited as *History*).

—— *The Western World and Japan*, New York, 1950.

SATOW, SIR ERNEST, *A Diplomat in Japan*, London, 1921 (here cited as *Diplomat*).

SCOTT, JAMES HENRY, *A Short Account of the Firm of John Swire & Sons Ltd.*, privately published, London, 1912.

SCOTT-JAMES, R. A., *The Influence of the Press*, London, 1919.

SHELDON, CHARLES DAVID, *The Rise of the Merchant Class in Tokugawa Japan 1600–1868*, Locust Valley, New York, 1958.

SHINJO HIROSHI, *History of the Yen: 100 Years of Japanese Money-Economy*, Kobe, 1962.

A Short History of The Japan Times (in commemoration of the 15,000th Issue of the Daily and Revision of its Title), Tokyo, 25 Mar. 1941.

SMITH, DAVID EUGENE, and MIKAMI YOSHIO, *A History of Japanese Mathematics*, Chicago, 1914.

SMITH, THOMAS C., *Political Change and Industrial Development in Japan: Government Enterprise, 1868–1880*, Stanford, Calif., 1955.

SOYEDA JUICHI, 'A History of Banking in Japan', in *A History of Banking in All Leading Nations*, ed. by *The Journal of Commerce and Commercial Bulletin*, 4 vols., New York, 1896.

STEAD, ALFRED, Ed., *Japan by the Japanese*, Tokyo, 1904.

STOCK, EUGENE, *The History of the Church Missionary Society*, 4 vols., London, 1899.

TAEUBER, IRENE B., *The Population of Japan*, Princeton, N.J., 1958.

TAKAKI MASAYOSHI, *A History of Japanese Paper Currency*, Baltimore, 1903.

TAKEKOSHI YOSOBURO, *The Economic Aspects of the History of the Civilization of Japan*, 3 vols., London, 1930.

THOMAS, W. T., *Protestant Beginnings in Japan 1859–1889*, Tokyo, 1959.

THOMPSON, H. P., *Into All Lands: The History of the Society for the Propagation of the Gospel in Foreign Parts 1701–1950*, London, 1951.

The Times, London, *The History of The Times*, 4 vols., London, 1935–52.
TREVELYAN, GEORGE MACAULAY, *British History in the Nineteenth Century*, New York, 1933.
TSUCHIYA TAKAO, *An Economic History of Japan*, trans. by Shidehara Michitaro, revised by Neil Skene Smith, *T.A.S.J*, Second Series, xv, Tokyo, 1937.
TUCKER, HENRY ST. GEORGE, *The History of the Episcopal Church in Japan*, New York, 1938.
UENO KIICHIRO, *A Hundred Years' History of Ships*, 2 vols., Tokyo, 1957–8.
UYEHARA SHIGERU, *The Industry and Trade of Japan*, London, 1936.
VERBECK, G. F., 'History of Protestant Missions in Japan', included in *Proceedings of the General Conference of Protestant Missionaries in Japan, Held at Osaka, Japan, April, 1883*, Yokohama, 1883.
VERY, Lieut. EDWARD W., U.S.A., *Navies of the World*, New York, 1880.
WARDE, EDWARD, Ed., *The House of Dodwell*, London, 1959.
WEI, W. P., *The Currency Problem in China*, New York, 1914.
WHITTINGHAM, PAUL BERNARD, *Notes on the Late Expedition against the Russian Settlements in Eastern Siberia, and of a Visit to Japan and to the Shores of Tartary and of the Sea of Okhotsk*, London, 1856.
WILLIAMS, H. S., *Tales of the Foreign Settlements in Japan*, Tokyo, 1958.
WILTON, GEORGE WILTON, *Fingerprints, History, Law and Romance*, London, 1938.
YAMAGUCHI KEN (UJI) [Shozan Yashi, pseud.] *Kinseishi Ryaku* (Summary History of Modern Times), Tokyo, 1872. Eng. translation by E. M. Satow, Yokohama, 1873, under title *Kinsé Shiriaku* (A History of Japan from the First Visit of Commodore Perry in 1853 to the Capture of Hakodate by the Mikado's Forces in 1869).
YANAGA CHITOSHI, *Japan Since Perry*, New York, 1949.
YEN, SOPHIA SU-FEI, *Taiwan in China's Foreign Relations 1836–1874*, Hamden, Connecticut, 1965.

Japanese

ASAHI SHIMBUN SHA, Ed., *Meiji-Taishō Shi* (Meiji-Taishō History), 6 vols., Tokyo, 1930.
BATCHELOR, JOHN, *Chikoro Utarapa ne Yesu Kiristo Ashiri Ekambakte, a Matteu Orowa no Asange Pirika* (Translation from the Ainu not available), Tokyo, 1889.
Daiichi Ginkō Hachijūnenshi Hensanshitsu (Committee for Compilation of Eighty Year History of the First National Bank), *Daiichi Ginkō Shi* (History of the First National Bank), 2 vols., Tokyo, 1957–8.
DENKICHI KOGA, *Hokkaidō Kyōdoshi Kenkyū* (A Study of the Local History of Hokkaido), Sapporo, 1932.
EBIHARA HACHIRŌ, *Nippon Ōji Shimbun-Zasshi Shi* (The History of European-language Newspapers and Magazines in Japan), Tokyo, 1934.
ETŌ KŌJI, 'Takashima Tankō ni Okeru Nichi-Ei Kyōdō Kigyō' (Japanese-British joint Enterprise at the Takashima Coal Mine) in *Bakumatsu Keizai Shi Kenkyū* (Study in Bakumatsu Economic History), ed. by Nihon

Keizaishi Kenkyūjo (Institute for Research in Japanese Economic History), Tokyo, 1935.

FUJIMOTO S., *Kaikō to Kiito Bōeki* (The Opening of the Ports and the Raw Silk Trade), 3 vols., Tokyo, 1939.

HINEYA YASUSADA, *Nihon Kinsei Kirisutokyō Jimbutsu Shi* (History of Christian Figures in Modern Japan), Tokyo, 1935.

Hokkaidō, *Hokkaidō Shi* (History of Hokkaido), 7 vols., Tokyo, 1937.

HONJŌ EIJIRŌ, *Meiji Ishin Keizai Shi Kenkyū* (Study of Economic History of the Meiji Restoration), Tokyo, 1930.

HORIE YASUZŌ, *Gaishi Yunyū no Kaiko to Tembō* (Retrospect and Outlook of Foreign Investment), Tokyo, 1950.

—— *Nihon Shihonshugi no Seiritsu* (The Formation of Japanese Capitalism), Osaka, 1939.

ISHII TAKASHI, *Bakumatsu Bōeki Shi no Kenkyū* (Study of History of Trade in the Late *Bakufu* Period), Tokyo, 1944.

—— *Meiji Ishin no Kokusaiteki Kankyō* (International Surroundings of the Meiji Restoration), Tokyo, 1957.

Japan. Gaimushō (Ministry of Foreign Affairs), *Nichi-Ei Gaikō Shi* (History of Japanese-British Relations), Secret, 3 vols., Tokyo, 1937–8. This is included in the Library of Congress microfilms of the archives of the Japanese Ministry of Foreign Affairs, 1868–1945 and is listed as SP 2.

Japan. Tetsūdōshō (Ministry of Railways), *Nihon Tetsūdō Shi* (History of Japanese Railways), 3 vols., Tokyo, 1921.

Kagoshima Ken (Kagoshima Prefecture, Japan), Compiler, *Kagoshima-ken Shi* (History of Kagoshima Prefecture), 5 vols., Kagoshima, 1939–43.

Kaigun Yushūkai (Naval Reserve Officers' Association), Compiler, *Kinsei Teikoku Kaigun Shi Yo* (Outline History of the Navy of Modern Japan), Tokyo, 1938.

KATSU SHIBA, *Nihon Rekishi Chizu* (Japanese Historical Atlas), Tokyo, 1923.

KATSU YASUYOSHI, Ed., *Kaigun Rekishi* (History of the Navy), 9 vols. (25 books), Tokyo, 1899.

KOIZUKA RYŪ, *Yokohama Kaikō Gojūnen Shi* (Fifty-Year History of the Opening of Yokohama), 2 vols., Yokohama, 1909.

Kōshaku Shimazu-ke Henshūjo (Editorial Office of the House of Prince Shimazu), Compiler, *Satsuma Kaigun Shi* (History of Satsuma Navy), 2 vols., Tokyo, 1929.

MATSUI KIYOSHI, *Kindai Nihon Bōeki Shi* (History of Modern Japanese Trade), Kyoto, 1959.

MATSUMURA KAN'ICHI, Compiler, *Mitsubishi Jūkōgyō Kabushiki Kaisha Shi* (History of Mitsubishi Heavy Industries), Tokyo, 1956.

MATSUMURA Y., Compiler, *Nihon ni Okeru Hyakunen Ei Ichiban Kan*, Ansei 6-nen—Showa 34-nen (Jardine's Centenary in Japan 1859–1959), Tokyo, 1959.

Meiji Zaisei Shi Hensankai (Association for editing financial history during the Meiji Period), *Meiji Zaisei Shi* (The Financial History of the Meiji Period), 15 vols., Tokyo, 1904–6.

The Mitsubishi Gōshi Kaisha (The Mitsubishi Company, Ltd.), Tokyo, 1911.

Bibliography 597

MURATA SEIJI, *Kobe Kaikō 30-nen Shi* (Thirty Years after the Opening of Kobe Port), 2 vols., Kobe, 1898.

Nagasaki, Shiyakusho (Nagasaki Municipal Office), *Nagasaki Sōsho* (A series about Nagasaki), 4 vols., Nagasaki, 1926.

NAKAMURA SEIJI, *Tanakadate Aikitsu Sensei* (My Teacher, Tanakadate Aikitsu), Tokyo, 1943.

Nihon Keizaishi Kenkyūjo (Research Institute for Japanese Economic History, Tokyo), Honjō Eijirō, Ed., *Bakumatsu Ishin* (Bakumatsu and Meiji Restoration Periods), Tokyo, 1942, vol. ii, Keizai Shiwa Sōsho (A Series of Accounts of Economic History).

Nihon Shimbun Kyōkai (Japan Newspaper Association), *Chihōbetsu Nihon Shimbun Shi* (History of Local Japanese Newspapers), Tokyo, 1956.

OKA YOSHITAKE, *Kindai Nihon Seiji Shi* (Political History of Modern Japan), Tokyo, 1962.

—— *Reimeiki no Meiji Nihon: Nichi-Ei Kōshō Shi no Shikaku ni Oite* (The Meiji Era: The Period of Dawn in Japan Viewed from the History of Negotiations with Britain), Tokyo, 1964.

OKADA KENZŌ, *Hakodate Hyakuchin to Hakodate* (One Hundred Facts and Historical Events of Hakodate), Hakodate, 1956.

OKADA SHUMPEI, *Bakumatsu Ishin no Kahei Seisaku* (Currency Policy at end of the *Bakufu* and early Meiji Periods), Tokyo, 1955.

—— *Meiji Zenki no Seika Seisaku* (Currency Policies in Early Meiji Period), Tokyo, 1958.

ONO HIDEO, *Nihon Shimbun Hattatsu Shi* (History of the Development of Japanese Newspapers), Tokyo, 1922.

—— 'Wagakuni Shoki no Gaiji Shimbun' (Early Period of Foreign Newspapers in Japan), which is the introduction to *Bakumatsu Meiji Shimbun Zenshū* (Collection of Late *Bakufu* and Meiji Newspapers), ed. by Osatake Takashi, Meiji Bunka Kenkyū Kai (Institute for Studying Meiji Culture), 5 vols., Tokyo, 1934.

OSATAKE TAKASHI, *Bakumatsu Gaikō Monogatari* (Tales of Late *Bakufu* Diplomacy), Tokyo, 1926.

OSATAKE TAKEKI, *Bakumatsu Gaikō Hishi Kō* (Secret Diplomatic History of the End of *Bakufu*), Tokyo, 1944.

ŌSHIMA FUJITARŌ, *Kokutetsu* (The National Railways), Tokyo, 1956.

OTSUKA TAKEMATSU, *Bakumatsu Gaikō Shi no Kenkyū* (Diplomatic History in Latter Days of Tokugawa Shogunate), Tokyo, 1952.

SAWA KANNOJŌ, *Kaigun Shichijūnen Shidan* (Seventy Years History of the Navy), Tokyo, 1942.

SAWA K. and HIFUMI T., *Kaigun Heigaku Ryō* (Institute of Royal Strategy), Tokyo, 1942.

TANABE TAICHI, *Bakumatsu Gaikō Dan* (Tales of Foreign Relations in the late *Bakufu* Period), Tokyo, 1898.

TANAKADATE AIKITSU, *Kuzu no Ne* (Selected Essays, Speeches, and other Works), Tokyo, 1938.

TOKUGAWA MITSUKUNI, *Dai Nihon Shi* (History of Japan), 243 *kan*, 100 vols., Yedo, 1851.

TOTSUKA SEIKAI, preface to 1837 edition of *Seimi Kaisō*.

598 *Bibliography*

TSUCHIYA TAKAO, *Hōken Shakai Hōkai Katei no Kenkyū* (A Study of the Disintegration of Feudal Society), Tokyo, 1927.
—— *Ishin Keizai Shi* (Economic History of the Restoration), Tokyo, 1942.
URAKAWA WAZABURO, *Urakami Kirishitan Shi* (History of Christians in Urakami), Osaka, 1943.
YAMAGUCHI KAZUO, *Bakumatsu Bōeki Shi* (History of Foreign Trade in the Closing Days of the *Bakufu*), Tokyo, 1947.
YAMAMOTO FUMIO, *Nihon Shimbun Hattatsu Shi* (History of the Development of the Press in Japan), Tokyo, 1944.
Yokohama Shiyakusho (Yokohama Municipal Office), *Yokohama-shi Shi Kō* (History of Yokohama City), 11 vols., Yokohama, 1931–3.
YUASA MITSUTOMO, *Kagakushi* (History of Science), Tokyo, 1961.

ARTICLES

Western

ANDERSON, WILLIAM, 'History of Japanese Art', *T.A.S.J.* vii, Pt. IV.
—— 'Kakke', *T.A.S.J.* vi, Pt. I.
ATKINSON, R. W., 'Analysis of Surface Waters in Tokyo', *T.A.S.J.* vii, Pt. IV.
—— 'Notes on Manufacture of O Shiroi', *T.A.S.J.* vi, Pt. II.
—— 'Notes on the Porcelain Industry in Japan', *T.A.S.J.* viii, Pt. II.
AYRTON, WILLIAM EDWARD, and PERRY, JOHN, 'The Specific Inductive Capacity of Gases'; 'The Importance of a General System of Simultaneous Observations of Atmospheric Electricity'; 'On a Neglected Principle that may be Employed in Earthquake Measurements', *T.A.S.J.* v, Pt. I.
BATCHELOR, JOHN, 'Notes on the Ainu' and 'An Ainu Vocabulary', *T.A.S.J.* x, Pt. I.
BLAKISTON, THOMAS WRIGHT, 'A Journey in North-East Japan', *T.A.S.J.* ii, Pt. I.
—— 'Zoological Indication of Connection of Japan with the Continent', *T.A.S.J.* xi, Pt. I.
BOXER, C. R., 'Sakoku, or the Closed Century', *History Today*, 1957.
BRUNTON, RICHARD HENRY, 'The Japan Lights', *Minutes of Proceedings of the Institution of Civil Engineers*, Session 1876–7, Pt. I, London, 1877 (cited here as *Japan Lights*).
CRAWCOUR, E. S., 'Japanese Commerce in the Tokugawa Period', *Journal of Asian Studies*, xxii, Aug. 1963.
DENING, WALTER, 'Modern Translation into Sinico-Japanese', *T.A.S.J.* xii, Pt. II.
DIVERS, EDWARD, 'Notes on the Amount of Sulphuretted Hydrogen in the Hot Springs of Kusatsu', *T.A.S.J.* vi, Pt. II.
DOUGLAS, ARCHIBALD C., 'The Genesis of Japan's Navy', The Japan Society, London, *Transactions*, xxxvi.
FAULDS, HENRY, 'Remarks on the Dojo' and 'Biological Notes', *T.A.S.J.* vi, Pts. I and II.
FLERSHEM, ROBERT G., 'Some Aspects of Japan Sea Trade in the Tokugawa Period', *Journal of Asian Studies*, xxiii, May 1964.

Fox, Grace, 'The Anglo-Japanese Convention of 1854', *Pacific Historical Review*, x, 1941.

Fujii Terugoro, Rear-Adm., 'Progress of Naval Engineering in Japan', *Transactions of the Institution of Naval Architects*, liii, Pt. II, Table 2.

Hashimoto U., 'An Historical Synopsis of Education and Science in Japan from the Meiji Restoration to the Present Day', *Impact of Science on Society*, xiii, 1963.

Horie Yasuzō, 'The Feudal States and the Commercial Society in the Tokugawa Period', *Kyoto University Economic Review*, xxviii, Oct. 1958.

'The Imperial Mint', Report of the Commissioners of the Imperial Mint for the Financial Year Ending 30 June 1881, *Japan Weekly Mail*, 22 Apr. 1882.

Jones, F. M., 'Foreign Influence on the Early Press of Japan', The Japan Society, London, *Transactions*, xxxii.

Kimura Ki, 'Yokohama, One Hundred Years Ago', *Contemporary Japan*, xxii.

Longford, Joseph H., 'The Growth of the Japanese Navy', *The Nineteenth Century*, lix, 1903.

Maclellan, J. W., 'Banking in India and China', photostat of article secured by Mr. John Keswick from Shanghai and Hong Kong Bank—journal not known.

McMaster, John, 'The Japanese Gold Rush of 1859', *Journal of Asian Studies*, xix, May 1960.

Milne, John, 'A Journey Across Europe and Asia', *T.A.S.J.* vii, Pt. I.

Ōkuma Shigenobu, 'A General View of Financial Policy during Thirteen Years', *Japan Weekly Mail*, 2 Apr. 1881.

—— 'The Industrial Revolution in Japan', *North American Review*, clxxi.

—— 'Revenues and Expenditures' (Report for eight fiscal years, 1868–June 1875), *Japan Weekly Mail*, 14, 21 Feb. and editorial comment upon this report, 5 June 1880.

Oya Shin-ichi, 'A Short Note on the History of Japanese Mathematics', *Japanese Studies in History of Science*, i, 1962.

Saigusa Hiroto, 'Japanese Astronomy in the Tokugawa Era', *Japan Quarterly*, v.

Sakai, Robert K., 'The Satsuma–Ryukyu Trade and Tokugawa Policy', *Journal of Asian Studies*, xxiii, May 1964.

Sakata Yoshio and Hall, John Whitney, 'The Motivation of Political Leadership in the Meiji Restoration', *Journal of Asian Studies*, xvi, Nov. 1956.

Smith, Sir Sidney, 'Finger Print Pioneer', *The Scotsman*, 21 Mar. 1961.

Smith, Thomas C., 'Introduction of Western Industry to Japan', *Harvard Journal of Asiatic Studies*, xi.

Tsiang, T. F., 'Sino-Japanese Diplomatic Relations 1870–1894', *Chinese Social and Political Science Review*, xvii.

Webb, Herschel, 'What is the Dai Nihon Shi', *Journal of Asian Studies*, xix, Feb. 1960.

Whitney, W. N., 'Notes on the History of Medical Progress in Japan', *T.A.S.J.* xii, Pt. IV.

Japanese

Ishii Takashi, 'Bakuchō Kōsenki ni Okeru Eikoku Kōshi Pākusu no Tain-ichi Seisaku' (The Policy of British Minister Parkes for Japan during the Bakufu–Chōshū War), *Bunka (Culture)*, xxvi, No. 3.

—— 'Saikōku Daimyō to Sakoku Kaikoku' (Western Daimyo and the Closing and Opening of the Country), *Nihon Rekishi (Japan History)*, July 1959.

Nezu Masashi, 'Meiji Shonen no Kirishitan Tsuihō to Teimei Kakkoku no Taido' (Exile of Christians in the early Meiji Period and the Attitudes of the Treaty Powers), *Shigaku Zasshi* (Journal of Historical Science), xlvi, June 1935.

Sakaguchi Masao, 'Seimi Kaisō no Kenkyū' (Studies on Seimi Kaisō), *Kagakushi Kenkyū (Journal of History of Science)*, lxxii, 1964, and lxxiii, 1965.

Shinobu Jumpei, 'Meiji no Gaikōshijō ni Okeru Pākusu no Ichi' (The Position of Parkes in Meiji Diplomatic Affairs), *Kokusaihō Gaikō Zasshi* (Journal of International Law and Diplomacy), xxvii and xxviii.

Tsuchiya Takao, 'Bakumatsu Dō Anki no Keizaiteki Bunseki' (Economic Analyses of the Restless Period of the End of Tokugawa), *Chūō Kōron (Central Review)*, Oct. 1932.

BIBLIOGRAPHIES, CHRONOLOGIES, DICTIONARIES, DIRECTORIES, INDEXES, REFERENCE BOOKS

Western

Association of Asian Studies, *Bibliography of Asian Studies*, 1955–66.

The Banking Almanac, Directory, Yearbook and Diary for 1862, ed. by D. M. Evans, London, 1862 (cited here as *The Banking Almanac*).

Bramsen, William, *Japanese Chronological Tables*, showing the date according to the Julian or Gregorian calendar of the First Day of Each Japanese Month from Tai-kwa 1st year to Meiji 6th year (A.D. 645 to A.D. 1873), Tokyo, 1880.

The Daily Press Chronicle and Directory, Hong Kong, 1865, 1866, 1868, 1869, 1870.

Dictionary of National Biography (D.N.B.) 1931–40, London, 1949.

Giuseppi, M. S., *Guide to the Contents of the Public Record Office*, Revised and extended (to 1960) from the Guide by the late M. S. Giuseppi, F.S.A., London, H.M. Stationery Office, London, 1963.

Great Britain, Foreign Office, *Catalogue of Printed Books in the Library of the Foreign Office*, London, 1926.

Great Britain, *General Index to the Bills, Reports, Estimates, Accounts and Papers Printed by Order of the House of Commons and to the Papers Presented by Command, 1852–1899*, London, 1909.

Japan Directory, 1879.

Japan Gazette, Hong List and Directory, 1872.

List of Japanese books on medicine, trans. from Dutch works before 1858, published by Suhavaya, Tokyo (no date).

The London and Provincial Medical Directory, inclusive of the Medical Directory for Scotland and the Medical Directory for Ireland & General Medical Register, London, 1863–83 (here cited as *Medical Directory*, London).

NACHOD, OSKAR, *Bibliography of the Japanese Empire 1906–26*, 2 vols., Leipzig, 1928.

PAPINOT, E., *Historical and Geographical Dictionary of Japan*, with 300 illustrations, 18 appendixes, and several maps, London, 1910.

PLARR, VICTOR GUSTAVE, *Plarr's Lives of the Fellows of the Royal College of Surgeons of England*, 2 vols., London, 1930.

The Times, Index, 1850–83.

UYEHARA, CECIL H., Compiler, *Checklist of Archives in the Japanese Ministry of Foreign Affairs, Tokyo, Japan, 1868–1945*, microfilmed for the Library of Congress, 1949–51, Washington, D.C., 1954.

VON WENCKSTERN, FRIEDRICH, *A Bibliography of the Japanese Empire*: vol. i, 1859–93, Leiden, 1895; vol. ii, 1894–1906, Tokyo, 1907.

Who Was Who 1897–1915, London, 1935.

YOUNG, JOHN, Compiler, *Checklist of Microfilm Reproductions of Selected Archives of the Japanese Army, Navy, and other Government Agencies, 1868–1945*, Washington, D.C., 1959.

Japanese

Dai Jinmei Jiten (Biographical Dictionary), 10 vols., Tokyo, 1954.

FUZAMBŌ's *Kokushi Jiten* (Dictionary of Japanese History), 4 vols., Tokyo, 1940.

IWANAMI, *Seiyō Jinmei Jiten* (Dictionary of Foreign Names), Tokyo, 1956.

Japan. Gaimushō (Foreign Office), *Nihon Gaikō Nempyō narabi ni Shuyō Monjo 1840–1945* (Chronological Table of Japan's Diplomacy and the Chief Documents), 2 vols., Tokyo, 1955.

Kokumin Hyakka Daijiten (National Encyclopedia), 12 vols., Tokyo, 1936.

Nihonshi Jiten (Dictionary of Japanese History), Tokyo, 1960.

Sekai Dai Hyakka Jiten (World Encyclopedia), 33 vols., Tokyo, 1955–63, xviii.

TAKENOBU YOSHITARO, Gen. Ed., Kenkyusha's *New Japanese–English Dictionary*, Tokyo, 1940.

INDEX

Abe Masahiro, 35, 36, 37.

Abe Masatō, dismissed, 166–7.

Actaeon, H.M.S., 66, 89.

Adams, Francis O., 275, 277–8, 496.

Adamson, W. R., and Company, 51, 316.

Admiralty, British, Board of, orders to naval officers in China, 9; instructions to Rear-Adm. Hope, 56; supports Alcock's request for increased protection, 79; instructions to Vice-Adm. Kuper, 124; order concerning instruction of Japanese officers, 255.

Ahrent Company, 261.

Ainu, 351–2, 528.

Aizu, Prince (daimyo of), anti-foreign sentiment, 195, 197; resistance to Imperial forces, 217, 231–3; ends northern rebellion, 235.

Akamatsu Noriyoshi, Adm., 293.

Albert, Prince, 4, 94 n. 1.

Alcock, Rutherford, 535, 536, 547; appointed consul-general for Japan, 53–7; accomplishments en route to Yedo, 58–60; selects quarters at Yedo, 60; refuses Yokohama as site for British settlement, 62–4; exchanges ratified texts of Treaty of Yedo, 64; states restrictions on use of force, 67; states grievances, threatens war, 75–6; protests and advises on currency policies 1859, 70–4, 76; views on Anglo-Japanese relations Jan. 1860, 76–7; personal isolation, 79, 80, 82; views on anti-foreign movement and *Bakufu* duplicity, 78–9, 83–4; requests greater naval protection, 79, 83, 86; audience with the Shogun, 82; concedes temporary postponement of opening of Yedo, 83; removes legation to Yokohama, 84–5; recognizes limits of Shogun's power, 85–6; recommends deferment of opening of more cities, 87–9; prohibits residence of British citizens in Yedo, 90; negotiations in Japan and England for London Protocol, 90–3, 94–5; views on same, 95–6;

advises attack on Satsuma by treaty powers, 102; recognizes need of Mikado's ratification of foreign treaties, 102; aids Russell in defining policy, 1863, 122–3; his instructions from Russell concerning use of force, 123–4; reports Japan's preparations for war, 127; decides on military action against Chōshū to enforce treaty rights, 128–30; reaction to Imperial orders for closing Yokohama, 129; develops cooperative policy with treaty powers, 130–2; states allied policy to Chōshū, 132–4; gives aims and justification for allied expedition, 136–7; negotiations with *Bakufu* following defeat of Chōshū, exaction of Shimonoseki indemnity, 141–3; is ordered home, 141; explains his policy and recommends additional powers for his successor, 145–6; his demands following murder of Baldwin and Bird, 147; leaves Japan, 147; supports Japan's request for military instructors, 148; his Chōshū policy approved in London, 148; his administration appraised, 148–50, 538–40; Minister Plenipotentiary to China, 150, 284.

Alt and Company, 327, 330.

Alt, W. J., 327, 385.

Amenomori, ——?, Mr., 511.

American Bible Society, 512, 527.

American Board of Missions, 511.

American Episcopal Church, 511.

American Episcopalians, 527.

Americans, in Yokohama, 63; in Hakodate, 65, 67; in arms trade, 109, 154; engaged in Japanese expedition to Formosa, 289–90, 291.

An Epitome of Chemistry, 466.

Anderson, Rufus, 6 n. 3.

Anderson, Dr. William, 478, 550.

Andō Nobumasa, 90, 92 n. 2.

Andō Tarō, 408.

Andrews, Walter, 507 n. 5.

Anglin, J. R., 422.

Anglo-Japanese Convention, 11–13, 52.

Richardson, C. Lennox, 98, 101.

Richardson, Henry, 331.

Rickard, J. G., 378.

Rickerby, Charles, 455, 549; commends Alcock's policy, 144; manager of Yokohama office of Central Bank of Western India, 378; edits the *Japan Times*, 422; publishes *Japan Times, New Series*, 427; edits the *Japan Mail-Times* papers, 431.

Ringdove, H.M.S., 86, 98, 99.

Rising Sun and Express, 433.

Robertson, John, 391, 394, 403.

Roches, Lèon, 131, 230; agreement for dockyard at Yokosuka, 155–6; and the Mikado's ratification of the treaties, 164, 166, 169, 172; reports British relations with daimyo, 176; arrangements for arsenal and French military mission, 198; demands following murder of French seaman fulfilled, 227, 228; withdraws French naval instructors, 253–4; and the imprisonment of Christians, 483–4; leaves Japan June 1868, 235.

Rodney, H.M.S., 235.

Rōjū (see also *Bakufu*), 106, 107; explained, 18–19; response to Western demands, 35–6, 38; currency orders, 69, 71; agree to expulsion of foreigners, 104; admit Shogun's inability to control anti-foreign forces, 121; oppose settlement of Shimonoseki indemnity at Osaka, 165; compromise re foreign ships in Straits of Shimonoseki, 188; apply for naval instructors 253–4.

Roman Catholic Church, at Nagasaki 1859–67, 482–4; proselytism at Urakami, 487, 490–1; converts by 1881, 512.

rōnin, 25, 77, 120, 164, 225.

Rover, U.S. bark, 576 and n. 2.

Royal Asiatic Society of Japan, *Transactions* of, 466, 528–9, 547.

Roza, F. da, 419, 442.

Russell and Company, 49.

Russell, Lord John, 4, 535; opposes Bowring's policy, 15; repudiates traders' behaviour, 74; defines use of increased naval force, 79; sanctions concession re opening of Yedo, 87; instructions 1861 on postponement question, 90; and the London Protocol, 94–5; objectives, peace and trade, 121; empowers Neale to treat with friendly daimyo, 122; prescribes conditions for use of force, 123–4; informs European courts Britain will not give up Yokohama, 126; opposes hostilities against Chōshū, orders Alcock home, 140–1; and the Satsuma envoys, 153; initial instruction to Parkes, 161; instructions re Mikado's ratification of the treaties and Shimonoseki indemnity, 164.

Russell, Revd. W. A., 504, as Bishop of North China 1872, 507.

Russia, 96, 258 n. 1, 278; and the Anglo-Japanese Convention, 10–12; treaties with Japan, 13 and n. 2, 37–8, 40; Malmesbury's orders concerning Alcock's policy, 54; activities in Yezo and Tsushima, 87, 88, 89; activities in the Sakhalin area, 176.

Russian (Greek) Orthodox Church, 482, 500, 512.

Russians, 65, 109.

ryō, 27 n. 4.

Ryūjō, Japanese warship, 259, 263.

Ryūkyū Islands, 173, 214, 271, 280; suzerainty and trade monopoly secured by Satsuma, 21; Satsuma's trade, 33–4; opened to British and French trade, 47 n. 1; relations with Meiji government, 282; Chinese and Japanese claims to suzerainty, 286–8.

Ryūkyūans, 281–2, 287–8, 296, 308, 577.

Ryder, Vice-Adm. A. P., 477, 523.

Sado, 207.

Saga, 251; rebellion in, crushed, 281.

Sagasa Tomoyasu, 472.

Saigō Jūdō (Tsugumichi), Lieut.-Gen., 299 n. 2; commands expedition to Formosa, 289, 291, 296–7; assumes responsibility for departure of troops to Formosa, 292–3.

Saigō Takamori, states conditions for opening of Hyogo and Osaka, 192–3; conversations with Satow, 193–4, 201, 204–5, 472; opposes British and French intervention in Japan's affairs, 205; to command Satsuma troops

PRINTED IN GREAT BRITAIN
AT THE UNIVERSITY PRESS, OXFORD
BY VIVIAN RIDLER
PRINTER TO THE UNIVERSITY